Jewish Funerary Customs, Practices and Rites in the Second Temple Period

Supplements
to the
Journal for the Study
of Judaism

Editor
John J. Collins
The Divinity School, Yale University

Associate Editor
Florentino García Martínez
Qumran Institute, University of Groningen

Advisory Board
J. DUHAIME — A. HILHORST — P.W. VAN DER HORST A. KLOSTER-
GAARD PETERSEN — M.A. KNIBB — J.T.A.G.M VAN RUITEN —
J. SIEVERS — G. STEMBERGER — E.J.C. TIGCHELAAR — J. TROMP

VOLUME 94

Jewish Funerary Customs, Practices and Rites in the Second Temple Period

By
Rachel Hachlili

BRILL
LEIDEN • BOSTON
2005

This book is printed on acid-free paper.

Library of Congress Cataloging-in Publication data

Hachlili, Rachel.
  Jewish funerary customs, practices, and rites in the Second Temple period/by
Rachel Hachlili.
     p. cm. — (Supplements to the Journal for the study of Judaism, ISSN 1384-
2161; v. 94)
  Includes bibliographical references and index.
  ISBN 90-04-12373-3
  1. Tombs—Palestine. 2. Burial—Palestine. 3. Jewish mourning customs.
4. Excavations (Archaeology)—Palestine. 5. Palestine—Antiquities. 6. Dead—
Religious aspects—Judaism. 7. Judaism—History—Post-exilic period, 586
B.C.–210 A.D. I. Title. II. Series.

DS111.9.H33 2005
393'.1'089924033—dc22   2004056754

DS
111.9
. H33
2005

ISSN 1384-2161
ISBN 90 04 12373 3

PRINTED IN THE NETHERLANDS.

CONTENTS

LIST OF FIGURES

LIST OF PLATES

Plate I–1. Jericho, general view of cemetery

Plate I–2. Qumran view of the site and of the cemetery

Plate I–3. Qumran general view of the cemetery

Plate II–1. Jerusalem, Monumental Tombs in the Kidron Valley

Plate II–2. Bene Ḥezir Tomb

Plate II–3. Tomb of Zechariah

Plate II–4. Absalom Tomb

Plate II–5. Jason's Tomb

Plate II–6. Tomb of Queen Helene of Adiabene, Lintel

Plate II–7. Nazirite family Tomb (Courtesy of the Department of Archeology, Hebrew University, Jerusalem)

Plate II–8. Sanhedriya tomb, facade

Plate II–9. Sanhedriya tomb, interior

Plate II–10. Frieze tomb, Lintel

Plate II–11. Jericho loculi tomb

Plate II–12. Jericho mourning enclosure (Photo. Z Radovan)

Plate II–13. Jericho miqveh (Photo. Z Radovan)

Plate II–14a,b. Jericho entrance and sealings (Photo. Z Radovan)

Plate II–15. Akeldama, Tomb 2, Chamber C (Courtesy of Israel Antiquities Authority)

Plate III–1. Jericho, Tomb D14 with wooden Coffin 113

Plate III–2. 'En Gedi wooden coffin (Courtesy of Israel Antiquities Authority)

Plate III–3. Naḥal David decorated wooden coffin

Plate III–4a–b. Decorated ossuaries: Type I (Courtesy of Israel Antiquities Authority)

Plate III–5a–d. Decorated ossuaries: Type II: a,b (Courtesy of Israel Antiquities Authority)

LIST OF TABLES

FOREWORD

This volume is intended to provide a comprehensive and instructive study of Jewish funerary customs, practices, and rituals in the Second Temple period, attitudes towards the dead, and the implications and significance of the beliefs are illuminated. The book is a collection of studies devoted to Jewish customs relating to death, burial and mourning, addressing the meaning of Jewish funerary art and tradition.

This survey is a compilation of the material excavated in the past few decades, especially the latest results, together with previous materials and studies.

The study outlines the material preserved in the ancient Jewish cemeteries of the Hellenistic and Roman periods at Jerusalem, Jericho, 'En Gedi, and Qumran, although it should be noted that many tombs were systematically robbed. This volume also explores the relationship with literary texts, and offers an interpretation of death and burial rituals.

The latent contribution of archaeology to the study of Jewish burial is vast, and is investigated here. As a result of many excavations in recent decades a large body of new material has come to light which now permits comprehensive treatment of ancient Jewish burial rites, art, and beliefs. The archaeology is dealt with in detail, with emphasis on various aspects of practices relating to death, particularly the manifestation of the burial rites.

The discussion takes the form of a general comparison, divided according to topics with specific themes and issues surveyed, reexamined, and redefined. Such topics are a description of the cemeteries, funerary architecture, inscriptions, interment receptacles and their ornamentation, assorted aspects of family tombs, the status of women in funerary relations, and more. Together, these subjects create what I hope is a conclusive case for the existence of distinctive Jewish burial customs and rites in Second Temple period. A comprehensive and illuminating interpretation of burial customs and rites is presented, and an overview of funerary art and insights into the social life of the Jews in the Second Temple period. An understanding of the heritage bequeathed to us by our ancestors can help penetrate the mists of time separating us from those periods.

Research of burials constitutes one of the main reliable sources of information related to various aspects of funerary practices and rituals, and offers a perception of ancient social life and community organization. Here the archaeological evidence is followed by a methodical account and interpretation, though there are some areas in the study where much remains to be done.

The survey and salvage excavations and the following research of the Jericho cemetery, conducted by Dr. Ann Killebrew and myself, on behalf of the Israel Department of Antiquities (now the Israel Antiquities Authority), and the Staff Officer for Archaeology in Judea and Samaria, were the essential initiation of this volume. The well preserved condition of many tombs and the exceptional state of preservation of the organic remains proved to be of significant importance for our knowledge of burial customs and material culture of the Second Temple period.

Several of the chapters included in the present collection have appeared as articles published previously, while others appear here for the first time. Some chapters have undergone extensive revision and expansion, and are revised and updated version of articles. Other chapters were written specifically for the present publication.

Rachel Hachlili
University of Haifa
November 2003

ACKNOWLEDGEMENTS

I had been researching and collecting material on this specific subject for the past years starting at the first excavation I conducted at the Jericho cemetery; I had now reached the stage when I wished to present the outcome of this labour.

Various people have contributed to my work. I should like especially to acknowledge my special gratitude to my friend, colleague and partner in the excavations at Jericho Dr. Ann Killebrew for her advice and encouragement, her reading and commenting on the manuscript. Some of the research was conducted together with her (see our joint articles). I am especially grateful to Dr. L.Y. Rahmani for his attention, support and assistance during the excavation and research of the Jewish burial practices at Jericho and his help with comparable material from Jerusalem.

I am likewise indebted to those who have helped me prepare this book: warm thanks are due to Prof. John J. Collins for his thorough editing; to Murray Rosovsky for his diligent work on the English; to Vered Raz-Romeo, my research assistant, for her help with some technical aspects, preparing parts of the tables and checking some of the bibliography. I thank particularly my colleagues Prof. Amos Kloner and Dr. Bo'az Zissu for the many significant and valuable studies of the necropolis of Jerusalem I relied on in this volume.

My sincere thanks are due to the following individuals and institutions who allowed me the publication and use of their photographs and drawings: Dr. G. Avni, Dr. G. Hadas, Prof. A. Kloner, Dr. L.Y. Rahmani; The Israel Antiquities Authority, Jerusalem for permission to publish some of the items and for many of the photographs from excavations in Israel; The Department of Archaeology, Hebrew University, Jerusalem for permission to publish some ossuaries photographs.

Affectionate thanks go especially to my husband Gad for all his help and to my children Guy, Sigal and Niv for their unfailing support and encouragement.

INTRODUCTION

Death is connected with mysterious perceptions; burial and graves express faith, belief, and ideas in different periods and diverse societies. The research and analysis of the tomb's form, the status and situation of the interred, the grave goods, the inscriptions, and significantly the burial customs, furnish us with evidence about the assumptions and notions regarding death in the given society.

Essential proof on the connection between the living and the dead is revealed by burial data. The mortuary rites and ceremonies, such as memorial architecture, inscribed texts, and effects belonging to the deceased placed in and around the burial place, evince a belief in a connection of the living with the world of the dead and provide enough elements to recreate past social organizations. The commemoration of ancestors appears regularly as a significant part of the present.

The deceased's relation to the grave goods preserved in tombs provide data on mourning customs and burial practices such as offerings, personal possessions, expression of grief, type of receptacle and fittings, the inhumation process, the individual's status in the community, family relations and burial status, monument construction, and the material culture of a given period.

The tombs offer ample data on the artistic taste evinced by funerary architecture and the ornamentation of receptacles and objects. Material culture is an important part of human contact and substance, articulating ideas and practices.

The skeletal remains preserved in tombs are almost the only source for anthropological data and research, providing information on the interred's ethnic origin, life expectancy, sex, gender, and age, medical condition, and cause of death.

Research into burial practices and the material remains of mortuary rituals is effective in reconstructing the history of a society, its religious beliefs and its social outlook. Burial customs might indicate the social status of the deceased, revealing social position as expressed in family tombs, their size, location, and the grave goods.

Changes in Jewish funerary practices did not alter the plan and architecture of the tombs. Though the funerary rites changed from inhumation in coffins and loculi to secondary burial by collection of bones in ossuaries the artifacts associated with these graves did not alter much and indicate that these were culturally and socially identical people. Most of the grave goods assemblages are shared by both sexes, with certain types found in graves that show gender association and trends, but not strict gender roles.

This study sets forth research based on material remains intended to reveal Jewish burial traditions, practices, and rituals, as well as the role the dead played in the life of the living.

The data gathered in this book include most of the published archaeological and epigraphic material, mainly from excavated tombs and graves. Architecture and decoration are discussed, as well as the finds, rites, and customs. The amount of data available from excavations is unfortunately limited to a restricted number of sites, especially Jerusalem. Enough evidence exists, however, to draw a picture of the Jewish funerary customs in the Second Temple period (first century BCE to first century CE).

The conclusions reached in this book are based on an analysis of excavation reports, the finds, and the research work of many scholars.

Several significant issues are raised in these pages: the particular Jewish customs identified by the material culture; family tombs, kin and ancestor relations; the interaction with earlier burial practices and with the neighboring cultures.

Chapter I describes the cemeteries, their location, and finds. Chapter II discusses the architectural and decorative features of the tombs; monumental tombs, tombs with ornamented façade, loculi tombs (tombs with a burial recess hewn in the tomb walls), acrosolia (tombs with arched niches) and other tombs, examining the characteristic features of tomb architecture. Chapter III is devoted to the portrayal of the burial receptacles: coffins, ossuaries, and sarcophagi; attention is paid to their manufacture and ornamentation. Chapter IV examines funerary art: compositions and styles are analyzed and the meaning and interpretations are discussed. Chapter V deals with selected funerary inscriptions on tombs, sarcophagi, and ossuaries, which are described and evaluated. Chapter VI records Jerusalem family tombs, priestly and high priestly tombs, Jericho family tombs; family relations are appraised. Chapter VII examines the status of women and their family relations. Chapter VIII discusses the *nefesh* as a funerary commemoration monument. Chapter IX focuses on the craftsmen and workshops that built the tombs and produced the ossuaries. Chapter X records the grave goods recovered in the tombs such as pottery, glass, iron, personal items, and coins, and considers their significance and meaning. Chapter XI describes and analyzes burial types, funerary customs and rites, protective measures, and 'magic' practices; it deals with the evolution of burial customs and the connection with the pagan world. Chapter XII places the material discussed in the book within a chronological framework and summarizes the evidence presented in this volume and draws conclusions about Jewish burial rites and customs.

The Second Temple period in general extends from the return from Babylon (mid 6th century BCE) until the destruction of Jerusalem and Masada (70 and 73 CE) or possibly until the Second War against the Romans, the Bar Kokhba war (132–135 CE). However, this book reports on the end of this period, the second century BCE to the end of the first century CE.

TERMINOLOGY

Terms for tomb and the receptacles (especially ossuary) appear on inscriptions on some ossuaries; some of the same terms are mentioned in Jewish sources of the period.

Terms for Tomb

Several terms such as קבר in Hebrew and τόπος in Greek (both words meaning 'tomb') are inscribed on ossuaries from Jerusalem (Rahmani 1994: 3). The word 'tomb' on these ossuaries was probably used in the sense of 'ossuary'; the word may also be a verb indicating 'buried'.

On an ossuary from French Hill, Jerusalem, the inscriptions in Hebrew מרי קבר and in Greek κυρε τυς τουπου refer to 'the masters of the tomb' (Rahmani 1994: Nos. 560). The Greek inscription also mentions the two brothers 'Mathia and Simon, sons of Yair', the masters of the tomb. Here the term 'tomb' possibly refers to 'ossuary'.

קיברא 'tomb' appears without a personal name on an ossuary from Abu Tor, Jerusalem (Rahmani 1994: No. 125). The word probably means either tomb or ossuary.

The term דה קוקא 'the *kokh*', a Palmyrene inscription, is engraved on an ossuary from Shu'afat. It probably means 'the sepulchral 'chamber' or perhaps a funerary urn (Abel 1913: 271, No. 11 Fitzmyer and Harrington 1978: No. 141; Rahmani 1994: 1).

Terms for receptacles: coffins, ossuaries

Greek terms for coffin (*aron* in Hebrew) and ossuary (a rectangular stone box for collecting bones) appear, and an Aramaic term was written or engraved on ossuaries found in Jericho and Jerusalem (Hachlili 1979: 55; Rahmani 1994: 3). Note that on some of the ossuaries the terms appear unaccompanied by the name of the deceased.

- The Greek word COPOC (*Soros*) was written in ink, on Ossuary VIII (Inscription 3a) (Fig. V–) found in the back of *kokh* 2, Chamber A at Jericho Tomb H (Hachlili 1979: 55, Figs. 41–42; 1999: 144, 153, Fig. IV.2, Table IV.1). This term appears for the first time on an inscription.

In the Hebrew Bible the word ארון (*aron*) has three different meanings: holy ark, container, and coffin. ארון *aron* meaning "coffin" occurs only once in the Bible (Gen 50: 26) and refers to the coffin used to transport Joseph's bones from Egypt to Israel. In the LXX this word is translated into Greek as σορος *soros* 'coffin or cinerary urn'. As coffins for burial were only used in the Second Temple period, the appearance of the coffin is probably a reflection of Egyptian practice (see Marcus 1975: 89–90, for the term 'coffin' in other Semitic languages). In Rabbinical sources dealing with ossilegium the term ארון (*aron*) is used to describe both large coffins (sarcophagi) and secondary burial containers (i.e., ossuaries). There are some problematic words, such as רוים (*TY Mo'ed Katan* I. 4), ארוים (*Sanhedrin* 6.12) and ירוין (*Semahot* 12. 8), which Lieberman (1962 V:1235) and Zlotnick (1966: 160, n. 8) interpreted as being mistranslations of the LXX word σορος (*soros*), here meaning ארון coffin (but see Meyers 1971: 60–61). Thus, σορός (*soros*) was a term for ossuary in use during the Second Temple period and was equivalent to ארון (*aron*) in Hebrew.

- *Ostophagos*. The Greek term ὀστοφάγος, "ostophagos", literarally "bone eater" (Strabo, 16.4.17), appears twice on an inscription scratched on a plain ossuary (Fig. 1) from a single-chamber tomb in the Kidron Valley, Jerusalem (Avigad 1967: 141, fig. 35).

It refers to the ossuary itself, as it apparently was the designation for ossuaries at this period (Sukenik 1937: 129–30, Pls. V:4, VI:4; Meyers 1971: 49–51; Avigad 1967: 141, fig. 35; Rahmani 1994: 3).

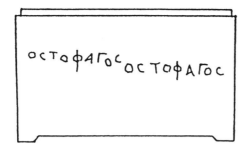

Figure I. Greek Inscription *Ostophagos* (after Avigad 1967: Fig. 35).

A similar term ὀστέον "osteon" occurs at Beth She'arim (Schwabe and Lifshitz 1974: no. 131).

- *Gloskoma* in Greek was a variant of γλῶσσκομον and was interpreted as a case for reed musical instruments (Liddell and Scott 1940 1:353. Klein 1908: 34, n. 2. Krauss 1910 1:398. 399, and n. 173). The term γλωσσκομον was found inscribed on a tomb wall in the Beth She'arim necropolis (Schwabe and Liftshitz 1974: no. 50, 78). In an inscription from Pamphilia *gloskomon* refers to a sarcophagus (Ormerod and Robinson 1910–11: 235). From these inscriptions and their contexts it is possible to conclude that the term *gloskomon* means burial or coffin (but see Meyers 1971: 53–54). The term נלוסקמא (*gloskoma*), which is probably a transliteration of the Greek into Aramaic, occurs several times in Rabbinic writings: נלוסקום (M. *Oho.* 9.15) and נלוסקום (T. *Oho.* 10.8), referring to thecoffin and its purifying laws (Meyers 1971: 55). The only place where the term דלוסקמא is connected with a container for collected bones is in Semaḥot 12.9. The same word דלוסקמא occurs once again in Semaḥot 3.2, where it refers to a child's coffin (Zlotnik 1966: 107, see note: "a small or simple casket, *aron*"). This term is spelled differently in each of the four citations presented.

The above data indicate that the Greek COPOC (*Soros*) in the Jericho inscription was the term for ossuary in use during the Second Temple period and is equivalent to ארון *aron* in Hebrew. *Ostophagos* (ὀστοψά-γος) may also have been used, but it was not the standard term for ossuary in Greek, as has been claimed (AvI-Yonah 1955: 799). The term נלוסקמא *gloskama* and γλῶσσκομον *gloskomon*, and its peculiar variants, when used in the context of secondary burials and bone collection is a later term used for coffin or burial, but not exclusively for ossuary, as this term is used in present-day Hebrew. However, it must be asked whether the term *gloskomon* means ossuary, i.e., a container for secondary burials. It may not necessarily refer to an ossuary, but to a box or a container ארון in the LXX or to burial or a coffin in the inscriptions.

Aramaic term for ossuary

The word חלת, חלתא is interpreted 'ossuary'; it appears on four Jerusalem ossuaries (in *status constructus* and the last one in *status emphaticus*):

An Aramaic protective formula on an ossuary lid from Jebel Hallat et-Turi mentions the word בחלתה (*Halat*) 'the ossuary' (Milik 1956–1957: 235, Inscription A1, Figs. 2, 3; Habermann 1956; Fitzmyer 1959; Rahmani 1994: 3).

The other inscriptions appear on ossuaries followed by the name of the deceased women buried in them (Fig. VII–6):

חלת שלום ברת שאול/די דשבחת שלום ברתה 'The ossuary of Shalom, daughter of Saul, who died from difficulties in child-bearing, Shalom her daughter' (Naveh 1970: 36–7; Rahmani 1994: 226; but see Fitzmyer and Harrington 1978: No. 88).

חלתא מרים ברת שמעון 'the ossuary of Miriam daughter of Shim'on' (Rahmani 1994: No. 502). חלת בלזמא 'Ossuary of Balzama' (Rahmani 1994: No. 461).

GLOSSARY

Arcosolium, arcosolia	*Arched niche, particularly to hold a coffin in a tomb.*
Distylos in antis	A façade with two columns flanked by two pilasters.
Halakha	Religious rules
Loculus, Loculi (*Kokh* in Hebrew)	burial recess hewn in the tomb walls. A loculus was semi-circular in shape and long (appr. 1.0 m. high, 2.0 m. long) enough to place in it a body or a coffin.
Miqveh	A ritual bath in which purification rites took place.
Mishna (M)	Collection of binding precepts which forms the basis of the Talmud and embodies the contents of the oral law. Compiled by Rabbi Judah Ha-Nasi, probably at Sepphoris, c. 200 CE.
Mortise and tenon joints	The coffin was assembled with mortised joints, that is, with wooden pegs called tenons which interlock with rectangular shaped cavities. The walls of the coffin were mortised to the four-corner posts and to the base of the gabled lid.
Ossilegium	An intentional act of collecting the bones of a relative individually and placing them into an ossuary (a specially prepared separate stone container), or into a separate heap of bones.
Talmud	Body of Jewish traditional law consisting of the Mishna and the Gemara. Two editions exist, the Jerusalem Talmud (JT) and the Babylonian Talmud (BT).
Tosefta (Tos.)	Collected corpus of traditions and teachings connected with the Mishna.

CHAPTER ONE

CEMETERIES

Several Jewish cemeteries have been found in the Land of Israel. Two main cemeteries of the Second Temple period are at Jerusalem and Jericho, and these furnish most of our data for funerary customs. Other smaller cemeteries were found around Jerusalem, in the Judean foothills, at 'En Gedi, Qumran, and some other sites in the Dead Sea area, and in the Galilee (Hachlili 2000c).

The necropolis was sited outside the town limits, in accordance with Jewish law. In the following sections the general outline and description of the cemeteries are summarized.

A. JERUSALEM

The Jerusalem necropolis consisted of tombs surrounding the city walls, all in important areas to the north, south, west, and east, concentrated in about a ring about five kilometers in circumference around the city limits of Jerusalem of the Second Temple period (Figure I–1) (Kloner 1980, 2000, 2001, 2003; Rahmani 1994; Zissu 1995; Geva and Avigad 1993; Kloner and Zissu 2003: 1–13). About 1000 tombs are known from excavations and surveys conducted in the last 150 years around the city (Table I.1). Few known tombs have been discovered within the Old City limits.

Table I.1: Tombs in Jerusalem

Area	No. of Tombs	%
North	309	38%
South	237	30%
East	124	16%
West	123	16%
Total	**793**	**100%**

Table I.1 (based on Zissu 1995: 149; Kloner and Zissu 2003: 10) indicates that the tombs were scattered all around Jerusalem, with

a much larger number in the north and south and fewer in the east
and west (Kloner 1980: 259–269; 2003: Table 1–2. On p. 33* he
mentions that approximately 950 Second Temple period tombs were
found, about 650 loculi tombs and 140 acrosolia tombs; Zissu 1995:
147–150; Kloner and Zissu 2003: 1–3). However, it is quite clear
that many of the original tombs were destroyed through the ages
and that the number of excavated and surveyed tombs (about 5%–10%,
Kloner 1980: 260) is only a fraction of the total number of tombs
in the Jerusalem necropolis. The most important areas of hewn tombs
were in the north and the south: in the north, they are in Kidron
Valley, Mount Scopus, the Mount of Olives, and the Hinnom Valley;
in the Sanhedriyya area many quarries for masonry were located,
and it was easier for tombs to be hewn and even ornamented.

The tombs were hewn and rock-cut out of *melekeh, mizi, helu* and
mizi ahmar of the *turon*. Others were cut in the chalk of *menuha* and
mishash formations. The monumental and decorated tombs were
carved in the harder Turonian rock and therefore were better preserved (Kloner 1980: 261–262, XVI; Kloner & Zissu 2003: 3–4).

Several crowded burial quarters and plots exist in the present-day
areas of Mount Scopus, the Mount of Olives ('Dominus Flevit'), and
French Hill, Sanhedriya and other parts of Jerusalem. The concentration and orientation of the tombs in Jerusalem indicate that they
were dispersed at random and depended on local topography and
the type of rock rather than on a central plan. They were generally hewn at a distance from the main roads out of the city.

There was no pattern in the arrangement of the tombs in specific
areas of Jerusalem, as is indicated by the various sites of the necropolis around all sides of the city (Figure I–1). The necropolis formed
a belt around the city that contained small agricultural settlements,
industrial terraces, fruit trees, guard houses, wine and olive presses,
as well as quarries, roads, aqueducts and pools. Various plants in
addition to the agricultural setting sometimes enhanced the sur-
roundings of the tombs (Kloner 1980: 262–270; Kloner and Zissu
2003: 11–13).

The majority of the tombs discovered in Jerusalem are small and
simple loculi tombs, as well as some acrosolia tombs; in many of
them burial in ossuaries was found, as well as a few sarcophagi.
Some of the tombs show continuous use and reuse by several generations, forming an intricate arrangement of burial chambers and

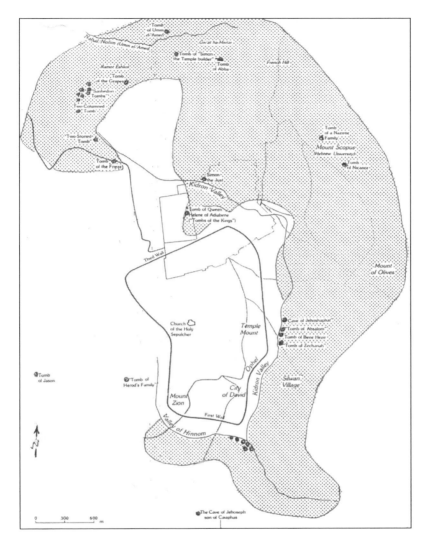

Figure I–1. Plan of the Jerusalem necropolis.

loculi. Many of the tombs were partly destroyed, plundered, and looted through the ages.

A group of monumental decorated rock-hewn tombs (see Chap. II) were discovered in Jerusalem: the Kidron Valley group consists of the tomb of Zechariah, the Bene-Ḥezir tomb, and the Monument of Absalom; the Jason Tomb and the Tomb of Helen and others probably belonged to prominent Jerusalem families; some have a memorial or *nefesh* in the shape of a pyramid or tholus standing above the ground and others have richly ornamented facades, while other tombs have a chamber wall faced with ashlars. The lavish ornamentation not withstanding, burial was probably similar to that of the simpler, undecorated loculi tombs. Many of the discovered tombs were found in disarray and looted.

During the Persian and early Hellenistic period Jerusalem Jews buried their dead in field and cist tombs (Zissu 1995: 170–172). A few such tombs were found in Jerusalem, perhaps indicating a simpler way of burial. The Jerusalem Jews also continued the use of bench tombs of the First Temple period. Zissu further suggests, that the Jewish cemetery of Jerusalem in this period was in the areas of Mamilla, Ketef Hinnom, and Mount Zion, to the west and southwest of Jerusalem.

Several tombs hewn into the soil, shaft ("dug-out", similar to the Qumran tombs) and field tombs, were found in several locations in Jerusalem (Kloner and Zissu 2003: 46–47). Two shaft tombs covered with stone slabs were discovered in East Talpiot, in proximity to other chamber tombs. In one of the shaft tombs the body of a male was found (Kloner and Gat 1982: 76).

Beth Zafafa (Zisso 1996, 1998) is a cemetery containing about 49 shaft graves, of which 41 were excavated (Figure I–2). The tombs date from the end of the Second Temple period to the Bar Kokhba period (possibly some of the tombs were also in use during the Roman and Byzantine periods).

The graves are hewn shaft tombs, half of them oriented north-south, the other half east-west; all are marked by stone tablets. In most tombs only one body was interred. The form and size of the tombs, as well as the custom of individual burial, are similar to the situation in the Qumran graves (see below).

B. Jericho

The Jericho cemetery is located on the eastern slopes of a chain of limestone hills bordering the Jordan valley on the west (Pl. I–2), not far from the winter palaces of the Second Temple period and west of the presumed site of the town of Jericho at that time (Hachlili and Killebrew 1999; several tombs were discovered in earlier exca-

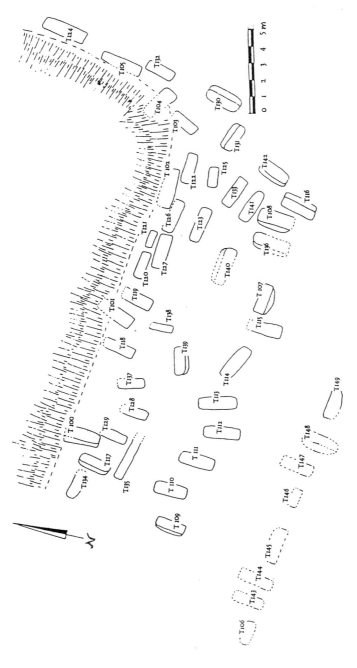

Figure 1-2. Beth Zafafa cemetery.

vations in Jericho: Bennet 1965). The borders of the cemetery seem to be Hill H in the south and Hills G and F (the two slopes of Wadi Tasun, below the Quruntul monastery) in the north. The hills are of different sizes and shapes: some are eroded and bare, such as Hill C, while others are covered with soil, dust, and debris. About 103 tombs were surveyed and excavated (Table I–2).

Table I.2. Jericho Tombs

Hills	A	B	C	D	E	F	G	H	Total
Excavated tombs	3	2		21		4	4	1	**35**
Robbed, surveyed tombs	3		32	2		3	5		**45**
Unexcavated tombs	1	2		4	12			4	**23**
TOTAL	**7**	**4**	**32**	**27**	**12**	**7**	**9**	**5**	**103**
Other tombs	1			1					**2**
One-kokh tombs	2		5	8	3	1	6		**22**
Type I tombs, burial in coffins				14					**14**
Type II tombs, bone collection				3		2			**5**
Type III tombs, burial in ossuaries	3	2	32	2				1	**40**

Most of the tombs were not exposed before the excavation, but the tombs on Hills C and H and on the lower levels of Hills G and F were discovered and robbed over the centuries (Figure I–3).

The cemetery extends over more than eight hills; although the excavations examined only a small part of this extensive area, rock-cut loculi tombs may have covered these hills almost completely. If this assumption is correct, the cemetery was huge and may have served the people of the entire Jericho region. These hills were chosen for burial because of the easily worked rock and because of their isolated location outside the population centers while still accessible from the city and the villages. The dry climate of the Jericho area preserved the tombs and their contents, including organic materials such as wood and leather.

The site of the Jericho cemetery was previously unknown and does not appear in any survey or description of the Jericho region. Survey

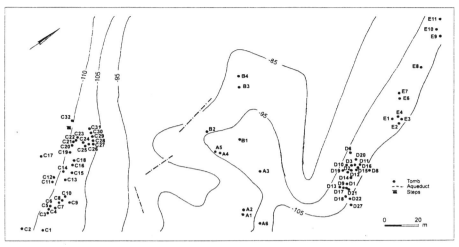

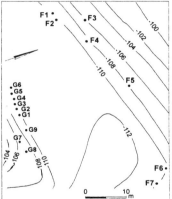

Figure I–3. The Jericho cemetery.

and salvage excavations were conducted at the Jericho site in 1975–
1979, when more than 100 tombs were recorded (see Table I–2).
Most of the surveyed tombs, especially those on Hill C, were robbed
and reused in antiquity and later times. The most important and
interesting of all the tombs in the cemetery is the tomb on Hill H,
named the 'Goliath family tomb' because of its inscribed ossuaries.

Eight hills (A–H) were surveyed and excavated in the Jericho cemetery
(Hachlili 1999: 5–44, Figs. II.1, 2). Hills A–E and H are located on
the east slope, west of the modern town of Jericho. Hill H probably

forms the border of the cemetery on the south, while Hills F and
G (Hachlili 1999: Fig. II.2), located respectively on either side of
Wadi Tasun, border the cemetery on the north.

On Hill A, seven rock-cut tombs were examined; of these, three
Type III tombs on the north slope were excavated; three others were
found robbed, and one was only surveyed. The entrances of all the
tombs faced north.

Hill B is located west of Hill A. Remains of the aqueduct from
'En Duyuq, which conducted water to the Herodian palaces of Jericho
(Tulul Abu el-Alayiq), can be traced along the top of the ridge. Two
tombs were excavated on the east side of the hill, with entrances in
the east. The roofs of these tombs had collapsed, resulting in debris-
filled tombs with few finds.

Hill C differs from the other hills surveyed or excavated in the
cemetery, because the bedrock is of a much harder stone than the
usual soft limestone, and because this is the only hill to the west of
the aqueduct, so that it runs through the cemetery; Hill C is the
southernmost and westernmost hill in the cemetery. All the tombs
on this hill have been robbed and looted continuously in antiquity
and until the present day.

Hill D (Hachlili 1999: Figs. II.21–22) is located to the north of
Hills A and B, between Hills A, B and E. A total of 29 tombs were
surveyed, most of which were excavated. All the excavated tombs
are located on the east-northeast slope, so that most of the tomb
entrances face east. About half of the excavated tombs were found
undisturbed in their original condition. Some of the excavated tombs
had only one *kokh*. Most of these tombs are grouped together and
probably constitute an expanded family complex. Most of the tombs
are one-*kokh* tombs. All consist of primary burials in wooden coffins,
with the exception of one tomb that was used for bone-collection
burials, stratigraphically and chronologically later than the tomb
complex.

Hill G consists of six one-*kokh* tombs, all robbed; only one tomb
was a three-*kokh* tomb on a higher level. No traces of coffins or
ossuaries were discovered in any of the tombs on Hills F and G.

Tomb H, the 'Goliath Family Tomb' (Hachlili 1999: 37–44, Figs.
II.67–83), is the most interesting in the Jericho cemetery. It had a
large courtyard with benches and an adjoining ritual bath (*miqveh*).
A corridor led to the tomb entrance, which was blocked by two

large stones reinforced with smaller stones. The first stone, which sealed the entrance, had been cut to fit the opening. This stone had a round hole in the right upper corner resembling a doorknob. The second, a rough rounded stone, rested against the first blocking stone, and together they hermetically sealed the tomb (Hachlili 1999: Fig. II.67–70). The entrance, built into the rock-cut opening in the hillside, consisted of a lintel and doorjambs. This is the only masonry entrance so far discovered in the Jericho cemetery. The tomb contained two connecting chambers. Chamber A had a standing pit, benches, eight kokhim and one bone repository, and its walls were covered with wall painting (see Chap. IV). A passage in the form of a *kokh* in the north wall connected Chamber A to the lower Chamber B.

Another tomb complex with a courtyard was excavated north of Wadi Quruntul, where several loculi tombs were uncovered (Bennett 1965: 521–530, Figs. 264–272). There were also several examples of secondary use of earlier tombs. Near the ancient tell, Kenyon uncovered shaft tombs, which had been reused in the Second Temple period. In Tomb G2, two small plain ossuaries were found. In Shaft Tomb G81, coffins and a leather pillow were discovered (Bennett 1965: Fig. 273). A group of simple graves also formed part of the Second Temple period cemetery. In one such grave (J41) a broken ossuary was found (Bennett 1965: 539, Fig. 271:4).

The Jericho necropolis salvage excavation and survey established the boundaries of the sixteen kilometer-long Second Temple period cemetery. The southernmost extent of the rock-cut loculi tombs was identified on Hills C and H; the tombs continue northward on Hills A, B, and D, until they reach Wadi Quruntul (Hills F and G), where burials were found on both sides of the wadi. Kenyon's excavations in the 1950s (Bennett 1965) indicate that the cemetery extended even farther north, past the tell of ancient Jericho. That part of the cemetery consisted of loculi tombs and reused shaft tombs and graves, containing wooden coffins or stone ossuaries.

Based on the surveys and excavations of the area, an estimated 250,000 people were interred in this cemetery during the first century BCE and through the first century CE.

The Jericho cemetery was located outside the town. On the hills flanking the Jordan Valley, approximately 120 tombs were discovered, all hewn loculi tombs, containing either primary burials in wooden coffins or secondary collected bone burials in ossuaries or in heaps.

The Jewish cemeteries of Jerusalem and Jericho of the Second Temple Period, as well as tombs in the Judean Desert, were located outside the town limits in accordance with Jewish law (M. *BB* 2, 9) and served the population of the surrounding area. Jews observed this prohibition against burial within the city boundaries, although in later sources exceptions are mentioned (e.g., JT *Naz.* 17, 5).

Open, rock-cut forecourts with benches are known from tombs in Jerusalem, some are small in size (Kloner 1980a: 210; Zissu 1995: 157). The courtyard of the 'Goliath' tomb (H) at Jericho, a large open courtyard with benches on three sides, was probably used for mourning and memorial services similar to the 'eulogy place' or house of assembly (Hachlili 1999: 37–38, Figs. II.68–69; Netzer 1999: 45–50, Figs. 78, 81, 82) mentioned in Jewish sources (BT *BB* 100b; Klein 1908: 51–52: Safrai 1976: 779).

Courtyards with benches dating to the third century CE are also found in the Beth She'arim Jewish necropolis and probably served a similar purpose (Avigad 1976a: 41–45, 81–82, Figs. 23–24, 35, 61, Pl. XXX:1). Comparable in plan, but differing in function, are the triclinia in the Nabatean cemetery at Petra (A. and G. Horsfield 1938: 31–39, Pls. 64:2, 66, 67:2, 71, 73) which served as a gathering place for commemorative meals on the anniversary of the deceased (but see Goodenough 1956 VI:169, 172, who suggests that Jews held similar feasts, an opinion refuted by Lieberman 1965: 509, 511).

In Jerusalem an aqueduct passed through the cemetery in close proximity to the tombs and even at times cut into them (Kloner and Zissu 2003: 7, Fig. 2). As noted, an aqueduct ran along the hilltops through the Jericho cemetery from 'En Duyuk (Na'aran) to ancient Jericho and the Hasmonean and Herodian palaces (Netzer 1977: 1). The ritual bath (*miqveh*) of the monumental 'Goliath' tomb was fed by this aqueduct. Jewish sources also mention aqueducts running through cemeteries (Sem. 14, 1 in Zlotnick 1966: 85, 165; M Yad. 4, 7; BT Hor. 13b, BT Meg. 29a; for a discussion of aqueducts in Jewish cemeteries see Patrich 1980).

The tombs found in the Jerusalem and Jericho cemeteries consist of rock-hewn tombs cut into the hillsides. Two basic tomb plans exist; one is known as the loculi-type (*kokhim*), the other, only in Jerusalem, as the arcosolia-type. Both types of plan are found in the

Jerusalem necropolis, but the Jericho cemetery consists of loculi tombs only. Occasionally, single-loculus tombs were constructed.

The form of the loculi tomb is of a square burial chamber, often with a pit dug into its floor deep enough for a man to stand upright. The rim of the pit forms three or four benches, along each side of the tomb. One to three arched loculi (1 m. high and 2 m. long) are hewn into three of the walls, the entrance wall being the exception.

The entrance to the tomb is rectangular; in Jerusalem it sometimes has a forecourt and an ornamented facade. The entrance is closed either by a blocking stone, sometimes in the shape of a large "stopper", or by mudbricks and small stones.

The evidence from Jericho proves conclusively that loculi tombs were first designed and used for primary, that is, permanent, burial in wooden coffins. The same tomb plan continued to be used in the case of ossuary burials. The origin of the plan for the rock-cut loculi tomb of the Second Temple period in Judea is to be found in Egypt, particularly in the Jewish tombs at Leontopolis, from as early as Hasmonean times.

Both types of burial, in the common loculi tomb, and in the arcosolia tomb, were in use at the end of the Second Temple period. These tombs served as family tombs, with provision for separate burial of each individual in the loculi, the arcosolia, and their containers.

C. 'En Gedi

Several tombs dated to the Second Temple period were excavated in the 'En Gedi area.

The Burial Caves of Naḥal David

Six small caves were used for first burials and re-interments (Avigad 1962b). In Caves 1 and 4 remnants of wooden coffins were discovered (one of them decorated with bone and wood inlays: see Chap. III). Other finds included a wooden bowl and cup, basket remnants, and fruits. Also a wrapped skeleton was preserved, still with leather shoes. In Caves 2 and 3 bones, pottery vessels, and bronze ladles were found. In Cave 5 several skulls, cooking pots, and a glass bottle were found. In the small Cave 6 only shards were discovered. These burials, probably of the inhabitants of 'En Gedi, are dated to the first century BCE, the Hasmonean period.

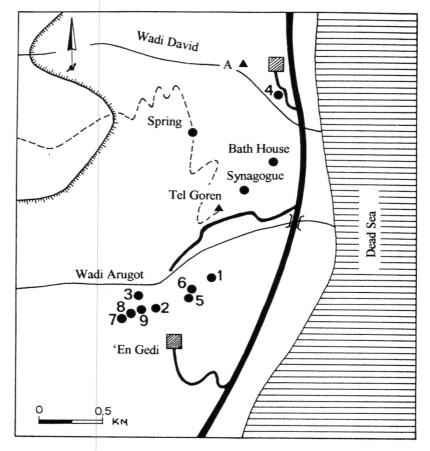

Figure I–4. 'En Gedi tombs.

Nine Tombs at 'En Gedi

The nine tombs found at 'En Gedi (Hadas 1994) were badly eroded;
some were found with the sealed entrance still intact (Figure I–4).
They consisted of loculi, a chamber, and central pit. The repository
of many skeletal remains was found. Most of the tombs contained
wooden coffins; one wooden ossuary was found in Tomb 3 and a
stone ossuary in Tomb 4.

About 40 coffins were found in the 'En Gedi tombs, different in
their construction from the technique used for the coffins at Jericho.
Other finds in the 'En Gedi tombs consisted of wooden vessels and

bowls; cosmetic items: ointment bowls, combs, a kohl tube; bronze objects: a jug, ladles, and kohl-sticks; pottery vessels; glass and stone beads; remains of palm mats and a basket; remains of textiles, possibly burial shrouds.

The 'En Gedi tombs are dated to the second-first centuries BCE. The burial customs in them exhibit several modes: the most prevalent was primary burial in wooden coffins. Others consisted of primary burial on the tomb floor with the corpse wrapped in mats or shrouds; secondary burial in wooden coffins; secondary burial in ossuaries. These modes of burial are based on few examples, so it is difficult to describe the actual practices and their chronological development. Note too that nothing was found to prove that the 'En Gedi burials were Jewish, except for finds and customs similar to those found at the Jewish cemeteries of Jerusalem and Jericho.

D. QUMRAN

The Qumran cemetery of the Second Temple period differs in burial customs from the Jerusalem and Jericho cemeteries. The site of Khirbet Qumran was established during the mid-second century BCE and destroyed in about 68 CE. The site was abandoned after an earthquake in 31 BCE (de Vaux 1953: 569),[1] and was eventually reoccupied (Period II), with repairs and rebuilding of the site around the time of the rule of Herod Archelaeus (4 BCE–6 CE). During this period under the rule of king Herod the inhabitants who left Qumran perhaps settled in Jerusalem possibly in the areas where similar tombs were discovered (see above Beth Zafafa). Magness (1995; 1998: 60) maintains that the settlement of Qumran was established later, in the mid-first century BCE (about 100 BCE) and was sectarian from the beginning.

The cemetery of Qumran consisted of a main and two secondary cemeteries (Figure I–5).

The main cemetery of Qumran, located about 35 m. east of the settlement, contains about 1200 graves arranged in ordered, regular and neat rows, separated by two paths into three plots (Pls. I–2, 3).

---

[1] But see Golb's (1995: 10) suggestion that the destruction could have been caused by a military attack during the Parthian invasion in 40 BCE.

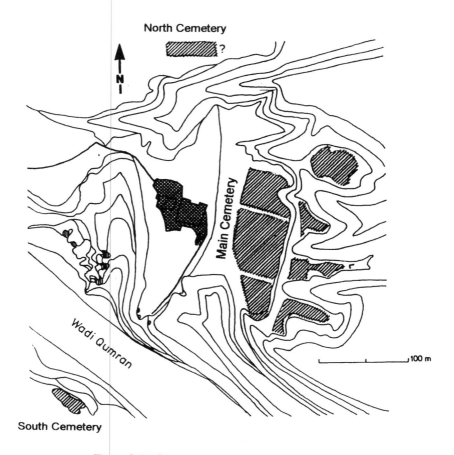

Figure I–5. Qumran cemeteries and tombs location.

East to the main cemetery smaller extensions of graves consist of the
North Hill and the North, Middle and South extensions or Fingers
(see Zangenberg 2000b, Kapera and Konik 2000 and Kapera 2000
for the number of tombs in Qumran). Recent survey and mapping
of the cemetery confirmed De Vaux estimate of about 1200 tombs
in the cemetery; see Eshel et al. 2002: 136, 141–143, note 4, Map
1, Table II).

Table I–3: Tombs in the Qumran Cemetery
(after Eshel et al. 2002: Table II)

	TOTAL	Oriented North-South	Oriented East-West	Identified by the GPR
Main Cemetery	**825**	727	3	95
North Hill	**81**	58	1	22
North Finger	**51**	50	1	0
Middle Finger	**129**	122	6	1
South Finger	**91**	42	43	6
TOTAL	**1177**	**999**	**54**	**124**

There are two secondary cemeteries, the northern (now destroyed) and the southern (some scholars argue the graves of this part are possibly Bedouin burials (see Chap. XI). The tombs are mostly oriented on a north-south axis.[2] The cemetery extends to the east of the site (Figure I–6). At the eastern edge of the Qumran Middle Finger a square building (de Vaux Building B) was re-excavated (Eshel et al. 2002: 147–153, Pl. III; Broshi and Eshel 2003: 31–33,71) dated to the Second Temple period and argued to be a 'mourning enclosure' used by the Qumran community.

Twenty-eight graves were excavated in the main cemetery, and seven more in the extensions (Tombs 1–8, 11–37). The northern cemetery contains twelve graves, of which two (T. 9, 10) were excavated. The south cemetery contains 30 graves of varying orientation, of which four (T. 1–4) were excavated; on the downward sloping hills seven more tombs were found with less regularity of orientation. A total of 56 tombs were excavated, 43 by de Vaux (1956: 569–575; 1973: 48–58), eleven by Steckoll (1968; but see Peuch 1998: 31 and Zias 2000: 240, note 56, for Steckoll unreliability) and two by Clermont-Ganneau (1873). Eshel et al. (2002: 140–141) were able to identify only thirty-six of De Vaux's tombs and one of Steckoll's, some other tombs were identified as having been excavated by grave robbers.

The proximity of the Qumran cemetery to the site, located about 35 m. away, is in accordance with Rabbinic law (M BB 2.9); the

---

[2] It should be noted, that the graves orientation is less consistent in the eastern extensions of the cemetery and in the secondary north and south cemeteries.

Figure I–6. Khirbet Qumran and the cemeteries.

distance of a cemetery from the site required for ritual purity is 50 cubits, which is about 25–30 m.[3]

The tombs and the interred at Qumran are oriented usually on the same north-south axis.[4] In the main cemetery area the excavated tombs contained males, while in the extended areas of the cemetery several skeletons examined were females and children. The recent data published by Eshel et al. (2002: App. A, Table V, which sum-

---

[3] Also Hachlili and Killebrew 1983: 110 and n. 3 p. 130; but see Golb (1994: 70; 1995: 34–5), who maintains that the cemetery is too close to the site: "it is impossible to believe that the purity-obsessed Essenes would build a cemetery so close to their settlement".

[4] The explanation suggested is that Paradise is located in the far north, and the dead will arise with their faces toward the north, walking on to the Heavenly Jerusalem (Kapera 1994: 107 and n. 47; Peuch 1993: 701).

marized the published results from the latest studies of the bones) report the identification of 24 males, five females and three children (see also Anthropological Table 6).

The Qumran north cemetery contained a group of 12 tombs, similar to the tombs in the main cemetery. Two (TA, TB) were excavated and contained one male and one female skeleton respectively.

The south cemetery consists of a group of 30 tombs of varying orientations. Four tombs were excavated; one contained a woman, the others children.

About 54 tombs oriented east-west are suggested to be Bedouin burials from the last centuries (Zias 2000; Eshel et al. 2002: Table V; Broshi and Eshel 2003: 32).

At the eastern edge of the middle extension or finger at the Qumran cemetery a square building (de Vaux Building B,) was re-excavated (Eshel et al. 2002: 147–153, Pl. III; Broshi and Eshel 2003: 31–33, 71) about 150 pottery body shards were found. The building is dated to the Second Temple period and argued to be a 'mourning enclosure', similar to the one at Jericho, for the use of the Qumran community. In the southern part of the building a pile of human bones identified as two women in secondary burial were discovered. Directly beneath these pile of bones (at about 3.5 feet) a male skeleton in primary burial oriented east-west was found, with a cooking pot above the legs and a couple of stones protecting the skull. The excavators date the burial of the two females and the male to the Second Temple period. Broshi and Eshel (2003: 31–33,71) identify the male skeleton buried in the building as the *mevaqqer* (overseer) an office referred to in the Dead Sea Scrolls; however, the orientation east-west and the cooking pot found with the deceased are not distinctive enough for this highly speculative identification.

The Qumran cemetery was used during the first century BCE until the end of Qumran in 68 CE. This dating is contemporaneous with the Qumran settlement community, which according to the pottery evidence was established only at the end of the second century BCE, probably around 100 BCE (Magness 1995).

The Qumran inhabitant's residence is in debate: Patrich (1994: 76) argues that two rooms on the second floor of the residential quarters could have served as dormitories. Magen and Eshel (1999: 328–335) maintain that their excavation points to the possibility that community members might have resided in the artificial caves dug in the marl terrace. They estimate that about twenty to forty artificial caves existed around in the Qumran settlement environs. These caves might have been occupied by one or more residents, which will also confirm the estimate of 150–200 inhabitants. The pottery found in these caves proves they were occupied during the first century BCE and the first century CE. The excavation has also found traces of tents, which might have been used for residence, for refugees or on the Sabbath (Magen and Eshel 1999: 336–339).

The community at Qumran possibly consisted of about 150–200 inhabitants (Broshi 1992: 113–4) or 50–70 inhabitants (Patrich 1994: 81–82). The cemeteries contains at least 1200 graves, and was probably used for about 190 years, the life period of the site. Nevertheless, it is also possible that the cemeteries of Qumran served as a central burial place for other similar sites in the area, as some scholars believe (Yadin 1983, I:324).[5]

A remarkable similarity can be detected in burial architecture between Qumran and the Nabatean cemetery at Khirbet Qazone in Jordan. The Qazone cemetery consists of over 3500 pillaged graves most of them oriented north-south, twenty-four were investigated, twenty-three of which were excavated. The cemetery is dated to the first and second centuries CE (Politis 1998b: 612, fig. 3; 1999, 2002).

The graves were dug into the natural al-Lisan marls, consisting of a single shaft with a side loculus covered by mud bricks. A few were constructed of stone cists. Each grave had a single burial, the bodies were laid out with their heads on the south side of the grave. No evidence of re-internment was detected. The interred included men, women and children in a balanced ratio. The corpses were well preserved. Some of the bodies were encased within decorated leather shrouds and reused textiles (mostly made of wool) raped around them (Politis 1998b: figs. 6, 7; 2002: 27–28, Figs. 7, 8, 11; Granger-Taylor 1999: 150, 160–161). Most of the textiles are Greek mantels, sleeveless Roman tunics, they are similar to slightly later textiles of the Cave of Letters and to the depicted dress in the Dura Europos synagogue wall paintings. A high proportion of the textiles found were used for children or babies. Most of the textiles were pieces of clothing, which were used as wrappings; but some were

---

[5] Bar Adon, 1981: 351, suggested that Qumran cemetery also served sites such as Khirbet el-Yahud and Rujm el-Bahr; But see Broshi 1992: 113.

made specifically for burial, such as decorated leather shrouds found in
seven excavated burials. Some grave goods were found: jewelry iron
bracelets, earrings, beads, a scarab; a wooden staff, a laurel wreath
and a pair of leather sandals were found in an adult male grave.

From the surface a few items were recovered: metal work, pottery and glass fragments of the 1st–2nd century CE. Five funerary
stelae from robbed-out tombs were discovered, four had engraved
rectangular signs (betyles or "Dusares blocks") and one was inscribed
in Greek. Two Greek papyri with Nabataean names were found by
tomb-robbers (Politis 1998b: 613, figs. 8–11; 2002: 27–28).

The Khirbet Qazone cemetery, with the possibility of comparable
period cemeteries at Khirbet Sekine, al-Haditha and Feifa, might
have belonged to the Nabatean community living near the Dead
Sea. Politis seems to identify Qazone as a Nabatean cemetery based
on its location roughly in Nabatea, on some finds like potsherds and
the stelae. Granger-Taylor (2000: 150) maintains that people buried
at Khirbet Qazone were ethnically mixed with no indication that
they were part of a particular religious grouping; tough the majority might have belonged to the local Nabatean population.

The interesting question is if there is any connection regional, ethnic
or cultural between the Qumran and the Qazone cemeteries (Shanks
1999). We are aware of connections between Jews and the Nabatean
in this period. However, it seems quite remarkable to find that both
Jews (Essenes?) and Nabatean buried their dead in the same manner
in this area. The possibility that both burial sites were Essene cemeteries or both Nabatean is unsustainable. Kapera (1995: 132) maintains that the Qumran cemetery "is an ordinary cemetery of the
period and area albeit a sectarian one". Zangenberg (1999: 214–217)
contends that the single shaft tombs are used by different groups in
the period with no proof that they are "Essene", nor are they a
regional feature as this type of graves were found not only in the
Dead Sea area but also at Beth Zafafa in Jerusalem (see also Zias
2000: 242–243). He further maintains that different types of burial
(single and multiple) were used at one and the same time in both
Jewish and Nabatean context; and that it is no longer possible to
consider this type of burial under one and the same religious concept. The Qumran single shaft tombs cannot prove that the inhabitants were Essene. Taylor (1999: 313) maintains that the shaft graves

reflect burial customs among the poor adopted by the Qumran community (see also Magness 2002: 96). Zias (2000: 243–244) suggests
that four shared criteria are needed to categorize a cemetery as
Essene: orientation of the tombs, the architecture of the graves, demographic disparity and few personal grave goods, all of which are
found in the cemeteries at Qumran and ʿEn el-Ghuweir (Hirschfeld
2003: 40 maintains that Qumran was the center of a rural estate
and the cemetery reflects a common burial practice of the period;
but see Eshel 2003: 59 and Broshi 2003: 64–5 who respond to
Hirschfeld's non-consensual theory).

The Qumran cemetery and the graves at other sites such as ʿEn
el-Ghuweir and Beth Zafafa indicate that the inhabitants there
employed different burial practices than those practiced by the inhabitants of Jerusalem and Jericho. The burial customs of Jerusalem and
Jericho were family oriented; burial was performed and sustained in
a family tomb while the Qumran type burial was a single individual burial with no indication of family context, probably a community burial. The form of the graves and the burial customs, as well
as the proximity to the site should be considered an essential factor
concerning the identification of the Qumran community in the Second
Temple Period (see Chap. XI). It seems much more research is
needed to comprehend and solve these issues.

E. ʿEN EL-GHUEWIR

The cemetery of ʿEn el-Ghuewir, where 17 tombs were excavated,
is located 800 m. north of a building (Bar-Adon 1977: 12–17). The
form of the tombs is similar to the Qumran tombs; their orientation is north-south, and each grave is marked by a heap of stones.
The interred lay supine. Remains of 13 men aged between 18 and
60–70, seven women aged between 18 and 34, and a child aged
seven were found. Some broken vessels and potsherds (a bowl and
three store jars) were found placed on the tombs. The shoulder of
a storage jar from tomb 18 was inscribed with the name (יהוחנן
Yehohanan) (Bar-Adon 1977: 17, figs. 21:3, 23). The dating of the
cemetery is first century BCE-first century CE, i.e., contemporary with
the Qumran cemeteries. The tombs' form is similar to the Qumran
tombs. Bar-ʿAdon maintains that the cemetery of ʿEn el-Ghuweir was
used by the settlement's occupants, and he asserts that the inhabit-

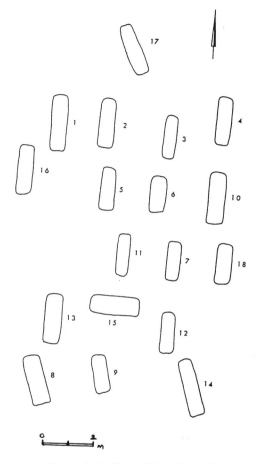

Figure I–7. ʿEn el-Ghuweir tombs.

ants of Qumran and ʿEn el-Ghuweir belonged to the same sect. Bar-Adon also believes that the large building at ʿEn el-Ghuweir served for ceremonial and assembly purposes much the same as the public center at Qumran. The community members probably lived in caves, tents, and booths. Some scholars have reservations about the relationship between Qumran and ʿEn el-Ghuweir.[6]

---

[6] de Vaux 1973: 89; Broshi 1992: 114–115, tested its pottery by neutron activation and the results are that there is no common source for the pottery discovered at the two sites; Golb 1995: 33–4 argues that the graves at ʿEn el-Ghuweir, like those at Qumran, are of the warriors who fought against the Roman army.

The cemetery of *Hiam el-Sagha* (Eshel & Greenhut 1993), located south of 'En el-Ghuweir, contains 20 shaft graves of which two were examined. Most of the tombs are oriented north-south; all are covered by stones. In one grave a 3–4-year-old child with a necklace of 34 glass beads was found; a 25-year-old man was interred in the second (Reshef & Smith 1993: 262–3).

Shaft tombs are quite rare in Jerusalem. Some are found as a single tomb among the common loculi tombs. Two graves were discovered: at East Talpiyot, one tomb oriented east-west (Kloner & Gat 1982: 171–2); and at Mamilla (Reich 1994: 117; Reich & Shukron 1994: 81).

The tombs at Beth Zafafa, East Talpiot and Mamilla in Jerusalem and at Hiam el-Sagha show no real proof that they are Jewish or "Essene" graves, except for their considerable similarity in form to the Qumran burials, which indicates a group with common burial customs (also Taylor 1999: 310–312. In Jericho, however, the shaft tombs are reused Middle Bronze tombs).

Some scholars suggest that these tombs were the burial places of individuals who belonged to the Dead Sea sect who lived in Jerusalem; others maintain that the shaft graves might have been in frequent use in Jerusalem and elsewhere, but did not survive as well as the rock-hewn tombs.

The Judean Desert Documents and burial practices

The Temple Scroll (11QT) is the only document of the Dead Sea Scrolls where burial customs are mentioned. It deals with the commandments regarding uncleanliness contracted from the dead, discussing (a) burial grounds (col. 48: 11–14); (b) the house of the dead person (col. 49: 5–21); (c) uncleanliness of a grave (col. 50: 5–9). The scroll bans random burials in dwellings and cities, instead one burial place should be assigned to every four cities (per tribe), so as not to pollute all the land. However, the archaeological finds indicate some different practices in this period: the cemetery of Qumran was found in the area east of the buildings; the excavated cemeteries of Jerusalem and Jericho of the Second Temple period are hewn on hills outside the cities.

Uncleanliness of a house, its residents and contents, and the manner of its purification and cleansing are treated in the Temple Scroll in detail (col. 49: 11–17). Uncleanliness occurs also through contact with or touching a dead man's bones or blood or a grave. Yadin asserts that the scroll intimates that all these proscriptions concerning uncleanliness contracted from the dead, usually applied to the priests, should apply to all the people of Israel.

There are no clear rules or laws indicated by the Dead Sea manuscripts. They seem, as observed by Yadin and Schiffman, to follow the usual Jewish laws with some modifications. The writings do not explain the significance of some of the Qumran burial customs.

F. Other Burials

The production of ossuaries ceased following the destruction of Jerusalem. *Ossilegium* was introduced by refugees from Jerusalem who settled in areas in the Jerusalem vicinity where the tombs contained ossuaries of a cheaper variety; soft limestone ossuaries were recovered from some sites in southern Judea, the Mediterranean coast and the Galilee. These later ossuaries are mostly plain; some later clay ossuaries were found (Rahmani 1994: 10; Sukenik 1930a: 124, No. 4, Pl. 1:3–3a). Various graves of the period were discovered in some areas around the country.

Tombs in South Judea

Judean foothills, South Mount Hebron ("Daroma")

The tombs in the cemeteries were sometimes loculi tombs, but later their plan changed into chambers with benches on which ossuaries and grave goods were placed. Such tombs, many of them with coarse sarcophagus-shaped ossuaries, were found in Yata, Eshtemoʻa, Thala, Ḥ. Kishor, Ḥ. Rimon, Susiya, Carmel, el-Aziz, and Ḥ. Anim. Dating of these tombs is difficult but probably most are of the second-fourth century CE. These sites indicate that the Jewish population either retained their land or perhaps returned to live following the Bar Kokhba revolt. The finds of the ossuaries from these tombs indicate that the practice of second burial in ossuaries survived in this area sporadically until the fourth century (Avigad 1967: 137–138; Kloner 1984; Rahmani 1994: 24; Guvrin 1997).

Eshtemoʻa

The cemetery at Eshtemoʻa, around the hills of the ancient Jewish settlement, contained tombs and mausolea. The only tomb published has an unusual plan with a central elliptical room. Twelve ossuaries were discovered, of which some were decorated and are typical to the Second Temple period; however, others are typical of the later more course ossuaries dated to the 2rd–3th century CE (Avigad 1967: 135–137; Zissu 2002: 166–168, Figs. 2, 3).

West Samaria, Migdal Tsedek

Several loculi tombs were discovered in the area of West Samaria at Migdal Tsedek, Aphek, and other sites. The tombs contained ossuary, pottery, and glass fragments, which designate a Jewish presence during the Second Temple period (Tsuk 1993).

Tel Goded, Judean Foothills

On the south and southwest slopes of Tel Goded in the Judean Foothills (Sagiv et al. 1998), salvage excavations and survey discovered plundered rock-cut tombs, among them 15 Iron Age II tombs, seven Hellenistic and early Roman tombs, and three Byzantine tombs. Of the four tombs excavated, Tombs 1 and 4 are dated to the first and early second century CE (down to the Bar Kokhba revolt):

Tomb 1 consists of a chamber with four loculi, three arcosolia, and one repository. The tomb contained fragments of eight plain ossuaries and fragments of jars and two lamps (see Table X–3.).

Tomb 4 consists of a chamber with eight loculi. The finds include fragments of five plain ossuaries, fragments of jars and bowls, and many lamps, glass bottles and beads (see Table X–3).

The finds in the tombs, such as the ossuaries, and their plan indicate that they probably belonged to Jewish families.

Several loculi tombs with ossuaries were discovered in the Galilee. The ossuaries are simple and coarse, and most of them are undecorated. The tombs were probably part of Jewish village cemeteries dated to the first–third century CE (Aviam 2002: 138, 180*).

Ḥorbat Ẓefiyya, Judean Shephelah

A rock-cut tomb was found as a result of salvage excavation at the eastern slope of Ḥorbat Zefiyya (Nahshoni et al. 2002). The tomb consists of two chambers: Chamber A with two regular and two shorter loculi, a passage leads to smaller Chamber B which has three regular loculi and a shorter loculus. Most of the finds were recovered from Chamber A, including thirty ossuaries all placed on the floor, 57 lamps, 13 cooking pots, etc. (see Table). Chamber B contained three ossuaries and few pottery vessels. The total finds in the tombs consisted of thirty-six ossuaries, ten of them decorated, 79 lamps, 21 cooking pots, three storage jars, two bowls, a jug, a piriform bottle and one glass bottle (Nahshoni et al. 2002: Table 1). The skeletal remains identify 49 individuals, most of them recovered from the ossuaries; the majority of them are children. Only three Greek inscriptions consisting of personal names were found on the ossuaries. The tomb is dated on the basis of the finds to the first–second century CE, probably up to the Bar Kokhba Revolt (132–135 CE), the ossuaries designate the tomb to a Jewish family which probably resided in the nearby village.

West Samaria, Migdal Tsedek

Several loculi tombs were discovered in the area of West Samaria at Migdal Tsedek, Aphek, and other sites. The tombs contained ossuary, pottery, and glass fragments, which designate a Jewish presence during the Second Temple period (Tsuk 1993).

Tell Abu-Shusha, Geva

Three tombs connected by a vaulted corridor were discovered, dated to the late first century BCE (Siegelman 1988). Although the tombs were robbed in antiquity many of the finds were still in them. The finds consisted of pottery: a large group of Eastern Terra Sigilata vessels – plates, bowls, and cups; cooking pots, unguenteria, lamps. Metal objects: three copper bowls, a fibula, a bell on a string, a key, copper parts of boxes, needles, an iron shovel, a spatula, an iron sickle, rings, and nails. Bone kohl stick and spoon, glass whorls; basalt bowls; a gold earirng, beads and shells.

Ḥuqoq

Four rock-cut loculi tombs were found, probably part of the cemetery of the ancient site (Kahane 1961). Tomb 1, dated to the first century CE, consisted of nine loculi; except for one loculus the tomb was robbed. Three undecorated limestone ossuaries and various objects, pottery vessels: ungunteria, lamps, glass bottles and beads, iron nails (Ravani and Kahane 1961: Fig. 3; see Table X–3). Tomb 2 was partly destroyed; it was probably in use for a short period. No objects were found in it. Tomb 3 was not opened. Tomb 4, dated to the second half of the first century CE (robbed and reused in the second-third century) had nine loculi. A few objects were discovered in the tomb most of them in the standing pit (Ravani and Kahane 1961: Fig. 4). Some skeletons, skulls, and bones were discovered.

Other Galilean Tombs

In a loculi tomb at Daburiyya four stone ossuaries were discovered (Aviam 2002a). The tomb is dated from the second half of the first to the third century CE. In the Kabul tomb two stone ossuaries, two clay ossuaries, and a clay coffin were found (Aviam 2002b). One ossuary from Kabul is decorated with a drilled design on its narrow sides (Aviam 2002b: 140–141, Fig. 5). Three ossuaries, one of them decorated, were found in a tomb at Sepphoris (Gal et al. 2002: 146–147, Fig. 2) with two other undecorated ossuaries. In tombs at Kafr Kanna two stone ossuaries and three clay ossuaries were discovered (Abu-Uqsa 2002: 156, Figs. 2–5).

Other similar stone ossuaries were found in Galilean sites. Most of them are simple and coarse, and only a few are decorated with similar designs to the earlier Jerusalem ones.

Burials in Caves in the Judean Desert

The Cave of the Skeletons, Masada: (Yadin 1965: 90–91). A pile of about 25 skeletons and bones (of men, women, and children) was found above objects such as pottery and fragments of mats and remnants of food. They seem to have been tossed down haphazardly, probably at the end of the Masada siege in 73 CE.

Several caves of Nahal Hever included burials, the remains are considered to belong to Jews who found refuge in these caves during the Second War against the Romans, the Bar Kokhba War (133–135 CE).

The Cave of Skulls (Cave 32), a secondary burial grave of seven skulls piled together and gathered bones beside them (Aharoni 1961b: 18).

The Cave of Horror (Cave 8). Several graves were found in this cave, with about 20 corpses including women and children (Aharoni 1961a:

161; 1962: 195–199). The finds consisted of fragments of cloth and two iron awls which were found beside the pelvis of a complete skeleton; ostraca, probably connected with the graves; three fragments of parchment with Hebrew writing. The skeletal remains correspond of 21 individuals, five males, five females and 10 children, one unidentified (Nathan 1961: 171–172). Pottery, spindle whorls and fragments of wooden combs were found in the cave (Aharoni 1962: 195–196).

The Cave of Letters. Burial Niche 2, in the eastern wall of Chamber III, contained secondary burials in three groups: (1) three baskets, each of which contained several skulls; (2) a group of graves, in which some of the bones were wrapped in cloth; (3) a single grave covered by cloth. Bone remains were found of nine women, four men and six children (Yadin 1961: 37–38; 1963: 34, 36). Some of the graves were of women and children. The graves indicate that the remains were collected and placed in and among the baskets. It is possible that the skeletons were collected by refugees. Among the finds in the cave was a purse which contained the archive of documents of a women named Babatha, some balls of linen thread a bronze mirror and its wooden case. Another mirror was found in some other area in the cave (Yadin 1963: 34–39, 125, 256). Another archive of a women Salome Komaise was found in the cave (Cotton 1995). Other finds in the cave included spindle whorls, wooden combs and beads as well as textiles, scarves, a hairnet (Yadin 1963: 130–131, 244–248).

The graves in the Judean Desert caves indicate that they were not part of organized or regular cemeteries, like those of the Second Temple period.

As the skeletal remains from these graves showed no signs of violence, the assumption is that they died of hunger and thirst during a long siege at the place they were hiding, probably in the second century CE, in connection with the Bar Kokhba War.

CHAPTER TWO

ARCHITECTURE OF ROCK-CUT TOMBS

Funerary Architecture, the nature and types of the tombs, the grave
plan and construction, as well as specific aspects of tomb structures
are discussed in this chapter. The architectural style of the Jewish
burial structures in the Jerusalem and Jericho necropoleis has features, elements of planning, and ornamentation in common with burial types of neighboring cultures, primarily of Greco-Roman origin.
However, the general composition and some details of the decoration are distinctive to the Jerusalem necropolis (Avigad 1950–51: 96).
The main groups of monuments characteristic of the Jerusalem and
Jericho tombs are distinguished by type and style. Their plan and
construction are outlined in the following sections.

A. Monumental tombs: Grand monumental structures, sepulchral
   rock-cut monuments above the ground or adjacent to the tomb's
   facade, with a complex of underground burial chambers. Some
   examples are only found in Jerusalem.
B. Tombs with ornamented façades.
C. Loculi tombs: Rock-cut underground tombs are the most common type of burial in all cemeteries. The rock-cut tombs found
   include tombs with chambers and loculi, with chambers only, or
   with loculi only.
D. Arcosolia tombs: These have chambers and arcosolia.

A. Monumental Tombs

Monumental tombs in Jerusalem are grand monolithic structures consisting of a sepulchral rock-cut monument above the ground with a
complex of underground burial chambers. They date to the Second
Temple period (second century BCE to first century CE). The style of
these monumental tombs is a mixture of classical Greco-Roman features and Egyptian features such as pyramids and cornices. However,
many details of decoration and composition are distinctive of the
necropolis of Jerusalem.

The ornamentation of the monumental tombs reveals the existence of a composite style, which sometimes combines the classical and Oriental, as in the Tomb of Zechariah, or even three styles. An example is the Monument of Absalom, which has a Doric frieze, Ionic capitals, and an Egyptian cornice (see Chap. IV).

The Greek distylos in antis (i.e. two columns flanked by two pilasters) characterizes several monumental tombs in Jerusalem such as: Bene Ḥezir, Tomb of Helene, Umm el-Amed, the Columns-Tomb near the tombs of Sanhedrin (see below). All the columns in these tombs were rock hewn, except for the Tomb of Nicanor where the pair of pilasters were built of stone (see below).

The monumental tombs of the Kidron valley and two others – Jason's Tomb and the Tomb of Queen Helene of Adiabene – are characterized by a partly rock-hewn and partly built free-standing monument (the *nefesh*) either above or beside the tomb's façade (see Chap. VIII). The monument usually has a pyramid or tholus surmounting a cube-shaped base.

Monumental Tombs in the Kidron Valley

A group of monumental tombs, located in the Kidron valley (Avigad 1954; Rahmani 1981: 46–48; Barag 2003) consists (from south to north) of the Tomb of Zechariah (late first century CE), the Bene Ḥezir tomb (dated to the Hasmonean period, second – early first century BCE), and the Absalom tomb (first century CE) with its adjacent Tomb of Jehoshaphat (Figure II–1; Pl. II–1). All the tomb names, except for Bene Ḥezir, later appellations from folklore.

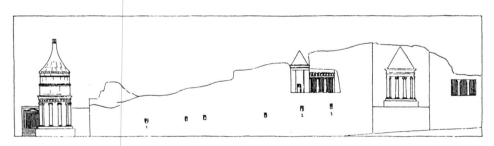

Figure II–1. Monumental tombs in the Kidron Valley.

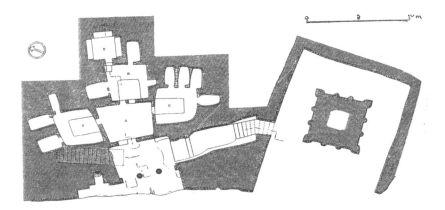

Figure II–2. Plan of the Bene Ḥezir and the Zechariah tombs.

The Bene Ḥezir tomb (the Sons of Ḥezir) is a rock-hewn tomb, consisting of a porch with a Doric style façade (Pl. II–2), a main chamber with three chambers branching off it, each with loculi; another small chamber has arcosolia on three sides (Avigad 1954: 37–78; Barag 2002: 39–44, 47; 2003: 79–95). A flight of stairs from the porch leads to the passage connecting the tomb with the nearby Tomb of Zechariah (Figure II–2). The tomb's porch facade is distylos in antis, with two baseless Doric columns between engaged antae crowned by an entablature with a Doric frieze. The tomb had another façade – a *nefesh* – attached to the side of the Doric façade (Figure II–3c), its hewn part including a faux entrance and a faux hexagonal window that have survived.

A first-century Hebrew inscription is incised in the architrave of the porch façade. It gives the names of several members of a family of "priests of the Sons of Ḥezir" (see Chap. V).

This monument is not only chronologically earlier than the others, its Doric ornamentation differs in that it is not in the composite style characteristic of the other Jewish tomb facades. The *nefesh* is hewn next to the tomb's façade perhaps similar to the hewn structure at Herod's tomb (see below). The arcosolia end chamber might have been a later addition to the original tomb dating to the first century CE. The Bene Ḥezir tomb is the earliest of the Kidron Valley tombs and probably belongs to the end of the Hasmonean period, to the latter half of the second century BCE.

The Tomb of Zechariah is a freestanding, solid, monolithic monument with a three-stepped base and no opening, to the south of the Bene Ḥezir tomb (Avigad 1954: 79–90; Barag 2002: 44–45; 2003: 95–99) (Figure II–3a; Pl. II–3). The tradition that it was the tomb of the prophet Zechariah gave it its name. The monument consists of two parts: a cube-shaped building rising on three steps, surmounted by a pyramid with a square base; the corners of the cornice are broken and might have once held metal spirals, a similar ornament might have issued from the pyramid's apex. The monument is decorated with an Egyptian cornice carried on engaged Ionic columns on all its four sides, with pilasters and attached quarter columns in the corners.[1]

This monument was intended not as a tomb but as a memorial, a *nefesh*, a sepulchral monument , either of the Bene Hezir tomb or more likely of a nearby unfinished tomb to the southeast. The Tomb of Zechariah is dated to the second half of the first century BCE.

The Monument of Absalom is named following the Jewish tradition in II Sam. 18, 18: "Now Absalom in his lifetime had taken and set up for himself the pillar which is in the King's Valley, for he said; I have no son to keep my name in remembrance; he called the pillar after his own name, and it is called Absalom's monument to this day".

The 'Monument of Absalom (7.00 × 6.80 m., and 20 m. high) has two parts (Pl. II–4):

(1) A lower rock-hewn square cube decorated with engaged Ionic columns bearing a Doric frieze and crowned by an Egyptian cavetto-cornice. This substructure contains a small chamber with two acrosolia and an entrance; this part of the monument is the actual tomb (Avigad 1954: 91–127, Figs. 49–75).
(2) An upper part built of ashlars consists of a round drum in the form of a pedestal topped by a concave conical roof, of Hellenistic-Roman style, built of ashlar stones crowned by a petalled flower. This *nefesh* was built as a type of tholus (Figure II–3b). This upper part was the *nefesh* for the lower tomb monument, and possibly also for the adjacent Tomb of Jehoshaphat (Avigad 1954: 112–117; Figs. 69–70, 72).

---

[1] The small hewn chamber under the monument should be seen as part of a chapel built in the 4th century (Rahmani 1981: 48).

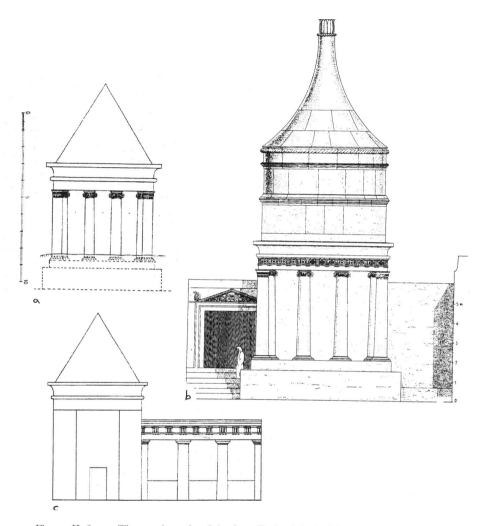

Figure II–3a–c. The tomb and *nefesh* of: a. Zechariah; b. Monument of Absalom
west façade; c. Bene Ḥezir.

The Tomb of Jehoshaphat is a family tomb complex of rock-hewn chambers (Avigad 1954: 134–138). It has an entrance hall and seven
chambers, with several loculi, arcosolia, and niches (Figure II–4). A
flight of steps attached to the Monument of Absalom leads to the
entrance of the Tomb of Jehoshaphat, and it is apparent that both
were hewn at the same time and according to a single plan. The large
entrance is surmounted with an ornamented pediment (see below).

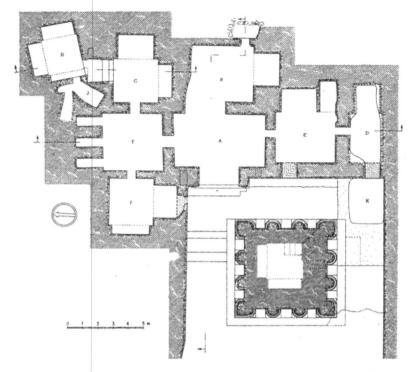

Figure II–4. Plan of the Tomb of the Monument of Absalom and the Tomb of Jehoshaphat.

The Monument of Absalom and the Tomb of Jehoshaphat are dated to the first century CE.

Jason's Tomb

Jason's Tomb in the western part of modern-day Rehavia, Jerusalem, is named after the person mentioned in the Aramaic inscription found on the porch wall (Rahmani 1967; 1981: 45–6). The tomb has three courts: a forecourt with an arched gateway built of ashlar, an ashlar-lined outer court, and an inner court entered through a heavy stone door. The porch entrance has a *mono-stylos in antis* facade, that is, a single Doric column located between two pilasters (on some fragments of a Corinthian capital and pilaster capital; see Foerster 1978). The tomb consists of two chambers: Chamber A has eight loculi, Chamber B served as a communal charnel. Both were originally sealed (Figure II–5).

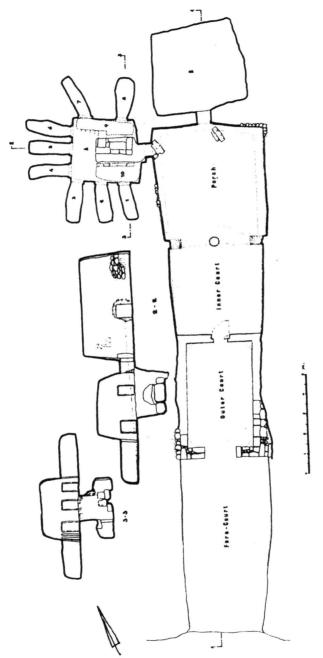

Figure II–5. Plan of Jason's Tomb.

The tomb is topped by a pyramid (Pl. II–5), of which only some
of the stones were discovered. The porch wall bears several charcoal drawings of ships, menoroth, and a stag, as well as several
Aramaic and a Greek inscriptions (Chap. V). A drawing of ships
and graffiti (see Chap. IV) on the porch's long wall seem to identify Jason, the father of the family whose tomb this was, as a war
captain in the days of King Alexander Jannaeus. Pottery vessels, mirrors, and coins were found in the tomb (see Chap. X), which is
dated to the Hasmonean period at the beginning of the first century BCE; the tomb was apparently looted in Herod's time, but continued to be in use until the early first century CE.

Tomb of Queen Helene of Adiabene

The so-called 'Tomb of the Kings' has been identified as the Tomb
of Queen Helene of Adiabene (a kingdom in northern Mesopotamia),
who with her family converted to Judaism during the reign of Claudius; they then settled in Jerusalem and built several palaces. Queen
Helene and two of her sons were buried there in a magnificent tomb
built ca. 50 CE. The tomb is mentioned already in antiquity by
Josephus (*Ant.* 20.17–95), who states that the Queen and her son
were buried "at the pyramids" (also Pausanias VIII, 16,4–5). The
tomb is the largest and most impressive tomb in Jerusalem (discovered in 1863 by de Saulcy, who attributed it by mistake to the Kings
of Judah, and named it 'Tomb of the Kings' (Kon 1947; Vincent
and Steve 1954: 346–362; Avigad 1956: 339–341; Rahmani 1981:
48–49; see also Clarke 1938). The tomb was robbed throughout the
ages and some of the remains were stored in the Louvre Museum,
Paris.

The tomb is situated north of the present day Old City. IT has
a rock-hewn forecourt, originally faced with dressed stones and a
wide staircase down to the hewn main courtyard, inner court and
porch (Pl. II–6). The tomb's porch façade is distyle in antis, with
Ionic columns. The tomb consists of a porch and a large main
entrance chamber, leading to eight chambers with niches and arcosolia (Figure II–6). A rolling-stone sealed the entrance to the tomb,
accessible through a depression in the porch's floor. Some unusual
mechanism moved the stone (Kon 1947: 60–63).

Three small pyramids similar to those found on the Tomb of
Absalom were originally located on top of the tomb (described by
Josephus in *Ant.* 20.95). Several stones belonging to one of the pyra-

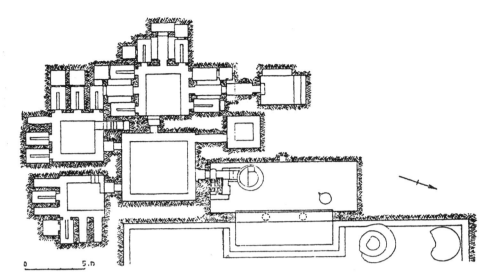

Figure II–6. Plan of the Tomb of Queen Helene of Adiabene.

mids' were discovered and partly reconstructed (Kon 1947: 74–77). The tomb façade was reconstructed (Vincent 1954: Fig. 100; Mazar, B., 1975: 231) with three monuments of *nefeshot* for Helene and her two sons (Figure II–7a, b).

The tomb has an impressively elaborate decorated façade. The opening is distyle in antis; enclosing this facade is an unfinished decorative band with leaves, fruit, and pine cones with a rosette in the centre. Surmounting it is a Doric frieze whose central motif is a triple bunch of grapes flanked by a pair of wreaths and a pair of acanthus leaves (see Chap. IV).

The tomb contained several sarcophagi (Chap. III). An undecorated one bore the inscription 'Queen Sadden' and had an elaborately decorated lid (Chap. V).

The Tomb of Herod's Family

The tomb (discovered in 1892 on the Nicophoria monastery site: Schick 1892: 115–120; Macalister 1901: 397–402; Avigad 1956: 346–347; Kloner 1980: No. 14–1) consists of an entrance sealed by a large rolling-stone leading into a small central hall with a barrel-vaulted ceiling, with four chambers around it. Their sealing stones were found lying about in the tomb. The chamber walls are faced with ashlar stones (Figure II–8a; Pl. II–7).

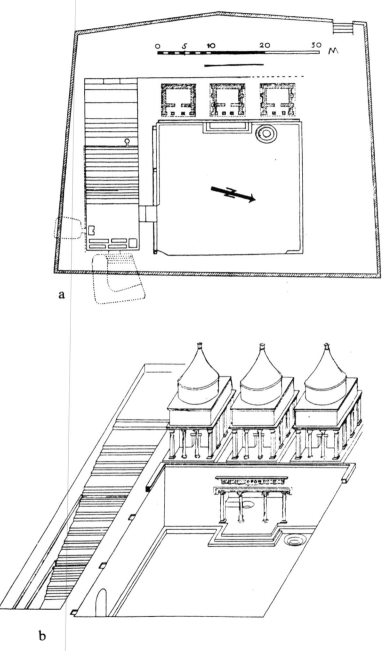

a

b

Figure II–7. Tomb of Queen Helene of Adiabene: Reconstruction of Façade.

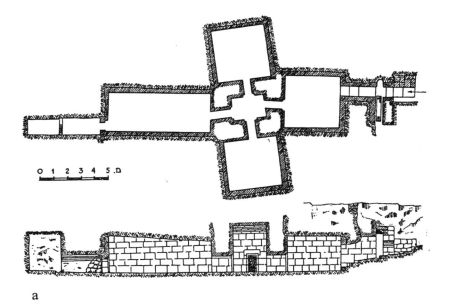

Figure II–8a, b. a. Plan of the Tomb of Herod's Family; b. Plan of the
Nazirite family tomb.

The plan is different from that in the other tombs but comparable to the plan of the Nazirite family tomb, Figure II–8). Discovered next to the tomb in front of the entrance were remains of foundations of a structure conjectured to be a monument base, probably the tomb's *nefesh*, Two stone sarcophagi were within, one plain, the other ornamented with a floral scroll and rosettes, and it had no lid; several decorated lids; were all found in the west chamber.

This tomb was identified as that of Herod based on Josephus' description (*War* 5, 108; 507); however, as King Herod was buried according to Josephus at Herodium it probably served some other member of his family.

Another claim for Herod's tomb was made for the scanty remains of a structure faced in *opus reticulatum* discovered north of Damascus Gate, Jerusalem. The excavators (Netzer and Ben-Arieh 1983: 171) thought it to be a monument and mausoleum, because of its location outside the city-walls. They further suggested that this mausoleum, like the round tomb of Augustus, was possibly Herod's burial monument mentioned by Josephus (*War* 5, 108, 507).

The debate over the burial place of Herod is still intense. Josephus (*Ant.* 17.195–199; *War* 1.667–673) describes the death of Herod at Jericho and that his body was carried in a funeral procession to Herodium but without specifying the exact the burial location. However, his tomb at Herodium was not found. Though scholars generally agree the tomb should be sought after in Herodium the main argument is if to locate it in Upper or Lower Herodium:

(1) The case for Herod's burial place in Upper Herodium is based on historical and archaeological evidence (Roller 1998:167). Magness (2001) maintains that the palace at Upper Herodium ceased to function after Herod's death, and the last reference to Herodium was the description by Josephus of his burial there. The next mention of the site is when rebels resided there at the time of the First Jewish War against the Romans (*War* 4.518–520, 555). Magness further argues that the absence of fine pottery ware types of the First Century CE at Upper Herodium support the contention that the site ceased to function after Herod's death, thus supporting the belief that Herod's tomb is inside Upper Herodium.

(2) Netzer and others (Netzer 2001: 114–116; Burrell and Netzer 1999: 709–711) locate Herod's tomb in Lower Herodium possibly in the area of the "Monumental Building". They argue that the domestic quarters at the Palace of Upper Herodium preclude the

possibility of Herod's tomb in that area. Hopefully the discovery of Herod's tomb some day will solve these arguments.

A tomb at Nicophoria located east of the Tomb of Herod's Family (Kloner 1980: No. 14–2; 1985a) contains four rooms and has a fifth external room, which served as an entrance; ossuaries and sarcophagi fragments were discovered in the rooms' fill. The entrance on the eastern side was faced with ashlar stones. The entrance to the tomb (between rooms I and II) was closed by a round rolling-stone. It was also an ornate and large tomb similar to its neighbor, the Tomb of Herod's Family.

The Nazirite Family Tomb

A burial-vault tomb on Mt. Scopus consists of a central chamber (I) and three smaller burial chambers (II, III, IV) branching from it (Figure II–8b; Pl. II–8). The entrance to the tomb (with its original sealing stone in place) is on the tomb façade but not on the axis of the upper arch; its the lintel is unusual in shape (Avigad 1971).

The central chamber had a barrel vaulting. Three openings lead to the burial chambers, originally closed by heavy stone slabs found lying on the floor in front of its respective openings.

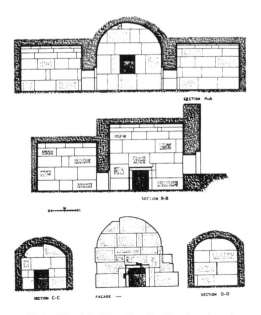

Figure II–9. The Nazirite Family Tomb, elevations.

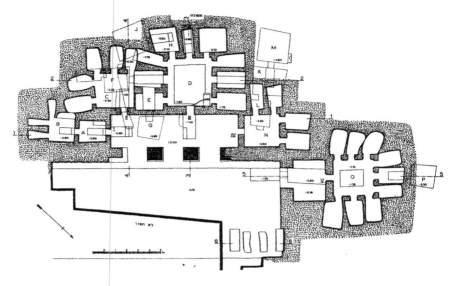

Figure II–10. Plan of the Tomb of Nicanor.

The walls and ceiling of the chambers are built of ashlar stones
(Figure II–9), and this fine masonry is comparable to the tomb of
Herod's family (above, Figure II–8a).

The Tomb of Nicanor

A large hewn tomb on Mount Scopus consists of a court, a porch,
and four burial hall-chambers with wide loculi or small chambers;
two of the entrances to the chambers are on floor level and two
descend under it (Avigad 1967: 119–125). Another hall-chamber was
hewn north of the court with a standing-pit and loculi (Figure II–10b).
The distylos in antis façade of the porch has two pillars, partly hewn
and partly built with ashlar stones, with no trace of an entablature.
The pillars were built not hewn out of the rock.

The finds contained some pottery, lamps, and many iron nails,
one sarcophagus and seven ossuaries, four of them decorated (Avigad
1967: 124, Pl. 21:2).

One of the ossuaries (now at the British Museum) is inscribed with
a bilingual inscription, referring to Nicanor of Alexandria, who
donated the famous door of Herod's Temple known as the 'Gate of
Nicanor' (see Chap. V).

The tomb apparently belonged to a famous and prominent Jewish family, whose head, Nicanor of Alexandria, was possibly buried in this tomb. Based on the inscription, the tomb is dated to the mid-first century CE.

B. Tombs with Ornamented Facade

The sepulchral monuments in the Jewish necropolis of Jerusalem have several characteristic features in their architecture and decoration. A feature common to many monuments is a Greek distylos in antis and ornamented façade (see also Chap. IV).

The façades of the tombs are classified by a typological not chronological survey, according to their main architectural features (following Avigad 1947, 1950–51). Their appearance from plain front to highly decorated facades is reviewed.

Classification of Rock-cut tombs by their façade ornamentation

Tombs entrances have several types of façade ornamentation. The most common façades in the necropolis of Jerusalem are:

1. Tomb entrance plain façade, unornamented
2. Tomb entrance moulded façade with the addition of a vestibule
3. Entrance façade ornamented with entablature and antae
4. Entrance façade with moulding and pediment
5. Columned porch (distylos in antis) façade with ornamented entablature
6. Columned porch (distylos in antis) façade with unornamented entablature
7. Tomb façade with three entrances

1 Unornamented, plain entrance in the center of the tomb façade; entry was directly from the forecourt. Some tombs had an additional porch; some tomb openings are surrounded by moulded stepped fillets (Figure II–11a; Avigad 1950–51: Fig. 1a, b, 2).

1.1. *Sanhedriya.* A large group of tombs was discovered at sanhedriya by the northern necropolis of Jerusalem (Pl. II–9) (Rotschild 1952; Rahmani 1961: 93–104).

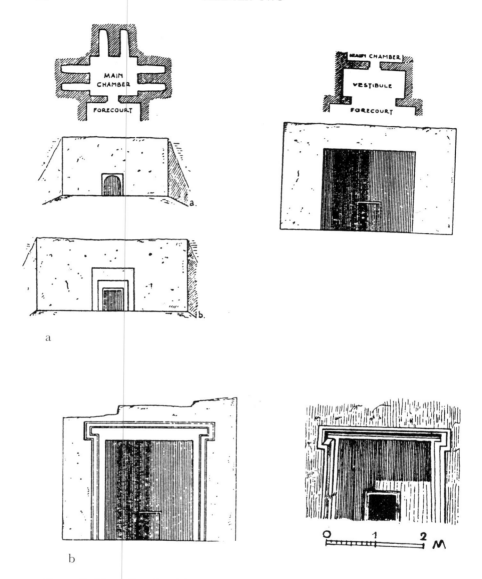

Figure II–11. a. Façade with small entrance; b. Façade with moulded frame.

Sanhedriya Tomb VII (Rotschild 1952: 33–34, Pl. VI, 7, VIII, 2, X, 1–2; Rahmani 1961: 120; Kloner 1980: 113–114, No. 25–7, Pls. 3–4) is part of three connected tombs, V, VI, VII. The tomb had a large forecourt leading to a vestibule, its opening surrounded by stepped fillets enhancing the function of the entrance.

2   Facade surrounded by a moulded frame appears in some tombs with a vestibule, these jambs and lintel emphasize the appearance of a gate (Figure II–11b; Avigad 1950–51: Fig. 3). Examples include the Grape tomb (4 below) and a tomb in the Hinnom Valley with a similar façade (Zissu 1995: 65, Fig. 35; Tomb 10–70).

2.1. *Ferdûs er-Rûm, Tomb in Hinnom Valley.* This tomb is large and elaborate, with several chambers, loculi, and arcosolia. The chambers had a domed ceiling. A small rolling-stone sealed the entrance to the inner chamber.

Some doorways have a moulded entrance surmounted by a gable (Figure II–12) (Macalister 1901b: 147–8, No. 38; Avigad 1956: Fig. 25; Kloner 1980: No. 10–8).

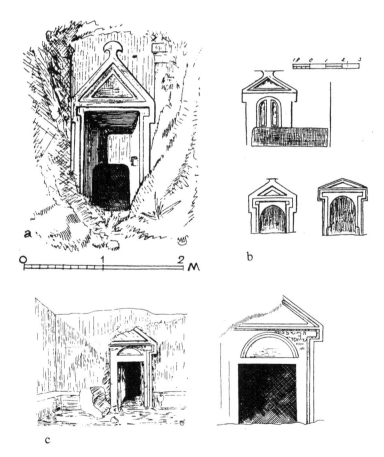

Figure II–12. Façade with moulded frame surmounted by a gable.

3   Tombs with decorated façades.

A few of the rock-hewn Jerusalem tombs have a façade with decorated entablature.

3.1. *The Frieze tomb*. The entrance of the tomb has a decorated façade with an entablature containing an architrave, a Doric frieze and a cornice carried by two *antae* flanking the opening (Pl. II–10) (Macalister 1902: 118–120; Avigad 1950–51: 100, Fig. 5; Kloner 1980: 108–109, No. 24–12). The Doric frieze is divided by triglyphs into five metopes, four of which decorated with rosettes, flank a central metope filled with a wreath. Surmounting it is an elaborately decorated Corinthian cornice (Figure II–13a). This is characteristic of Roman architecture, which is usually more elaborately ornamented than Hellenistic.

3.2. *Tomb in Hinnom Valley*. This is a destroyed and restored tomb (now integrated into the chapel of the monastery of Akeldama), its doorway ornamented with a Doric frieze divided by triglyphs into eight metopes containing rosettes and some other motifs (Figure II–13b). The tomb has several chambers with loculi and arcosolia. Some have a moulded entrance surmounted by a gable (Macalister 1901b: 154–5, No. 50; Vincent and Steve 1954: Fig. 94; Kloner 1980: No. 10–19).

4   Tombs with decorated façade with mouldings and a pediment

Several tombs have a moulded facades surmounted by ornamented pediments.

The tympanum of the pediment ornament is filled with floral or plant motifs, consisting of a central focus, which spreads to both sides of the triangle. The pediment is completely filled in accordance with the Oriental notion of *horror vacui*. Gables with plain tympana surmount some tombs with smaller entrances. This decoration can be likened to the sarcophagi ornamentation.

4.1. *The Grape Tomb* has a moulded frame surrounding the wide doorway with a superimposed pediment. The tympanum of the pediment is decorated with a central rosette flanked by vine branches and two bunches of grapes; all three corners of the pediment are crowned with acroteria (Figure II–14a). The soffit at the entrance is decorated with plants and geometric motifs in the metopes. The capital jambs of the entrance are also ornamented (see Fig. IV–2). Pilasters in the corridor and a moulded band across the ceiling are

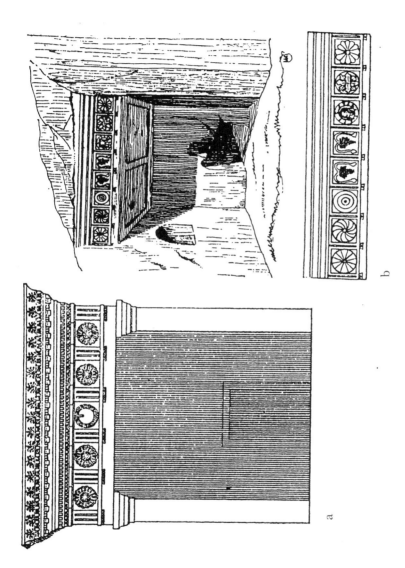

Figure II–13. Decorated façades: a. 'Frieze Tomb'; b. Hinnom Valley Tomb.

also unusual. The tomb consists of a main chamber leading to three chambers each with nine loculi. The south chamber leads to another arcosolia chamber with a ceiling ornamented with a carved rosette in a circle, and decorated pilasters beside the arcosolia (see Fig. IV–2) (Macalister 1900a: 54–61, Fig. 00; Avigad 1956: 336; Kloner 1980: 180–181, Pl. 20, No. 26–8).

Figure II–14. Façades of: a.'Grape' tomb; b. 'Sanhedrin' Tomb; c. The Tomb of Jehoshaphat.

4.2. *Sanhedriya*: the so-called *'Sanhedrin Tomb'* or *'Tomb of the Judges'* – (Tomb XIV).

This elaborate tomb, known as the 'Sanhedrin Tomb' consisted of 63 burial places and several cubicles and loculi for bone collections. This figure accords with the tradition of the number of Sanhedrin members, hence the name given to the tomb. However, the members of the Sanhedrin were buried in their ancestors' tombs, not alltogether in a separate tomb. This tomb, the largest in this group in the northern necropolis, was more likely the burial place of a prominent and wealthy family. It consists of a large court hewn into the rock with benches, cut from the rock, along three of the sides (south, west and north). A square pillar and a large basin were found in the forecourt (Rotschild 1952: 30–31; Rahmani 1961: 93–104, Fig. 4; 1981: 49; Kloner 1980: 117–119, No. 25–14). There is a porch (vestibule) and a large main chamber with loculi in a double row, one above the other, which leads to two other chambers with loculi and arcosolia.

Two decorated pediments crown the central, outer entrance and the entrance to the porch (Figure II–14b). The tympanum of the entrance pediment is decorated with a stylized acanthus calyx (the usual three acanthus leaves) centrally placed; from this issue two stylized acanthus scrolls symmetrically placed in opposite directions; pomegranates and fruits fill the space. Acroteria decorate only two of the corners of the gable; the central one was destroyed (Rotschild 1952: 33, Pl. IX,2; Guide 1956: Pls. 5,2; 6,1). The pediment of the porch is ornamented with two long and two wide acanthus leaves, meeting in the center in an ornamented circle, with acroteria decorating all three corners of the gable.

As stated, this tomb probably belonged to a prominent Jerusalem family and was used until the destruction of Jerusalem in the first century CE.

4.3. *The Tomb of Jehoshaphat*, which is adjacent to the Absalom Monument, has a flatly carved gabled façade and acroteria (Avigad 1954:). The pediment is decorated with a highly stylized design of branches growing out of a central acanthus leaf creating medallions which are filled with fruit (Figure II–14c–d).

5 Ornamented porch entrance.

In some cases the tomb has a porch entrance in the form of a Greek distylos in antis façade, without a gable. The most common of the tomb entablatures consists of a Doric frieze, sometimes with an addition in the centre and around the entrance as at the Tomb of Queen Helene of Adiabene, and usually combined with Ionic columns. Some rock-hewn tombs portray a combination of features, of Hellenistic and Roman styles, the Doric and Ionic, a mixed style which characterize Jewish funerary art in Jerusalem (Avigad 1950–1951: 98–103). These structural elements seem to have been borrowed from the façade of classical buildings.

5.1. *The Bene Ḥezir tomb* porch façade is in the style of distylos in antis, with two columns between *antae* carrying a simple Doric entablature, consisting of a plain frieze carried by Doric columns (Watzinger 1935, II:61; Avigad 1950–51: 101; 1954: 42–46) (Figure II–15a).

5.2. *The Tomb of Helene, Queen of Adiabene ('Tomb of the Kings')*

The Tomb of Queen Helene of Adiabene, who as noted earlier settled in Jerusalem after she and her family converted to Judaism, was used for burial probably ca 50 CE. Situated north of the present day Old City, the tomb is large and impressive (Kon 1947). It has a rock-hewn court, a staircase, an ornamented façade, and chambers with niches and arcosolia.

The tomb of Queen Helene of Adiabene has a richly decorated facade. The entrance façade is distylos in antis, with Ionic columns. Enclosing this façade is an unfinished decorative band with leaves, fruit, and pine cones, with a rosette in the centre. Surmounting it is a Doric frieze whose central motif is a triple bunch of grapes flanked by wreaths and acanthus (Figure II–15b). The impressively elaborate composite style of this tomb's façade is unique.

5.3. *Umm el Amed.* The rock face of the tomb's façade is carved with imitation of ashlar stone masonry (Avigad 1950–51: 103, Fig. 7). The tomb has a distylos in antis porch. The entablature runs above the entire façade and consists of a Doric metope frieze containing rosettes, above which is a row of dentils, which is an Ionic feature; below it are Doric guttae (Figure II–15c). The architrave is relatively low in relation to the frieze, which is characteristic of Hellenistic architecture. The Ionic capitals are a hypothetical reconstruction.

5.4. *Two-Storied Tomb.* The rock-hewn façade of the tomb (Figure II–16a) consists of two stories. The lower story has a distylos in antis porch with a Doric style entablature (Avigad 1950–51: 105–106). The Doric frieze and part of the upper storey survived; the excavator proposed a flat or gable roof (Galling 1936: 118, Fig. 5).

Figure II–15. Tomb facades of: a. 'Bene Ḥezir'; b. 'Queen Helene of Adiabene'; c. Umm el-Amed.

The Two-Storied Tomb attests to an important link between Jewish sepulchral art and that of Petra. Two-storied facades are the rule in Petra tombs, albeit much more imposing than this one.

5.5. *Sanhedriya* Tomb VIII, *'The Two-Columned Tomb'*

The tomb has a large courtyard with benches on both sides. It leads into a porch with a distylos in antis façade, and through a small narrow and low entrance into a main chamber leading into three small chambers. The east chamber has loculi and acrosolia (Rotschild 1952: 33–34; Avigad 1947: 119–122; Rahmani 1961: Fig. 3; Kloner 1980: 114–115). The two-columned façade of the tomb is preserved except for the right-hand column, which has disappeared. The façade also lacks a moulded entablature; the existing column has no base and has sturdy proportions (Figure II–16b). The *antae* and its capitals are different in the quality of their execution, which shows inferior workmanship in details. The tomb probably was used during the first century CE (Avigad 1947: 119–122, Fig. 5).

5.6. *The Tomb of Nicanor*, on Mount Scopus is a large hewn tomb with a court, a porch, and four burial hall-chambers with wide loculi or small chambers (see above; Avigad 1967: 119–125). The distylos in antis façade of the porch has two pillars, partly hewn and partly built with ashlar stones, with no trace of an entablature (Figure II–16c).

5.7. *Tomb in Hinnom Valley*. This is a large and elaborate tomb system, There are several chambers with loculi and arcosolia; the porch has a distylos in antis façade. Some doorways have a moulded entrance surmounted by a gable (Macalister 1901b: 157–8, No. 56; Kloner 1980: Nos. 10–25, 26, 27).

6   A façade in stylos in antis.

The façade of the Jason's Tomb porch is stylos in antis, a Doric column flanked by two pilasters (antea) (Pl.). (Rahmani 1967: 64, Fig. 1, Pl. 13). Several other tombs in the Kidron valley have the same façade (Kloner 1980: 51–52, 55, Nos. 7–14, 7–22, 7–49).

7   Façade with three entrances.

Tomb in Hinnom Valley. A large and elaborate tomb with a unique façade of three entrances. The central one is the largest and is surmounted by an arch decorated with a western conch (Figure II–17a). (Dalman 1939; Macalister 1901b: 216–218, No. 60; Avigad 1950–51: 104–106, Fig. 9; Kloner 1980: 62–63, No. 10–31).

a

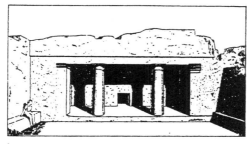

b

c

Figure II–16. Tomb facades: a. 'Two-Storied' Tomb; b. 'Sanhedriya' Tomb VIII; c. Nicanor Tomb.

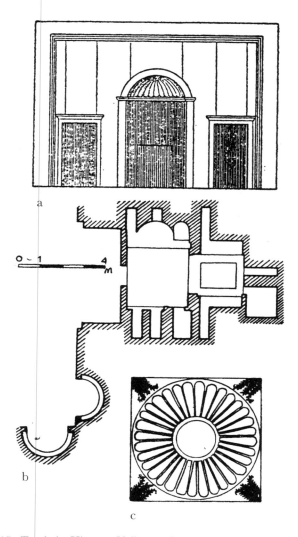

Figure II–17. Tomb in Hinnom Valley: a. Façade; b. Plan; c. Decorated dome.

The tomb has two main chambers and one lower chamber (Figure II–17b). The principal chamber had three *kokhim*, two of which were concealed by a movable sealing stone, similar to the one at Ferdûs er-Rûm (see above). The ceiling of this tomb has a dome decorated with a carved rosette (Figure II–17c) (Vincent and Steve 1954: Fig. 95). Similar facades are typical of Syro-Roman architecture. This tomb seems to show early Roman influence, and thus is assigned by Avigad to a date in the first century CE.

C. LOCULI TOMBS

Tomb Plan, Formation, and Dimensions

The typical underground tomb in the Jerusalem and Jericho cemeteries was hewn into the hillside and consisted of a square chamber, often with a square rock-cut pit in the floor. The height of the
chamber was usually less than that of a person and a pit was cut
only when the ceiling was not high enough to permit a person to
stand upright (some tombs are without a pit: see Jericho Tombs D9,
D22; Hachlili 1999: 16, 18–19, 21; 29–30). In tombs with standing
pits, benches were left along three sides of the chamber and the
kokhim were hewn level with the tops of the benches. Some rock-cut
tombs had only a chamber (Kloner and Zissu 2003: 42–3) which
contained either sarcophagi or a pile of bones, or were at times used
as a storage place for ossuaries; see, for example, a tomb on Mt.
Scopus (Fig. VI–10).

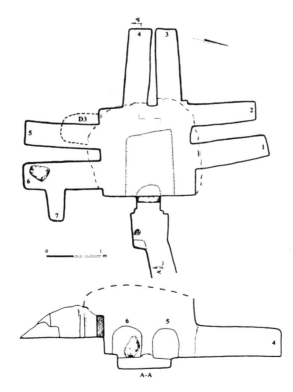

Figure II–18. Plan of loculi tomb.

The loculi had roughly vaulted ceilings and were cut into the walls, with the exception of the entrance wall. Usually there were one to three loculi in each wall. Some single-loculi tombs were also uncovered (Pl. II–11); of these, a number have a small open area in front of the loculus (Figure II–18). Some of the tombs have rock-cut courtyards in front of the entrance.

The small square opening was usually sealed with a blocking stone. In cases where the entrance was at a higher level than the chamber floor, one or more steps facilitated descent from the entrance down into the chamber.

These loculi tombs are similar in plan and execution to other contemporaneous tombs.

Formation of Rock-Cut Tombs

Most of the tombs were hewn into the soft, local, *meleke* limestone. The initial work was probably carried out with an iron hammer and a pick (some were found in loculi tombs in Jerusalem: Jotham-Rothschild 1952: 26, 31; Rahmani 1961: 100, Pl. XIV, 2; Kloner and Zissu 2003: 4). The tomb chambers and *kokhim* were then smoothed with a flat chisel 2–3 cm in width. Such chisels were recovered in Tomb H, Chamber B (Hachlili 1999: Fig. III.84:1–3; for stone-cutting see Nylander 1970: 22–28; 47–53). Tool marks are seen in many of the tombs, and on the *kokhim* walls in Jerusalem (Kloner and Zissu 2003: 4) and Jericho (Hachlili 1999: Figs. II.38, 40, 44, 57, 58).

After the chamber and the standing pit were hewn, the loculi were cut in a counterclockwise direction, from right to left (see comments on Jericho Tombs D3 and D27: Hachlili 1999: 16, 31, Figs. II.27–28, 55, 58). The process of burial and reburial was evidently also followed from right to left. Some double loculi (for two burials) were found in Jerusalem. From the irregularity in the number and location of the loculi, the chamber and the occasional standing pit seem to have been cut first and the *kokhim* later, according to the requirements of the tomb owners.

Dimensions of Loculi

Loculi measurements are recorded in rabbinical sources, e.g., M BB, 6.8; Tos. BB 6.22; BT BB 100b–101a:

והכוכין ארכן ארבע אמות ורומן שבעה (טפחים) ורוחבן ששה טפחים

"the length of the *kokhim* is four cubits, their height seven [spans] and their width six [spans]". The number of loculi that should be hewn on each side of the tomb is also mentioned, but this seems general and unrealistic. The number and measurements of the loculi were determined by the needs, size and economic situation of the families (for Jerusalem, see Kloner 1980: 231; Kloner and Zissu 2003: 27–29). In Jericho the sizes of the *kokhim* vary, even within the same tomb (Hachlili 1999: 53, 57, Table II.5).

Scholars have devoted studies to the metrology of the loculi tombs, attempting to establish the existence of common set of dimensions, namely the application of a standard cubit by tomb workers in Jerusalem. Apparently, the common measure used was the Egyptian cubit (long cubit = 52.5 cm; short cubit = 44–45 cm).[2] Evidently, cubits were used in the Second Temple tombs only as general guidelines. The dimensions of the loculi were usually determined by the size of the coffin or of the deceased. These nicely match the dimensions related by the Mishna for a loculus length of four cubits, referring to either the long or short Egyptian cubit (M BB 6:8; Tos. BB 6:22).

The loculi in Jericho first accommodated primary burials in wooden coffins in the first century BCE and were later used for bone collection in ossuaries and repositories in the first century CE. This evidence gains support from similar conclusions set forth for the Jerusalem necropolis, where *kokh* tombs were first used for primary burials (Kloner 1980: 224–225). It has also been maintained (Avigad 1954: 47, 1976: 259; Lieberman 1962: 1235; Kutcher 1967: 273–275; Meyers 1971: 64–69) that the *kokh* tomb was used for ossilegium. However, it seems unlikely that a 2 m long *kokh* would be hewn to contain ossuaries measuring some 0.70 m. It is much more probable, especially at Jericho, that the loculi were originally hewn for primary burials either in coffins or directly in the loculi (Kloner 1980: 224–225; Hachlili and Killebrew 1983a: 110).

"Mourning Enclosure", Courtyard, Forecourt

The most impressive "Mourning Enclosure" was discovered at Jericho 'Goliath Tomb' (Pl. II–12) (Tomb H: Hachlili 1999: 37, Fig. II.68;

---

[2] The long Egyptian cubit had seven spans, the short one six spans; a span equals 7.50 cm (Petrie 1892: 30; Klein 1908: 69–82; Kloner 1980a: 218–219; Ussishkin 1993: 285)

Netzer 1999: 45–48, Figs. II.78–81). This "Mourning Enclosure" complex consisted of the Goliath tomb, a large courtyard with benches in front of the tomb, adjoined by a ritual bath (*miqveh*), and an upper gallery with broad steps situated atop the tomb.

The large courtyard in front of the tomb was approached through a wide entrance close by the northeast corner. Another entrance was probably at the southwest corner, leading into the ritual bath complex (Figure II–19). The courtyard (measuring ca. 12 × 12 m) had masonry walls on three sides; in the west a hewn wall was erected with an upper gallery above. The courtyard had three or four rows of benches along the walls built of small fieldstones and white plastered; on the west side only one bench was found, which might have served as a shelf for placing artifacts. The courtyard was not roofed.

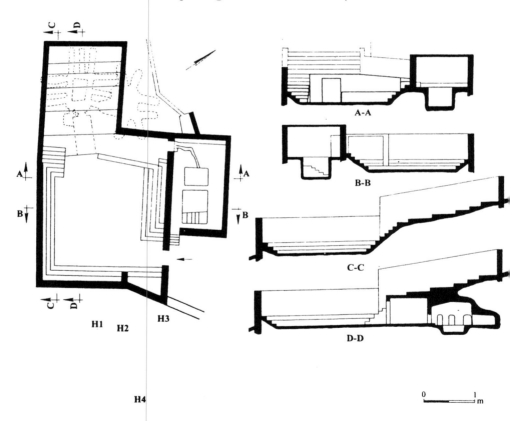

Figure II–19. Jericho, The Goliath Tomb (tomb H): schematic plan and sections of Courtyard, Upper gallery and Ritual bath.

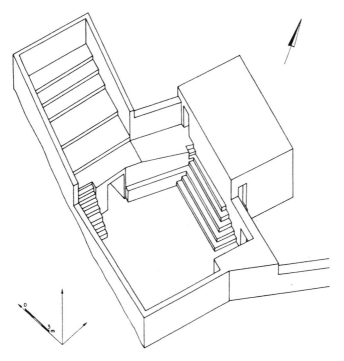

Figure II–20. Jericho. The Goliath Tomb (tomb H), Mourning
Enclosure reconstruction.

The Upper Gallery of the Goliath Tomb at Jericho is a unique
unroofed structure situated atop the main tomb chamber along the
southern part of the courtyard's west edge (Figure II–20; Pl. II–13);
resting on the natural slope, three broad steps were preserved and
two more may have originally existed (Netzer 1999: 45, Figs. II.78, 80).

The Ritual Bath (miqveh)

A few ritual baths (*miqveh*) were found in tomb complexes. In Jerusalem,
two ritual baths were located in the lower part of the courtyard of
the Tomb of Helene of Adiabene (Kon 1947: 37; Reich 1990: 243–5,
419) and next to several tombs on Mt. Scopus (Reich 1990: 246,
401, Fig. 17:1). At the Mt. Scopus Observatory a ritual bath was
uncovered, probably hewn with Tomb A and the cistern in stage 1;
its role is unclear (Weksler-Bdolah 1998: 27*, 51*).

At Jericho the *miqveh*, located north of the main courtyard, is constructed of a rectangular chamber with two entrances, one on the eastside from the main courtyard and the other from the entrance square on the south; the walls are not well preserved (Hachlili 1999: 37; Netzer 1999: 47, Figs. II.78–83). The chamber contains a bench on the west wall and two pools: the west pool undoubtedly served as a water storage tank, the *osar* (אוצר); the larger east pool, of the same depth, includes a stairway of six steps on its east wall. Both pools were plastered with a hydraulic, grey, ash-lime plaster (Pl. II–13). Although the top of the common wall between the pools has not been preserved, by analogy with some of the ritual baths in the Jericho Hasmonean winter palaces complex, a narrow channel may be restored, built into the missing top of the common wall. The ritual bath was located in covered rooms, as in the Jericho palaces and at Masada.

The bench runs along the east face of the west wall. It is plastered with the same hydraulic plaster as the floor and the pools. It might have served the bathers for changing their clothes.

The water supply for the pools was along a small channel that entered the chamber at the southwest corner and continued across to the west pool. The channel originated in the major water channel from Na'aran and ended just west of the chamber in a small tank. This tank probably served to reduce the speed of water-flow due to the difference in elevation from the Na'aran conduit.

The role and function of the *miqveh* in a cemetery is intriguing, since according to the *Halacha* a person could not be purified from contamination by the dead in a cemetery (Reich 1990: 119–121; Kloner and Zissu 2003: 16). However, in Qumran sources (the Temple Scroll and 4Q414) immersion in the *miqveh* on the first day is recommended for purification.

The "mourning enclosure" at Jericho shows no evidence that the courtyard and upper gallery were roofed, however, the ritual bath was usually located in covered rooms (Fig. II–20; Netzer 1999: 48, 50). The upper gallery situated atop the two chamber tomb indicates an apparent intention to include also the tomb in the "mourning enclosure" complex. The large size of the Jericho complex and its location at the south end of the cemetery was probably expected to serve not only the Goliath family but a much larger community.

These upper structures with their benches functioned as assembly halls and were regarded in this context as a "mourning enclosure" used for burial rites, mourning and funeral ceremonies (Hachlili 1988a: 91–92; Netzer 1999: 49–50).

The closest parallel to Jericho's upper gallery are the overlying upper structures at the later necropolis of Beth She'arim, Catacomb 14 and Catacomb 20 (dated to the third-fourth centuries CE; Avigad 1976: 58–62, 111–114, 124, Figs. 24, 51; Weiss 1989: 96–100; Netzer 1999: 49–50).

Similar forecourts with benches were found at Sanhedriya Tombs VIII and XIV, and at a few tombs at the Valley of Hinnom (Kloner 1980, Kloner and Zissu 2003: 15–16, Nos. 4–27, 5–1, 10–31, 25–8, 25–14). At the Tomb of Helene of Adiabene a large courtyard and two ritual baths were found (see above). Smaller forecourts were hewn in front of many Jerusalem and Jericho tombs.

Rock cut courtyards with steps similar to the upper gallery at Jericho were found at Kafr 'Uzeiz (Amit 1991) and at Ḥurvat Burgin (Zissu and Ganor 1997), where a rock-cut stairway led down into the courtyard.

At Qumran eastern edge of the Middle Finger a square building (de Vaux Building B,) was re-excavated (Eshel et al. 2002: 147–153, Pl. III; Broshi and Eshel 2003: 31–33,71) dated to the Second Temple period and argued to be a 'mourning enclosure', similar to Jericho, used by the Qumran community. The arguments for the Qumran 'mourning enclosure' are not convincing.[3] The location of the building at the extreme end of the middle extension, though higher than the tombs, does not make sense, it is very far and difficult to reach from the settlement or the main cemetery; there are no benches or any other indication for the use of the structure except for the burials at the southern part of the building. The similarity with the Jericho structure is deficient. The Jericho 'mourning enclosure' has benches and is built above a large, elaborate two chambers tomb structure, as is the case at Beth She'arim. The additional conclusion that the Middle Finger thus was the burial place of important personalities seems far-fetched.

---

[3] Eshel et al. (2000: 147–153) report that the building size is 4.50 × 5.05 m, they found pottery shards of the second temple period. In the southern part of the building (Tomb 1000) they found a pile of bones in secondary burial, identified as the remains of two women dated to the second temple period. Under this pile of bones (at a depth of 3.5 feet) a skeleton in primary burial oriented east-west was found, above the skeleton's legs a cooking pot was placed. (Broshi and Eshel 2003: 32).

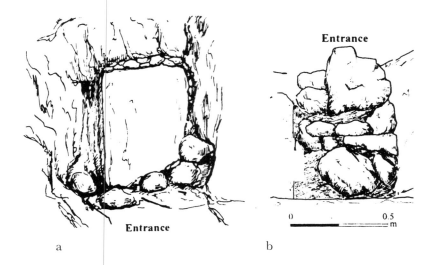

Figure II–21a–b. Tomb entrances.

The Entrance

The façade of Second Temple tombs in Jerusalem are carved in the rock and ornamented, the decoration is found on Monumental tombs and Façade ornamented tombs (see above, Figs. II–11–17; Chap. IV).

The entrance to the ordinary loculi tombs is relatively small and a person wishing to enter would need to stoop (Pl. II–14). No particular orientation of the tomb entrances was observed; usually they face all directions. No consistent method of sealing the tombs could be discerned.

The entrance could be sealed with a large sealing stone (Figure II–21a) or a number of small stones and rubble mixed together to seal the opening (Figure II–21b).

Sealing of the entrance

Several types of blocking stones were identified (Hachlili 1999: 51, 52, Table II.4):

- Slabs specially prepared to block the entrance completely. These have a protuberant 'stopper', which fits into the opening (Figure II–22, 1,2,6). After the blocking stone was set in place, the opening was further sealed with small stones and plaster. The sealing of the tomb was done in a way that blended with the surrounding hillside (see for example, Jericho tombs: Hachlili 1999: 29, 51, 53: Figs. II.27, 52, 56, 84:1, 2, 6; Jericho Tomb D27 was closed with the 'stopper' incorrectly placed outside).

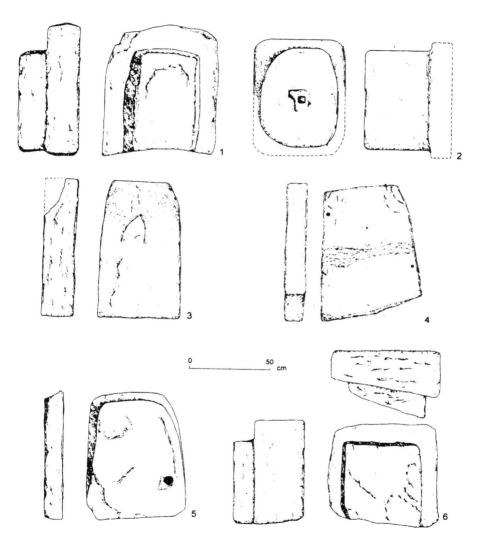

Figure II–22. Sealing stones examples: 'stopper' and flat.

It is noteworthy that at Jericho these blocking slabs are not of local
rock so they must have been brought from another area. Several
blocking stones found not *in situ*, but scattered on Jericho Hills A
and E, were reused architectural elements, probably taken from
abandoned buildings or from where they had been left as rejects.

- Flat blocking stones, either rectangular or with a rounded top
  (Figure II–22, 3–5). The space between the blocking stone and the
  entrance was sealed with small stones and plaster (Hachlili 1999:
  Fig. II.85:3–5). Some tombs had a recessed door frame (tombs in
  Jerusalem, Kloner 1980: 213, Pls. 4, 9; Jericho tomb D17: Hachlili
  1999: Fig. II.51).
- Some of the tombs were sealed with small stones, bricks and plaster instead of a blocking stone (Figure II–21b). At Jericho most of
  the tombs with this kind of sealing had a single *kokh*.
- Two slabs, one leaning against the other, blocked the entrance of
  the Goliath Tomb at Jericho (Pl. VI–3); these were possibly the
  'Dophek' and 'dophek dophkin' mentioned in the Mishna (*Ohalot*
  2,4) (Kloner 1980: 216; Kloner and Zissu 2003: 24–25).
- A round rolling-stone גולל, closing the entrance was found in several rock-cut tombs, dated to the end of the first century BCE and
  the first century CE. At the door a slot was cut to hold a round
  stone; the stone was rolled into the slot away from the entrance.
  The following tombs in Jerusalem were sealed by means of rolling
  stones: the Tomb of Helene, Herod's family tomb (Pl. II–7), the
  Nicophoria tomb (east of Herod's family tomb), a tomb on Mt.
  Scopus, a tomb in the Kidron Valley, and the Hinnom Valley
  tomb. Similar rolling stones were discovered at a tomb at Horvat
  Midras (Kloner 1980: 161, nos. 2–4; 215–216; 1978, 1985a: 60–63,
  n. 27, Pls. 11, 12, 13,1; Kloner and Zissu 2003: 23–24); and at
  the cemetery of Hesban (Waterhouse 1998: 72–76, Fig. 5.4; Pls.
  5.15, 5.16).

Some of these methods seem to have been used for the final sealing of the tomb, while the other methods, with the easily moved
stones, may have been used when the intention was to return to the
tomb for further burials.

Stone Doors, which blocked some chambers inside the tombs, were
quite rare but some were discovered in Jerusalem (Kloner and Zissu
2003: 25–26):

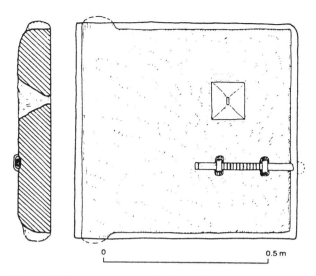

Figure II–23. Stone door, Akeldama Tomb 2, Chamber C.

- Four pivoting stone doors were used in the Akeldama tombs 2 and 3; they are an unusual sealing feature in Jerusalem. They probably date to the original burial phase of the Second Temple period. One door at tomb 2 has preserved its iron locking device, still found *in situ* (Avni and Greenhut 1996: 32; Figs. 1.31, 32).
- A hinged stone door blocked the opening to Akeldama Cave 2, Chamber C, (Figure II–23; Pl. II–15). Extended from the top and bottom of the door were two rounded pivots, which fit into rock-cut sockets in the lintel and threshold. In the center of the door an iron locking device was attached by staples set in lead, with the keyhole 15 cm above the lock (Avni and Greenhut 1996: 19, Figs. 1.30–32).
- A pivoting stone door closed the entrance to Akeldama Cave 3, Chamber C, connecting Chambers A and C. The door was decorated with four rectangular panels carved in sunken relief, in imitation of a wooden door. Carved in the upper right-hand panel was a representation of large rounded doorknocker suspended from a hook. The door was locked by a stone inserted into it through a narrow crevice (Avni and Greenhut 1996: 26, 32, Figs. 1.44–45, 47; Winter 1996: 113,b).
- A pivoting stone door closed the entrance to Akeldama Cave 3, Chamber D, identical to door 2. The door's upper stone hinge

was set into a socket penetrating Trough II in Chamber C. The door was locked through a narrow slanted opening in Trough II (Avni and Greenhut 1996: 30, Figs. 1.48, 55–56).
• Fragments of a stone door with pivoting hinges were found in Akeldama Tomb 1, Chamber A, near the passage to Chamber B, with fragments of an iron door-lock nearby (Avni and Greenhut 1996: 6, Figs. 1.5; Winter 1996: 113,a; Fig. 7.3).

Similar doors (Avni and Greenhut 1996: 37, note 6) were discovered in the Tomb of Helene (Kon 1947: 68–70); a decorated stone door was found in a tomb at Bethlehem (Macalister 1902b) and in later burials at Beth She'arim (Mazar, B. 1973: 221–222; Avigad 1976: 18, 48–51, 91–92, 117, 263, Catacombs. 15–23, Figs. 37 and others).

Some depictions of decorated doors appear on the façade of some tombs (mentioned by Avni and Greenhut 1996: 32; Clermont-Ganneau 1899: 298; Macalister 1900a: 1901; Dalman 1939; see above and Chap. IV).

The architecture of the loculi tombs did not undergo any changes in the first century CE, although the tombs were then also used for ossuaries and bone collection. The loculi tomb was the common burial form in use during the Second Temple period, first for primary and later for secondary burials.

Origins and Comparison of Loculi Tombs

The origins of the loculi tombs should be studied with regard to burial in the First Temple Period and compared with tomb architecture of neighboring countries (Hachlili 1999: 57–59).

Rock-cut tombs of the First Temple Period in Judah are relatively common. The tombs usually consist of a passage leading to the entrance and a burial chamber surrounded by benches, which served as resting places. A repository pit for transferred bones was often present (Loffreda 1968; Ussishkin 1993: 300–303; Barkay 1994a). The most extensive necropolis of this period was excavated in Jerusalem, where the tombs were hewn into the hilly terrain, and are similar to tombs in other areas of Judah.

In the necropolis at Silwan, about 48 tombs of three architectural types were surveyed (Ussishkin 1970; 1993: 257–268, 293–294): gabled tombs; monolithic above-ground tombs, and flat ceiling tombs. A common feature is the cornice carved in the join of the ceiling and the walls. Repository pits are completely absent from the Silwan tombs. Tombs similar to the third group are found on other hillsides around Jerusalem. The Silwan tombs were hewn in the eighth century BCE (Ussishkin 1993: 293–294, 316–317) and their architectural style can be traced to Egypt and Phoenicia. Ussishkin maintains (1993: 328–331) that the three architectural styles served three different groups of burials. The tombs with gabled ceilings and the monolithic tombs were used for single or double burials (at most three), probably of upper class individuals, whereas tombs with flat ceilings were used for a larger number of burials, possibly for a family. These tombs are different from the loculi tombs of the Second Temple period, but already point to the beginning of individual burial in a family tomb, which characterizes Jewish burial customs in the Second Temple period.

Rock-cut loculi tombs were widespread in the Semitic world in the Hellenistic and Roman periods, from approximately the second century BCE to the third century CE (see Galling 1936; Avigad 1956: 323; Rahmani 1961, 1967a, b; Kloner 1980: 213; Kloner and Zissu 2003: 34–36).

The comparative material can be divided into loculi tombs earlier than the Jerusalem and Jericho tombs, and those contemporary with them (Hachlili and Killebrew 1983a: 110–11, 125–128).

• Earlier rock-cut tombs are found in: Phoenicia (Renan 1871: 401–505, Pls. XX–XVI; Perrot and Chipiez 1885: 149–153, 226); Egypt: Alexandria and Fayum (Noshy 1937: 21); Judea: Hellenistic Marissa, ca. 200 BCE (Peters and Thiersch 1905: 81–84).
• Contemporary loculi tombs: Dura Europos (Toll 1946: 7–19, 47); Nabatean tombs at Petra (the Petra cemetery had mainly chamber tombs and shaft tombs: Jaussen and Savignac 1909: Tomb B20, Fig. 157; Tomb A3, Fig. 174; Tomb B6, Fig. 183; Horsfield G. and A. 1938: 93–115; McKenzie 1990); several Nabatean stone cist tombs with wooden coffins at Kurnub (Negev 1971: 117–119, n. 41); Palmyra (Watzinger 1932: 79–80; Gawlikowski 1970: 107–128; Schmidt-Colinet 1989); sundry Syrian tombs (Sartre 1989).

The loculi tomb in Egypt (Noshy 1937: 21–22 suggests a Phoenician origin) – one of several types of burial – was particularly prevalent at Alexandria, Fayum, and Leontopolis (also called the city of Onias), a Jewish colony dated to the second century BCE–first century CE

(Jos. *Ant.* 12.387; 13.62–73; 14.99, 131–133; *Wars* 1.31–33; 7.420–432).
The Jewish cemetery at Leontopolis consisted of rock-cut loculi tombs
with a central chamber, which was probably sealed by stelae (Naville
1890: 13; Griffith 1890: 51–53), eighty of which bore Greek inscriptions (Frey 1952: 378–381, Nos. 1450–1530; Lewis 1964: 145ff.). As
relations are known to have existed between the Jewish communities in Egypt and Judea (Jos. *War* 1.33; 7.422–425; *Ant.* 12.387;
Kasher 1978: 113–127), a connection can be traced between the
rock-cut loculi tombs of the Second Temple period in Judea and
those in Egypt, especially at Leontopolis. These connections go back
at least to Hasmonean times (*Ant.* 18.63, 67; 14.99, 133; see also
Tcherikover 1970: 278–287). However, this does not rule out the
Phoenician origin of this tomb type in the Hellenistic and Semitic
world, both in Egypt (Noshy 1937: 22) and in Judea (Marissa: Peters
and Thiersch 1905: 15–35).

The comparable loculi tombs at Marissa and Palmyra are rectangular, with the loculi arranged symmetrically along a long and
narrow corridor, while the Jerusalem and Dura Europos tombs are
centrally focused and arranged around a square chamber. Moreover,
the Dura Europos tombs have a dromos and loculi in the entrance
wall as well, and usually a larger number of loculi.

Scholars hold opposing views on the origin of loculi tombs. Some
posit an Egyptian origin, probably Alexandria (Watzinger 1932:
79–81; 1935: 19; Barag 1978: 55; Kloner 1980: 228–229); others a
Phoenician origin, which influenced Alexandria and the Hellenistic
world (Thiersch 1904; Schreiber 1908: 160–177, 1914: 3–14; Noshy
1937: 39).

The validity of the debate over Egyptian *vs.* Phoenician origin can
be questioned on three counts: (a) basic differences in ground plan;
(b) a considerable time gap between the comparative material and
the Jewish tombs; (c) the burial customs in these tombs.

a. *Basic Differences in Ground Plan*: Most of the loculi tombs in
Phoenicia and Egypt consist of a narrow chamber with the loculi
arranged symmetrically on both sides; many of the loculi at Alexandria
had gabled ceilings, as at Marissa. These tombs are generally higher
and more spacious than the Jewish loculi tombs. At Dura-Europos
there is a dromos leading into the tombs, and loculi were hewn on
all sides of the chamber, including the entrance wall (Toll 1946: 7–8,
Pls. II–XX). In the Jewish tombs the loculi were cut into three walls

of a central chamber, and some of the tombs had a courtyard. The loculi had vaulted ceilings.

b. *Time Gap.* – The Phoenician loculi tombs are dated to the Iron Age (eighth-seventh centuries BCE). Persian and early Hellenistic loculi tombs were found at Sidon and 'Amrit (Renan 1871: 401–405, Pls. XVI, XVIII–XX). In Egypt the loculi tombs first appear in the Hellenistic period but were common in the Roman period. They were used for primary burial, and no evidence of secondary burial or bone collection was noted. The loculi tombs in Dura Europos are mainly dated to the second-third centuries CE, although Toll (1946: 132–139) assumed that they began to be used in the second century BCE. Palmyrene loculi tombs are dated to the second-third centuries CE. The Jewish loculi tombs first appear in the late second century BCE, continuing into the late first century CE, with sporadic occurrences noted in the second century CE as well. They were thus evidently contemporary with the later Egyptian loculi tombs.

c. *Burial Customs*: Burial practices in Palmyra and Dura Europos were probably similar. Families may have hewn the tombs but they also sold them to others as burial plots. The basic character of the Jewish loculi tombs, with interment either in coffins or ossuaries, is the family burial. It should again be stressed that loculi tombs at Jericho (and probably also at Jerusalem) were originally hewn for first burials in wooden coffins or loculi, and continued to serve for ossuary burials.

Jewish rock-cut loculi tombs of the Second Temple period in Jerusalem and Jericho evidently bear regional influence, especially those of the Jewish cemetery at Leontopolis. At this particular time they satisfied the need for individual burial in family tombs.

D. Arcosolia Tombs

Arcosolia tombs began to appear sporadically during the first century CE; as many as 100 such tombs are found in Jerusalem). The arcosolia is a bench-like aperture with an arched ceiling hewn into the length of the wall. Three arcosolia were hewn, one in each wall of the chamber (Figure II–24a; Pl. II–15). These were more expensive burials as there were only three burial places in a chamber, instead of six or nine loculi. The deceased was placed on the arcosolium bench. Some arcosolia tombs served to store ossuaries (Kloner 1980: 232–236; Avigad 1976: 259–261, Zissu 1995: 45–46, 153–157; Kloner and Zissu 2003: 36–40). Many of the Jerusalem arcosolia tombs also contain loculi.

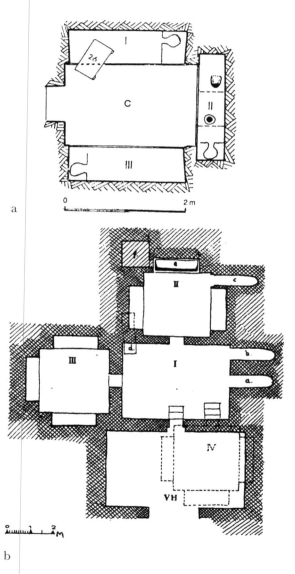

Figure II–24 Acrosolia tomb plans: a. Akeldama Tomb 3, Chamber C; b. Pilaster Tomb.

This type of tomb might have served prominent and more affluent Jerusalem families (e.g., the Bene Ḥezir tomb, the 'Sanhedrin Tombs', Tomb of Helene, the Pilaster tomb (Figure II–24b, Figure II–25), and Ḥorvat Midras in the Judean Shephela (Kloner 1978). Scholars proposed that acrosolia tombs served for the burial of prominent members in the family (Macalister 1999: 54–61; Avigad 1954: 79–90). However, others (Kloner 1980: 234–5; Kloner and Zissu 2003: 39–40) refute this, and suggest the acrosolia served for the placing of ossuaries and that the origin of the acrosolia could be found in the development of various burial forms in Second Temple Jerusalem.

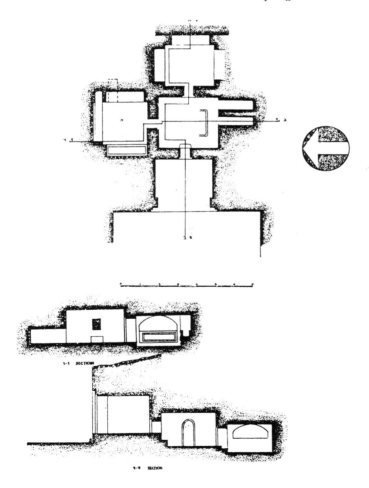

Figure II–25. Sanhedriya Tomb 7.

Note especially Akeldama tombs 1–3 with arcosolia and burial
troughs, which were among the latest to be hewn in Jerusalem in
the Second Temple period. They consisted of chambers with arcosolia, shelves for ossuaries, or burial troughs for primary burial (Avni
and Greenhut 1996: 32–33, Plan **1**. 12). Troughs for primary burial seem to have been introduced in Jerusalem only about the mid-
first century CE (Kloner 1980: 235) but are known from monumental
tombs in Jerusalem in the Iron age (Barkay 1994a: 116–117, 150–151,
Figs. 1, 5–8, 11). The troughs and headrests probably were evoca-
tive of sleeping arrangements in the house of the living.

In the third century CE the arcosolia burial constituted the most
common architectural form for primary interment at the Beth She'arim
necropolis, and was usually reserved for more expensive burials
(Avigad 1976: 259–261). In several cases the deceased was interred
in a trough grave hewn in the arcosolium. From the third century
on, the trough grave became a common type of burial.

Headrests

Headrests are fairly rare in Second Temple burial; one example is
the carved headrests at one end of each of the three troughs in the
arcosolia of Chamber C of Akeldama Tomb 3 (Avni and Greenhut
1996: 27, Fig. 1.12). Some Iron Age tombs in Jerusalem and Judea
display similar headrests. They possibly originated in the first century rock-cut tombs (Kloner 1980: 27; Barkay and Kloner 1986;
Barkay 1994a: 150–151) and served as a kind of pillow or head support as well as a decorative element.

E. OTHER TOMBS

Field tomb and cist tombs. Some evidence of a simpler way of burial
was discovered in Jerusalem, namely a kind of field tomb and cist
tombs dug in the ground (Kloner 1980: 244–246; Zissu 1995: 97,
153). About 18 hewn field tombs, consisting of individual inhuma-
tions in small rock-cut troughs covered by stone slabs, and sometimes
also faced with slabs were discovered in the Mamilla neighbourhood.
In the tombs, only pottery, coins, and glass vessels were found dated
to the first century BCE–first century CE, probably serving the poor
of the city.

Another type of burial consisted of vertical *shaft tombs* with several burial niches at the bottom. Reich (1994: 117) suggests that tombs dated to the second century BCE represent a form of burial common in Jerusalem prior to the loculi tomb. However, these were individual tombs, not family tombs.

The shaft tombs with loculi found at Mamilla, might have been a development in the later first century in addition to the regular loculi tombs (Reich 1994: 106–107). Some shaft tombs were discovered in the northern part of the Ketef Hinom hill, which were used during the late Roman period probably by Jewish residents of Mount Zion.

Several shaft ("dug-out") tombs, similar to the Qumran tombs, were found in several locations in Jerusalem. For example, two shaft tombs covered with stone slabs were discovered in East Talpiot (Kloner and Gat 1982: 76) in proximity to other chamber tombs.

The *Beth Zafafa* graves are hewn shaft tombs (Zisso 1996), marked by stone tablets (Fig. I–2). In most tombs only one body was interred. The form and size of the tombs, as well as the custom of individual burial, are similar to these features in Qumran graves

Cist tombs dug into the ground covered with stone slabs were found on the slope of the Hinnom Valley (Barkay 1994b: 92–93). No skeletal remains were discovered, only several coins. These tombs are dated to the first-second century CE. In some of the First Temple period tombs (tombs 34 and 51) evidence of continuous use in the Second Temple period was found.

CHAPTER THREE

INTERMENT RECEPTACLES

The receptacles used for the interment of the deceased consist of wooden coffins, stone and clay ossuaries, and stone sarcophagi.

A. WOODEN COFFINS

Wooden coffins were not well preserved but some were found in Jewish cemeteries and tombs in the Land of Israel for example, at Jericho, 'En Gedi, Qumran and in the Dead Sea area.

Table III–1: Jericho, Wooden Coffins

Coffin No.	Tomb No.	Coffin Type	Loculi Dimns. (cm)			Coffin with Lid Dims. cm			Type of Lid		Coffin Decoration		Items in Coffin
			H	L	W	H	L	W	Hinged	Gabled	Painted	Incised	
59	D9–3	B	115	220	60	77	190	50		+	+		+
78	D12–Pit	B				85	190	45		+	+		+
84	D12–w bench	B								+	+		
85	D12–s bench	B								+?	+		
94	D12–3	B	40	200	60	90	180	50		+?	+		
102	D9	B											
103	D12–1	?											
104	D12–2	B										+	
109	D9	B											
113	D14	A				70	190	50	+				
128	D15	?											+
184	D27–2	C	92	190	50					+			
185	D27–5	C	98	200	65					+		+	+
187	D27–6	C	95	170	50	81	190	52		+		+	+
190	D27–4	C	96	200	50	75	190	42		+		+	
198	D27–3	C	96	210	50					+		+	

Jericho Wooden Coffins

Wooden coffins were discovered in Jericho in about 14 tombs on
Hill D (Table III–1; Hachlili 1999: 60–92, Table III.1). Several of
the tombs probably had wooden coffins in all the loculi, though only
a few have survived. The one-loculus tombs, with the exception of
D14 (Coffin 113, fairly well preserved), contained only poorly preserved fragments of wood (see Table III–1, for coffin type, decoration and dimensions).

One coffin was usually placed in each loculus, with the exception
of loculus 2 in Tomb D12, which contained two coffins, one of a
woman and next to it a smaller coffin for a child (Hachlili 1999:
Figs. II.39, 43). As a rule, the coffins contained one individual; however, sometimes several individuals were buried together in one coffin
(see Anthropological Table, Hachlili and Killebrew 1999: 192–194,
for details regarding skeletal remains).

The deceased were laid supine in the coffins with the head usually to one side, and the arms close to the sides (Hachlili 1999: Figs.
II.35, 39, 41, 55).

In Jericho, the coffins were used only for primary and not for secondary burials. This is in contrast to 'En Gedi (Avigad 1962b: 180;
Hadas 1994: 12, 18, 57, except for Tomb 1, Hadas 1994: 45), where
wooden coffins were reused (like ossuaries?) for the burial of collected bones (see below). Several species of timber used for the coffins
were identified (see Tables III–2 and III–3 for details on the timber
used of all parts of the coffins).

Description and Carpentry

The Jericho coffins consisted of two parts, the chest and the lid. The
coffin chest comprised two long and two short side boards, a bottom, and four corner posts whose lower part served as feet. The
corner posts and lids differed in size and form from coffin to coffin;
the lids were also of different types, gabled and hinged (Table III–1).

The chest sides were made of two or three long horizontal boards
and two or three short horizontal boards; their ends were shaped as
a tenon, a flat projection to fit into the mortise of the post (Hachlili
1999: Fig. III.2). The chest parts were joined by mortising and pegging (Figure III–1b).

Each of the four well-carved corner posts had two mortises (sockets) on two sides, into which the tenons of the long and short chest

Table III-2: Jericho, Timber of Wooden Coffins

Coffin no.	CHEST Corner Posts	CHEST Side Boards	Bottom	Boards	LID Pediment Parts	LID Ridge	LID Hinges	Planks, Framing Decoration	FRAGMENTS, MISC. Misc.	FRAGMENTS, MISC. Dowels, Pegs
59	Christ-thorn			Sycamore	Cypress Sycamore	Sycamore		Sycamore		Christ-thorn Euphrates poplar
78	Sycamore				Sycamore	Sycamore		Sycamore	Sycamore Kermes oak (charcoal) Christ-thorn	
84	Sycamore				Sycamore	Sycamore			Date palm (string) Sycamore	Christ-thorn
85	Sycamore			Cypress				Sycamore	Euphrates poplar Pine sp. (charcoal)	Christ-thorn
94	Sycamore	Sycamore Cypress	Sycamore					Sycamore		Christ-thorn
102									Sycamore Pine sp. Christ-thorn	
103		Sycamore								
104					Sycamore			Sycamore (charcoal)	Sycamore	Euphrates poplar Christ-thorn
109										
113	Christ-thorn Olive Sycamore	Aleppo pine Cypress	Cypress Euphrates poplar	Cypress			Olive Atlantic pistachio	Cypress	Cypress Christ-thorn Tamarisk	
128		Cypress			Sycamore			Sycamore Cypress	Pine sp.	Christ-thorn
183										
184				Sycamore Calabrian pine						
187	Christ-thorn	Christ-thorn Calabrian pine	Sycamore	Calabrian pine	Euphrates Calabrian pine	Cypress Christ-thorn Calabrian pine		Calabrian pine	Christ-thorn	Christ-thorn
190	Sycamore	Cypress		Cypress	Cypress	Sycamore		Cypress	Cypress	Christ-thorn
198	Sycamore	Sycamore	Sycamore	Sycamore	Sycamore	Sycamore		Sycamore		Sycamore

sides were inserted (Hachlili 1999: Fig. III.2:2); every mortise joint
was secured by wooden dowels. and was clean and well cut, presumably with a very sharp mortise chisel. The horizontal boards
were pegged together by round wooden dowels. One coffin had decorated corner posts (Hachlili 1999: Coffin 94: Figs. III.18:2; 19:1,3).

The holes into which the wooden dowels in all the coffin parts
were inserted show marks of a drilling tool (Hodges 1964: 116–117).
The wooden dowels were small and round (Hachlili 1999: Figs.
III.2:2, 14:1,3; 20:3; 21:9–11; 30:15; 37:8).

The standard of the carpentry as observed on the Jericho coffins
is fairly advanced and varied (Hachlili 1999: 85–87), and is comparable to the carpentry of the wooden coffins of the fourth–third
centuries BCE found in Egypt and South Russia (Watzinger 1905;
Vaulina and Wasowicz 1974; for ancient carpentry, see Richter 1928:
94–95, 154–155; Singer et al. 1956: 233–239; Hodges 1964: 112–122).

Several types of timber were used for the Jericho coffins: sycamore,
cypress, Euphrates poplar, Christ-thorn, olive, Aleppo pine and
Calabrian pine (Table III–2). Most coffin parts were made either of
sycamore or cypress timber, which is easily worked (Liphschitz and
Waisel 1999: 88–92, Table III–2).

Coffin Types

Three coffin types could be distinguished at Jericho (Table III–1;
Hachlili 1999: 60–85, Table III.1):

Type A – One coffin of this type was discovered (Coffin 113, found
in one-kokh Tomb D14; Pl. III–1) and it is the only one with a flat
hinged lid (Figure III–1a).

The chest of Coffin 113 was constructed of four corner posts and
boards rectangular in section; all survived, although some were in
poor condition (Hachlili 1999: Fig. III.1–5). Each side of the chest
consisted of three to four horizontal boards pegged together. The
lower board, which is joined to the bottom, has depressions for the
iron fittings. Two of the surviving boards of the short side indicate
that a shallow horizontal recess ran along the middle of these boards.

This coffin is also unusual in having iron parts as supporting elements. Four iron corner sheets and four iron nails (Figure III–2b),
one fairly large (Hachlili 1999: 67, Fig. III.7–9), may have been used
to secure fittings for joining the bottom boards to the lower long

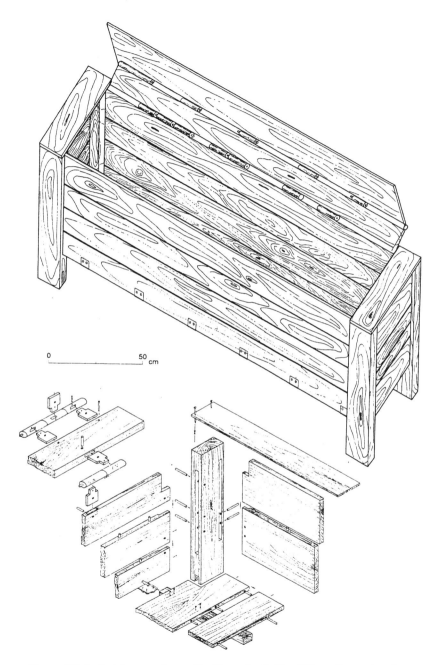

0   50 cm

Figure III–1. Jericho wooden coffin Type A, Coffin 113: a. Reconstruction;
b. Carpentry of the coffin.

boards (Hachlili 1999: Fig. III.3). Each of the iron corner sheets has four round protruding nails, which probably fixed them to the side and bottom boards. Similar fittings, several iron plaques with remains of wood and a nail, were discovered in tomb 1–15 on Mt. Scopus, western slope (Vitto 2000: 92). Comparable bronze angles fixed to the corners of wooden coffins were found in tombs at Dura Europos (Toll 1946: 99).

The iron lock plate with a perforated L-shaped opening (Figure III–2c), was probably attached to one long side of the coffin as a decoration (?) or may have once been used as a lock, if the coffin was originally a cupboard, or as a symbol of protection (see Chap. XI).

The most interesting features of this coffin are the well-preserved flat lid (Hachlili 1999: 63, Figs. III.6) made of two horizontal boards, connected by wooden hinges (Figure III–2a). The lid consists of two boards: a narrow board with grooves on either side for hinges to connect the lid to the long side board and to the second, wider board of the lid (Hachlili 1999: Fig. III.5:1–4), which has grooves for hinges on one side only. Both side boards and the narrower board of the lid bear four grooves indicating that four hinges had connected the lid to the chest (Hachlili 1999: 65, Figs. III.5:1, 4).

Ten round wooden hinges have survived, as well as one especially long hinge (Hachlili 1999: Fig. III.6); some still have part of the wooden strip which connected the hinges to the boards (Figure III–2a). Three of the hinges are 'male', with projecting points at both ends, two are 'female', with sockets at both ends, five are 'mixed', with a socket at one end and a projecting point at the other. The long hinge is also of this kind (Hachlili 1999: 66, Fig. III.6:1–10).

The grooves on the lid sides and the long side of the chest seem to indicate that five hinges connected the chest to the narrow board of the lid, as well as the long hinge (Hachlili 1999: Fig. III.6:10) placed at one end of the coffin (Hachlili 1999: Fig. III.3); seven hinges connected the two boards of the lid (Hachlili 1999: Figs. III.3; III. 5:3), totaling thirteen hinges. The arrangement of hinges on this coffin is unusual; in comparable wooden coffins, the boards of the lid are connected by a row of hinges pinned together end-to-end, and another row of hinges joining the lid and the long side of the chest. They usually have alternating hinges with sockets and projecting parts (Watzinger 1905: 24, Coffin No. 1, Ills. 27–32, p. 32,

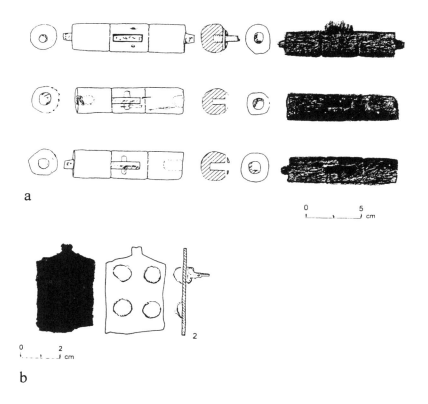

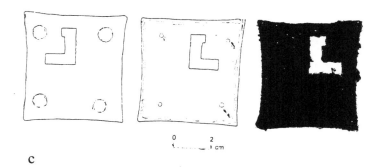

Figure III–2. Jericho Coffin 113: a. Wooden hinges; b. Iron corner sheets; c. Iron plate.

Coffin No. 8, Ill. 56). The hinges of our coffin are similar to those of Egyptian coffins and of coffins from Yuz-Oba Barrow (Vaulina 1971: 58, Figs. 2–3; Vaulina and Wasowicz 1974: Fig. 43).

Though the row of hinges is incomplete, it is quite certain from the almost completely preserved parts of Coffin 113 that the lid was workable even without the full row of hinges (Hachlili 1999: 67, Fig. III.2a; also Hodges 1964: Fig. 26).

Type B – This coffin type has a chest and a high gabled lid (Figure III–3). Five coffins of this type survived (Coffin 59, Tomb D9–3; Coffins 78, 84, 85, 94, Tomb D12).

The chest was constructed of several boards and four corner posts. Coffin 94 (Hachlili 1999: Figs. III.18, 19:1–3) corner posts have a mortise, which shows the method of joining one of the horizontal boards to the leg; its tenon had two holes for the securing dowels. The short sides probably consisted of two boards pegged togather with a projecting decorated frame (Figure III–3).

Coffins 59, 78, 84, 85 and 94 have high gabled lids with side boards and tympana. The lateral boards along the gable top are pegged together by a decorated ridge with black and red paint (Hachlili 1999: Figs. III.10; 11,12:3,4; 17:2; 23:3–5).

The lid tympana are triangular panels composed of three (or more) horizontal boards, pegged together by dowels; and joined to the lateral boards diagonally by dowels (Hachlili 1999: Fig. III.14: 1–4, 23). The tympana are decorated with painted black and red bands (Hachlili 1999: Figs. III.10; 12:5; 14; 17:6–9; 22:4). The sloping lateral boards are sometimes also similarly decorated (Hachlili 1999: Fig. III.20:7–13; see below).

Type C – This coffin type has a chest with gabled lid. Coffins of this type were found only in Tomb D27 (Coffins 184, 185, 187, 190, 198) (Figure III–4).

The coffin chest is framed with thin, narrow planks decorated with incisions (Hachlili 1999: Fig. III.30:7–12; 35:6–7).

Some of the corner posts and the ridges of these coffins were probably turned on the lathe (Singer et al. 1956, II:232–233; Hodges 1964: 117–118), while two of the coffins (187 and 190) have boards with recesses for hinges which are difficult to explain (Hachlili 1999: Figs. III.29:6,7; 35:4–6).

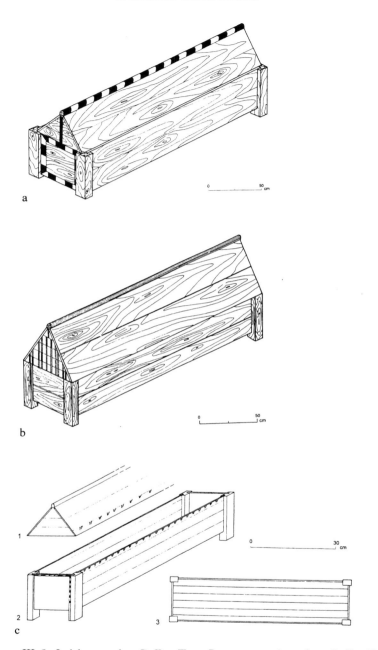

Figure III–3. Jericho wooden Coffins Type B, reconstruction of: a. Coffin 59; b. Coffin 78; c. Coffin 94.

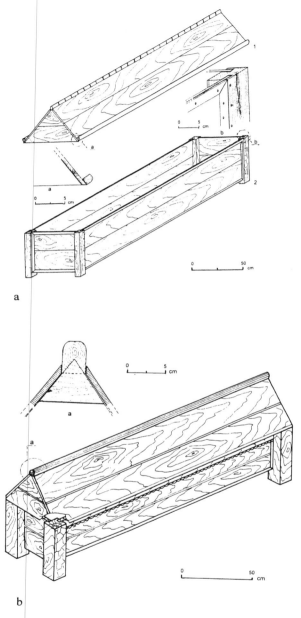

Figure III–4 Jericho wooden Coffin Type C, reconstruction of: a. Coffin 187; b. Coffin 190.

The coffins of Type C had gabled lids constructed of back and front tympana and side boards, secured by one or three ridges; the sides of the chest were framed by thin planks with incised designs. The gabled lid of Coffin 187 had three ridges: a central ridge decorated with groups of three incised lines and two lateral, plain(?) ridges joining the side boards of the lid; these were probably glued, since no dowel holes were found. The tympana boards were pegged together by dowels and the boards covered these joints (Hachlili 1999: Figs. III.27; 29:10–12; 30:14,16; 34:5–6).

Three wooden coffins were uncovered in Tomb G.81 at Jericho (Bennett 1965: 532–533). They had gabled lids, with doweled boards of the chest. Although few details have been published, these coffins were probably similar to the Jericho coffins.

The wooden coffins at Jericho were sometimes decorated on the narrow side of the chest, on the gabled lid's tympana and ridge, and on the corner posts (see Table III–1, Chap. IV).

'En Gedi Wooden coffins

Wooden coffins found in tombs 1–6 at 'En Gedi were preserved (Pl. III–2; about 40; 35 registered) (Table III–3; Hadas 1994: 4–5, 18, 22, 24–32, 34–36, 41–50; 3*–5*, Figs. 3–13, 33–49, 52, 71–78; one of these is on display in the Israel Museum). The wooden coffins and vessels were preserved due to the climate and the high salinity of the soil (Hadas 1994: 5*).

Hadas defines two types of wooden coffins A and B, and two sub-types, A1 and B1 (Table III–3; Hadas 1994: 45, Table 3):

Type A: The most common of 'En Gedi wooden coffins is a rectangular chest with four legs and a gabled lid (Figure III–5a), of which about 30 were found (Table III–3, eight coffins, tomb 1; two coffins, tomb 3; three coffins, tomb 4; fourteen coffins, tomb 5; three coffins, tomb 6? (Hadas 1994: Fig. 71).

Type A1: One coffin was found (Coffin 2, Tomb 6) its planks are connected by saddle-joints, and it has no legs (Figure III–6b): (Hadas 1994: Fig. 52).

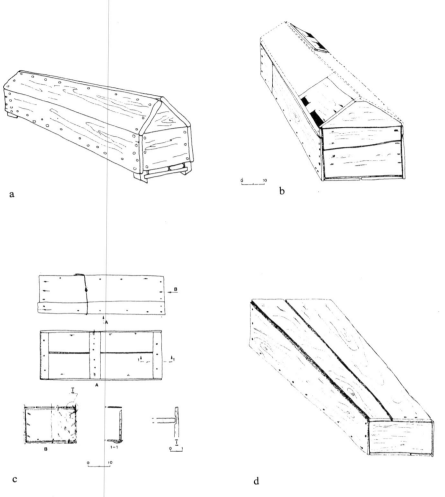

Figure III–5. ʿEn Gedi wooden coffin: a. *Type A*; b. *Type A1*; c. *Type B*;
d. *Type B1*.

Type B One wooden coffin (Coffin 7, discovered in Tomb 5) (Figure
III–5c), was made as a rectangular pine box, with a flat lid (Hadas
1994: Fig. 42–43,73). Hadas (1994: 45) suggests this is an ossuary.
However, on p.27 he reports that it contained the primary burial of
two children; so this appears to be a small coffin for the interment
of children, not an ossuary. Hadas adds the limestone ossuary to
this type and suggest that these wooden ossuaries were the origin of
the stone ossuaries.

Type B1: Three coffins with plain asymmetrical chest, their side a single plank, with a flat lid and bottom made of two joint planks (Figure III–5d) were found: Coffin 3, Tomb 3; Coffin 4, Tomb 4; Coffin 3, Tomb 6 (Hadas 1994: Fig. 74).

Table III–3: 'En Gedi, Wooden Coffins (after Hadas 1994: Tables 2–3).

Tomb No.	Coffin No.	Type	Coffins Dimensions						Timber	No. of interred Individual
			L	Chest W	H	H	Lid Plank	Bottom		
1	1	A	50+	35	21	13	21/19	30	Sycamore	1
	2	A	130+	33	22	?				2
	3	A?	88+	34	28	?				3
	4	A	81+	35	18	9	20/19	33	Sycamore, Tamarix	2
	5	A	184	36	18	10	19/18	31		1
	6	A?	140	32	18	?				3
	7	A	100	23	?	10	15	23		2
	8	A	120/118	26	12	17	24		Sycamore, Tamarix	2
2	Frags. of 4 coffins									61
3	1*	A	111+	20+		?				5 Skulls
	2*	A	135+	36	26	?				3
	3*	B1	62	20						3
4	1*	A?	115+	20+	10+	?				1
	2*	A	175	34	23					5
	3*	A?	185	34	20	?			Coniferous?	3
	4*	B1	55	20	20					2
	Oss.	B1	62	24	28	Pencil case lid			Limestone	
5	1	A	175	36	22	10	22/20	34	Sycamore, Christ-thorn	5
	2	A	174	36	24	23	22	33	Sycamore	2
	3	A	103	25	23	14	19	22	Sycamore	1
	4	A	177	35	22	9	16	21?	Sycamore	3
	5	A	172	35	20	11	20	31	Sycamore	4
	6	A	184	38	28	12	18	28	Sycamore	7
	7	B	57	23	15				Pine, Sycamore, Cypress	4
	8	A	173	36	18	12	22	36	Sycamore	5
	9	A	182	35	17	12	21	33	Sycamore	3
	10	A	76	23	16	4	10	19	Sycamore	2
	11	A	177	36	24	12	20	33	Sycamore	3
	12	A	177	39	20	12	22	36	Sycamore	2
	13	A	?			10	20	34		
	14	A	?			7	14	25		
	15	A	181	35	23	8	19	35	Sycamore	2
6	1	A?	110+	35	?	?			Sycamore	1
	2	A1	183	34	24	13	20	36	Sycamore	7
	3	B1	165	16/28	21/17				Sycamore	4
	4	A?	?	30	20					
	5	A?	?	32	20					

* No lid was found and these coffins do not necessarily belong to the type.

The 'En Gedi Wooden coffins are simply constructed as plain chests with four legs and a gabled lid (Pl. III–2) and should probably be dated to the first century BCE (Hadas 1994: 45–49; 2002: 25–27). The chest was assembled of thin boards, one board for each side of the chest, joined at the corners and pegged into the inside of the corner posts, which provided support and functioned as legs (Figure III–6). Tapered wooden pegs were used to join all sections of the coffins; they connected the long, side, and bottom boards to the legs. The gabled lid is constructed of two boards pegged to both triangular pediments and to the chest with concealed pegs. Edge joints between panels were made with concealed dowels. It is possible that some joints were glued as no pegs were found.

Occasionally support for the underside was provided (Hadas 1994: Figs. 75, 76).

Metal nails were used in three coffins: two bronze nails secured a mortise joint between two lengths of planking (Hadas 1994: fig.77, Coffin 15, Tomb 5). Iron nails were found with an impression in the wooden coffin in Tomb 3, and a single nail in Tomb 5 (Hadas 1994: 18, 32).

Almost all coffins were bound by a 10 mm thick, triple-braided date palm rope (see Chap. XI). The coffins are usually made of sycamore, the pegs also of tamarisk. Some other woods were used such as cypress, cedar, pine and jujube; all except for cedar and pine are native to the region (Table III–3; Hadas 1994: 49, Tables 1, 3; 72, App. 3, Table 1).

Some of the 'En Gadi coffins were decorated (Figure III–7).

Naḥal David caves, 'En-Gedi

Wooden coffins were found in two of the Naḥal David caves in the 'En-Gedi area (Avigad 1962b: 181–183). In Cave 1, the coffins had completely disintegrated. Several remnants of wooden coffins were discovered in Cave 4. They had been used for first burials in the cave, but later more skeletons were interred in them. In one coffin seven skulls had been placed. A coffin found in this cave was decorated (see Chap. IV, Pl. III–3). The side of the chest were dovetailed boards (Avigad 1962b: 182, Pl. 22A); the coffin contained a cup and a small wooden bowl, remains of a small plaited basket with peels of two pomegranates and the shells of two walnuts. Another coffin contained a skeleton wrapped in disintegrated cerements and

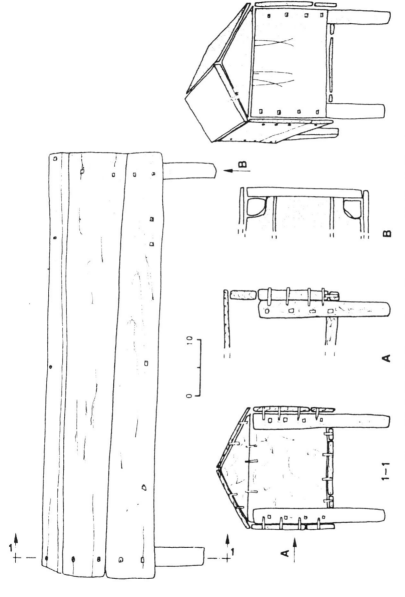

Figure III–6. 'En Gedi wooden coffin carpentry (Coffin 10, Tomb 5).

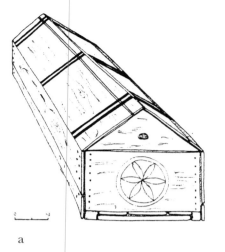

a

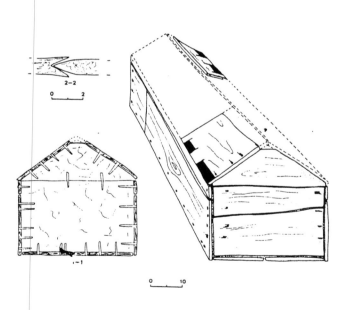

b

Figure III-7a,b. ʿEn Gedi wooden coffin decoration.

embroidered leather shoes. The coffins are dated to the first century BCE (Avigad 1962b: 185) and seem to be contemporary with the Jericho coffins.

Qumran Wooden Coffins

Remains of wooden coffins were discovered in the main Qumran cemetery, in two of the single, individual tombs (de Vaux 1973: 46–47). The data are insufficient for a description, but wood fragments and dust as well as the structure of the tomb indicate that the coffins were rectangular.

Comparative Material

Wooden coffins most similar in construction, decoration and other details those discussed above were found in Egypt and South Russia; these were published and discussed by Watzinger (1905), Edgar (1905), Minns (1913: 322–329) and Vaulina (1971). Most of these coffins were much larger and more elaborately decorated; they were constructed of four corner posts tenoned into the mortised side boards of the chest (Figure III–8, Figure III–9; Figure III–10).

These coffins usually had gabled lids with one or three ridges or with hinges, which allowed one sloping side of the lid to open (Watzinger 1905: 24–28, 30–31, 43–44; Ills. 27–50, 56, 76–78, 127; Edgar 1905: 1–2, Pl. III; Vaulina 1971: 57–58, Figs 2–3; Vaulina and Wasowicz 1974: 35–75, Types I and II).

The coffins are dated to the fourth-third centuries BCE, and may have served as prototypes for the Jericho coffins.

Some wooden coffins were also found in the Dura-Europos cemetery. They had gabled lids, boards and corner posts, probably joined by dowels (Toll 1946: 99–101). Some bronze angles were discovered nearby, explained by the excavator as fixed at the bottom and corners to secure the joints. Some of the coffins were decorated with a layer of painted plaster (Toll 1946: Fig. 6, Pl. 58).

They were probably used during the Hellenistic period until the second century CE. Remains of coffins were reported in some tombs at Petra (Murray and Ellis 1940: 12).

Wooden coffins are quite rare in ancient cemeteries in Israel. However, in some areas remnants of coffins were discovered: in the Nabatean necropolis of Mampsis some shaft tombs (Negev 1971:

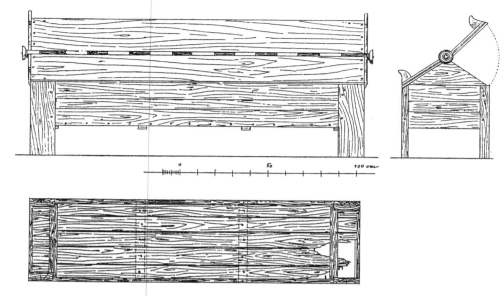

Figure III–8. Wooden coffins from Egypt.

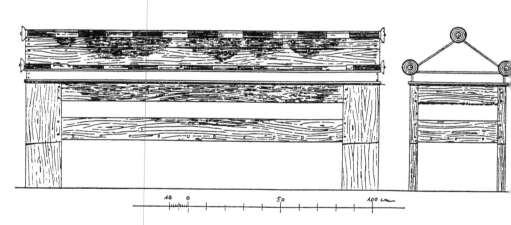

Figure III–9. Wooden coffins from Egypt.

117–118, Fig. 6, Pl. 248, Tombs 100, 112, 117, 118, 121) yielded
several wooden coffins. The best-preserved coffin, from Tomb 100,
is made of cedar wood, decorated with simple design incisions (Figure
III–11).

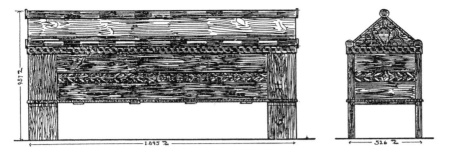

Figure III–10. Decorated wooden coffin from South Russia.

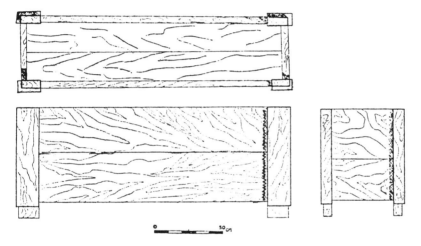

Figure III–11. Wooden coffin from Nabatean Mampsis, Tomb 100.

In size it is larger than the Jericho coffins, and the corner posts are dovetailed to the side boards, like the Naḥal David coffins. The tombs and the coffins are dated to the first century BCE – second century CE.

A fairly well preserved lidless cedar wood coffin was found at Yotvata in the Negev (Meshel 1991: 25, photo in Zevulun and Olenik 1978: 91, Fig. 233). It was constructed by the corner posts being joined to the side boards.

At Tel Malhata four wooden coffins were reported, in one of which leather shrouds were found (Eldar and Nahlieli 1983: 39). Several remains of wooden coffins were discovered at Kfar Giladi

(Kaplan 1967: 107) and Heshban (Waterhouse 1973: 118). Iron rings assumed to come from wooden coffins were discovered in (Stern & Gorin Rosen 1997: 7).

In the Beth-She'arim Jewish necropolis (third-fourth centuries CE) a group of iron nails and some iron corner pieces were found (B. Mazar 1973: 222–224, reconstructed as parts of wooden coffins on Pl. 30, 5, and as wooden ossuaries on Fig. 27, without sufficient evidence).[1] Wooden coffins may have been used at Beth She'arim for primary burial.

No wooden ossuaries have so far been found in any tomb in the Land of Israel (see comments on 'En-Gedi Type B, above). As can be observed from the Jericho coffins, iron nails and fittings may have been used as supporting elements of wooden coffins in a manner different from that described in the reconstruction at Beth She'arim.

The comparable wooden coffins, though some are contemporary in time and culture, are different in construction. The Jericho coffins are made with mortise joints, decorated with either paint or incisions, and they had a variety of lids. The other local coffins such as those from 'En Gedi are either simply joined or dovetailed and some are too fragmentary to identify their structure. The Jericho coffins most closely resemble those from Egypt and South Russia in their construction and quality of workmanship.

B. Ossuaries

The Ossuaries: material, technique, form

Most of the ossuaries of the Second Temple Period so far discovered the Land of Israel are from Jerusalem. Several groups of ossuaries were found in Judea, at Jericho (including six ossuaries discovered north and northwest of Tell Jericho; Bennett 1965: 516–517), as well as in Samaria, Galilee, and the Jezreel valley (Hachlili 1988a; 1999: 93).

Ossuaries were hand-hewn from large blocks of limestone (Pl.

---

[1] It should be noted that fragments of three wooden coffins were found in the upper part of tomb 1, chamber A, at Akeldama, dated to the Byzantine period (5th–7th centuries CE) (Avni & Greenhut 1996: 7, plan 1.3).

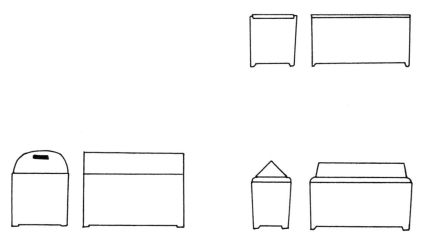

Figure III–12. Stone ossuary forms.

III–4) by stonecutters, using mallet, hammer and chisel. Usually they were in the shape of a rectangular box resting on four short feet (Figure III–12). The ossuaries were most likely produced in stone quarries situated around Jerusalem.

Unfinished ossuary fragments were discovered in a stone workshop on Mt. Scopus in Jerusalem (Amit et al. 2000: 356–357). Other quarries at Hizma, Jebel Mukabbar, and Tel el-Ful did not yield any ossuary fragments, only large stone blocks, which some scholars suggest have been used for the production of ossuaries (Magen 2002a: 133).

No standard dimensions seem to have been used (they were ca. 60 × 35 × 30 cm. for adults, smaller for children). The stone lid was flat, vaulted or gabled (Figure III–12). Many ossuaries were decorated, incised or chip carved usually on the front and sides (see below).

A smoothed surface is found only on ossuaries of quality workmanship or with a special decorative front. Ossuaries of poorer workmanship lack smoothed surfaces, and the cutting tools marks are clearly visible. The surface was cut vertically and these visible tool marks show that two tools of different widths were used (for example, Hachlili 1999: Figs. III.42b, 55, 61a, 65a–c, 70a, 73b). The designs were usually incised, seldom painted (For the supposed cost of ossuaries, see Chap. IX).

Inscriptions in Jewish script and/or in Greek were scratched, incised or written in ink on some of the ossuaries, on the front, back, sides, and lid. The inscriptions usually gave the name of the interred person and his family relations; sometimes the inscriptions noted a profession or a status. Special kinds of inscriptions were sometimes found, such as an abecedary or a unique, inscribed funerary bowl, found in an ossuary tomb in Jericho (See Chap. V). Out of 897 ossuaries included in the catalogue published by Rahmani (1994: 11, 13) about 227 are inscribed, with the addition of about 50 not published in his collection and some discovered recently.

Some of the ossuaries had drilled holes in the lid and upper part of the chest, with incised lines or crosses as direction marks to indicate the place for the holes (Hachlili 1999: Figs. III.62b, 75a–c). At one time these were erroneously taken for an early record of Christianity (Sukenik 1947: 12–15, 21–26, 30; refuted by Tzaferis 1970: 27; Smith 1974: 65; Rahmani 1982: 112). The marks served to designate the position of the lids on the ossuaries, and the holes served to fasten the lid to the ossuary with ropes or metal pieces.

Ossuary Ornamentation

Many of the recorded ossuaries from Jerusalem and Jericho are decorated (Pl. III–4). The location of the decoration on the ossuaries was usually on the long side, the front, the sides and sometimes the lids (Hachlili 1988a; 1999: 111–114).

The ossuaries were possibly produced in the quarry and ornamented in Jerusalem workshops (Magen 2002a: 133).

The designs are incised or carved in the soft limestone of the

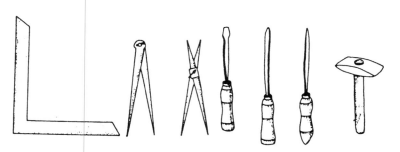

Figure III–13. Tools used to produce Ossuaries.

ossuaries with various tools such as compass, ruler, straightedge, carving knife, gouge, mallet, and chisel (Figure III–13).

The decorated ossuaries in Jerusalem and Jericho can be divided into three main types (Hachlili 1988a: 7).

Type I

The common and basic type of ornament was arranged symmetrically in a bipartite manner. The front of the ossuary has a frame of incised or chip-carved zigzag lines, usually divided on the façade (long side) into two metopes (or panels), although three or more do occur. The two metopes are generally filled with an identical pair of six-petalled, or multi-petalled rosettes, sometimes with added floral designs filling the space between the rosettes (Figure III–14; Pl. III–4). Most of the decorated ossuaries belong to this type.

Figure III–14. Decorated Type I ossuaries.

Type II

A framed tripartite design consisting of two identical six-petalled
rosettes; sometimes highly stylized multi-petalled rosettes flank a central motif. The ornament was arranged symmetrically on both sides
of the design in bipartite manner (Figure III–15; Pl. III–5). Sometimes
the two side depictions comprise various other motifs flanking a
rosette in the center. The motifs are: plants (Rahmani 1994: Nos.
382, 893), discs (Rahmani 1994: Nos. 388, 445, 736), and geometric patterns (Rahmani 1994: No. 399, 635) (Figure III–15).

Type III

The ossuary front is completely covered with a design, usually lacking rosettes Figure III–16; Pl. III–6a–b). (Rahmani 1994: Nos. 17,
41, 58, 60, 79, 121, 160, 175, 176, 191, 217, 220, 236, 290, 298,
308, 352, 353, 362, 420, 455, 481, 476, 480, 482, 487, 494, 730,
735, 835, 841; but sometimes an unusual addition of rosettes (see
Pl. IX–12).

Figure III–15. Decorated *Type II* ossuaries.

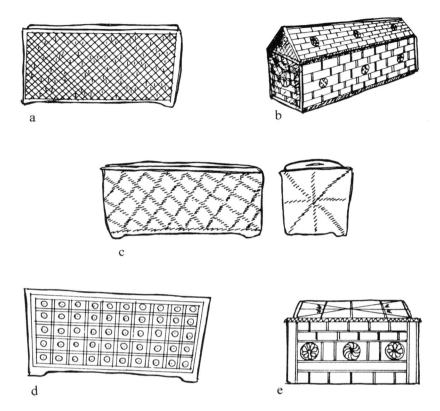

Figure III–16. Decorated *Type III* ossuaries.

Type IV

This type show variations and unusual decorations that do not fit the above three types, such as rosettes in groups (Figure III–17; Pl. III–6c–d); an unusual relief carved six-pillared tomb facade (see below); and others (Rahmani 1994: Nos. 478L, 478Lid, 482, 490, 815).

Repertoire of motifs

The arrangement of the repertoire of motifs decorating the ossuaries follows Figueras (1983: 36–77; also Hachlili 1988a: 10; 1999: 111–113). Rahmani (1994: 28–52) organized the repertoire of ossuary motifs according to his interpretation of the meaning of the ornamentation.

The motifs are similar to those appearing in other arts of the Second Temple period. Figurative motifs are absent from ossuary

Figure III–17. Decorated *Type IV* ossuaries.

ornamentation, in accordance with the aniconic art of that period (Hachlili 1988: 110–115).

Geometric motifs

Geometric motifs appearing on ossuaries contain rosette, wreath, disc, concentric circle, half circle, lozenge, zigzag lines, and checker board (Figure III–16–17).

Zigzag, was a simple pattern, executed often as a frame to the whole design borders the metopes and encloses the rosettes (Pls. III–4–5). Half circles at times appear in zigzag. Similar designs are present on many ossuaries (Rahmani 1982: 113–14; 1994: 36–7, Figs. 59–60; Figueras 1983: Pls. 11:307, 207; 12:17, 185).

Rosettes – The geometric rosette have an almost limitless number of variations (Figueras 1983: 36–41; Hachlili 1988a: 10–11; 1999: 112, Fig. III.53; Rahmani 1994: 39–41, Figs. 72–85; For rosette carving see Smith 1973: 73–75; 1983: 177–179.)

The main types of rosettes include the usual six-petalled rosette; the multi-petalled rosette (eight, twelve, sixteen, twenty-four petals) and the whirl rosette, which occurs in two forms, geometric and floral (Figure III–18; Figure III–19; Pls. III–4–5).

Figure III–18. Various rosettes decorating ossuaries.

Figure III–19. Examples of rosettes decorating ossuaries.

The majority of the rosettes on the ossuaries are either simply incised lines or lines filled with zigzag patterns. Some rosettes are chip-carved (Hachlili 1999: Fig. III.84, ossuaries Nos. 4, 6, 12, 23, XVI, XXII), and a few are painted (No. 3). There are also variants of rosettes such as the petals of one rosette forming the side of another so as to create an endless rosette pattern or an 'all-over' pattern. The six-petalled rosette in the circle sometimes has its lips linked by petals; heart-shaped leaves and dots or small circles are carved between the rosette petals.

Plant motifs

The main types of plants decorating ossuaries (Figure III–20; Pls. III–4–6) consist of acanthus leaf, palm tree, palmette, wreath, garland, grape and vine, acanthus, lotus flower, pomegranate, almond, pine-cone, lily, tree, branches, plants, and leaves (Rahmani 1994: 41–42).

Stylized Palm-tree are known to ornament Jerusalem ossuaries (Rahmani 1982: IV 115; 1994: 48–50; Figueras 1983: 42, 91–116). A similar stylized plant is incised on a Jericho ossuary (Hachlili 1999: Fig. III.85b, Ossuary 23).

Wreath ornamentation appears rarely on ossuaries and sarcophagi.

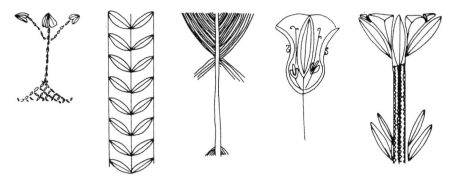

Figure III–20. Plant motifs decorating ossuaries.

Architectural motifs

Motifs of architectural nature consist of tomb monuments or facades, tomb entrance and door (Pl. III–7a), columned porch, gates, *nefesh*, columns, arcosolium, and ashlar walls (Figure III–21).

Figure III–21. Architectural motifs decorating ossuaries.

Tomb façade and entrance

Some ossuaries are decorated with a stylized tomb façade structure, such as a tomb entrance showing a paneled door, or a decorative motif. Such structures of three types are represented on a group of ossuaries for which several different interpretations have been proposed (Hachlili 1997; Chap. IX, group 1).

An elaborately ornamented hard limestone ossuary (Pl. III–7b) (from Mount Scopus southern slope, Jerusalem; Kloner 1993: No. 14, Rahmani 1994: No. 482) is decorated with a monumental six-pillared tomb facade (for details see Chap. IV).

An *ashlar wall* motif appears on a group of ossuaries. A wall is depicted in a header and stretcher arrangement, which is similar to tomb façades in Jerusalem, from which this motif was probably selected (Rahmani 1994: 35); on some of the ossuaries this motif is overlaid with rosettes.

Other architectural elements engraved on ossuaries include gates, arches, column, and the *nefesh*.

Figure III–22. Amphora motifs decorating ossuaries.

Other motifs

Various other motifs decorating ossuaries appear rarely. They include kantharos, dagger, and amphora (Figure III–22; Pl. V–5c, d), probably used as mere ornamentation. Pagan motifs such as altar and libation, sun and moon, are also found (Rahmani 1994: 34, 52).

A few ossuaries are decorated with a five-branched menorah-like plant (Figure III–23) (Rahamani 1994: 51–52, Figs. 127–128; Hachlili 1999: Fig. III.54f).

Frames – The majority of the frames are parallel lines, incised or carved in a zigzag pattern (Rahamani 1994: 36–37; 1999: 113–114;

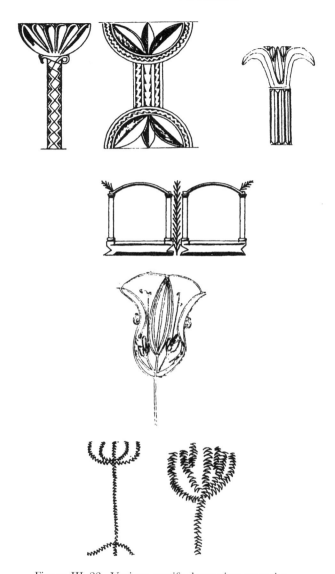

Figure III–23. Various motifs decorating ossuaries.

Fig. III.53). Some frames consist of dotted incised lines. Some ossuaries have two frames (Hachlili 1997); a double frame of chip-carved zigzags is found on one ossuary front (Figure III–24; Pls. III–4–6).

Elaborately carved or notched frames occur on some ossuaries: a palm-trunk pattern, a simple triangle pattern, and a special carved

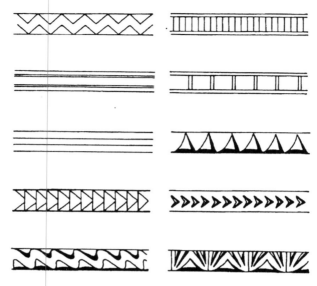

Figure III–24. Frames Decorating Ossuaries.

design in the upper frame line. Branches and plants sometimes with fruit and leaves appear as frames on ossuaries or in upright position in between the metopes; at times the motif is abstract and appears as a plant-like design (Rahmani 1994: 42).

Carved relief decoration

A small group of about 28 ossuaries discovered in tombs in Jerusalem are made of hard limestone; 21 of them have carved relief ornamentation (Rahmani 1994: 7) (Pls. III–4–6). These ossuaries are fashioned from local hard limestone and their decoration is in high relief; they usually were decorated with a sunken panel inside a profiled frame; their repertoire of motifs is similar in content and execution, usually consisting of plant and geometric designs in raised or sunken panels: a great variety of rosettes (Rahmani 1994: Nos. 12–14, 60:F, L; 153, 282:L; 294:R, L; 604:F, R, L; 736:L, R; 893:R; Avigad 1971: ossuary No. 1, Pl.), wreaths composed of flowers and leaves tied at the top by a fillet, usually depicted on the narrow side of the ossuary (Rahmani 1994: 41–42, Nos. 14:R, 60:R, 282:F, B; 308:R; 893:L), pomegranates (Rahmani 1994: Nos. 60:F; 308:L), lily (Rahmani 1994: No. 308:L), branch flanked by two grape clusters (Rahmani 1994: No. 893:F), running scroll, each spiral ending in a lily (Bagatti and Milik 1958: Sarcophagus 2 lid, Pl. 18, fot. 38, 39; Rahmani 1994: No. 587 lid).

Other motifs are geometric designs in raised or sunken panels: raised rectangle resembling an ashlar (Rahmani 1994: Nos. 14:F, 121:F; 294:F, B; 408:F, B), rhomb, (Rahmani 1994: No. 121:L), disc (Rahmani 1994: Nos. 14:L; 392:R; 393:R; 408:L; 587 lid; 597:L; 736:F, B, Lid), ring (Rahmani 1994: Nos. 596:L; 736:F, B, Lid), profiled frame (Bagatti and Milik 1958: Sarcophagus 2 front, Pl. 18, fot. 39; Rahmani 1994: Nos. 154, 308:F; 393:F, B, L).

These ossuaries were fashioned from local hard limestone and made by Jerusalem stonemasons, and "their relative rarity must be attributed to the degree of skill required for their manufacture, and the consequent high cost" (Rahmani 1994: 7). Bagatti and Milik (1958: 45–46) maintain that hard limestone chests should be regarded as sarcophagi. Rahmani (1994: 6) rightly disagrees, and argues that unless these decorated ossuaries are long (about 1.8m.), they should still be considered ossuaries (see also Foerster 1998: 303ff.).

Carved relief decoration also appears on twelve soft limestone ossuaries with patterns copied from tomb facades, sarcophagi, and hard limestone ossuaries (Rahmani 1994: 7, Nos. 160, 251, 326, 366, 388, 445, 569, 587, 601, 654, 679, 681, 831, 841).

Painted ossuaries

A few ossuaries are painted; an ossuary (from a tomb at Shemuel Hanavi St., Jerusalem; Rahmani 1994: 7–8, 126–128, No. 209) is the only one with elaborate polychrome ornamentation (Figure III–25a). The ornamentation consists of three semi-circular red garlands with red dart-shaped objects, round fruit, and lily-shaped flowers all in red and yellow; the motifs and their execution differ from the other local ossuaries and seem to represent foreign influence. Some decorative elements seem inspired by styles III and IV on Pompeian wall paintings and certain designs on Roman altars and sarcophagi, as well as by elements in Asia Minor.

At Jericho an ossuary has a red-painted design (Figure III–25b) consisting of two six-petalled rosettes in circles, a branch between them, and a similar branch in the left corner (Hachlili 1999: 93, Ossuary 3, Tomb A1, Fig. III–40).

Front

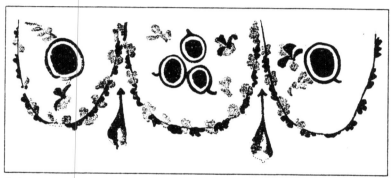

Back

a

b

Figure III–25. Ossuaries with painted decoration.

Three ossuaries from Jerusalem are decorated by a wash (Rahmani 1994: Nos. 464, 758).

A group of ossuaries from the Hebron Hills(?) displaying decorative motifs that might indicate an external origin were cited in the catalogue by Rahmani. One of them has a unique motif in the center, which probably represents a nefesh or a tomb-facade, flanked by two rings, each with a small central disc. Rahmani (1994: 177, No. 445) suggests that this ossuary, probably dated to the mid-second century CE, might have been carved by a craftsman from Syria. Another has on the front a depiction of an aedicula-shaped structure topped by a dome containing a similar smaller structure. On the back is an incised representation of a structure (?) or featureless human figure (?) with an object, possibly a jar or lyre, to its left. Rahmani (1994: 195–196, No. 555) suggests that the representation on this ossuary, probably dated to the second century CE, may indicate the origin of the deceased as Palmyra or Dura Europos. A group of ossuaries from the Hebron Hills (?), probably dated to the second century CE (Rahmani 1994: 52, 134, 138, Nos. 234, 251, 463, 635), seems to be pagan in its style of ornament. The designs on these ossuaries include altar and libation, sun, and moon. As it is quite implausible that Jews of the Second Temple period would have used representations of heavenly bodies; the ossuaries of this group seem locally produced, so they might have belonged to Nabataeans or other pagans influenced by the Jewish custom of ossilegium.

Interpretation of Motifs

Scholars differ over the meaning and interpretation of ossuary ornamentation (Rahmani 1994: 25–28). Goodenough (1953 III:119, 133; 1964 XII:68) maintains that the designs possessed symbolic value, possibly representing the hope of an afterlife. Figueras (1983: 78–86), following Goodenough, proposes that ossuary decoration reflected eschatological beliefs. Others suggest that it expressed beliefs of Judeo-Christians and detect hidden mystic meanings (Testa 1962: 426–513). Rahmani contends (1982: 115–118; 1994: 27–28) that the ornamentation on the ossuaries was non-symbolical and represented contemporary funerary art and architecture in Jerusalem. The motifs are not connected with Jewish everyday life; the decoration was inspired by "the tombs of the Jerusalem necropolis, their monuments, gates, courtyards, the trees and flowers seen outside them as well as elements of the tombs' interior". No symbols are depicted on the ossuaries except possibly the menorah, nor do any of the motifs represent the Temple (Hachlili 1988: 110–113; 1988a: 8).

The designs on Jewish ossuaries are part of an ensemble of decorative patterns used in the art of the Second Temple period, despite the fact that some of the motifs are found only in funerary art. Since ossuaries bearing different designs are found in the same tomb, the ornamentation seems to have been chosen by the family, and frequently a different design was used for each family member.

It is noteworthy that the ossuaries were ornamented on the front, sometimes elaborately, even though in most cases nothing would be seen of the decoration after the ossuaries had been placed in the tomb. Ossuary ornamentation should probably be seen as a response to the deep psychological needs of the living and the ideas current at that time about death and resurrection.

The ossuaries from Jerusalem and Jericho are similar in size, style, and decorative motifs. However, most of the Jericho ossuaries seem to have been made locally, though some might have come from Jerusalem. Several alternative explanations for the relationship between the Jericho and Jerusalem ossuaries can be suggested (Hachlili 1997: 247): the ossuaries were all made in Jerusalem and transported to Jericho; artisans and apprentices came from the Jerusalem workshops to work in Jericho; local Jericho artisans learned their trade in Jerusalem and following their return to Jericho set up their own workshops; patterns may have been copied by artisans from a common pattern book, and a Jericho artisan might have copied the pattern and made his own changes in the ornamentation of the ossuaries.

Sarcophagus-shaped ossuaries

The sarcophagus-shaped ossuaries were made of local hard limestone; they are large, crudely fashioned, usually plain; a few decorated ossuaries have a rosette in relief-carving or sunken relief. The lid was gabled with corner acroteria. The form and shape of the ossuaries was apparently copied from contemporary sarcophagi; the acroteria-shaped lids indicate that the original form was lost. These ossuaries were discovered in tombs in several Jewish settlements located in the southern part of Mount Hebron ("Daroma") and southern Judea: Carmel, el-Aziz, el-Kirmil, Eshtemoʻa, Ḥ. Anim, Ḥ. Kishor, Ḥ. Rimon, Ḥ. Thala, Susiya, and Yatta (see Chap. I, pp. 23–24).

The ossuaries are dated to the mid-second to mid-third century CE (some date them to the early fourth century), indicating that the practice of second burial in ossuaries survived in this area albeit sparsely (Avigad 1967: 137–138; Kloner 1984; Rahmani 1994: 24, Nos. 681–690, 857–862; Baruch 1997; Guvrin 1997).

Undecorated ossuaries

Large coarse undecorated ossuaries were found at the Hebron Hills, Horvat Thala in the southern Shephelah, Ḥuqoq in the Galilee, and some other sites (recorded in Rahmani 1994: Nos. 683–690, dated to the second to the early fourth century; Kloner 1984: 330–331). These ossuaries are different, later in date, and survived outside Jerusalem and Judea. The find of these ossuaries indicates that the custom of secondary burial in ossuaries might have survived until the later date of the fourth century.

Aviam and Syon (2002: 184) maintain that the custom of ossilegium in stone ossuaries arrived later to Galilee in the late first to mid-second century, their poor quality attests to their later production after decorative tradition disappeared. Only four decorated ossuaries were recovered from the Galilee (Daburiyya, Kabul, Kefar Kana, and Sepphoris; Aviam and Syon 2002: 152–153). Three are decorated on the short side a schematic wreath is depicted. On two of the ossuaries the other short side is decorated with a façade of a building with a gabled roof. The Sepphoris ossuary is decorated with on the long sides with architectural designs. Three other ossuaries from the Galilee bear inscriptions.

Clay ossuaries

A few clay ossuaries were produced; none predate 70 CE and most date from 135 CE to the mid-third century CE. The custom of ossilegium was introduced by waves of refugees to Judea and other areas after the destruction of Jerusalem.

The clay ossuaries are made of reddish-brown clay with a straw temper and a black core, usually poorly fired. Ribs reinforce the edges of the chests, with slightly inverted rims. Chest walls often knife-pared, and an inner ledge below the rim of the chest supports the lid. The lids are crudely modeled imitations of roof tiles with strap handles applied lengthwise along the center (Figure III–26; Pl. III–8). Fifteen clay ossuaries are cited in Rahmani's catalogue. Most

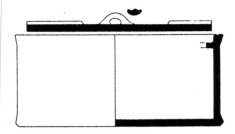

Figure III–26. Clay Ossuary.

of them were found in southern Judea and the Galilee and locally purchased, supposedly from the Hebron hills (Rahmani 1994: 10, 24; Table 1: Groups B5b, C1b, C2; Ossuaries Nos. 39–40, 187, 339, 340, 471, 754–6, 805, 806, 853, 864, 866, 895; only one clay ossuary of a child is reported to come from a Jerusalem tomb: Sukenik 1930a: 124: Ossuary 4, Pl. B:3,3a).

Aviam and Syon (2002: 153–185, Table 1) list about seventy stone and clay ossuaries recovered from loculi tombs located in thirty sites in the Galilee, most of these are known or assumed to be Jewish villages, dated between the late first and the third century CE. They classify the clay ossuaries into five general types and the lids into three types (ibid.: 155). They conclude (ibid.: 184–185) that the Galilee ossuaries were probably manufactured in a local small cottage industry that appeared in Galilee after the fall of Jerusalem. They were produced in similar technology to clay coffins. It seems clay ossuaries were a cheaper option in comparison to the limestone ossuaries, or were used as replacement because the stone production ceased to exist. The distribution of the ossuaries in the Galilee supports the postulation that *ossiligium* was a Jewish custom.[2]

Some Jewish ossuaries are known from the Diaspora. They include a number of clay examples from North Africa, dated probably to the second-third centuries CE (Ferron 1956: 107, Pl. 11; Rahmani 1994: 10, n. 24).

(For the chronology and geographic distribution of ossuaries, see Chap. XII: 520).

---

[2] The Ḥurvat ʿUza tomb where a clay ossuary was found with eleven clay coffins (Ben-Tor 1966: 22–24; Rahmani 1994: no. 187) has no evidence of being a Jewish tomb (Aviam and Syon 2002: 183, Table 1).

Comparable Material

Comparable material consists of ossuaries found especially in Asia Minor, these being groups of ossuaries from Ephesus, Sardis, and their environs as well as Rhodian cinerary caskets.

A large group of ossuaries (about 109 are recorded) was discovered in Ephesus and its environs, produced during the late Hellenistic period to the end of the second century CE. Their use precedes the increased Roman utilization of sarcophagi for inhumation burial (Thomas 1999). These ossuaries were rectangular containers, made of thick coarse white marble, with small feet and a flat or gabled lid. They were used for calcified bones left after cremation of a corpse, identical in function to the *cineraria*, ash chests discovered in Italy. More than half of the ossuaries bear their owners' names, usually on the front face, indicating classes of Roman citizens, freed persons who tended to use the garland-decorated ossuaries (Thomas 1999: Pl. 132:1–3). Only a few of the ossuaries were found in the context of burial, mostly were discovered in secondary use in building or as fountain basins.

The Ephesian ossuaries are divided into two types: the earlier plain type and the later garland-decorated type. The main decoration is the garland and semi-finished garland, consisting of a standard motif of two garlands, composed of autumn fruits: grapes, pomegranates and figs, carried between two rams' heads in the corners, and a bull's head (*boukephalion*) in the center. This design usually ornaments the long sides of the chest, while the narrow sides bear only one garland (Thomas 1999: Pl. 132:1–4). The semi-finished garland ossuaries designate the inclination of the workshops or purchasers to leave one or more of the sides unfinished. Their production seems to have been prevalent in the fifty years before sarcophagus production (Thomas 1999: 552, 553 – diagram, Pl. 132:3–4; the ossuaries are dated to the second half of the first century BCE). Some of the ossuaries were also decorated with paint. The iconography of the design, the garland, the rams, and the bulls reflected the same motifs on monumental architecture and indicated sacrificial aspects and offerings of fruit. Roman influence was designated by the introduction of a small funerary chest, suitable for cremation.

Another type of comparable ossuary is the so-called 'Sardis type', characterized by the decoration of a lock flanked by two discs on the front of the ossuary, giving the impression of a jewelry box (Fraser 1977: Pl. 29; Thomas 1999: 551, Pl. 131:4).

The Rhodian rectangular cinerary caskets are made of white limestone with a gabled lid (similar to sarcophagi); they are undecorated, sometimes inscribed on the short side or on the lid, and dated to the later Hellenistic period (Fraser 1977: 12–13; Pls. 25–28). These chests contained ashes of cremated dead; they were placed in loculi or in chamber tombs in the necropolis with sarcophagi burial. There seems to be no link between the Rhodian and the Asia Minor caskets.

The Asia Minor and Rhodian ossuaries evidently differ fundamentally in shape, decoration, and function from the Jewish ones. Moreover, the cultural, geographical, and religious differences created an enormous gap between the pagan and Jewish worlds.

Although Hellenistic individualistic concepts left their mark on Judaism, the "actual concept of a physical, personal and individual resurrection as found in late first century BCE Jerusalem is clearly Jewish . . ." (Rahmani 1986: 99; 1994: 53–55). Furthermore, the custom of ossilegium, as well as the ornamentation of the ossuaries, is distinctly indigenous, and should be considered as "fundamentally Jerusalemite, being conceived without any direct foreign influence". Jerusalem probably strongly influenced the customs and practices of the Jews of Jericho and Judea as a whole.

Origin of Ossuaries

An attempt was made to determine the origin of the ossuaries by comparing them with earlier bone containers, as remote as the Chalcolithic period (Meyers 1971: 27–31). Rahmani (1973: 121–123) justifiably refuted this approach and also ruled out a possible connection with Persian bone containers (1986: 98–99; 1994: 56–57). He rejected the possibility of Persian influence on Jewish ossilegium and ossuaries; he maintained that the date for the introduction of ossilegium and bone containers in Persia seems to be the mid-first century CE. Evidence for communal charnels probably occurs only in the late first or early second century CE and ossuaries are prevalent only in the Sassanian period. In Rahmani's opinion, the clay and stone ossuaries found in Central Asia, which date from the third-second centuries BCE, did not influence Jewish ossuaries because of lack of any contact.

The possibility of Hellenistic influence has also been probed extensively. The standard shape of the ossuary as a rectangular chest is based on similar household furniture, and it was used throughout the Hellenistic and Roman world (Rahmani 1994: 58–59).

(For scholars' debate on the causes and origin of the custom of secondary burial in ossuaries, see Chap. XI).

C. Stone Sarcophagi

Stone sarcophagi are quite rare in the Second Temple period. Only about twenty were discovered in the Jerusalem necropolis, most of them from five tombs of royal and prominent families (Rahmani 1994a; Foerster 1998).

The sarcophagi were large and heavy, had a rectangular body, and a gabled or vaulted lid; Rahmani (1994: 4) suggests, regarding both sarcophagi and ossuaries, that they were made in the form of a wooden household chest. Many of the sarcophagi were decorated especially on the long side, sometimes on the narrow sides and on the lid (see Table III–4 for sarcophagi measurements, decoration, and inscriptions).

As a rule sarcophagi could be used for primary burial. However, either no bones were found in them or the condition of the bones was such that was difficult to determine if the deceased were interred in primary or secondary burial. For some of the sarcophagi, scholars suggest the burial of the head of the family was primary and the bones of close relatives were later placed in the same sarcophagus (No. 14).

Many sarcophagi were found together with ossuaries in the same tomb. This might indicate that the majority functioned as large ossuaries for secondary burial rather than as sarcophagi for primary burials.

The 'cushion' or headrest, the special recess and ledge found in the interior of some of the sarcophagi (Nos. 4, 5, and possibly 13), is similar to some early Roman sarcophagi and is considered as an early element (Brandenburg 1978: 282, 285; Foerster 1998: 303). Some of the decorated sarcophagi possibly were intended to be visible to the living by their position inside the tomb (like some Roman stone sarcophagi: White 1999: 88–90; see Tyre, Chehab 1983–6). (For a discussion of the ornamentation of the sarcophagi, see Chap. IV).

Description of Sarcophagi

These decorated sarcophagi were found in several Jerusalem tombs:
1. A sarcophagus at Akeldama, Jerusalem (Tomb 2, chamber B, in loculus II in the south corner of the chamber) could not be removed; its lid had been removed in antiquity and was found in the chamber (Avni and Greenhut 1996: 18; Shadmi 1996: 46, No. 19, Fig. 1.29b–c; Foerster 1998: No. 13, Taf. 124,1). Only the narrow side of the sarcophagus is exposed and is decorated with a circular wreath of flowers and fruits in high relief, enclosing a round-petalled flower, all framed in a sunken panel (Pl. III–9). Above the wreath is a Greek inscription recording the two interred: 'Eros and Hermione of Doras'. The sarcophagus is dated to the first century CE by means of stylistic comparisons.

Two sarcophagi were uncovered in the Nazirite family burial vault on Mount Scopus:
2. Nazirite Sarcophagus 1 was made of hard limestone, its decoration being in relief (Avigad 1971: 191–192, Fig. 4. Pls. 38–39; Foerster 1998: No. 10, Taf. 122,1; 142, 2). The sarcophagus front has a molded frame enclosing a floral design in shallow relief arranged symmetrically (PL. III–10). In the center is a stylized lily(?) (or acanthus calyx) with a double volute and a central petal. From within the lily an acanthus scroll issues on each side, with ivy leaves, blossoms, and bunches of grapes. Small rosettes with four, six, or twelve petals fill the spaces. The form of the acanthus scrolls is comparable to the sarcophagus found in the tomb of Herod's family (Figure III–29).

The ornamentation of this sarcophagus, especially in the treatment of the leaves and grapes, may still be regarded as of naturalistic nature. The bunches of grapes motif on the sarcophagus is common in the repertory of Jewish art of the Second Temple period, and a close parallel appears in the center of the Doric frieze on the façade lintel of the Tomb of Queen Helene of Adiabene ("Tomb of the Kings"). The gabled lid of the sarcophagus bears a broad, dense band of ivy garland leaves, entwined with ribbons. A rosette decorates each of the tympanon. An exact parallel appears on the lid of sarcophagus from the Mount of Olives (Bagatti and Milik 1958: 48, PL. 17). Possibly the lids originated in the same workshop. The sarcophagus has perforated holes at the bottom (similarly to ossuaries) probably for the drainage of body fluids (Figure III–27).

Figure III–27. Sarcophagus 2.

Avigad (1971: 191) maintains that sarcophagus No. 1 from the Nazirite family tomb and the sarcophagus found in the tomb of Herod's family were both undoubtedly produced at the same workshop, with the Nazirite sarcophagus possessing the finer motif.

3. Sarcophagus No. 2, from the Nazirite family tomb (200 cm long, 57 cm wide, 51 cm high) (Avigad 1971: 192–193, fig. 5; Foerster 1998: No. 9, Fig. 5), is larger and heavier, made of hard limestone, plain with no ornamentation, with a vaulted lid (201 cm long and 26 cm high). An irregular hole was crudely punched near the bottom on one of the narrow sides.

In the "Tomb of Herod's family" two sarcophagi (Nos. 4 and 5) and several richly decorated lids were found on the floor in the same room (Figure III–28).

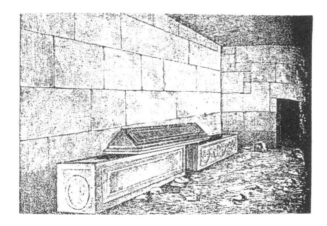

Figure III–28. Tomb of Herod's family: chamber with sarcophagi.

4. A sarcophagus made of hard limestone carved in relief (Schick 1892: 119–120; Macalister 1901: 401; Vincent and Steve 1954: 345, fig. 96, Pls. 84–85,1; Watzinger 1935: 68, Taf. 29, abb. 67; Avigad 1956: 346–7, Fig. 28; Foerster 1998: No. 8, Taf. 121,3–4; 122, 2–3). The sarcophagus front has a molded frame enclosing a floral design in shallow relief arranged symmetrically. In the center is a stylized acanthus calyx with a double volute and a central petal; issuing from it are stylized acanthus scrolls in two opposite directions. Small rosettes with twelve petals alternate between the scrolls (Figure III–29a; Pl. III–11).

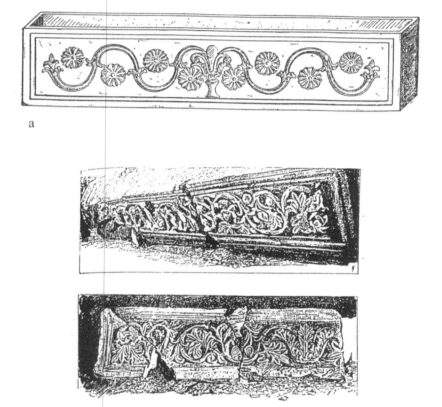

Figure III–29. Sarcophagus 4: a. front; b. decorated lid (two sides).

The motif on this sarcophagus is stylized to the point of lifeless-
ness. The form of the vines is comparable to the Nazirite sarcophagus No. 2). The short sides and the interior are similar to sarcophagus
No. 4 from the same tomb.

A gabled lid probably belonged to this sarcophagus although it is
decorated in a different style (Schick 1892: 119; Vincent and Steve
1954: 346, Pl. 85; Goodenough 1953: 238; Foerster 1998: No. 8,
Taf. 122,2,3). The lid is adorned (Figure III–29b) with lifeless and
stylized acanthus scrolls on both sides of the gable, which issue from
a three-leaved acanthus calyx in the center; the scrolls stems termi-
nate in fruits, leaves, and flower buds. This design is comparable to
decorated gables of some tombs in Jerusalem.

5. A plain molded sarcophagus with gabled lid (Schick 1892: 119–120;
Watzinger 1935: 69; Vincent and Steve 1954: 345, fig. 96, Pls. 82;
Foerster 1998: No. 7, Taf. 121,3). The short sides are decorated,
one with a rosette, the other with a protruding disc (Figure III–30).

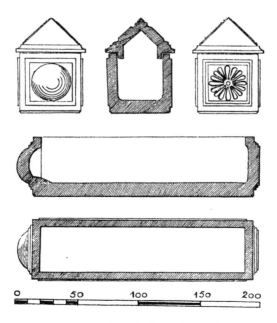

Figure III–30. Sarcophagus 5.

The interior has a carved raised ledge or 'cushion' for the head.
The sarcophagus has a gabled lid.

The Tomb of Helene of Adiabene ("Tomb of the Kings") yielded
the largest group of sarcophagi and some lids (Nos. 6–11):

6. A sarcophagus (now in the Louvre: Inv. AO 5036) has its front
and vaulted lid decorated with a continuous row of five dissimilar
rosettes, with eight small discs which fill the empty space between
the larger ones on the front (Figure III–31). The sides of the sarcophagus are ornamented with a rosette in a wreath on one side
and with a double lined circle on the other (Dussaud 1912: 46, No.
30; Kon 1947: 70–72; Avigad 1956: Fig. 20; Foerster 1998: No. 2,
Figs. 2,3, Taf. 120:1–3).

7. A sarcophagus chest, now situated in front of the Islamic Museum
on Temple Mount in Jerusalem, its front decorated with several
rosettes is similar to sarcophagus No. 6; the side is ornamented with
a rosette in a double lined circle (Rahmani 1994a: 231; Foerster
1998: No. 3, Taf. 120, 4,5). Foerster (1998: 298) suggests that a frag-

Figure III–31. Sarcophagus 6.

ment of a vaulted (semi-circular) lid in the Louvre (Inv. AO 5046) with the same decoration (Figure III–32) and dimensions plausibly belongs to this sarcophagus and derived from this tomb.

Figure III–32. Sarcophagus 7, lid.

8. This sarcophagus, now in the Louvre (Inv. AO 5029), has sunken panels with six blocked-out discs on all sides of the chest: two discs on the front and back and one on each side. It has a gabled plain lid (Dussaud 1912: 43, No. 28; Kon 1947: 71, Fig. 17; Goodenough 1953: 237; Vincent and Steve 1954: 351, abb. 98; Foerster 1998: No. 4, Taf. 125,2). On its front, two inscriptions are engraved in Aramaic: צדה מלכתא and Syriac צדן מלכתה 'Sadah [or Sadan], the Queen' (Figure III–33). Scholars identified the inscription as relating to Queen Helene of Adiabene.

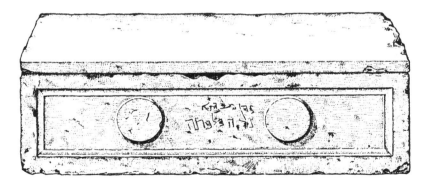

Figure III–33. Sarcophagus 8.

9. An unfinished sarcophagus (now serving as the water trough of the fountain in Ha-Gai St., Jerusalem) believed to originate in the Tomb of Helene of Adiabene has blocked-out panels and three blocked-out discs on the long sides (Pl. III–12a), one on a short side and phiale on the other. At the end of the sarcophagus a headrest is carved inside as an elevated ledge (Clermont-Ganneau 1899, I:129, 138, 232; Rahmani 1994a: 233; Foerster 1998: No. 5, Taf. 121,1).

10. A sarcophagus chest is set into the lower part of a Mamluk structure dating to 1482; this is the Qayat-Bay fountain on Temple Mount, Jerusalem (Goodenough 1953, III: Fig. 240; Jacoby 1989: 284, Fig. 1; Rahmani 1994a: 232–233; Foerster 1998: No. 6, Taf. 121, 2). It is decorated by a band of six multi-petalled rosettes separated by lotus buds, with an ovolo on top and two bands on the lower part (Figure III–34; Pl. III–12b).

Figure III–34. Sarcophagus 10.

11. A vaulted sarcophagus lid, made of hard limestone (now in the Louvre, Inv. AO 5057) is decorated with an elaborate and rich design of vine scrolls, acanthus leaves, various flowers, and fruits in several bands framed by a molded running medallion scroll (Figure III–35); it is reconstructed from two fragments (Kon 1947: Fig. 14; Goodenough 1953, I:134, III:232, 233–235; Foerster 1998: No. 1; Taf. 125,1).

Two sarcophagi were discovered on the Mount of Olives ('Dominus Flevit') although the excavators recorded seven sarcophagi (Bagatti and Milik 1958: 45–49):

12. A sarcophagus with a gabled lid from Mount of Olives tomb 301 ('Dominus Flevit') is decorated on its long side with a projecting panel; the short side has a square projecting panel and a disc (Bagatti and Milik 1958: No. 3, Pl. 17: Fot. 37; Foerster 1998: No. 12, Taf. 123, 1–2). The gabled lid has an ivy-leaf garland on its front sloping gable (Pl. III–13), similar to the decoration of the lid on Sarcophagus No.2 from the Nazirite tomb.

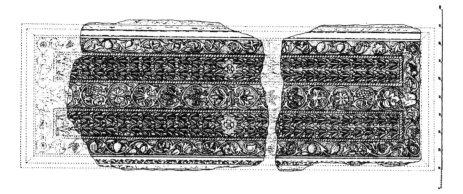

Figure III–35. Decorated lid of Sarcopagus 11.

13. A sarcophagus with a hemispherical lid from the Mount of Olives ('Dominus Flevit') tomb 299; its chest front is decorated with three blocked-out discs. One of the short sides has a hemispherical disc, similar to Sarcophagi 4 and 5 from Herod's family Tomb (Bagatti and Milik 1958: No. 4, Pl. 18: Fot. 40; Foerster 1998: No. 11, Taf. 125,3).

Several large ossuaries (Nos. 14–16) may have been used as sarcophagi, mainly because of their dimensions. Vincent and Steve (1954: 345) argue that these sarcophagi contained a single deceased person. Rahmani (1994: 217, No. 666) maintains that it is likely that some of these sarcophagi were used as ossuaries, which means that bones of close relatives would have been added to the primary burial.

14. A sarcophagus was recovered with several ossuaries from a tomb on the southern slope of Mount Scopus,and was used as an ossuary (Kloner 1993: 99–101, No. 27, Fig. 21; Rahmani 1994: No. 490). Its ornamentation consists of a central row of seven multi-petalled rosettes (Pl. III–14).

Each narrow side is decorated with a rosette within a grooved ring. The gabled lid is decorated with of a central row of five multi-petalled rosettes, flanked by two rings with rosettes within, and an ashlar design at the base. A Greek inscription records: "Of Phasael, and of Iphigenia, of Phasael his son". The same hand apparently incised the names of wife and son. It seems that Phasael, the head of the family, was interred first, and the bones of his wife and son (of the same name) were added later. Kloner and Rahmani prefer to regard this as a large ossuary.

15. A sarcophagus or large ossuary, found with a sarcophagus (No. 16) and an ossuary, were looted from a tomb on the eastern slope of Mount Scopus (Rahmani 1994: No. 668). The sarcophagus is ornamented with an ashlar-wall pattern on all sides; on the front there is a row of sixteen rosettes framed by a line circle; similar rows of rosettes are present on the narrow sides (Pl. III–15). The gabled lid is decorated with ashlar-wall pattern and a row of eight rosettes. Two holes appear on the lower part of the left side.

These two sarcophagi (Nos. 14 and 15) have a similar feature, the deep depression (handgrip) for handling on the narrow sides of the gabled lid.

The similar ornamentation on sarcophagi Nos. 14 and 15 is also comparable to two ossuaries found in tombs on the Mount of Olives ('Dominus Flevit') (Bagatti and Milik 1958: No. 26, Pl. 19: Fots. 41–42; No. 88, Pl. 19: Fots. 44–45).

16. A plain sarcophagus or large ossuary was found in a tomb on Mount Scopus, eastern slope, with a sarcophagus (No. 15) and an ossuary (Rahmani 1994: No. 666).

17. Two 'sarcophagi' are carved into the rock in the left chamber of Tomb VII at Sanhedriya (Rothschild 1952: 33, Pl. 8:2; Rahmani 1961: 100–101, Pl. 13:2, 13:1).

Figure III–36. Sarcophagus carved into the left-hand chamber of Tomb VII at Sanhedriya.

These were uncommon arcosolia that had been arranged as 'sarcophagi'; they are part of the rock and are immovable (Figure III–36). The 'sarcophagus' opposite the entrance was adorned with three rosettes. Several fragments of sarcophagi were discovered at Sanhedriya: three hard limestone fragments of sarcophagi chests with raised or molded panels were also discovered in Tomb VII.

A fragment of a rounded sarcophagus lid decorated with a plain raised disc was found in Tomb XIV (Rahmani 1961: 101, Pls. 13:2, 13:1).

18. Fifteen fragments of sarcophagi and lids were discovered in the fill of the rooms of a tomb east of 'Herod's family tomb' (Kloner 1985: 61, Pl. 13,2).

Table III–4: Stone Sarcophagi

No	Provenance	Dimensions cm L W H	Lid	Decoration	Inscription	Reference
1	Akeldama, Tomb 2			Front, side	Greek	Shadmi 1996: 46
2	Mt. Scopus Nazirite Tomb	188 × 45.5 × 42.5	gabled	Front, lid		Avigad 1971: 191–192
3	Mt. Scopus Nazirite Tomb	200 × 57 × 51	Vaulted			Avigad 1971: 192–193
4	Herod's family Tomb	180 × 50	Gabled decorated	Front		Schick 1892: 119–120
5	Herod's family Tomb	180 × 50	Gabled	sides		Schick 1892: 119–120
6	Helene of Adiabene	200 × 47	Vaulted decorated	Front, sides		Dussaud 1912: 46, No. 30
7	Helene of Adiabene	200 × 55	Vaulted decorated	Front, sides		Rahmani 1994a: 231
8	Helene of Adiabene	205 × 57	gabled	Front, back, sides	Aramaic Syriac	Dussaud 1912: 43, No. 28
9	Helene of Adiabene	190/200 × 55/60 × 54/56		Front, back, sides		Rahmani 1994a: 233
10	Helene of Adiabene	202 × 62.5		Front		Jacoby 1989: 284, Fig. 1
11	Helene of Adiabene	195 × 55	Vaulted decorated			Kon 1947: Fig. 14
12	Mt. of Olives 'Dominus Flevit'	150 × 45 × 63	Gabled decorated	sides		Bagatti & Milik 1958: No. 3
13	Mt. of Olives 'Dominus Flevit'		hemispherical			Bagatti & Milik 1958: No. 4
14	Mt. Scopus	170 × 51.5 × 53	Gabled decorated	Front, sides	Greek	Kloner 1993: No. 27
15	Mt. Scopus	184 × 48.5 × 55 + 28	Gabled decorated	Front, sides		Rahmani 1994: No. 668
16	Mt. Scopus	165 × 46.5 × 47 + 21				Rahmani 1994: No. 666
17	Sanhedriya Tomb VII	2 sarcophagi carved into the rock				Rothschild 1952: 33, Pl. 8:2
18	East of Herod's family Tomb	15 fragments				Kloner 1985: 61

CHAPTER FOUR

FUNERARY ART

The funerary art of the Second Temple period is rich and varied. It consists of ornamentation of tomb façades, sarcophagi, and ossuaries, as well as wall paintings and graffiti.

The architecture and decoration of the sepulchral monuments in the Jewish necropolis of Jerusalem have several characteristic features. Common to many monuments is a Greek distylos in antis and ornamented façade.

Jewish funerary art as expressed in ornamented tombs reflects a Hellenistic tradition, executed locally. Rahmani (1981: 49) contends that the architectural features of the Second Temple period tomb façades in Jewish Jerusalem have a purely ornamental value. These carvings should not be seen as intended to represent entrances to an 'Eternal House'. Moreover, no symbolic value was intended in these ornamentations.

A. Tomb Ornamentation

The composite style is characteristic of ornamented tombs in Jerusalem, and its execution is typical generally of Jewish art of the Second Temple period. This style, an amalgamation of stylistic features influenced by Hellenistic-Roman architecture and by Oriental elements, consists of combines common Doric and Ionic styles with an Egyptian cornice and pyramid. It is found on monumental tombs and on the façade of ornamented tombs; distinctive illustrations are the two free-standing monuments of Zachariah and Absalom. Espcially impressive is the unique composite style of the façade of the Tomb of Queen Helene of Adiabene. Similar monumental tombs, which combine both a tomb and a *nefesh* memorial, have been found in some other Jerusalem tombs (Avigad 1950–1951; 1954: 112–117; 1956; 1975). The façade and the molded frame of the doorway are carved in the rock and ornamented in many tombs in Jerusalem of the Second Temple period and are comparable to façades of Nabatean tombs at Petra (McKenzie 1990).

Ornamentation in the Jerusalem necropolis consists essentialy of two main elements. (a) Tomb ornamentation outside: façade and porch decoration, ornamentation on entablature, frieze and pediment; some tombs have an addition of the *nefesh* ornamentation. (b) Tomb ornamentation inside: carved and painted parts of the grave as well as wall paintings.

Jerusalem tombs contain an ornamented façade and porch. A feature common to many monuments is a distylos in antis façade. The characteristic decoration of the façade is a molded entablature with the frieze elaborately ornamented (see also Kloner and Zissu 2003: 16–22). Ornamented tomb façades appear on the Frieze tomb and the Tomb in the Hinnom Valley (see Chap. II, pp. Nos. 3.1, 3.2). Tomb façades with ornamented moldings and pediment occur on the the Grape tomb, Sanhedriya XIV and the Tomb of Jehoshaphat. These two tombs have acroteria decorated with floral design (see Chap. II, pp. Nos. 4.1, 2, 3) (McKenzie 1990: 97).

Some tombs have a porch decorated with a Doric frieze; the metopes are filled by discs at the Two-storied tomb; at the Tomb of Helene of Adiabene a special design decorates the center of the frieze; a comparable façade appears at the Urn Tomb at Petra, decorated with a similar frieze and an undecorated pediment (McKenzie 1990: Pl. 40b–c). Carved rosettes decorate the metopes of the Umm el-Amed tomb. The tombs of Helene of Adiabene and Umm el-Amed have Ionic columns on attic bases in the distyle-in-antis porch. The façade of the Frieze tomb has a Doric frieze, its metopes filled with rosettes and a wreath in the central metope. The Bene Ḥezir tomb has no decoration in the metopes. Sanhedriya Tomb VIII and the Tomb of Nicanor bear an unornameted porch.

Similar tomb façade ornamentation occurs in group no. 7 of the Petra tombs, among them the Roman Temple, the Obelisk and the Khasneh Tombs, dated to the first and second century CE (McKenzie 1990: 2–9ff., Table 1).

Some particular architectural features occur on Jerusalem tombs: ashlar masonry decorating the façade and inner walls of tombs; decorated ceilings and domes; and other distinctive ornamentation.

Ashlar masonry decoration

Ashlar masonry appears on walls and sometimes on ceiling; the chambers of the Nazirite family tomb are built of ashlar stones (Pl. IV–1)

(Avigad 1971: 186, 188, Fig. 3, Pls. 33–35). The walls of the tomb of Herod's family are faced with ashlar stones (Schick 1892: 120; Vincent 1954: Pl. LXXXIV:1).

The fine masonry is quite similar on these two tombs, and is also comparable to the following examples: the two chambers in a tomb in Kidron Valley are lined with masonry (Mayer 1924; Savignac 1925; Clermont-Ganneau 1899, II: 341ff.). The façade of Umm el-Amed tomb (Fig. II–15c; Avigad 1950–51: 103, Fig. 7) has rock drafted masonry, indicating a wish to imitate a building.

Ornamented dome and ceiling

Several of the Jerusalem tombs are adorned with a decorated ceiling: the Absalom Tomb burial chamber has a ceiling ornamentation (Figure IV–1), consisting of a square relief ornamented with a large circle (or wreath) enclosing a star, and four discs in the four corners (Avigad 1954: 102, Figs. 63, 64).

Figure IV–1. Decorated ceiling of Absalom Tomb chamber.

The arcosolia chamber of the Grape tomb has a ceiling (Figure IV–2a) ornamented with a carved rosette in a circle (Macalister 1900: 54. see below.)

A tomb in Hinnom Valley has a domed ceiling in the entrance chamber (Figure IV–2b), decorated with a rosette and a calyx in its

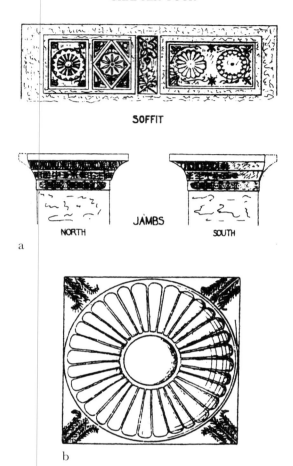

SOFFIT

JAMBS

NORTH   SOUTH

a

b

Figure IV–2a,b. a. Grape tomb decorated soffit and jambs; b. Rosette decorating domed ceiling of Hinnom Valley Tomb.

four corners (Macalister 1901b: 217, No. 6; Vincent 1954: Fig. 95B) Another tomb at the Hinnom Valley (*Ferdûs er-Rûm*) has a domed ceiling (No. 2.1, see below).

Architectural decoration

Mount of Olives Tomb (the 'Sisters of Zion') has a unique architectural feature; in the corridor leading from the main chamber to the second chamber, two columns were engraved as pilasters with Doric capitals (Fig. VI–32; Vincent 1902b: 279).

At a Silwan village tomb (Figure IV–3), the façade of the entrance to the passage is decorated with carved architectural elements consisting of a gable with three acroteria and two flanking pillars (Avigad 1967a: 126–129, Tomb 29/1; Fig. 10,11).

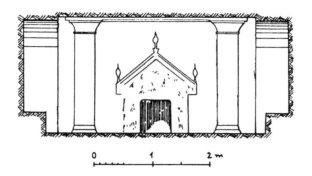

Figure IV–3. Carved decoration on Silwan village tomb.

Some comparable carved architectural decorative elements appear on tombs in the Kidron and Hinnom valleys (Macalister 1900a; 1901; Dalman 1939).

The architectural features of the Jerusalem rock-cut tombs have similar basic features:

- Many of the Jerusalem tombs display the colonnaded porch type in the form of a Greek distyle in antis front; This porch façade borrowed from the front of a Doric temple but without its gable (Watzinger [1935: 61] explains the omission of the gables to match the form of the local roof, which is usually flat; Avigad 1950–51: 101–104; 1954: 51–52). The Bene Ḥezir porch façade is created in the pure Hellenistic style and thus is the earliest of the Second Temple period, probably dated to the mid-second century BCE (Avigad 1950–51: 57–59).

- An adjacent or topped pyramid = *nefesh* is part of the architecture of several tombs the Kidron Valley tombs, the Jason's tomb, the Tomb of Helene of Adiabene, the Tomb of Herod (see Chap. II). Sources mention the story of Simon the Hasmonean (142 BCE) who erected a memorial of seven pyramids (*nefeshot*) over his parents and brothers tomb at Modiʿin (I Macc. 13. 25–30; Josephus, Ant. 13. 6. 5).

- An ornamented façade with a pediment is rare in the Jerusalem
  necropolis, found only at three Jerusalem tombs: the Grapes tomb,
  Sanhedriya Tomb XIV, and the Tomb of Jehoshaphat (Pl. IV–2).

The Kidron Valley monuments (Avigad 1954: 131–133) are an important step in the development are marked by: of the monumental
tomb, reflecting the tradition of erecting a memorial to the deceased
soul. The main chronological stages in this development: the Tomb
of Pharaoh's Daughter and other Silwan tombs, in the form of a
simple Egyptian chapel; the Tomb of Zechariah, a solid monument
in the form of an Egyptian chapel with Ionic columns surmounted
by a conical pyramid; the Tomb and *nefesh* of Bene Ḥezir are a
combination of a colonnaded façade with the pyramid borrowed
from ancient Egypt; lastly, Absalom's Tomb is an example of the
peak development of the Hellenistic-Roman monumental tomb, consisting of an ornamented square substructure (which is the tomb),
surmounted by a Hellenistic cylindrical tholos representing the nefesh
(replacing the conical pyramid), similar to Nabatean funerary art at
Petra.

Comparisons to the ornamented tombs of Jerusalem can be found
in Asia Minor tombs cut into the rock face and often at a considerable height. Some contain stone *klinai*. In their earlier phase, these
tombs are wholly non-Greek (Kurtz and Boardman 1971: 286–288,
297, Pl. 77). In Lycia, some tombs, not earlier than the fourth century BCE, are rock-cut with architectural façades, a massive podium,
a colonnaded façade with a gabled or pyramidal roof, imitating the
construction of timber, rectangular or with a high roof similar to
the Lycian sarcophagi; at Xantos only one tomb has a Greek colum-
nar façade, more common later at Telmessos. "The architecture and
art of Lycia were formed by the confluence of three quite distinct
traditions, the local, the Near East and the Greek" (Childs 1978: 4).
The decorated tombs of Lycia are the primary preserved art found
there. They share two characteristics with the Jerusalem tombs, they
are above ground and they are sizeable monuments. Many were
located near or at the centers of towns and might have served more
than a simple funerary function; occasionally they might also have
a votive or propaganda character. The tomb could serve as an expression of dynastic, religious, and eschatological power.

The funerary architecture of Jerusalem reflects "architectural features in various styles, pure and hybrid, they reveal both an ancient Oriental tradition of sepulchral building and the influence of contemporary Western architecture" (Avigad 1954: 144). The Kidron Valley monuments reveal this hybrid style, composition and inspiration containing Egyptian, Hellenistic, and Roman features. It is illustrated in the Tomb of Zechariah, with its Egyptian cornice and pyramid and its Hellenistic ornamentation of Ionic columns; at the Tomb of Bene Ḥezir, with its in Hellenistic portico in the Doric style – a rock-cut distyle in antis – and its adjoining façade bearing a pyramid – the *nefesh*; in Absalom's Tomb, where a mixture of styles survives: Ionic columns, Doric frieze capped by an Egyptian cavetto cornice, surmounted by the tholos, and a concave conical roof.

B. Wall-Painting

Paintings decorate the walls of the monumental Goliath Tomb at Jericho, dated to the first century CE (Figure IV–4). This provides a unique example of Jewish funerary art (Hachlili 1985). The walls of both chambers of the Goliath tomb (Hachlili 1979; 1999: 37–44) were white plastered but only Chamber A was subsequently decorated.

This wall-painting provides a new and important source for Jewish funerary art in the Land of Israel and the surrounding area during the first century CE.

Description

Traces of painting appeared on three walls of chamber A (Figure IV–5). The wall-painting was executed in various shades of red, brown, and black. The loculi and passage to the second chamber were outlined by three alternating lines, a thick black line flanked by two thinner red ones, began at floor level forming an arch above each loculus.

The main motifs of the wall-painting appear above the loculi on the north, south, and west walls. The painting on the north wall is the best preserved and consists of the vine-branches motif depicted by bunches of black grapes, red vine leaves and tendrils enclosed by a red frame (Figure IV–5 right, Figure IV–6; Pl. IV–3). The thick brown stem of the vine branches begins between loculi 1 and 2 and extends outside the red frame. The branches spread and grow mainly

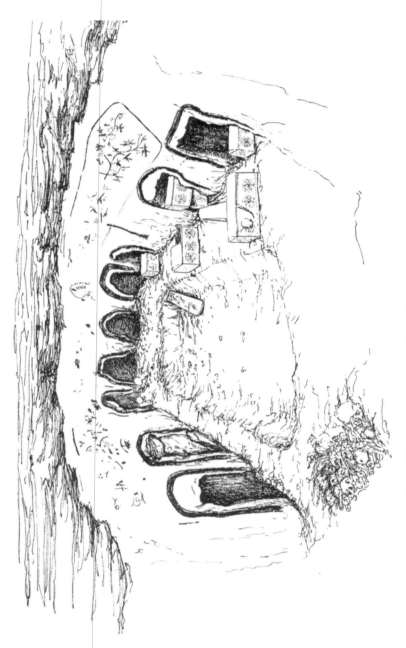

Figure IV–4. Jericho, Goliath Tomb Chamber A with wall paintings.

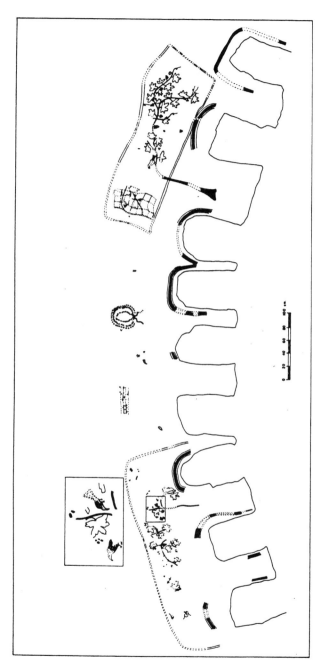

Figure IV–5. Jericho, Goliath Tomb Chamber A wall paintings.

to the east. On the main branch close to the stem, fragments of a bird (the tail and beak) appear. To the west of the stem only a leaf and two clusters of grapes remain. In the upper left corner an unusual geometric design, resembling squares, may represent a pergola.[1]

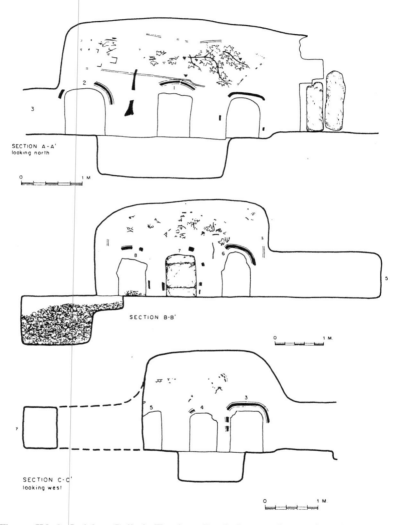

Figure IV–6. Jericho, Goliath Tomb wall-painting on the north wall (section A–A), on the south wall (section B–B); on the west wall (section C–C).

---

[1] Compare a pergola and grape-vine in the wall painting of Boscoreale (Lehmann 1953: 205, Pl. XXII.).

The painting on the south wall (Figure IV–5 left; Figure IV–6 section B–B) was more damaged than that on the north wall, but the similarity of the theme on the two walls makes it possible to determine with certainty the subject originally depicted. Fragments of three sides of the frame remain, and the west line of the frame continues down past the middle of loculus 6. The thin stem of the vine seems to begin between loculi 6 and 7, and the majority of the vine spreads towards the east side of the wall. Two birds, one missing its tail and the other with only a body and its legs, are executed in shades of brown. The birds appear to be perched on the main branch or in mid-air (Pl. IV–4). Considering all the remaining pieces of the three birds on the north and south walls, an entire bird can be reconstructed. On both walls the birds are drawn close to the main stem, near the western wall.

Although the painting on the west wall opposite the entrance is the least preserved, this was probably the centre and focal point of the three wall-paintings. From the few remaining fragments on the west wall the subject is obviously completely different from that on the north and south walls. Three courses of ashlar stones or brick masonry, probably portraying a structure, are visible on the left section (Figure IV–5 center; Figure IV–6 section c–c). The margins are painted in black and the bosses of the stones are red. To the right of the masonry motif are two fragments of floral design. Next to the masonry a long narrow leaf has survived which may be part of a floral design, and at the far right a wreath of red leaves and black dots is depicted. The base is tied with a black ribbon in the occidental bow-knot.

Style and Technique

The wall-painting was well-executed and freely drawn in a naturalistic style; only the birds seem to differ stylistically. The central motif, a vine consisting of branches, leaves, clusters of grapes, tendrils, and birds, is successful in conveying a naturalistic impression, but the details are stylized. The stem on the north wall is a mature, large vine with curled tendrils extending from it. The leaves and bunches of grapes appear at irregular intervals on the branches. All the vine leaves are rendered *en face* with uneven edges, usually pointing downwards in accordance with gravity (Pl. IV–3). They were first drawn in outline and then filled in with the same red colour. All the leaves extend from the branches, each on a single, short and slender stem.

The dominant leaf has five folioles, with no veins, but at times it is depicted with fewer folioles. Similar leaves can be found on a painted wall in a first- or second-century CE tomb of Clodius Hermes in Rome (Levi 1947: 512, Fig. 187 who describes it as a painting in the advanced Antonine style of the first-second centuries CE).[2]

The triangular bunches of grapes consist of a large cluster flanked by two smaller clusters shown by a series of black dots, each dot representing a grape (Pl. IV–5). These are similar to grape bunches which appear on Nabataean pottery from Khirbet Tannur (Glueck 1959: 11.24). The bunches are small in proportion to the leaves. The stem always supports a single cluster of grapes which hang downwards. In contemporary art, grapes are usually elliptical in shape. Grapes in Jewish art usually appear as a central bunch flanked by a smaller cluster on each side, which Avi-Yonah (1981: 70, Figs. 24–25) considered to be prevalent on Jewish monuments and refered to as the 'Jewish type'; they are usually more stylized than the Jericho grapes.

The birds in the Jericho paintings, are shown perched on branches or in mid-air (Pl. IV–4). They were drawn first in outline, and then the details of the head, legs, and wings were added in brown. The lines and dots appearing on the body indicate feathers. The depiction of the birds is very different from that of contemporary birds.

Stylistically the wall-painting can be compared to the Jericho painted pottery found in the cemetery (Hachlili 1979b: 66; Killebrew 1999: Fig. 57:4,6), the 'Painted Jerusalem Ware' bowls from Jerusalem (Avigad 1983: Fig. 201; Mazar 1975: Pl. I), and the painted Nabataean pottery (Glueck 1965: Pl. 30A). The wall-painting should probably be associated with the Eastern naturalistic Flower Style described by Rostovzeff (1919) and dated to the first and second centuries CE (a style described by Vitruvius VII, 5, 3; for a discussion of the style, its date, and its connection with the Siq el Bared painting, see Horsfield 1938: 23; Glueck 1956: 21).

Motifs

The main motifs in the wall-painting are the vine branches, birds, wreath and masonry.

---

[2] Rahmani (1994: 43, n. 90) asserts (without providing any proof) that the vine in this wall painting was influenced by Jews from abroad.

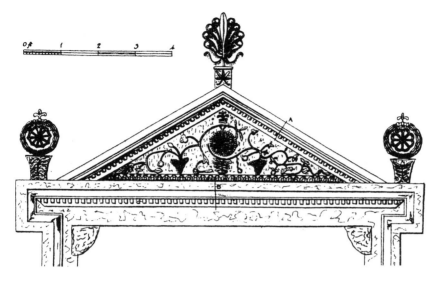

Figure IV–7. Decorated pediment of 'Tomb of the Grapes', Jerusalem.

The vine-branch motif in Jewish funerary art of the first century CE was rare and each example is different (Avi-Yonah 1961: 23; 1981: 69–71, 79–82); it appears on Jerusalem tomb pediments, ossuaries and sarcophagi. The stylized vine-branch motif on the pediment of the 'Tomb of the Grapes' (Figure IV–7) (Macalister 1900: Pl. III) spreads symmetrically from the centre to the sides. The grapes are of 'Jewish type' (Avi-Yonah 1981: 79).

The vine motif also appears on ossuaries. The vine branches engraved on an ossuary from French Hill create a narrow frieze above the rosettes (Strange 1975, Fig. 1:4: Rahmani 1994: No. 600); the stylized vine-branch motif is seen as a frame, with some leaves unfinished, on an ossuary located at the Israel Museum (IM 74.36.34; Rahmani 1994: No. 816). Two triangular bunches of grapes beautifully executed appear flanking a branch on the front of an ossuary from Mt. Scopus, Jerusalem (Rahmani 1994: No. 893) (Pl. V–13a).

More examples appear on sarcophagi. One is found on the front of a first-century CE sarcophagus (see Pl. III–11) discovered in the Nazirite burial on Mount Scopus (Avigad 1971: 191, Pls. 38a, 39b). The stylized and symmetrical design has a floral centre with the branches issuing from it. The leaves appearing on the vine are unusual. The grapes are similar to those on the 'Tomb of the Grapes' (Fig. II–14). A similar motif appears on a sarcophagus lid from

Dominus Flevit, consisting of five scrolls with alternating leaves and grapes (Bagatti and Milik 1958: Pl. 16, Photo 35, similar to the French Hill ossuary). The vine-branch decoration in these examples, is executed in a well-defined area and is centrally organized (except on the ossuaries), beginning from the centre and continuing in a symmetrical fashion on each side.

In non-funerary contexts, the motif appears on coins from the time of the First Jewish Revolt (67–68 CE; Meshorer 1982, II:112–13; Pl. 18:11–13). Vine branches decorate the ceiling of a dome on the Double Gate, Jerusalem (Mazar, B. 1978: Fig. I) and are found stamped on the shoulder of a storage jar from the Jewish quarter. A Herodian lamp bearing this motif was found in the excavations of the Gush Halav synagogue (Meyers et al. 1979: 56, Fig. 21c).

The closest contemporary parallel to the Jericho motif, is the vine-branch motif on a wall-painting found on the vaulted ceiling of the 'Painted House' at Siq el Bared (Horsfield 1938: 21–24, Pl. 50; Glueck 1956: 13–23, Figs. 1–2; 1965: Pls. 203, 204, 209).

Figure IV–8. Painted vaulted ceiling of a House at Siq el Bared.

The detailed painting was arranged as a tapestry-like scene of vines, flowers, birds, and mythological figures (Figure IV–8) (Glueck 1965: Fig. 203b), including a greater variety of motifs and details than is found on the Jericho painting. Not only are mythological figures added, but there are several types of birds, some standing, some flying. Glueck (1956: 23) suggests an early first century CE or later date for the painting, and that it was executed by an Alexandrian draughtsman (Glueck 1965: 291).

Outside Israel, similar examples of these motifs are found in Nabataean Syria, usually decorating lintels and door jambs of temples, gates, and other public structures (Butler 1903: Pls. 317, 332, 334; 1915–19, V: Fig. 317b; VII: Figs. 323, 326–27, 330d, 339–42, 346, 367, 371, 376–77).

Later, during the second century CE, the vine branches constituted a very popular motif on tomb decoration. Other comparisons come from the Roman East, on the ceiling of a Roman tomb near Tyre (Lasseur 1922: 17–18, Pl. 111a) and on the tympanum of another Roman tomb dating to the second century CE, also near Tyre (Dunand 1965: 11–12, Pls. 11, 111). Vine branches with bunches of grapes and birds appear in fragments of a wall-painting from the interior of a second- to third-century CE tomb at Massyaf, Syria (Chapouthier 1954: Pl. B:1–2, Figs. 11, 14).

The motif appears in both funerary and architectural decoration at Palmyra. In funerary art the motif appears on the decorated ceiling in the exedra of the 'Tomb of Abdastor' (dated 98–239 CE; Ingholt 1938: 139, Pl. I:2–3). Another example is found on a wall-painting in the Tomb of Hairan (mid-second century CE), where a man and a woman stand framed by vine branches with grapes (Ingholt 1932, Pls. II, III). Two pilasters from the Tomb of the Three Brothers (c. 142 CE) were decorated with vine branches and grapes (Kraeling 1961: 16, Pls. II, XV).

The vine-branch motif also occurs on architectural elements at Palmyra, mainly from the 'Temple of Bel' (Seyrig et al. 1975: Pl. 20: 1). All the Palmyran examples were executed in narrow, well-defined areas and the grapes are depicted in the shape of a central bunch flanked by two smaller clusters. The vine branches appear in the form of a scroll (with one exception), the majority consisting of alternating leaves and grape bunches, with tendrils filling the spaces among them. The grapes are executed horizontally, or parallel, to the observer (Seyrig 1940: Pls. XXIX:I, 2, 5–9; XXXII:21; XXXIII:27).

During the third to fourth centuries CE, the vine-branch motif continues to appear in tombs as a vine which grows freely and fills the surface of the plastered tomb interior. One example comes from a painted tomb near Ashkelon where the interior of the vault was decorated with a vine executed on stucco plaster (Ory 1939: 41, Fig. 2, Pls. XXVII–XXIX).

Another wall-painting is from the 'Tomb of the Birds' on the Mount of Olives, where the ceiling and acrosolia are decorated with vine branches, bunches of grapes, and a variety of recognizable birds, including peacocks (Kloner 1975: 29, Pls. B–C).

In later Jewish art of the third and fourth centuries CE onwards, the vine-branch scroll was popular, occurring mainly on architectural reliefs in synagogues. The motif is confined to a well-defined area, usually long and narrow in shape. It has the form of a geometric scroll with alternating leaves and grapes issuing from a central object, usually an amphora (Avi-Yonah 1981: 80–81).

The same composition decorates three lead sarcophagi from Beth She'arim. The running scroll contains leaves, bunches of grapes, amphorae, and birds drinking from a vessel (Avigad 1976: 173–182, Figs. 89:1–2, 90, Pls. LXII–LXVII). The motif is stylized and geometric also on the stone 'Shell Sarcophagus' (Avigad 1976: 143–44, Pl. XLII:I, 2).

In sum, the vine-branch motif first appeared toward the end of the first century BCE and gradually spread and grew in popularity. The motif decorated architectural elements as well as appearing in funerary art among the Jews, and Nabataeans, and at Palmyra. The various ways in which the vine-branch motif was depicted and its means of execution depended on the allotted space and the material used (paint, stucco, stone, etc.) more than on different artistic styles. In later Jewish art the motif is stylized, issuing from a vessel usually at the centre of the defined area on which the relief is carved. Birds seldom appear as part of the scene.

The bird motif has few comparisons. Birds, though different in style, appear in a later tomb at Beth Jibrin (Guvrin) where they decorate the spandrels of the arches (Bliss and Macalister 1902: 201, Pl. 98f.). An incised bird, slightly resembling the Jericho birds, appears on a tombstone from a catacomb in Rome (Goodenough 1953, III: Fig. 729). The motif continues to appear on the walls of later Jewish catacombs in Rome, but the birds can be identified clearly as ducks, peacocks, etc. (Goodenough 1958, VIII: Figs. 27–59). In non-funerary contexts, birds frequently appear on the wall frescoes of Pompeii but are more naturalistic in style (Jashemski 1979: Figs. 169–76, 391–95, 401, 418, 420). The bird rarely appears in contemporary first-century CE wall-paintings and reliefs. More numerous examples date from later periods. However, they differ greatly in style from those appearing in the Jericho wall-painting.

The wreath appears on the west wall of the Jericho tomb. It occurs occasionally in contemporary Jewish funerary art where it is usually depicted as a stylized, round wreath used to decorate tomb facades in Jerusalem (Kon 1947: Pl. 8a), or on ossuaries, where it decorates one of the sides (Rahmani 1994: 41–2, No. 14R, 60R, 206L, 282F, 308R, 464F, 893L). Fragments of a wreath appear in the fresco from the House of Caiaphas in Jerusalem (Broshi 1972: Pl. 7). These wreaths are tied with the occidental bow-knot (Avi-Yonah 1981: 76–76). The wreath in the Jericho painting is distinctive in its being a more naturalistic depiction. The wreath is a common representation in painting or reliefs on graves in the Hellenistic period (Peters and Thiersch 1905: 87, Pls. VI, IX–XI, XIV).

The masonry (or ashlar stones) depicted on the west wall of the tomb is a less-known motif. Several contemporary examples appear: masonry carved into the rock, covering the side walls of the façade, occurs on the first-century CE Jerusalem Umm el-Amed tomb, in an apparent attempt to imitate a structure (Avigad 1947: 118, Figs. 2–4; 1950–51: 103, Fig. 7; Vincent 1954: Figs. 109–110). Other examples come from Jason's Tomb (Rahmani 1967: 19, Pls. 13B,C) and the tomb of Deir ed Derb (Savignac 1910: 125, Fig. II). The facade of the Tomb of the Nazirite family is actually built of ashlar stone (Avigad 1971: 186, Fig. 3, Pl. 33b).

The same ashlar stone motif also decorates several ossuaries from Jerusalem (see Chap. IX, Group 3). The ashlars are incised, filling the entire ossuary front, sometimes with overlayed rosettes (Bagatti and Milik 1958: Pl. 19: 41, 42, 44; Rahmani 1994: 35, Fig. 42).

A similar depiction of masonry decorates the back wall of the triclinium of the 'Painted House' at Siq el Bared (Horsfield 1938: 21, Pl. XLIV:1, 2). The wall is moulded in low relief on a stucco panel. The joints are incised and coloured red while the panels are painted yellow to imitate masonry.

It is likely that the Jericho wall-painting not only attempts to depict a building, but more specifically imitates a tomb façade of the Umm el-Amed type.

The motifs appearing on the wall-painting are either geometric or floral. No human or animal figures, except for several birds, appear in the wall-painting, as is the case with Jewish art of the Second Temple Period. The repertoire of motifs dating to the Second Temple Period is known mainly from ossuary and tomb decoration and has quite a variety of floral, geometric, and architectural elements (Rahmani 1967: 120–122).

Significance of the Motifs

The significance of motifs appearing in Jewish funerary art has been the subject of discussion and debate. Scholars have suggested that the vine branches in funerary art represented a symbol of the sacred wine, drunk by the *mystae* in a feast supposed to represent life after death (Ory 1939: 41). Goodenough (1956, VI, 67–68, I 72–73, Fig. 243) suggests that the vine at Palmyra had funerary importance apparently as a guarantee of future life. He supported this suggestion with the wall-painting appearing in the Tomb of Haran and added that personal immortality seemed to be indicated by the birds eating grapes from the vine. Figueras (1983: 82) maintains that the vine and grape cluster possibly had symbolic significance connected to the afterlife. Rahmani (1994: 43) argues that the literature of the period makes no mention of a significance associated with the vine in funerary customs.

It is difficult to accept a symbolic funerary meaning for this motif. The evidence previously discussed indicates that this motif was common in Oriental art, and appeared on various types of architectural elements and structures, as well as on pottery (Avi-Yonah 1961: 23). It differed only in style and means of execution, not in meaning or symbolism. It is possible that the rarity of the motif is due to the difficulty of its execution. The fact that this motif seldom appears during the first century CE provides further evidence for the claim that it lacks any symbolic meaning. It seems more probable that the vine-branch motif was used as a decorative and filling motif without any symbolic meaning.

The bird motif too has been endowed with symbolic significance by scholars. Goodenough (1958, VIII:24, 41, 42; Avi-Yonah 1960:

29, n. 16). holds that the bird was associated with the soul of the deceased in Jewish sources, which mention the bird in connection with death: "Whilst the soul can say: the body has sinned, that from the day I departed from it I fly about in the air like a bird..." (BT Sanhedrin 91a). However, the appearances of this motif (often associated with vine branches) in non-funerary contexts also rule out a symbolic significance attached to the depiction of birds.

The appearance of the wreath was probably associated with the custom of placing wreaths on graves. As the motif was common in Hellenistic art, while considerably less so in first century CE Jewish art, it is doubtful that a symbolic meaning can be attached to the wreath (Goodenough 1953, III: Fig. 30, 119; Figueras 1983, 255; but see Rahmani 1994: 43).

The masonry motif, which has been associated with the depiction of tomb façades, has also been considered symbolic (Goodenough 1953, I: 117–18, n. 65). Figueras (1983: 82) interprets it as the house where the dead rested. Rahmani (1967: 189), who once agreed with this interpretation, now disagrees (Rahmani 1994: 35) and points out that several representations of masonry incised on ossuaries were unfinished and lacked windows or doors and therefore cannot be a house.

The motifs decorating the Jericho tomb walls appear in both funerary and non-funerary contexts in Jewish and non-Jewish art throughout the region. Hence, these motifs should not be interpreted as having any symbolic significance in connection with Jewish funerary rites or death. It can be concluded that while not exclusively funerary in context, these motifs seem to be the favoured repertoire appearing on tomb architecture, sarcophagi and ossuaries, as well as on the Jericho wall-painting.

The paintings were most likely executed shortly after the workmen had finished hewing out the tomb, in the early first century CE.

Contemporary fragments of wall-paintings have been discovered in Jewish structures, usually in the villas and palaces of the Jewish Quarter in Jerusalem (Avigad 1983: 149–50, Figs. 105–106), the House of Caiaphas on Mt Zion (Broshi 1972: 106, Pls. 7–8), the Hasmonaean and Herodian palaces of Jericho (Netzer 1974: Pls. a, b), and at Masada (Yadin 1966: 44, 46, 47, 79, 82). Most of these wall-paintings consist of a rich variety of brightly coloured geometric designs and occasionally architectural and floral patterns; however, the vine-branch motif does not appear. No humans nor animals, except for birds in the Mount Zion painting, have been found.

Conclusions

The importance of this wall-painting and its motifs can be summarized as follows:

(1) Although wall-paintings commonly appear in palaces and villas in the Jerusalem and Jericho area during the Herodian period, the painting discovered in the monumental Goliath tomb is the first found in a Jewish tomb of this period. As this tomb is located in Jericho, one of the main Jewish centres of the period, it is difficult to imagine that it was a unique occurrence. The fact that to date only one decorated tomb has been found may be a matter of chance or due to favourable conditions of preservation.

(2) The main motif, the vine branches, was one of the popular decorative motifs throughout the region, appearing both in secular and sacred contexts. In each of the early examples the composition, style, and means of execution differ. However, in Jewish funerary art the motif rarely occurs.

(3) The wall-painting was most likely executed at the time of the hewing of the tomb, at the beginning of the first century CE, evidently for the benefit of the tomb's visitors as well as to indicate the family's prominent position. It should be differentiated from tomb graffiti that occasionally appear on tomb walls and seem to have been executed by visitors to the tomb. The Jericho tomb wall-painting thereby displays the earliest dated vine-branch motif found in a tomb painting in the Semitic-Roman world.

The wall-painting with its motifs, especially the vine branches, is related to the neighbouring arts, and attests to the similarities among and the relationship of Jewish, Palmyran, and Nabataean art (Avi-Yonah 1961: 25, 65–95). In other areas of Jewish funerary practice and art the same relationship is evident.

Wall painting in other tombs

Several tombs display wall-painting decoration and usually only parts of the paintings have remained.

Akeldama

Elaborate architectural decoration with a high standard of work-manship is found inside Akeldama Tomb 3, Chamber C (Pl. IV–6) (Avni and Greenhut 1996: 26–27, 33; Figs. 1.46–50, 53, colored photos p. 2). The ornamentation consists of wall decorations of carved and incised panels and geometric designs painted red, as well as architectural elements carved in low relief. A delicate design of rectangles and lozenges painted dark red was incised above the passage from Chamber A. Carved pilasters in low relief with imitation of pseudo-Doric capitals in low relief flank the acrosolia in the four corners of the chamber; a frieze of three fasciae is incised above the columns. Rectangular panels in sunken relief are carved under the acrosolia emulating chamber doors which seem to imitate wooden doors The combination of incision and red paint is quite rare and may be compared to the Mokata 'Abud loculi tomb (see bellow). The excavators point out that the origin of the decorative style may be sought in Jewish art of the Second Temple period in Jerusalem, or better in North Syrian funerary architecture (Palmyra, Galikowski 1970; Browning 1979:192–213).

Wall painting remains in the Judean Shephelah tombs

Several tombs surveyed or excavated in the Judean Shephelah were decorated with wall paintings (Kloner 1994a):

Mokata 'Abud. A two-chamber tomb with loculi (Conder and Kitchener 1882: 362–363; Kloner 1994a: 168, fig. 4) has a portico surmounted by a sculpted frieze rendering wreaths, rosettes, and bunches of grapes (Figure IV–9) similar to the lintel of the Tomb of Helene of Adiabene (Fig. II–15b). The right chamber's walls were plastered and decorated with a strip of geometric designs of four black lozenges and red rectangles alternately on the white background; above is a wavy strip in red, yellow and white. Between the loculi the panels are painted in red. The tomb is dated either to the first-century CE or Byzantine period. The similarity to the Akeldama painting tends to make the earlier date more plausible.

Ḥorvat Midras. This is a first/second-century CE Jewish burial tomb that displays a façade decorated with wall painting. Remains of colored plaster were found in the courtyard (Kloner 1994a:169).

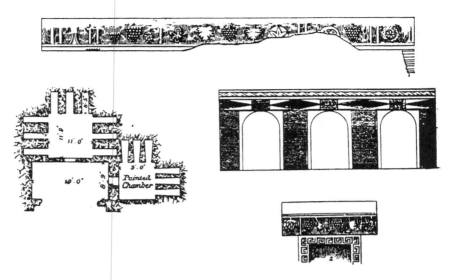

Figure IV–9. Mokata ʿAbud wall decoration.

Givʿat Seled – A first-century CE two-chamber tomb containing a main
chamber with loculi and an inner chamber with arcosolia was discovered at Givʿat Seled (Kloner 1991: 162, Figs. 4, 5). Fragments
of wall paintings appear on the western wall of the main chamber:
a long narrow brown strip consisting of irregular cross-hatching bor-
dered by horizontal lines is painted on either side of the entrance
to the inner chamber. Above it are painted panels and designs.
Apparently most of the wall had been ornamented with floral patterns. A perpedicular green stem with pair of double leaves painted
on the white plaster is preserved. Above it is a basket-like object
with a curved handle in brown-red. To its left is a brown-colored
object (Kloner 1991: Fig. 4 and color plate). Two dark-brown circles are painted close to the ceiling aligned with the left doorpost of
the entrance (Kloner 1991: Fig. 5). Fragments of painted Ionic capital, dark-red plaster, and floral patterns were also discovered.

C. DRAWING AND GRAFFITI

Several drawings and graffiti appear on the porch walls of Jason's
Tomb. Three ships are drawn on the western wall, a stag is drawn
on the northern wall, and graffiti of seven-armed menoroth are
scratched on the porch's eastern wall (Rahmani 1967: 69–75).

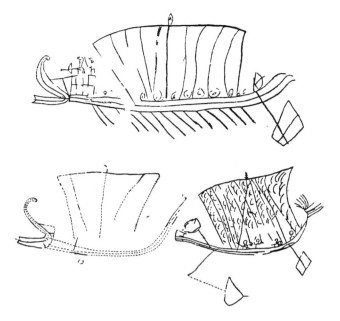

Figure IV–10. Jason's Tomb drawings: Ships.

Three drawings in charcoal of ships, two warships, and a merchant (or fishing) vessel appear on the western wall of the porch at Jason's Tomb (Rahmani 1967: 69–73, 97, Fig. 5a,b).

One is a swift warship with a large mainsail (Figure IV–10a); 14 oars are seen, and at the bow two warriors stand. A smaller warship with no remnants of oars and a high stern is badly preserved (Figure IV–10b). The third ship is a merchant (or fishing) vessel with a full-blown mainsail (Figure IV–10c).

The drawings are fully detailed, possibly indicating that the drawing was executed by a person who was familiar with ships and boats. Different interpretations are suggested for the depiction of ships in burial context: Rahmani assumes that the original occupant of the tomb was in some way connected with the naval exploits off the coast of Palestine in 100–64 BC. In a literary text,1 Macc. 26–9, Simon directs that Jonathan's bones be reburied in Modein "... he carved ships, so that they could be seen by all who sail the sea". Kurtz and Boardman (1971: 207–8) contend that warships found in warriors' graves at Argos around 700 BC, in Cyprus, and in Crete "are not indicative of local interest in marine warfare, as has been suggested for Argos, nor are they symbolic of the voyage to the other world, which was not a concept popular with the Greeks (Charon had a punt, not a warship)". Toynbee (1971: 38) maintains that . . . "ships symbolize journeys, and death has been viewed as a journey in innumerable cultures". Death has been viewed as a journey on a ship or ferry, across a river that seperates the world of the living and the world of the dead. By the time of the Maccabean, death had come to be understood as an extended process or journey leading to a new world, and it was represented by a ship which might have been a particular death symbolism (Kraemer 2000: 17–18, 52, 102–103) ". . . The drawings of ships express in pictures instead of words, the notion that death is like an over-water passage. Only when payment is made and the passage accomplished will the deceased find her final rest".

Ships already appeared in funerary art in the Land of Israel at the end of the eighth century BCE. At Ḥurvat Loya, two simple sailships are engraved on the tomb's wall (Barkay 1994: 132, fig. 18). At Beth She'arim (Mazar, B. 1973: 52, 75, 117, 227; Fig. 12; Pls. VII:3, IX:4; XX:2; XXIII:1,2) painted ships and an incised boat appear on the catacomb walls.

Some other drawings and graffiti were discovered on the walls of Jason's Tomb (Figure IV–11).

A drawing of a resting stag appears over the entrance to Room B (Rahmani 1967: 73, Fig. 6, Pl. 21B). Graffiti of several sevenbranched menoroth (Rahmani 1967: 73, Figs. 7, 8; Pls. 22A, C) were incised on the eastern wall of the porch, a palm branch and a chalice. Rahmani (1967: 96–97) contends that the porch drawing served as identification of one of the interred, and is meant to indicate the occupation of the deceased. The stag may represent a symbol of strength or refer to a family name. Thus, the graffiti in Jason's tomb were drawn as a reference to those interred in the tomb and not as a purely decorative embellishment at the time the tomb was being hewn, as is the case with the Jericho wall painting.

D. ORNAMENTATIONS OF COFFINS, OSSUARIES AND SARCOPHAGI

Wooden Coffin Decoration

Wooden coffin decoration consisted of painted or incised geometric patterns.

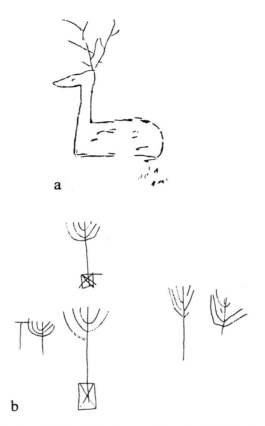

Figure IV–11. Jason's Tomb drawings: a. Stag, b. Graffiti of menoroth.

Several of the Jericho wooden coffins were decorated (Table III–1): the short side of coffin 113 (type A) has an indication of a shallow horizontal recess which might have been originally decorated (Fig. III–1; Hachlili 1999: 63, Figs. III.2:1, 3:3).

Type B coffins are decorated with painted alternating black and red bands bordred by grooves on the narrow sides of the chest, the gable lid tympana and the ridge (a–c). On some of these coffins the corner post is also decorated with painted alternating black and red bands (Fig. III–3; Hachlili 1999: 68, Figs. III.10; 11, 12:5; 15; 17:6–9; 18; 19, 20:12; 22:4; 23:3–6).

Type C wooden coffins, are decorated with incisions on the chest's framed thin, narrow planks, with similar engravings decorating the ridge of the gabled lid (Fig. III–4; Hachlili 1999: 71, Figs. III.27:1, 30:7–12; 35:6–7).

Some of the 'En Gadi wooden coffins are decorated: Coffin 11
(Tomb 5) has a six-petalled rosette incised on the narrow side; a
double incision, probably a carpenter's mark, is on the narrow side
of Coffin 10 (Hadas 1994: Tomb 5; figs. 45, 46). Two coffins were
painted: the lid of Coffin 11 (Tomb 5) was decorated with three
pairs of black stripes bordred by grooves; Coffin 2 lid (Tomb 6) was
ornamented by horizontal black lines bordred by grooves (Hadas
1994: figs. 46, 48, 52); A red band decorated a panel of a coffin
from Tomb 5.

An exceptional decorated wooden coffin with a gabled lid was
found in Naḥal David Cave 4 (Avigad 1962b: 182, Pl. 22A, now
on display at the Israel Museum). The ornamentation consisted of
bone and wood inlays with patterns of circles, rosettes and pomegranates. (Pl. IV–6).

Ossuaries ornamentation

A large number of Jerusalem and Jericho ossuaries are decorated
typically on the front long side, on the sides and occasionally on the
lid (Hachlili 1988a; 1999: 111–114). The ossuaries were apparently
made in a quarry and the ornamentation was done in workshops
(Magen 2002: 133).

The designs are carved or incised on the ossuaries soft limestone
of the with tools such as carving knife, compass, chisel, ruler, gouge,
mallet and straightedge. The ornamentation consists of a zigzag frame
enclosing two metopes decorated with rosettes; six-petalled rosettes
or multiples of six, executed by compasses or with a ruler (Avi-Yonah
1961:16–21; 1981:96–100; 107–109). Some of the ossuaries are decorated with a pattern covering the whole front or sides (see ossuary
types, Chap. III).

The chip-carving technique is frequently used and is characteristic of ossuary decoration (Figueras 1983: 27ff.; see Rahmani 1988:
56–62, 73–74; 1994: 7 for the chip-carving technique); this method
was probably derived from woodcarving. The surface of the chest
and lid of the ossuaries were smoothed, whereas the base and sometimes the lid were roughly dressed. Some of the ossuary surfaces are
covered with red paint, but ossuaries with painted designs are rare.
The main ornamentation is on the front, while the sides often bear
the design of one rosette in a frame; the back is sometimes decorated; inscriptions incised or written in charcoal or ink appear on
all sides of the ossuary.

The decorative technique is similar to the special technique of local stone carving that developed in the Second Temple period (Hachlili 1988a: 8). In Jerusalem, stone carving developed into a skilled craft, which created a local style based on local artistic traditions. Stone quarries and workshops have recently been found in the Jerusalem area (Avigad 1983: 165–183; Magen 1994). Local stonemasons produced architectural elements and ornamention of items such as lintels, tomb façades, sarcophagi and ossuaries, as well as stone vessels.

The workshops probably advertised their repertoire by means of some form of pattern book (Hachlili 1988: 112–115).

The ossuary ornamentation typically covers all of it probably as a result of the distaste for empty spaces (*horror vacui*). The patterns decorating the ossuary usually consist of an "all-over" or "endless" designs. The ornament generally is arranged symmetrically on both sides of the design in bipartite type; tripartite or quadripartite decoration is found in only some cases. The deep gouging of the pattern produces a sharp contrast, an alteration of shade and light.

Some decorated ossuaries are of particular interest: An elaborately ornamented hard limestone ossuary (from Mt. Scopus southern slope, Jerusalem; Kloner 1993: No. 14, Rahmani 1994: No. 482) is decorated on the front with a six-pillared tomb façade set on a high stylobate; the pillars carry entablature with moulded cornice and unfinished central acroterium. In the centre, is a high, narrow doorway, above it a pediment. Between the pillars are arched niches, each with a floral ornament issuing from an eight-petalled rosette. The back of the ossuary has a similar design, but the tomb façade is unfinished. The left narrow side is decorated with a tomb-entrance façade consisting of an arch resting on pillars with a moulded doorway composed of two-leaved door. Above the doorway is a decorated gable. Four discs are carved between the arch and pedimnet. The right narrow side is decorated with a tomb-entrance façade with 'Syrian' gable resting on four pillars; the doorway is composed of a two-leaved door; above the doorway is a pediment crowned by a central floral ornament. The tomb façades carved on the front and back of the ossuary resemble Nabataean tomb façades from Petra, whereas tomb façades from Jerusalem are similar to those carved on the sides of the ossuary. Rahmani maintains that the Nabataean influence on this ossuary may have derived through family members (possibly of Nabataean origin) using this tomb. The front and back of the ossuary are decorated with arched niches between pillars, with a doorway in the centre. Each of the arched niches on the front of the ossuary only is decorated with a floral ornament. The back decoration of the ossuary is incomplete; the last niche carved is gabled. Kloner (1994b: 238) concludes that the artist who produced this ossuary worked from a pattern book; the inspiration for his work on the ornamentation of this ossuary was no doubt from the similar structures he saw in the Jerusalem necropolis and on monuments from Petra and from some elements he saw in Alexandria.

All the sides and the lid of an ossuary from the western slope of Mt. Olives, ("Dominus Flevit") (measuring 114 × 46 × 72 cm.) are ornamented with several motifs; the excavators thought it a sarcophagus (Bagatti amd Milik 1958: Sarcophagus 1, Pls. 14–16, fot. 28–35), Rahmani (1994: 6, n. 3) an ossuary. The front contains by a branch with leaves flanked by two wreaths encircling rosettes. The back is ornamented with three stylized rosettes. The right side is decorated with a whirling rosette within a wreath, whereas the left side has a wreath. The arched lid is ornamented on both sides, one side by a scroll of vine leaves and grapes, the other by a running scroll with leaves and pine cones.

An ossuary discovered in Tomb 2, Chamber B at Akeldama, Jerusalem (Shadmi 1996: 45, No. 17 Fig. 2.12) is of hard limestone decorated in high relief. Its front, finely executed, consists of two eight round petalled rosettes, with pistils at the center, each enclosed in a square profiled frame. The two narrow sides are ornamented with a bucranium, carved in schematic outline, perhaps intentionally left in this state. These bucrania are unique in the repertoire of Second Temple period ossuaries.

The repertoire of motifs decorating the ossuaries is quite extensive (see also Figs. III–16–23). It consists of geometric motifs such as rosette, disc, concentric circle, half circle, lozenge, zigzag lines and checker board. Plants decorating ossuaries consist of acanthus leave, palm tree, palmette, wreath, garland, grape and vine, lotus, pine-cone, pomegranates, almond, lily, tree, branches, plants, leaves and flowers.

Architectural motifs consist of tomb monuments or façades, tomb entrance and door, columned porch, gates, *nefesh*, columns, arcosolium, and ashlar walls. Motifs such as amphora, kantharos, dagger, and five-branched menorah decorate a few ossuaries.

Many of the patterns and designs were derived from earlier Iron Age local pottery and Greek architectural forms and are comparable to decorative Parthian art, especially ornamented stucco. Avi-Yonah (1960: 21) maintained that Jews returning from the Babylonian exile introduced these designs of Mesopotamian origin to Judea. Most motifs are similar to those appearing in other arts of the Second Temple period (Hachlili 1988: 110–115). No figurative motifs are present in ossuary ornamentation, in accordance with the aniconic art of that period.

Sarcophagi ornamentation

Most of the sarcophagi are decorated. The motifs are aniconic, the decoration contains deeply carved folioles, symmetrical arrangement of flowers, leaves and rows of rosettes (Avi-Yonah 1961: 16, 21, 23). Symmetrical stylization is the ornamentation's most dominant feature. The sarcophagi are decorated with carving in high relief; the style, technique, and motifs are generally similar to the engraved ossuary ornamentation, especially on some of the hard limestone ossuaries (see Figs. III–29–32). Many of the Jerusalem sarcophagi are ornamented with a moulded frame for a sunken panel; sometimes further decorations are added.

The repertoire of motifs decorating the sarcophagi is limited and consists largely of geometric and floral patterns: rosettes, acanthus scrolls, acanthus calyx, wreath, grapes, fruits, and discs. The stylized vine-scroll is a favorite design. The sarcophagi also show distaste for empty spaces, *horror vacui*.

Rahmani (1994: 57–59) maintains no proof exists that direct foreign influence was exerted on Jewish funerary art, or on sarcophagi and ossuaries. Foerster (1998: 303, and n. 54) argues that the sarcophagi pattern of ornamentation and the interior 'cushion' are similar to Early Roman sarcophagi and seem to indicate a relation between these groups.

As stated, this ornamentation is closely related to the ossuary decoration, and apparently derives from the same sources as those for the Jerusalem monumental tombs and their environs (Avigad 1971: 191; Rahmani 1982a; 1994: 27–28; Hachlili 1988: 113; but see Foerster 1998: 304, who suggests that the architecture and decorative ornamentation of funerary monuments, sarcophagi, and ossuaries in Jerusalem derives from pagan funerary monuments of the Hellenistic and Early Roman periods).

An essential unity exists in the basic repertoire of the sarcophagus and ossuary ornamentation. Nevertheless, some significant differences are evident in their decoration technique: the sarcophagi are fashioned in high relief, whereas the ossuaries (except the hard limestone ossuaries: see Chap. III) are incised with tooling such as compass, drill, and carving knife, or are chip-carved. The sarcophagus ornamentation shows the greater technical ability of the craftsmen, who might have been more familiar with Hellenistic and Roman art. The richer and beautifully reliefed sarcophagi were probably much more expensive so that only wealthy, prominent Jerusalem families would have the means to afford them. The sarcophagi are frequently comb-dressed, and have a much narrower range of stylistic and design possibilities. The distinctive form, ornamentation and execution of the sarcophagi might indicate a single creative master (Smith 1973: 81 reaches this conclusion for the group of sarcophagi he discusses).

Jewish funerary art consists mostly of tomb decorations, façades, pediments, and friezes in Jerusalem and tomb wall-painting at Jericho, as well as funerary receptacles, richly ornamented ossuaries, and sarcophagi. The art is aniconic art, with geometric, floral and architectural motifs. The origin of this art is Hellenistic, with execution by local stone masons and artists.

E. Intentional Imperfection in Jewish funerary art

The phenomenon of the incomplete ornamentation is encountered in the funerary art of the Second Temple period on tomb façades, sarcophagi, and ossuaries in Jerusalem. In the Beth She'arim cemetery the same idiosyncrasy occurs in carvings which are half-finished on tomb walls and in sarcophagi ornamentation (Hachlili 1988: 380–382).

Tombs

Several Jerusalem tombs have incomplete architectural decoration: The façade of the Tomb of Queen Helene of Adiabene consists of ornamented lintel and jambs, with the carved ornament on each side of the door jamb left partially incomplete (Fig. II–7). A sarcophagus, found in this tomb, bears an inscription mentioning Queen

Saddah, identified as Helen of Adiabene, flanked by two discs (Fig. III–33); Goodenough (1953, I:134) maintains that the artisan left these discs to be carved later with rosettes, at the discretion of the client. A two-columned uncompleted entrance to a tomb is found south of the Tomb of Zechariah in the Kidron Valley.

Ossuaries

Several ossuaries exhibit the similar unfinished carved ornamentation. Many of the motifs, the rosette in particular, are incomplete.

About forty ossuaries have some decorative details left unfinished, most of them on the ossuary front but some have incomplete ornamentation on sides, back, or lid also (Pls. IV–7–8) (Rahmani 1994: 8–9). Occasionally two rosettes are depicted on the ossuary: one is beautifully chip-carved whereas the other is only schematically outlined (Figure IV–12).

Sometimes the ossuary front decoration is incomplete: the carving of both rosettes on an ossuary is unfinished (Rahmani 1994: no. 106). Some ossuaries have completely carved rosettes, but one of them shows a rudimentary ornamental element between the rosette leaves, never finished (Hachlili 1988: Fig. XIV.1a–b). Ashlar stones carved on an ossuary, though meant to cover the front of the ossuary entirely, are partly uncompleted (Rahmani 1967: 189, ossuary 17, Pl. 39:1; 1994: no. 184, pl. 25; Hachlili 1988: Fig. XIV.1c). In some cases details of the ossuary ornamentation are incomplete: the central lily motif on an ossuary is not finished, only the roots were chip carved (Rahmani 1994: no. 129). The decoration is unfinished on an ossuary front, with two incised circles prepared for superimposed rosettes (Rahmani 1994: no. 455). On an ossuary decorated with two unfinished rosettes only the carving of only three petals of the right-hand rosette is finished (Rahmani 1994: no. 474). The design on an ossuary reveals the gable façade on left side with the cornice under the rim unfinished (Rahmani 1994: no. 482, Fig. 100). On the right-hand narrow side of an ossuary the motif is sketched, partly carved but left unfinished (Rahmani 1994: 9, no. 224). An ossuary's left-hand narrow side bears an unfinished disc (Rahmani 1994: no. 392).

Some ossuaries show incomplete ornamentation on the left side: the left-hand chip-carved rosette carving is incomplete (Rahmani 1994: no. 112).

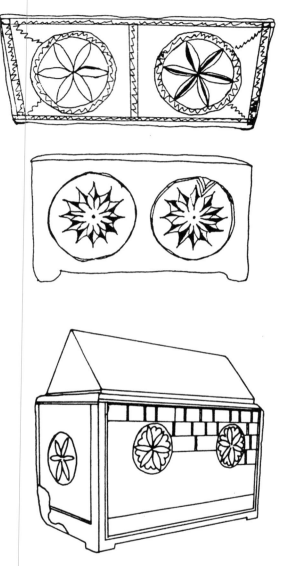

Figure IV–12. Ossuaries with unfinished carved ornamentation.

Ornamentation on the left is unfinished (Rahmani 1994: no. 182). The left-hand rosette is unfinished, lacking the segments that link the petal-tips of right-hand rosette (Rahmani 1994: 9, no. 346). The left-hand rosette is only sketched, not finished, on the ossuary back (Rahmani 1994: no. 417).

Other ossuaries show incomplete ornamentation on the right side: The right-hand rosette lacks the small discs between petals, which decorate only the left-hand rosette (Rahmani 1994: no. 131). The right-hand rosette is only outlined in incision whereas the left-hand is chip-carved (Rahmani 1994: no. 202). The front ornamentation of the ashlar façade and arched gate on the right is incomplete, and the right-hand rosette is only outlined, its carving unfinished (Rahmani 1994: no. 384). The right-hand rosette is unfinished, lacking the segments linking the petal-tips of the the left-hand rosette (Rahmani 1994: no. 593). The circle around the rosette is missing the wavy pattern on Akeldama, Ossuary 24 (Shadmi 1996: 47, fig. 2.18). The rosettes on the right are unfinished on Ossuary 6, in the collection of the German Protestant Institute of Archaeology (Fritz and Deines 1999: 230, fig. 6).

On a Jericho ossuary front, the left-hand rosette has one unfinished petal (Hachlili 1988: Pl. 19; Hachlili 1999: 111, Ossuary XXI, Pl. III.51).

Some lids with only sketched decoration of rosettes were placed on fully ornamented ossuaries (Rahmani 1994: Nos. 160, 184, 377, 446, 588).

Motifs arranged in unidentical symmetry

Seldom are unidentical motifs depicted on ossuaries, but a few examples are observed: Three different unidentical rosettes are carved on an ossuary. One ossuary is incised with a central menorah-plant flanked by a rosette on the right and a vase on right (Rahmani 1994: No. 37, 197, 815). An ossuary found in the Nazarite family tomb on Mt. Scopus has two completely different rosettes carved on its front (Avigad 1971: Pl. 41:A, Ossuary 8). A beautiful, unusually rendered front is depicted on ossuary from tomb C at the Har-Hazofim Observatory (Mt. Scopus, Jerusalem). The front of the ossuary is decorated with an encircled chip-carved rosette on the right, some flowers in the center, and an elaborate encircled design on the left; the upper part has a geometric design (Weksler-Bdolah 1997: 40*, oss. C6, Fig. 25).

The Beth She'arim cemetery shows the same phenomenon, where several sarcophagi have incomplete decorations (Figure IV–13): Sarcophagus 25, the "Daughters" sarcophagus (Avigad 1976: Hachlili 1988: fig. XIV.2a), has an incomplete left-hand wreath. On the

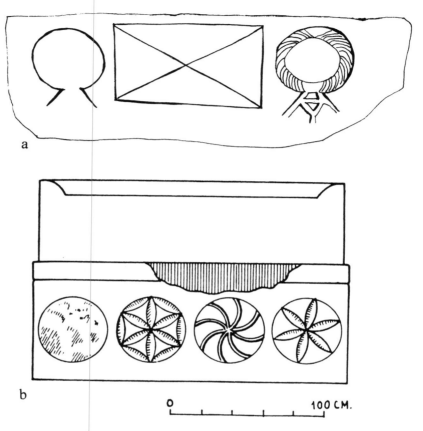

Figure IV–13. Beth She'arim Sarcophagi with incomplete ornamentation.

"Shell" sarcophagus, the left-hand wreath adjacent to the eagle aedicula is unfinished (Avigad 1976).

On Sarcophagus 87 (Avigad 1976: Hachlili 1988: fig. XIV.2b) the rosette is outlined by a circle and is incomplete. Only the first few eggs of the egg and dart patterns on the rim of the "Acanthus B" sarcophagus are carved (Avigad 1976: 152, Pl. 48,1; Hachlili 1988: fig. X.14). The "Menorah" sarcophagus has a plain front with two columns, on which two thin red painted lines are marked. Avigad (1976: 149) contends that this was in preparation for carving.

Unfinished work is rare on Roman sarcophagi except for the portrait heads on their lids which were presumably to be finished on the purchaser's order (Koch and Sichterman 1982: 613, Figs. 68–71; Rahmani 1994: 9, n. 14). The unfinished condition of early Roman sarcophagi indicates that they were often not completed until they were purchased, or were finished only when there was an immediate need (Smith 1973: 82). See also unfinished decoration on some Ephesus ossuaries (Thomas 1999).

A few examples of imperfection, namely incomplete carving, found not in a funerary context are the following. A sundial, found in the Palatial Mansion in the Jewish Quarter of Jerusalem (Avigad 1983: 119, Fig. 116), made of soft limestone ornamented on one side with a series of carved rosettes, the upper one on the left is unfinished. An ornamented rectangular stone table found in the 'Burnt House' in the Jewish Quarter of Jerusalem (Avigad 1983: 125, Fig. 141), has unfinished ornamentation on the edge of the table on the left and right sides. A Corinthian capital found in the Jewish Quarter of Jerusalem (Avigad 1983: 151, Fig. 157), has unfinished ornamentation under the lily scrolls.

Rahmani (1994: 9, who estimates that about 15% of the ornamentation of ossuaries is unfinished) proposes several possible interpretations for the non-completion of the carved ornamentation: the client needed the ossuaries urgently for immediate use. The artist was negligent in the execution of the ossuary's decoration. "Parsimony, which might have arisen from a condemnatory attitude toward the superfluous expediture of money or labour on the dead" (cf. Sem. 9.23). Rahmani prefers the negligent execution of the ossuaries ornamentation as the reason for the unfinished state rather than ideological or religious significance, noting that it is paralleled also by the careless execution of the inscriptions. Rahmani contends (1977: 25) that the ossuary work shows indifference on the part of the artists and their clients towards the quality of the finished ossuary. This is explained further by the civil strife and the exigency of the time, during the war against the Romans when many of the workshops were either completely closed down or were operating at a reduced level of workmanship. Both demand and quality consequently suffered.

This unusual trait of partly incomplete ornamentation, which recurs quite often in funerary art, seems to suggest more than mere negligence in craftsmanship, or indifference on the part of the clientele, as suggested by Rahmani (1977: 25; 1994: 9). It would appear to be intentional, and also to carry some significance. One may conjecture that

it is associated with a desire to avoid competition with a perfection
that only God can achieve. On the other hand, it may have been
due to the character of Jewish popular art, and to the artists' standards of composition and their cultural environment, which did not
traditionally demand perfection.

CHAPTER FIVE

INSCRIPTIONS

The inscription was a form of commemoration of the dead, part of the symbolic structure of society and an important part of death rituals. Inscriptions might be an extension of the burial ceremony. The funerary inscriptions were possibly formulated to suit the needs of the living participating in the funeral rituals. The relationships expressed in the epitaphs were mainly what those burying their dead felt was appropriate in the context of the family. In most inscriptions the deceased's nuclear relatives commemorated him or her, and they regarded the inscriptions as part of the rites separating the living from the dead. Some unusual inscriptions honored their ancestral home or family by stating their wish to be taken back for burial. Inscriptions may be treated as evidence of the social structure of family relations (Saller and Shaw 1984: 139–145; Morris 1992: 156–165).

The inscriptions convey that the duty of providing a memorial to the deceased was fulfilled, possibly out of feelings of affection, with emphasis on the nuclear family and its social structure.

The inscriptions were engraved with chisels or nails (found in tombs such as the Goliath and Nazarite tombs) or written in ink or charcoal. It is possible to infer that well carved inscriptions on ossuaries or sarcophagi were engraved outside the tomb, as they needed light, perhaps in the workshop, whereas careless inscriptions were possibly carved or written inside the tombs. Many of the inscriptions are apparently the work of the deceased's relatives, although 'professional' scribes presumably engraved some of them.

A. Selected Inscriptions on Tombs, Sarcophagi and Ossuaries

Inscriptions on Tombs

1. Jason's Tomb Inscriptions

The Tomb of Jason (Alfasi St., Jerusalem) contained two courts, a porch, a burial chamber with loculi, and a repository chamber (see

Chap. II). On the porch walls some charcoal graffiti drawings and several Aramaic inscriptions and one in Greek were discovered. The tomb is dated to the beginning of the first century BCE and it continued in use until the beginning of the first century CE (Rahmani 1967a; Avigad 1967b; Benoit 1967; Fitzmyer and Harrington 1978: No. 89).

The four-line Aramaic inscription (Figure V–1) was found on the plastered northern wall of the porch, written in charcoal to the left of the entrance. It reads

קינא עלמא עיבד ליסון בר פ. . . [אחן] שלם די בנת לך קבור סבא הוה שלם
ס. . . . .
כדנין קינא עלמא רחמיא למעבדא לך זי הוית שוא. שלם
חני . . . סני מח . . קינא היכלין שלם

A powerful lament make for Jason, son of P . . . (my brother), Peace! . . . Who hast built thyself a tomb, Elder, rest in peace!/ . . . s/ Such a powerful lament will thy friend make for thee, who hast been . . . Peace/ Honiah . . . great . . . lament like these, Peace! (Avigad 1967b: 105).

Another translation (Fitzmyer and Harrington 1978: No.89) reads: "Make an everlasting lament for Jason, son of P . . ., my brother. (It is) Salome who has built for you an elder's tomb. Be (at) peace!./ . . . s/ Friend are joined to make an evelasting lament for you who were worthy (of it). Peace/ Honi . . . very much *mh* . . . a lament *hykylyn.* Peace!"

Puech (1983: 483–485) argues that קינא עלמא should be interpreted as "eternal dwelling", similar to בית עלם in Eccl 12:5; and that the sentence ends with "be at peace in [Jeru]salem".

The Jason inscription is an Aramaic funerary lamentation using a borrowed Hellenistic formula. It is a unique in its language, its attitude to a monumental tomb, and its palaeographic details (Avigad 1967b: 106). The inscription begins with an appeal to the visitor to lament the death of Jason; it then wishes the deceased, who was evidently the elderly head of the family or a public figure, to rest in peace within the tomb he had built for himself. Next the scribe expresses the sorrow of Jason's friends conveyed by a lament; the last line may be a lament by Honiah, the scribe of the inscription, to his brother Jason. Fitzmyer and Harrington (1978: No. 89) argue that the end of the first line states that his sister Salome built the tomb. Puech's (1983: 486–7; 494–9) interpretation concludes that

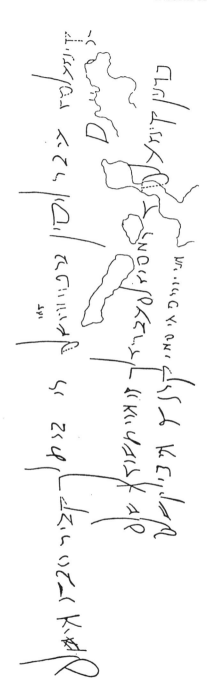

.1 מקד חזק על אמק חד חזק על חדה ... ם ... הו חדה חזק ... אבא אלעזר אבא דלא

.2 ... ם

.3 מקד אבא דמך חדה אלע דזל לק אבא חזק על ... מך חד לק אלעזר בית חדה אבא דמך קבר אלעזר דזנה

.4 מקד אלע ... מרין ... דבה מרין חזק

Figure V–1. Jason's Tomb, Aramaic inscription.

Figure V–2. Jason's Tomb, Greek inscription.

Jason's remains were brought from abroad and buried in Jerusalem in this tomb; he suggests that Jason's family lived in exile, possibly in Alexandria, since the deposition of his grandfather the high priest Jason (see also Park 2000: 30, 72, 96).

Avigad (1967: 110) maintains this is the oldest inscription written in a Jewish cursive script found so far. He dates it to the beginning of the first century BCE.

The two-line Greek inscription in Jason's Tomb is written in charcoal on the porch wall (Figure V–2) and was difficult to decipher, it reads

εὐφραίνεστε οἱ ζῶντες
[τ]ό δέ (λοι)πό[ν. .]πεῖν ομα φα[γεῖν].

Rejoice, you living, It remains to drink and to eat (Benoit 1967: 113).

Lifshitz (1966: 248–249) argues that the inscription follows the theme of enjoying life. Puech (1983: 492–3) reads the inscription, "Feast, you living brothers, and drink at the same time (or together). No one is immortal"; he interprets the words as reflecting actual commemorative funerary meals. They also explain the pottery finds and remains of fire in the tomb. Park (2000: 67–72) rightly concludes that the more simple interpretation "as an exhortation to the living to enjoy life before the onset of death" is correct, and it also implicates the fact of universal mortality and the swiftness and finality of death. Rahmani (1967a: 97) concludes that the tomb with its finds, and more especially the inscriptions, represents a tomb of "a wealthy Sadducee priestly family living in the late Hasmonean period".

2. The Abba Inscription

A unique Aramaic inscription written in paleo-Hebrew characters (Pl. V–1) was found in an arcosolia tomb on the northern slope of

Giv'at Ha Mivtar, Jerusalem. The inscription was carved on the wall above a small loculus entrance in Chamber II.

The late first century BCE inscription in paleo-Hebrew includes seven lines within a rectangular frame (Rosenthal 1973; Naveh 1973; Tzaferis 1974; Fitzmyer and Harrington 1978: No. 68), it reads:

אנה אבה בר כהנה א

לעז[ר] בר אהרן רבה אנ

ה אבה מעניה מר/ד

פה די יליד בירושלם

ונלא לבבל ואסק[ת] למחת

י בר יהוד וקברתה במ

ערתה דזבנת בנטה

I, Abba, son of the priest Eleaz[ar], son of Aaron the elder, I Abba, the oppressed and the persecuted, who (was) born in Jerusalem and went into exile to Babylonia, brought (back to Jerusalem) Mattathi(ah), son of Jud[ah]; and I buried him in the cave which I had acquired by the writ.

The inscription records a man named Abba of priestly descent, born in Jerusalem, who was persecuted and had to leave his home for exile in Babylon. He later returned and brought back the bones of Mattat (Mattathiah?) son of Judah; he then buried them in the tomb he had acquired by writ. However, no bones were discovered in the small sealed loculus.

Several suggestions as to the author's origin were put forward: a Samaritan priest who converted to Judaism (Lieberman 1974); a first-century Jewish origin (Rosenthal 1973). Naveh (1973: 91) maintains that Abba was a heterodox and separatist of some kind, who might have been persecuted by the government or by the official Jewish establishment.[1]

3. *The Sons of Ḥezir Inscription*

A three-line Hebrew inscription (109 cm. long, 19 cm. high) was carved in the center of the façade's architrave of the Bene Ḥezir tomb, in the Kidron Valley, Jerusalem (Avigad 1954: 37–59; see Chap. II, Fig. II–3c).

---

[1] In chamber I of the Abba tomb, which was possibly hewn earlier than chamber II, an elaborately decorated ossuary was found (Rahmani 1994: No. 350). It was suggested that the ossuary belonged to the Hasmonean king Mattathias Antigonus (*Ant.* 15.1.2) (Mattathias, son of Judah, of the inscription) (Grintz 1974); however, the remains in it were principally those of an older woman (Smith 1977).

The letters show remains of red paint (Figure V–3). The inscription was discovered by de Saulcy (1854, II:206) and published by de Vogue (1864: 200ff., Pl. 7). They and other scholars tried to decipher the inscription; the final and most reliable reading was given by Avigad (1954: 61).

זה הקבר והנפש של אלעזר חניה יועזר יהודה שמעון יוחנן
בני יוסף בן עובד יוסף ואלעזר בני חניה
כהנים מבני חזיר

> This is the tomb and the *nefesh* of El'azar, Ḥaniah, Yo'ezer, Yehudah, Shim'on, Yoḥanan sons of Yosef son of Oved; Yosef and El'azar, sons of Ḥaniah, priests of the Sons of Ḥezir.

The inscription records a four generation family buried in the tomb, who belonged to the priestly family originating in the 'house of Ḥezir', the 17th priestly course serving in the Jerusalem Temple in the First Temple period (I Chr. 24:15, Neh. 10:21) and probably also in the Second Temple period (Avigad 1954: 59–66; see Chap. VI, No. XII).

De Vogue (1864: 46, 130) and Klein (1920: 15) argued for the identification of El'azar, Yo'ezer and Shim'on named in this inscription with the three brothers of the Boethos family, who were high priests in Herod's time (*Ant.* 15, 3; 19, 6,2); they proposed the replacement of the 'sons of Yosef' by the 'sons of Boethos'. However, this identification is unacceptable, as it has no substantial evidence (Avigad 1954: 61).

Sarcophagi Inscriptions

Only two inscriptions engraved on sarcophagi were found to date.

4. Aramaic Inscription on a Sarcophagus

An Aramaic and Syrian inscription is engraved on the front of a sarcophagus retained from the Jerusalem tomb of Queen Helene of Adiabene, (Figure V–4):

'צדה מלכתא' and Syrian 'צדן מלכתה' 'Sadah [or Sadan], the Queen'.

The meaning of the name is not clear. Scholars identified the inscription with Queen Helene of Adiabene (Josephus *Ant.* 20. 95; Lidzbarski 1898: 117; Avigad 1956: 341; Kutscher 1956: 351. Fitzmyer and Harrington 1978: No. 132, suggest reading the name 'Saran' and 'Sarah').

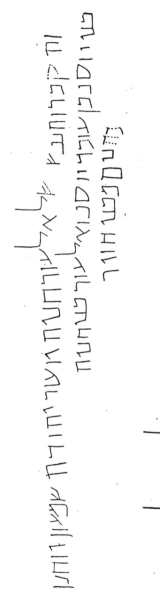
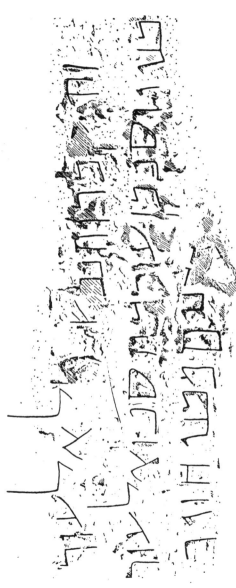

Figure V-3. The Bene Hezir inscription.

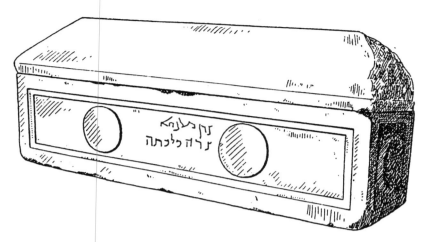

Figure V–4. The 'Sadah Queen' inscription on Sarcophagus
(after Avigad 1956: 341).

5. *A sarcophagus Inscription from Akeldama*

A hard limestone sarcophagus (No. 19) discovered in Akeldama
(Jerusalem) Tomb 2, Chamber B, Loculus II, had not been removed
from its place; on its narrow side above a wreath decoration it bears
a Greek inscription (Pl. V–2) mentioning two members of the Eros
family (Avni and Greenhut 1996: 18, Fig. 1.29a–c; Ilan 1996: 62,
No. 9; Shadmi 1994: 46, No. 19), it reads:

᾿Ερωτος κάι ῾Ερμιόνης Δώρατος

Eros and Hermione of (or: [children] of) Doras.

Selected Ossuary Inscriptions

Inscribed ossuaries are found mainly from the Jerusalem and Jericho
area, and only rarely from other areas (Rahmani 1994: Nos. 145,
290, 425, 464, 465, 610). The proportion is about a 25% of inscribed
ossuaries out of the complete corpus of ossuaries. However, there is
no distinct directive governing the proportion of the inscribed ossuaries. Rahmani (1994: 11) sums it up "in some tomb groups, the majority of ossuaries seems to have been inscribed and in other groups
about half of them bore inscriptions. Some groups have a single
inscriptions or none at all".

Inscriptions are usually carelessly executed, sometimes with mis-
takes; generally they are not incorporated into the decoration of the

ossuaries. The inscriptions were probably executed outside or inside the tomb at the time of the burial by relatives of the deceased. The Greek inscriptions written in ink on an ossuary from the Goliath tomb at Jericho is a rare example of a carfully written and well-spaced executed inscription (below; Hachlili 1999: 144, Inscription 3a, Fig. IV.1a). The majority of the inscriptions were frequently incised; some were finely written in ink, charcoal, and painted; some of the carving tools, such as a chisel or a nail were found discarded in the tomb (Rahmani 1994: 11–13; Hachlili 1999: 139).

The inscriptions appear on the front, rear, long, and narrow sides of the chest and on the lid of the ossuary, with preference for undecorated spaces. Little consideration was given to the placement of the inscription on the vacant surface. However, inscriptions were also executed on or across the decoration, even when unadorned areas were available. Many inscriptions are repeated on the ossuaries at least twice, and sometimes three or more times on the front back and the lid, in different languages and scripts, for example, most of the inscriptions from the Goliath tomb at Jericho (Hachlili 1999a: 144, inscription nos. 3, 4, 6–9, 11–13). In most cases the inscriptions are written horizontally, but a few appear vertically, ascending or descending, due to lack of skill or carelessness.

The languages used in the inscriptions are Aramaic, Hebrew, and Greek. Little difference can be seen in the use of Hebrew or Aramaic. In the bilingual inscriptions the main text was in Greek and the Hebrew was a summary, or the names had a Greek form.

Jewish and Greek scripts are used on the 233 inscribed ossuaries published by Rahmani (1994). Of these, 143 inscriptions bear Jewish script only, 73 Greek script only, 14 both Jewish and Greek scripts, two Latin script, and a single one bears Palmyrene script.

The Jerusalem and Jericho ossuary inscriptions indicate that the Jewish script was prefered, with considerable Greek additions (Rahmani 1994: 304–307, Table 2). These inscriptions intimate that the Jewish population knew Greek, probably just for everyday speech.

The inscriptions on ossuaries are brief or lengthy and informative, like similar epitaphs and representations on Greek and Roman funerary monuments (Kurtz and Boardman 1971: 260–266; Koch and Sichtermann 1982: 582–617). Altough the local ossuary inscriptions are simpler and tend to brevity (Rahmani 1994: 20–21).

Most ossuary inscriptions bear the full name of the deceased and his/her family relationship; a few record the age, place of origin, profession, or title of the deceased. These inscriptions expressed pride in the family and demonstrated their social standing. The repetition of the names of the deceased may indicate an expression of bereavement, grief and consolation. Moreover, the inscriptions and epitaphs might remind visitors of the deceased virtues. In some cases the inscriptions may have designated the burial place within the tomb of some person. The names helped to determine a resting place for a relative of the person already buried in a particular receptacle (cf. *Sem.* 13:8).[2] Some rare inscriptions include 'magic' and formulae for the protection of the deceased (see Chap. XI).

Selected ossuary inscriptions are discussed below, more inscriptions are examined in Chap. VI.

6. *The Nicanor inscription*

A bilingual inscription (Figure V–5) consisting of three Greek lines and two names in Hebrew are engraved on one of the ossuaries (now at the British Museum) found in the tomb of Nicanor; the inscription is dated to the mid-first century CE (Avigad 1967a: 124–125, Pl. 21:1; Frey 1952: No. 1256; Fitzmyer and Harrington 1978: No. 108; Kane 1978: 279–282):

> ὀστᾶ των τοῦ Νεικά-
> νορος Ἀλεξανδρέως
> /ποιήσαντος τὰς θύρας
> נקנר אלכסא

> The bones of the [sons or descendants?] of Nicanor the Alexandrian who made the doors. Nicanor Alexa.

The inscription most likely refers to Nicanor of Alexandria, who donated the famous door of Herod's Temple known as the 'Gate of Nicanor' (M Midot 2:4, 2:3; Yoma 3:6; BT Yoma 38a; JT Yoma 41a). The ossuary apparently contained the bones of some members of Nicanor's family, and he also might have been interred in the

---

[2] In the Beth She'arim and Jaffa public cemeteries the consolatory inscriptions seem to have been little more than personal, often spontaneous, expressions of bereavement and love for the deceased (Mazar 1973: 193; Schwabe and Lifshitz 1974: 219). The main purpose of these inscriptions and epitaphs are slightly different and may have been aimed to guide the bereaved or visitor to the place of mourning and to demonstrate the ownership; to designate the burial places of a person within the catacomb; to indicate and demonstrate the ownership of a tomb, hall or burial vault.

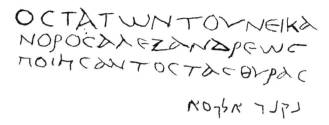

Figure V–5. The Nicanor inscription.

tomb. Kane (1978: 281) suggests that the inscription in Hebrew refers to two sons, Nicanor and Alexas, who might have been interred in the tomb.

7. *The 'Simon Builder of the sanctuary' Inscription*

On an ossuary from Tomb 1, Givʿat Ha Mivtar, Jerusalem (Figure V–6; Pl. V–3) the inscription records:

> סימון בנה הכלה 'Simon, builder of the sanctuary' (Naveh 1970: 34; Rahmani 1994: 20–21).

Simon is identified as one of the builders, a master-mason or engineer who took part in the construction of Herod's sanctuary: the Temple in Jerusalem.

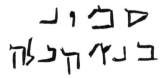

Figure V–6. The 'Simon' inscription.

8. *The Yehoḥanah inscription*

An ossuary, bought and possibly originating at Hizmeh (?) (Barag and Flusser 1986: 39; Rahmani 1994: No. 871), is engraved with a Hebrew inscription (Figure V–7; Pl. V–4) that reads:

יהוחנה ברת יהוחנן
בר תפלוס הכהן הנדול

Yehoḥanah, daughter of Yehoḥanan, son of Thophlos the high priest.

This ossuary evidently contained the bones of Yehoḥanah the grand-daughter of Theophilos the high priest, who served ca. 37–41 CE (Josephus *Ant.* 18.123; 19.297), it seems it was important to mention the high social rank of this woman (see Chaps. VI and VII).

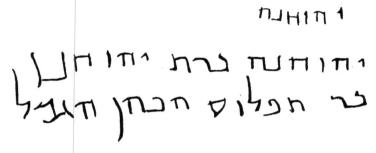

Figure V–7. The 'Yehoḥana' inscription.

9. *An Ossuary Inscription on a 'Burial in Jerusalem'*

On an ossuary found in a tomb on Mt. Olives, Jerusalem, a long Aramaic inscription was engraved (Figure V–8):

יוסף בר אלעשה ארתכה איתי נרמיה די אמכא אמה לירושלם

Joseph son of Elasa, a chariot (or a name) brought the bones of his mother to Jerusalem (Puech 1982: 355–358).

It is the only inscription mentioning the later custom of moving bones of the deceased to be buried in Jerusalem. On another ossuary from the same tomb the word *Haliba* (*Halifa*?) is inscribed six times. Peuch (1982: 368–372) suggests that the inscriptions written in the Palmyrene and east Aramean indicate that the interred origin had been in North Syria or North Mesopotamia. Consequently, Joseph perhaps brought his mother's bones from there to be buried in Jerusalem.

10. *The list from Beth Phage*

The inscription was engraved on an ossuary lid discovered in a tomb at Beth Phage (on the eastern slope of Mount of Olives, Jerusalem).

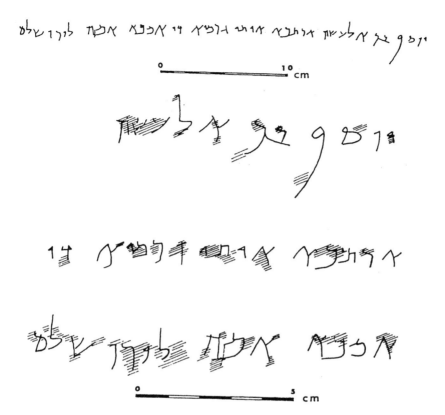

Figure V–8. The 'Burial in Jerusalem' inscription.

The tomb consisted of a courtyard in the south, a main chamber with a standing-pit with one ossuary placed on the bench. The east chamber had a standing-pit and four ossuaries placed on the benches; one loculi with four ossuaries, and an ossuaries repository chamber on a lower level with two ossuaries. Eleven ossuaries were found in this tomb all together (Orfali 1923).

The ossuary lid (Figure V–9) found in the tomb was inscribed with a Hebrew list of names and numbers containing 27 lines written in cursive script (Sukenik 1924; 1935: 104–107; Frey 1952: No. 1285; Milik 1971; Naveh 1990: 111–112) (now in the collection of the Musée de Louvre, no. AO 7487). A similar published list (Dussand 1923; Sukenik 1924; 1935: 107–108; Frey 1952: No. 1286) is a modern forgery (Naveh 1990: 111–112, note 11).

The List

1. 'son of the Painter'	1 drachma, 2 obols	בן הציר ר 1 מ
2. Thina	4 obols	בן תחנא מ 4
3. son of Yehuda	3 obols	בן יהודא מ 3
4. 'son of Yehoyamed	1 1/2 obol	בן יהויעמד מ 1 ף
5. 'The Galilean'	2 obols	הגלילי מ 2
6. son of Rabbi (of Kalibi)	2 obols	בן רבי מ 2
7. son of Azariah	3 obols	בן עזריה מ 3
8. son . . .		בן . . .
9. son of Madik	2 drachma	בן מדך ר 2
10. Simon son of Saltu (Salman)	1 1/2 obol	שמעון בן שלטו (שלמו) מ 1 ף
11. son of Yehohanan	3 obols	בן יהוחנן מ 3
12. son of Qarnu (qarkas)	2 obols	בן קרנו (קרקס) מ 2
13. son of Halafta	2 obols	בן הלפתא מ 2
14. 'Yehosef the Galilean'	2 obols	יהוסף הגלילי מ 2
15. 'Yasnuq the Babylonian'		ישניק הבבלי
16. Yehosef	1 obol	יהוסף מ 1
17. son of the Ogi (the Levi)	3 obols	בן העני (הלוי) מ 3
18. 'the Comber (of Linen)'	3 obols	השורק מ 3
19. Yadua	2 drachmas	ידוע ר 4
20. son of Fazzi	3 tetradrachmas (?)	בן פזי ר 3
21. son of Aftalmayos	1 obol	בן אפטלמיס מ 1
22. Nomos	1 drachma	נומש ר 1
23. Levi	3 obols	לוי מ 3
------------------		--------------------------------
24. Levi		לוי
25. son of Rabbi		בן רבי
26. son of Saltu (Salmu, Salman?)		בן שלטו
27. Yadua	4 obols	ידוע מ 4

The 27-line list, written in cursive script, is inscribed in two columns;
names on the right and numbers on the left, apparently recording
payment in (denarius (drachma) and obolus); to the right of the
names are short diagonal lines, possibly meaning 'paid'.

The document is a list of names of a group of Jewish ossuary
workshop craftsmen, perhaps employed in the ossuary workshop and

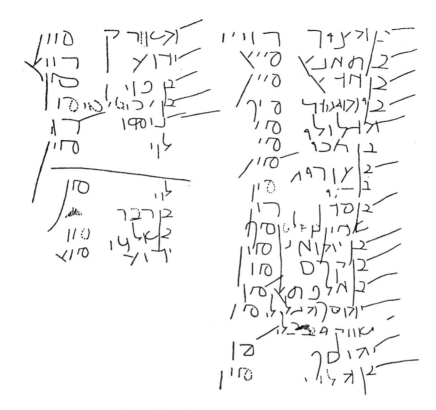

Figure V–9. The list from Beth Phage.

probably written by the employer (Sukenik 1924: 171); each name in
the list is followed by numbers and letters; short diagonal lines before
and sometimes after the names. The abbreviated form of the numbers
mean: (רבע) ר, a 'quarter' (of a sheqel), i.e. a denarius; (מ =) מעה,
'obolus', one sixth of a dinarius; (פ =) פלג, 'half' an obolus (Naveh
1990: 111). Dussand suggested the strokes were the letter *lamed* = L,
while Sukenik argues that the master made the marks indicating
verification or that the reckoning in each case was exact.

The list possibly documents the workmen daily wages with the
additional note (the diagonal line) whether they have been paid or
not. Sukenik (1935: 109) wrongly contends that perhaps the number might indicate the quantity of ossuaries the craftsmen prepared.

The document indicates that such a workshop apparently employed
quite a number of workers. It also might imply that many of the

ossuaries were prepared in advance and kept in storage for future purchases. However, some ossuaries might have been specially ordered, and their design chosen by the clients.

Nearly all the names in the lists appear as patronymics ('son of X') and nicknames without their personal name. Some names, such as Yehosef, Yehohanan, Levi, and Yadu'a, are common and recurring. Several consist of personal names followed by an epithet based on the place of origin: יהוסף הגלילי 'Yehosef the Galilean' (line 14), 'the Galilean' (line 5); 'Yasnuq the Babylonian' (line 15). 'Son of Aftalmayos' (line 21) might be a transcription of a nickname 'The Ptolemean' (Milik 1971: 84–85). Others include occupation designations: בן הציר 'son of 'the Painter' ('or Hunter') (line 1), השורק *ha-Soreq* (line 18) 'the Comber (of Linen)' (Sukenik 1935: 106) (see below).

The list records twenty names, four of them repeated at the end of the list. Fourteen of the names begin with 'son'; eight are patronymics without a personal name; five times 'son' is followed by a nickname of the person or his father. Three are personal names; twice personal names appear with a nickname, twice only a nickname is recorded, and only once a full name.

This list of names and nicknames is an example of a group of people who are on familiar terms in their own social circle, perhaps people who lived in a familiar and circumscribed location (Naveh 1990: 111). Kutscher suggested (1956: 355) that in daily life people, especially poor people, seldom used their full name, and that this list is an indication that Hebrew was spoken in Jerusalem.

A stone vessel workshop was recently discovered on the slope of Mount Scopus, Jerusalem (Amit et al. 2000: 358). The excavators suggest that this was the workplace of the workers mentioned in the Beth Phage inscription.

Ossuary Inscriptions from Jericho

11. Inscriptions from the Goliath Family Tomb (Table V–1)

Thirty-two inscriptions engraved on fourteen ossuaries were found in the Goliath tomb (Hachlili 1979; 1999:142–155, Inscriptions 1–14, Table IV.1; Rahmani 1994: Nos. 782–803). Seventeen of them are in Greek and the remaining fifteen are in the Jewish script. Bilingual inscriptions are found on three ossuaries (Nos. XVIII, XX, XXI) all placed in loculus 14 (Hachlili 1999: 40, Fig. II.77). Inscriptions are written on the front, sides, and lids of the ossuaries. They contain the deceased's name and family relationship, with the exception of Inscriptions 3a–b and 14. Most of the inscriptions were incised into the soft limestone with a chisel (or nail?); others are written in ink (Inscriptions 3a–b) or charcoal (Inscription 14). Many inscriptions are repeated on the ossuaries at least twice, sometimes three times or more.

Table V–1. The Goliath family inscriptions and anthropological data.

Insc. No.	Oss. No.	Location of ossuary L = Loculus	Inscription	Translation	Sex	Age in years	Note
			Chamber A				
1	I	Before L1	Μαριάμη γυ Ιούδου	Mariame, wife of Judah	F?	20. 6–11 m	
2a	II	Before L1	יהועזר בן אלעזר נליה	Yeho'ezer son of Ele'azar Goliath	M??	4 10 m	
2b			יהועזר בן אלעזר נליה	Yeho'ezer son of Ele'azar Goliath		6 m	
3a	VIII	In L2 (back)	Θεοδότου ἀπελευ-/ θέρου βασιλίσσης-/ Ἀγριππείνης-σορός	Theodotos freed-man of Queen Agrippina – Ossuary	M	50–60	Tall
3b			Θεοδότου ἀπελευ-/ θέρου βασιλίσσης-/ Ἀγριππείνης-σορός	Theodotos freedman of Queen Agrippina			
4a	XII	Before L12–13	Ἰωέζρος	Yeho'ezer			
4b			Ἰωέζρος/Ἰσμαήλου	Yeho'ezer son of Ishma'el	M	40	Cripple
4c			Ἰωέζρος/Ἰσμαήλου	Yeho'ezer son of Ishma'el			
5a	XIII	On floor	Μανάημος	Menaḥem	M	18–20	Tall
5b			Σίμων	Simon	M	40–50	
6a	XIV	On floor	Σίμων	Simon			
6b	XIV	On floor	Σίμων				
7a			מריה ברת נתן[נ]אל שלמשן	Maria daughter of Nat[an]el Shlamsiyon	M	40	
7b	XV	On floor	מריה בריה נתן[נ]אל בת שלמשן	Maria daughter of Nat[an]el daughter of Shlamsiyon			
7c			מריה ברת	Maria daughter of			
8a			יהועזר אקביא/אזביא	Yeho'ezer Aqaby'a/Azaby'a			

Table V-1 (cont.)

Insc. No.	Oss. No.	Location of ossuary L = Loculus	Inscription	Translation	Sex	Age in years	Note
			Chamber A				
8b	XVI	On floor	אקביא/אזביא	Aqabyʾa/Azabyʾa	M	4 yrs	
8c			יהועזר אקביא/אזביא	Yehoʿezer Aqabyʾa/Azabyʾa			
8d			יהועזר אקביא/אזביא	Yehoʿezer Aqabyʾa/Azabyʾa			
9a		In L14,	Ἰωέζρος Ἰωέζρου	Yehoʿezer son of			
9b	XVIII	front, right	Γολιάθου	Yehoʿezer Goliath	M	20–50	
9c			יהועזר בן יהועזר נלית	Yehoʿezer son of Yehoʿezer Goliath			
			Ἰοέζρος Ἰοέζρου Γολιάθου	Yehoʿezer son of Yehoʿezer Goliath			
10	XIX	In L14, front, left	Σαλώμη γυνή Ἰωέζρου Γολιάθου/καί Ἰσμαήλος υιός καί/ Ἰωέζρος υιός	Salome wife of Yehoʿezer Goliath and her son Ishmael and her son Yehoʿezer	F M	40–50 3–4	
11a		In L14,	Σελαμσιους μητρός	Shlamsiyon mother	F	50–60	
11b	XX	back, right	Ἰοέζρου Γολιάθου	of Yehoʿezer Goliath			
11c			שלמשיון אמה די יהועזר נלית	Shlamsiyon mother of Yehoʿezer Goliath			
			Σελαμσιους μητρὸς Ἰοέζρου Γολιάθου	Shlamsiyon mother of Yehoʿezer Goliath			
12a	XXI	In L14,	יהועזר בר אלעזר	Yehoʿezer son of	M	25–35	Exceptional height 1.885 m
12b		Back, left	Ελεάζαρος	Eleʿazar			
13a	XXII	In L15	יהועזר אקביא/אזביא	Yehoʿezer Aqabyʾa/	M	5–6 m	
13b			קנמומא	Azabyʾa Cinnamon			
			אקביא/אזביא	Aqabyʾa/Azabyʾa			
14	VI lid	In the pit	ΑΒΓΑ/ΕΖ/ΗΘ/Φ				

The most interesting inscriptions are discussed.

Four ossuaries (XVIII, XIX, XX, XXI) located in Chamber B, *kokh* 14, engraved with Inscriptions 9–12 (Figure V–10a–b; Pls. V–5–8). In these inscriptions the important construction of three generation of the Goliath family are found (Hachlili 1999: 149–152; Figs. IV.10–13).

Two ossuaries (XX and XXI) placed at the back of *kokh* 14 are engraved with Inscriptions 11 and 12. Inscription 12 refers to the father of this family, who was exceptionally tall: יהועזר בר אלעזר 'Yehoʿezer son of Eleʿazar', and bears on the side "Eleʿazaros" written

יהועזר בר
אלעזר

ΕΛΕΑΖΑΡΟC

a

INS. 11a

CEΛΑΜCΙΟΥC ΜΗΤΡΟC ΙWΕΖΡΟΥ ΓΟΛΙΑΘΟΥ

שלמשיון אמה די יהועזר גלית

CEΛΑΜCΙΟΥC ΜΗΤΡΟC ΙΟΕΖΡΟΥ ΓΟΛΙΑΘΟΥ

b

Figure V–10a–b. Jericho, Goliath family, Inscriptions 11–12.

in Greek (Inscription 12b) (Figure V–10a; Pl. V–5). Inscription 11 refers to his wife שלומשיון אמה די יהועזר נלית 'Shelamsiyon, mother of Yeho'ezer Goliath' (Figure V–10b; Pl. V–6).

Two ossuaries (XVIII, XIX) found in the front of the same *kokh*, held the remains of יהועזר בן יהועזר נלית 'Yeho'ezer son of Yeho'ezer Goliath' (bilingual Inscription 9 (Figure V–11a; Pl. V–7) and his wife

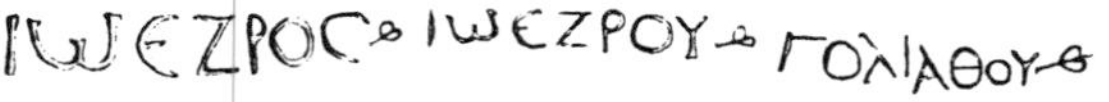

IWEZPOC IWEZPOY ΓΟΛΙΑΘΟΥ

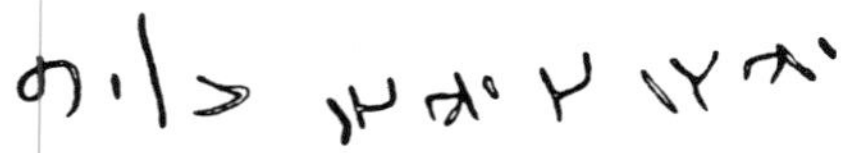

יהועזר בן יהועזר גלית

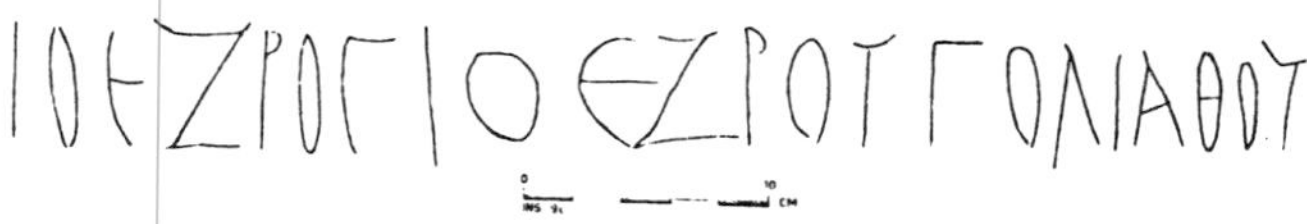

IOEZPOC IOEZPOY ΓΟΛΙΑΘΟΥ

a

CΑΛΩΜΗ ΓΥΝΗ IWEZPOY ΓΟΛΙΑΘΟΥ
KAI ICMAHΛOC YIOC KAI
IWEZPOC YIOC

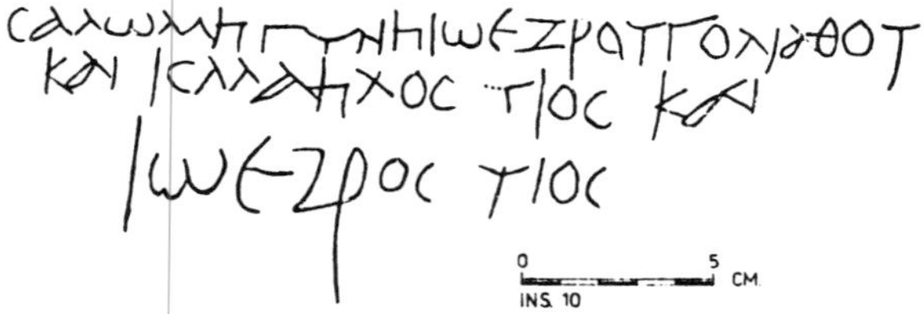

b

Figure V–11a,b. Jericho Goliath Family, Inscriptions 9–10.

Salome (Inscription 10: Σαλώμη γυνή Ἰωέζρου Γολιάθου/καί Ἰσμάηλος υἱός καί/ Ἰωέζρος υἱός 'Salome, wife of Yeho'ezer Goliath, and Ishmael (her) son and Yeho'ezer (her) son' (Figure V–11b; Pl. V–8).

The bilingual Inscriptions 9 and 11 in Jewish and Greek script are written in the same cursive style and may have been executed by the same hand. These four inscriptions refer to the founders, the father and mother, of the family, their son, his wife, and their two grandchildren.

- Inscriptions 3 (Ossuary VIII) was found in Chamber A, Kokh 2) is the most interesting in the Goliath tomb. The Greek inscriptions were written in ink on the upper corners of the ossuary back (Figure V–12; Pl. V–9) (Hachlili 1979a: 46–47, Figs. 41–42; 1999: 142, 144–145, Fig. IV.1, Table IV.1):

ΘΕΟΔΟΤΟΥ ΑΠΕΛΕΥ/ΘΕΡΟΥ ΒΑCΙΛΙCCHC/ΑΓΡΙΠΠΕΙΝΗC
– COΡΟΣ

The ossuary of 'Theodotos, freedman of Queen Agrippina'.

The inscription contains the personal, servile name of Theodotos, followed by the status indication (his manumission) and his patron's name, Queen Agrippina. This inscription, written in the form customary for funerary inscriptions of freedmen, indicates the legal fact of Theodotos' manumission by Queen Agrippina and that he was an 'imperial freedman'; it also confirms that the events recorded in this inscription were considered by the family to be important, indicating Theodotos' special status as a Roman citizen.

Theodotos/Nat[an]el, a member of a prominent Jewish family in Jericho, was probably enslaved after being taken a prisoner of war (perhaps during a civil disturbance in Judea). Then he may have been taken to Rome, where he adopted his Greek servile name Theodotos, a translation of his Hebrew name Natanel (see below, Inscription 7). The association between these two names is supported by the fact that many slaves adopted Greek names at the time of their enslavement (Gordon 1924: 100, 105; Westermann 1955: 96; Duff 1958: 56).

Theodotos' status ΑΠΕΛΕΥΘΕΡΟΥ (= freedman of) indicates that he was manumitted by Queen Agrippina (for other Agrippina inscriptions, see Weaver 1972: 47, 64–65, 72). It is likely that he was taken as a 'political slave', since he came from a prominent family. Many

ΘΕΟΔΟΤΟΥΑΠΕΛΕΥ-
ΘΕΡΟΥΒΑCΙΝCCΗC-
ΑΓΡΙΠΠΕΙΝΗC-COΡΟC

ΘΕΟΔΟΤΟΥ ΑΠΕΛΕΥ–
ΘΕΡΟΥ ΒΑCΙΛΙCCΗC–
ΑΓΡΙΠΠΕΙΝΗC–COΡΟC

0   5
                    cm

ΘΕΟΔΟΤΟΥΑΠ ΛΕΥΟΕΡΟΥ-
ΒΑCΙΛΙC ΗCΑΓΡ ΠΕΙΝΗC

ΘΕΟΔΟΤΟΥ ΑΠΕΛΕΥΘΕΡΟΥ–
ΒΑCΙΛΙCCΗC ΑΓΡΙΠΠΕΙΝΗC

0   2
           cm

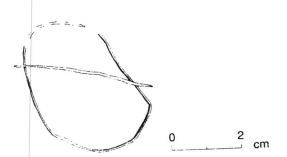

0   2
          cm

Figure V–12. Jericho, Goliath family: Theodotos Inscription 3.

Roman slaves were war captives (Westermann 1955: 84; Treggiari 1969: 4). Jews were often sold into slavery following rebellions. There is an inscription mentioning a captive from Judea in the reign of Claudius (Bang 1910: 233). Josephus records (*War* 1, 180) the selling of Jews into slavery on several occasions; in the time of Cassius in 53 BCE; during the revolt in Judea at the time of Varus, Legate of Syria (*War* 2, 39–54; *Ant.* 17.254–269); and at the time of the Jewish Revolt (*War* 3.62).

Queen Agrippina in this inscription should be identified with Agrippina the Younger (15–59 CE), daughter of Agrippina the Elder and Germanicus, who in 49 CE married Emperor Claudius, her uncle (Tacitus, *Ann.* XII 1–8). She acquired the title of 'Augusta' in 50 CE and was the owner of a large number of slaves in her own right (Weaver 1972: 64). It is believed that she poisoned Claudius in 54 CE in order to ensure the succession of her own son Nero. In the first years of Nero's rule she continued her co-regency (Tacitus, *Ann.* XII 64; XIII, 21–22). Later she lost her power and was murdered in 59 CE by a freedman (Tacitus, *Ann.* XIV 3–9; Jos. *War* 2.249; *Ant.* 20.148, 151).

Theodotos may have been a domestic slave in Queen Agrippina's household (Hachlili 1979: 46; for the legal status of Theodotos as a freedman of Queen Agrippina, see Piatelli 1987; 1990). It is tempting to suggest that he was in charge of Roman interests or property of the Empress in Jericho itself, or in some neighboring area, but there is no evidence for this suggestion (Hachlili 1979: 63, n. 2). Later, during Agrippina's reign (51–55 CE), he gained manumission, perhaps due to Agrippina's close relations with the king of Judea Agrippa II and his family. After his release Theodotos returned to his home in Jericho, where he died and was placed in the family tomb. Inscriptions 7a–b (on Mariah's ossuary No. XV) established his position in the family, i.e., Theodotos/Nat[an]el, the freedman of Queen Agrippina, is the son of Shelamsiyon and father of Mariah (see below).

The Greek term COPOC (*Soros*) at the end of Inscription 3a appears here for the first time in an ossuary inscription (Hachlili 1979a: 55; 1999: 153). The word ארון (*aron*) meaning "coffin" occurs only once in the Hebrew Bible (Gen 50:26) and refers to the coffin used to transport Joseph's bones from Egypt to Israel. In the LXX this word is translated into Greek as σορος (*soros*), meaning 'coffin or cinerary urn'. It seems that *soros* according to the Jericho inscription was a term for ossuary in use during the Second Temple period and was equivalent to ארון *aron* in Hebrew (see Chap. III).

• Inscriptions 7a,b (Ossuary XV) cites מריה ברת נת[נ]אל בת שלמשׁיׂ 'Mariah, daughter of Nat[an]el and granddaughter of Shelamsiyon' (Figure V–13; Pl. V–10).

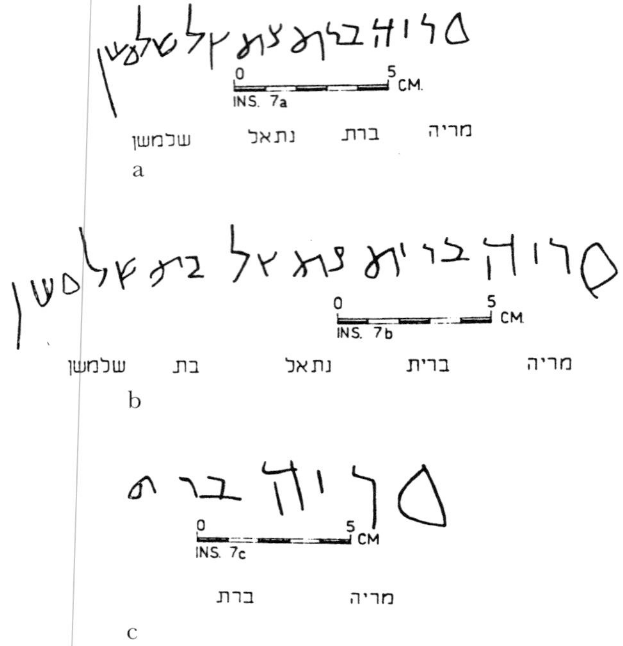

INS. 7a

שלמשון   נתאל   ברת   מריה

a

INS. 7b

שלמשון   בת   נתאל   ברית   מריה

b

INS. 7c

ברת   מריה

c

Figure V–13. Jericho, Goliath Family: 'Mariah' Inscription 7.

In this inscription Mariah is recorded as the daughter of Nat[an]el, i.e. Theodothos, who is mentioned in Inscription 3 (above); it is unusual in the fact that Mariah, of the third generation, traces her ancestry back to a woman, Shelamsiyon her grandmother (Hachlili 1979: 57; 1999: 142). (See below Inscription 16b 'Ishmael bar Palta', where *bar* in this case means 'grandson'; Hachlili 1978: 45, 48).

• Inscriptions 8a–d (ossuary XVI) יהועזר אקביא/אזביא 'Yeho'ezer Aqa-by'a/Azaby'a' and Inscription 13a (ossuary XXII) יהועזר אקביא/אזביא קנמומא 'Yeho'ezer Aqaby'a/Azaby'a Cinnamon' are inscribed on children's ossuaries and mention two identical names, probably written by the same hand (Figure V–14, 15; Pl. V–11a,b).

These two ossuaries held the remains of child and an infant, both with the same name Yeho'ezer Aqaby'a (or Azaby'a?). The endearment nickname 'Cinnamon' was added to the infant inscription probably to differentiate him from the other Yeho'ezers in this tomb.

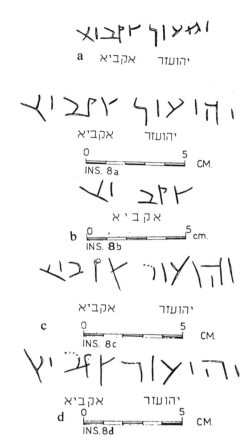

Figure V–14. Jericho, Goliath family: Inscription 8.

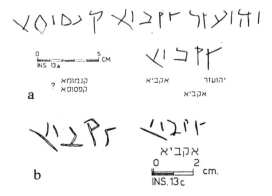

Figure V–15. Jericho, Goliath family: Inscription 13.

• Inscription 14 was written in charcoal on a lid, which probably belonged to Ossuary VI (Hachlili 1979: 47–48; 1984a; 1999: Fig. IV.2).
The inscription is a Greek abecedary, consisting of nine letters of
the alphabet, in four lines: ΑΒΓΔ/ΕΖ/ΗΘ(?)/Φ (see Fig. XI–19).

The lid was found standing in the northwest corner of the pit, with
the inscription facing the tomb entrance (see Fig. IV–4) (Hachlili
1999: Figs. II.73,74). Sometime while the tomb was in use the lid
was probably removed from the ossuary, the letters were inscribed
on it, and it was intentionally placed facing the entrance (see discussion Chap. XI).

(For other inscriptions of the Goliath family members see Chap. VI).

14. *Jericho Inscriptions of a Family 'from Jerusalem'*

Four funerary inscriptions were discovered in Tomb D1 at Jericho
(Hachlili 1978; 1999: 155–158, Figs. IV.16–19); two are written on
a bowl (Inscription 15a,b) and two on ossuaries 19 (Inscription 16)
and 20 (Inscription 17), all found in the same kokh. The two ossuaries were found *in situ*, placed one on top of the other. The bowl,
which was resting on debris close to the corner of Ossuary 19, originally might have been placed on top of Ossuary 20 and later fell
onto the debris. The inscriptions on the bowl and Ossuary 19 are
in Jewish script while Ossuary 20 bears a Greek inscription.

The bowl Inscriptions (Inscriptions 15a,b; Pl. V–12) are two short
texts in cursive Jewish letters (height 1.0–1.5 cm.) inscribed in ink
on the bowl, one inside and one outside.

Inscription 15a, on the inside, (Figure V–16a) begins with a slant-
ing line which seems to indicate the starting point of the inscription.
It reads

ישמעאל בר שמעון בר פלטא [מן] ירשלם

Ishmael son of Shim'on son of Palṭa [from] Jerusalem

Inscription 15b, on the outside, consists of two lines (Figure V–16b):

ישמעאל בן פלטא / שמעוו מן ירשלם

Ishmael son of Palṭ'a/Shim'on from Jerusalem

The two other inscriptions appear on ossuaries 19 and 20.

Inscription 16 (Ossuary 19) contains two lines of formal Jewish
script lightly incised with a chisel (Figure V–17a). It reads

Figure V–16a–b. Jericho, bowl inscriptions 'from Jerusalem' (Inscriptions 15a,b).

Figure V–17a,b. Jericho, Ossuary Inscriptions 16, 17.

Pelaty'a from/Jerusalem פלטיא מן ירשלם

Bones of an adult male were found inside this ossuary.

Inscription 17 (Ossuary 20) (Figure V–17b) reads

CIMWNOC L MA Simon aged 41

The bones of a male aged between 40 and 50 years were discovered inside this ossuary (Hachlili 1999: Appendix, Anthropology Table 2). The age of the deceased is indicated by the sign *L*, which stands for ετων ("years"), whereas *MA* are the Greek numerical symbols for 41. Although the *L* sign indicating the date is frequent on coins and weights (Hestrin and Israeli 1973: nos. 230–32), it is rare on ossuaries as a sign indicating age; only one other such example is known from an ossuary inscription from the Kidron Valley, Jerusalem (Avigad 1962b: 6–7, fig. 7, Ossuary 6, Inscription 4a,b, maintains that the use of the *L* sign on the inscription "follows a practice probably introduced from Cyrenaica"; but see Demsky (2002: 16, note 13), who suggests reading the text '*Simonos [s]lma*'; the *Slma* is a quasi-consonantal spelling of Solyma (for Shalem, i.e., Jerusalem.)

The ossuary inscriptions in this tomb indicate that the three men – Ishmael, Shim'on/Simon, and Pelaty'a/Palt'a – were related, belonged to the same family and were 'from Jerusalem'. Their relationship is evident only from Inscription 15a on the inside of the bowl.

The genealogical order is not the same in the two bowl inscriptions. Inscription 15a seems to be the correct order of the family names: 'Ishmael son of Shim'on, son of Palt'a from Jerusalem'. Inscription 15b is more problematic as it cites 'Ishmael son of Palt'a/Shim'on from Jerusalem'.

Inscription 15a emphasizes that Ishmael, the third generation, is "from Jerusalem". Inscription 16 mentions that the first-generation Palt'a (whose bones were found in Ossuary 19) is also "from Jerusalem". The Greek inscription No. 17 on Shim'on's ossuary gives only his name and age. Perhaps Ishmael, the author of bowl Inscriptions 15a and 15b, realized that Inscription 17 did not mention the origin of his father; therefore, he omitted the name Shim'on, which should have been in the first line of Inscription 15b, and added a separate second line with the information that Shim'on was "from Jerusalem" (for the paleography of these inscriptions see Hachlili 1978: 49–55).

The main inscription seems to be 15a, which contains the complete genealogy and origin of Ishmael, who placed the bowl at the site of his father's and grandfather's ossuaries, all in one kokh. Inscription 15b is an addition, which again mentions the author and his relationship to the family, adding that Shim'on was from Jerusalem, as this information was missing from Shim'on's ossuary inscription.

מן ירשלם 'from Jerusalem' appears in Inscriptions 15a, b, and 16. Parallels to the expression מן *min* followed by a place name include a two-line ostracon from Masada (Avi-Yonah et al. 1957: 59–60) and two occurrences in a Bar Kokhba letter (Yadin 1962: 250–51, document 44). Parallels from later periods include an Aramaic papyrus (Milik 1954: 183), a synagogue mosaic floor (Sukenik 1935: 48, fig. 15), and the use of the Aramaic form דמן in the Talmud to indicate the non-Israeli place of origin of a Rabbi (BT Ketubot 7; BT Berakot 29a). On the basis of the above examples it can be concluded that the word *min* followed by a place name indicates place of origin and that this expression does not occur frequently in this period. This is indicated usually by the addition to the person's name of his place of origin in the adjectival form, as is customary in the Bible (for example, 1 Sam 14:3, 18; Jud. 12:7). In later sources, when Jerusalem is mentioned as a place of origin it is written in the adjectival form preceded by the word 'š (Levi 1879: 266; Kasowski 1972: 588; Safrai 1972: 62–78).

Jerusalem (ירשלם *yršlm*) appears in Inscriptions 15a and 15b without vowel letters, whereas in inscription 16, Jerusalem (ירושלם *yrwšlm*) appears with one vowel letter, the *waw* (for the origin and spelling of the name Yerushalayim see Klein 1992: 15–17; Demski 2002: 15–18). There are several other known inscriptions where Jerusalem is mentioned (with the same spelling): on a literary text found on the wall of a tomb at Khirbet Beit Lei, dated to the sixth century BCE (Naveh 1973: 84, pl. 13, and n. 14; 92). The place-name Jerusalem appears also on an inscription on Ossuary 1 from the Mount of Olives (Puech 1982: 35; see Chap. VI), and in the Paleo-Hebrew Abba inscription (see above; Rosenthal 1973; Naveh 1973). The spelling (ירשלם *yršlm*) occurs also on Paleo-Hebrew stamps (fourth century BCE; Hestrin and Israeli 1973: no. 155) and on coins of the first revolt (Meshorer 1967: coin nos. 148, 151), but some appear with the full spelling ירושלם.

The spelling of Jerusalem is rare in contemporary inscriptions. There are some examples in commentary texts from Qumran where the name Jerusalem occurs written in its full form (Barthélemy and

Milik 1955: 82, pl. 15; Baillet, Milik and De Vaux 1962: 127, pl. 27:5, no. 4; pl. 26:13, line 6).

Since these Jericho inscriptions are short and deal only with a family genealogy, it is difficult to conclude whether they are Aramaic or Hebrew.

In summary, it seems that the main inscription 15a contained the complete genealogy and origin of Ishmael, who placed the bowl at the site of the ossuaries of his father Shim'on and of his grandfather Palt'a, all in one loculus. From these first century CE inscriptions it is possible to conclude that this was the tomb of members of a family, originally from Jerusalem, but who probably resided, died, and were buried at Jericho.

The four inscriptions reveal that this was a family tomb, and they trace its genealogy for three generations. The importance of this find is that it is the first time a bowl with funerary inscriptions accompanying ossuaries has been found. The bowl seems to serve as a memorial recording the family genealogy, since the bones of Ishmael, the author, were not found in the loculus. Three of the inscriptions also state that this family was originally from Jerusalem. Within the corpus of tomb inscriptions of the period, this is the first time that Jerusalem appears as a person's place of origin, and it is only the second inscriptional occurrence of the name Jerusalem.

Expressions of Consolatory and Sorrow

Few consolatory expressions appear on epitaphs inscribed on tombs or ossuaries, though they are quite common in Greek and Roman epitaphs. At Beth She'arim about 40 out of the 220 inscriptions include consolatory expressions (Rahmani 1994: 17–18).

Several ossuary inscriptions display formulae of an exclamation of sorrow.

The word חבל 'Woe' is an exclamation of sorrow (Rahmani 1994: 18) and of love for the deceased; it appears in Palmyrene script on Ossuary 11 from Shuafat, Jerusalem דה קיקא. . ./. . קימו ... חבל/. . .זיטר וסרה ובדתה/. . .חבב 'this is the ossuary(?) of . . . Kaiamu Ḥabab . . . Zitar and Sara and her daughter . . . Woe . . .'

(Abel 1913: 271, Pl. 1, No. 11; Frey 1952: No. 1222; see Chap. VI, pp.). On an ossuary from Jerusalem an exclamation of sorrow might be implied by the phrase 'who failed to give birth' (Rahmani 1994: 18, No. 226) (see Chap. VII, pp.). A similar formula appears on a painted Hebrew and Palmyrene inscription at Beth She'arim (Mazar B. 1973: 201–2, 207) and is added to a Greek inscription (Schwabe and Lifshitz 1974: Nos. 117, 119).

The term שלום *Shalom* (peace) is lacking in the formulaic use of ossuary inscriptions, and the examples that do occur obviously indicate the deceased's name (Rahmani 1994: Nos. 13, 23, 24, 226, 286, 582, 682, 694; Park 2000: 87–89). The only exception is the use of *Shalom* as a blessing at the end of each sentence in the inscription of Jason's Tomb, which might have a symbolic meaning (Avigad 1967: 103; Park 2000: 96–7). At the end of the first line the blessing הוה שלם 'be in peace' or 'rest in peace' occurs, and it refers to the deceased. It seems the use of the term in the funerary context came later, in examples at Beth She'arim and the Diaspora.

The inscriptions were found on tomb walls, sarcophagi and ossuaries, they usually record the name of the deceased and his/her family relationship; a few record the age, place of origin, and profession or title of the deceased. Some rare inscriptions include special epitaphs, 'magic' formulae for the protection of the deceased, and texts expressing the sorrow of the bereaved (see also Chaps. VI, and XI).

B. Personal Names, Nicknames and Family Names

Personal names, nicknames, and family names are an important source for the study of ancient Jewish life and society, as well as for a general picture of major onomastic trends and elements of Jewish names in the Second Temple period (Hachlili 1984b, 2000a).

The sources for names in the Second Temple period are vast: non-literary sources such as funerary inscriptions, mainly on ossuaries but also on tombs, tombstones, and sarcophagi; papyri and ostraca from Masada, the Judean Desert, Wadi Murabaat, and the Bar Kochba letters; the Dead Sea Scrolls. Literary sources for names are the Bible, the New Testament, the Maccabean books, and the writings of Josephus Flavius. Research into the onomasticon of the names of this period reveals an interesting historical and social picture (for a study of the Jewish onomasticon and the question of identifying ancient Jews by their names, see Mussies 1994).

Rahmani (1994: 13–15) in his catalogue (which is restricted to the ossuaries in the collection of the IAA) lists 147 names, nicknames, and probable names inscribed on ossuaries: 72 are Jewish, 51 are Greek, seven are Latin, four are Palmyrene, of which two names seem to be 'Arab', and one is a Nabatean name in Greek script.

Names in the Second Temple period take several forms: single personal names יהודה Yehudah; full names in the patronymic form of 'X son of Y', 'Yehoezer son of Eleazar' יהועזר בן אלעזר; a full name with a nickname, 'Yehoezer son of Yehoezer Goliath' יהועזר בן יהועזר נלית; a patronymic: 'son of Y', בן יהודה, 'son of Yehudah'; a matronymic: בן החורנית 'son of the Horanit [woman]'; a single nickname, הגלילי, 'the Galilean' and a nickname as a patronymic בן העני 'son of the poor' (for a group of various names see the list from Beth Phage, above).

A woman's full name is 'X daughter of Y', שלום בת יהודה 'Shalom daughter of Yehudah'; a married woman is named 'X wife of Y' מרים אשת (אתת) יהודה 'Miriam wife of Yehudah'; sometimes a woman is named 'X mother of Y', שלמשיון אמה יהועזר 'Shlamsion mother of Yehoezer', or an abbreviated form שלמציון אמנה 'Shelamziyon our mother'. Sometimes the inscription includes a woman's name and her son's: שלם ומתיה בנה 'Shalom and Mattya her son' (see also Chap. VII, pp).

The full name was the official and formal name of a person, commonly used on burial inscriptions, where it also served as a commemoration, a memorial for the dead; on jars the full names designated ownership; and on legal documents a formal name was required. The abbreviated name, where the personal name or patronymic is deleted, are found mainly on lists, but sometimes also on ossuary inscriptions.

Choosing a Name

Different customs determined the choice of name in the First and Second Temple periods. The reasons behind the choice in the Second Temple period were different from those in the First Temple period, when names were given in honour of special events that befell the family or the nation; examples are Isaac (Gen. 17,17–19), the sons of Jacob, where every name has its reason (Gen. 29,32; 30,23; 35,18),

Imanuel (Isa. 7, 14–17) and others (Hachlili 1984b: 192). By contrast, during the Second Temple period, naming children after an ancestor was prevalent. Most common was paponymy and metronymy, that is, naming a son after his grandfather and a daughter after her grandmother (Ilan 1995: 53). This custom was prevalent in the Egyptian, Phoenician and Greek world. The Elephantine and Assuan Aramaic papyri indicate that the custom first arose among the Jews in fifth century BCE Egypt (Buchanan-Grey 1914: 163–164, 172). There is some suggestion that the custom was also common in Eretz Israel: טוביה 'Tubias' was a common paponym in בית טוביה 'the House of Tubias' (from the sixth century to 200 BCE); and for both sons and daughters in prominent families such as the Hasmonean dynasty (Hachlili 1984b: 192, Figure 2). One of the few literary sources for the custom of paponymy indicates that a child is named Abram after his dead grandfather (*Jubilees* 11, 14–15).

The custom of patronymy was apparently common among the royal Hellenistic dynasties. From the first century BCE on, the practice became increasingly prevalent among prominent Jewish families in Eretz Israel, resulting in a small number of personal names appearing for several generations in a single family (Hachlili 1979: 53, fig. 49; 1984b: 192–194).

Another practice (derived and influenced by Greek and Roman customs) was giving a daughter the name of the father with a feminine ending. This was prevalent in the Hasmonean and Herodain dynasties (Ilan 1995: 53–54), for instance, Alexandra after Alexander and Herodias after Herod; another example is Yohanna as a feminine form of Yehohanan, inscribed on ossuaries from Jerusalem. It sometimes occurs also with sons named after their mother.

In choosing the names for their children, members of the general public might have preferred the names of high priests, aristocrats, and priests.

Double names appear chiefly among Hebrew-Greek names, but there are also double Hebrew names for instance, Miriam-Johana or Salona-Mariame (Rahmani 1994: 14). These are similar to classical *signa* (Horsley 1984: 89–96).

Contracted names occur sometimes, such as Martha and Mara, Yeshu‘a and Yeshu (Rahmani 1994: 15, Nos. 468, 469).

Personal Names

Men's Names

The personal Hebrew biblical names שמעון, יהוסף, יהודה, אלעזר, יהוחנן,
יהושע, חניה, יונתן, מתתיה Shim'on, Yehosef, Yehudah, Ele'azar, Yehoḥanan, Yehosu'a, Ḥananiah, Yonathan, and Mathathiah (Table V–2a)
are the most common Jewish names in the onomasticon of the late
Second Temple period (Hachlili 1984b: 188–191; Ilan 1987: 138;
2002: 4–8, 59–238, Table 7; see also Kane 1978: 270–271); these
include the names on funerary inscription (mainly on ossuaries)
(Rahmani 1994: 14), the personal names of the Qumran sect members (Eshel 1997: 52), the names found at Masada (Hachlili 1999a:
49–50) and the Judean Desert documents on ostraca and papyri
(dated to the early second century CE. The frequency of the names
in these later documents is slightly different, see Table V–2a). Some
Greek names appear on ossuaries[3] the most frequently used are
Alexander (on 8 ossuaries), דוסתס Dositheus (6 ossuaries) תדא, תדיון,
Thaddaius (on 3 ossuaries), Theodotus (on 3 ossuaries), and Philo
(on 3 ossuaries.

In the biblical onomasticon, although enormous, the frequency of
the names is low. In the Second Temple period the onomasticon is
much smaller but the rate of recurrence of the names is high.

The popularity and the frequency of men's names, especially the
five most common, is probably a result of their being the typical
names of the Hasmonean dynasty (Hachlili 1984b: 188–191; Ilan
1987: 238–241; 2002: 6–8; see especially her interesting suggestion
about Yehosef being another Hasmonean brother), as well as the
custom of patronymy, naming a son after his father, which was
prevalent during this period among the Jewish population (Hachlili
1979: 53; 1984b: 195). Note also the most common names among
high priests: Shim'on, Yehosef, Ele'azar, Yehosu'a, Yehonathan,
Mathathiah, and Ishmael (each appears three times).

יהודה Yehuda was a common Hebrew name and had some variations such as יהודא ידן יהוד יהודן (Rahmani 1994: 293, 327(?), 370,
464, 477) as well as the Greek Ἰούδας. The name Yehuda was
adopted by proselytes (see below). Note also that members of the

---

[3] For Jews bearing Greek, Latin and Semitic names, see Ilan 2002: 10–14.

Qumran sect were called יהודה Yehudah, whereas opponents of the sect were given the names מנשה Manasseh and אפרים Ephraim (Eshel 1997: 40); some scholars maintain that Manasseh could be identified with the Saducees, and Ephraim with the Pharisees.

The majority of the names (including nicknames) on ossuary inscriptions are common in the onomasticon of the period.

It is interesting to consider that names such as those of the Patriarchs – Abraham, Isaac and Jacob – were rarely used in the Second Temple period; only the name יעקב/יעקוב Ya'acov appears on several ossuaries from Jerusalem (Table V–2a; Rahmani 1994: Nos. 104, 290, 396, 678, 865). Equally scarce are most of the Israelite tribal patronymic and names of the prophets (Klein 1930: 325; see also the study by Cohen 1976; Hachlili 1984b: 188–9; Ilan 1984: 11–16; 2002: 5–6).

Proper names were those in full, that is, a personal name with a patronymic, and many of the funerary inscriptions and other sources have them. Most of the ossuary inscriptions refer to the full name, while patronymics unaccompanied by the deceased's personal name are rare (Rahmani 1994: 15). Note that in the Second Temple period the names were used in their longer theophoric version, יהוסף Yehosef, יהושע Yehosu'a, יהוחנן Yehohanan, which might have been the correct, official form of the name.

On several name-lists the most common are patronymics 'בן ה. . .' 'son of Y' or 'son of' plus nickname' without a personal name. Instances are many of the names on the list incised on an ossuary lid from Beth Phage (see above pp; Figure V–7): בן הציר 'son of the painter', בן עזריה 'son of Azariah'. The name-lists on ostraca from Masada bear mostly a patronymic or single nicknames, such as הגדריאן 'from Gadara', בר ישוע 'son of Yeshu'a' (Naveh 1990: 112–115; Hachlili 2002).

On several ossuaries patronymics appear lacking the deceased's personal name: בני אלעזר, בני חנן, בר יהודא, בר נחום 'sons of Ele'azar', 'sons of Ḥanan', 'son of Yehuda', 'son of Naḥum' (Rahmani 1994: 15, Nos. 75, 76, 464, 571; Hachlili 2002: 95–97; for further examples see Chap. VI).

On a list of officers in the temple, many of the names are referred to by a patronymic only, or nickname such as בן אחיה 'Ben Ahijah' נחוניא חופר שיחין 'Nehuniah the trench-digger' (Mishna Shek. 5.1; Tos. Shek. 2:14; Naveh 1990: 109–111). It seems that in daily life

people in particular social groups might have called each other by
a proper name, a nickname, or 'son of Y', where Y was a personal
name or a nickname (Naveh 1990: 113).

Women's Names

The personal Hebrew names Salome, Mariam, Maria, Shelamziyon,
Martha, Yehohana, Shipra/Shapira (Table V–2b; also Ilan 2002:
Table 8) are the most common female names in the onomasticon
of the late Second Temple period (Hachlili 1984b: 188–191; Ilan
1987: 138; 2002: 239–256; 418–429).

Women's names consisted of single personal names, although a
woman's proper full name was 'X daughter of Y' (the father) שלמציין
בת אלעזר 'Shelamziyon daughter of Eleazar' (Rahmani 1994: No.
342). However, frequently in the inscriptions a women's name included
the husband's name מרים אשת מתיה 'Mariame wife of Mattiah'
(Rahmani 1994: No. 559) or a son's name שלמשיון אמה די יהועזר גלית
'Shelamsiyon mother of Yeho'ezer Goliath' on an ossuary from
Jericho (see above; Hachlili 1979: 57, Inscription 11a–c; 1999: 153,
Inscription 11a–c, Fig. IV.11). At other times a woman was referred
to only as אנתת אלעזר 'wife of Eleazar' (Rahmani 1994: No. 74).
Rare exceptions are a father identified by the name of his daugh-
ter, inscribed on an ossuary from Jerusalem (Bagatti & Milik 1958:
99, no. 41); a granddaughter identified by her father's and grand-
mother's names, on an ossuary from Jericho (Hachlili 1979: 57,
Inscription 7a,b, Figs. 14–16; 1999: 153, Inscription 7a,b, Fig. IV.8);
and men identified by their mothers' names (Ilan 1992) (see Chap.
VII, pp.).

Women names constituted about 10% of the named population
in the Second Temple period (Ilan [2002: 8–9, 239–256, Table 8]
lists 16 biblical women's names). This adds to other evidence indicating the social status of women in the period (Ilan 1989: 186–87;
1995: 53–56). The most common female names in the Second Temple
period were Mariame מרים, Mariah מריה, Shalom/Salome שלום and
Shelamziyon שלמציון in several variations; about 50% of the entire
female population bore these names (Hachlili 1984b: 191; Ilan 1989:
191–92; 2002: 9). The majority of women used only eleven Hebrew
names in this period (Table V–2b) and less than half the women
had names in Aramaic, Greek or Latin, Persian, and Nabatean (Ilan
1989: 191). At Beth She'arim six Hebrew names appear in this order

of frequency: Sara, Miriam, Esther, Ruth, Rachel, and Hana (Hachlili 1984b: 191).

On the Masada ostraca (Hachlili 2002: 98–100) the women were recorded only as 'wife of . . .' or 'daughter of . . .' with only the husband's or father's name inscribed in Hebrew and Aramaic: אתת[ז]בידא 'wife of [Ze]bida' and בת דמלי 'the daughter of Domli' (Yadin & Naveh 1989: 21–22, nos. 399, 400, 402, 403, 405). The exception is [שלום הגלי]לית 'Shalom (or Salome) the Gali[lean]' (Yadin & Naveh 1989: 22, no. 404) who was called by her personal name and an epithet.

The above-noted commonest Jewish women's personal names of the period מרים Mariam, מריה Mariah, שלום Shalom/Salome and שלמציון Shelamziyon (the one which is not a biblical name), their popularity is probably due to their being typical names of the Hasmonean dynasty (Hachlili 1984b: 191; Ilan 1987: 240; 1995: 55; 2002: 9). However, we do not know if matronymy was a custom practiced by women, as the mother's name is not mentioned in the name of a daughter, and only rarely in the name of a son. Ilan (1989: 191–192, 196–200; 1995: 55; 2002: 239–256) lists most of the examples. Almost all funerary inscriptions have these names, with a few others recorded once or twice. Scholars maintain that Salome and the longer version Shelamziyon are the same name (Ilan 1989: 196–97, 198–99 lists Mariah as a form of Mariam, and Shelamziyon as a form of Salome; but in her report on the inscriptions from Akeldama she notes (1996: 70; also 2000: 9) that Salome and Shelamziyon are not the same name. Salome and Shelamziyon were apparently not the same name; Mariam and Maria might have been the same name, Maria a diminutive (Cohen 1974; Hachlili 1984b: 191, note 8; Mussies 1994: 253). A possible other variation of the name is מריאמנה Mariamne (Rahmani 1994: No. 108). The name Martha מרתה מרה, מרתא Μάρθα, Μάρα appears on several ossuaries from Jerusalem (Rahmani 1994: Nos. 45, 67, 220, 256, 287, 290, 354, 468, 648, 701, 868).

Shelamziyon was perhaps used most frequently around the time of the reign of the Hasmonean queen (first century BCE), whereas Salome was used more frequently in the later Second Temple period (first century CE). In later times these names were no longer in use. In Jericho a variation of the name appears שלומשיון שלמשן, שלמשיון Shelamsiyon both in Jewish script and in Greek (Hachlili 1999: Inscriptions Nos. 7, 11; Figs. IV.16, 17, 27, 28, 29; Table IV.2).

Table V–2. Comparative Table: Frequency of Hebrew Personal Names among Jews in the late Second Temple Period

a. *Men's Names*

Name	Total	Total %	Ossuary or Tomb Inscriptions	Masada Ostraca Papyri	Josephus	New Testament	Judean Desert Documents
שמעון Shim'on סימון Simon	174	16.0	63	22	29	11	49
יהוסף Yehosef	163	15.0	47	12	20	6	78
יהודה Yehudah Judah	121	11.1	44	20	15	6	36
אלעזר Ele'azar	115	10.6	34	10	19	2	50
יהוחנן Yehohanan	89	8.2	26	11	9	2	41
יהושע, ישוע Yehoshu'a, Yeshu'a	83	7.6	23	5	14	1	40
מתתיה/מתתיהו Mattatiah	55	5.1	17	1	12	2	23
יהונתן Yehonatan	53	4.9	14	1	14	–	24
חנניה Hananiah/ Ananias, חנינא Hanina	51	4.7	18	6	10	3	14
מנחם Menahem	33	3.0	6	1	2	1	23
יעקב Ya'aqov	29	2.7	6	4	4	5	10
חנן Hanan	25	2.3	6	1	6	–	12
יהועזר Yeho'ezer	24	2.2	18	2	3	–	1
ישמעאל Ishmael	23	2.1	9	1	3	–	10
זכריה Zechariah	20	1.8	5	4	5	2	4
לוי Levi	17	1.6	5	1	4	2	5
חזקיה Hisqiah	16	1.5	7	3	3	–	3

b. *Women's names*

Name	Total	Total %	Ossuary or Tomb Inscriptions	Masada Ostraca Papyri	Josephus	New Testament	Judean Desert Documents
שלום Salome	56	25.2	41	3	3	1	8
מרים Mariam	44	19.8	29	1	6		8
שלמציון Shelamziyon	30	17.5	25	–	2	–	3
מריה Mariah	22	12.1	14	1	1	6	–
מרתה Martha	18	9.9	17		–	1	–
יהוחנה Yehohana	11	6.0	7		–	1	3
שפירה/שפרה Shapira	11	6.0	9		–	1	1

Recurrence of Names in a Family

The custom of patronymy (and sometimes matronymy), even when the son was not born after the father had died or the daughter after the mother had died, seems to have been prevalent during this period among the Jewish priesthood and aristocracy, especially among the families of the high priests as well as amid the Hasmonean and Herodian dynasties. Originally it was a foreign custom, used by the Hellenistic royal dynasties, which was evidently adopted by the Jews (Stern 1960: 8, nn. 43–47).

As a result of the increasingly common use of paponymy, patronymy and matronymy, the recurrence of names down three generations was prevalent in the Second Temple period.[4] It might even be possible to identify a family by its characteristic recurrent name (Hachlili 1984b: Table 2). Moreover, the names recur because the individual is not important except as a member of the collective that identifies itself by a small number of names (Rubin 1994: 258). This three-generation, or longer, recurrence of names is indicated by literary sources and inscriptions.

During the Second Temple period the prevalent custom among the royal dynasties was paponymy, apparently from the end of the fourth century BCE. In the Hasmonean dynasty the names Mattathiah, Yehohanan, Yehudah, and Yonathan are repeated for ten generations, these being paponymics or names of some other kinsmen, usually uncles (Hachlili 1984b: Figure 2).[5] In the House of Tobias (third century BCE) this name and the Greek name Hyrcanus are repeated for four generations, each individual being named after his grandfather (Maisler 1941: 122). In the Herodian dynasty recurrent names are Herod, Joseph and Agrippa (Hachlili 1984b: Figure 1). In the Hasmonean and Herodian dynasties the names Shelamziyon, Salome, Mariamme, and Cypros were also given to daughters after their mothers' or grandmothers' or sometimes aunts' names.

In the high priestly families the same trait is found: the 'House of Onias' (332–165 BCE) has the recurrent names Onias and Shim'on for six generations, until in the last generation Onias turned into

---

[4] A similar custom appears in Palmyra in the 1st century CE, see Ingholt 1974: 43.

[5] It is interesting to note that the name Shim'on the most common in this period, does not recur in the Hasmonaean dynasty after Shim'on the Hasmonaean.

paponymy (Jos. *Ant.* 11, 77; 20, 261; 22. 5; Buchanan-Grey 1896: 2, and notes 4, 5; 1914: 165, n. 4; Hachlili 1984b: Fig. 5). In the Hanan (Ananus or Annas) family of high priests (first century CE) recurrent names are Hanan (Ananus), a patronymy repeated for three generations, and Matthias (Jos. *Ant.* 18, 2, 1; Hachlili 1984b: Figure 4; Stern 1966: 250–251; 1976: 606; Barag and Flusser 1986: 42, Table 1). In the Boethus high-priestly family (late first century BCE–first century CE) the recurrent name is Shim'on son of Shim'on (*Ant.* 19.297; Stern 1976: 604–6). The Phiabi family of high priests (first century CE) has the name Ishmael son of Ishmael repeated (*Ant.* 15.3; Stern 1976: 607–8, n. 4).

Repeated names were customary also in priestly and other noble families, and might have been prevalent also among Jews of all classes. In the priestly family of Josephus Flavius (Yehosef son of Mattathiah), the repeated names are Mattathiah by patronymy, Shim'on, and Yehosef (Jos. *Vita* 1. 1–5; 8; Schürer et al., 1973: 43–46, n. 3; Hachlili 1984b: Figure 6). Several inscriptions recording three generations of priestly families encompass recurring names (see Chap. VI, pp.). In the Goliath Family tomb the repeated names of three generations include seven different individuals named Yeho'ezer by patronymy, Ele'azar, and Ishm'ael (Hachlili 1979: 53, 66, fig. 49). In the Babtha family (of the Bar Kokhba Letters) the recurrent names are ישוע Yeshu'a and Yehudah (Yadin 1971: 234). In the family of the president Hillel (first century CE on) the custom of paponymy is evident, and the repeated names are Hillel, Gamliel, Shim'on, and Yehudah (Buchanan-Grey 1896: 2; Klein 1929: 327).

A few examples of the custom of patronymy among the Jewish general population is attested in ossuary inscriptions from Jerusalem: 'Mattiah son of Mattiah' (Sukenik 1928: 121); 'Yehudah son of Yehudah' (Frey 1952: no. 1283c); 'Saul son of Saul' on an ostracon from the Judean Desert (Aharoni 1962: 196, Pl. 29A); 'Yehudah son of Yehudah' in letter no. 29, and 'Yehosef son of Yehosef' in letter no. 42 from Wadi Muraba'at (Benoit et al., 1961: 156). On a marriage contract the name of the groom is 'Eleazar son of Eleazar', and the name of a witness is 'Yehudah son of Yehudah' (Milik 1954: 183).

Priests' Names

Most of the names are relatively common in this period, but scholars suggest that some personal names occur frequently among priests and especially in high priestly families. One such example is Ele'azar, which was used mainly by priests (Stern 1961: 21, n. 119). Yeho'ezer is considered to be a name of priests (Grintz 1960). Other names such as Yehosef, Yehoshu'a/Yeshu'a, Shim'on and Mattathias are common in high priestly families (see Table V–2a). The use of a name in consecutive generations in the family was a custom characterizing prominent and priestly families. As with the commonest women's names, the popularity and the frequency of these priestly names is possibly a result of their being the typical names of the Hasmonean dynasty (Hachlili 1984b: 188–191; Ilan 1987: 238–241; 2002: 6–7, Table 5), as well as the prevalent customs of paponomy and patronomy in the Jewish population (Hachlili 1979: 53; 1984b: 195).

Family Names and Family relations

Surnames (family names) were not common in ancient times. They appear usually in the form of the word 'House of' with the addition of a name, 'son of Y', or an ancestor's name. A family name could also develop from a title, a profession, an appellative, or a nickname, and could be inherited by subsequent generations (Hachlili 1984b: 202–203).

House בית. Royal and priestly oligarchies of the Second Temple period are sometimes referred to as 'House of ' followed by the name of the first ancestor, who was a prominent figure after whom his progeny were named (Bichler 1966: 138, n. 48). An example is the royal House of Hasmonean; the high priestly families were frequently named House of Boethus, House of Phiabi, House of Hanan (Annan) and House of Cantheras קנתרס or Cathros קתרס (*Ant.* 12.265; Jeremias 1969: 194–198).[6] The priestly family name קיפא Qypha, Qopha (or Caiaphas) on three ossuaries from the "Caiaphas' tomb in North Talpiyot, Jerusalem, is possibly equated with the high priestly house of Cathros, meaning 'basket-carrier' (Reich 1992: 75–6; Peuch 1993; Horbury 1994; see Chap. VI, pp.). The 'daughter of Cathra' בת קתרא found on an inscription from Masada (Yadin & Naveh 1989: 22, no. 405; Naveh 1990: 117) might also belong to this family.

---

[6] The name 'son of Cathros' בר קתרס was found inscribed on a stone weight in the 'Burnt House' in Jerusalem (Avigad 1983: 129–131).

Sometimes the name was used for disgrace (Klein 1929: 348) for example 'בית הפגרים' 'House of Corpses'.

'Son of X' The appellative 'son of X' or 'sons of X', where the X is not a personal name but a family name, usually appears in families of the twenty-four priestly courses (the full list: 1 Chron. 24, 7–18). Genealogical lists of priest were kept and used in the Second Temple period in order to maintain the priestly customs and the purity of their pedigree (1 Chron. 9, 10–13; Jos. *Vita* 6; *Against Apion* I, 31–36; Jeremias 1969: 275–283). Some examples of such families are: 'Meremoth the son of Uriah, son of Hakkoz' הקוץ (Neh. 3,4), a priestly family of the seventh course; they might have served as the Temple treasurers, an inherited office in the family of Hakkoz (Stern 1976: 590–591; Benoit et al., 1961: 223). The name appears possibly also in an inscription on a stone found in Nazareth (Eshel 1991). It is possible that the name בן סירא 'son of Sira' also belongs to the same Hakkoz family (Klein 1929: 341; 1930: 267), as the meaning of both these names in Hebrew is 'thorn'. The family of the priests of 'sons of Hezir' בני חזיר the 17th course, is inscribed on the lintel of a tomb in the a Kidron valley (see above). The name מנחם בן בנא יכים כהן 'Menahem son of sons of Jachim', of the 21st priestly course, is inscribed on an ossuary found in a tomb at Dominus Flevit (Bagatti & Milik 1975: 89–92). An Aramaic marriage contract of 117 CE (Benoit et al. 1961: 112) cites the name מנשה מן בני אלישיב 'Manashe of the sons of Elyashiv' which is the name of the 11th priestly course.

An ancestor's name. The name of a progenitor was occasionally used by subsequent generations as a family name. Klein (1929: 329) suggested that a family name deriving from an ancient ancestor, is 'חניכת אבות' 'ancestor surname' (*Mishna, Gitin* 9), which might be kept for at least ten generations. In the high priestly families שמעון בן ביתוס 'Shim'on son of Boethus', 'Ishmael son of Phiabi', ישמעאל בן פיאבי 'Mattathias son of Hanan' מתתיהו בן חנן were named after an ancestor of some generations back. Scholars maintain that a personal name (of an ancestor?) could also serve as a family name; for instance an ossuary inscribed שמעון בוטון 'Shim'on of (the family of) Boethos' (see Chap. VI) apparently eludes to a priestly family.

Nicknames

Nicknames appear frequently during the Second Temple period; they were added to personal names and were an organic part of a person's name.

Nicknames were given because of the frequency of some of the personal names and to distinguish individuals bearing the same name especially in a single family. For instance, two ossuaries from the same tomb in Talpiyot in Jerusalem bear the name Jesus; the name Judas/Yehuda is present on two ossuaries from the same tomb on the Mount of Olives (Rahmani 1994: Nos. 32, 35; 113, 114). The names 'Yeho'ezer 'Aqabiya/'Azabiy'a' and 'Yeho'ezer Cinnamon' are recorded on three ossuaries from the Goliath tomb in Jericho (Hachlili 1979: 48, 56; 1999: Inscriptions 8 and 13). Another reason was the need of a family to have the same identifying nickname, sometimes down several generations. Frequently a nickname was given as an endearment or a pet-name, or to disgrace a person. Nicknames often described a title, a profession, or a physical aspect of the individual, sometimes becoming a family name (Hachlili 1984b: 195–204).

Some families used a surname deriving from their ancient ancestor nickname. Occasionally a nickname was given after death in memory of an event, and the next generations used this same nickname. Special nicknames were given to priests, especially those who had a common personal name; sometimes they were derogatory nicknames aimed at denouncing hated priests (Klein 1930: 262). Others were called after their disablities, or their office, for instance the nicknames given to the officers in the temple (*Mishna, Sheq.* 5,1; *Tos. Sheq.* 2,14 (Klein 1929: 330, 333, 338). In some cases the nicknames were given in order of the alphabet, such as בן אילפא, בן־נימל, בן הא or according to their order of birth, such as בן־בוכרי, בן־לקיש, בן פטירא (Klein 1929: 334, 340). It is possible that a matronymic appended to a person's name is a nickname, as usually the proper name included the father's (or grandfather's) name. The name-form 'son of Y', בן יהוחנן, 'son of Yehohanan', בן הציר 'son of the painter' without a personal name might be a nickname. Such names appear on the Bethphage ossuary lid (see above) and on several Masada ostraca name-lists (see below). Some of the officers of the temple are also named in the same way בן־נבר, בן־ארזה (*Mishna, Sheq.* 5,1). Klein (1929: 330) maintains these were the son's nickname rather than the father's.

Others (Bichler 1966: 127, n. 16; Clines 1972: 282–287) contend
that this form was a nickname of the young, while the elderly were
called by their full name; or that this form meant that the person
belonged to a guild (Mendelsohn 1940: 18). It might have been a
family name too, as many of the guild professions were inherited.

Nicknames of the Hasmonean Dynasty

In the early Second Temple period nicknames are found in the
Hasmonean family: "At this same time there was a man living in
the village of Modai (Modin) in Judaea, named Mattathias, the son
of Yohanan, the son of Shim'on, the son of Asamonias, a priest of
the course of Yehoyarib, and a native of Jerusalem. He had five
sons, יוחנן הקרוי הגדי 'Yohanan called Gaddes', שמעון הקרוי התטי
'Shim'on called Thatis', יהודה הקרוי המכבי 'Yehudah called Maccabaeus'
אלעזר הקרוי החורי 'Ele'azar called Auran', and יונתן הקרוי החפי
'Yonatan called Apphus' (*Ant.* 12.265–266; also I *Macc.* 2,1, with few
changes).

Hasmonaean is possibly a family name used as a nickname only
by Josephus (instead of the name Maccabaeus: (Jeremias 1969:
188–189 n. 132). Other scholars (Abel 1949: pls. III–IV) maintain
it was the nickname of the father or the grandfather of Mattathias.

Scholars are divided on the meaning of the nicknames of Mattathias's
sons. Some contend that they were given to them at birth. Others
maintain that these nicknames were added as they grew up after
their deed or characteristic was known (I *Macc.* 104–105; I *Macc.*
18, notes to the Hebrew translation). יוחנן הקרוי הגדי 'Yohanan called
Gaddes', or Gaddis, might according to some scholars be the name
Gad, the Semitic god of fortune (Abel 1949: 31; *Ant.* 12.265, Marcus
note i).

שמעון הקרוי התטי 'Shim'on called Thatis' is suggested as deriving
from Aramaic and meaning 'the Zealot' (*Ant.* 12, 265, Marcus note j);
in the Syrian translation it is התרס' which means 'the provider'.

The most widely accepted etymology proposed for יהודה הקרוי
המכבי 'Yehudah called Maccabaeus' is from the Hebrew מקבת 'hammer', hence 'Yehudah the Hammerer' describing his prowess. Others
suggest that the nickname was given to him at birth because of the
shape of his head. Still others argue that the letters מכבי *m q b y*
are an acronym of the hemistich in Exodus 15,11 (Hachlili 1984b:
196). The nickname חורן 'Horan', of אלעזר המכונה חורן/עורן 'Ele'azar

called Ḥoran/Auran', has been interpreted in several ways. Some scholars maintain that it was given after his death, on account of the חוֹר *ḥor* 'hole' he opened in the elephant (I *Macc.* 6,46), hence 'the Borer'. Others contend that Eleʿazar, like his brothers, was given his nickname at birth (*1 Macc.* 2,5, note Hebrew translation), meaning his being עוֹרֵן 'Auran', 'vigorous', 'forceful', 'alert' (Schürer et al. 1973: 158, n. 49).

יונתן הקרוי החפי 'Yonatan called Apphus': the interpretation of this nickname is the Hebrew חפש, 'the Searcher', or 'the Digger' (*Ant.* 12.266, Marcus note there).

Another nickname in the Hasmonean dynasty is that added to Alexander Jannaeus: "and as a result of his excessive cruelty he was nicknamed Thrakidas (the 'Cossak') by the Jews" (*Ant.* 13, 383; Marcus notes that the Thracians were known for their great ferocity; also Stern 1960: 209).

Nickname types

Nicknames are of several types:
• The addition of the nickname to the personal name, for example, יוסף הגלילי 'Joseph the Galilean'; יחוני החרש 'Yeḥoni the artisan', craftsman' or possibly 'smith', (or 'deaf, mute').
• The nickname belongs to the father of the interred person, for example, שלומציון בת שמעון הכהן 'Shelamziyon daughter of Shimʿon the priest' (Clermont-Ganneau 1899: Nos. 1–2; Frey 1952: No. 1317).
• The nickname belongs to the grandfather of the interred person, for example, יהוחנה ברת יהוחנן בר תפלוס הכהן הגדול 'Yehoḥanah daughter of Yehoḥanan son of Theophilus the high priest'.
• The nickname is added to the full name of the interred person (X, son of Y, + nickname) for example, two inscriptions on the same ossuary from Jerusalem: יהודה הסופר; יהודה בר אלעזר הסופר 'Yehudah the scribe', 'Yehudah, son of Eleʿazar, the scribe' (Clermont-Ganneau 1899: Nos. 3–4; Frey 1952: no. 1308; Klein 1920: 19–20).
• The nickname is added to the name of the father of the interred person (X, son of Y + nickname), as indicated by inscriptions on two ossuaries from Mount Scopus, Jerusalem: one on that of חנניה בר יהונתן הנזר 'Ḥananiah, son of Yehonathan, the Nazirite', the other on his wife's ossuary: 'Shalom, wife of Ḥananiah, son of the Nazirite' שלום אנתת חנניה בר הנזר (Avigad 1971: 196–198). The nickname 'the Nazirite' belongs to Yehonathan, the father of Ḥananiah, as indicated

on the first inscription and proved by the second inscription where
the father is recorded only by his nickname 'the Nazirite'.
• The personal name is followed by a nickname, which is either the
father's nickname or a family name, for example, שמעון בר סבא
'Shim'on, son of the elder' inscribed on an ossuary from Talpiot,
Jerusalem (Sukenik 1945: 31).
• A nickname added to the names of several members of the family, signifying a family name, for example, a Jerusalem family named
"Kallon"; Kallon might have been an ancestor whose name evolved
into a family name (See Chap. VI, pp. No. XIII). Tomb H in Jericho
is the burial place of the 'Goliath' family according to a group of
inscribed ossuaries (see above).
• The name of the head of the family became a family name, for
example, Kallon קלון (Avigad 1956: 331).
• Nicknames used as patronymics without the addition of a personal
name, for example, הגלילי 'The Galilean' on the Bethphage list (see
above).

Nicknames as Family names

A surname could be a nickname given to one (or more) of the ancestors by virtue of title, occupation, place of origin, physical characteristic and defects, and positive or negative qualities (Goitein 1970;
Hachlili 1984b: 203; 2000: 93–95). Many families are known whose
nickname evolved into a family name.

Surnames deriving from titles such as הכהן 'the priest' (1 Sam. 11,
2–3; 22, 11) or הסופר 'the secretary' or 'the scribe', for example
שפן בן אצליהו בן משלם הספר 'Shaphan the son of 'Azaliah, son of
Meshullam the secretary' (2 Kgs 22,3), were acquired by virtue of
an inherited office and title, so that it became the surname of suc-
cessive generations.

Place of origin was sometimes a nickname that turned into a family name, for example, הבשני 'from Beth She'an', a nickname that
appears on ossuaries of three members of a family from Jerusalem
(see Chap. VI; Frey 1952: nos. 1372–1374; Rahmani 1994: No. 139).

Family names stemming from physical characteristic are found in
several instances: In the Goliath family monumental tomb, in every
inscription where the name Goliath appears it is added to the personal names and family relation of the interred individual (Hachlili
1979: 52; 1999: 148–9; see below). The first-generation and second-

generation Yehoʻezer had 'Goliath' added to their personal name. It seems that 'Goliath' was not the name of an individual but a nick-name describing a physical characteristic (at least four male mem-bers of this family were exceptionally tall: Hachlili and Smith 1979: 69–70) that became a surname. The physical characteristic, being tall, and the nickname were inherited in this family.

Appellatives added to a personal name sometimes became a sur-name or a nickname; for example, 'The poor' עניה appears on an ossuary from Schneller: יהוסף בר אנין עניה/אבא קבר 'Joseph, son of Hanin, the poor/father, his son buried him' (Klein 1920: Nos. 12; Frey 1952: nos. 1373; Rahmani 1994: No. 139). Two possibly related Greek inscriptions from Beth Sheʻarim cite: Σαμουέλ Ἰσαάκου πεν-ηχρου 'Samuel, son of Isaac the poor' and [Σα]μουήλο [υ υἱου] Γερμα-[νου π]ενι- [χρ]ου '[The tomb] of Samuel, son of Germanus the poor' (Schwabe & Lifshitz 1974: Nos. 99, 206), probably a nickname indicating the family's modest way of life.

In the bible some surnames evolving from appellatives, based on negative character traits, appear in families returning from Babylon, for example, בני חגב 'sons of Ḥagab' (locust, grasshopper) (Ezra 2, 46) and בני פרעש 'sons of Parosh' (flea) (Ezra 2,3; 8,3; 10,25; Nehemiah 3,25; 6,8; 10,15).

Occupations are also found as nicknames that became surnames. Examples are fishermen family from Jaffa inscribed as בית החרמים 'House of Haharamim' (Schwabe 1937: 86–89); 'house of linen work-ers' בית עבדת הבץ (1 Chron. 4,21), probably weavers; 'Son of gold-smiths' חנניה בן הרקחים and 'son of perfumers' עזיאל בן חרהיה צורפים (Nehem. 3,8).[7]

Nicknames forms

In the following, nicknames are listed according to place of origin, title, occupation, physical characteristics and defects, honorific or age-related titles, disabilities, positive and negative qualities, and endear-ments. It is likely that some of these are in *status emphaticus* as nicknames (or surname) and were occasionally derogatory.

---

[7] But see Mendelsohn (1940: 18–19) who maintains that the term *ben* here, does not refer to blood relation but means 'organization' or 'guild', thus 'the guild of the weavers'.

Place of Origin

The place of origin is the most common nickname in the period, and is also frequent in biblical times as well as in the Mishna and Talmud periods (Hachlili 1984b: 200). The nickname usually derives from the name of a place, to a lesser degree from a tribe, or a sect. It usually appears with ה 'the', and sometimes ד׳ ,מן, מ, 'from X' is added to the name; also found is איש 'man from'. Naveh (1979: 21–23) and Rahmani (1994: 139, No. 257) argue that names like סוכיא Sokhite 'from Sokho', as well as nicknames such as 'the Galilean' and 'the Babylonian' are names based on their birthplaces.

Ossuaries from Jerusalem and Jericho record the place of origin of the deceased. Only selected examples are listed (Figure V–18; Pl. V–13):

יוסף הגלילי 'Joseph the Galilean' (Frey 1952: no. 1285 (the Beth Phage list lines 14, 15, see above). הגלילי 'the Galilean' also appears on papyrus 52 from Murabb'at (Benoit et al. 1961: 169).

אמיה הבשנית, חנין הבשני, פפיס הבשני 'Amiah, Ḥanin, and Papis from Beth She'an' (Scythopolis), three members of a family, their names and nicknames in Greek and Aramaic inscribed on three ossuaries from Schneller, Jerusalem (Klein 1920: Nos. 11–13; Frey 1952: nos. 1372–1374; Fitzmyer and Harrington 1978: No. 145; Rahmani 1994: no. 139).

יהוד בר שבט מין בת אלון 'Yehud son of Shevat [or *shevet* 'rod'?], from Bet Alon' inscribed on an ossuary from Ammunition Hill, Jerusalem (Figure V–18a). 'Bet 'Alon' might refer to Bet 'Alonim, identified with Ramat el-Khalil, near Hebron (Rahmani 1994: 146, no. 293).

מרתה בת יהוסף בן יעקב אתת יהוסף מנחין 'Marta, daughter of Yehosef, son of Ya'aqov, wife of Yehosef from Hin', inscribed on an ossuary from Jerusalem (?) (Figure V–18b). Hin, the origin place of of Martha or her husband, could be identified with Bet Hini near Caesarea or Hini in Babylonia, near Kufa (Rahmani 1994: 145, no. 289).

ישמעאל, שמעון ופלטיא מן ירושלם 'Ishmael, Shim'on, and Pelatya from Jerusalem': this three-generation family is cited on a bowl from Jericho and on an ossuary from the same tomb (see above, Figure V–16; Hachlili 1978: 45–47; 1999: 155–158, Inscriptions 15–17).

Ἰουδά Ἰούδου Βεθηλέτου 'Judah son of Judah from Beth-El' is inscribed on an ossuary from the Mount of Olives (Vincent 1902: 102–103).

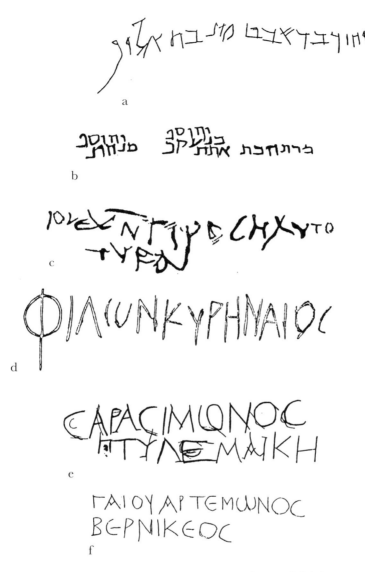

Figure V–18. Nicknames mentioning Places of Origin.

Several ossuaries record individuals originating in the Diaspora:
Babylon, Egypt, Cyrenaica and Syria:

ישניק הבבלי 'Yasnuq the Babylonian' inscribed on the Beth Phage
  list, line 15 (see above, Milik 1971: 78, 82–84).

בן אפטלמיס 'son of Aftalmayos', inscribed on the Beth Phage list, line
21, might be a transcription of a nickname 'The Ptolemean' (see
above, Milik 1971: 78, 84–85).

אלכסנדרוס קרנית 'Alexander (son of Simon) the Cyrenian', inscribed
on an ossuary lid from the Kidron valley, Jerusalem (Avigad 1962:
10–11; Kane 1978: 278–9; see below for the other interpretation,
occupation or trade) (see Chap. VI). The same place of origin
appears on some other inscriptions: הלל הקיריני 'Hillel from
Cyrenaica' (Benoit et al 1961: 220) הקרני 'the Qaranaite' or 'the
Cyrenian' (Yadin & Naveh 1989: 26, no. 424).

ארסטון אפמי 'Ariston of Apamea' and יהודה הגיור 'Yehudah the proselyte': these inscriptions are inscribed on an ossuary from Akeldama,
Jerusalem (Ilan 1996: No. 19, ossuary 31). The interred person
bears two names: Ariston, his Greek name, with the addition of
his place of origin in Apamea, Syria; and his Hebrew name Yehudah, seemingly adopted after his conversion (Ilan 1996: 66) (see
Chap. VI)

Πεποίηκεν Ἀζᾶ Βεροῦτος 'Aza[ria] son of Berous (or: of Beirut) made
(it)' is inscribed on another ossuary from Akeldama; it records the
name of the artist who made the ossuary. The Greek 'Beroutos'
may signify the place of origin as the Syro-Phoenician city of
Beirut (Ilan 1996: 60–61; No. 7, ossuary 17, Fig. 3.7) (see Chap. VI).

Φίλων Κυρηναῖος 'Philon from Cyrenaica' is inscribed on an ossuary
from 'Dominus Flevit' on the Mount of Olives, Jerusalem (Figure
V–18d; Bagatti & Milik 1975: 81, Oss. 10, insc. 9).

Ιουδα ν προσήλυτο[ ] τυρα 'Yehuda the proselyte, from Tyre' is inscribed on an ossuary likewise from 'Dominus Flevit' (Figure V–18c;
Bagatti and Milik 1958: 84, ossuary No. 21, Inscription 13; interpretation also by Lifshitz 1962: 79; Puech 1983: 519, No. 27).

Σάρα Σίμωνος/Πτυλεμαικὴ 'Sara (daughter) of Simon of Ptolemais' is
inscribed on an ossuary from the Kidron valley (Figure V–18e;
Avigad 1962: 8, No. 5: Rahmani 1994: No. 99).

Γαίου Ἀρτέμωνος/Βερνικέος 'of Gaius, (son) of Artemon, Berenikaian
(from Berenike)' is inscribed on an ossuary from Ramat Eshkol,
Jerusalem (Figure V–18f.); the interred person probably hailed
from Berenike in Cyrenaica (Rahmani 1994: No. 404).

Ιουστος Χαλκίδηνος 'Justus of Chalcedon' is inscribed on an ossuary
from north Jerusalem (Abel 1913: 275; Frey 1952: No. 1233).

Μαρία Ἀλεχάνδρου γυνὴ ἀπό Καπούης 'Maria wife of Alexander from
Capua', is inscribed on an ossuary from the Mount of Olives
(Vincent 1902: 106–107).

On Masada ostraca some single nicknames appear without a personal name:

הגדריאן 'the person of Gadara', 'the Gadarian' (Yadin & Naveh 1989: 24, no. 420,2);

העמקי 'of the Valley' (Yadin & Naveh 1989: 28, no. 434), or a village near Acco (Naveh 1992: 44);

ציפון 'north' (Yadin & Naveh 1989: 28, no. 436).

שמעון בר נוטוס 'Shimeon son of Notos': 'Notos' is Greek for south or southern (Yadin & Naveh 1989: 40, no. 462), or possibly the name בנימון? Benyamin?. A similar name

חנניה נותוס 'Ḥananiah Notos', appears on a Qumran document 4Q477 (Eshel 1997: 51). Also found are

הלל הנוסי 'Hillel the . . . Nusian (?), 'of a place named . . . Nos' (Yadin & Naveh 1989: 41, no. 473).

שלום הגלי[לית] 'Shalom (or Salome) the Gali[lean]' (Yadin & Naveh 1989: 22, no. 404).

Josephus mentions several nicknames of place of origin, such as יוחנן מגוש חלב 'Yohanan from Gush Halav' (in the Galilee); ניקולאוס מדמשק 'Nikolaus from Damascus', Herod's philosopher and court historian; מלתקה השומרונית 'Meltaka the Samaritan', one of Herod's wives; יהודה איש הגולן 'Yehudah a man from the Golan' (War 1, 562, 2, 567; Vita: 189–196; Ant. 15, 185; 18, 4).

Josephus records several sect members: יהודה האיסי, יוחנן האיסי 'Yehudah the Essene' and 'Yoḥanan the Essene (War 1, 78–9; 2, 567); מנחם האיסי, שמעון האיסי 'Menaḥem the Essene' and 'Yohanan the Essene;' צדוק הפרושי Zadok the Pharisee', who was one of the founders of the zealots' sect (Ant. 15, 373–379; 17, 346–348; 18, 4).

Title

Title nicknames indicate the person's class, status, and office. Some were given to the individual for his own role but many of the titles were inherited with the office. The most common titles were הכהן 'the priest' and הסופר 'the scribe/secretary' (Figure V–19).

הכהן 'The priest'

This nickname was very important, as it was intended to preserve the purity of the priests, but only few of these titles have been found (on the genealogy of the priests see Josephus, Vita 6, Against Apion 1,7; Klein 1939: 30–50; Jeremias 1969: 213–214). On Jerusalem ossuaries several inscriptions appear with these titles (Figure V–9):

אנה אבה בר כהנה אלעז[ר] בר אהרן רבה... 'I, Abba, son of the priest Ele'az[ar], son of Aaron the elder' . . . This Aramaic inscription in paleo-Hebrew script was discovered on a wall of a tomb at Giv'at Ha Mivtar (see above, Pl. V–1; Rosenthal 1973, Naveh 1973, Tzaferis 1974).

פנחס ויעקביה כהנה 'Pinhas and Yak'aviah the priests' (Figure V–19a; Abel 1913: 268; Frey 1952: No. 1221; Puech 1983: 499–500).

מנחם מן בנא יכים כהן 'Menaḥem of the sons of Yachim the priest', inscribed on an ossuary from 'Dominus Flevit' (Figure V–19b; Bagatti & Milik 1958: 89–92, Ossuary 83, Inscription No. 22, Pl. 81). The interred belonged to a priestly family of the house of Yachin, the 21st priestly course (I Chr. 24:17).

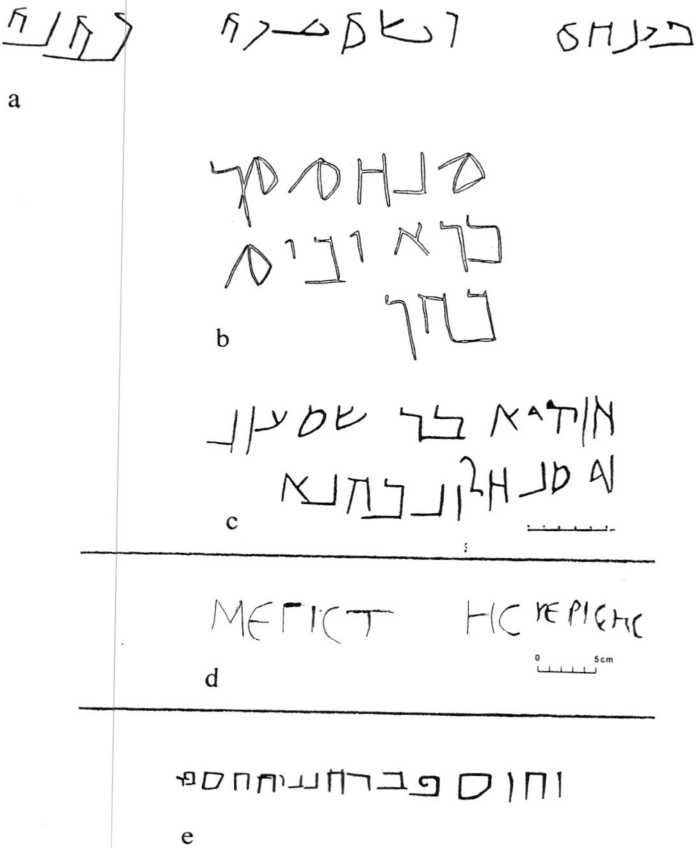

Figure V–19. Title Nicknames.

שלומציון בת שמעון הכהן 'Shelamziyon daughter of Shim'on the priest'
(Clermont-Ganneau 1899: Nos. 1–2; Frey 1952: No. 1317).

בן שמעון הכוהן... 'the son of Shim'on the priest' (Slousch et al. 1925:
101, Fig. 35).

יהוחנה ברת יהוחנן בר תפלוס הכהן הגדל 'Yehoḥanah daughter of Yehoḥanan son of Theophilus the high priest' (see above, Pl. V–4;
Barag and Flusser 1986: 39; Rahmani 1994: No. 871).

חזקיא בר שמעון זי מן חלון כהנא 'Ḥizqia son of Shim'on from Ḥalvan,
the priest'; probably a priest originating in Halvan, a town in
Babylonia, who died in Judea, or died in Babylonia and his bones
were brought to Jerusalem for burial (Figure V–19c; Naveh 1992:
192, fig. 131).

ח[נני]ה כהנא רבא עקביא בריה 'A[nani]as the High Priest, Aqavia his
son'; inscribed on a vessel found in Masada, probably designates
priestly shares authorized by Aqavia the son of the High Priest
(Yadin 1965: 111; Yadin & Naveh 1989: 37–39, no. 461).

Μεγίστης ἱερίσης 'Megiste the priestess': this Greek inscription is on
an ossuary from Akeldama, Jerusalem. Like the other ones of
women (above), this one probably records the wife or daughter of
a priest, not a woman with a religious function or an official position (Figure V–19d; Ilan 1991/2: 157–159; 1996: 61–62).

Similar titles are also found on inscriptions from the necropolis in
Beth She'arim. The Greek inscriptions mention 'Yehudah the priest',
and 'Sarah the daughter of Nehemiah, mother of the priestess'. The
title כהנים 'the priests' appears in Greek and Hebrew (Schwabe &
Lifshitz 1974: nos. 49, 66, 181). The Greek 'Cohen from Beirut'
might be a family name, not a title (Avigad 1976: 30).

סופר 'Secretary, Scribe'
The title was the person's office and possibly was inherited. Some
scholars maintain that all officials were thus titled (Hachlili 1984b:
201, and n. 230; for the term in rabbinic literature see Ayali 1984:
89–90).

Several inscriptions on ossuaries from Jerusalem mention the title:
יהודה הסופר, יהודה בר אלעזר הסופר 'Yehudah the scribe', 'Yehudah
son of Ele'azar the scribe' appears on an ossuary from Jerusalem
(Clermont-Ganneau 1899: Nos. 3–4; Frey 1952: no. 1308; Klein
1920: 19–20).

יהוסף בר חנניה הסופר 'Yehosef, son of Ḥananya, the scribe' is inscribed
on an ossuary from Mount Scopus, Jerusalem (Figure V–19e; Pl.
V–13a; Sussman 1992: 94; Rahmani 1994: No. 893).

יועזר בן יהוחנן הסופר 'Yoʻezer son of Yehoḥanan, the scribe' is inscribed
on the front, and יועזר הסופר 'Yoʻezer the scribe' on the side, of
an ossuary from Gophna (about 20 km north of Jerusalem; now
at the University of Chicago; Wolff 1997).

Other titles such as חלקיה שומר האוצר 'Ḥylkiah the keeper of the
treasure' probably the temple treasurer, and יוסף סוכן הבית 'Joseph
the house steward' are cited by Josephus (*Ant.* 20, 194; 15, 185; Alon
1966: 51; Jeremias 1969: 160–167; Stern 1966: 244, n. 56). Officers
in the temple are listed in the Mishna and Talmud (M Sheq. 5,1
and JT Sheq. 5, 49a), where they appear with their personal name
and title. Among them are נביני הכרוז 'Gabini the herald';

נחוניה חופר השיחין 'Neḥuniah the trench-digger'; פנחס המלביש 'Phineas
the dresser' who possibly was in charge of the vestments (Bichler
1966: 88, 101). The most important office in the temple after the
high priest was

חנינא סגן הכהנים 'Ḥaninah the priests-deputy' 'the temple strategus'
(M Sheq. 6,1; Alon 1966: 256; Bichler 1966: 88; Jeremias 1969:
160–167; Schürer et al. 1973: 371), who was a permanent officer
in the temple serving as substitute high priest.

Διδάσκαλος *didaskalos*, 'Teacher' or 'Rabbi' appears on three ossuaries from the same tomb on the Mount of Olives, Jerusalem (see
Chap. VI; Sukenik 1930: 140–141, 143); on another ossuary רב
חנא 'Rab Ḥana' is inscribed (Abel 1913: 269, Pl. 1,9).

Various titles were used in the First Temple period and in synagogue inscriptions of the fourth-sixth centuries CE (Hachlili 1984b:
202), such as חזן 'caretaker', פרנס warden, גזבר 'treasurer', and ארכון
'head of the community'.

Occupation and Trade

This nickname is given to a person on account of his occupation
and trade, or it derives from a profession, that was common in the
period. Frequently it was inherited and became a family name or
nickname (Figure V–20a) (for occupation and trade terms in rabbinic literature see Ayali 1984: 57–68, 78, 104).

On two ossuary inscriptions from Jerusalem interesting nicknames
appear, which are connected to the building of the temple:

סימון בנה הכלה 'Simon builder of the sanctuary' (Pl. V–2,3) is probably one of builders or engineers who took part in the construction of Herod's sanctuary (see above; Naveh 1970: 34).

ניקנור עושה הדלתות 'Nicanor who made the doors' is inscribed on an
   ossuary from the Nicanor family tomb on Mount Scopus (see
   above; Avigad 1967: 124–5).

It is difficult to determine if these nicknames were used by the people during their lifetime or given to them after their death in order
to commemorate their pursuits.

יחוני החרש 'Yeḥoni the artisan, craftsman' or possibly 'smith', (or
   'deaf, mute') is inscribed on an ossuary from 'Dominus Flevit',
   Jerusalem (Bagatti & Milik 1975: 83, insc. 12, fig. 22, phot. 80).
   A similar nickname appears on an ostracon from Masada בר חרשא
   'son of artisan, craftsman' (it could also mean 'deaf', see below)
   (Yadin & Naveh 1989: 26, no. 421,5).[8]

בן הציד (הציר) 'Son of the hunter' or 'the painter' is inscribed on
   the Beth Phage list (see above). צידא 'the hunter' appears on an
   ostracon from Masada (Yadin & Naveh 1989: 29, no. 440; for
   the term in rabbinic literature see Ayali 1984: 31, 95–96).

השורק 'the Comber (of Linen)' (The Beth Phage list, line 18; see
   above; Sukenik 1935: 106; Frey 1952: 278, no. 1285).

יהונתן קדרה Yehonatan the potter (or the 'pot') (Figure V–20a; Naveh
   1970: 34–5; Rahmani 1994: No. 222), or the pot-seller, or the
   black (Fitzmyer and Harrington 1978: No. 86). Yadin (Naveh
   1970: 35, n. 1) argued that it could mean a derogatory nickname
   'the pot' = pot-bellied.[9]

תרפט הנשבה 'The captive physician'(?). תרפט could be used here as
   a reference to a healer or a physician (Figure V–20b; Rahmani
   1994: no. 80).

Several similar nicknames appear on Masada ostraca (Hachlili 2002:
102).

---

[8] See also 'לעמא הנסך 'to 'Ama the craftman' (Phoenician?), inscribed on a
Phoenician tombstone (Hestrin & Israeli 1973 no. 143).
[9] Cross (1969: 24*–26*) suggests that some of the 'Yahud' seal impressions from
Ramat Rachel on which the word (פהרא =) פהוא meaning 'the potter', are potters
seals.

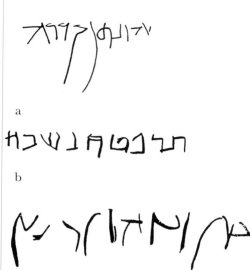

a

b

c

Figure V-20. Nicknames with Occupation and Trade.

אלכסנדר קרנית 'Alexsander *Qornyt*', meaning 'Alexander the druggist', is inscribed on an ossuary lid from the Kidron valley, Jerusalem (Avigad 1962: 10–11). It possibly reflects his occupation as a scent or spice merchant (see Chap. VI) This term is similar to a sage's name

[יהו]דה בר בשמ[א] '[Ju]dah son of the druggist' or maker of ointment, perfumes' is inscribed on an ostracon from Masada (Yadin & Naveh 1989: 41, no. 471). Also יהודה בן ישעיה הבשם 'Yehudah son of Yeshiah the druggist'. Similar is אלעזר הקפר 'Eleazar Ha-Qapar', who according to some scholars is a 'druggist'. 'Qapar' is a spice from which drugs were made (Naveh 1978: 26).

יהוסף בר אנרה, טוביה בר אנרה, מריה ברת אנרה 'Yehosef, Toviah and Mariah sons and daughter of Agrah' (Bagatti and Milik 1958: 96–97, inscriptions 32–34). Milik suggests that 'Agrah is a nickname meaning 'day-laborer' or 'hired-hand' (see Chap. VI).

יהוסף קני 'Yehosef (the) Zealot', or '(the) silversmith' on an ostracon at Masada (Yadin & Naveh 1989: 41, no. 474).

קצבא 'the butcher' is a nickname, or else the jar belonged to a butcher (Yadin & Naveh 1989: 43, no. 512). ר' זכריה בן הקצב

'Zachriah son of the butcher' was a priest at the end of the Second Temple period (Margaliot 1945: 270–71; Bichler 1966: 7,10).

בנ הנחתם 'son of the baker' is inscribed on a Masada ostracon (Yadin & Naveh 1989: 28, no. 429).

יהודה הנחתום 'Yehudah the baker' is a nickname of a sage (*TJ. Hagiga*, 2a).

שלמיה נגרא 'Shelamiah the Carpenter' is written on a name-list on a fourth century BCE document from Ketef Yeriho (Eshel & Misgav 1988: 171; Eshel 1997: 42).

בר בניה 'The son of Benaiah' or 'The son of the builder' on an ostracon at Masada (Yadin & Naveh 1989: 26, no. 421,6; 423).

Ιουδα ω προσήλυτο[ ] τυρα 'Yehuda the proselyte, cheese-maker' (Bagatti and Milik 1958: 84, ossuary No. 21, Inscription 13; Puech 1983: 519, No. 27; see other interpretation by Lifshitz 1962: 79).

Physical characteristics

Some nicknames alluded to physical characteristics, and they frequently occurred in *status emphaticus*. Several of these nicknames originated in terms of mockery and abuse and may have been later used as family names (Rahmani 1994: 14). An example already noted is the name Goliath, which originally was a nickname probably meaning 'Giant' and which eventually, served as a family name (Figure V–21) (but see Naveh 1989: 10, n. 20).

גלית Goliath

This name is inscribed in Jewish and Greek scripts on four ossuaries found in the Goliath Tomb in Jericho (see above; Hachlili 1979: 52–53; 1999: 148–9). In these inscriptions Goliath is added to the personal name and family relation of the interred individual. The references to this name in the Bible and rabbinical sources all emphasize Goliath's stature, his most outstanding physical characteristic (see above). The examination of the skeletal remains of four male members of this family indicated they were exceptionally tall (Hachlili 1979: Table 1). The height of Yeho'ezer son of Ele'azar, mentioned in Inscription 12a (Hachlili 1999: Figs. IV.13a,b, Ossuary XXI; Hachlili and Smith 1979: 67) is estimated at 1.885 m., close to Goliath's height in LXX. In antiquity Yeho'ezer bar Ele'azar, possibly the first of the line to be nicknamed Goliath, might have been considered a giant in stature. Note that it is rare for a Jewish family to bear the name of a historical enemy. Only one such occurrence, 'the sons of Sisera', is found, among the families returning from the Babylonian exile (Ezra 2, 53; Neh. 7, 55).

Josephus mentions a similar nickname, 'Eleazar the Giant': "Among which included a man, 7 cubits tall, a Jew by race, named Eleazar, who on account of his size, was called the Giant' (*Ant.* 18.103). Columella, a Latin author (first century CE) describes "a man of the Jewish race who was of greater stature than the tallest German" (Stern 1974: 426–7, possibly identified with Eleazar referred to by Josephus).

The Biblical Goliath the Philistine, is described as "a mighty man . . . of Gath, whose height was six cubits and a span" (I Sam. 17:4). In the LXX and 4QSam[a] his height is given as four cubits and a span, approximately 2m. In the Babylonian Talmud the name Goliath is explained thus: "Goliath (was so named) said R. Johanan because he stood with effrontery before the Holy One" (BT Sot. 42b). It is also stated that Goliath means, as in the Bible, "coming from Gath". In later Jewish legends Goliath is described as "Goliath the giant, being the strongest and greatest of Orpah's four sons" (Ginzberg 1946, III:414; IV:85–88; VI:250). All the above references emphasize Goliath's most outstanding physical characteristic, his stature.[10]

נאיס נניס 'Gaius the small' is inscribed on an ossuary from Mount Scopus, Jerusalem; the nickname נניס probably derived from the Greek νάνος 'dwarf' (Figure V–21a; Rahmani 1994: 172, no. 421). The name of a sage שמעון בן ננס (Semahot 8,7; Zlotnik 1966: 138) has the same meaning.

Σαλώμνα κατανα 'Little (*katana*) Salomna' is inscribed on an ossuary from El-Jib; the word *katana* is a Greek transliteration of קטנה 'little one' in Hebrew (Figure V–21b; Rahmani 1994: no. 552).

זומלית זערא 'small soup-ladle' is inscribed on an ostracon name list at Masada (Yadin & Naveh 1989: 25, no. 420,4; Hachlili 1984b: 197).

---

[10] Recent research into stature of males and females at the Qumran cemetery report that stature for males from the main cemetery is ca. 159–168 cm. (Röhrer-Etrl 1999: 43, Table 4; Zias 2000: 232–3, Fig. 2).

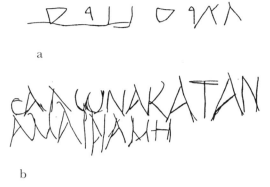

a

b

Figure V–21. Physical Nicknames.

Several appelatives designating short stature appear in the Beth She'arim inscriptions: 'The short' אנינא הקטן, יהודה הקטן, יוסף הקטן, דומיניקה הקטנה (Mazar B. 1973: No. 137; Schwabe & Lifshitz 1974: No. 175; Avigad 1976: Nos. 10, 11). This nicknames is interpreted as signifying short in stature or an endearment for children, or as an appellative chosen by a prominent person to designate modesty. In the Talmud several Aramaic epithets designating short stature are mentioned: זעירא, קטינא, מר ינוקא, מר קשישא, מר זוטרא (Margaliot 1945: 648–9).

Disabilities and Defects

Nicknames derived from a physical defect in a person were undoubtedly personal as the defects were not inherited. They were especially important in priestly families as disabled priests could not serve in the temple. Josephus (*Vita* 1:3–4) when recounting his ancestry describes two forebears, 'Simon the stammerer' (Ψελλός) and 'Mattaias the hunchback' (Κυρτός) whose nicknames refer to their physical defects, their disabilities. On another occasion he mentions 'the lame one' (*War* V, 474). Several of these nicknames originated as terms of mockery and abuse (Rahmani 1994: 14) and may have been later used as family names (Figure V–22).

יהודה בן אלמא 'Yehuda, son of Ilma = 'the mute', inscribed on an ossuary from Jerusalem, Mount Offence (Figure V–22a; Rahmani 1994: no. 117). See also יהוסף בן האלם 'Joseph son of Ellemos', which is the name of the father of a high priest who served only one day (Jos. *Ant.* 17.166).

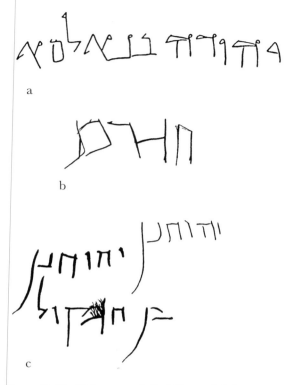

Figure V–22. Nicknames of disability and defects.

הגדם 'The amputated', 'the one-handed' is inscribed on an ossuary from the Kidron Valley; it possibly is in *status emphaticus* as a nickname (Figure V–22b; Pl. V–13b; Rahmani 1994: No. 62). In the Wadi Murabaʿat inscription a similar nickname occurs (Benoit et al. 1961: 220, 232; Hachlili 1984b: 197–8; see also Noth 1928 227–228 for similar names in the bible).

יהוחנן בן־הנקול (= העקול) 'Yehoḥanan son of the hanged with knees apart' is inscribed on an ossuary from Tomb 1, Givʿat Hamivtar (Figure V–22c); this interpretation of the nickname is in debate, some scholars maintaining that it is a nickname meaning 'the crooked'. If it is a nickname it was given to the interred after his death referring to the manner of Yehohanan's crucifixion (Naveh 1970: 35; Yadin 1973; but see Rahmani 1994: 130, no. 218). But Puech (1993: 505–6, No. 11) holds that the name is יהוחנן בן־חזקיל 'Yehoḥanan son of Ḥizqiel'.

חרש 'deaf, mute' (or 'artisan, craftsman, smith') is found on an ossuary
(Bagatti & milik 1958: 83, Inscription 12) and on a Masada ostracon
בר חרשא (Yadin & Naveh 1989: 26, no. 421,5).

Honorific or Age-related titles

Nicknames designated to honor individuals or praise a person's character or action are recorded by Josephus (*Ant.* 12.157; 18.273): שמעון
הצדיק 'Shimeon the Just' חלקיה הנדול 'Ḥilkiah the Great' (Hachlili
1984b: 197, n. 85 (Figure V–23; Pl. V–8)).

Two inscribed ossuaries from Mount Scopus, Jerusalem, record:
חנניה בר יהונתן הנזר 'Ḥananiah son of Yehonathan the Nazirite' and
שלום אנתת חנניה בר הנזר 'Shalom wife of Ḥananiah son of the Nazirite'
which was an honorific nickname (Avigad 1971: 196–198) (see
Chap. VI).

אבונה שמעון סבא יהוסף ברה 'our father, Shim'on (the) elder, Yehosef
his son' is inscribed on an ossuary from the Kidron valley, Jerusalem
(Figure V–23a; Pl. V–13c). סבא is interpreted as 'elder' or as an
honorific title (Rahmani 1994: No. 12). The funerary lament inscription, written in charcoal on a wall in Jason's tomb, includes the
appellative סבא, which was also used as an appellative for the
sages (Avigad 1967: 104).

שמעון הזקן 'Shim'on son of the elder' is inscribed on an ossuary from
Talpiot, Jerusalem. Sukenik (1945: 31) maintains this Shim'on the
elder was a member of the Sanhedrin.

שמעון הזקן 'Shim'on the old' is inscribed above a loculus in a Kidron
valley tomb (Sukenik 1947: 357).

אנה אבה בר כהנה אלעז[ר] בר אהרן רבא 'I, Abba, son of the priest
Ele'az[ar], son of Aaron the elder'. This is an Aramaic inscrip-
tion in paleo-Hebrew script carved on a wall of a tomb at Giv'at
Ha Mivtar (see above, Pl. V–1; Rosenthal 1973, Naveh 1973,
Tzaferis 1974).

יעקב בירבן 'Ya'aqov Birbbi' is the first appearance on an ossuary
of the honorific title *Birbbi* 'Great one' (lit. 'son of the great')
(Figure V–23b; Rahmani 1994: 258, No. 865). This title occurs
also on tombstones at Jaffa (Frey 1952: 892, 893, 951) and later
on mosaic floors.

רב חנא 'rabbi Ḥana' is inscribed on an ossuary from north Jerusalem
(Abel 1913: 269; Frey 1952: no. 1218).

a

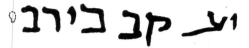

b

c

Figure V–23. Nicknames with Honorific and Age-related titles.

רבא 'great, large, senior, the elder' appeared on ostracon from Masada
(Yadin & Naveh 1989: 21, no. 391).

מר, מרא and the Greek equivalent κύριος indicating the title 'master'
occur, on ossuary inscriptions (Rahmani 1994: Nos. 327, 560).
They also appear at Beth she'arim (Schwabe & Lifshitz 1974: No.
130). From the third century they became the usual honorific title
for father, superior or teacher.

יהוסף בר אנין/אבא קבר בריה 'Joseph, son of Hanin, the poor/father,
his son buried him' appears on an ossuary from Schneller (Figure
V–24c; Klein 1920: Nos. 12; Frey 1952: nos. 1373; Rahmani 1994:
113); a different translation is: 'the father buried his son' (Fitzmyer
and Harrington 1978: No. 145). עניה 'The poor' is possibly also
an appellative that became a surname or nickname.

Two possibly related Greek inscriptions from Beth She'arim are
carved: Σαμουέλ Ἰσαάκου πενηχρου 'Samuel, son of Isaac the poor'

and [Σα]μουήλο [υ υἱου] Γερμα- [νου π]ενι- [χρ]ου '[The tomb] of Samuel, son of Germanus the poor' (Schwabe & Lifshitz 1974: Nos. 99, 206), probably a nickname indicating the family's modest way of life.

יוחנן חטלא 'Yoḥanan Ḥtl' is inscribed on a jar from Qumran; the epithet Ḥtl' is difficult to explain. It was interpreted by Yadin (1957: 62) as 'Yoḥanan the Youth'; see also תחנה חטלא on a fourth-century BCE name-list from Ketef Jericho (Eshel H. & Misgav 1988: 171, and n. 41; Eshel E. 1997: 42).

Negative qualities (derogatory nicknames)

Many of these nicknames were designated to insult, when people wished to express their disgust for famous or prominent persons (Figure V–24). Examples are בן כלבא שבוע 'son of the sated dog', or בן הרצחן 'son of the murderer' (Klein 1929: 339, 347; 1939: 35–6; Hachlili 1984b: 198–199). Clines (1972: 282–287) maintains that calling a person by his patronymic alone is an offesnive form.

נרידא 'the dour', a nickname possibly referring to a hard, dry person, is inscribed on an ossuary from Mount Scopus, Jerusalem (Figure V–24a; Pl. V–13d; Fitzmyer and Harrington 1978: No. 125; Rahmani 1994: No. 44). נרידא 'Gerida', meaning 'rind', 'dour', or 'crust' appears on a Masada ostracon; perhaps it is a nickname for a rough person (Yadin & Naveh 1989: 28, no. 432).

Several odd nicknames perhaps alluding to obesity or gluttony are found:

מרים אתת העגל 'Maryam, wife of the calf', inscribed on an ossuary (Figure V–24b), is possibly a derogatory nickname derived from עגול 'round' implying 'paunchy' (Rahmani 1994: No. 821).

שפירה בת יהוחנן בן רביך 'Shappira, daughter of Yehohanan, son of Revikh (?)' is inscribed on an ossuary from Jerusalem (Figure V–24c). רביך 'Revikh' is difficult to decipher, but it might indicate an oil-soaked cake of unleavened dough, thus alluding to obesity (Rahmani 1994: No. 198).

Ἰουλία Τρωξαλλίς 'Julia Grasshopper' is inscribed on an ossuary (Figure V–24d). Rahmani (1994: No. 498) maintains it is a strange nickname, which could refer to a personal trait of Julia or indicate that she belonged to a family named חגב *Ḥagav*. This insect nickname also appears on an ancient seal; בני חגב, בני חגבה (grasshopper

a

b

c

d

Figure V–24. Nicknames with negative qualities.

in Hebrew) was used as a family name among the returnees from
Babylon (Ezra 2:45, 46; Neh. 7:48).

לוי בר מלשה בנפיה 'Levi, son of Malosha, by himself' is incised on
an ossuary from Ben Shemen. The name מלשה is perhaps a nickname meaning 'kneading trough' (Rahmani 1994: No. 610).

יהוד בר שבט מין בת אלון 'Yehud son of Shevat (or *shevet*, from Bet
Alon' is inscribed on an ossuary from Ammunition Hill, Jerusalem).
Shevat or *shevet* might be a nickname in the sense of 'rod', referring
to an aggressive or forceful character (see above; Rahmani 1994:
No. 293).

Similar nicknames are inscribed on Masada ostraca (Hachlili 2002: 103):

בן כנבון 'a round cake' and בת קרזלה 'son of Qarzela', 'rounded,
rolled', are both nicknames for a fat person (Yadin & Naveh 1989:
28, no. 430; 22, 28; nos. 408, 420:3, 421:7).

בר קסא 'son of Qasa', may be a nickname meaning 'son of the
wooden stick or chip' (Yadin & Naveh 1989: 25, no. 420:6).

Positive qualities

These Nicknames praise a person's character or action, or commemorate an event or a vow by an individual. Examples of such positive nicknames appear in literary sources (Hachlili 1984b: 198).

Persons bearing nicknames such as גר in Hebrew and גיורא in
Aramaic are identified as proselytes (Hachlili 1984b: 198). The most
common name for proselytes was apparently Yehudah (Ilan 1991/2:
154–5; 2002: 50), which occurs on several ossuaries (Figure V–25;
Pl. V–8):

יהודה הגיור 'Yehudah the proselyte' and ארסטון אפמי 'Ariston from
Apamea' are inscribed on an ossuary from Akeldama (Figure
V–25a; see above and Chap. VI). It seems that this was his Hebrew
name, added to his Greek name Ariston after his conversion (Ilan
1996: 66, No. 19).

מריה הגיורת הדולקת 'Mariah the proselytess the one who lights' or
'from Dolek' or 'of Dolichene' or 'from Delos' is inscribed on a
stone fragment of an ossuary or a sarcophagus (Figure V–25c).
Frey (1952: No. 1390) suggests she might have been the one
who lit lamps for Jews on the Sabbath (see also Bagatti and Milik
1958: 95).

Three ossuaries from Dominus Flevit, Jerusalem, are inscribed with
names of proselytes:

שלם הגיורת 'Shalom the proselyte', Ἰουδα προσήλυτο[ ] 'Yehudah the
proselyte', and Διογένης προσήλυτος 'Diogenes the proselyte' (Figure
V–25b; Bagatti & Milik 1958: 84, 89, 95; Inscriptions Nos. 13,
21, 31; Kane 1978: 276–7).

Ἰούδατος Λαγανίωνος Προσηλύτου 'Yeodatos, son of Laganion, the
proselyte' is inscribed on an ossuary from Jerusalem (Figure V–25d;
Frey 1952: No. 1385).

שמעון בר גיורא 'Shim'on bar Giora' (*War* 2, 521), meaning 'son of
the proselyte', was from a family of proselytes (Klein 1929: 333).

ישוע נירא 'Yeshu'a the proselyte' occurs on an inscribed Masada list-
name (Yadin & Naveh 1989: 25, no. 420,7).

Both these last nicknames might be lineage or family names, possibly indicating that these persons came from a family of proselytes.

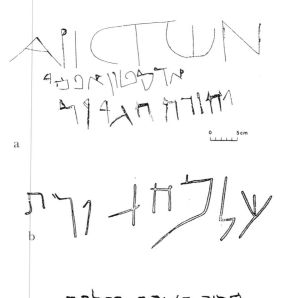

a

b

בריה הדירת הדלקת

c

ΙΟΥΔΑΤΟΣ
ΛΑΓΑΝΙЛΝΟΣ
ΠΡΟΣΗΛΥΤΟΥ

d

Figure V–25. Nicknames with positive qualities.

סבורא *Savor'a* is carved on an ossuary from wadi el-'Ahmediya in Jerusalem area. Avigad (1967: 131) contends that it is a nickname meaning a sage, a scholar.

יואב Jo'ab, inscribed on a Masada ostracon, is an extremely rare name, probably applied to a man who was very brave (Yadin & Naveh 1989: 29, no. 439).

Endearment

Nicknames were used as endearments or pet-names for children or adults (Figure V–26). Some of these nicknames derived from aromatic plants.

קנמומא אזביא/אקביא יהועזר 'Yehoezer Akabia/Azabia the Cinnamon' is inscribed on a child's ossuary from Goliath tomb in Jericho (see above; Hachlili 1979: 55–57; Figs. 25–26; 1999: 149–150, Fig. IV.14). 'Cinnamon' should be seen as an endearment for the child 'Yeho'ezer 'Akaby'a/'Azaby'a', probably meaning 'sweet', was added to differentiate him from another child with the same name interred in another ossuary (No. XVI) in the same chamber (Hachlili 1979: 55–57; Figs. 18–23; 1999: 142, Fig. IV.9; but see Puech 1983: 509–511).

Cinnamon (Greek Κυνναμωμον, Hebrew קנמון) occurs in the Bible several times: Ex. 30:23; Prov. 7:17; Song of Songs 4:14; Jer. 6:20, as well as in Ben Sira 24:25 (for later references see Levi 1879, IV:340). Cinnamon is a high evergreen tree, whose bark served for the manufacture of the spice or a perfume (Jos. *War* 4. 390; *Ant.* 3.197). Cinnamon at that time was considered to be associated with a sweet smell (in the LXX and Theodotian, Κυνναμωμον in Jer. 6:20 is translated as "sweet cane").

Examples of personal names derived from plants and trees occur already in the Bible (Noth 1928: 230–231) as well as in later periods.

ΘAMAP *Tamar*, is inscribed on an ossuary (Frey 1952: No. 789). This common name derived from the palm tree appears in several variations in both Greek and Hebrew: תמריא *Tamaria* (Cowley 1923: No. 8 [111]); דיקלא *Dikla* (Jastrow 1926: 319), תמרא Tamra (Jastrow 1926: 1679), תאנה *Teana* "fig tree" is an example of names derived from Hebrew words and transliterated into Greek. On an ossuary the same name is spelled differently, Θεέννας (Abel 1913: 275; Frey 1952: No. 1233), and Θινος appears on a funerary inscription (Schwabe 1941: 931).

בלזמא חלת 'ossuary of Balzama' is inscribed on an ossuary from Jerusalem(?) (Figure V–26a; Rahmani 1994: No. 461). Balsam is an aromatic plant and the name here might be considered as an endearment. Cinnamon and balsam appear together as plants of paradise (*Levitucus Rabbah* 31,10; Rahmani 1994: 180, 245).

'Jesus aloe'(?) is inscribed in Greek on an ossuary from Talpiyot, Jerusalem; aloe might be a nickname related to an aromatic plant (Sukenik 1947; Kane 1971: 103–105; 1978: 272; Rahmani 1994: No. 114).

קרנית אלכסנדרוס 'Alexander *Qarnyt*', where '*Qarnyt*' is identified with 'thyme' and is mentioned among medical plants. It might have

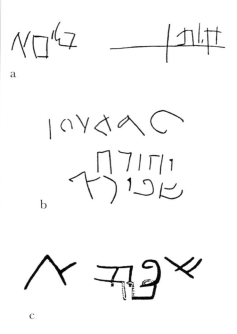

Figure V–26. Nicknames of Endearment.

been a nickname for Alexander (Avigad 1962: 10–11) or his trade
(see above).
קרקם 'saffron', (Clermont-Ganneau 1891: 242; 1899: 406, no. 15).

Another example of a tree species used as a name occurs in inscriptions 75 and 76 from the Beth She'arim cemetery: ΙΑΚΩΒ ΘΟΥΘΑ.
'Jacob (son of) Thoutha' (Schwabe and Liftshitz 1974: 49, *thoutha*
is the Aramaic form of the Hebrew word *thuth*, 'mulberry'). There
are similar examples of this practice of using endearment in the
Bible: בשמת, יבשם, מבשם Noth (1928: 223), translates these words as
"balsam".
שפירא 'the beautiful' is a nickname designated as an endearment for
    men (Figure V–26c; Hachlili 1984b: 199; Rahmani 1994: No. 455).
יהודה שפירא 'Yehudah Shappira' is inscribed on two ossuaries from
    Jerusalem, Mount of Olives (Figure V–26b; Sukenik 1928: 196–7,
    No. 2; Rahmani 1994: No. 35) and 'Dominus Flevit' (Bagatti
    & Milik 1958: 84–85, No. 13b). On another ossuary appears
    אבישלום אבא יהותנ שפר[א] (Frey 1952; No. 1393). שפירה 'Shappirah'
    in Hebrew appears twice on an ossuary (No. 16, in the collection

of the German Protestant Institute of Archaeology; Fritz and Deines 1999: 230, fig. 14).

קלון 'Kallon' a family name inscribed on a group of ossuaries from Jerusalem (Grimme 1912: 533; see Chap. VI) may originally have been a nickname meaning beautiful -*Kallon* in Greek, although in Hebrew it has a negative meaning of 'disgrace' and 'shame'.

Names signifying endearment such as 'Ammia' or אמא Imma, 'mother' (and its variations derived from 'mother'), and Πάπος Pappos, 'Pappias' from 'papa' for father, which derived from baby talk (*Lallnamen*) were occasionally added to a person's first name (Rahmani 1994: 14, Nos. 21, 51, 71, 139, 256, 257); see also Τάτης Tate, derived from the term of endearment τατα ('daddy' 'papa') on an inscription from Beth She'arim (Schwabe and Lifshitz 1974: No. 128).

Summary and Conclusions

The reasons for the choice of names in the Second Temple period were different from those of the First Temple period, when names were given in honour of special events occurring in the family or in the nation. By contrast, during the Second Temple period, naming children after an ancestor was prevalent. Most common among the Jews in fifth-century BCE Egypt was paponymy, naming a child after his grandfather. From the first century BCE on, patronymy, naming after the father, apparently became increasingly common. Matronymy, naming a son after his mother, was also sometimes practiced, but only by men, not women. Patronymy was especially prevalent among prominent Jewish families in Eretz Israel, resulting in a small number of personal names appearing for several generations in a single family. This custom had some social implications, for example, families could be identified by their recurring personal names. It seems to indicate the strong status of the family and its position in Jewish society in the Second Temple period.

Did patronymics alone, or *ben* with a nickname, or a nickname alone, which constitute many of the names on the Beth Phage list and on Masada ostraca, signify 'nameless' people? Naveh (1990: 111–113) contends that these names were characteristic of persons living in a familiar social circle. These were abbreviated names, but names all the same, and people knew to whom they referred: their family

connection, their social standing and milieu, or their status in the
family tomb. They possibly had the same personal name and needed
the nickname or the patronymic to differentiate and identify them.
At Masada the ostraca shards are very small and contain only a single name. Thus, only a person with no name at all should be designated 'nameless', like שמעון ואתת 'Shim'on and (his) wife' (Rahmani
1994: No. 150), where the unnamed wife is interred in the same
ossuary with her husband.

Funerary inscriptions on ossuaries attest to names of prominent
figures as well as of common people. On ossuary inscriptions more
men than woman had their names inscribed (the ratio of male to
female names is about 3.5 to 1). Frequently a women's name includes
the father's, husband's, or son's name. In Ilan's list (1989: 189) 43
of the 152 women found in burial inscriptions have at least one
additional male family member listed. Sometimes a husband's name
appears alone, even though his nameless wife is buried in the ossuary
with him, as noted above.

A large number of Second Temple Jews bore the same name,
and the need to distinguish them resulted in the added nicknames.
Frequently the original nickname, or an ancestor's name, was attached
to the names of sons, wives, daughters, and grandchildren, and so
it became a family name.

The use of nicknames was common at the time. These alluded to
place of origin, especially when the deceased came from outside
Jerusalem in the case of local Jerusalem tombs, or Jericho when they
originated in Jerusalem. Nicknames referring to title record rank and
religious status; occupation alludes to social standing, professionals,
and artisans; physical characteristics, which are denoted frequently,
sometimes derive from terms of abuse; nicknames of praise or positive traits sometimes originated in deeds that marked events in Jewish
life, such as הגר 'the proselyte'; nicknames for endearment sometimes
derived from aromatic plants, such as קנמומא 'cinnamon'; negative
traits were also used as nicknames alluding to abusive behavior and
terms of derision. The most common nicknames are those designating place of origin. Abbreviated nicknames without a personal
name are frequently used on the Beth Phage list and on ostraca at
Masada.

Among priestly families nicknames of physical characteristics and
especially disability are notable; it was important to identify them as
disabled priests, as they were forbidden to serve in the Temple. Some

of the priestly families that grew rich through exploitation of the public retained derogatory nicknames intended to identify them in the community.

The nicknames, especially the inherited ones, were commonly given to the person at birth, for example, the Hasmonean sons. However, physical characteristics, especially disabilities, were given when they became evident. Endearments and derogatory nicknames were designated during a person's lifetime. Some of the endearment nicknames found on ossuaries most likely were used to distinguish family members bearing the same name.

Nicknames of title, profession, and office were conferred at the time their bearers began to practice it, unless it was inherited. Endearments and occupation nicknames might have been inscribed on funerary inscription in order to identify and commemorate the deceased; for instance, 'Simon builder of the Sanctuary' and 'Nicanor who made the doors' express social standing.

Family names could also evolve out of a title, a profession, or appellative nicknames, and could be inherited by subsequent generations.

CHAPTER SIX

FAMILY TOMBS

A. Description of Family Tombs

The tombs described below (arranged by subject and in alphabetical order), some of them monumental, shed light on social life during the Second Temple period, especially regarding family relations, life and death, as well as on the problem of secondary burial in ossuaries during the first century CE. This particular group of tombs (many other tombs which have only a small number of inscriptions are not discussed here) were chosen because of their architectural plan and the inscriptions engraved on the ossuaries, which indicate that these were family tombs; usually a three-generation family was buried in them, and from the inscriptions and the anthropological data it is sometimes possible to reconstruct a family tree.

The significant number of inscriptions in each of these tombs indicates that the families were Jewish, literate, bilingual, and in some cases prominent. Moreover, the evidence at times suggests that some of these families could have been of the priestly families known to reside in Jerusalem and Jericho. Other tombs provide evidence of eminent individuals who were buried in Jerusalem and are known from the archaeological record, namely tomb, sarcophagi and ossuary inscriptions, as well as from ancient sources. Some of the described tombs designate the burial of Jews from or originating in the Diaspora.

The small select group of tombs (about twenty, described below) were discovered in various parts of Jerusalem and two in Jericho. They contain evidence which proves that they served as family tombs. For ossuary decoration and inscriptions, see Table VI–1.

Family Tombs at Jerusalem

I. *A tomb at Ḥallet et-Turi*

A tomb discovered south of the Silwan village (Milik 1956–57: 232–267; Kloner 1980: No. 7–20) contains two chambers, the outer one with five loculi. The inner chamber contained one loculus; 30 ossuaries and about 10 lids were found, some of them with inscriptions (Figure VI–1).

Most of the ossuaries were decorated, and engraved with 15 inscriptions and five signs, they read:

שלמציון Σελμασιων; שלמנה ו[בת]ה 'Shelamziyon'; possibly 'Shlomna and her daughter' (two inscriptions on ossuary B13). יהוחנן בר שמעון 'Yehohanan son of Shim'on' (ossuary B14). שמעון בר הדקא 'Shim'on son of Hidka' (ossuary B25). מתתיה בר יהוסה 'Mathatiah son of Yehose' (ossuary B26) שמעו]ן בר יוחנן 'Shim'on son of Yohanan' (ossuary B15), מתתיה 'Mathatiah' is repeated three times (ossuary B28); the name שלמציה 'Shlamziya' (probably a variation of Shelamziyon) is engraved on ossuary B10. The name שמעון 'Shim'on' is carved twice, on Ossuaries B29 and B11; עקיבא 'Aqib'a' (ossuary B31).

A protective inscription which warns against secondary use of the ossuary is engraved on the lid of ossuary B24 (Milik 1956–57: 235–239, Figs. 2–3; see Chap. XI).

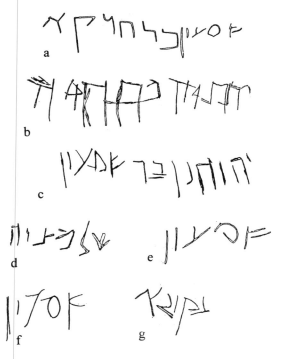

Figure VI–1. Inscriptions on ossuaries found at Ḥallet et-Turi.

The ossuaries found in the same tomb and the inscriptions including the recurring names of Shimʿon (4 examples), Yehoḥanan,
Mathatiah, and Shelamziyon allude to the deceased being members
of the same family, who were interred in this family tomb.

II. *Kidron Valley (Wadi el Ahmadieh, northern slope)*

A loculi tomb with a courtyard and two burial chambers I, II (Figure
VI–2) was discovered in the Kidron Valley with the sealing stone
still in situ (Sukenik 1945a: 26–31; Kloner 1980: Nos. 7–11). Chamber
I has a slightly barrel-vaulted ceiling. Two loculi are hewn into the
first chamber's north wall; the western one is blocked by a sealing
slab. The eastern wall contains a niche which held human bones
and was blocked by a stone slab. Chamber II was probably hewn
later as a result of widening a loculus.

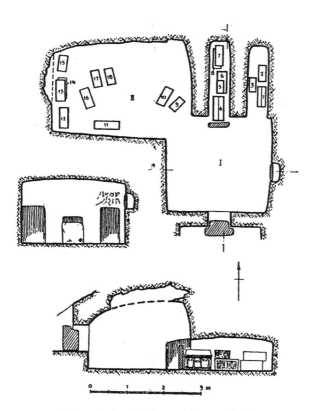

Figure VI–2. Kidron Valley tomb plan.

Eighteen ossuaries were found (Rahmani 1994: Nos. 106–110), three (Nos. 1–3) in the loculus 1, five (Nos. 4–8) in loculus 2, and ten (Nos. 9–18) scattered on the floor of chamber II. Most ossuaries are decorated, eight are plain (Nos. 3, 7–11, 15, 17). One ossuary is unusual in its decoration and inscription (Sukenik 1945:28–30, No. 4, inscription 1); its front is decorated with four Ionic columns enclosing three *tabulae ansatae* with three inscriptions in Greek script.

A charcoal inscription in Jewish script was found engraved above the eastern loculus: שמעון הזקן 'Shimeon the elder'; Sukenik (1945: 29–31) suggested that he was one of the elders of the *Sanhedrin*.

The ossuaries were carved with inscriptions in Greek and Jewish script (Figure VI–3): inscription 1 (ossuary 4) has three inscriptions in Greek script: Σαλω Μαρία 'Salome' 'Maria'; Ἰωσήρ καὶ Ἐλιέζερ δίδυμοι 'Joseph and Eliʿezer the twins'; Ἰωσήφ Κορσιον 'Joseph the maiden'.

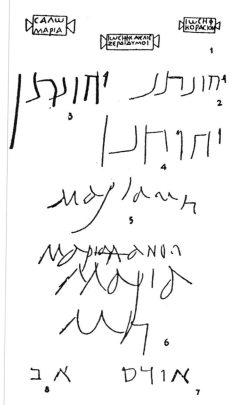

Figure VI–3. Inscriptions on ossuaries found in the Kidron Valley tomb.

Sukenik maintains that they all probably belong to the same family: Salome was the mother's name, Joseph was the father's name, Maria and 'the maiden' (the younger daughter, possibly named thus because she died young) were two daughters, and the twins Joseph and Eliʿezer were two sons. Yet note that the ossuary contained the bones only of two adults.

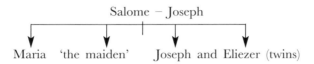

Inscriptions 5–6 record Μαριάμη 'Mariame', which appears three times on the lid of ossuary 13. Inscriptions 2–3, 4, 7–8 are engraved on ossuaries 6, 12, and 16 with the names אידס, יהוחנן, יהונתן.

III. *Kidron Valley*

The rock-cut tomb situated on the lower slope of the Kidron Valley consists of a porch and a square courtyard, with a niche in its northwest corner, partly hewn and partly constructed in masonry, and sealed by a stone slab (Mayer 1924; Savignac 1925; Kloner 1980: No. 7–13). Through the courtyard doors one descends to a rectangular south chamber (B) and an east chamber (C), their walls lined with masonry; a standing pit was cut in the floor forming three benches; in chamber B the ossuaries were arranged on the benches one above the other. In chamber C groups of bones were found on the benches and no ossuaries (Figure VI–4). Mayer suggests that the bones found on the benches (and the complete absence of ossuaries) in chamber C indicates that the dead were placed in this room until the flesh decayed; afterwards the bones could be collected into the ossuaries.

Nineteen ossuaries (12 decorated, seven plain) were found in the tomb (Rahmani 1994: Nos. 12–27), placed together on the shelves of the southern chamber (B). Three are decorated hard limestone ossuaries.

Thirteen of the ossuaries bear 14 inscriptions (Figure VI–5), all in Jewish script and one bilingual (Mayer 1924: 59–60, inscriptions 1–14; Savignac 1925: 258–266; Rahmani 1994: Nos. 12–27): אבונה שמעון סבא/יהוסף ברה / 'Our father, Shimʿon the Elder, Yehosef his son' (inscription 1; Rahmani 1994: No. 12); Yehosef is mentioned

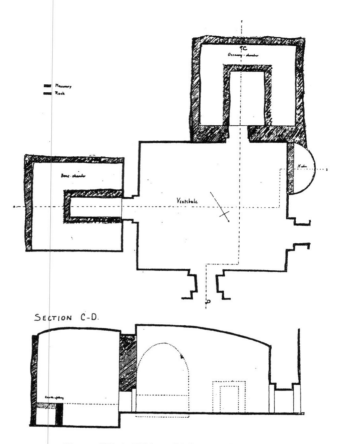

Figure VI–4. Kidron Valley tomb plan.

on this ossuary specifically as the son who interred his father's remains
(see below); he himself is interred in another ossuary (inscription 2;
Rahmani 1994: No. 22). Possibly אמא 'Imma' (inscription 14; Rahmani
1994: No. 21) was the grandmother of this family, the wife of 'Shim'on
the Elder. 'Shelamziyon daughter of Shim'on' שלמציון ברת/שמעון
(inscription 3; Rahmani 1994: No. 26) might be either the daughter of 'Shim'on the Elder' and the sister of Yehosef (Mayer 1924:
59, No. 3, suggests she is the daughter because of the similarity in
the carving of inscriptions 1 and 3); or Shelamziyon could be the
wife of Yehosef, if she was the daughter of the other Shim'on son
of Alexa (inscription 6). 'Yo'ezer [son of Ye]hosef' יועזר]בר ו[הוסף
(inscription 4; Rahmani 1994: No. 15) is the son of Yehosef and
grandson of Shim'on the Elder.

Another branch of the family (inscriptions 5, 9–13) mention Elʿazar, son of Shetʾ אלעזר בן שת (inscription 8; Rahmani 1994: No. 17); Puech (1983: 504, No. 7) suggests reading אלעזר בן קשת Elʿazar, son of archerʾ. שלום אשת אלעזר 'Shalom wife of Elʿazar' is his wife (inscription 13; Rahmani 1994: No. 13), and possibly their three children are שלון בת ליעזר 'Shalon daughter of Liʿazar' (Liʿazar is possibly a contraction of Elʿazar; inscription 9; Rahmani 1994: No. 27), 'Elʿazar' אלעזר and שלום Σαλώμη 'Shalom' (inscriptions 10–11 and 12; Rahmani 1994: Nos. 20, 23; Puech 1983: No. 22).

Figure VI–5. Inscriptions on ossuaries from the Kidron Valley tomb.

A third branch of the family is found (inscriptions 6, 7): שמעון בר
אלכסא 'Shim'on son of Alexa' (inscription 6; Rahmani 1994: No.
18) or Puech (1983: No. 8) suggests שמעון בר אלעסא 'Shim'on son
of Alasa' and his son יהוסף בר שמעון 'Yehosef son of Shim'on' (inscription 7; Rahmani 1994: No. 16); Mayer and Sukenik read יחזק
'Yehezeq'. Another ossuary is carved with two inscriptions, שלום אשת/
יהודה and שלום אתת/יהודה 'Shalom wife of Yehuda' (inscription 8;
Rahmani 1994: No. 24; this is a rare example of both Hebrew and
Aramaic inscribed on the same ossuary). It is difficult to place her:
perhaps she was the wife of a son of this family who was buried in
an ossuary without an inscription.

> • Shim'on the Elder – Imma
> ↓
> Yehosef ↔ 'Shelamziyon, daughter of Shim'on
> ↓
> 'Yo'ezer son of Yehosef
>
> • El'azar ben Sheth ↔ 'Shalom wife of El'azar
> ↓
> Shalom, El'azar, Shalon
>
> • Shim'on son of Alexa
> ↓
> Yehosef son of Shim'on

Several Hebrew men's names recur in the family: Shim'on, Yehosef,
El'azar, Yo'ezer, and two women's names, 'Shelamziyon and 'Shalom'.
It is notable that two deceased in this family were named Shim'on
with a son named Yehosef. Shelamziyon daughter of Shim'on might
have been the connection, being the daughter of one Shim'on and
the wife of Yehosef the son of the other Shim'on.

IV–V. Mount of Olives – "Dominus Flevit"

The "Dominus Flevit" necropolis is situated on the western slope of
the Mount of Olives. About 500 various types of tombs of diverse
periods were discovered at the site (Bagatti and Milik 1958). The
types of tombs include 44 late Roman period tombs and 20 arcosolia tombs (of the fourth century CE). Nineteen loculi tombs of the
Second Temple period were excavated; they consist of one or two
chambers, loculi, standing-pits, and a small entrance. These tombs

contained 129 plain and decorated ossuaries. Seven of them are large hard limestone ossuaries, referred to as sarcophagi by the excavators. The ossuaries bear 43 Aramaic, Hebrew, and Greek inscriptions (Milik 1958: 45–100). The onomasticon in these tombs includes eleven Greek, eleven Aramaic, and seven Hebrew names.

Two family groups are of special interest due to their inscribed ossuaries.

IV. *Tomb of Monogramma, Mount of Olives ("Dominus Flevit")*

The tomb consisted of a central chamber, with loculi on all sides (Figure VI–6) (Bagatti and Milik 1958: 6–9, Tomb 65–80, Fig. 3, Ossuaries 6–30; inscriptions 6–15; Kloner 1980: No. 3–3). A wide loculus (65) contained three ossuaries (Bagatti and Milik 1958: Ossuaries 6–8); five ossuaries were placed in loculus 70 (Bagatti and Milik 1958: Ossuaries 26–30), two were placed in loculus 74, and one in loculus 66 (Bagatti and Milik 1958: Ossuaries 9–11). A small pit (76) leads into a lower plastered chamber (79), used as a storeroom for 14 ossuaries placed on three levels (Bagatti and Milik 1958: Ossuaries 12–25).

Twelve inscriptions (5–16) are engraved on Ossuaries 19–21, 23, and 25 found in loculus 79, on Ossuaries 10–11 found in loculus 74, on Ossuaries 26–27, 29 in loculus 70, and on ossuary 8 in loculus 65 (Figure VI–7).

Among the inscriptions are personal names of males: שמעון 'Shimeon' (inscription 5), 'Eshmael' אשמעל (inscription 6). יהוני החרש 'Yehuni the artisan (inscription 12); female names are 'Martha' מרתה 'Miriam' מרים (inscriptions 7 and 15) and 'Shalom and her son' שלום ובנה (inscription 8).

The following two inscriptions might indicate that some deceased from this tomb originated in the Diaspora: 'Philon from Cyrenaica' Φίλων Κυρηναῖος (inscription 9) and 'Yehuda the proselyte' Ιουδα ν προσήλυτο[ ] τυρα; שפירא *Shapira* appears on the same ossuary and is probably a nickname meaning 'beautiful' (inscription 13).

V. *Tomb of the 'Agra family', Mount of Olives ("Dominus Flevit")*

Consisted of three chambers (Figure VI–8), one with three loculi, a lower one (431) in which two ossuaries were discovered, and chamber 437, which contained 22 ossuaries; this chamber seemed to be a storage room for ossuaries (Bagatti and Milik 1958: 18–19, 96–97,

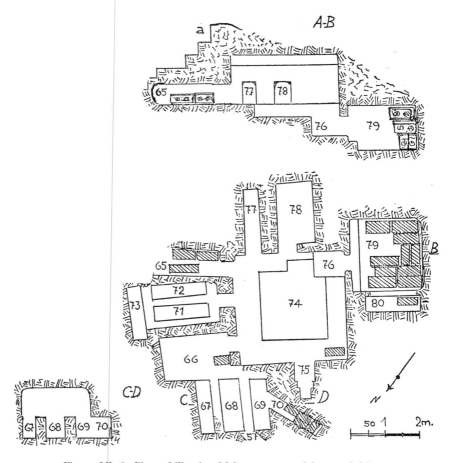

Figure VI–6. Plan of Tomb of Monogramma, Mount of Olives.

Tomb 427–438, fig. 8, ossuaries Nos. 95–120, inscriptions 30–40; Fitzmyer and Harrington 1978: Nos. 80–82; Kloner 1980: 3–16).

Nine inscriptions are engraved and painted on eleven of the ossuaries from this chamber (Figure VI–9):

יהוסף בר אנרה, טוביה בר אנרה, מריה ברת אנרה ,מ 'Yehosef, Toviah and Mariah sons and daughter of 'Agrah' (inscriptions 32, 33, 34, Ossuaries 99, 106, 107). Milik suggests that 'Agrah is a nickname meaning day-laborer, hired-hand; possibly it was the name of the father or a family name. Milik dates the inscriptions to the end of the first century CE. The inscriptions 'Mariah daughter of 'Agrah'.

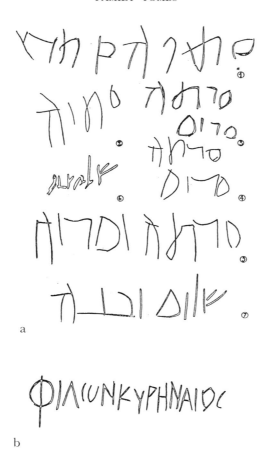

a

ΦΙΛΙΩΝΚΥΡΗΝΑΙΟϹ

b

Figure VI–7. Inscriptions on ossuaries from the tomb of Monogramma,
Mount of Olives.

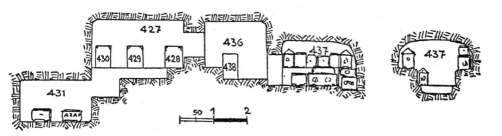

Figure VI–8. Plan, tomb of the Agra family, Mount of Olives.

מריה ברת אגרה and 'Ḥananiah son of Shim'on' חנניה בר שמעון appear on the same ossuary (No. 107, inscriptions 34a–c). Milik maintains that the ossuary contained the couple Mariah and Ḥananiah who may have lived with the father-in-law's family; alternatively, Mariah might have been the mother of Ḥananiah, since as a rule a wife was buried in her husband's family tomb.

טוביה בר אגרה 'Toviah son of 'Agrah' (inscription 33) was a scion of the 'Agrah family. The mother of the family was probably 'Martha our mother' מרתא אמנו (inscription 39).

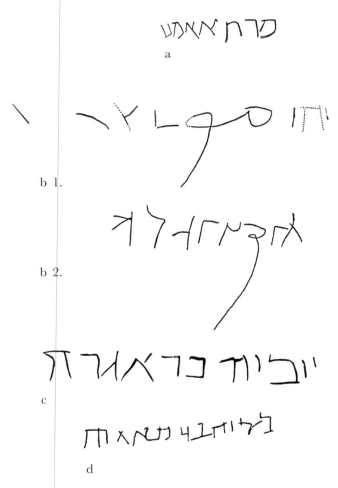

a

b 1.

b 2.

c

d

Figure VI–9. Inscriptions on ossuaries from the tomb of the Agra Family, Mount of Olives.

'Agrah – Martha 'our mother'

Mariah, daughter of 'Agrah; Yehosef, son of 'Agrah; Toviah son of 'Agrah

Ḥananiah 'son of Shim'on'

Other inscriptions in this tomb consist of two inscribed ossuaries, each found in a separate loculus. The inscriptions are the following. 'Shalom the proselyte'.

שלם הגיורת (Bagatti and Milik 1958: 95, inscription 31, ossuary 97); in her ossuary a glass bottle was found (ibid.: pp. 18–19). 'Azariah, Zechariah' Αζαρτας Ζαχαριου (inscription 30, ossuary 95). The same names 'Azariah son of Zechariah' עזריה בר זכריה appear on another inscription (inscription 36, ossuary 112). 'Yeshu'a' ישוע (inscription 40, ossuary 120). 'Shalom wife of Shappir'.

שלום אתת שפיר (inscription 38, ossuary 118); *shappir* שפירא שפיר might be a name derived from a nickname meaning 'beautiful' (see below, pp.). The recurrent names in this tomb are Zechariah, 'Azariah, and the woman's name Shalom.

VI. *Tomb of the* didaskalos *family, Mount of Olives*

The tomb on the slope of the Mount of Olives (Sukenik 1930b; Kloner 1980: Nos. 1–27) consists of only one chamber (no loculi) with a dome ceiling; an entrance sealed with stones is on the south. A standing pit was cut in the center creating three benches; two narrow depressions were hewn on the two corners of the east bench (Figure VI–10a).

Thirteen ossuaries were found in the tomb (Figure VI–10b), of which twelve had been placed on the benches and one in the depression (Sukenik 1930b: 140–141, 143; Pls. C:2, 4; E, 2).

Eight of the ossuaries are engraved with ten inscriptions, most of them in Greek, which reveal that this was a family tomb (Figure VI–11): ossuary 12 has two inscriptions: a name in Hebrew, תדטיון 'Theodotion' (inscription 1) probably the Greek name Theodotos; and the Greek term Διδάσκαλος *didaskalos* interpreted as the 'Rabbi', or 'the teacher' (inscription 2). Ossuary 9 bears the Greek name Θεύμνας, probably short for Θεόμνηστος (inscription 3) equivalent to the Hebrew name Zechariah. Ossuary 7 shows the Hebrew name

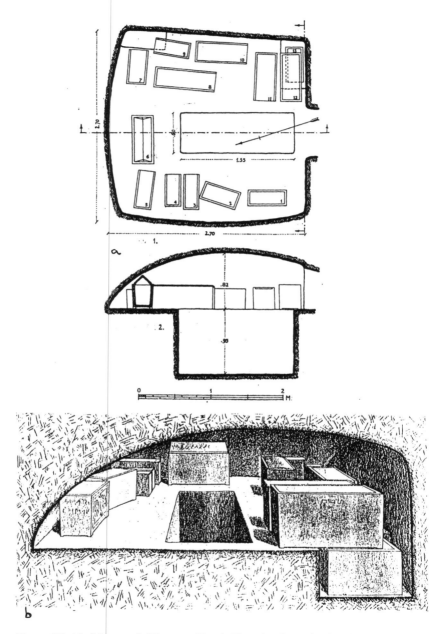

Figure VI–10. Mount of Olives: a. Tomb Plan, b. Ossuaries inside the chamber.

שלמציון בת תדיון 'Shelamziyon, daughter of Thedayon', short for Theodotion (inscription 4); she was apparently the daughter of Theodotion of inscription 1. Two Greek inscriptions are engraved on ossuary 6: the name Θεόδοτιωνος 'Theodotos' (inscription 5), probably the same name as the one on inscription 1; and Δεσδέκαλλου *didaskalos* (inscription 6). On ossuary 5 are the name Σαπίρα, the transliteration of the Hebrew female name 'Shapira', and Ἀνδρούς 'Androus' (inscription 7), probably two names for the women interred in this ossuary. On ossuary 3 are inscribed the Greek name Θεμντσδε 'Theomnisde' short for Θεόμνηστος 'Theomnstos', and δεσκαλου *deskalou* 'teacher' (inscription 8). On ossuary 2 the name אלעזר 'Elazar' is engraved (inscription 9). Ossuary 1 has two names inscribed on it: Ἀμάτο, probably Ἀμάτου 'Amatu', and Σημων probably 'Simon' (inscription 10).

Διδάσκαλος *didaskalos*, 'Rabbi', the term for 'the teacher' appear on three inscribed ossuaries in the tomb: (inscriptions 2, 3, on ossuary 12); on two others (inscriptions 6 and 8, Ossuaries 3, 6) the term appears in Greek letters but in a Semitic phonetic form: Δεσδέκαλλου and δέσκαλου. Sukenik maintains that the people interred in the ossuaries belonged to a family of teachers, *didaskalos*, which might have been a family name. The family probably consisted of the father Theodotion (ossuary 12), his daughter Shelamziyon (ossuary 7), a son Theodotion with the same name as his father (ossuary 6); two other sons are probably buried in the tomb with similar names, Themntosde, also mentioned as a teacher (ossuary 3), and Theomnas (ossuary 9), both probably a short variation of the Greek name Theomnestos.

VII. *Mount Offense (Bât'n el-Hawa)*

This is a tomb of one rectangular chamber with a central standing pit and five loculi (Chaplin 1873: 155–156; Clermont-Ganneau 1874: 7–10; 261–280; 1899: 381–412; Frey 1952: Nos. 1304–1330; Kloner 1980: No. 3–31; Barkay 1989; Gibson and Avni 1998) (Figure VI–12a). The three loculi in the west wall contained primary burials in situ and some ossuaries. The other two loculi might have been used as repositories for secondary burials (Gibson and Avni 1998: 163–165, Fig. 2, Tomb 1). About 30 ossuaries seem to have originated in this tomb.

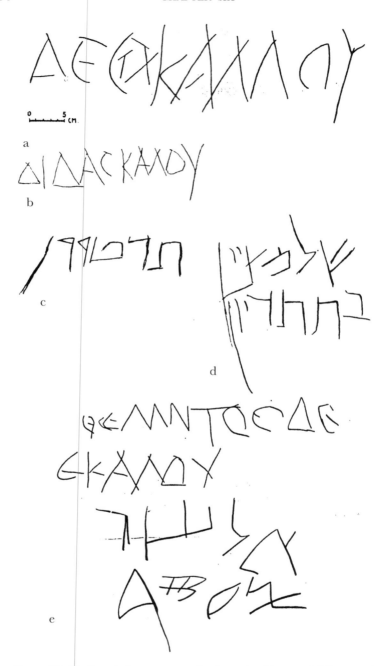

Figure VI-11. Inscriptions on ossuaries from the Mount of Olives tomb.

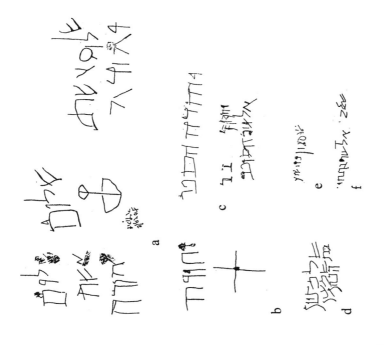

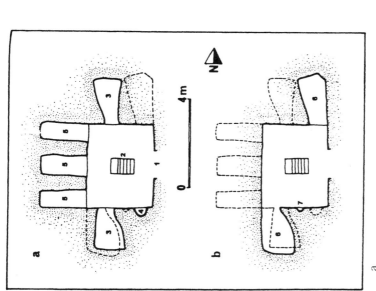

Figure VI-12a,b. Mount Offense tomb: a. plan; b. Inscriptions on ossuaries.

The inscribed ossuaries were carried off and displaced so it is difficult to make out their origin location. The ossuaries apparently belonged to a family of several generations. Clermont-Ganneau (1899: 381, 386) suggested incorrectly that a single *crux immissa* engraved on one of the ossuaries was evidence that the inscribed ossuaries belonged to the earliest Jewish-Christian community in Jerusalem. Gibson and Avni (1998: 163, 173–4) argue that this stylized Christian cross was carved by Christians re-using the tomb in the Byzantine period.

Thirteen ossuaries were engraved with 19 Hebrew and Greek inscriptions (Figure VI–12b). Some family relations can be discerned: three individuals named 'Yehudah' were interred in this tomb: (1) יהודה 'Yehudah' (Clermont-Ganneau 1899: Nos. 8, 11), (2) יהודה בן חנניה 'Yehudah son of Hananiah' (Clermont-Ganneau 1899: No. 190); (3) יהודה הסופר, יהודה בר אלעזר הסופר 'Yehudah son of Ele'azar, the Scribe' (Clermont-Ganneau 1899: No. 3), who might have been the son of 'Ele'azar son of Natai' אלעזר בר נתי (Clermont-Ganneau 1899: Nos. 3–4 and 6; Puech 1983: No. 2a,b; Barkai 1989). שלום אשת יהודה 'Shalom wife of Yehudah' (Clermont-Ganneau 1899: Nos. 9, 10, 10A) was probably the wife of Yehudah the Scribe and Yehudah (1) was perhaps their son.

שלמציון בת שמעון הבהן 'Shelamziyon daughter of Shim'on the Priest' was probably the daughter of שמעון בר ישוע 'Shim'on son of Yeshu'a' and perhaps unmarried, thus buried in her father's tomb (Clermont-Ganneau 1899: 394, Nos. 1–2 and 5).

1. Ele'azar son of Natai
↓
'Yehudah son of Ele'azar, the Scribe → Shalom, wife of Yehudah
↓
Yehudah

2. Shim'on son of Yeshu'a
↓
Shelamziyon, daughter of Shim'on the Priest

Two titled family members are recorded:

שלמציון בת שמעון הבהן 'Shelamziyon daughter of Shim'on the Priest' and יהודה הסופר, יהודה בר אלעזר הסופר 'Yehudah son of Ele'azar, the Scribe' (Clermont-Ganneau 1899: Nos. 1–2 and 3–4).

The recurring names in the family are Yehudah, Ele'azar, Shelam-ziyon, and Shalom.

VIII. *The 'Nazirite' family tomb, Mount Scopus*

This is a burial-vault hewn tomb consisting of a central chamber (I) with three smaller burial chambers (II, III, IV) branching from it (Avigad 1971; Kloner 1980: Nos. 1–11). The chambers' walls and ceiling are built of ashlar stones, and this fine masonry is compara-ble to that of the tomb of Herod's family.

The façade had an the unusually shaped lintel; the opening was closed by the original sealing stone. The central chamber had a bar-rel vaulting, and three openings led to the burial chambers, originally closed by heavy stone slabs found lying on the floor before their respective openings (Figure VI–13a; Pl. VI–1).

The tomb contained two sarcophagi, 14 ossuaries, and two odd ossuary lids.

In room I, two ossuaries, one of hard stone, and a separated lid were found (Nos. 1–3). Room II contained two sarcophagi and ten ossuaries (Nos. 4–13) probably transferred at a later phase from the other rooms. In room III one ossuary and a lid (Nos. 14–15). Two ossuaries were placed in room IV (Nos. 16–17).

Three of the ossuaries were inscribed (Figure VI–13b), two record-ing husband and wife. The two were found together in Room II:

Inscription 1 (on the front of ossuary 7) reads: חנניה בר יהונתן הנזר 'Ḥanania son of Yehonathan the Nazirite'. Inscriptiion 2 (incised on the narrow side of ossuary 8) is: שלום אנתת חנניה בר הנזיר 'Shalom wife of Ḥanania son of the Nazirite'. The Nazirite is an appellative indicating its bearer's abstinence from wine and cutting the hair for a certain period because of a vow. Avigad (1971: 193, 198) contends that 'Yehonathan the Nazirite' was the head of a prominent and aristocratic family, probably buried in the plain sarcophagus, while his wife was apparently interred in the ornamented sarcophagus; in both these sarcophagi decomposed bones were found. Each contained an adult interment and bones later thrown in. Their son Ḥanania and his wife Shalom were interred each in their respective inscribed ossuaries.

'Yehonathan the Nazirite'

'Ḥanania, son of Yehonathan the Nazirite' ↔ 'Shalom, wife of Ḥanania son of the Nazirite'

Figure VI–13a,b. Nazirite family tomb: a. plan; b. inscriptions.

Another inscription records אשוני בר שמעון בר אשוני 'Ashuni son of Shimʿon son of 'Ashuni, engraved on the lid of ossuary 16 found in room IV.

This monumental tomb (dated to the first half of the first century CE) apparently belong to one of Jerusalem aristocratic families. In its architectural and artistic standards it is akin to the royal tombs of Queen Helene and Herod's family (see Chap. II, pp.).

IX. *The 'Betshanite/Scythopolitan' Family Tomb, Schneller*

This tomb, discovered in 1905 near the Syrian orphanage at Schneller, contained two chambers; the first chamber has a standing pit and benches, with no finds. The second chamber has five loculi with their original sealing stones; two of the loculi contained three ossuaries each, with another two ossuaries on a bench. In all, there were eight ossuaries (Schneller 1905; Kloner 1980: No. 24–8).

Three ossuaries inscribed in two languages (Figure VI–14) were found in the tomb (Figure VI–14; Lidzbarski 1908, II:191–199; Klein 1920: Nos. 11–13; Frey 1952: Nos. 1372–1374; Fitzmyer and Harrington 1978: No. 145; Rahmani 1994: no. 139).

On the first, three inscriptions are engraved. Two of them record the same person in two languages, in Greek on the front of the ossuary: Ανίν Σκυθοπολείτης 'Anin the Scythopolitan', and in Hebrew on the narrow side: חנין הבשני 'Ḥanin the Betshanite'. Under the latter the third, unusual, inscription is carved (Figure VI–14b): יהוסף בר אנין עניה/אבא קבר 'Yehoseph, son of Hanin, the poor/ father, his son buried him' (Rahmani 1994: No. 139; Misgav 1997: Fig. 1). A different possible translation is: 'The father buried his son' (Fitzmyer and Harrington 1978: No. 145). Rahmani's interpretation is probably right, in light of inscription above it, חנין הבשני 'Ḥanin the Betshanite'. This was probably the ossuary of the father Ḥanin, who was buried there by his son Yehosef. עניה 'The poor' is probably the son's nickname (see Chap. V).

The second ossuary has two bilingual inscriptions: one on the narrow side in Hebrew: אמיה הבשנית 'Ammia the Betshanite' (from Beth She'an), and one on the lid in Greek: Αμμία Σκυθοπολιτίσσα 'Ammia the Scythopolitan' (Figure VI–14a).

On the third ossuary are three inscriptions (Figure VI–14c), two on the narrow side: Παπίας, and פפיס הבשני 'Papias the Betshanite',

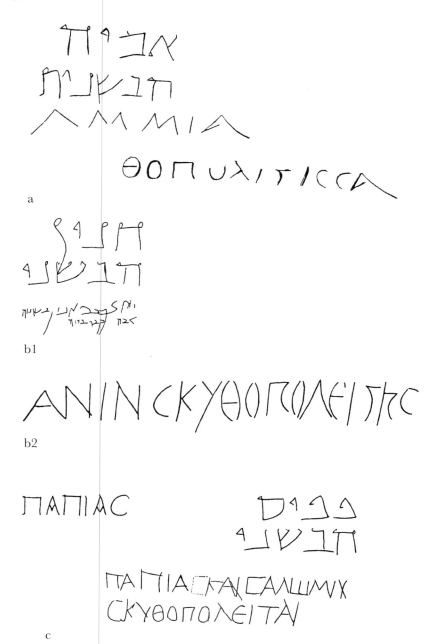

Figure VI–14. Inscriptions on three ossuaries from the Schneller tomb.

and one on the lid: Σαλώμιχ/Σκυθοπολεῖται 'Papias and (his wife)
Salomich' (probably a transcription of Σαλώμη 'Salome') the Scythopolitans'.

The interred members of this family mention their origin, Beth
She'an/ Scythopolis. All three inscriptions seem to be written in the
same hand.

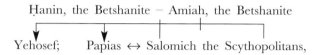

Ḥanin, the Betshanite – Amiah, the Betshanite

Yehosef;   Papias ↔ Salomich the Scythopolitans,

These three ossuaries possibly record a family consisting of Ḥanin,
his wife 'Amiah', and their son Yehosef, who buried his father as
mentioned on the father's ossuary; Yehosef was probably buried in
one of the other uninscribed ossuaries discovered in this tomb. It is
likely that Papias was the other son who was interred with his wife
Salomich in their own ossuary. This family originated in Beth She'an
(Scythopolis), and eventually 'the Betshanite'/'the Scythopolitan'
became their surname or nickname.

X. *Talbiyeh, south slope*

The Talbiyeh tomb consisted of a square court, an entrance leading to an upper chamber with a standing-pit, and two arcosolia: one
on the west wall and the other on the south wall (Sukenik 1928:
113–121; 1929; Savignac 1929; Yellin 1929; Fitzmyer and Harrington
1978: Nos. 95–98; Kloner 1980: No. 23–19). On the north wall is
a niche with a standing-pit, possibly a repository for bones. A lower
chamber hewn under the court contained twelve ossuaries (Figure
VI–15). This chamber was originally vaulted and might have been
formerly an earlier tomb, reused later (Sukenik 1928: 113–115, Pl. 1).

Twelve ossuaries (Rahmani 1994: Nos. 70–79) were found in the
lower chamber, and were probably moved about. Nine of the ossuaries had inscriptions (Figure VI–16) representing a three-generation
family (Sukenik 1928: 121). The family consisted of several members:

אבא דוסתס, דוסתס אבונה ולא למפתח 'Dostas our father, and not to be
opened' engraved on the front and lid of ossuary 1 – apparently the
father of the family; his wife אמא שלמציון, שלמצין אמנה 'Shelamziyon
our mother' engraved on the front and on the lid of ossuary 2; their

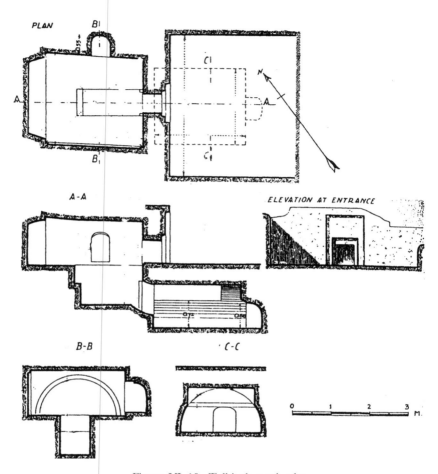

Figure VI–15. Talbiyeh tomb plan.

son מתתיה 'Mattatya' on the front and lid of ossuary 3; his wife 'Shalom and Matya her son' שלם/ומתיה ברה אתת מתיה וברה on the front and lid of ossuary 4.

Two other inscriptions record the 'wife of Elʿazar' אנתת אלעזר (on the front and lid of ossuary 5) and the 'sons of Elʿazar בני אלעזר (on the front and lid of ossuary 6). These were probably the wife and sons of Elʿazar, son of Dostas and Shelamziyon. The 'sons of Ḥanan' בני חנן (inscribed on the front of ossuary 7) are probably also grandsons of Dostas and Shelamziyon; Dostas דוסתס (on the front of ossuary 8) could be another son or a grandson. Hence, the fam-

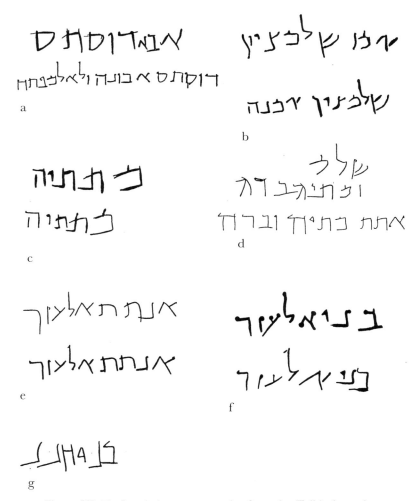

Figure VI–16. Inscriptions on ossuaries from the Talbiyeh tomb.

ily of Dostas and Shelamziyon had three or four sons, three of them married, and they had several grandchildren.

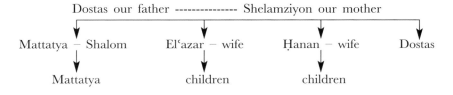

Dostas דוסתם is a contraction of the name Dositheos, which has the same meaning as מתתיה Mattatya – 'gift of God'. These recurring names of a son, a grandson and of the grandfather in Greek all have the same meaning.

The recurring female names are Shalom and Shelamziyon. Note that the personal names of El'azar's wife and children and of Ḥanan's wife and children are not given.

XI. *Talpiyot Tomb*

The loculi tomb at Talpiyot (Figure VI–17) comprises a courtyard and an entrance on its southern side, with a rectangular sealing stone found in front (Sukenik 1947; Kloner 1980: No. 13–1). The burial chamber has a rectangular standing-pit in front, which left benches on the three sides around the pit. Five loculi are hewn into the chamber walls, two each in the south and east walls, and one in the west wall. This single loculus is divided into two stories by a number of stone slabs.

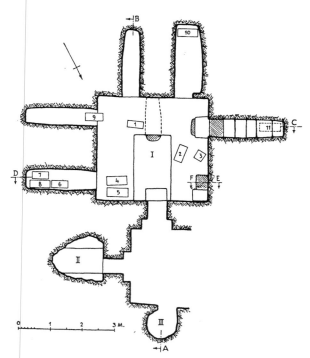

Figure VI–17. Talpiyot tomb plan.

Fourteen ossuaries were discovered in the tomb (only three were retained by the IAA; Rahmani 1994: Nos. 113–115). Ossuaries 1–5 were placed on the benches; osuaries 6–8 were in loculus 5; ossuaryossuary 9 was at the entrance to loculus 4, ossuary 10 was in loculus 2, ossuary 11 in loculus 1. Ossuaries 12–14 were taken out by the workmen before the excavation.

Of the 14 ossuaries five had inscriptions. Among the decorated ossuaries (Table VI–1) two (ossuaries 10 and 12) have some similarities in their motifs. Nevertheless, each ossuary was seemingly chosen individually as even the similar designs display diverse workmanship in their decoration (see Chap. IX). Ossuary 8 (Sukenik 1947: 26, Fig. 10) has unique charcoal cross-like marks in the middle of all the sides, possibly in preparation for some decoration which was never completed (Smith 1974: 58–60; Puech 1982b: 50; Rahmani 1994: 19, No. 114).

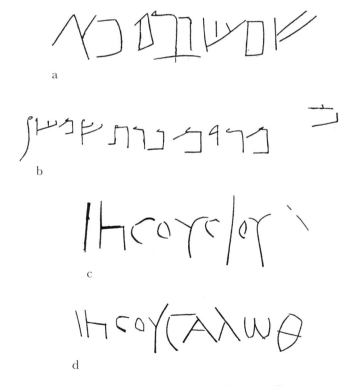

Figure VI–18. Inscriptions on ossuaries from the Talpiyot tomb.

Five of the ossuaries had inscriptions (Figure VI–18): three in
Jewish script, mentioning 'Shim'on the elder' שמעון בר סבא (ossuary
1) and his daughter 'Miriam, daughter of Shim'on' מרים ברת שמעון
(ossuary 4). The name Matti מתי (on ossuary 10) is an abbreviation
of Mattathias. Two ossuaries found in the same loculus were each
inscribed in Greek script with the same name 'Jesus' Ἰησοῦς ἰού.
Sukenik (1947: 16–20, Figs. 17–26, 30) incorrectly interpreted these
inscriptions and the cross-marks as an expression of lamentation for
the crucifixion of Christ. Possibly the name Jesus was followed by
the name of his father Judas (ossuary 7); the second inscriptions is
'Jesus Aloe' Ἰησοῦς ἀλώθ (ossuary 8), possibly a nickname serving to
distinguish the two individuals named Jesus (see below; Kane 1971;
1978: 271–273; Rahmani 1994: 106, No. 113).

Priestly and High-Priestly Family Tombs

The inscriptions on a tomb façade and on ossuaries attest to the
relation of some individuals to a priestly family or to a high priestly
family.

The Temple ritual required the division of the priesthood into 24
courses each of which served two weeks during the year (Stern 1976:
587, 594–595). Several of these courses are mentioned on funerary
data discussed below.

Stern (1976: 603) maintains that "at the close of the Second Temple
period, any distinguished priest, distinguished by reason of his social
standing, and in the majority of instances, one who belonged to the
group of oligarchical priestly families of the high priesthood, could
be called a high priest. Hence, in effect the principal officers of the
Temple could be called high priests. Thus, the term high priests
serves as an expression par excellence of the social hierarchy that
prevailed at the end of the Second Temple period".

Some family tombs include inscribed ossuaries mentioning a priestly
relation. The women recorded in these inscriptions appear as wives
and daughters of priests (Ilan 1995: 72–74). Marriage into priestly
families was considered a great honor. Priests generally tended to
marry daughters of other priests.

XII. The 'Bene-Ḥezir' family tomb

The Bene-Ḥezir tomb in the Kidron Valley, consists of an entrance
hall, a central hall (A) and chambers B, C, D with several loculi,

and chamber E with arcosolia (Avigad 1954: 37–59; see Chap. II; Fig. II–2).

A three-line Hebrew inscription was carved in the center of the façade's architrave (Fig. V–3).

זה הקבר והנפש של אלעזר חניה יועזר יהודה שמעון יוחנן
בני יוסף בן עובד יוסף ואלעזר בני חניה
כהנים מבני חזיר

This is the tomb and the *nefesh* of El'azar, Ḥaniah, Yo'ezer, Yehudah, Shim'on, Yoḥanan sons of Yosef son of Oved; Yosef and El'azar, sons of Ḥaniah, priests of Bene Ḥezir (Avigad 1954: 59–66)

The inscription records a four-generation family, who belonged to the 17th priestly course (I Chr. 24:15, Neh. 10:21).

The family tree of the Bene Ḥezir family includes: the forebear Oved, his son Yosef, the latter's six sons El'azar, Ḥaniah, Yo'ezer, Yehudah, Shim'on, and Yehoḥanan, and Ḥaniah's two sons Yosef and El'azar.

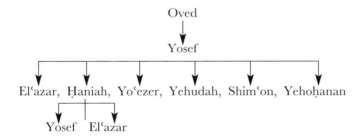

The recurring names in this family are El'azar and Yosef.

XIII. *The 'Boethos' priestly(?) family tomb*

The tomb, in Mount Scopus, western slope, consists of a courtyard with two entrances: the one on the east wall leads to a square empty chamber; the other entrance, on the north wall, leads to another chamber with three loculi and two small chambers (Figure VI–19) (Sukenik 1934; Kloner 1980: Nos. 1–8).

Twenty-three ossuaries were found in the tomb, most of them placed in the loculi and small chambers (Sukenik 1934: 62–64, Fig. 1; the IAA retained five ossuaries, Rahmani 1994: Nos. 41–45).

Four of the ossuaries were inscribed (Figure VI–20): שמעון בוטון 'Shimon of (the family of) Boethos' is inscribed on ossuary 10. Sukenik

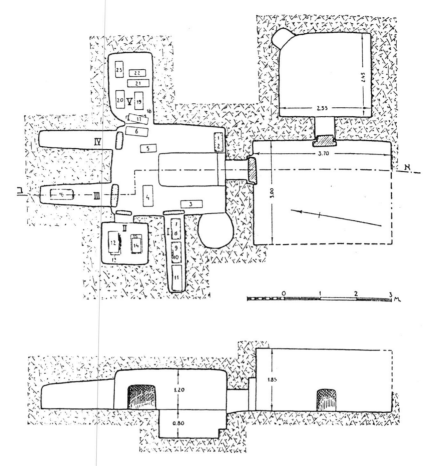

Figure VI–19. 'Boethos' family tomb plan.

(1934: 70–73) links this tomb to the priestly family of Simon son of Boethos of Alexandria (Josephus *Ant* 15:320), based on the ossuary with the family name בוטון and the name Μάρθας Martha (on ossuary 3). He suggests that the family lived in Jerusalem at the time of King Herod.

The names in this family are Mattathiah מתיה, מתתיה (on ossuary 13), Martha (on ossuary 3), and a nickname Greida גרידא (on ossuary 12).

XIV. *The 'Caiaphas' family tomb.*

This tomb, in north Talpiyot ('Peace Forest'), is a single burial chamber with four loculi and a standing-pit (Figure VI–21). The entrance

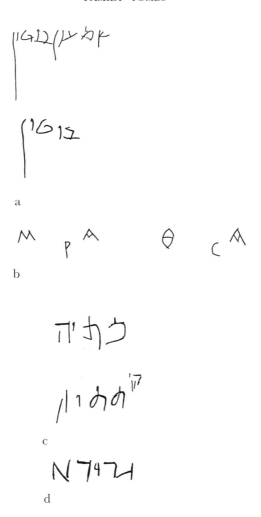

Figure VI–20. Inscriptions from the 'Boethos' family tomb.

was blocked by a large slab and small stones. In the northeast corner a repository is hewn into the chamber floor (Greenhut 1992;
Reich 1992; Flusser 1992; Puech 1993; Horbury 1994; Kloner &
Zissu 2003: Nos. 11–53). Pottery fragments were strewn throughout
the tomb.

Six decorated ossuaries were discovered, only two (5, 6) in situ,
in loculus IV. The other four were found in the chamber, apparently removed from loculi I–III. Six more ossuaries and three lids,
some of them broken, were found in the fill of the chamber and in

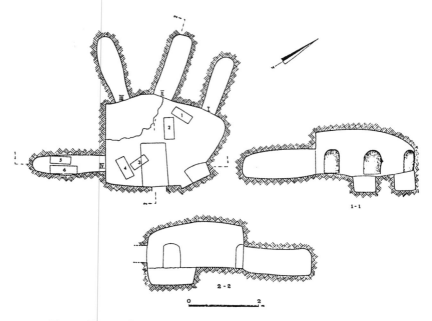

Figure VI–21. Caiaphas tomb plan and inscriptions on ossuaries.

the standing pit. In all, twelve ossuaries and four broken lids were found (Greenhut 1992: 63–68, Plan 1, Table 1, Figs. 1–7).

Seven of the ossuaries have inscribed names and letters (Figure VI–22). Two of the inscriptions, 5 and 6 (on ossuary 6), record: יהוסף בר קיפא 'Yehosef son of Caiaphas' and inscription 2 (on ossuary 3) has קפא, a similar name. Two inscriptions, 4 and 7 (on ossuaries 5 and 8), are incised with names of women: מרים ברת שמעון 'Miriam daughter of Shim'on' and שלום 'Shalom'.

The meaning and interpretation of the name קיפא, קפא 'Caiaphas' is in dispute. Some scholars consider it the nickname of an ancestor, possibly related to a high priestly family (Reich 1992: 72–76, Figs. 1–7). Puech (1993a: 43; 1993b: 193–195) suggests the name is Qoppa or Qefa, and not Qayyapha. He contests the proposal that this tomb belonged to a high priestly family for the following reasons. The term 'priest' is not recorded on any ossuary, and the tomb is too small to be considered a tomb of a high priestly family. Thirdly, the high rate of infant mortality makes it unlikely that the family was of a high rank. Lastly, ossuary burial seem unsuitable for

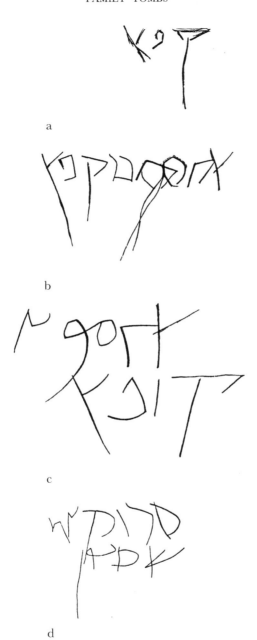

Figure VI–22. Inscriptions on ossuaries from the 'Caiaphas' tomb.

Sadducees. Horbury (1994: 46) maintains that "the ossuary inscriptions can not be said to correspond directly to the name Caiaphas, and Inscription 5 and 6 do not, therefore, clearly attest the Joseph surnamed Caiaphas of Josephus and the New Testament". Horbury further suggests it is an Aramaic name 'Joseph bar Qopha', also a priestly name probably related to the name Qayyapha.

XV. The 'Kallon' family tomb

This Chamber-tomb, in Qatamon, Jerusalem, consisted of a small courtyard and an entrance with its sealing stone in situ. The chamber (A) had one wide loculus (D), three collecting loculi, and a standing-pit. The latter was divided into two parts, the upper part consisting of slabs for standing on, the lower leading to an ossuary chamber (Figure VI–23). To allow passage to the ossuary chamber the slabs were lifted. The ossuary chamber (C) had a standing-pit, creating three benches, on each of which two ossuaries were placed; six ossuaries altogther were discovered in the tomb (Grimme 1912; Hänsler 1913; Klein 1920: 8–13; Frey 1952: Nos. 1350–1355, with photos; Fitzmyer and Harrington 1978: Nos. 90–94; Kloner 1980: No. 23–18; Misgav 1991: 42–47).

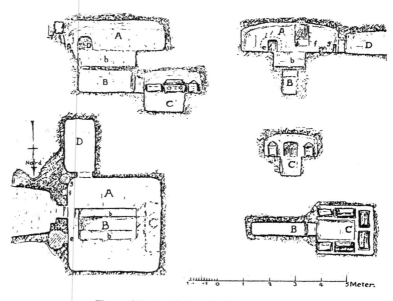

Figure VI–23. Kallon family tomb plan.

All six ossuaries were inscribed (Figure VI–24; Figure VI–25) (Grimme published only four inscribed ossuaries, nos. 1–4; Hänsler, Klein and Frey published all six inscribed ossuaries. Misgav (1991: 47) discribes a seventh inscribed ossuary. However, the tomb plan (Figure VI–23) shows only six ossuaries in Chamber C.

Inscription 1a,b (on the front and the lid of ossuary 1; Figure VI–24,1) consists of two Hebrew inscriptions: מרים יועזר שמעון בני יהוק בן קלון מבני ישבאב 'Miriam, Yo'ezer, and Shim'on, children of Yeḥzaq, son of Kallon, of the sons (?) of Yeshb'ab'. These inscriptions record the three generations of the family, their family name, and priestly decsent.

Inscription 2a,b (on the front and on the lid of ossuary 2; Figure VI–24, 2) consists of two Hebrew inscriptions: יהועזר/יועזר בר שמעון בר קלון 'Yeho'ezer/ Yo'ezer son of Shim'on, son of Kallon'.

Inscription 3a,b,c (on the front of ossuary 3; Figure VI–25, 3) consists of three Hebrew inscriptions: a,b – שמעון בר יהועזר בר קלון 'Shim'on son of Yeho'ezer, son of Kallon'; c – שמעון בר יועזר 'Shim'on son of Yo'ezer'.

Inscription 4a,b (on the lid and on the short side of ossuary 4; Figure VI–24, 4) consists of a Hebrew inscription: a – יהוסף בר שמעון 'Yehosef son of Shim'on', and a Greek inscription: b – Ἰώσηπος Κάλλων 'Joseph Kallon'.

Inscription 5a,b (the front and the lid ossuary 5; Figure VI–25, 5) consist of two Hebrew inscriptions: a – שלמציון ברת נמלא 'Shelamziyon, daughter of Gamla' and b – שלמציון אתת יהועזר בר קלון ברת נמלא 'Shelamzion, daughter of Gamla (Gamliel?), wife of Yeho'ezer son of Kallon' (Hänsler 1913: 134–5; Klein 1920: 9, No. 5; Frey 1952: No. 1353, see above). This inscription, recording both the original name of Shelamziyon and her married status, might designate that she belonged to a prominent family, being identified as the sister of 'Yehoshu'a son of Gamla' the High Priest in the reign of Agrippa II (Josephus, *War* 20, 213; Sukenik 1931: 17).

Inscriptions 6 a–d (on the lid of ossuary 6) consist of four Greek inscriptions mentioning two members of the Kallon family: a,c – Σίμωνος Σίμωνος Κάλλωνος 'Simon' 'Simon Kallon'; and b, d – Ἰώσηπος Κ[ά]λλωνος; Ἰώσηπος Κ[ά]λλωνος 'Joseph Kallon' (Hänsler 1913: 136; Klein 1920: 9, No. 6; Frey 1952: No. 1353).

Another inscription (on the side of ossuary 7) mentions [-]יה בר שמעון בר קלון, '[. . .]ya son of Shim'on, son of Kallon' is described by Misgav (1991: 47). Yet, in the tomb plan only six ossuaries appear

Figure VI–24. Inscriptions 1, 2 and 4 on ossuaries from the Kallon family tomb.

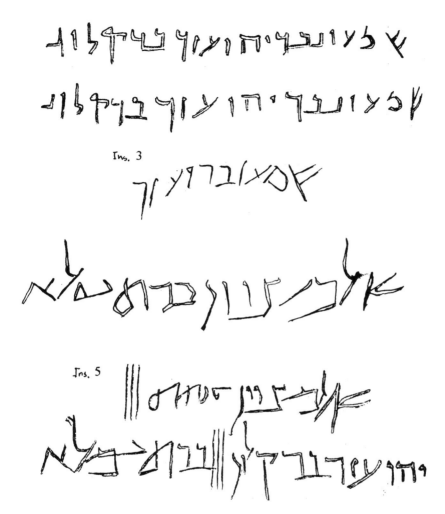

Figure VI–25. Inscriptions 3 and 5 on ossuaries from the Kallon family tomb.

(Figure VI–23) and this ossuary is not mentioned in any of the other publications.

These inscriptions record a three-generation family, mentioning the father Yeḥzaq, son of Kallon; they were descendants of the priestly family 'Yeshb'ab', the 14th course of the Temple priests (I Chr. 24:13). 'Kallon' might have been an ancestor whose name evolved into a family name. The surname קלון 'Kallon' derives either from a derogatory Hebrew nickname meaning 'disgrace', 'shame', or a positive Greek nickname meaning 'beautiful' (see below).

Scholars suggest different family trees for this family (see also the suggested family tree presented by Misgav 1991: 48).

1. Hänsler (1913: 136):

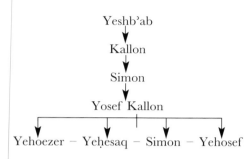

2. Klein (1920: 10–11):

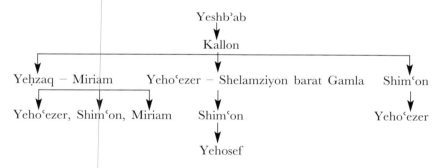

My suggestion for the family tree is determined by:

• 'Kallon' is the family name, based on the Hebrew and Greek inscriptions on all the ossuaries.

• The most revealing and complete inscription is No. 1 on ossuary 1, refering to Miriam, Yeho'ezer, and Shim'on, the three children of Yehzaq son of Kallon, of Yeshb'ab (the priestly course). This inscription includes the family name and is the only one which records the family's priestly decsent. Thus, this inscription is the primary reference to the family relations.

• Shim'on (ossuary 1) had two sons: 'Yehosef son of Shim'on' (ossuary 4) and 'Yeho'ezer, son of Shim'on, son of Kallon' (ossuary 2).

- Yoʻezer (ossuary 1) had a son, ʻShimʻon son of Yehoʻezer son of Kallon' (ossuary 3), who possibly had a son ʻ[ ]ya son of Shimʻon son of Kallon' (ossuary 7).
- Yehoʻezer (ossuary 2) had a wife ʻShelamziyon daughter of Gamla' (ossuary 5) and possibly two sons Simon and Yehosef (ossuary 6).

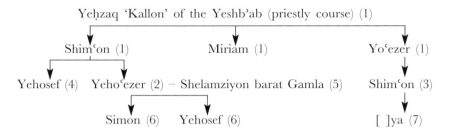

Yeḥzaq 'Kallon' of the Yeshbʼab (priestly course) (1)

Shimʻon (1)   Miriam (1)   Yoʻezer (1)

Yehosef (4)   Yehoʻezer (2) – Shelamziyon barat Gamla (5)   Shimʻon (3)

Simon (6)   Yehosef (6)   [ ]ya (7)

The recurring male names in this family are Shimʻon and Yehoʻezer; the female names in the family are Miriam and Shelamziyon.[1]

Family Tombs of Interred Jews from the Diaspora

Several tombs discovered in Jerusaelm include ossuaries with inscriptions indicating the origin of the deceased in places in the Diaspora. The question is if the deceased were brought from the Diaspora to be buried in Jerusalem or if their family had originated in the Diaspora (see Gafni 1981) and it was important enough for them to mention the fact on their inscriptions. Pilgrimage to Jerusalem and the absorption of Diaspora Jews in Jerusalem is known from literary sources (Stern 1976: 570–571). The presence and final resting place of Jewish immigrant families from the Diaspora in Jerusalem (Ilan 1991–1992: 150–154; 1996: 68) is attested by the following tomb groups. Regev (2002: 50–55) argues that the three Jerusalem tombs (Nos. XVII, XVIII, XX) were not familial tombs but the burial place of Diaspora Jews, immigrants and proselytes, who probably were buried together in a loculi tomb as a community since they had no relatives in the city. Nevertheless, the following are family

---

[1] The name [Bi]lgah was inscribed on the corner of the north wall of a tomb near Gophna (near the Jerusalem-Nablus highway, about 20 km. north of Jerusalem), probably referring to the priestly family of the house of Bilgah, the 10th course of the Temple priests (I Chr. 24:17) (Sukenik 1933–4: 7–9; Ilan 1995: 73, note 60).

tombs since they have inscriptions attesting to family relations among the interred, as well as several recurring names in the family.

XVI. *The 'Eros' Family Tomb, Akeldama (Tomb 2)*

At Akeldama in the Kidron Valley three tombs were discovered. The courtyard of tomb 2, shared with tomb 1, led to its entrance, which was closed by a square sealing stone; three steps led to the floor of the main chamber A (Avni and Greenhut 1996: 15–21, Plans 1.6–1.8; Kloner & Zissu 2003: No. 7–77). This main chamber A has ten loculi, and the tomb has two more chambers, B and C, at a lower level. Chamber C contained loculi and acrosolia. A staircase descended from chamber A into chamber B (Figure VI–26). The small chamber B served as an ossuary repository. The single loculus in the south corner contained a decorated hard limestone sarcophagus, its lid thrown across the chamber. In a small cell carved in the west corner of chamber B three decorated ossuaries (nos. 9, 11, 12) were found; seven more ossuaries (nos. 10, 13–18) were stacked one above the other in the chamber, which was apparently disturbed in antiquity (Avni and Greenhut 1996: Plan 1.8).

Eleven ossuaries and a sarcophagus were found in chamber B; nine had inscriptions in Greek script except one which was bilingual. All probably belonged to the 'Eros' family (Ilan 1996: 57–63).

Ossuary 11 found in Chamber B records 'Eiras of Sel[e]uc[ia]', (or: daughter of Sel[e]uc[us] (Ilan 1996: 59, Inscription 3). Eiras (a feminine name) was probably a native of one of the Syrian Seleucias.

One of the inscriptions reads Πεποίηκεν Αζά Βερούτος/ Έρώτας 'Aza[ria] son of Berous (or: of Beirut) has made (it)' (Ilan 1996: 60–61, inscription 7); apparently the artist himself was not buried there; it was he who decorated the ossuary (17) with a unique design (Pl. VI–2) of bucrania carved in a schematic outline on the two narrow sides and of naturalistic flowers on the front (Shadmi 1996: 45, Fig. 2.12) (see Chap. IV p. 27). This might signify that contact with the Syrian community was still maintained (Ilan 1996: 60–61). The name of the deceased, Έρώτας 'Erota', is engraved on the front of the same ossuary.

The 'Eros' family inscriptions (Figure VI–27) indicate that they preferred to use Greek names and the Greek language. Only one Hebrew name, 'Jesu'a' ישׁוע, is found in a bilingual inscription (no. 5). The recurring Greek name Erota in the 'Eros' family appears here for the first time in local Jewish onomastics.

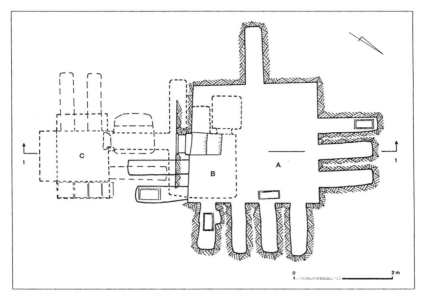

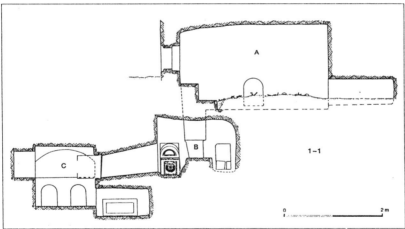

Figure VI–26. The 'Eros' family tomb, Akeldama (Tomb 2) plan.

XVII. *The 'Ariston' Family Tomb, Akeldama (Tomb 3)*

Akeldama tomb 3, located in close proximity to tomb 1, consists of four chambers: A and B had six loculi each; C was a passage-chamber with three arcosolia and shallow burial troughs; and D was a back chamber used as an ossuary repository (Figure VI–28) (Avni and Green-hut 1996: 22–31, Plans 1.9–1.13; Kloner & Zissu 2003: Nos. 7–78).

Figure VI–27. Inscriptions on ossuaries from the 'Eros' family tomb 2, Akeldama.

Fourteen ossuaries were discovered: one each (nos. 22, 26) in Chambers A, and C; three in Chamber B (nos. 23–25) and eleven in Chamber D (nos. 27–37). Almost all the ossuaries were inscribed with the names of the deceased, some with their family relations (Figure VI–29).

Fourteen inscriptions on the ossuaries (Ilan 1991/2: 149–157; 1996: 68–69) reveal that in Chambers A, B, and C only women, called Hannah, Auge daughter of Do[ras], Erous, Kyria, and Helene, were interred in the ossuaries; these individuals might have belonged to

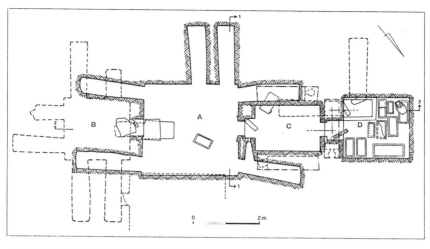

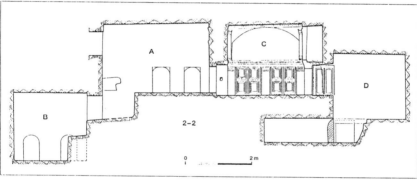

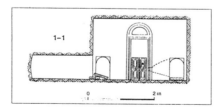

Figure VI–28. The 'Ariston' family tomb 3, Akeldama, plan.

another family who leased these chambers for a short period from the 'Eros' family. The inscriptions on the ossuaries in Chamber D (Figure VI–30) mention the 'Ariston' family, a Syrian family from Apamea.

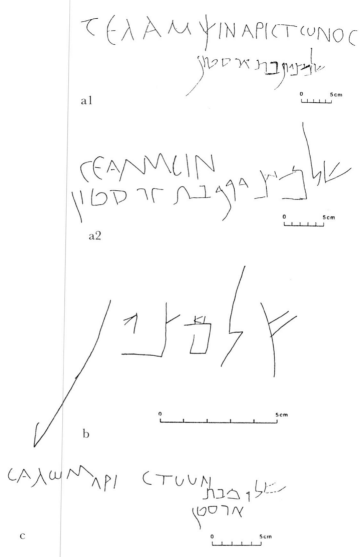

Figure VI–29. Inscriptions on ossuaries from the 'Ariston' family tomb 3, Akeldama.

The inscriptions on ossuaries from tomb 3 use Greek, Aramaic, and Hebrew names (Figure VI–29; Figure VI–30). One inscribed ossuary (no. 31, inscription 19) contains the bilingual inscriptions of Ἀρίστων ארסטון אפמי 'Ariston of Apamea' and יהודה הגיור 'Yehudah the proselyte'. The interred person bears two names: Ariston, a Greek name, and Apamea, his place of origin in Syria; it seems that his Hebrew name Yehudah was adopted after his conversion (Ilan 1996: 66). Ariston's two daughters are also found in this chamber: שלמציון בת ארסטון Σελαμψίν Αρίστωνος 'Shelamziyon, daughter (of) Ariston' (inscriptions 16–17, ossuary 28) and Σαλώ(ν) Αρίστωνο(ς) 'Shalom, daughter (of) Ariston' (inscription 22, ossuary 35).

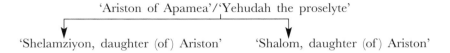

'Ariston of Apamea'/'Yehudah the proselyte'

'Shelamziyon, daughter (of) Ariston'   'Shalom, daughter (of) Ariston'

Two other women, named Shelamziyon (in Jewish script, inscription 18) and Salom(e) (in Greek script, inscription 15), and two men, 'Shabtai son (of) Nehemiah' (inscription 20) and 'Natira' (inscription 21), were also interred in this chamber and may have belonged to the 'Ariston' family. The female names Shelamziyon and Shalom recur in this family; the name Kyria appears in both the Ariston and Eros families.

The inscriptions on the Akeldama ossuaries indicate that the families using these tombs came from the Diaspora, most likely originating from three places, Apamea, Beirut, and Seleucia in the Roman province of Syria (Ilan 1996: inscriptions 3, 7, 19; Misgav 1991: 140–141). The Eros family (tomb 2) seems to have come from Seleucia in Syria, while tomb 3 was used by the converted 'Ariston' family and perhaps also shared by the 'Eros' family (Avni and Greenhut 1996: 34; Ilan 1996: 68–69). The inscriptions specify the deceaseds' place of origin in addition to their names, and if they were born Jews or were proselytes – as attested by the inscription of Ariston of Apamea'/'Yehudah the proselyte' – from the Diaspora who migrated to Jerusalem, where they lived and were buried in family tombs.

XVIII. *A Kidron Valley Tomb*

This rock-cut tomb is situated on the south-western slope of the Kidron Valley. It consists of one chamber with a standing-pit forming three benches ; the entrance on the north side was blocked by a stopper stone (Avigad 1962; Kloner 1980: Nos. 7–8).

Eleven plain ossuaries (Rahmani 1994: Nos. 95–104) were found in the tomb, ten placed together on the eastern bench and one on the corner of the western bench (Figure VI–31).

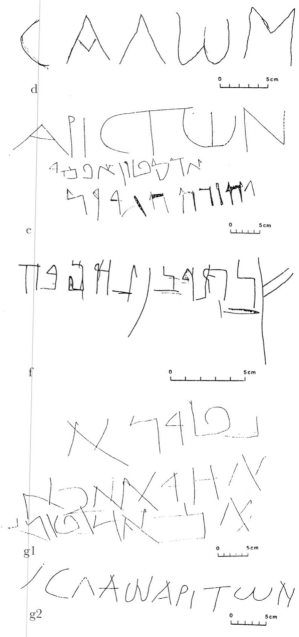

Figure VI–30. Inscriptions on ossuaries from the 'Ariston' family tomb 3, Akeldama.

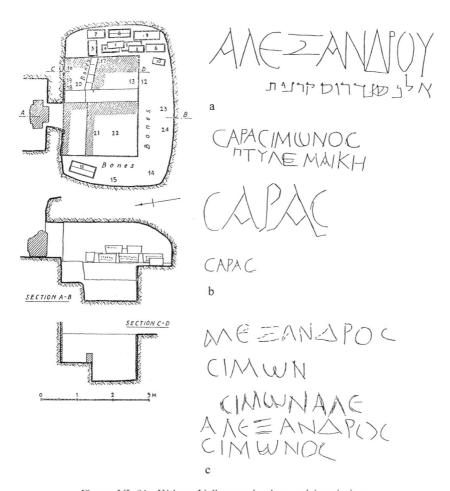

Figure VI–31. Kidron Valley tomb plan and inscriptions.

Nine ossuaries bear inscriptions, of them eight in Greek script, one bilingual, and one in Jewish script (Figure VI–31). Twelve personal names appear; eight of them are Greek, three are Hebrew names in Greek transcription, and one is in Hebrew. Some of the Greek names are especially common in Cyrenaica and some of the others are in use chiefly among Diaspora Jews. Two of the inscriptions (nos. 7, 8 on ossuaries 5 and 9) record Ἀλεξανδρος Σίμωνος אלבסנדרוס קרנית 'Alexander son of Simon from Cyrenaica' and his sister Σάρα Σίμωνος/Πτυλεμαικη 'Sara of Ptolemais'. They are the son and daughter of Simon, whose inscription is not found in the tomb (Powers [2003: 51] believs that very likely Simon of Cyrene was the one who carried Jesus cross at the crucifiction). It seems that the tomb contained a family originating in Cyrenaica who now belonged to the Jewish community that existed in Jerusalem.

XIX. *Mount of Olives Tomb (The 'Sisters of Zion')*

The tomb consists of a main chamber with three loculi, an arcosolium with head support; on the south wall there is a depression-like room, which was used as a repository for bones or ossuaries, and two arcosolia with head supports (Figure VI–32). In the corridor leading from the main chamber to the second chamber two columns were engraved as pilasters with Doric capitals (Vincent 1902b: 279 CD). The second smaller chamber has three arcosolia; several ossuaries were discovered in this chamber (Vincent 1902a, 1902b; Frey 1952: Nos. 1283–1284; Kloner 1980: No. 3–27).

The Greek inscriptions on the ossuaries (Figure VI–33) mention 'Judah son of Judah of Betel' Ἰουδά Ἰούδου Βεθηλέτου, and 'Jose son of Judah Pheidros' Ἰωσής Ἰούδου Φαίδρου; possibly two brothers 'Jose' and 'Judah' are interred in the same ossuary. Their father was also 'Judah' and their grandfather had a Greek name, 'Pheidros' (Schwabe 1956: 365). The other ossuary is inscribed 'Maria, wife of Alexander of Capua' Μαρία Ἀλεξάνδρου γυνή ἀπό Καπούης, probably recording a Jewish women from the Diaspora. It seems possible to infer that this family, with its inscriptions in Greek script, originated in the Diaspora.

XX. *A Tomb at Shuafat (Arad el-Beida), North Jerusalem*

This tomb consists of a chamber with fourteen loculi; the walls were covered with ashlar stones (Figure VI–34). Fragments of 25 ossuaries were discovered with 16 inscriptions in Greek, nine in Hebrew, and two in Palmyrene (Abel 1913; Frey 1952: Nos. 1215–1239; Kloner 1980: No. 30–13).

Several inscriptions mention names and nicknames (Figure VI–35):

One of the inscriptions mentions 'Justus of Chalcedon' Ἰουστος Χαλκίδηνος with a nickname Θεέννας, the Hebrew word תאנה *te'ana* ('fig tree') transliterated into Greek. This may mean that he was an

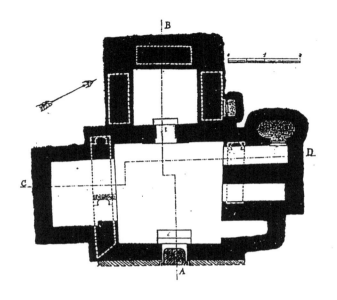

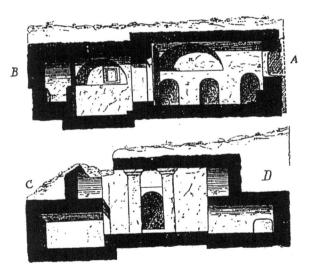

Figure VI–32. Mount of Olives tomb (the 'Sisters of Zion'): plan.

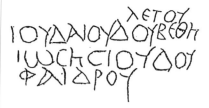

c

d1

MAPIAΓYNHAΛEZAN
APOYAΠOKAΘOYHC

d2

Figure VI-33. Mount of Olives tomb (the 'Sisters of Zion'): inscriptions
(after Vincent 1902a: 104, 106-7).

expert on figs. (Abel 1913: 275; Frey 1952: no. 1233; Schwabe 1956: 366).

Other inscriptions include כהנה (שמעיה) פנחס ויעקביה 'Pinḥas and Ye'aqaviah (or Shama'yah) the priests' (Puech 1983: 499–500, No. 1; see pp. . . .); 'Rabbi Ḥana' רב חנא or possibly תחנא (Misgav 1997: 127).

Abel (1913: 276–7) proposes that three groups of names appear on these inscriptions: (1) Jewish names (engraved in Hebrew and Greek) common in priestly families: Pinḥas, Yakaviah, El'azar, Yehudah, Ezekias, Ḥiskiah, Jesus, Benjamin, Martha, and Shelamziyon. (2) Palmyrene and other immigrant names: Alexandrin, Elhanan, Kaiamos, Nehemiah, Sarah, Salami and Salamath. (3) Greek-Latin names: Africana, Africanus, Anius, Aristobula, Catula, Epictete son of Pheidon, Juste of Chalcedon', Philon.

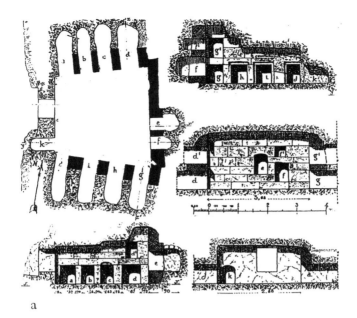

Figure VI–34. Tomb at Shuʿafat (Arad el-Beida): plan.

Figure VI–35. Tomb at Shuʿafat (Arad el-Beida): inscriptions.

It seems possible that this family with its Hebrew, Greek, and Palmyrene names and script, with two titled members, originated in the Diaspora, possibly in north Syria.

XXI. *The Tomb of Nicanor*

This tomb, discovered in 1902 on Mt. Scopus, is one of the most monumental tombs in Jerusalem, with a plan similar to that of the Tomb of Bene Hezir (see Chap. II, pp.; Fig. II–10). Seven ossuaries were found not in situ. The finds in the tomb included pottery and iron nails (Clermont-Ganneau 1903: 131; Avigad 1967: 119–125, Pl. 21:1; Kloner 1980: No. 2–5–9).

The Nicanor bilingual inscription engraved on ossuary 4 (now in the British Museum) records: "The bones of the [sons or descendants?] of Nicanor the Alexandrian who made the doors. Nicanor the Alexandrian" (Frey 1952: No. 1256; Fitzmyer and Harrington 1978: No. 108; Kane 1978: 279–282) (see Chap. V, 172–3, Fig. V–5). The inscription most likely refers to Nicanor of Alexandria, who donated the famous door of Herod's Temple known as the 'Gate of Nicanor' (M Midot 2:4, 2:3; Yoma 3:6; BT Yoma 38a; JT Yoma 41a). The ossuary apparently contained the bones of some family members of Nicanor the Alexandrian, and he himself might have been interred in the family tomb.

Burial of Jews originating in the Diaspora is characterized by the following features (Rahmani 1994: 17, Ilan 1996: 68).

- Inscriptions mentioning a place of origin (origin-name, ethnic-name) in the Diaspora in addition to personal names.
- Greek names not popular in local circles but frequently used by Diaspora Jews.
- More correct Greek grammar on the ossuaries.
- Use of foreign script: Palmyrene and Latin script might have been used by Jews from Rome living in Jerusalem and adopting local burial customs (Rahmani 1994: Nos. 579, 197, 202, 497).
- The proselytes were a phenomenon of the times, namely the conversion of Diaspora Gentiles to Judaism. Some went to live in Jerusalem; this particular status was noted on the inscriptions, with the recurrence of the name Yehuda for a male proselyte (see Chap. V, 227).

In addition to foregoing family tombs nos. XVI–XXI, the following is a list of names of deceased persons in ossuary inscriptions mentioning the place of origin in the Diaspora (see also Chap. V):

- 'Philo from Cyrenaica', inscribed on an ossuary from a tomb on the Mount of Olives (Bagatti and Milik 1958: 81, No. 9)
- 'Gaius, (son) of Artemon, from Berenike' in Cyrenaica, a Greek inscription engraved on an ossuary from a tomb in Ramat Eshkol, Jerusalem (Rahmani 1994: No. 404)
- 'Judah, a proselyte' who was perhaps a native of Tyre in Phoenicia, inscribed on an ossuary from a tomb on the Mount of Olives (Bagatti and Milik 1958: 84, No. 13)
- 'Martha, daughter of Yehosef, son of Ya'akov, wife of Yehosef, from Hin', inscribed on an ossuary. It is suggested that Hin is Martha's or her husband's place of origin, identified either with Hini in Babylonia, mentioned in the Talmud (*TB Git.* 80a), or with Beth Hini east of Caesarea (Rahmani 1994: No. 290:5)

The inscriptions confirm the connection to the Diaspora of two groups of interred: Jewish families originating in the Diaspora and converts who immigrated to Jerusalem to live there, and were later buried in family tombs.

Family Tombs from Jericho

XXII. *The 'Goliath Family Tomb' (Tomb H), Jericho*

The Goliath tomb in the Jericho cemetery consisted of a large courtyard with benches, an adjoining *miqveh*, and two chambers with loculi (Hachlili 1999: 37–44, Figs. II.67–83; Netzer 1999: 45–50). A corridor led to the tomb entrance, built into the rock-cut opening in the hillside, consisting of a lintel and doorjambs. Two large sealing stones reinforced with smaller stones blocked the entrance. The inner stone, which sealed the entrance, had been cut to fit the opening; the second, a rough rounded stone, rested against the first blocking stone (Pl. VI–3). Together these stones sealed the tomb hermetically. The tomb contained two connecting chambers (Figure VI–36). Chamber A had a standing pit, benches, eight loculi, and one bone repository. A passage in the form of a loculus in the north wall connected Chamber A to the lower Chamber B.

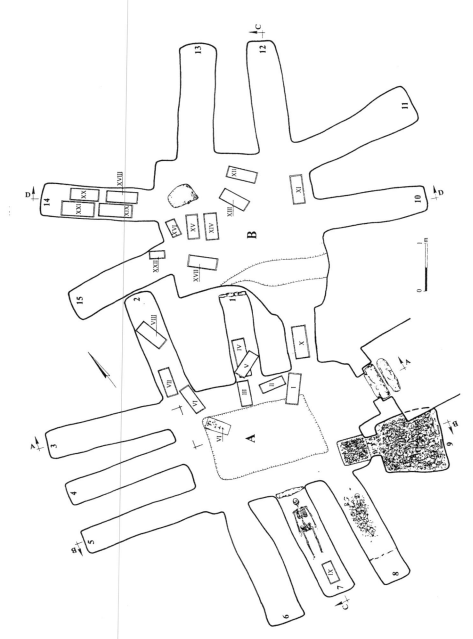

Figure VI–36. Jericho, Goliath tomb plan.

Chamber A had two loculi in the north wall next to the passage, three loculi in the west wall, three loculi in the south wall, and a bone repository in the east wall (loculus 9), next to the entrance (Pl. VI–4a; Hachlili 1999: Figs. II.71–74). The walls and ceiling of the tomb were plastered white and the walls were decorated with painted designs. On the north and south walls the paintings were well preserved, while on the west and east walls very little remained. The red and black painted design included vine branches and leaves, birds, and probably a pergola.

Nine ossuaries (I–IX) were uncovered in Chamber A, placed in loculi 1–4 and on the benches in front of them. The small ossuary IX was found at the back of loculus 7. In front of the ossuary was a primary burial of a female with her feet towards the loculus opening. Bone repository 9, next to the entrance, is lower than the loculi and was cut deep into the rock with a low ceiling. It contained the bones of close to 100 individuals in a large pile, seemingly arranged similar to the way to that of the bones in the ossuaries.

Chamber B (Hachlili 1999: 40–44, Figs. II.71, 75–77) was connected to Chamber A by a loculus-shaped passage ending in two steps. Ossuary X had been placed in this passage. Chamber B had six loculi, two each in the east, north, and west walls (Pl. VI–4b). The ceiling was high enough to stand, so that no pit was necessary. The walls and ceiling were plastered white. loculi 14 and 15 were higher than the chamber floor.

Twelve ossuaries were found in chamber B. Ossuaries XVIII–XXI were found in loculus 14 and ossuary XXII in loculus 15; all other ossuaries (XI–XVII) were uncovered in a group on the floor. Ossuary XVI, which stood on the floor next to the wall under loculus 15, is similar to ossuary XXII in shape and inscriptions, and was probably originally placed together with ossuary XXII in *kokh* 15. 22 ossuaries were found in the tomb and one outside (Pl. VI–5). This tomb seems to have been disturbed in antiquity, as indicated by the removal of the ossuaries from their original places in the loculi, and by the lack of pottery (only a few fragments were found); the pottery vessels may have been removed at some time in antiquity. However, someone who had entered the tomb for a reason other than robbing must have done it, as the bones inside the ossuaries were not disturbed and the tomb was carefully resealed.

The Inscriptions

Fourteen ossuaries engraved with 32 inscriptions were found in the Goliath tomb at Jericho (Table V–1; Hachlili 1979; 1999: 142–155, inscriptions 1–14, Table IV–1).

The information about the family relations obtained from the inscriptions can be summarized as follows.

The nucleus of the Goliath family is established by inscriptions 9–12, engraved on four ossuaries (XVIII, XIX, XX, XXI) placed in loculus 14 (Figure VI–36; Pl. VI–6). In these inscriptions the important construction of the three-generation Goliath family is found. Ossuaries XX and XXI, placed at the back of *kokh* 14, is engraved with bilingual inscriptions 11 and 12. It refers to 'Yehoʿezer son of Eleʿazar' the father of the family, who was exceptionally tall, and his wife 'Shelamsion, the mother of Yehoʿezer Goliath' (Fig. V–10). The two ossuaries XVIII and XIX, at the front of the loculus, held the remains of 'Yehoʿezer son of Yehoʿezer Goliath' (bilingual inscription 9) and his wife 'Salome, wife of Yehoʿezer Goliath, and Ishmael (her) son and Yehoʿezer (her) son' (inscription 10) (Fig. V–11).

Ossuary VIII, engraved with inscription 3 (Fig. V–12), records that it is 'The ossuary of Theodotos, freedman of Queen Agrippina' (Hachlili 1979a: 46–47, Figs. 41–42; 1999: 142, 144–145, Fig. IV.1). Theodotos/Nat[an]el was probably enslaved after being taken a prisoner of war to Rome, where he adopted his Greek servile name Theodotos, a translation of his Hebrew name Natanel. He may have been a domestic slave in Queen Agrippina's household. Inscription 7a–b (ossuary XV) citing 'Mariah, daughter of Nat[an]el and granddaughter of Shelamsiyon' (Fig. V–13) establish his position in the family: Theodotos/Nat[an]el, the freedman of Queen Agrippina, was the son of Shelamsiyon and the father of Mariah (Hachlili 1999: 143–144, Table IV.1 and family tree, Fig. IV.34).

Theodothos' inscription mentions a historical figure, Queen Agrippina, for the first time in an ossuary inscription. In addition, the Greek word for ossuary, *copoc*, appears at the end of inscription 3a.

Two ossuaries, XVI and XXII, containing the remains of a child and an infant, were engraved with inscription 8a–d: 'Yehoʿezer 'Aqabyʾa/'Azabyʾa', and inscription 13: 'Yehoʿezer' Aqabyʾa/'Azabyʾa Cinnamoma' (Figs. V–14, 15). The two children had identical names; the endearment nickname 'Cinnamon' was added to the infant's inscription.

Ossuary I with inscription 1 (Figure VI–37) records: 'Mariame wife of Judah'. The inscription mentions Judah, probably another son of Yeho'ezer son of Ele'azar and his wife Shelamsion; the ossuary contained only the remains of his wife Mariame and those of her infant.

Ossuary II contained three children and is engraved with inscription 2 recording 'Yeho'ezer son of Ele'azar Goliath' (Figure VI–38). Inscription 4 on ossuary XII refers to Ἰωέζρος Ἰσμαήλου 'Yeho'ezer son of Ishmael' (Figure VI–39a).

Inscriptions 5a–b (ossuary XIII) Μανάημος, Σίμων 'Menahem, Simon' and 6a–b (ossuary XIV) Σίμων 'Simon' (Figure VI–39b) may have been incised by the same person, as indicated by their similar cursive Greek script and their unusual position at the edge of the ossuary front; both are written vertically from top to bottom. The individuals in these ossuaries were a father and son, probably Simon and Menahem, son of Simon.

ΜΑΡΙΑΜΗ ΓΥ ΙΟΥΔΟΥ

Figure VI–37. Jericho, Goliath tomb, Inscription 1.

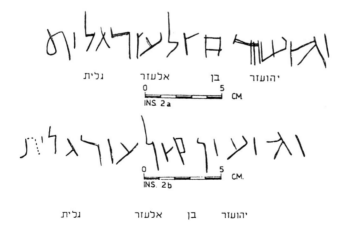

גלית   אלעזר   בן   יהועזר

INS. 2a

INS. 2b

גלית   אלעזר   בן   יהועזר

Figure VI–38. Jericho, Goliath tomb, Inscription 2.

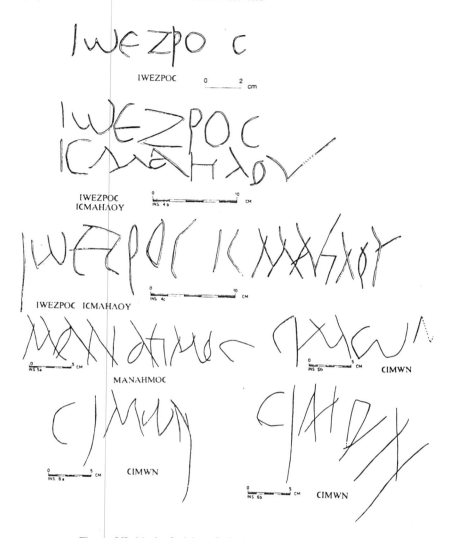

Figure VI-39a,b. Jericho, Goliath tomb, Inscriptions 5-6.

Inscription 14, written in charcoal on the lid of ossuary VI, was probably a 'magic' formula (see Chap. XI).

Goliath family members' names

Thirteen personal names appear in the Jericho tombs, of which three appear in this tomb for the first time: Nat[an]el, ʼAqabyʼa/ʼAqabyʼa and Goliath. Most of the other names appear in contemporary sources, and are often spelled in the same way, but occasionally there are slight variations. Many names are written in both Jewish and Greek script, and only a few are in Greek script alone.

The names of the male members in the Goliath family (Ele'azar, Judah, Yeho'ezer, Ishmael, Menaḥem, Nat[an]el, and Simon), as well as the female names Mariah, Mariame, Salome, and Shelamsiyon (Hachlili 1979: Table 2), are common names in the onomasticon of this period. Most are biblical names, with the exception of 'Aqaby'a/ 'Aqaby'a, which appears here for the first time (for a discussion of names and nicknames, see Chap. V; Hachlili 1984b, 2000). The group of the Jericho ossuary inscriptions is exceptional in the recurrence of the names Yeho'ezer, Ele'azar, Ishmael, and Yeho'ezer 'Aqaby'a/'Aqaby'a. The name Yeho'ezer recurs down the three generations of this family, with seven different individuals so named (Hachlili 1979: Table IV.3 and Fig. IV.34). The custom of naming a son after his father, even when the son was born when the father was still alive, seems to have been prevalent in this family (Hachlili 1984b: 192, 194–195, 2000). In the Goliath family, children were also named after relatives (inscriptions 2a,b, 4b,c, 10, Hachlili 1999: Figs. IV.7a,b, 8, 10a,b, 11a,b, 26a,b), i.e. that is, uncles or grandfathers, as is the case with the names Ele'azar and Ishmael (Fig. VI–40).

The name Yeho'ezer 'Aqaby 'a/'Aqaby'a (inscriptions 8a–d, 13a–c, ossuaries XVI and XXII; Hachlili 1999: 146, 149–150; Figs. IV.9a–d; 14a,b) should be considered a name belonging to both children interred in these two different ossuaries, probably to differentiate them from the other Yeho'ezers in the Goliath family.

The Family Relations

The family relations in the Jericho Goliath tomb determined by the inscriptions, the anthropological data, and the placement of the ossuaries are summed up in the family tree, Figure VI–40 (Hachlili 1979: 56–58, fig. 49; 1999: 153, Fig. IV.15; Hachlili and Smith 1979). The four ossuaries (XVIII, XIX, XX, XXI) found in situ in loculus 14 of Chamber B contain in their inscriptions most of the important details for constructing the basic outline of the family tree (see Chap. V).

Inscriptions 9, 10, and 11 establish the family relationship of Shelamsiyon, Yeho'ezer son of Yeho'ezer Goliath, and Salome. Inscription 11 informs us that Shelamsiyon is the mother of Yeho'ezer Goliath, and inscription 10 indicates that Salome is the wife of

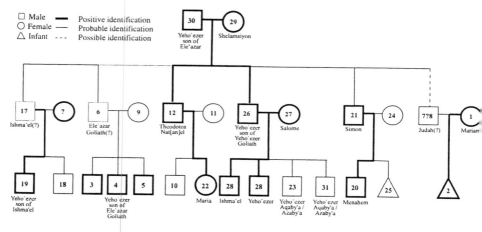

Figure VI–40. The Goliath family tree.

Yehoʿezer Goliath. The relationship of these three – a mother, her son, and his wife – is thereby established.

Yehoʿezer son of Eleʿazar is the only individual in loculus 14 whose inscription, no. 12, does not include reference to his family relationship. However, from the placement of his ossuary with the other three, and from inscription 9 on his son's ossuary (Yehoʿezer son of Yehoʿezer Goliath), Yehoʿezer son of Eleʿazar must clearly be the father of the family and husband of Shelamsiyon.

Another identification is evident from inscription 7a–b: ʿMariah, daughter of Nath[an]el, daughter of Shelamsiyon' (i.e., the grand-daughter of Shelamsiyon). Nath(an)el in inscription 7 is to be identified with Theodotos, the freedman of inscription 3 interred in ossuary VIII, hence Theodotos/Nath[an]el is Shelamsiyon's son and Mariah's father.

The placement of several of the ossuaries, along with the infor-mation revealed in their inscriptions, indicates that those contained in these ossuaries are also members of this family: Simon and Menahem (ossuaries XIII and XIV), who are father and son, Simon possibly being a son of the tomb's founders Yehoʿezer and Shelamsiyon. Miriam, wife of Judah and mother of an infant (ossuary I), was prob-ably related to the family through her husband, who most likely was a son of Shelamsiyon and Yehoʿezer son of Eleʿazar.

Ossuary II contained three children whose inscription reads ʿYehoezer son of Eleazar Goliath'. Evidently they were members of this family, one or all of them being the sons of Eleʿazar Goliath.

Ele'azar Goliath probably was a son of Shelamsiyon and Yeho'ezer son of Ele'azar (but see Misgav 1997: 128–130).

The same name Yeho'ezer 'Akaby'a inscribed on two small ossuaries (XVI and XXII) held the remains of young children. The name may have been reused after the death of one of the children. From the name Yeho'ezer and the placement of these two ossuaries in close proximity to the group of ossuaries in loculus 14, it may be concluded that the two children were probably grandchildren of Yeho'ezer and Shelamsiyon and the offspring of Yeho'ezer son of Yeho'ezer Goliath.

In conclusion, the information about the family relations obtained from the inscriptions, in conjunction with the anthropological data, can be summarized as follows (Figure VI–40). The tomb contained three generations of a family: the founders of the tomb, Yeho'ezer son of Ele'azar (possibly the first to be nicknamed Goliath, and Shelamsiyon, and their six sons. The six sons and their wives were buried here, as well as fourteen of their offspring. It is evident from this and other tombs that only the sons and their families were buried with their parents. Daughters of a family were considered members of their husbands' family on their marriage, and were probably buried in their husbands' family tomb (for women's status in the family see Chap. VII).

Was Goliath a Priestly Family?

Literary sources mention that a large community of priests resided in Jericho and served in the Temple in Jerusalem (see BT. Ta'an. 27a: "Twenty-four divisions of priests were in the Land of Israel and twelve of them were in Jericho" (Luria 1973: 13–16 on the priestly divisions, especially at Jericho; Schwartz 1988). Several factors indicate that the Goliath family may have been a priestly family:

(1) The tomb was an unusual monumental tomb in comparison with the other excavated tombs in the Jericho cemetery. The tomb contains two large chambers, including a spacious courtyard surrounded by benches and with an attached *miqveh* (ritual bath). While the courtyard may have been used by the community as a 'mourning house' (Chap. II; Hachlili and Killebrew 1983a: 112–113; Netzer 1999: 45–50) it may have formed part of the tomb as this was a priestly family which required its own purifying bath.

(2) The use of the same name Yeho'ezer for three consecutive generations was a custom current mainly among prominent Jewish

families, especially the priestly oligarchy (Grintz 1960: 340; Rahmani 1961: 107, n. 12; Hachlili 1984b: 192–194).

(3) Most of the names of the family members are relatively common in this period; furthermore they occur frequently among priests (Stern 1961: 21, n. 119, where he suggests that the name Ele'azar was used mainly by priests; Hachlili 1984b: 194–195).

XXIII. *Jericho, Family 'from Jerusalem'*

Jericho tomb D1 consists of remains of a chamber with three loculi and a standing pit (Hachlili 1978; 1999: 12–14, 155–158, Fig. II.24). The south side had collapsed completely (Figure VI–41). Three ossuaries were found in the tomb; ossuary 18, with bones of a woman, was found in a small loculus. The other two are inscribed ossuaries (nos. 19 and 20, Hachlili 1999: 97, 100; Fig. III.43, III.55, VIII.2) and were found *in situ*, one placed on top of the other in loculus 2, together with an inscribed pottery bowl.

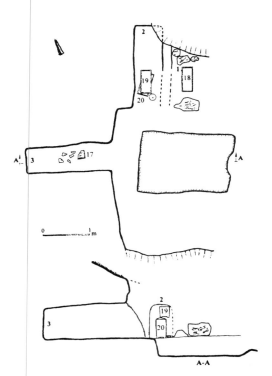

Figure VI–41. Jericho tomb D1, plan.

Two inscriptions were written on a bowl and two were carved, one on each of the two ossuaries (inscription 16, ossuary 19; inscription 17, ossuary 20; Hachlili 1978; 1999: 155–158, Figs. IV.16–19). The bowl, which rested on debris close to the corner of ossuary 19, may have been originally placed on top of ossuary 20 and later fell onto the debris.

Pelaty'a/Palṭ'a 'from Jerusalem'
↓
Shim'on/Simon 'from Jerusalem'
↓
Ishmael 'from Jerusalem'

All four inscriptions mention a three-generation family consisting of Ishmael son of Shim'on/Simon and his grandfather Pelaty'a/Palṭ'a and the fact that they are all 'from Jerusalem' (Figs. V–16, 17). The inscriptions also indicate that all three men were related and belonged to the same family. However, the relationship between them is evident only from main inscription 15a, the inner bowl inscription. This sets out the complete genealogy and origin of Ishmael, who had placed the bowl at the site of his father's and grandfather's ossuaries, all in one *kokh*.

These inscriptions suggest that this was the tomb of a family originally from Jerusalem, but whose members probably resided, died, and were buried in Jericho. It is unlikely that 'from Jerusalem' is an indication of the family's residence and that they had come to Jericho to be buried. The unique inscirbed bowl served as a memorial tracing the genealogy of the family and commemorating their origin 'from Jerusalem'. The bones of the two men, Palt'a and Shim'on, were found each in his own ossuary, but the bones of Ishmael, the third generation, were not found; he may have been buried in the collapsed southern part of the tomb.

Table VI–1: Family Tombs, Their Ossuaries and Inscriptions

Tomb No.	Provenance and Name of Tomb	No. of Oss.	Decorated Ossuaries	Plain Oss.	No. of Insc.	Male Insc.	Female Insc.
	Jerusalem						
I	Ḥallet et-Turi	30	7	23	15	13	2
II	Kidron Valley, Wadi el Ahmadieh	18	10	8	9	5	4

Table VI–1 (*cont.*)

Tomb No.	Provenance and Name of Tomb	No. of Oss.	Decorated Ossuaries	Plain Oss.	No. of Insc.	Male Insc.	Female Insc.
III	Kidron Valley	19	12	7	14	8	6
IV	'Monogramma tomb', Mt. of Olives, "Dominus Flevit"	12	–	11	12	8	4
V	'Agra' family tomb, Mt. of Olives, "Dominus Flevit"	24			11	7	4
VI	Mt. of Olives	13	2	11	8	6	2
VII	Mt. of Offence, (Bât'n el-Hawa)	30			19	7	6
VIII	'Nazirite' family, Mt. Scopus	14	11	4	3	2	1
IX	"Batshanite" family, Schneller	8			5	3	2
X	Talbiyeh	12	4	5	9	5	4
XI	Talpiyot	14	10	4	5	4	1
XII	'Bene Ḥezir', Kidron Valley				1	1	–
XIII	'Boethos' family, Mt. Scopus	23			4	3	1
XIV	'Caiaphas' Tomb, Talpiyot	12	6	6	7	3	2
XV	'Kallon' Family, Qatamon	6	1	5	6	4	2
XVI	'Eros' family, Akeldama	13	12	1	9	2	7
XVII	'Ariston' family, Akeldama	16	14	2	12	4	8
XVIII	Kidron Valley, 'Cyrenaica'	11		11	9	6	3
XIX	Mt. Olives				3	2	1
XX	'Nicanor' family, Mt. Scopus	7	4	3	1	1	–
XXI	Shu'afat (Arad el-Beida)	25			24	19	5
	Jericho						
XXII	'Goliath' tomb (Tomb H)	23	22	1	14	10	4
XXIII	Family 'from Jerusalem' (D1)	4	4	–	2	2	–

The description of the family tombs and Table VI–1 indicate that many of the ossuaries were decorated; in most cases only some of the ossuaries were inscribed with the names of family members, but see Tombs IV, XV, XXI were almost all the ossuaries had inscriptions. The Table also designates that male inscriptions acount for almost double the number of female inscriptions.

Other Jerusalem tombs with inscribed ossuaries were found; however, in most of these tombs only personal names of members of a family are recorded, though sometimes inscriptions of husband and wife or father and son are registered. Some examples: On a sarcophagus (No. 27) discovered in a Mt. Scopus tomb, the Greek inscription records a father and son with the same personal name and probably the wife of the son, all interred in the same sarcophagus (Kloner 1993: 100–101). In a tomb at Ramat Eshkol the names of husband and wife appear on their respected ossuaries (Tzaferis 1970: 29–30, Tomb IV, Nos. 12, 14; Rahmani 1994: Nos. 226, 227). One ossuary from French Hill is inscribed with two personal names probably refering to husband and wife (Rahmani 1994: No. 354). Among a group of ossuaries found in a tomb at Abu-Tor, four ossuaries were inscribed each with the name of husband, his wife, a father and his son (Spoer 1907: 356–357, Nos. 4, 5, 6, 7). In a tomb in East Talpiot inscriptions on two ossuaries (Nos. 2 and 4) record a father and son (Kloner 1997: 18).

The selected list of Jerusalem and Jericho tombs described above are all family tombs as indicated by: a) the loculi-tomb architecture demonstrates family relationships; b) the inscriptions reveal family relations and associations which are an important social element, as well as attesting to the occasional practice of near relatives buried together in the same ossuary; c) the recurring names in these families designating family relations were the same name occurs in several generations; d) The burial custom of *Ossilegium*, an intentional procedure of gathering the skeletal remains of the individual deceased by his or her close relatives into an ossuary, while retaining this burial within the family tomb (see Chap. XI).

Prominant individuals buried in Jerusalem and Jericho are identified from the archaeological record of tomb architecture (see the tombs of Bene Ḥezir, Nicanor, Helen of Adiabene), by sarcophagi, ossuary, and tomb inscriptions, as well as from ancient sources (see also Avni and Greenhut 1996: 35, note 7; Ilan 1991/2: 153, note 11).

The list records prominent deceased persons mentioned on funerary inscriptions and discussed in the family tombs:

- The Bene Ḥezir priestly family in the inscription from tomb XII are priests of the house of Hezir, the 17th priestly course serving in the Temple (I Chr. 24:15 and Neh. 10:21).
- 'Shim'on of (the family of) Boethos' inscribed on an ossuary from tomb XIII. Sukenik (1934: 67) links this tomb to the priestly family of Sim'on b. Boethos of Alexandria (Josephus, *Ant.* 15.320).
- Inscriptions on ossuaries found in tomb XV indicate that the interred family in this tomb belonged to a priestly family of the house of Yeshb'ab, the head of the 14th course of the Temple priests in the period of David (I Chr. 24:13), who were buried in this tomb and related their family pedigree (Stern 1976: 591).
- The inscription of 'Shelamziyon daughter of Gamla wife of Yeho'ezer son of Kallon' who belongs to the Kallon family, (tomb XV), is identified as sister of Yehushu'a son of Gamla the High Priest in the reign of Agrippa II (Josephus, *War* 20,213; Schwabe 1956: 366).
- Caiaphas the High Priest is known from an inscription on an ossuary from a tomb XVI.
- 'Ariston of Apamea' from Akeldama, inscribed on an ossuary in tomb XVII, may possibly be identified with the person noted in the Mishna (*Halla* 4:11) who bears gifts to the Jerusalem Temple from abroad.
- 'Alexander son of Simon Qarnit', tomb XVIII, might be identified with Alexander son of Simon of Cyrene mentioned in the New Testament.
- 'Nicanor of Alexandria', who donated the gates of the Temple, is inscribed on an ossuary found in tomb XXI.
- Theodotos/Nathel 'the freedman of Agrippina' inscribed on an ossuary from tomb XXII (Jericho) was probably a prominent individual as a freedman of the royal family who aquired the Roman citizenship.

Other inscriptions which cite prominent persons are:

- The front of a sarcophagus from the tomb of Queen Helene of Adiabene was inscribed in Aramaic and Syriac 'Sadan (or Saran) Malkta' who is identified as Queen Helene (Josepus, *Ant* 20. 95;

Lidzbarski 1898: 117; Avigad 1956: 341; Fitzmyer and Harrington 1978: No. 132).

- 'Mattathias son of Judah' recorded on the Abba inscription (see below) was identified by some scholars with Mattathias Antigonus, the last Hasmonean king (Rosenthal 1973: 72–81; Grintz 1974), but the identification is refuted.
- 'Yehoḥanah daughter of Yehoḥanan son of Theophilus the high priest' is known from an inscription on an ossuary (See Chap. V), Barag and Flusser 1986: 39; Rahmani 1994: No. 871).
- 'Menaḥem of the sons of Yachim the priest' inscribed on an ossuary belonged to a priestly family of the house of Yachin, the head of the 21st course of the Temple priests (I Chr. 24:17) who were buried in a tomb on The Mount of Olives (See Chap. V; Bagatti & Milik 1958: 89–92, ossuary 83, inscription No. 22, Pl. 81).
- The name [Bi]lgah was inscribed on the corner of the north wall of a tomb near Gophna, probably referring to a priestly family of the house of Bilgah, the head of the 10th course of the Temple priests (I Chr. 24:17) (See Chap. V; Sukenik 1933–4: 7–9; Ilan 1995: 73, note 60).

B. Family Tombs and Relations, Discussion

The tomb plans and inscription data shed light on family types and the period's social life. Those interred in these family tombs apparently constituted extended families of parents, sons, and their families (Saller and Shaw 1984: 124–145; Shaw 1984; 1991; 1996; Meyer 1990). The inscriptions evidently designate an act of commemoration, indicating the social relationship between the deceased and the commemorator; in particular, family members seem to have been the ones who engraved the inscriptions, implying affection, love, and a sense of duty, as well as the aspiration to preserve some memory of oneself after death. These include commemoration of the elderly, of children, and of members of the nuclear family generally. The relation within the family is disclosed in the funerary commemoration of wife by husband, of husband by wife, of children by parents, and of parents and sometimes siblings by children. Men are more frequently the commemorators, although women had various ritualistic roles in funerary rites. A study of Christian inscriptions from the City of Rome designated that the proportion of males and females commemorating inscriptions is almost equal, however, this is peculiar to Christians and characteristic through the whole population (Shaw 1996: 107). The prevailing impression from the data is the centrality of the family as the fundamental social unit, with the father-mother-children triad as the main focus of family duty.

Burial in a family tomb as well as the importance of individual burial is evident in Jewish burial practices of the late Second Temple period . This is represented in the plan of the loculi tomb, which provides for individual burial of coffins, or ossuaries in loculi, and at the same time allows family members to be buried in the same tomb. This is noticeably attested by the inscriptions found on tombs, sarcophagi, and ossuaries. The perception of individual burial for the entire population and not just for the upper classes, as in the Israelite period, is probably related to the increasing importance placed on the individual in contemporary Hellenistic society as a whole (Kurtz and Boardman 1971: 273) and to the Jewish belief in the individual resurrection of the body. The concept of individual resurrection is reflected in sources as early as the second century BCE (Dan. 12:2; 2 Macc. 7:9–23; 12:38–45; 14:46; Jos. *Against Apion* II, 218; Finkelstein 1940: 145–159; Rahmani 1961: 117–118, n. 6: 1978: 102–103; 1981 I; 1982, III). The importance of the family, combined with that of the individual in his family and society, is evident in the Jewish funerary practices of the period.

Location of the ossuaries in the tomb

The location of ossuaries, as well as the inscriptions, verifies the notion that the loculi tombs are family tombs. Ossuaries of family members were placed in a group, close togather in the same loculus or chamber in several tombs; for example, in the Kallon family tomb (No. XV) all six ossuaries were located on the benchs of Chamber C (Fig. VI–23); in the Goliath family tomb (No. XXII) four ossuaries of the core family members were positioned in Chamber B, loculus 14 (Fig. VI–36, also see above).

The location of the ossuaries in the tomb indicates that some tombs had a special place hewn for the repository of ossuaries; some tombs show signs of disturbance in antiquity, revealing that the ossuaries were taken out of the loculi and placed in some other location; other tombs have ossuaries scattered in various locations.

- In some of the above listed tombs ossuary chambers were found: see above, tombs II, IV, VI, VII, XI, XVI, XIX, XVIII. At times, special chambers were apparently hewn for the purpose of storing ossuaries (Zissu & Kloner 2000: 107). Some examples of repositories for ossuaries are found in Jerusalem: in a tomb on the western slope of Mount Scopus, fourteen of the twenty-four ossuaries were stored in tightly sealed chambers, nos. 13–15, and a pit, no. 16 (Vitto 2001: 98, Plan 1). Another tomb at Neveh Ya'aqov had a repository chamber for ossuaries; it contained five ossuaries placed on a wide shelf (Vitto 2001: 114, Plan 6).

- Several chambers, loculi, and arcosolia were at later stages used as ossuary storerooms. For example, in a Dominus Flevit tomb (nos. 427–438) a chamber (437) served as a storeroom for 22 ossuaries (Bagatti and Milik 1958: 18–19, Fig. 8). At Mount Scopus Observatory, Tomb C, chamber CV had eight ossuaries placed on the benches (Weksler-Bdolah 1998: 28–9). In Giv'at Shapira tomb I, eight ossuaries were placed in *kokh* E, which apparently had been made into an ossuary storage room (Gershoni & Zissu 1997: 45–6). In Mount Scopus tomb I, chamber C, three arcosolia functioned as an ossuary storage in the last stage. Twelve ossuaries were placed first on the arcosolia with their decorated sides outward, and later on the floor. In Mount Scopus tomb II, chamber E was used to store 20 ossuaries (Kloner 1993: 80, 84).

- A number of tombs contain scattered ossuaries in various locations in no particular order (see tombs nos. I, III, X, XII, XIII, XV, XXI).

- Tombs with both an ossuary repository and scattered ossuaries in various locations (tombs V, XVIII).

- Several tombs seem to have been disturbed in antiquity, as indicated by the removal of the ossuaries at some stage from their original places in the loculi (see tombs IX, XIV, XVII, XXII).

- Some arcosolia were also used as ossuary depositories as they were not fit for primary burial (Kloner 1980a: 234–5). In Mount Scopus tomb, Chamber C with three arcosolia (Kloner 1993: 80–81) contained seven ossuaries and a sarcophagus (used for bone collecting).

Family relationship

About half the inscriptions refer to the name of the deceased and his family relationship, usually mentioning the father (Rahmani 1994: 15–16). Patronymics unaccompanied by the deceased's personal name

are rare. In a few inscriptions a grandfather is cited. In Jericho
inscription 7b a grandmother is referred to (Hachlili 1999: 153). In
some inscriptions of women their name is accompanied by the name
of their husband, hence the relationship is stated. In other inscriptions the name of the woman's father follows or precedes that of
the husband. On some the name of the wife is omitted (see below).

The majority of of the inscriptions found in the family tombs
record a three generation family (see Tombs III, V, VII, X, XII,
XIII, XXII, XXIII). Many reflect family relations by recurring names
in the same family (see Tombs I, III, XII, XVIII, XXII).

Most of the inscriptions refer to the father of the deceased (73
inscriptions listed in Rahmani's catalogue).

Patronymics unaccompanied by the deceased's personal name rarely
occur (see the Bethphage list, Chap. V; Benoit et al. 1961: No. 45,7;
Rahmani 1994: Nos. 75, 76, 464, 571; Masada ostraca, Hachlili
2002: 94; Beth She'arim, Schwabe and Lifshitz 1974: Nos. 89, 97;
see also Naveh 1990). A few inscriptions mention a grandfather; one
commemorates a woman (Rahmani 1994: Nos. 57, 198, 290, 327,
520, 871). The simple inscription אבא denotes father and not an
actual name, The words אבא 'father', or אבונו 'our father' and אמא
'mother', 'our mother, or mother Maryam', each inscribed on an
ossuary (Family Tombs III, X; Rahmani 1994: Nos. 12, 21, 344,
351, 561; inscription 21 at Akeldama, Ilan 1996: 67), were probably dedications engraved by their children (see tomb II and X above;
Rahmani 1994: Nos. 70, 334; Also Avigad 1961: 143). סבא, הזקן
might mean 'elder' (Family Tombs II, III). Likewise the Greek
ἀδελφός indicates either a brother or a name (Rahmani 1994: No.
135); אחוה (brother) is inscribed on an ossuary at Akeldama (Ilan
1996: 67, inscription 21). Sometimes a sibling relationship was indicated in addition to the patronymic, or implied by the inscriptions
'sons of X' (Rahmani 1994: Nos. 75, 76, 570, 584?). Two brothers
were interred in the same ossuary (Family Tombs II, XIX; Rahmani
1994: No. 560). A married couple were sometimes placed in a single ossuary, possibly also when the name of man is followed by that
of a woman even though the relationship is not explicitly stated
(Rahmani 1994: Nos. 150, 139, 354, 455). In a few cases the name
of wife and son were added to name of the head of the family
(Family Tombs II; Rahmani 1994: Nos. 354, 490); children were
interred with their mother (Family Tombs I, IV, XXII; Rahmani
1994: Nos. 73, 800, 868), or father (Ossuary 12 from a tomb on

the western slope of Mount Scopus, Rahmani 1994: No. 396; Vito 2000: 78, Fig. 29c; Ossuary 2 from a tomb on the eastern slope of Mount Scopus, Rahmani 1994: No. 469; Vito 2000: 105). Two brothers were interred in an ossuary, with the wife of one of them laid in a separate ossuary (Family Tomb XIX). Two brothers were interred each in a seperate ossuary (Sukenik 1925: 76, 78, Ossuaries 1, 12). A sibling relationship is implied by 'sons of N' (Family Tomb X; Rahmani 1994: Nos. 75,76). Relatives sometimes indicate a sibling relationship in addition to a patronymic (Rahmani 1994: No. 570) which is different from מן בנא, מבני which possibly indicate membership of a priestly clan (see the Kallon family, Tomb XV, Inscription 1).

In the Goliath family, a unique inscription records the mother of X without mentioning the name of her husband (Tomb XXII, Inscription 11; see also Chaps. V, and VII). In the Kallon family (Tomb XV) Shelamzyion is recorded as both daugther and wife.

When the name inscribed on the ossuary is of the deceased's son this might indicate the son buried the father (see below; Rahmani 1994: Nos. 12, 139, 370, 573; at Beth She'arim, Schwabe & Lifshitz 1994: 183:4–5; 219:8–9; and at Jaffa, Frey 1952: No. 927).

Although not many of the inscriptions on the tombs and ossuaries record dedications from family members, they still provide a memorial to the deceased, whilst also indicating the relationship within the immediate family:

Dedication to parents by children:
A son who interred a relative's remains

The practice of interment of relatives, primarily children interring their parents' remains, is revealed in several tomb and ossuaries inscriptions:

• On the ossuary from tomb IX three inscriptions were engraved, the third being unusual: יהוסף בר אנין עניה/אבא קבר 'Joseph, son of Hanin, the poor/father, his son buried him' (Rahmani 1994: No. 139; but see a different translation: 'the father buried his son', Fitzmyer and Harrington 1978: No. 145). Rahmani's interpretation is probably the right one, namely the ossuary was of the father Hanin חנין הבשני, mentioned in the other inscription, who was interred by his son Yehosef.

• The inscription on an ossuary from tomb III refers to 'our father, Shim'on the Elder, Yehosef his son' (Rahmani 1994: No. 12);

Yehosef undoubtedly figures on this ossuary as the son who interred his father's remains. Yehosef himself is probably interred in another ossuary inscribed with his name (Rahmani 1994: No. 22).

- On an ossuary from French Hill the inscriptions mention יהודה/יהודה 'Yehudah' and on the lid של אמו של ידן 'of (his) mother of Yudan'; the name may possibly refer to a son who interred the bones of his unnamed mother in this ossuary (Rahmani 1994: No. 370:4).

- On an ossuary from the tomb on the western slope of Mount Scopus, Jerusalem, the inscription reads: פינחס בר יוסף קבר אמה 'Pinhas son of Yosef buried his mother'. The bones in this ossuary were probably those of the unnamed mother of 'Pinhas son of Yosef'; the addition of his name to the inscription was probably meant to confirm that he had fulfilled his filial duty (Rahmani 1994: No. 573:3).

- The inscriptions אבא קבר 'father, his son buried him' and קבר אמה 'buried his mother' designates a son burying one of his parents; the addition of their name to the inscriptions means that they had fulfilled their filial duty (Rahmani 1994: 3, 16; Nos. 139, 573). The word קבר 'tomb' inscribed on these ossuaries was probably used in the sense of 'ossuary'.

The two following inscriptions record individuals whose relatives possibly died in the Diaspora (Babylon, Syria, or Mesopotamia). They re-interred their bones in tombs in Jerusalem. These are the only inscriptions dated to the Second Temple period mentioning the later custom of transferring bones to Jerusalem (Safrai 1974: 194; Gafni 1981; Puech 1982: 367–371). These inscriptions are different from those found in tomb groups XVI–XXI. Those are of families originating in the Diaspora who moved to Jerusalem where they live and were buried, and their inscribed ossuaries record their origin abroad.

- A unique Aramaic paleo-Hebrew inscription carved above a loculus entrance on a Givat ha-Mivtar tomb (Rosenthal 1973; Naveh 1973; Tzaferis 1974; Fitzmyer and Harrington 1978: No. 68) reads (Chap V, Pl. V–1): 'I, Abba, son of the priest Eleaz[ar], son of Aaron the elder, I Abba, the oppressed and the persecuted, who (was) born in Jerusalem and went into exile to Babylon, brought (back to Jerusalem) Matta-thi(ah), son of Jud[ah]; and I buried him in the cave which I had acquired by the writ.'

The inscription records a man named Abba, of priestly origin born in Jerusalem, who was persecuted and had to leave his home; later he returned to bury the bones of Mattat (Mattathiah? a relative?) in the tomb he had acquired.

- An Aramaic inscription engraved on an ossuary from a Mount of Olives tomb (dated to the late first century BCE or the first century CE; Allegretti 1982: 353–354):

יוסף בר אלעשה ארתכה איתי נרמיה די אמכא אמה לירושלם

'Joseph son of Elasa, a chariot [or a name, "Artakes"] brought the bones of his mother, 'Amma [or 'Amka], to Jerusalem' (Puech 1982: 355–372; 1983: 517, No. 26). Puech suggests that the inscription written in the Palmyrene and east Aramean script indicates that the interred hailed from North Syria or North Mesopotamia; Joseph brought his mother's bones for burial in the tomb in Jerusalem.

Josephus (*Ant.* 20. 92–96) relates a similar practice: Monobesos sent the bones of Helene of Adiabene and her son (his brother) Isates to Jerusalem to be buried in their tomb, probably in 65–66 CE. It is possible that the bones of Helene of Adiabene were interred in the plain sarcophagus, inscribed in Aramaic and Syriac 'Queen Zadda', which was discovered in her tomb.

Dedication to children by parents

- The relationship in the family is also indicated by the commemoration of the children, 'sons of El'azar', and wife, 'wife of El'azar' possibly by their father and husband, although he omitted their personal names (see above Tomb X).
- An ossuary recording 'The bones of the [sons or descendants?] of Nicanor the Alexandrian who made the doors' indicates that members of the family, possibly the parents, commemorated the sons (see tomb XX above).

Dedication of siblings

Commemoration of brothers and sisters is rare: on two ossuaries 'brother' is inscribed (Rahmani 1994: 15, Nos. 135, 570), and 'Mariah daughter of Yehohanan'; 'Maryam, my sister' is inscribed on an ossuary lid (Avigad 1961: 143) possibly indicates that the brother (or sister?) buried his sister. It is interesting to note that in the Kallon family two brothers and their sister are buried together in one ossuary (see tomb XV, Ossuary 1, Inscription 1).

Note that fathers are referred to usually as part of the personal name of the sons or daughters. Husbands are mentioned by the recording of their name on the wife's inscription, or when the inscription includes the names of both the husband and his wife. Conversely, women's inscriptions occasionally mention the father and or the husband.

Grandparents are rarely mentioned but some names include three generations. Six ossuaries from Jerusalem (Rahmani 1994: Nos. 57, 198, 290, 327, 520, 871) bearing the names of men and women record a grandfather too:

יהודה בר יהוחנן בר יתרא 'Yehuda, son of Yehoḥanan, son of Yitro;

יהוסף מרה בר בניה בר יהוד[ה 'Master Yehosef, son of Benaya, son of Yehud[a]'; אשוני בר שמעון בר אשוני 'Ashuni, son of Shim'on, son of 'Ashuni';

שפירה בת יהוחנן בן רביך 'Shappira, daughter of Yehoḥanan, son of Revikh';

מרתה בת יהוסף בן יעקב אתת יהוסף מנהין 'Martha, daughter of Yehosef, son of Ya'akov, wife of Yehosef, from Hin';

יהוחנה/יהוחנה ברת יהוחנן בר תפלוס הכהן הגדל 'Yehoḥana/Yehoḥana daughter of Yehoḥanan son of Theophlos, the high priest' (see above). Likewise an ossuary from Jericho Goliath tomb (Hachlili 1979: 33, 46–47, 57; 1999: Fig. IV.8, Jericho inscription 7b, see above) is inscribed מריה ברת נתאל שלמשן 'Maria daughter of Nathel [grandaughter of] Shelamsiyon'.

Family relations based on the information acquired from the family tombs can be summed up as follows. Family tombs containing ossuaries with inscriptions usually contain no more than three generations of a family, and even these are rare. Examples include the 'Kallon' family (tomb XV), three generations interred in ossuaries are found in several family tombs, for instance a tomb in the Kidron valley (tomb III), the 'Dositheus' family from Jerusalem (tomb X), and the Goliath family tomb from Jericho (tomb XXII); the Bene Ḥezir (tomb XII) is an example of a four-generation family tomb (see also tombs V, VII, XIII,). The unique inscirbed bowl found in a Jericho tomb traces the three generations of the family commemorating this family 'from Jerusalem' (tomb XXIII).

The information obtained from the records above attest to the great emphasis on the relationship between husband and wife and between parents and children (see also Shaw 1996: 109–110).

It is evident from the data that only the sons and their families were buried with their parents. Daughters of a family, upon marriage, were considered members of their husband's family and were most likely buried in their husband's family tomb.

Marks and emblems designating family rank

Several marks and emblems might have signified the family rank or profession of the deceased, or may allude to a personal characteristic (Rahmani 1994: 20):

- Priestly rank of the deceased may be indicated by an incised altar on an ossuary (Rahmani 1994: No. 41), or by representations of the menorah on ossuaries (from Jerusalem, Rahmani 1994: no. 815, 829, lid; from Jericho, Hachlili 1999: ossuary No. V, Fig. III.54f.).
- The occupation of the deceased's family might be intimated: incised scales on a child's ossuary might indicate a money-changer (Rahmani 1994: No. 3); a fish-shaped mark on an ossuary (Rahmani 1994: No. 348, fig. on p. 156) might indicate that the deceased was a fishmonger. An incised representation of a plow (Bagatti 1971: Fig. 102:3) may signify that the deceased was a smith or a farmer.
- The depiction of a large fig leaf and figs, and a fig tree as part of the ossuary decoration (Rahmani 1994: no. 742), might be a punning device representing a personal or family emblem alluding to the name חאנה 'fig' in Hebrew (see ossuary lid, Milik 1956/7: fig. 22, top left).

Conclusions

The tombs and the finds examined above reveal family tombs; the inscriptions portray relations among family members, the bond between them, the honor bestowed on elders in the family, children's commemoration of their father and sometimes their mother, and the status of women in the family. Also indicated are the position and rank of priestly families and prominent individuals; the origin of some families in other parts of the land but buried in Jerusalem.[2] The unique inscirbed bowl found in a Jericho tomb traces the genealogy and served as a memorial to this family 'from Jerusalem'. The Diaspora origin of some Jewish families that immigrated to the Land of Israel to live and were eventually buried in Jerusalem.Then there were the families of proselytes, converts to Judaism who went to live in Jerusalem; they seem to have had a special status as they noted the fact of their conversion on their inscriptions. The name Yehuda was apparently frequently adopted by a proselyte.

The family was the core of the social structure, and the surviving members of the family arranged and passed on the funerary rituals and ceremonies.

Family burial was conducted in a loving atmosphere; interment in a family tomb maintained the succession of the generations in a traditional society (Bar-Ilan 1994: 213–225). The children, the younger generation, were eager to continue the tradition, especially to fulfill their proper and ceremonial duties, adding memorial inscriptions to the interred, designating their status, their family relationship, and sometimes their occupation, title, and so on. They were obliged to protect their ancestors and family status, by guarding the site of the tomb and the position of those buried in the grave. The family tomb was considered a house and the necropolis as the city of the dead. The entire populace expressed respect and commitment to those resting places of the family.

It should be noted that the decorated ossuaries in the family tombs are different in their design, which indicates that the ossuaries were randomly collected or ordered from the workshops. They were probably chosen by family members according to their diverse tastes.

---

[2] Bar Ilan (1994: 221) contends that proselytes were buried in separate tombs. Regev (2002: 52–55) suggests that immigrants and proselytes did not use family tombs, but were buried together since they had only part of their family or no family at all; sometimes they were buried with a family of immigrants.

CHAPTER SEVEN

WOMEN

A. The status of women in the family

The status of women in the family from birth to death was one of dependence and subordination. Women were inferior to and dependent on men; a woman's standing in the society was through association with her father, brothers, or sons. An important fact to consider is that a woman's "marginality in society was marked at the start of her life by the absence of any rite of initiation into her tribe or religion" compared with the rite of circumcision for a boy (Archer 1990: 261).

Women's position in the family was insecure and weak. The father controlled his daughter until her majority (at age twelve years and a half); all that time she was a burden on him (Ben Sira 7.25). Her marriage, usually arranged by the father and future husband, resulted in her relocation to her husband's house, where she lived under his authority; she raised their children, and at last won respect in her role as a mother. A childless woman's position was fragile, although children could support their widowed mother (Archer 1990: 261).

Ancient Jewish funerary rituals and inscriptions reflect attitudes towards women as well as revealing their social position.

Women's status and family relationship as conveyed by inscriptions

The archaeological data add significant evidence regarding the burial of women. These data include funerary inscriptions (names and nicknames, family kinship and genealogies) as well as skeletal remains of the deceased.

Inscriptions sometimes mark women's burials, yet they might also be identified by anthropological data, or by personal belongings, such as cosmetic items (mirrors, needles, and spindle whorl), which are commonly suggested to indicate women's graves (see Table VII–1).

The inscriptions mentioning women's names and their family relationships are the best evidence of women's interment and burial. Occasionally they might attest to a woman's status and social standing.

The inscriptions from family tombs indicate that quite a number of women also had inscribed ossuaries; sometimes half of the inscriptions belong to women and at times even more (see Table VI–1). The inscriptions frequently mention the status of women, signifying the deceased woman as being a daughter, mother, or wife.

Several observations should be made:
- Some family inscriptions ignore women completely, for example, the four-generation genealogy list of the Bene Ḥezir priestly family.
- Only inscriptions about male indicate trade or profession.
- Marriage into priestly families was considered a great honor. Priests generally tended to marry daughters of other priests (Ilan 1995: 72–74).
- It seems that separation of men and women was often practiced in burial customs. The man and wife were buried each in his or her own ossuary placed in close proximity. Yet there are instances of burial in the same ossuary.

The ossuary catalogue (Rahmani 1994: 11, 14–15) lists 897 ossuaries, with 227 inscriptions; women's names appeared only in 96 inscriptions on 76 ossuaries. The inscriptions bear 153 women's names, compared with 513 men's names, about 23% of the total. However, the numbers are unbalanced as many of the women's names include the name of husband or children (Ilan 1996: 38). Nevertheless, some exceptions are noted in family tombs such as the Akeldama tombs, where more inscriptions of women were discovered. In other family tombs the ratio between men's and women's inscriptions is interesting; women's names, as well as men's, with a grandfather's name are rare (Rahmani 1994: male names, Nos. 57, 327, 520; for female names see below).

The most common practice of naming a woman was to denote her marital status; women are referred to as daughter, wife, or mother, the male equivalent of which was not acknowledged in the case of a man. This points to the subordinate position of a woman to that of her husband (Archer 1990: 267–8).

The following are some examples of inscriptions mentioning women's names and their family relationship (see Table V.1):

Personal name (or double name) (Figure VII–1):

מריה Mariya (Rahmani 1994: No. 706). Miriam מרים (Bagatti and Milik 1958: inscription No. 15); מרים יחנה Miriam, Yoḥana (Rahmani

1994: No. 31); מרחא Martha (Rahmani 1994: Nos. 220, 468);
Shelamziyon שלמצין (Bagatti and Milik 1958: inscription No. 17;
Rahmani 1994: No. 243) Shelamziyon שלמציון (Abel 1913: No. 8;
Frey 1952: No. 1223). Yoḥana, Yehoḥana יהוחנה, יוחנא (Rahmani
1994: 270).

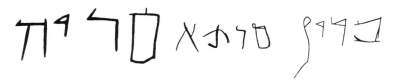

Figure VII–1. Women's personal name.

Personal name with nickname of status, title, or origin:
שלם הגיורת 'Shalom the proselyte' attests to the status of this woman
as a proselyte (Figure VII–5) (Bagatti and Milik 1958: 95, ossuary
97, inscription 31).

Μεγίστης ἱερίσης 'Megiste the priestess' is a Greek inscription carved
on an ossuary from Akeldama, Jerusalem. It probably records the
wife or daughter of a priest, and not a woman with a religious function or an official position (Ilan 1991/2: 157–159; 1996: 61–62).

Several inscriptions state the origin of women:
אמיה הבשנית in Greek Ἀμμία Σκυθοπολιτίσσα 'Ammia the Betshanite'
(from Beth She'an), 'Ammia the Scythopolitan' (Chap. VI, Tomb
IX). יוחנה שבאה Ιουλια ἀσιανή Ιουδι [θ], 'Yeḥonna from Sheba (?),
Julia, asiatic, Judith'. The name 'Yeḥonna from Sheba' probably
refers to her origin in Kush (Puech 1983: No. 32). Σάρα Σίμωνος/Πτυλε-
μαική 'Sara (daughter) of Simon of Ptolemais' inscribed on an ossuary
from the Kidron valley (Chap. VI, Tomb XVIII); 'Maria of Capua'
(Frey 1952: No. 1284).

Daughter (patronym)

In general the personal name of both women and men mention the
father.

• *X daughter of Y, woman's name followed by father's name*, is the most
common identification in inscriptions and documents. Some examples are as follows (Figure VII–2; Pl. VII–1):
ידית בת נדב 'Judith, daughter of Nadav' (Rahmani 1994: No. 572).
מריה ברת אגרה 'Mariah daughter of 'Agrah', probably a nickname

(Chap. VI, Tomb V). מרים ברת שמעון 'Miriam daughter of Shim'on' inscribed on an ossuary from Talpiot (Sukenik 1947: 17, Figs 20, 21). מרים ברת שמעון 'Miriam daughter of Shim'on' inscribed on an ossuary from The Caiaphas Tomb (Chap. VI, Tomb XIV). חלהא מרים ברת שמעון 'the ossuary of Miriam daughter of Shim'on' (Rahmani 1994: No. 502). מרחא ברת חניה 'Martha, daughter of Hananya' (Sukenik 1936: 92–3; Rahmani 1994: No. 67).

שלום ברת יהוחנן 'Shalom daughter of Yehohanan' (Sukenik 1932: No. 4; Frey 1952: No. 1245). שלום ברת עוי 'Shalom daughter of Awiy' (Bagatti and Milik 1958: inscription No. 19). שלון בת ליעזר 'Shalon daughter of Li'azar' (Chap. VI, Tomb III). שלמציון בת שמעון הכהן 'Shelamziyon daughter of Shim'on the Priest' (Clermont-Ganneau 1899: 394, Nos. 1–2; Frey 1952: No. 1317).

שלמציון ברת שמעון 'Shelamziyon daughter of Shim'on' (Mayer 1924: 59, No. 3). שלמציון בת תדיון 'Shelamziyon daughter of Thadion' (Sukenik 1930b: No. 4; Frey 1952: No. 1265). שלמציון בת ארסטון Σελαμψίν Αρίστωνος Shelamziyon daughter (of) Ariston From Akeldama, Jerusalem (Chap. VI, Tomb XVII). שלמצי בת שמי Shelamzi daughter of Shamai (Frey 1952: No. 1258).

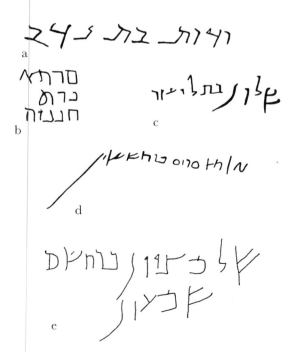

Figure VII-2. Examples of daugthers' names followed by father's name.

Archer (1990: 267–270) contends that women identified by their father' rather than their husband name were either divorced or widowed and had returned to their father's house. Ilan (1995: 55 and Note 35) is right in arguing that according to the great number of women known by their patronymics this is statistically improbable. It is also plausible that these women were unmarried and therefore were buried in their father's tomb, namely their family tomb.

• *Woman's name followed by father's and grandfather's names*: יהוחנה ברת יהוחנן בר תפלוס הכהן הנדול 'Yehoḥanah daughter of Yehoḥanan son of Theophilus the high priest' on an ossuary (Barag and Flusser 1986: 39; Rahmani 1994: No. 871).

מרים (יועזר, שמעון) בני יהזק בן קלון מבני ישבאב 'Miriam, Yeho'ezer (or Yo'ezer), and Shimeon, children of Yeḥzaq, son of Kallon, of the sons(?) of Yeshb'ab' (see Chap. VI, Tomb XV). שפירה בת יהוחנן בן רביך 'Shappira, daughter of Yehohanan, son of Revikh (?)' (Rahmani 1994: Nos. 198, above). Μάρθα Ιωση Μωαηρος 'Martha, daughter of Yose, daughter of Moaeros'; the last name is probably a Nabatean, Palmyrene, or Hatrean name (Puech 1983: No. 40).

• *Woman's name followed by father's and grandmother's names*: This inscription in which the grandmother is cited, is unique.

מריה ברית נתאל בת שלמשן 'Mariah, daughter of Nath[an]el, daughter of Shlamsion'. It is carved on ossuary XV from the Goliath Tomb in Jericho (see Chap. VI, Tomb XXII).

• *Woman's name followed or preceded by her father's name and accompanied by her husband's name* appears on several ossuary inscriptions from Jerusalem: שלמציון אתת יהועזר בר קלון ברת נמלא/שלמציון ברת נמלא 'Shelamziyon, daughter of Gamla (Gamliel?), wife of Yeho'ezer son of Kallon' (See Chap. VI, Tomb XV).: מרתא בר פפיס/אתת יהוסף 'Marta, son (!) of Pappias wife of Yehosef' is inscribed on an ossuary possibly from Jerusalem.

מרתה בת יהוסף בן יעקב אתת יהוסף מנחין 'Marta, daughter of Yehosef, son of Yaaqov, wife of Yehosef from Hin' appears on another ossuary (Figure VII–3c; Pl. VII–2). Three similar Greek inscriptions on the same ossuary from Silwan, Jerusalem record Δωτούς γυνή Πρωτάτος θυγάτηρ Τειμείωνος 'of Doso, wife of Protas, daughter of Timision' (Rahmani 1994: Nos. 236, 256, 290).

• *Daughter's name identifies the Father*: Χρήσιμος πατήρ Δημαρχ(ία)ς 'Chersimos' is identified as 'the father of his daughter Demarchias' (Bagatti and Milik 1958: No. 41). This is a unique occurrence; Ilan (1995: 55–56) maintains that it might indicate that the mourners were more familiar with the daughter than with the father.

Wife

• *X wife of Y: woman's name followed by that of her husband's*, sometimes with the addition of a nickname, stating family name, or origin (Figure VII–3):

אלישבע אתת טרפון 'Elisheva wife of Tarfon' (Pl. VII–3); מרים אתת יחקיה 'Miriam wife of Yeḥkiah/Yehiskiah' (Spoer 1907: Nos. 3–4; Frey 1952: Nos. 1338, 1341). מרים אשת מתיה 'Miriam wife of Matya' (Rahmani 1994: No. 559).

Μαράμη γυ(νή) ʼΙούδου 'Mariame, wife of Judah' carved on ossuary I from the Goliath Tomb in Jericho (Chap. VI, Tomb XXII). Μαρία Ἀλεξάνδρου γυνή ἀπό Καπούης 'Maria, wife of Alexander of Capua' from a Tomb on the Mount of Olives (Chap. VI, Tomb XIX).

שלום אשת/יהודה 'Shalom wife of Elʿazar'; שלום אשת אלעזר and שלום אתת/יהודה 'Shalom wife of Yehuda' (Chap. VI, Tomb III). שלום אנתת חנניה בר הנזיר 'Shalom wife of Ḥanania son of the Nazirite' from the Nazirite family burial-vault on Mount Scopus (Chap. VI, Tomb VIII). שלום אתת שפיר 'Shalom wife of Shappir' (Bagatti and Milik 1958: inscription No. 38). שפירא אנתת שמעון 'Shapira wife of Shimon' (Sukenik 1931: 19; Frey 1952: No. 1384).

מרים אתת העגל 'Maryam, wife of the calf', or 'the paunchy'; this name of a wife, followed only by her husband nickname, which might be derogatory (Rahmani 1994: No. 821).

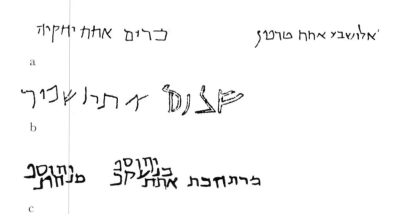

Figure VII–3 Examples of names followed by 'wife of . . .'

• *Woman's name 'X wife of Y' followed by the names of her children*: Σαλώμη γυνή Ἰωέζρου Γολιάθου/καί Ἰσμάηλος υἱός καί/Ἰωέζρος υἱός 'Salome wife of Yo'ezer, son of Goliath, and Ishmael (her) son and Yo'ezer (her) son', this inscription is carved on ossuary XIX from the Goliath Tomb in Jericho (Chap. VI, Tomb XXII).

• *Name of a woman following the name of a man*: this might indicate man and wife although their relation is not distinctly recorded. הנניה מרתא 'Ḥananya' and 'Martha' inscribed on an ossuary are probably husband and wife (Puech 1983: 515, No. 20; Rahmani 1994: No. 354); Παπίας καί Σαλωμιχ/Σκυθοπολεῖται 'Papias and Salomich/the Scythopolitans' were buried in the same ossuary (Chap. VI, Tomb IX).

לא סכל אנש למעלה ולא אלעזר ושפירה 'Nobody has abolished his entering, not even Ele'azar and Shappira' (Naveh 1980; Rahmani 1994: No. 455).

• *Name of woman, a man and son*: Inscriptions engraved on a lid of a large ossuary (sarcophagus?) mention a man, his wife, and his son of the same name: Φασαήλου, καί Εἰφιγενείας, Φασαήλου υἱού 'of Phasael, and of Iphigenia, of Phasael his son'. The same hand incised the name of the woman and son. The bones of the wife and son seemingly were added to the father's receptacle at a later date (Kloner 1993: 101, No. 27; Rahmani 1994: No. 490).

• *No personal name of woman, only her relationship as a wife*: a man's name accompanied only by 'wife' is inscribed on several ossuaries: 'wife of El'azar' אנתת אלעזר (Sukenik 1928: 119, ossuary 5; Rahmani 1994: No. 74). 'El'azar and his wife' אלעזר ואשתו (Frey 1952: No. 1247). 'Shim'on and (his) wife' שמעון ואתת (Rahmani 1994: No. 150).

Mother

• *Woman's personal name* (sometimes full name 'X daughter of Y') *followed by 'mother of N'* (Figure VII–4; Pl. VII–5):
אמה ברת הנניא אמה זי/סוכיא Imma, daughter of Ḥananya, mother of the Sokhite, inscribed on an ossuary (Naveh 1979: 21–23; 1994: 139, No. 257).

של אמן של ידן 'of (his) mother of Yudan' on an ossuary from French Hill, Jerusalem. Ἀλέξας Μάρα μήτηρ/Ἰούδας Σίμων υἱός αὐτης 'Alexa Mara, mother of Judas Simon, her son' (Figure VII–4b), on another ossuary from Jerusalem (Rahmani 1994: 15, Nos. 257, 370, 868). Σαβατίς/μήτηρ Δάμωνος 'Sabatis mother of Damon', is inscribed

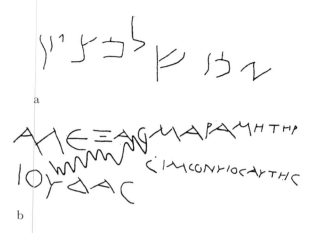

a

b

Figure VII–4 Examples of Names followed by Mother

on an ossuary from a Kidron Valley tomb, Jerusalem (Avigad 1962: 2; Rahmani 1994: No. 98). The Aramaic and Greek inscriptions שלומשיון אמה די יהועזר גלית Σελαμσιοῦς μητρός Ἰωέζρου Γολιάθου 'Shelamsiyon, mother of Yehoʿezer Goliath', are carved on ossuary XX from the Goliath Tomb in Jericho (Chap. VI, Tomb XXII).

• *Name preceded by 'mother', or followed by 'our mother'*: 'Mother Miriam' אמה מרים (Rahmani 1994: No. 351). 'Shelamziyon our mother' אמא שלמציון, שלמציון אמנה (Figure VII–4a; on front and lid of ossuary 2; Chap. VI, Tomb X). 'Martha our mother' מרתא אמנו (Chap. VI, Tomb V).

The simple inscription אמא, denoting 'mother' and not an actual name, is found on an ossuary from the Kidron Valley (Chap. VI, Tomb III). Μητέρα 'mother' inscribed on an ossuary (Frey 1952: No. 1376).

• *Women's name followed by unnamed 'her son' or 'her children'*: סרה וברתה 'Sara and her daughter' (Abel 1913: No. 11; Frey 1952: No. 1222). שלום ובנה (Bagatti and Milik 1958: No. 8). שלם/ומתיה ברה, אתת מתיה וברה 'Shalom and Matya her son' (on front and lid of ossuary 4; see Chap. VI, Tomb X). שלמנה ו[בת]ה 'Shelomna and her daughter' on Ossuary B13 from Jebel Hallet et-Turi, Jerusalem (Chap VI, Tomb I; Milik 1956–57: 240–241, Inscription 2, Fig. 5). The crude inscription on an ossuary, probably from Jerusalem, Ποπέλι/Ἰωσῆς/Ἰησοῦς 'Popili (a), Joses, Jesus', records a mother Popilia, and her two infants Joses and Jesus who were interred in the same ossuary

(Rahmani 1994: No. 56). On an ossuary found in a Ramat Rachel tomb the inscription reads: Μαρύλλας των παιδιων 'Marylla and her small children' (Kochavi 1963: 72, Fig. 29). Salome and her children Yehoezer and Ishmael are mentioned in an ossuary inscription from the Goliath Tomb in Jericho (Chap. VI, Tomb XXII).

• *Daughter's name followed by mother's name* (matronym): Σαλων Σαφιρα 'Salon (daughter of) Shappira' (Puech 1983: No. 30); these might possibly be two names of the same woman; or perhaps Shappira was a nickname meaning in Hebrew 'the beautiful'.

Women's names including 'daughter of' are similar to men's names men with 'son of'.

Marital status is given, or emphasized significantly, by the insertion of 'Wife of', while the status 'husband of' does not appear.

'Mother' is more common than 'father' (Rahmani 1994: 12) though it appears also with men's names, for example, Abba, 'father' or a name, on a plain ossuary from Ramat Eshkol (Rahmani 1994: No. 334). יהוד אבון 'Yehud, our father', is inscribed on an ossuary from French Hill (Rahmani 1994: No. 561). Πατήρ 'father', is found on ossuaries from Ramat Eshkol and Sanhedriya (Rahmani 1994: Nos. 567, 751).

Names of endearment such as 'Ammia' or אמא 'Imma' = meaning mother, and 'Pappias' which derives from baby talk (*Lallnamen*) were sometimes added to a person's first name (Rahmani 1994: 14, Nos. 21, 51, 139, 256, 257). Also, at Beth She'arim, 'Tate' in Greek is found (Schwabe and Lifshitz 1974: No. 128).

Inscriptions on the Jerusalem and Jericho ossuaries attest that only sons' families were buried with their parents. Daughters on their marriage were considered members of their husbands' family, and were accordingly buried in their husbands' family tomb.

Women's Status in the family

The status of two women Shelamsiyon and Mariah, indicated in ossuary inscriptions from the Goliath family tomb in Jericho, are of special interest. One inscription reveals the prominent status in this family of Shelamsiyon, the wife of the tomb's founder. Her inscription (Hachlili 1999: Inscription 11a–c) refers to her as the mother of Yeho'ezer Goliath and does not mention her husband, contrary to the custom in funerary inscriptions of women. Mariah's inscription

(Hachlili 1999: Inscription 7b) relates that she was the daughter of Natanel and the granddaughter of Shelamsiyon (but see Rahmani 1994a: 242). These unusual inscriptions can perhaps be explained as follows. From the anthropological examination, Yeho'ezer son of Ele'azar died at the young age of approximately 35 years, while his wife, Shelamsiyon, died at the age of approximately 60. This may explain her important status in the family: having outlived her husband by many years she was responsible for raising the family. Therefore it is her name that appears in the inscriptions of other family members instead of her husband's name.

Mariah's inscription attests that she was the third generation to be interred. Examination of her remains showed that she died at age 40. Her father, the manumitted Theodotos/ Nath[an]el, is inscribed, as is, uniquely, citing of her grandmother Shelamsiyon.

The interment of Mariah in her father's and grandmother's family tomb (instead of in her husband's family tomb as was customary) evidently means that she was unmarried (*Sem.* 14, 5–7; Rubin 1977: 228, 1994: 258), a widow with no children, or a divorcee who returned to her father's house and was then buried in her father's family tomb. Archer (1990: 268–270) suggests that a woman on the death of her husband was forced (by his heirs) or chose (*Sem.* 4.3) to return to her father's house and was then buried in the family tomb and inscribed by her original name 'X daughter of Y'.

Several inscriptions mention the special status of women who came from prominent priestly families, which in fact demonstrates that it was important to cite the rank. Apparently descent from (or marriage into) priestly families was considered a great honor. Two examples stand out.

'Yehohanah daughter of Yehohanan son of Theophilus the high priest' (Barag and Flusser 1986: 39; Rahmani 1994: No. 871). Mariam, Yeho'ezer (or Yo'ezer), and Shim'on, children of Yehzaq, son of Kallon, of the sons(?) of Yeshb'ab". This inscription records a three generation family, and priestly descent: they belong to the family of Yeshb'ab, the 14th course of the Temple priests (I Chr. 24:13). Priests generally tended to marry daughters of other priests (Ilan 1995: 72–74).

Women proselytes

The conversion to Judaism of women and men was common, but only a few were known by name or nickname (Ilan 1995: 211–214).

Women primarily converted for the purpose of marriage, which affected their status in the Jewish community. The most famous convert in the Second Temple period was Queen Helene, who together with her two sons Izates and Monobazus arrived in Jerusalem from Adiabene around the year 46 (*Ant.* 20.51; Shiffman 1987: 293–312). Only two women proslytes are mentioned on funerary inscriptions: מריה הגיורת הדולקת 'Mariah the proselytes the one who lights' or 'from Dolek' or 'of Dolichene' or 'from Delos', inscribed on a stone fragment, either of an ossuary or a sarcophagus (Frey 1952: No. 1390 suggests she might have been the one who lit for Jews on the Shabath; Bagatti and Milik 1958: 95).

שלם הגיורת 'Shalom the proselyte', inscribed on an ossuary (Figure VII–5) from Dominus Flevit, Jerusalem (Bagatti & Milik 1975: 84, 89, 95; Inscriptions Nos. 13, 21, 31).

Figure VII–5. Inscription of 'Shalom the Proselyte' from the Mount of Olives.

The inscription data demonstrate that the most common practice was to list women as daughter or wife (seldom as mother), depending on their status and on the circumstances of their death. The husband and children were responsible for the funeral and burial of women, including widows and divorcees.

A woman was buried with the husband's name even if she died a widow. Her marital status (which was not stated in the case of a man) as wife or mother reinstated the male lineage of the family.

B. BURIAL OF WOMEN AND CHILDREN

Women dying in childbirth

Several funerary inscriptions and data preserve specific examples of information on Women who might have died in childbirth. An inscription on an ossuary from Giv'at Hamivtar in Jerusalem records (Figure VII–6):

חלת שלום ברת שאול/די דשבדת שלום ברתה 'The ossuary of Shalom, daughter of Saul, who died from difficulties in child-bearing', or 'who failed to give birth' (Figure VII–6). (Naveh 1970: 36–7; Rahmani 1994: No. 226; Ilan 1995: 117); but see Fitzmyer and Harrington (1978: No. 88) who read, 'who hoped for (?) Salome her daughter.' The ossuary contained the bones of a woman with those of her fetus in her pelvis (Hass 1970: 48).

Figure VII–6. Inscription from Giv'at Hamivtar.

As noted, Naveh interprets דשבדת by as 'she had difficulties in child-bearing' or 'she failed to give birth'. The fact that the ossuary contained the woman's bones with those of her infant still in her birth canal indicates that she indeed died in the last stages of her pregnancy. Mother and daughter apparently had the same name.

Another funerary inscription from Byblos in Phoenicia is Ζαλομη ἡ ἐτ(ε)κεν Αρτήρ (Frey 1952: No. 874; Ilan 1995: 118, notes 56–61). As the inscription mentions the names of the woman and of her children, it possibly indicates a woman who died in childbirth. Although the date is unknown the inscription probably suits the Second Temple period.

In Jericho a wooden coffin (no. 59 found in tomb D9) contained the remains of a female with a fetus at her feet, accompanied by a small wooden bowl and a large bronze ring fragment (Hachlili 1999: 18). It seems that the woman died while giving birth.

Individual burial of women and children

Evidence for the individual burial of women and children is found in Jerusalem, Jericho, and 'En Gedi. It is proven by anthropological data as well as by inscriptions.

The numbers of identified individuals interred in Jerusalem tombs according to the anthropological data published (many of the skeletal remains were destroyed or are unpublished; for the published data, see Appendix and Anthropology Tables) show that nearly the same number of females and males were buried in many Jerusalem and Jericho tombs. Zias (2000: 250) contends that in a regular Second Temple period Jewish cemetery 50% of the skeletons will be sub-adults, not sexed, and the rest will be male and female.

In Jericho, women and sometimes children were interred in their own individual coffins or ossuaries. Other data indicate several cases in which women were interred with their children in the same coffin or ossuary (see Appendix and Anthropological Tables; Hachlili & Killebrew 1999: 192–195).

In one instance discovered in Jericho a woman and a child were buried each in an individual wooden coffin. One of the two coffins (Nos. 104a and 104b, in tomb D12) placed in the same loculus contained the primary burial of an adult female with fragments of leather and a sandal placed next to her. The second smaller coffin contained the remains of a child, three or four years old. At the child's feet was a glass amphoriskos and two wooden vessels (Hachlili 1999: 22, 24, Fig. II.43).

Eight women were interred in ossuaries in the Goliath tomb (Ossuaries VI, VII, X, XV, XX); three of them were buried with their children in the same ossuary (ossuaries I, XVII, XIX). The inscriptions (1, 7, 10, 11) identify four of the women, one as a mother and two as wives.

Twelve children were found interred in ossuaries (no identification of sex by anthropology, only age): three were buried with their mothers (ossuaries I and XIX with two children). Two groups of three children each were buried in one ossuary, one group in small ossuary IX with no inscription; three children were interred in large ossuary II bearing inscription 2. Each of the two children had his own small ossuary and is identified by the inscriptions (ossuaries XVI, XXII, inscriptions 8 and 13). Five of the children are identified as males by their inscriptions. In this tomb were interred twelve men, of whom six are identified by inscriptions.

At 'En Gedi some coffins contain only a child (tomb 1, coffins 1, 5; tomb 4, coffin 1; tomb 5, coffin 3); several contains a women and a child (tomb 1, coffin 2; tomb 3, coffin 3; tomb 4, coffin 3; tomb 5, coffins 4, 11; Hadas 1994).

At times children were buried in their own individual ossuary with their own inscription, as described above. However, several other inscriptions relate different situations:

Children without names, only with the name of their father, are recorded in ossuary inscriptions from a Jerusalem tomb (Chap. VI, Tomb X): 'sons of El'azar' (on the front and lid of ossuary 6), and 'sons of Hanan' (on the front of ossuary 7).

An ossuary has three inscriptions in Greek script. One reads 'Joseph and Eliezer the twins', citing the children with mother or father unnamed. However, the other two inscriptions might be of the father and the mother (Chap. VI, tomb II, ossuary 4).

The number of identified women buried in Jerusalem, Jericho and 'En Gedi tombs is only slightly lower than that of the identified number of men, while child mortality seems greater (see Anthropological Tables 1–5).

Women and the Cemetery of Qumran

A small number of Qumran tombs were excavated with finds of a large number of men in the main cemetery while a small number of women and children were found only in the extensions and secondary cemeteries. The facts are controversial: some scholars argue that the finds attest to the celibate character of the Qumran community (de Vaux 1973: 45–47; see Hachlili 1993: 251, and bibliography in note 9; Golb 1994: 58); others maintain that women were buried in all of the Qumran cemetery sectors (Taylor 1999: 309; Zangenberg 2000: 73–75; on the subject of women at Qumran in literary works, see Elder 1994, Schuller 1994, Magness 2002a: 163–187; 2002b). In Taylor's catalogue (1999: 305, 307–310, Tables 1–40; see also Magness 2002a: 172–173) the evidence (from de Vaux's excavations) shows that in the western side of the large cemetery, three females were interred in tombs T7, T22 and T24 (with a male), oriented N/S; another six – were in tombs T32–T37 in the southeastern sector, oriented E/W. However, Zias (2000: 230, 247) considers these to be Islamic burials.[1] Taylor (1999: 292–296; 319–321)

---

[1] The suspect evidence from 11 graves from the excavation by Stekoll (1966–7) four females were interred in tombs 6–8, 11, oriented N/S; In the northern cemetery two graves had one female and one male, in the southern cemetery the four graves had one female.

challenges the belief in the marginality of women in the Qumran community, based on the finds in the cemetery and the texts of the DSS. She suggests that the gendered finds such as one spindle whorl and some bronze items from T24 (but see Magness 2002a: 177–8), as well as the careful reanalysis of skeletons from Qumran and DSS study, might indicate women's presence in the communities of Qumran. Taylor (1999: 323) explains the high number of males buried in the western sector of the main cemetery as a result of a massacre (a fact that is unproven, Hachlili 2000b: 666–667). It is apparent that women were present in Qumran, but in a minimal number (at the most three females in the main cemetery – T22, T24a, TA) compared with the number of males (see Anthropological Table 6; also Magness 2002a: 178–9, 182–185; 2002b: 93–95); women and children were found in graves in the south cemetery, and Zias might be right in suggesting that the burials in the Southern and extension cemeteries are Bedouins. But see Zangenberg (2000: 74–75) who argues that on the basis of the original and current research that 16 females and 26 males individuals are identified in Qumran, which is quite common sex ratio.

'Gendered' finds from the Qumran settlement which might indicate burial of women consist of only one spindle whorl and four beads; three beads and fragments of a wooden comb were discovered in the Qumran scroll caves (Taylor 1999: 318–319; Magness 2002b: 97–102). In comparing the 'gendered' finds from Qumran with those found at Masada and the Judean Desert Caves Magness (2002b: 108) concluded that the archaeological evidence presented verifies "only minimal female presence at Qumran".

Nevertheless, it is important to consider that the anthropological facts, the form of the shaft tombs and burial practices indicate that the Qumran cemetery did not include families (Hachlili 2000b: 666), which might also reflect on the settlement.

C. Burial Rites Involving Women

The participation and role of women in funeral and mourning rituals is discussed in literary sources. Studies tried to examine the difference gender made in funerary and mourning rituals as well as inspecting if a woman's death repeated or restated her social status in life (Archer 1990: 264). Sources indicate that burial of and mourning over women were conducted in the same way as for men (T MK 20b; Sem. 4.1–2). Sons and daughters mourned father and mother equally, above other relatives (Sem. 9.3f.; JT MK 3.8, 83d; MK. 22ab). Men and women joined those accompanying the funeral procession (Safrai 1976: 778; Archer 1990: 264, also Humphreys 1980: 99–100).

Considerable differentiation in rituals of the funeral and mourning were practiced according to gender, as evinced from literary sources (Archer 1990: 271–275) and summarized below.

In the case of a deceased male the bier was laid on the ground and eulogies and memorial addresses were delivered over the body. The bier of a woman, by contrast, was not set down on public ground out of respect or for reasons of uncleanness (M Nidd. 10.4; MK 3.8; MK 27b). A eulogy was probably not spoken for a woman. Public officials accompanied only the cortège of a man (Sem. 11.2; Safrai 1976: 778). The duties of a husband at his wife's death included the arranging for the funeral, her burial place, and two flute players and one wailing woman for the funeral procession (M Ket. 4.4). Funerary eulogies and memorial addresses mentioned in the Talmud focus on men and are considered a very public affair. They were not suitable for a woman's lifestyle, consisting usually of domestic isolation. However, in some cases a husband eulogized his wife (Sem. 14.7) or in others praises were sung not for her but for the qualities of her male relatives (Sem. 3.5). Archer (1990: 278–280) contends, "Women's work and deeds were not individuated or regarded as having an equal merit to the activities of men in the public arena . . . women at death remained in a sense marginalized from the concerns of the larger community. It is important to note that the woman, in death as in life, was regarded as a source of special uncleanness" (see also Sem. 11.1).

The funeral rituals were preferably performed by the sons, not daughters (4 Maccabees 16.6–11). However, the help of women in some burial rituals was required (Ohol. 3.9), chiefly "as it did not matter if they incurred the corpse uncleanness, as they were not obliged to participate in the feasts. Women were not under religious obligation to attend the 'house of mourning' but were allowed to attend funerals" (Archer 1990: 278–280).

Women, both relatives of the deceased and paid professional keeners (*mekonenot*), were present at funerals, usually engaging in general, public, and vocal lamentation for the dead, which was an expected and integral part of the proceedings. They performed the graveside ritual of keening (Archer 1983: 281–283; Safrai 1976: 778–779), in addition to which their grief was displayed in beating the chest, hand clasping, and chanting dirges (*kinot*). This kind of lamentation stood out from other burial rituals in its loudness and emotionality. Some of it was perhaps intended to drive away spirits, a task better performed by women who were usually associated with superstitious magic and other popular practices. It was suitable for women to take on the role of keening as it was not a religious obligation and they did not represent the community or any official act.

D. Women's graves marked by personal belongings

Grave goods of a personal and gendered type were usually associated more commonly buried with women than with men. They commonly consist of cosmetic items, the spindle whorl, and jewelry (Ilan 1995: 185; Taylor 1999: 318–319; Magness 2002: 97–8). Typically they might signify a woman's grave (Hachlili & Killebrew 1983: 116, 121). The spindle whorl found in some of the burials is a reminder of the description of the virtuous woman in Prov. 30:19: she "layeth her hands to the distaff and spindle". The presumed connection of cosmetic items with women's burials is confirmed by some of the finds in the Jerusalem, Jericho, and 'En Gedi tombs and ossuaries. Several tombs contain women interred with such objects (Figure VII–7; Table VII–1):

In a tomb on Mount Scopus in Jerusalem (tomb 1–21) an ossuary (no. 17) contained bones of a woman and a kohl stick (Kloner 1980: 160–161, Fig. 30:1).

Jason's Tomb in Jerusalem contained items belonging to women such as four round bronze mirrors (Pl. VII–4), a spindle whorl, a spindle hook, a cotton hairnet, and an iron key.

Rahmani (1967: 76, 91, 93, 96) suggests that these items possibly belonged to a woman, as attested by the depiction of wealthy ladies' tomb-monuments as an indication of status (Hairnets discovered at Masada are described as a typical garment among women (Sheffer and Granger-Taylor 1994: 220).

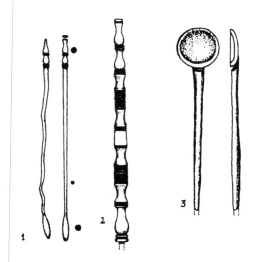

Figure VII–7. Personal Belongings of Women from Jerusalem Tombs.

In a tomb on Ruppin Road in Jerusalem were found a bronze kohl stick, a round bronze mirror, a bone needle, and some pottery, which the excavator took to indicate a woman's burial place (Rahmani 1961: 110, Pl. XVII:2). French Hill Tomb 6 (Tomb 29–15 contained a burial of a skeleton with a mirror, a kohl stick, and two beads (an ossuary rested on the upper part of this burial); it is suggested that the skeleton was probably female (Strange 1975: 40).

A glass bottle was found in the ossuary inscribed 'Shalom the proselyte' from the Mount of Olives, Jerusalem (Bagatti and Milik 1958: 95, ossuary 97, inscription 31).

Coffin 78, discovered in the pit of tomb D12 in Jericho, contained the primary burial of a woman and a child. Several objects (Figure VII–8) were placed inside the coffin next to the woman's head. They included a bronze decorated kohl stick found with a bead at its end, a bone spatula, a basalt weight, leather fragments in the shape of flowers (buttons?), a leather string, and two iron nails (Hachlili 1999: 22, 139, Figs. III.79, 82, 85, 86:3, 89).

A decorated glass amphoriskos was found in a child coffin next to a woman's coffin in Tomb D12 in Jericho (Pl. VII–5) (Hachlili 1999: 22–24, Fig. II.43).

Wooden coffins discovered at 'En Gedi containing women, men, and children sometimes included personal belongings such as beads and

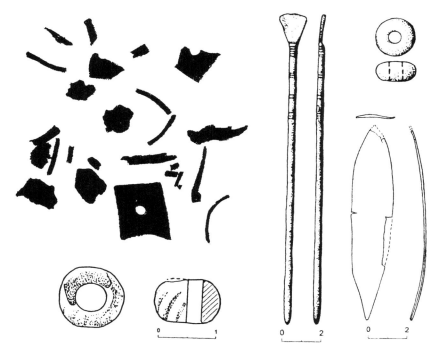

Figure VII–8. Personal belongings of a woman and a child from Jericho, Coffin 78.

various wooden vessels and objects (Figure VII–9) (see Table X–6; Hadas 1994: 4–5, Figs. 14, 15: tomb 1, coffins 1, 2, 6, 7, 8).

In the center of tomb 6 at ʿEn Gedi several cosmetic vessels were discovered, including wooden bowls, a wooden comb, a hair-pin, and beads (Figure VII–9); these items probably were placed originally inside a basket or a mat of a woman buried without a coffin (Hadas 1994: 34, Fig. 61). However, coffin 4 (tomb 1) contained the bones of a man and a child together with a wooden bowl, the lid of a box, a comb, many beads, and fragments of leather shoes and of textiles (Hadas 1994: 4–5, Figs. 14, 15). Inside coffin 15 (tomb 5) were the remains of a man, and a wooden kohl tube and a bronze kohl stick (Hadas 1994: 32, color Pl. 8). Beads were found in several coffins in Tomb 1 and 6 made of glass and stones (Hadas 1994: 11, Figs. 15:27; 56, 7*).

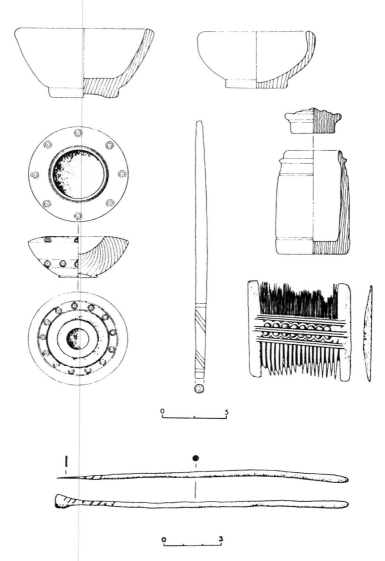

Figure VII-9. Personal Belongings of Women from 'En Gedi, Tomb 6.

Table VII–1: 'Gendered' Grave Goods in tombs, possibly related to Women

Tomb	Reference	Spindle whorl	bracelet	Beads pendants	Ring	mirror	Kohl stick	spatula	Spoon comb	needle pin	Spin hook	key	Misc
Jerusalem													
1–15	Vitto 2000: 91 Kloner & Zissu 2003				copper								Fibula Plaque copper
*1–21	Kloner & Zissu 2003						bronze						
1–35, 36	Kloner & Zissu 2003					1							
1–39	Sussnan 1992: 95 Kloner & Zissu 2003				1 iron + gem								
2–16	Rahmani 1980; Kloner & Zissu 2003				1 iron + glass bezel								
2–42	Edelshtein & Zias 2000; Tomb C Kloner & Zissu 2003	1 glass		Bone beads									
3–24	Kloner & Zissu 2003							1					
3–28	Kloner & Zissu 2003			+ iron bronze									
12–5	Kloner & Gat 1982; Kloner & Zissu 2003						1 bronze						
12–44	Kloner & Zissu 2003						bronze						
13–9	Stekelis 1935 Kloner & Zissu 2003							1 bone					

Table VII-1 *(cont.)*

Tomb	Reference	Spindle whorl	bracelet	Beads pendants	Ring	mirror	Kohl stick	spatula	Spoon comb	needle pin	Spin hook	key	Misc
13–33	Bilig 1995 Kloner & Zissu 2003	1 bone		+					2				
19–4	Sukenik 1930a Kloner & Zissu 2003	1	2 silver	+		1				1 bone pin			
19–13	Kloner & Zissu 2003		metal frag.										
21–1	Sussman 1982 Kloner & Zissu 2003							1 bronze					
*21–18?	Rahmani 1961: 110–114; Kloner & Zissu 2003					1	1				bone needle		
23–3 **Jason Tomb**	Rahmani 1967; Kloner & Zissu 2003	1	2 glass		3 rings	4 bronze					1	1	Hair-net
*25–6	Rahmani 1961: 104; Kloner & Zissu 2003	1 hematite											
25–13	Rahmani 1961: 104; Kloner & Zissu 2003			pendant									
26–9	Kloner & Zissu 2003							1 bone	1 bone				
28–4	Kloner & Zissu 2003				1 bronze								
28–7	Kloner 1981; Kloner & Zissu 2003							1 bone					

		beads	bracelet/bone			iron	wooden/other
29–15	Strange 1975: Tomb 6; Kloner & Zissu 2003	2 beads		1	1		Wooden bowl
30–22	Kloner & Zissu 2003		Bone bracelet				
30–23	Wolff 1996; Kloner & Zissu 2003					1 iron	

Jericho

*Coffin 59, D9	Hachlili 1999: 16, 18	1 bronze				Wooden bowl
*Coffin 78, D12	Hachlili 1999: 22	1 faience 1 glass	1	1		Glass
*Coffins 104a, b, Tomb D12	Hachlili 1999: 22, 24 (child & woman coffins)					Wooden bowls, leather

'En Gedi

		beads	bronze	wood	
Tomb 1	Hadas 1994: 4–11	129 beads	bronze	wood	wooden tube
Tomb 6	Hadas 1994: 36–40; 3*–5*	88 beads	bronze	wood	wooden bowl
					wooden tube, pin

* items found with woman's bones.

As stated at the beginning of this section, the gendered items found
in the tombs and considered to be related to women include the
spindle whorl, cosmetic objects such as mirror, kohl stick, spatula,
needle, spoon, and comb. and various articles of jewelry: bracelet,
beads, pendant, ring (Table VII–1).

Spinning was regarded as a typical women's activity; the spindle
whorl, used for spinning wool, was a small stone, glass, or clay disc
with a hole pierced through the center into which a wooden stick
was inserted. The spindle whorl (*pika* in Rabbinic Hebrew) served
as the flywheel of the tool. It generally preserved well and has been
found in many of the tombs and sites all over the ancient world
(Peskowitz 1997a: 164–165, 1997b: 112–115; Reich 2001: 149–150).
Some of the spindle whorls were placed with interred women; others
were placed with interred of unclear sex. Peskowitz (1997a: 167–9)
maintains that spindle whorls were tools used by women as spinning
was an occupation exclusive to women in ancient Judea. The spindle and the loom symbolized the essence of womanhood. At times
the spindle "was used to commemorate and compliment women . . .
these spindles buried with the dead can be said to represent ancient
women and/or to represent familiar figures used to represent ancient
women".

In several Jerusalem tombs spindle whorls were discovered (Table
VII–1); a Haematite whorl found in Sanhedriya tomb 6 had been
placed beside a women. Rahmani (1961: 104, Pl. XIII; 7, left) suggests that it may have been buried with the women for reasons of
"intense grief" or perhaps to show that the deceased was a virtuous woman, who, in accordance with the depiction, "layeth her hands
to the spindle" (Prov. 30,19). Whorls were found in several tombs
(Jason's Tomb, Rahmani 1967: 90, Pl. 23C; Sukenik 1930: 124, Pl.
III,6; Zizzu 1995: Tomb 13–33, Bilig 1995: 70–71). A fragment of
a spinning hook was discovered in Jason's Tomb (Rahmani 1967:
91, n. 89) (Compare the large number of 384 spindle whorls of various materials found at Masada [Reich 2001]).

Cosmetic items found in the tombs consist of kohl stick, spatula,
mirror, needle, spoon, and comb. The kohl stick and spatula were
used to prepare cosmetics, creams, or kohl by braying it as well as
being utilized to spread cream and apply paint to the eyes. Kohl
sticks were discovered in several tombs (Table VII–1): in Mount
Scopus tomb 1–21 a kohl stick was buried with the bones of a
woman inside ossuary 17 (Kloner 1980: 160–161, Fig. 30:1). In tomb

21–18, *kokh* 1, a bronze kohl stick was found, with a round bronze mirror and a bone needle and some pottery, indicating a woman's burial (Rahmani 1961: 110, Pl. XVII:2). A bone kohl stick and spoon were found in a tomb in Ramat Eshkol (Kloner 1980: 161, Fig. 30:2, 3, Tomb 26–9). A bronze decorated kohl stick with a bead at its end was discovered inside coffin 78 in tomb D12 in Jericho with a primary burial of a woman and a child. The kohl stick was decorated with incised grooves and bands at the top (Hachlili 1999: 22, 139, Fig. III.82). A bronze kohl stick was found inside coffin 15 in tomb 5 at 'En Gedi with a male remains (Hadas 1994: 32, color Pl. 8).

Bronze mirrors discovered in several Jerusalem tombs are considered items associated with women. Some mirror were found (Table VII–1) in Jason's Tomb (Rahmani 1967: 91, Pl. 24C); a fragment of a bronze mirror, silver plated, was found in a tomb on Mount Scopus (Zissu 1995: 20, Tomb 1–36).

Jewelry, mainly single beads and a few rings, was discovered in tombs and coffins, which are also usually associated with women's burial (Table VII–1).

Summary and Conclusions

The family relation is indicated by the woman's name usually followed by the name of the father, which was customary with both men and women; however, only 'wife of' or 'mother' signifies the family status. Archer (1990: 266) maintains that the inferior or secondary status of women continued in death is supported by the archaeological data.

The inscription data convey the woman's relationship and status in the family by her connection to a male in the family: father, husband, or son. A woman as wife is cited as 'X wife of Y', where her name is followed by her husband's; or a woman's name 'X wife of Y' is followed by the names of her children. Other examples show the name of a woman following the name of a man; in one case the inscription included the name of woman, a man, and a son. Several dedications had no personal name for the woman, only her relationship as a wife.

The funerary data and inscriptions related to women designate that fewer names of women than of men appear; more women are unnamed. More men's than women's ossuaries have been discovered, meaning that more men than women had their names inscribed.[2]

It is possible that at times husband and wife were buried in the same ossuary but only the husband's name was carved (Ilan 1995: 47–48). Many ossuaries with inscription only list the woman's first name. The names consist of personal name, sometimes a name with nickname of status, title, or origin; in one case the mother and the daughter had the same name. However, in general the personal name of both women and men includes the father's name (patronym). Many women's names appear as 'X daughter of Y', that is, the woman's name followed by her father's. A few have the woman's name followed by the father's and grandfather's names; in one case the woman's name is followed by her father's and her grandmother's names. Several women's names are followed or preceded by the father's name and accompanied by the husband's name. In one instance the daughter's name identifies the father (see above).

The family relationship of a woman as mother is evinced by her personal name (sometimes in full) followed by 'mother of N'; in some cases a woman's name is preceded by 'mother' or is followed by 'our mother', or a woman's name is followed by 'her son' or 'her daughter', unnamed.

Many of the women's names on funerary inscriptions included their father's, husband's or son's name, thereby adding male names to the onomasticon. This is unique, since in Josephus and rabbinical sources the name alone is given alone (Ilan 1995: 47–48).

Apparently the woman is the one who continues the lineage of her husband and his family. Furthermore, when a woman is buried with her children, the inclusion of a son's name strengthens her motherhood and childbearing identity. The inscription of a woman who has given birth commemorates childbearing as a value in women's lives (Ilan 1995: 57–60, 111–121; Peleg 2002: 67–71). Inscriptions about males usually offer more social details such as origin, occupation, profession, and status.

---

[2] The number of Jewish women known by name from sources is 261, compared with about 2300 men's names, that is 11.3% of the total (Ilan 1995: 47–48, notes 8–11); tomb inscriptions yielded 487 male names and 152 female names (Ilan 1989: 189). Mayer (1987: 101–125) lists 769 Hebrew, Aramaic, Palmyrene, Greek, Latin, Egyptian women's names from Israel and the Diaspora, However all recent ossuary inscriptions are missing; the list includes names dating from the Second Temple period until the sixth century CE).

Evidence for the individual burial of women and children in Jerusalem, Jericho, and 'En Gedi is provided by anthropological data as well as by the inscriptions. Some inscriptions cite a women dying in childbirth; in Jericho a female with a fetus interred in a wooden coffin possibly indicates that the woman died in those circumstances.

In these tombs women and sometimes children were interred in their own individual coffins or ossuaries, while other examples show women interred with their children in the same coffin or ossuary.

Burial and mourning of women were conducted, according to our sources, in the same way as for men. Sons and daughters mourned both parents equally. Men and women accompanied the funeral procession.

Nevertheless, women, in death as in life, was regarded as a source of special uncleanness.

Some differentiation in funerary and mourning rituals existed according to gender. At the funeral the rituals were performed by sons rather than daughters. However, women did participate in funerary rituals and were present at funerals. They usually engaged in general, public, and vocal lamentation for the dead as an integral part of the funerals women were. These women were relatives of the deceased as well as paid professional keeners. Grief was also expressed by the women in hand clasping, beating the chest, and chanting dirges.

Grave goods of a personal and gendered type were more frequently buried with women than with men; the items usually consisted of cosmetic items, mirrors, spindle whorl, and needles. Typically they marked a woman's grave. Some simple grave goods, wooden or pottery vessels, accompanied the burial of children.

In conclusions, the situation of the woman in burial reflects the gender social order. She depended on men, and many of the inscriptions emphasize the significance of her marital status. The active role of a woman in funeral and mourning was mainly the graveside ritual of keening. Based on the anthropological data and the inscriptions it seems that women in death were treated in the same manner as men. The same burial rites were applied; they were interred in the same tomb, and in their individual receptacles, coffins or ossuaries, sometimes together with their child or children, or with their husband; many had inscriptions carved on their individual ossuary, though such recordings are less frequent than on men's ossuaries.

CHAPTER EIGHT

THE *NEFESH*

The *nefesh*, or funerary marker, consists of a monument, object, stone, stele, or building, and is known from Semitic funerary customs, both from inscriptions and monuments (Hachlili 1981). Among the Syrians and the Nabataeans, the *nefesh* was believed to be both a monument as well as the dwelling-place of the spirit after death (Gawlikowski 1970: 27ff. and 1972: 15). Literally, the word *nefesh* means 'soul', but in a funerary context it is the term applied to a form of funerary monument, the marker on a tomb, a stele or it might indicate the tomb itself, a funerary building or mausoleum (Jastrow 1926: 926, Sukenik 1945: 84–85; Avigad 1954: 66, 72; Rahmani 1994: 32; Park 2000: 152–157).

In Second Temple Period sources, grave markers and pyramid-capped obelisks are mentioned (I *Macc.* 13:27–29; *Ant.* 13, 211; 16, 182; 20, 95). In descriptions of the tombs of the Jewish nobility, the pyramid shape is also emphasized as the mark of a tomb, I *Macc.* 13.27–30 reads, ". . . Moreover he set up seven pyramids, one against another for his father and his mother and his four brethren . . ." The seven pyramids mentioned in this passage are equated with seven *nefesh* and probably took the form of obelisks (Horsfield 1938: 39, Pl. 67:2; Avigad 1954: 69; Gawlikowski 1972: 7–8). This would imply that *nefesh* and pyramid were synonymous (Avigad 1954: 69). An additional passage appears in Josephus's description of the tomb of Helene, Queen of Adiabene (*Ant.* 20, 95): "Monobazus sent her bones and those of his brother to Jerusalem with instructions that they should be buried in three pyramids . . ." These are identified with the Tomb of Helene, Queen of Adiabene (The 'Tomb of the Kings') in Jerusalem.

So far no inscribed tombstones have been found in a Jewish funerary context of the Second Temple period (Sukenik 1945: 84–86, fig. 2, Pl. 6:1, 6:2, where these tombstones date to the fourth century CE; Avigad 1954: 69). In later rabbinical literature, grave marking is mentioned (*Mishna, Shekalim* Ia; *Moed Katan* Ib; *JT, Moed Katan* Ib).

A. The Finds

The *nefesh* appears in Jewish funerary art of the Second Temple period as (a) a monument or (b) a decorative motif.

The nefesh *as a funerary architectural monument*

The *Nefesh* on Jerusalem Monumental tombs is characterized by a partly rock-hewn and partly built free-standing monument, above or next to the loculus tomb façade. The monument usually has a pyramid or tholus surmounting a cube-shaped base (Fig. II–3). Examples of this type are found in rock-cut tombs in the Kidron Valley, namely Zechariah's Tomb, the Bene Hezir tomb, and Absalom's tomb, as well as Jason's Tomb, Herod's Family Tomb, and a tomb near Herod's Tomb (Kloner & Zissu 2003: 14–2; see Figs. II–3, 7; Pls. II–4, 5). In the Tomb of Helene of Adiabene a three-dimensional fragmented stone was found measuring 84 cm. in height (Kon 1947: 80: fig. 25). Rahmani (1977: 50) explained the stone fragment as the upper part of a monumental pyramid. This is possibly an obelisk, comparable to the Nabateans 'Tomb of the Obelisks' (Horsfield 1938: 39, Pl. 67:2, note 7; Clarke 1938: 88–89, 102–104; McKenzie 1990: 156–7. See reconstruction of all three pyramids similarly to the pyramid on top of Absalom's tomb, Fig. II–7).[1]

The *nefesh* of the Zechariah and Bene Hezir Tombs as an architectural symbolic pyramid apparently followed the tradition of the pyramid as a tectonic expression to the deceased soul. The unusual combination of a tomb's portico (a colonnade, a distylus in antis) with a pyramid adjacent is unique to the Bene Hezir tomb, which has comparisons in the much earlier (15th–13th century BCE) Egyptian wall paintings in the Thebes necropolis (Avigad 1954: 76–7, figs. 29, 42; see also suggested reconstruction of the *nefesh* as a tower-like monument by Barag 2003: 88–89, Fig. 14).[2]

---

[1] At a tomb at Givʿat Shahin fragments of roof tiles and pottery pipes were found which suggest the remnants of some superstructure, perhaps a sort of *nefesh* (Rahmani 1958: 101: 1981: 49).

[2] Tomb 40b at Khirbet Fattir "has two small square arched openings at the southern wall, it was probably surmounted by a funerary monument (*nefesh*) of which only a large recess overlapping the façade remains" (Strus 2003: 93).

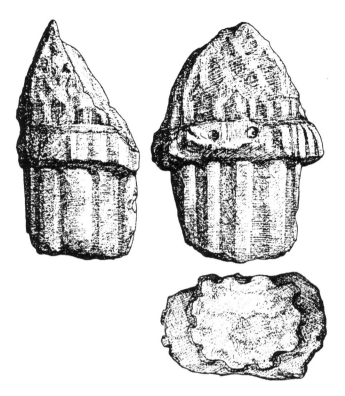

Figure VIII–1. The Jericho Stone *Nefesh*.

The stone *nefesh*: A three-faceted stone was found on the surface of Hill D at Jericho, out of its original context and in a damaged condition (Hachlili 1981: 34, Fig. 2; 1999: 162, Fig. VI.2). It consists of three parts. The lower section appears to be a fluted column. This is topped by a thicker, vertically fluted ring, which in turn is capped by a cone decorated with lozenge-shaped geometric forms (Figure VIII–1; Pl. VIII–1).

One especially interesting detail appears on the front of the thickened ring: a flattened portion containing two man-made holes might have served to attach a metal plaque bearing Ionic volutes. This stone was probably used as a grave marker in the cemetery.

In Jericho, on a wall drawing in a nine-loculus rock-cut tomb, F4, the *nefesh* appears as a decorative motif portrayed as a pyramid-capped column. The charcoal drawing was discovered in the northeast corner of the wall between loculi 3 and 4 (Hachlili 1981: 33–34, Fig. 1; 1999: 33, 162, Figs. II.62, VI.1).

Figure VIII–2. The Jericho Drawing of *Nefeshot*.

It depicts three columns and part of a fourth (Figure VIII–2), each column consisting of the following elements: a fluted shaft on a raised rectangular base, with an Ionic capital surmounted by a pyramid. One column and part of another have hatched filling, and the whole design is interspersed with various tree-like designs, Especially noteworthy is the palm tree design on the lower left portion of the drawing (for comparisons of palm trees appearing with a *nefesh*, see Dalman 1908: 245, abb. 185, tomb 402).

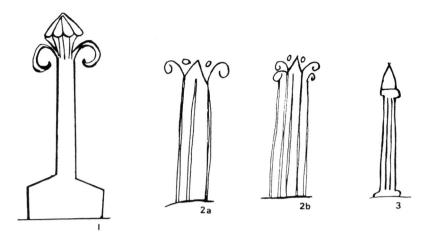

Figure VIII–3. Column-*Nefesh* carved on Ossuaries.

The *nefesh* as a pyramid-capped column is engraved on several ossuaries from Jerusalem and Jericho as part of their ornamentations. The motif of the nefesh as fluted columns topped by a pyramid below which two volutes are attached, inscribed on some ossuaries (Figure VIII–3; Pl. VIII–2).

On the front panel of an ossuary from Mount Scopus, a fluted column is incised, standing on a base with a pyramid or cone on its top (Pl. VIII–2a; Rahmani 1994: No. 122). Two columns topped by pyramids appear on the front panel and on the lid of ossuary from French Hill (Rahmani 1994: No. 599). Another ossuary from French Hill bears a depiction of a base supporting an unfluted column topped by a decorated cone. A volute is attached to each side of the column (Pl. VIII–2b; Rahmani 1994: No. 601).

On the lid of an ossuary from East Talpiyot, Jerusalem (Figure VIII–4), a *nefesh* is represented as a column-form monument (Rahmani 1994: No. 730: lid).

On an ossuary (possibly from Jerusalem) the *nefesh* is rendered in a similar form (Figure VIII–5); a fluted column set on four steps, topped by an ashlar-built pyramid which has a dot or an anchor-shaped ornament at the apex; spirals rise from each side of the base (Rahmani 1994: 133, Nos. 231:F, 231:L; Fig. 26). Similar pyramid-capped obelisks are known from the Tomb of the Obelisk, Petra (Pl. VIII–5; Horsfield 1938: Pl. 67,2; McKenzie 1990: 156–157, Pl. 122).

Figure VIII–4. *Nefesh* carved on an Ossuary lid.

Figure VIII–5. *Nefesh* carved on an Ossuary.

B. The Form of the *Nefesh*

The *nefesh* is represented in basic forms as a mark on a grave (Avigad 1954: 66; Mazar 1973: 198; Rahmani 1994: 31–32).

A rectangular, pyramid-capped monument

The Jewish tombs in the Kidron Valley, Jerusalem, are the best examples of this form of *nefesh*. They appear as a rectangular, pyramid-capped monument (Pl. II–1). Similar forms of *nefesh* decorate ossuaries, with the addition of a dome-capped column (Rahmani 1994: 31–32). The *nefesh* as a tomb monument in Jerusalem stood above (Jason's Tomb) or beside the tomb; set on steps (Tomb of Zechariah) or on a monolithic base (Tomb of Absalom, and the Tomb of the Obelisk at Petra; Rahmani 1994: 31–32).

The Tomb of Zechariah (Pl. II–2) is a free-standing monument with a small rock hewn chamber. It consists of a cube-shaped building surmounted by a pyramid. This monument was intended to be a memorial, a *nefesh*, either of the Benei Hezir tomb or of a nearby unfinished tomb.

The tomb of Absalom (Avigad 1954: Fig. 51; Pl. II–4) consists of a lower rock-hewn cube, an upper drum, and a cone built of ashlar stones. The lower cube is decorated with engaged Ionic columns bearing a Doric frieze and an Egyptian cornice. The drum and conical roof are crowned by a petalled flower. The upper built part is the *nefesh*, the monument, a type of tholus (Avigad 1954: Figs. 69–70). The two free-standing monuments of Zechariah and Absalom are examples combining a tomb and a *nefesh* memorial.

Above the Tomb of Bene Ḥezir (Avigad 1954: Fig. 25) a rock-cut platform has survived. It probably was the base for a similar *nefesh*, which the inscription on the façade of the tomb identifies. In the tomb of Queen Helene part of an obelisk was discovered which probably served as a similar *nefesh* (Kon 1947: 80, Fig. 25; see also parallels: Rahmani 1977b: 49–50; 1978: 107; 1981c: 47).

Similar depictions of a *nefesh* are inscribed or carved in relief on Nabataean tombs (Figure VIII–6) (Dalman 1908: figs. 145–48, 155–60, 184, 295–97, 313; Brunnow and Domaszewski 1904: 321, figs. 352, 353, 459–60; Browning 1982: Figs. 49, 52; McKenzie 1990: 87–92; Horsfield 1938: 39, Pl. 67:2, who suggests that the tomb of the obelisks resembles the description in I Macc. 13:27–30).

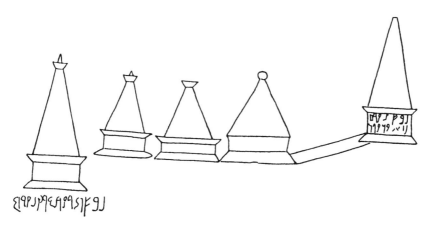

Figure VIII–6. Nabatean inscribed *Nefesh*.

The form of *nefesh* as a rectangular, pyramid-capped monument similar to the monuments of the Kidron Valley, is depicted on ossuaries. On an ossuary from Jerusalem (?) (Rahmani 1994: 133, figs. 26, No. 231:L) the *nefesh* is formed as a number of columns set on four steps, topped by a frieze, with an ashlar built pyramid which has an anchor-shaped ornament at the apex and spirals rising from each side of the base (Figure VIII–5). The spirals at the sides possibly represent metal ornaments. Such ornamentation was probably affixed to all four corners of the base of the pyramid on the Jerusalem Tomb of Zechariah, which was broken already in antiquity. The anchor at pyramid apex resembles those on Jewish coins (Meshorer 1967: Nos. 8, 11, 50–53, 56–57; Rahmani 1994: 31). These ornaments on the Jewish examples may have been used as a local replacement for the statues or sometimes vessels found on the base and apex of tomb monuments abroad (Gabelman 1973: Fig. 40:1–2; Rahmani 1994: 31).

A detached column, cone-formed, obelisk-shaped

A detached column is sometimes fluted and may stand on a base surmounted by cones or small pyramids (Figure VIII–2).

Both the three-faceted sculptured stone cone on top of a truncated column and the charcoal drawing from Jericho belong to this form of grave marker (See above). Comparisons between the Jericho stone grave marker and the charcoal drawing reveal that both incorporate fluted columns topped by decorated cones. The Ionic capital, which is seen in the drawing, appears on the stone marker as the two holes drilled to attach a metal plaque bearing Ionic volutes. Reconstructing the grave marker on the basis of the drawing would lead one to assume that the stone originally had a base.

Similar contemporary representations of a pyramid-capped nefesh are depicted on ossuaries (Figure VIII–3) (Rahmani 1994: 32–3, figs. 13, 28, 29; Ossuaries 122, 231:F, 231:L, 486(?), 599 Lid, 601).

A fluted column is incised, standing on a base with a pyramid or cone on its top (Pl. VIII–2a; Rahmani 1994: No. 122). Two columns topped by pyramids appear on the front panel and on the lid of an ossuary (Rahmani 1994: No. 599).

These representations include fluted columns topped by a pyramid below which two volutes appear to be attached (Figure VIII–4; Pl. VIII–3). A depiction of a base supporting an unfluted column topped by a decorated cone, with a volute attached to each side of the column, appears on another ossuary (Pl. VIII–2b; Rahmani 1994: No. 601). Another possibly unfluted column is inscribed on an ossuary (Rahmani 1994: No. 486). A curious form of a column-form monument, a *nefesh* (Figure VIII–4), is represented on the lid of an ossuary (Rahmani 1994: No. 730: lid, Fig. on p. 227, Pl. 104). Similar pyramid-capped obelisks are known from the Tomb of the Obelisk at Petra (Pl. VIII–5).

Some versions of the *nefesh* consist of hybrid forms (Figure VIII–7; Pl. VIII–4) appearing as a fluted column set on steps culled from the pyramid-capped *nefesh*; sometimes they have ashlar-built or decorated steps and are topped with a conch or various capitals of unusual design (Rahmani 1994: 33, 262; Figs. 31–35; Ossuaries Nos. 44, 78, 110, 445, 600, 746; fig. 33 = Avigad 1976a: 640 bottom left).

Note that an ossuary from Jerusalem displays a similar set of steps, which are surmounted by an amphora (Rahmani 1994: 34, Fig. 36, No. 325).

A simple detached column-formed tombstone or obelisk appears also on Nabataean and Palmyran tombs (Pl. VIII–5) (Avigad 1954, 69–70; Gawlikowski, 1970: 34, fig. 12).

A cubical construction surmounted by domes

Another form of *nefesh* is depicted on a group of ossuaries mainly from the Hebron Hills (?); the design consists of a pyramid-capped cube shaped *nefesh* entirely overlaid with reticulate pattern (Figure VIII–8).

The pyramid-capped *nefesh* is flanked by trees on one of the ossuaries from the Hebron hills (Rahmani 1994: 32, Fig. 27, Nos. 199, 465, 473, 555(?), 631, 814, 825F, 837:R). The ossuary renditions flanked by trees may represent the domed tombs typical of the Hebron Hills and foothills in which these ossuaries originated. In one ossuary (Rahmani 1994: 631R) the depiction derives from a dome probably resting on corbels, capping a cubic construction. One ossuary depiction may be based on aedicule-shaped *nefesh* or huts, which stood near a *nefesh* (Rahmani 1994: 555F and R). Another ossuary (Rahmani 1994: 445) seems to refer to tower tombs or similar monuments in Syria, dated to the Hellenistic period in the first century CE (Gawlikowski 1970: 16, n. 36). Another possibility is that it is a distorted representation of a Nabataean tomb façade.

Figure VIII-7. Variation of Column-*Nefesh*.

A graffito possibly of a *nefesh*, was inscribed on a small limestone found in one of the dwelling quarters at the Galilee city, Yodfat, and dated to the first century CE (Aviam 1999: 99–101). The graffito consists of a cubic construction capped by a gabled roof standing on three steps, flanked by two trees(?). Aviam suggests that it is possibly unique individual and authentic testimony to the siege and conquest of Yodfat, similar to a nefesh design carved on an early Roman tomb wall found in the survey of Aseqa.

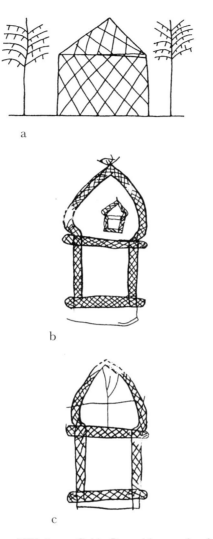

Figure VIII–8a–c. Cubic Pyramid-capped *nefesh*.

C. Discussion

The representations of the *nefesh* consist of two main types, all depicted in funerary contexts: as part of tomb structures or as a column-pyra-mid grave marker. These types have certain basic structural simi-larities: a rectangular base supports either an architectural monument or a fluted column topped by volutes and a cone, and all were found in funerary contexts.

Littmann (1914: xi–xii) and Gawlikowski (1972: 6) consider the erection of a *nefesh* and its use as a grave marker as a Nabataean custom, which was adopted by the Jews. Avigad (1954: 72–73) believes that the evidence in support of this view is insufficient.

The elaborate examples of the tomb structures consisting of architectural monuments, with similar monuments depicted in ossuary ornamention, appear in Nabataean, Palmyrene and Jewish funerary art (Avigad 1954: 71; Gawlikowski 1970: 22–30; 1972, 8ff.; McKenzie 1990).

Past research has emphasized the pyramid as the most important and necessary element of the *nefesh*. It is believed that this shape symbolized the dead man's soul according to local custom coming originally from Egypt, but continuing in use through the Hellenistic-Roman Period in the Eastern Mediterranean. At Soueida the remains of a first century BCE square structure with Doric columns and architrave surmounted by a stepped pyramid were discovered, with an inscription in Greek and Nabatean mentioning a *nefesh* (Brünnow and Domaszewski 1909, III:98; Avigad 1954: 67, Fig. 38). It means that this kind of solid structure is a *nefesh* (Figure VIII–6). In Nabatean art the obelisk and the shape of a pyramid became a symbol for the *nefesh* (Avigad 1954: 69). The Nabateans used a similar shape of a square base topped by pyramid or a cone (Figure VIII–9; Pls. VIII–5–7), engraved on the rock at Petra, sometimes with a Nabatean inscription mentioning a *nefesh* (Brünnow and Domaszewski 1904, I: No. 825, Fig. 459; Avigad 1954: 68, Fig. 39; McKenzie 1990: 140–143, 156–157, 159–161; Pls. 79, 122, 138).

These forms were apparently used by the Nabateans as a kind of schematic symbol and motif instead of a built architectural *nefesh* (Avigad 1954: 69). Another Nabatean *nefesh* consists of a stone-stele placed before a tomb with the inscription of the name of the deceased, sometimes with the addition of the term *nefesh* (Butler 1907: Fig. 186; For a detailed and comprehensive discussion of this subject see Avigad 1954: 66–78, 131–132; Gawlikowski 1970: 22–23).

Columns as grave markers are not unique to Jewish and other Semitic funerary art. Grave markers in the Graeco-Roman world usually had one or two functions: to mark the position of the grave or to commemorate the dead by a monument (Boardman and Kurtz 1971: 218–19; Toynbee 1971: 245). Columns were sometimes used

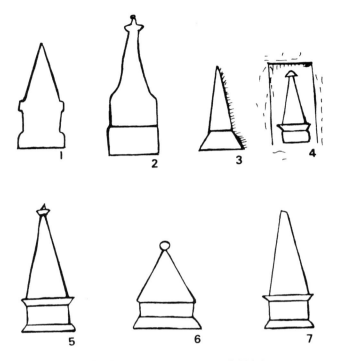

Figure VIII–9. Nabatean engraved *Nefesh*.

to mark graves in place of stelae. The name of the deceased was often inscribed on the base or capital of the column (Boardman and Kurtz 1971: 129). These columns usually supported a statue of a sphinx, a lion, or korai, or objects such as bases or tripods (Collignon 1911: 37–41, fig. 41; 97–98, fig. 49; Boardman and Kurtz 1971: 241, fig. 26, Pl. 29).

In the Hellenistic period the *columella* or *kioniskos* (= the small column) was used, as found in Attic cemeteries; these columns might have been topped by a garland or other form of decoration (Boardman and Kurtz 1971: 166–67, fig. 27A). Note that in the Roman period the funerary column (*cippus*) served as a stele, as in the Sidon examples (Figure VIII–10) with the inscription on the base and the garland on top (Contenau 1920: 49–51, fig. 14; 287–89, fig. 85). Similar *cippi* were found in Palmyra with an inscription mentioning a *nefesh* (Avigad 1954: 70).

The key importance of the pyramidal capital is underlined by Jewish sources, funerary art, and the finds. However, other essential

Figure VIII–10. Funerary columns (*cippi*) from Sidon.

elements are included in these *nefesh* forms: a fluted column, a base, and a capital with volutes. It is thus highly tempting to conclude that other combinations of these elements, such as the columns depicted on ossuaries are also grave markers. Some elaborate columns are depicted on ossuaries; they stand on some steps upon which is a fluted column topped with what seems to be a capital usually made up of two parts: the lower part is wider and is filled with geometric patterns. The capital ends in two volutes (Goodenough 1953, III: Figs. 160, 162, 165, 167, 170; II, 12; Bagatti and Milik 1958: Pl. 20:46, 49, p. 58. But see Rahmani 1968: 224; 1994: 33, where he sees these examples as representations of monuments or tholoi, such as Absalom's tomb; Rahmani 1977: 51–54). Monumental structures and the column appear also as designs on ossuaries imitating actual structures. Even though no column has been found in a funerary context, it is more than probable that they existed. But see Rahmani (1977: 54; 1994: 33–34) who strongly opposes to seeing these columns as a *nefesh*; he also refutes suggestions by Figueras (1983: 61–62) that there was a relation between the column motif and the much earlier Greek tomb stelae, where only the steps are a common feature.

It would seem that in the structural representations on ossuaries, and in the Jericho examples, elements exist which can be compared and referred to the same reality: a marker or a monument to the dead, that is, a *nefesh*. From these examples it is clear that the column as a grave marker was itself of little importance and served merely to support the statue or other object placed on it.

The Jericho *nefesh*, and some of the ossuary representations rendered as a column topped by a pyramid, may be compared to the Greek and Roman examples discussed above. The main difference lies in the object placed on top of the column: a pyramid instead of the statue or other object as in the Graeco-Roman world. The Jews, in adopting the symbolic *nefesh*/pyramid from the pagan world, probably discarded its original meaning (Avigad 1954: 76; Meyers 1971: 12–13; Gawlikowski 1972: 15). But combined with the column it came to be a uniquely Jewish grave marker. Due to prior lack of evidence, the Jewish *nefesh* was considered invariably to be a monumental structure. This has been shown from the archaeological evidence in Jerusalem and from written sources: Josephus (in Ag. Ap. II, 205, when writing about burial customs) speaks against the erection of a monument, or a *nefesh*. In rabbinical sources *nefesh* also means a tomb structure (see M Ohol., VII, I; T Ohol., X, 7–8 – 'a solid tomb structure'; Shek., 11, 5: 'from what was left over of the appropriation for funeral expenses we built a monument', and T Ohol., XVII, 4). But the finds from Jerusalem and Jericho enable us to conclude that the Jews, together with the surrounding cultures, recognized several forms of *nefesh*, and that besides monumental structures they also employed a free standing column, topped by a pyramid.

CHAPTER NINE

WORKSHOPS AND CRAFTSMEN

Several crafts were common and specific to Jerusalem, above all the art of working the stone utilizing local raw material available naturally. The architectural engraving and ornamentation of the tombs, stone sarcophagi, and ossuaries of the Second Temple period especially attest to the stone carving craft.

Stone quarry-based workshops of limestone, containing wasters of stone vessels, are reported in Jerusalem and environs (Mt. Scopus, the Abu Dis-Beth Sajur region and Hisma, Kloner 2003: 35*–37*) where some ossuary fragments were recovered (Gibson 1983: Fig. 1:14). Ossuaries, sarcophagi, and stone vessels were apparently produced at the quarry, though the finish and decoration might have been added in the workshops of the city (Magen 1978: 9–18; 1994: 245; Rahmani 1994: 3).

The local hard limestone used to produce ossuaries and sarcophagi was of three kinds: reddish (*mizzi ahmar*), grayish (*mizzi yahudi*), or whitish (*meleke*).

A. Ossuaries and Sarcophagi Production and Workshops

Ossuary Production

Hard limestone ossuaries fashioned from local stone and made by Jerusalem stonemasons (Rahmani 1994: 7) are relatively rare, possibly due to the degree of skill required for their manufacture, which consequently incurred high cost to the purchasers.

Several methods were employed to produce the relatively limited repertoire of motifs decorating the ossuaries and sarcophagi. The ossuaries were decorated by incision, relief carving, and chip-carving; the workmanship gradually deteriorated into poorly executed incised decoration, some of it done freehand. Contrary to Goodenough's opinion (1953: 120) it should not be considered that the work was by relatives of the deceased or had symbolic meaning (Rahmani 1994: 7–8). The incised ornamentation was marked by compass and ruler and then engraved, frequently in zigzag lines.

About a third of the decorated ossuaries are wholly or partly ornamented by chip-carving (Rahmani 1988; 1994: 7–8). This technique
was used by many cultures for the ornamentation of various materials such as clay, wood, stone, and metal. The tools for chip-carving
were a carving knife, a chisel, a gouge, and a string; a ruler was
used to sketch charcoal guidelines on the surface of the ossuary; a
compass to measure circles and curves; the burin incised straight
lines. The basic technique of chip-carving consisted of four cuts: the
furrow; the *almond* or *leaf*; the *triangular* and the *zigzag*.

Many of the ossuaries had a red or yellow wash covering their
surface; some were decorated with a red painted design. Copying
and imitation of ornamentation from hard limestone ossuaries to
other ossuaries occurred in a few cases (Rahmani 1994: 9).

A motif evolved when artisans borrowed motifs unaware of their
original meanings, or even imitated previous copies without reference to their origin. They chose and used motifs while mixing, reduc-
ing, and changing some or all of their elements (Rahmani 1982:
112; 1994: 9). An example is the amphora motif (Rahmani 1994:
34, Fig. 36–41; Nos. 120, 183, 213, 325, 378, 399, 815; Kloner
1998). It is possible that the amphora topped monuments in Jerusalem
Herod's family tomb (Schick 1892: 118, Fig. 11) and possibly Absalom's
Tomb (Avigad 1954: 114–117). Some tombs at Petra are also crowned
with an amphora (McKenzie 1990: 127–172). The amphora in the
Greek and Hellenistic world was also associated with a *loutrophoros*,
a vase related with rites of marriage and death; stone *loutrophoros*
appeared in funerary architecture as well as on relief decoration,
serving as a grave marker and later linked to a funerary urn for cremation (Kurtz and Boardman 1971: 111, 127–129, 152, 167, 241,
Fig. 21, Pl. 36). The amphora in Jewish funerary art and architecture has several renderings: simple and clear, ornamented, and stylized with incised zigzag lines (Rahmani 1994: 34, Figs. 36–41). It
probably began to appear on top of tombs and in the ornamentation of ossuaries after the amphora lost its original significance and
turned into a mere ornament; Kloner (1998: 52–3) suggests that the
amphora is used as signifying marking a tomb and a *nefesh*.

Other examples include the palm tree motif, which evolved into
a sword (see below group 2).

The tools used to prepare and decorated the stone ossuaries (Figure
IX–1) were a compass, the *circinus* (*pargol*, M Kelim 19.5) for circles

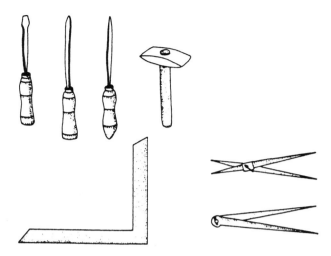

Figure IX–1. Tools used to produce Ossuaries.

and curved lines; the *linea*, probably the *kan* (M Kelim 12.8), namely a string, chalked or reddened, to mark straight lines; the *regula* for the same purpose but possibly also a ruler; the *kintra* (M Kelim 14.3) used for engraved lines. Tools used for chip-carving and deep cuts were the scalprum (perhaps the *ismel:* M Kelim 13.4), the *caelum* (possibly the *maphseleth*: M Kelim 13.4), a carving knife, a gouge with an angular or rounded edge, and a straightedge (Smith 1973, 1983; Rahmani 1982: 113; 1994: 7; Hachlili 1988a).

An example of the use of these tools in the decoration of ossuaries is the frame design of the ossuary. This was probably carved freehand, while the rosettes were laid by geometric means with a compass and a straightedge.

The inscriptions on ossuaries and sarcophagi were engraved with chisels or nails, or written in ink or charcoal. Some well-carved inscriptions were engraved outside the tomb, as they needed light, perhaps by 'professional' scribes prepared in advance in the workshop. However, the many careless inscriptions were possibly carved or written inside the tombs apparently by the deceased's relatives.

Sarcophagi Workshops

The sarcophagi were apparently produced in Jerusalem, in the same ossuary workshops or similar workshops probably in the Jerusalem area, as attested by the concentration of the purchases, and the finds of sarcophagi in the Jerusalem tombs.

The technique of sarcophagus manufacture followed several stages: rough hewing of the stone, relief carving decoration, and the exterior dressing.

Scholars incline to conclude that the same workshops produced all the sarcophagi in view of the similarities in decoration: Avigad (1971: 191) maintains that Sarcophagus 2 (from the Nazirite family tomb, No. 1) and Sarcophagus 4 (found in the of Herod family tomb) were undoubtedly produced at the same workshop, although the Nazirite exemplar shows the finer motif. This conclusion is based on the similar decoration of the sarcophagi front.

The lid of Sarcophagus 2 (from the Nazirite family tomb, No. 1) is similar to the decoration on the lid of Sarcophagus 12 (from the Mount of Olives).

The ornamentation on Sarcophagi 14 and 15 is quite similar, as is that on two comparable ossuaries found in tombs at 'Dominus Flevit' (Bagatti and Milik 1958: No. 26, 88, Pl. 19: Fots. 41–42, 44–45). Kloner (1993: 101) maintains that these sarcophagi might have been manufactured in the same Jerusalem workshop, purchased there, and probably placed in tombs on the area of the Mount Olives – and Mount Scopus. These sarcophagi are quite different in their ornamentation from the group of early Roman sarcophagi published by Smith (1973).

Evidence of local workshops lies in the ornamentation of ossuaries portraying similar or even identical elements (perhaps by the use of pattern books), in addition to some rare inscriptions.

B. Artists and Craftsmen

Ossuaries and sarcophagi were probably produced by two main groups of local stone workers (Rahmani 1982: 212): Stonemasons, who carved the tomb façades, hard stone sarcophagi, and ossuaries using mallet and chisel; stone carvers, who prepared all kind of stone vessels: cups, dishes, jars, boxes and table tops (Magen 1976; 1994; Avigad 1983: 165). Another possibility is itinerant craftsmen trained in a school or a workshop, who then traveled all over the country executing tomb decorations, sarcophagi, and ossuaries for various clients. Yet it seems more likely that the workshops were in Jerusalem and/or vicinity, on account of the availability of the local limestone material, the clientele on the spot, and the cemetery close by.

The craftsmen used the local limestone and employed lathes for large vessels, and manual work with mallet and chisel for ossuaries and some smaller vessels. This was a flourishing stone industry, which produced other types of stonework too, such as tables and household vessels. Only few ossuary fragments were found in the quarry-based workshops, but in some of them the spaces found in the stone correspond to an average ossuary. Also, the tool marks on ossuaries resemble those on the hand made stone vessels.

The artists chose to ornament ossuaries with various motifs and elements, which reflected the funerary environment. The chip-carved ossuaries represent the work of the more skilled among them. The sarcophagi and the hard limestone ossuaries may have been produced in the same workshop.

The skill and ability of the local stone working craft is evident in the ornamentation carved on tomb façades, the stone sarcophagi, and the ossuaries, which in time developed into a typical Jewish form.

Inscriptions that mention artists

Artists are mentioned by name in a list inscribed on an ossuary lid, and two craftsmen are possibly known from their names engraved on ossuaries.

A list inscribed on a lid of an ossuary was discovered in a tomb near Beth Phage (Mount of Olives, eastern slope) (see Fig. V–9). The document is a ledger listing 23 craftsmen, possibly employed in five teams in an ossuary workshop. This might imply that many of the ossuaries were prepared in advance and kept in storage for future purchases, yet it is also possible that some were specially ordered and their design chosen by the clients. The list records the names of a group of Jewish ossuary craftsmen, probably written by the employer; each name is followed by numbers and letters, possibly a register of their wages with an additional note of whether they had been paid or not. The range of the recorded wages may indicate the variety of the work in the workshop, from preparation of the ossuary to the carving of the ornamentation (Rahmani 1994b: 7–8).

Two ossuaries from Jerusalem display similar signs to those of the

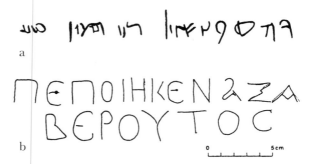

a

b

Figure IX–2. Ossuary Inscriptions mentioning Craftsmen: a. East Talpiyot;
b. Akeldama Inscription on Ossuary 17.

Beth Phage list (Figure IX–2): an ossuary from Mount Scopus, eastern slope; the signs stand for a quarter sheqel, = equal to one drachma and four obols (Rahmani 1994: No. 696).

An ossuary from East Talpiyot, Jerusalem is inscribed with יהוסף 4 [עה]מן מעין 2 [בע]שאול ר בר 'Yehosef the son of Sha'ul, drachma 2, obols, obol 4' (Figure IX–2a); the inscription apparently gives the artist's name and the price tag possibly for the ossuary decoration. Rahmani (1994: 10, No. 730) maintains that the name inscribed on the ossuary is that of the artist, but on another ossuary (No. 716) from the same tomb, the name Sha'ul is recorded and is identified by Rahmani as the father of the above-mentioned Yehosef. So the name may indeed have been that of the deceased, and the amount of money noted was the price of the ossuary. The signs on these ossuaries probably represent a price-tag, most likely the sum paid to the craftsmen.

An unusual Greek inscription on an ossuary found in Akeldama, Jerusalem (Tomb 2, Chamber B) cites 'Aza[ria] son of Berous (or: of Beirut) made (it)' (Figure IX–2b). The inscription records the name of an artist (of Syrian origin) who apparently made or decorated the ossuary, but he was not buried in it. Possibly the Greek 'Beroutos' indicates the place of origin as the Syro-Phoenician city of Beirut (Ilan 1996: 60–61, 68 No. 7, ossuary 17; Fig. 3.7). The other inscription on the ossuary notes the name of Erota, a female interred in this ossuary. The decoration of this hard limestone ossuary is unique (Shadmi 1996: 45). It renders two eight-petalled rosettes in high relief on the front, and bucrania on both narrow sides. These two designs are of different style and quality from most of the ossuaries found in this tomb.

C. Ossuary Groups with Similar Design

The following discussion of the ossuary groups concentrates on some designs, patterns, and motifs that recur on a number of ossuaries and some sarcophagi. Three such groups are discussed; each consists of a number of ossuaries decorated with an identical or similar design.

Group 1

A group of ossuaries found in various tombs in Jerusalem and its environs and an ossuary found in Jericho Tomb A2 (Pl. IX–1) (Hachlili 1997; 1999: 6–8) seem to be decorated with the same design and executed in similar form, which suggest a common source.

The shared design consists of two incised frames, most in order A and a few in order B, enclosing a tripartite decoration. On the outside there are two chip-carved rosettes, of types A and B, which flank a central motif. The ornamentation has three characteristic designs designated types 1, 2, 3 (Figure IX–3).

Frames

Two incised frames enclose the front panel of every ossuary design:

Order A comprises an outer frame depicted by closely spaced carved lines (fluted frame) with squares at all four corners (Figure IX–3a–b; Pl. IX–2). The inner narrower frame is rendered by pairs of widely spaced incised lines (metope frame). Most of the ossuaries have this order of frames (Hachlili 1997: Figs. 2, 4–5, 7–10).

Order B has the pattern of the frames reversed (Figure IX–3c, left; Pl. IX–1): the outer frame has widely-spaced pairs of lines and the inner one has closely-spaced vertical lines. There are several ossuaries with this order of frames. One of them is the Jericho ossuary and four more are from Jerusalem (Rahmani 1994: Nos. 263, 309, 318, 330, 891; Hachlili 1997: Figs. 1, 3, 9.1; Figs. 1.2; 4.3; 7.1; 8.2). Three ossuaries have only a single fluted or metope frame (Figure IX–3c, right) (Rahmani 1994: Nos. 46, 56, 432; Hachlili 1997: Figs. 9.2. Figs. 1.3; 8.1, 8.3).

Rosettes

Two types of rosettes are depicted on these ossuaries:

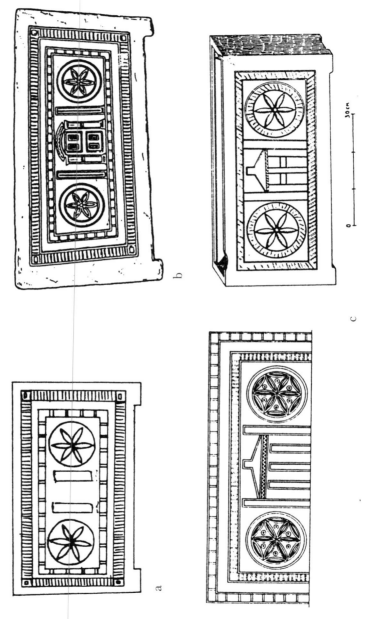

Figure IX–3. Ossuaries from Jerusalem: a. Type 1; b. Type 2; c. Type 3, ossuaries from Jericho and Jerusalem.

A. Simple chip-carved six-petalled rosettes, framed by incised concentric circles, which appear on the majority of the ossuaries (Figure IX–3a–b; Pls. IX–1, 2, 7).

B. Six-petalled chip-carved rosettes with ends joined by six leaves and with six additional small circular depressions between the petals, framed by incised concentric circles (Figure IX–3c, left; Pl. IX–4, 5). These rosettes appear on the Jericho ossuary (Hachlili 1997: Fig. 1) and on five Jerusalem ossuaries (Rahmani 1994: 891, 185; Shadmi 1996: Fig. 2.25. Ossuary 31; Hachlili 1997: Figs. 9.1, 10.1–3).

Central Motif

The main variation in these ossuaries is the design of the central motif, which displays three types of architectural structures (Figure IX–4):

Type A. On the majority of the ossuaries two or more columns are depicted (Pls. IX–1–3). Rahmani (1994: 29, ill. 32) suggests these are representations of columned porches of local tombs. Two columns appear on nine Jerusalem ossuaries and on one ossuary from Beth Nattif (Rahmani 1994: Nos. 107, 113, 228, 254, 263, 329, 330, 469, 715, 869; Figs. 2–5; Hachlili 1997: 243, Figs. 2–5, 7). These ossuaries are almost identical in their ornamentation: two frames enclosing two similar rosettes that flank two columns. Exceptions are one ossuary where the order of the frames is reversed and another from Akeldama, which has type B rosettes. Two other Jerusalem ossuaries with identical ornamentation are one in the Hebrew University collection and one from Dominus Flevit (Jacoby 1987: Nos. 100, 168).

A three-columned porch appears on one ossuary, a five-columned porch decorates another one (Rahmani 1994: Nos. 381, 250), and on a third a seven-columned porch is carved (Rahmani 1994: No. 58). A similar ossuary with a seven-columned porch was found in Tomb B in the Har-Hazofim Observatory (Mount Scopus, Jerusalem) (Weksler-Bdolah 1997: 40*, Ossuary B2, Fig. 17). One unusual ossuary from Romema, Jerusalem (Figure IX–4, Type A), belonging to this group, displays frames similar to those described above. It differs, however, in its panel design, it lacks rosettes, and it has five columns with arrows filling the spaces between them (Pl. IX–3) (Hachlili 1997: Fig. 8). Rahmani (1994: 29, No. 175) maintains that it is an abstract representation of a tomb façade.

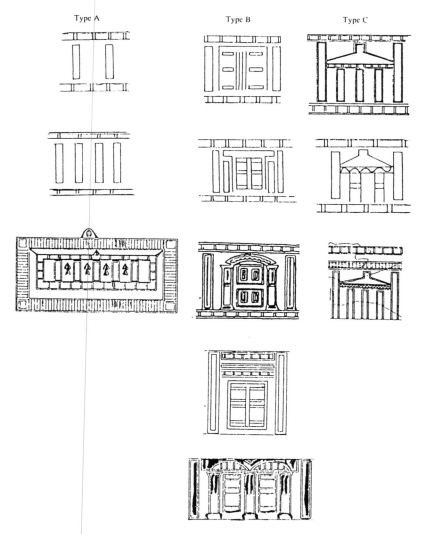

Figure IX–4. Central motif Types A, B, C.

Type B (Figure IX–4; Pls. IX–4, 5). This motif consists of a paneled door, usually with two leaves, sometimes with metope frieze above the door jambs and entrance, or a double gate with partially fluted columns on the bases and Doric capitals supporting a low arch, flanked by the same pair of columns as in Type A (Hachlili 1997: 244–6, Fig. 10).

Type B ossuaries are identical in ornamentation, central motif, and frames; they differ only in their rosettes, one being of type A and the other of type B. Type B central motif appears on seven ossuaries from Jerusalem (Rahmani 1994: nos. 185, 241). Four ossuaries belong to the Hebrew University collection (Avigad 1967: 131, no. 8, Pl. 22,5; Hebrew University collection no. 1523; Spoer 1907: 354, plate, below; Goodenough, vol. III: Figs. 216, 219).

Type C (Figure IX–4; Pls. IX–6, 7). This architectural design portrays a façade of a three-columned porch surmounted by a frieze, decorated either with metopes or with a zigzag pattern, and a gabled roof with a square acroterium. The central façade is flanked by two columns, which are probably extended antae, indicating side acroteria (Rahmani 1994: 29; Hachlili 1997: 243–244; Figs. 1, 9). On two ossuaries, panels connecting the three columns might indicate a two-leaf door. This motif, which is akin to Type A, probably represents a tomb façade (Rahmani 1994: 29). It appears on four Jerusalem ossuaries (Rahmani 1994: nos. 46, 90, 711, 891; Hachlili 1997: Fig. 9) and on the ossuary fragment from Jericho (Hachlili 1999: 97, Ossuary 12, Fig. III.42).

Interpretations of these motifs vary: they have been considered a Torah shrine (Avi-Yonah 1981: 36; Goodenough 1954, IV:120); the Temple porch (Figueras 1983: 57); a representation of the "Eternal House" or "everlasting home" (Figueras 1983: 85). Rahmani (1994: 28–29, 47), who rejects all these, is correct in maintaining that these designs, representing tomb façades, entrances, and doors, have no symbolic significance. Rahmani (1994: 45–46) believes that this motif represents a tomb entrance showing a paneled door or door frames.

Motifs such as the Torah shrine and the menorah evolved into Jewish symbols only after the destruction of the Temple, probably at the end of the first or early in the second century CE (Hachlili 1988: 234–236, 285).

The basic design seems to consist of two frames (orders A and B, fluted and metope) and the two rosettes flanking two columns. Other examples have additional columns or an architectural motif (Types B and C) in the center, between the innermost pair of columns, thus creating a design that combines all the elements. This is also the most common design and it appears on the greatest number of ossuaries (about 34).

On a few ossuaries, inscriptions are carved not on the front, but only on the side and back; in this category one ossuary is exceptional (Spoer 1907: 354, plate, below), having an inscription carefully carved on the front above the outer frame of the design. It seems as if the inscription carvers took pains to avoid damaging the design on the front of the ossuaries.

Only in two cases were the ossuaries found in the same tomb or adjacent ones. Three ossuaries come from a tomb on the western slope of Mount Scopus, Jerusalem (Hachlili 1994: Figs. 2, 4, 7) and two (Hachlili 1994: Figs. 8, 10:3) were found in Romema in two adjacent loculus tombs. The sites indicate that these ossuaries were common in tombs throughout the Jerusalem area and as far as Beth Nattif and Jericho.

Interestingly, the motifs described, such as tomb façade, tomb entrance, gate, and the simple columned porch, are found only on this group of ossuaries. Moreover, the artists who produced these group seem to have restricted their repertoire of designs merely to these motifs.

The question arises as to whether the Jericho ossuary was imported from a workshop in Jerusalem, and if so, whether all the ossuaries found in the Jericho tombs were manufactured in Jerusalem workshops and then transported to Jericho. Alternatively, artisans or apprentices might have come from Jerusalem to work in Jericho, or a craftsman from Jericho might have worked in the same workshop, which produced the identical Jerusalem ossuaries. An artisan from Jericho might have copied the pattern and made his own changes. Whatever the answer, the artist who decorated the Jericho ossuary must have been contemporary with the Jerusalem craftsmen and familiar with the patterns and motifs used for the ornamentation of the ossuaries.

Group 2

A group of ossuaries with similar decorative elements and affinity of execution seems to have been produced in one workshop, or this workshop used a pattern book for the similar design. This group consists of several Jerusalem ossuaries (Goodenough 1953: Figs. 205, 206, 207; Rahmani 1959; 1982: 117; Figueras 1983: Pls. 33:420; 34; 422).

Figure IX–5a–d. Ossuaries with Stylized Palm-tree Design.

The façade decorations of these ossuaries consist of the following identical elements (Figure IX–5):

- A chip-carved zigzag single or double frame usually incised on all four sides. Occasionally the bottom line of the frame is single.
- Within the frame are depicted two chip-carved six-petalled or multi-petalled rosettes.
- In the centre between the rosettes a stylized depiction of a palm tree in the shape of an upright triangular motif appears, representing a single branched palm tree ('triglyph'), sometimes with several small lines chip-carved into the bottom frame designating the roots of the tree; this motif occasionally evolved into a knife or sword (Rahmani 1982: 115 and Fig. on p. 117; 1994: 49, Figs. 120, 121).
- An interesting element common to some of these ossuaries is the two vertical lines incised from the lower part of the two rosettes to the bottom frame, which may have functioned as aids to the mason in carving the triangles. Two of the ossuaries are decorated in a slightly different way: one has two twelve-petalled rosettes (Goodenough 1953: Fig. 206) and the other has a different central motif, a stylized triangle (Figueras 1983: Pl. 33:420).

Fourteen ossuaries, all found in Jerusalem, are decorated with the design and are divided into three types (Figure IX–6; Pls. IX–8–11):

Type A. The central motif is a single branched palm tree ('triglyph'), with a small notched triangle (Figure IX–6:1–5; Pl. IX–8) carved close to the bottom line of the frame, designating the roots of the tree, or described as a pointed arrow-like design carved in the upper part between the rosettes (Rahmani 1994: 49, Fig. 120; Nos. 216, 367, 387, 485, 741; Sukenik 1947: Ossuaries Nos. 4, 9, 13; Goodenough 1953, III, Figs. 205–207; Figueras 1983: Pl. 34: No. 422; Shadmi 1996: 49, Fig. 2.24, Ossuary 30, Akeldama).

Type B. The central motif is an upright triangle, which is interpreted as a stylized palm tree represented by a single upright branch, supplemented by the representation of a sword handle (?) (Figure IX–6:6; Pl. IX–10). This transforms the motif, giving it a new implication. The only indication left of the original motif is the lines of the tree's root. The design appears on four ossuaries from Jerusalem (Pl. IX–9) (Rahmani 1994: 49, Nos. 146, 306, 317; Shadmi 1996: 44, Fig. 2.9, Akeldama, Ossuary 13).

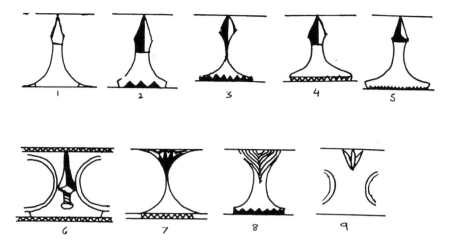

Figure IX–6. Group 2, Types A, B, C.

Type C. This central motif appears on three ossuaries and is unique, rendered in a different way in each of them (Figure IX–6:7–9). A distinctly stylized palm tree is represented by three or more ascending stylized branches. Only on one of them do the small notched triangles appear, indicating the tree's roots; on another ossuary the palm branch issues from the apex of a stepped gable or pyramid top of a *nefesh* (Pl. IX–11) (Rahmani 1994: Nos. 49, 83, 883). Sometimes it appears as leaf or foliage, which could represent the top of a tree or of a plant, with a stylized root shown as an indented carving at the base.

Interpretation of the motif varies: Rahmani (1959; 1994: 9, 49) maintains that the design's central motif is a stylized palm tree, with the roots sometimes visible. The foot of the tree trunk is represented by small incised vertical lines. The original form is completely lost. Sometimes it appears as "a single ascending branch in upper centre representing the tree's crown", frequently with small triangular notched lines delimiting the tree's root (Rahmani 1994: Nos. 216, 485, 367, 205–207; 422? with some variations on Nos. 83, 315, 741). At other times an indication of the trunk remains (Rahmani 1994: No. 49).

The stylization of the motif on several ossuaries so obscured its origin, that the palm tree branch was transformed into the representation of an upright sword with a handle, "providing the motif

with an entirely new meaning . . . which may perhaps be attributed
to the prevalent strife of the period . . ." (Rahmani 1959: 189; 1994:
49, Nos. 146, 306, 317; Shadmi 1996: ossuary 13). Figueras (1983:
48) describes this motif as the 'Arrow-Type' in the group of plant
motifs; he further maintains that once a dagger design, it degener-
ated into a mere hint of this motif.

Group 3

A group of ossuaries with similar decorative design and affinity of
execution was discovered in Jerusalem. The design consists of an
ashlar wall motif, arranged in header and stretcher design similar to
façades of Jerusalem tombs and buildings (Rahmani 1994: 35, Fig.
42; see ashlar wall in façade of tombs Chap. II). The design decorates the front and sides of two sarcophagi and several ossuaries,
sometimes overlaid with encircled rosettes (Figure IX–7).

The Ashlar wall motif consists of four types in which the motif
decorates all sides of the ossuaries and sarcophagi including the
gabled lid; some ossuaries are ornamented with the addition of overlaid rosettes and others are adorned with variations of the motif:

a. Unadorned ashlar-wall pattern covering the ossuary front and
sometimes sides; the ossuaries have a flat, sliding, or gabled lid (Figure IX–7a; Pl. IX–12). The pattern appears on Jerusalem ossuaries
(Rahmani 1994: Nos. 217, 420, 481, 487, the last two from the same
tomb; Jacobi 1987: No. An. 1987: 127–8; Sukenik 1942: 30, Fig. 3,
Ossuary 2).

b. Unadorned ashlar-wall pattern covering the ossuary front and
sides (Figure IX–7b; Pl. IX–13); its gabled lid is decorated with an
added pair of engraved overlaid rosettes on both ends (Rahmani
1994: Fig. 42, Nos. 353, 455, 730).

c. Ashlar-wall motif with variations incised on all sides. On the
front and back they are overlaid with a row of two or more superimposed six-petalled or multi-petalled rosettes, the sides with one multi-
petalled rosette. The lids are flat, vaulted, or gabled incised with
rosettes and other patterns. (Figure IX–7c). (Rahmani 1994: Nos.
34, 164, 184; the chest is decorated with unfinished ashlar wall motif
on front; No. 384 right side is unfinished; No. 478 is rendered with
superimposed rosettes in the center of the ossuary's front and back;
Gershuny and Zissu 1996: Fig. 25, Ossuary 218; Bagatti and Milik
1958: Nos. 26, 88, Pl. 19: Fots. 41–42, 44–45). On one ossuary the
ashlar wall motif is overlaid with three encircled rosettes only on the

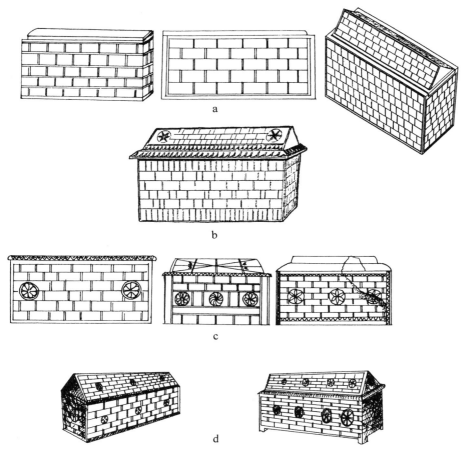

Figure IX-7. Ossuaries Decorated with Ashlar Wall Motif.

gabled lid, while the chest is decorated with two eight-petalled rosettes
(Pl. IX-14) (Rahmani 1994: No. 407). A variation of the design of
ashlar-wall pattern overlaid by a row of six-petalled or multi-petaled
rosettes is rendered on the front of sarcophagi from Mount Scopus;
on the sides the rosettes are framed by a high relief carved ring.
The gabled lid is decorated with the ashlar-wall pattern and a row
of eight rosettes; the two at the ends are also framed by a high relief
carved ring (Sarcophagi Nos. 14, 15, Chap. III) (Rahmani 1994:
Nos. 490, 668). The other sarcophagus is decorated with sixteen
superimposed rosettes, each in a circle. The gabled lid with the
wedge handle is similar in both sarcophagi, which might indicate
the same artist or workshop (Rahmani 1994: No. 668).

Three of the ossuaries and the sarcophagus ornamented with the ashlar wall motif on their chest only (and one on the lid) were discovered in the same tomb in Jerusalem (Kloner 1993; Nos. 6, 12, 24, 27 = Rahmani 1994: Nos. 478, 481, 487, 490).

The interpretation suggested by Goodenough (1953, I:117–118), shared by Figueras (1983: 53–55), and in the past also by Rahmani (1962: 74; 1967a: 190–191), is that the ashlar wall motif was intended to represent the deceased's 'Eternal House'. The ossuaries with the superimposed rosettes were 'mystic shrines' that protected the deceased. Rahmani (1994: 35) counters this assumption and claims that the ashlar wall motif was merely selected from the architecture of local tombs.

*

The similar or identical ornamentation and the elements portrayed on all these ossuaries suggests that they were produced in the same workshop, possibly in the Jerusalem area (Rahmani 1967: 190; Hachlili 1988a: 112–114, Fig. IV, 16; 1988b: 23. Rahmani [1994: 9] contends that it is difficult to prove that ossuaries with common motifs are from the same workshop, but see ibid. 259, No. 869). Alternatively, it has been suggested that a pattern book was used by artists to copy the same design. However, the close similarities among many of the ossuaries discussed here – not only in the almost identical design, but also in the similar execution (see Rahmani 1994: Nos. 113, 228, 254, 329, 715, 869) – seem to favour the first interpretation.

Several explanations for the connection between Jerusalem ossuaries and those found in other sites in the country such as Jericho can be offered (1) The ossuaries were made in Jerusalem and transported to Jericho and other sites (above Group I). (2) Artisans and apprentices came from the Jerusalem workshops to work in Jericho. (3) local Jericho artisans learnt their trade in Jerusalem and following their return to Jericho set up their own workshops. (4) patterns may have been copied by artisans from a common pattern book (Hachlili 1997: 247); a Jericho artisan might have copied the pattern and made his own changes in the ornamentation of the ossuaries. Note Kloner's assumption (1994b: 238) that the artist who produced the ossuary with the monumental façades (Rahmani 1994: No. 482) worked from a pattern book. The inspiration for his work on the ornamentation of this ossuary included the similar structures he saw in the Jerusalem necropolis, some elements he saw in Alexandria, and on the monuments from Petra. Rahmani suggests that the members of the family who used this tomb possibly were of Nabatean origin.

It is possible that the same workshops manufactured all the decorated ossuaries: incised, chip-carved, and relief-carved. The incised ossuaries might have been produced by apprentices or less skilled craftsmen (Rahmani 1994: 8).

Of the location of ossuary workshops we know little, except that the ossuaries were probably produced in Jerusalem, which was renowned for the skill of its stonemasons in the Second Temple period (Avigad 1980: 165–176; Rahmani 1994: 7; Magen 2002: 133). The local craft of stone cutting can be attested by the architecture, carving, and ornamentation of the rock-cut Jerusalem tombs and by the carved ossuaries and sarcophagi, as well as stone tables and vessels.

Marketing of Ossuaries

The purchase of ossuaries from the workshop, or where and how they were obtained, is not apparent (Rahmani 1994: 10–11). It is possible that ossuaries were acquired from the craftsman at his workshop (Sukenik 1935b: 109).

The value and price of the ossuaries might have been linked to the complexity of their ornamentation, in various degrees of prices: plain ossuaries were possibly the cheapest, incised ones were slightly more, and the relief and chip-carved were still more expensive; the hard limestone ossuaries were the most expensive, since they were produced by skilled artists.

Some ossuaries yielded 'price tags'. The Beth Phage list records the daily average wage that some of the workers earned; it matches the price of a plain ossuary, which was recorded on one of them. Its price was one drachma (*dinar*) and four obols; while a decorated ossuary cost only one *dinar* more. This was possibly the price, as recorded on another ossuary, for the ornamentation alone rather than for the whole ossuary (Rahmani 1994: 10, Nos. 696, 730). Minimum daily wages ranged between one obol (one sixth of a *dinar*) as a very low wage, which still might have supported a person, to one and two *dinars*. Thus, it is possible that two or three days were needed to produce an ossuary and about the same for a client to pay for it (Rahmani 1994: 7, and n. 8; Teitelbaum 1997: 152, n. 85).

It is a reasonable assumption that two different craftsmen worked on the ossuary manufacture; one prepared the chest and lid, the other the artist who decorated it, and each was paid separately.

The majority of ossuaries were bought already made; the finely ornate ossuaries were probably made to order only in rare cases. It is possible that some inscriptions on the ossuaries were prepared in advance.

The choice of a plain or a decorated ossuary by the deceased's family, which meant spending money on a burial, depended on religious and social concerns (Rahmani 1994: 11): whether to pacify the dead, to alleviate the mourner's feelings, or to impress the living, all those considerations were frequently condemned in this period, as attested by literary sources (Sem. 8:2–6; 9:23; BT Ket. 8b).

Only wealthy families could afford costly ossuaries; however, cheaper ones, plain or incised, should not be regarded as a sign of poverty or parsimony. Simple and elaborately decorated ossuaries were found together in the same tomb (see the tomb of Helen of Adiabene, tomb of Nicanor, and other family tombs), which refutes the proposition that the choice was a result of wealth, frugality, or lack of care about the deceased.

GRAVE GOODS

Grave goods as part of the burial assemblage can enlighten us partially about mortuary rituals and practices. Grave goods were placed by the buriers as part of the ritual process of disposing of the dead, and were often observed by the mourners and the visitors to the grave. Sometimes, although "the grave goods were significant they might have been removed after being displayed, or in Athens were given away as prizes in funeral games or the like" (Morris 1992: 104–108). Diverse reasons are given to explain the offering of grave goods: they were supposed to nurture the dead and to fulfill symbolic as well as functional roles.

Studies of grave goods evaluate the nature of the assemblages in funerary deposits, assess the symbolic value of some artifact types, and consider their value to society both living and dead. Analysis of the objects may reveal the processes of selection of grave goods; some objects were suitable for burial whereas others were rarely used as grave goods. Frequently the possessions of the deceased were tainted, and the living had to obliterate them or leave them with the corpse. Discovery of grave goods does not inevitably indicate belief in afterlife, although some items might indicate some requirement by the dead (Pearson 1993: 207, 224). Everyday objects placed as grave offerings might evince "an inner need to satisfy a sense of loss or reluctance to credit total separation from the dead, rather than any positive belief in the value of the offerings to the departed" (Kurtz and Boardman 1971: 206). The grave goods were generally frugal and sparing, displaying restraint; the custom in Jewish tombs was to bury with few belongings or offerings, signifying that the buriers in most cases were trying not to demonstrate affluence and suggesting eschewal of display (Morris 1992: 118).

Several proposals have been presented to interpret artifacts buried with the dead (Avigad 1956: 334–335, Fig. 10; Rahmani 1961: 118–119; 1967: 95–96; Kloner 1980: 254; Kurtz and Boardman 1971: 207–212); three categories are suggested:

1. Personal possessions interred with both men and women including jewelry, weapons, strigils, mirrors, cosmetic vessels, and spindle whorls. It is quite difficult to decide whether these possessions
   belonged to the dead or were offerings by the living, and therefore "not always appropriate to sex. The number of apparently
   inappropriate offerings is considerably reduced when we reflect
   that mirrors and even earrings need not be unmasculine, that
   adults keep their toys, even that some women might wash or
   exercise and use strigils" (Kurtz and Boardman 1971: 209).

2. Items of everyday use were placed in the tombs, but in the burial context they might have assumed a funerary significance; they
   usually were items related to some ritual in the burial. Some vessels were placed in the tomb for functional purposes. Scholars
   maintain that objects were set in some Jewish graves in order to
   provide for food and drink, jewelry, and accessories for the deceased
   in his or her afterlife; these customs, abandoned later, were a
   continuation of an earlier custom and tradition of the First Temple
   period. Rahmani (1967: 95–96) maintains, "The social structure,
   as well as the concept of afterlife, as reflected in the tombs of
   the Hasmonean period, definitely conforms with what is known
   of the Sadducees . . . and their denial of resurrection after death.
   This evidently included the need to provide nourishment for the
   deceased, as well as utensils, clothing and ornaments".

The most common items found in the tombs were unguentaria (see
Tables X–1–7): vessels such as bottles containing oil or funerary
spices used for tending the deceased, for anointing the body or bones
of the dead; "but the offering of oil after the burial seems also to
have been a regular practice, at least in Athens, and at the time of
burial the offering of one or more oil flasks may have become a
normal practice for kin or guests" (Kurtz and Boardman 1971: 209).
Other everyday vessels found in graves include cooking pots, jars,
and storage jars, all probably utilized to satiate the thirst of the dead.
Lamps were used for illumination in the grave but they might have
had some symbolic meaning such as lighting the way for the dead.
In a few cases, following the Greek practice of Charon's obol, small
coins were buried with dead for symbolic payment of the ferryman
who took them across the river Styx into Hades. Sandals or shoes

may have been regarded as needed on the deceased's journey, or they had some symbolic meaning. Some vessels were placed as a symbolic expression of "intense grief"; offerings placed in the grave served to arouse people's compassion and to intensify grief (Rahmani 1961: 104; Allon 1976; Lieberman 1965). De Vaux (1958: 95) contends that the grave goods had only a symbolic meaning; the offerings had no intent of worship of the dead.

3. Objects made especially for the grave are seldom found in connection with Jewish burials. Nevertheless, the carinated bowls with handles (Type C, Killebrew 1999: 116, Fig. III.56:6–8, 12–15) found only in association with the Goliath tomb and mourning enclosure in Jericho, might have been especially produced for burial purposes; likewise the wooden bowls and plates, which might have been made for the grave. In Athens (Kurtz and Boardman 1971: 212–213) some pottery was created especially for the grave such as certain funerary *hydriai*, series of vases and other clay artifacts, as well as jewelry.

The grave goods discussed in this chapter include pottery, glass, wood, iron, leather, and textiles, as well as personal effects of the deceased, which generally comprised toilet articles, accessories, jewelry, wood and metal vessels, and ceramic wares.

A. POTTERY

Grave goods found in burials are mostly pottery vessels; many, especially unguentaria, are often intact or only partly damaged.

The assemblage of the pottery placed in the tombs is of a limited repertoire. It represents the common, simple ware of the same types in use in daily life at this time. Most of the pottery is a selection of everyday repertoire, not luxury ware like Terra Sigilata or other imported vessels. Imported pottery was rarely found (see the Geva tomb, Sieglman 1988).

Pottery vessels placed next to bones in the tomb might have served as humble offerings to the deceased (Avigad 1967: 133).

Kahane (1952: 125–127) in researching the origin of the pottery types and their geographic distribution regarded the central issue as the Hellenization of Jewry in the Herodian period. Considering the pottery types, he asks: (a) Can this type be derived from earlier local types? (b) Has it been found outside Palestine? If so, is it before, contemporary with, or later than the corresponding local type? In which cultural area – Oriental Greek, or Roman? (c) Can the type also be traced in non-Jewish tombs and settelments in Palestine?

Deformed pottery found in tombs might indicate concerns such as contamination or strife; pottery fragments may have been deliberately broken, or thrown into the tomb as an expression of pain, sorrow, or grief (Kloner 1980: 257–258; Hachlili & Killebrew 1999: 168). Pottery was scattered in the tomb, found in places such as the standing pit, loculi, and benches, and seldom inside a coffin or ossuary.

The pottery vessels commonly associated with tombs of the Second Temple period (first century BCE–first century CE) are an important aspect of burial practices during this period. The pottery assemblage found in Jerusalem and Jericho tombs (Tables X–1–7) consist of bowls, kraters, cooking pot, jugs, store jars, unguentaria (spindle bottle, piriform bottle, globular juglet, aryballos, alabastron), and lamps (Killebrew 1999: 115–133). A few pottery vessels were discovered at 'En Gedi (Hadas 1994: 54–55, 6*).

Several other vessels have been found only infrequently in tombs, such as a flask (one complete flask recovered in Jericho Tomb D22, Killebrew 1999: 129, Fig. III.67,1; also in Jerusalem, Gershoni & Zissu 1996: 46*, fig. 19,6, in the pit of Tomb 1).

The pottery is now discussed typologically.

Bowls

A small number of different types of bowls characteristic of the Second Temple period were discovered in tombs (Killebrew 1999: 115–117): a small deep or shallow bowl with an incurved rim and a large deep bowl with a flaring rim and carinated body. A shallow carinated bowl with an everted rim, flat base and two handles was found only in association with Jericho tomb H and the mourning enclosure (Figure X–1; PL. X–1).

The function of these bowls in the funerary context is explained

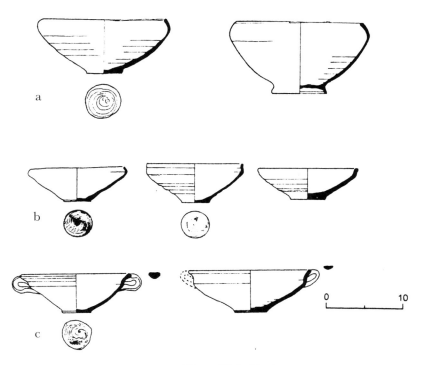

Figure X–1. Bowls.

as having contained liquids to wash, rinse, or anoint the deceased (Kloner 1993: 86).

An exceptional case is the inscribed bowl found in Jericho tomb D1, which apparently served as a funerary memorial, tracing the genealogy of a family 'from Jerusalem' (Hachlili 1978; 1999: 155–158).

Krater

Two types of kraters have been found (Killebrew 1999: 117): a plain globular krater with vertical handles, and a larger one with horizontal handles and a ridge on the shoulder, decorated with red painted designs (Figure X–2; Pl. X–2). These kraters were discovered only in ossuary tombs (Type III) in Jericho. They might have served as offerings specially placed for the deceased.

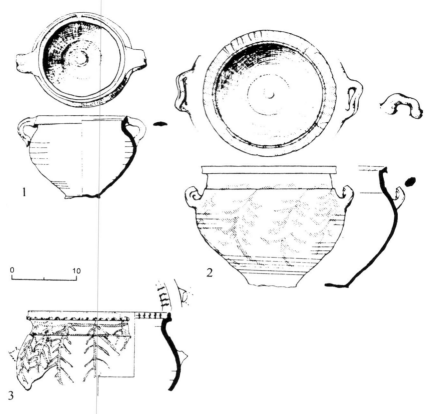

Figure X–2. Kraters.

Cooking pots

Several types of cooking pots were found in Jerusalem and Jericho tombs (Killebrew 1999: 117–119): high-necked bag-shaped cooking pots with two handles with several sub-types; low-necked globular cooking pots with carinated shoulder (Figure X–3; Pl. X–3); and shallow carinated casseroles, which are a rare type. In Jerusalem tombs a wide-mouthed open carinated cooking pot was discovered (Vitto 2001: 90, Fig. 47:4). The squat globular shaped cooking pot is the most common found in the Jericho cemetery and appears in Tomb types I and II, particularly abundant in collected bone burials. It is not found in ossuary burials in Jericho. It is also the common type found in the ʿEn Gedi tombs, especially Tomb 2 (Hadas 1994: 12–17, Fig. 22).

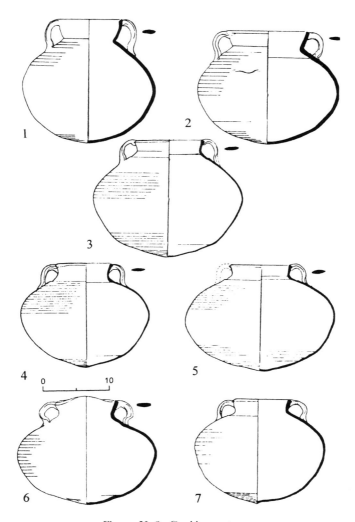

Figure X–3. Cooking pots.

The function of the cooking pots in a funerary context is subject to debate, and various proposals have been made. Avigad (1956: 334) suggests that cooking pots were used for water to wash hands; they were easily broken and this is why many pottery fragments are found in the tombs. Another proposal argues that cooking pots were used to heat water for burial functions such as washing the deceased's body (Kloner 1980: 255–256; 1993: 86). The cooking pots were brought as offering to the dead (Kahane 1952: 86, Avigad 1970: 240).

The cooking pots contained oil and wine, which were poured onto the bones while an ossilegium was conducted (Rubin 1977: 240). An early custom of putting food in the tomb is suggested; the large number of cooking pots (80) and bowls (50) for about 35 deceased in Jason's Tomb, and the presence of soot on the bottom of cooking pots, indicate "that these vessels were intended to provide for the deceased food cooked on the spot", probably in the courtyard, and then placed in the tomb loculi (Rahmani 1961: 118, nn. 12, 13). Alon (1977: 103–104) contends that vessels of the deceased and belonging to the mourners were placed in the tomb: "it was forbidden to remove them which was considered robbery of the dead. This might have been seen in popular belief as a justification to give food to the dead without incurring the accusation of idolatry". This was possibly an early custom of placing food and drink in the tomb, which later was abandoned (Bloch-Smith 1992: 122–126; also Lieberman 1965: 509).

Possible commemorative meals are suggested (Zissu 1995: 160) for instance by a pile of ashes before the entrance to tomb 1 at Givʿat Shapira, which included cooking pots blackened fragments (Gershuny and Zissu 1996: 46*); or at Ras el-Jami, Isawiye, where a cooking pot was found with ashes in a niche close to the courtyard stairs. No bowls or other vessels were found there (Kloner 1980: 18, No. 2–22).

Some symbolic rite may well have been associated with the placing of cooking pots in the tomb as indicated by the following examples: Four cooking pots were discovered placed in four corners of the chamber in a Jerusalem tomb (Zissu 1995: 79, no. 12–45). In Jericho, cooking pots were placed next to wooden coffins 78, and 85 (tomb D12) as well as in front of the sealing slab of tomb D12–2 (Hachlili 1999: 22, Fig. II.42). At Qumran, in Building B, a skeleton in primary burial was found with a cooking pot placed just above the legs (Broshi and Eshel 2003: 32).

No general agreement exists regarding the practice of funerary meals in Jewish tombs. The cooking pots were not used for a mourning feast, as such a feast was not conducted in Jewish tombs, especially not inside the tomb (Lieberman 1965: 495–532; Rubin 1977: 386–379) as suggested by some scholars (Goodenough 1953, I:107–8); this custom was prevalent in the Greco-Roman world. Even when a reference to a feast appears in an inscription (see Jason's Tomb

Greek inscription) it could imply enjoyment of life before death (Park 2000: 69–72).

It is possible that the cooking pots might have been placed inside the tomb, next to coffins or beside the deceased deliberately as a symbol for the commemorative meals.

Unguentaria

Unguentaria (also termed *lacrimaria* or *balsamaria*) consisted of clay vessels such as spindle (fusiform) bottle, piriform bottle, globular (piriform) juglet, aryballos, and alabastron. Such bottles were made of glass. The term *lacrimarium* was used for unguentaria on the assumption that it was used to collect the tears of mourners, which is dismissed as unlikely by most scholars. *Balsamaria* was used to describe the content – balsam – of the vessels (Anderson-Stojanovic 1987: 106).

The unguentaria vessels (Figure X–4) found in Second Temple tombs (Killebrew 1999: 119–121) consist of small globular juglets with flat or rounded base and handleless; and flat-based piriform bottles, small and large, some with painted lines. In Jerusalem tombs spindle bottles appear as early as the second century BCE. Less frequently found in tombs are aryballos and two types of alabastra with pointed or flat base; flat-base alabastra were found inside two ossuaries in a Jerusalem tomb (Vitto 2001: 78, Fig. 44:3–7).

Unguentaria are common in tombs of the Second Temple period, especially in those containing primary or collected bone burials. In tombs that contain only ossuary burials, ceramic unguentaria are less frequent and appear to be replaced by glass bottles. Unguentaria are often intact or only partly damaged; they are quite commonly found in tombs' chambers, benches and pits, but seldom in the loculi or in ossuaries. However, as unguentaria vessels are not found in all burials (see Tables X–1–7) it might indicate they were not an essential part of the funerary ritual. Many of the unguentaria found in tombs are of poor manufacture; it is suggested that these were inexpensive and mass-produced vessels for funerary use (Anderson-Stojanovic 1987: 120).

The function of the unguentaria is in dispute and diverse suggestions have been made; unguentaria shapes and forms indicate that they served as a container for liquids, which might include unguents, water, wine, oil, or honey (Kahane 1952: 131; 1953: 48) though the

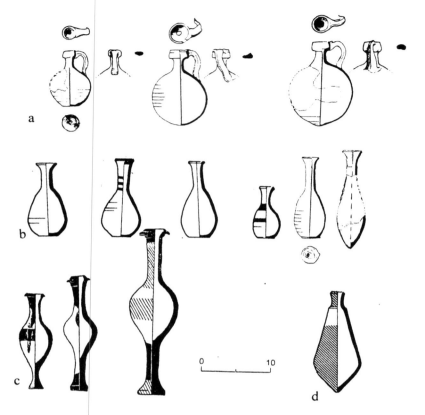

Figure X–4. Unguentaria.

contents of unguentaria might have also contained powdered or granular substance like spices or incense (Anderson-Stojanovic 1987: 116). "The bones may be sprinkled with wine and oil. So Rabbi Akiba. Rabbi Simeon ben Nannas says: 'Oil but not wine, because wine evaporates'. 'Neither wine nor oil' say the Sages 'because these only invite worms, but dried herbs may be put on them" (*Sem.* 12.9; Zlotnik 1966: 82, 161).

Some scholars suggest that unguentaria were filled with oil for illumination (Avigad 1956: 334) or perhaps were used as candle holders (Forbes 1966, 6:140). Others argue that unguentaria vessels contained oil and perfumes brought into the tomb for funerary rituals; they served several functions in various burial stages: for sprinkling perfume on the deceased's body (BT Sanhedrin 48b); the body was cleaned, purified, and anointed with water and oil in preparation for burial before being wrapped in shrouds (M. Shabat 23,5 and Bichler 1936: 48); funerary spices were sprinkled on the burials and the tomb, and then for fear of contamination the vessels were left in the tomb or placed next to the bones (Klein 1908: 31–32; Rahmani 1961: 118; Rubin 1977: 202; Kloner 1980: 255; 1993: 86).

Other possibilities are that the liquid contained in the unguentaria could help decompose the body; the perfume in some of the vessels could add a pleasant scent and prevent the bad odor (BT Brachot 53A; Rubin 1997: 123–128). Another suggestion is that ceramic unguentaria, common in the grave goods of the Greek, Hellenistic, and early Roman periods, functioned as a popular offering through-out the Mediterranean world (Anderson-Stojanovic 1987: 106).

The substance in the unguentaria might have been used in the funeral rites only for a short time, and then placed in the burial. Water, oil, or wine could have been used for short-term purposes in Greek and Roman funeral rites (Anderson-Stojanovic 1987: 121). Wine was used on the deceased's remains (Toynbee 1971: 50, n. 173), as was oil, and with inhumation the custom of oil or wine libation at the graveside was practiced (Kurtz and Boardman 1971: 144–145; Toynbee 1971: 44). The empty unguentaria might have been placed in the grave after the funeral rites as a symbol of the honor paid to the dead at the time of burial. Some unguentaria were not intended to contain anything, but might have been mass-produced for symbolic use only, as a simple grave offering (Anderson-Stojanovic 1987: 121–122).

The perfumes and the lamp were symbols representing the continuation and the graduation from living to death. They were meant to ease the great crisis; BT Brachot 53A states that the lamp was not to be lit but to honor the dead, and the perfumes were not to be smelled but to prevent the bad smell of the dead (Rubin 1997: 123–128).

Jugs and Jars

Jugs found in tombs consist of two main groups (Killebrew 1999: 121–123): squat globular jugs, often decorated, with rounded bases, and small spherical jugs with flat bases (Figure X–5). An unusual

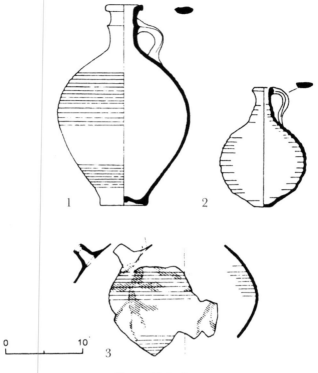

Figure X–5. Jugs.

spouted jug with a red floral pattern painted on the outside, similar to the decoration on the kraters, was found in Jericho tomb D1
(Figure X–5:3).

Storage Jars

Several complete bag-shaped storage jars with a broad, rounded base
were found in the Jericho cemetery (Killebrew 1999: 123, 125), usually in association with coffin burials, where they had been placed
outside the tomb entrance (Figure X–6:1, 3; Pl. X–4).

Other types consist of cylindrical broad-shouldered and cylindrical bag-shaped jars found in and outside a number of tombs.

The storage jars found inside the grave may have held water used
for the dead; those jars placed outside the grave either signified of
a last rite or were used for purification after the tomb was sealed.

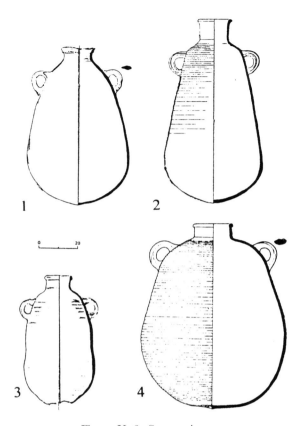

Figure X–6. Storage jars.

Lamps

Several types of lamps are found in tombs (Killebrew 1999: 125, 129) (Figure X–7): A folded lamp commonly appears in first century BCE contexts. In Jericho it was recovered in association with Type I burial (coffin). Also found are a Judean radial molded (or 'sunburst') lamp (second–first century BCE) and a wheel-made knife-pared ('Herodian') lamp; this is the main lamp of the first century CE (at least until 70 CE), found at all sites of this period. In Jericho it was found with ossuary burials. A round disk lamp with flat base decorated with an ovolo pattern in relief was common in the late first-second centuries CE.

Lamps were found in funerary context, in the courtyards, chambers, and loculi of graves. Lamps were intended first of all for the

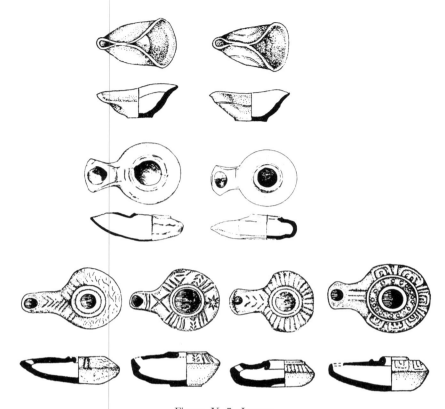

Figure X–7. Lamps.

living, to illuminate, as there is no life without light. Several functions of lamps could be discerned:

a) A lamp was used to light up the tomb for the funerary ceremony, for the act of burial, and for the mourners. It was necessary
to light the tomb at the time of burial or while collecting bones
(Rahmani 1961: 118).

In some tombs a special niche for the lamp was discovered (see
Jerusalem, Mt. Scopus Observatory Tomb D, loculus IV, Weksler-
Bdolah 1998: 50*).

b) A lamp was lit out of respect and commemoration of the dead,
as indicated by lamps placed beside a burial or inside the ossuary.
The lamp was lit for the dead (M. Berachot 8,6); in JT, Berachot
8,6, the sages note a distinction between the lamps for the dead and
those for the living (Weksler-Bdolah 1998: 50*).

c) The lamp in a funerary context may be considered a symbol
of life and of a person's soul (Prov. 20, 27). The lamp had perhaps
a symbolic meaning (see Jericho tomb A2, where a lamp was placed
on the deceased's skull, Hachlili 1999: 8). It could be placed above
the deceased's head or bed, symbolizing both life and death (Rubin
1997: 124).

The lamp used by the living might have been place in the tomb
at the time of the funeral, of the burial, or later on during the visit
by mourners. It is also possible that the buriers might have taken
some lamps out after the funeral.

Other ceramic vessels found in the tombs (Killebrew 1999: 129)
consist of a flask, found at Jericho, tomb 22 and in the pit at Givʿat
Shapira, tomb 1 (Gershoni & Zissu 1996: 46*, fig. 19,6), a cup, a
funnel (Figure X–8), and other utensils found in Jerusalem and Jericho
tombs.

*

Pottery vessels constitute the bulk of the grave goods found in Second
Temple tombs. They are of particular importance because of the

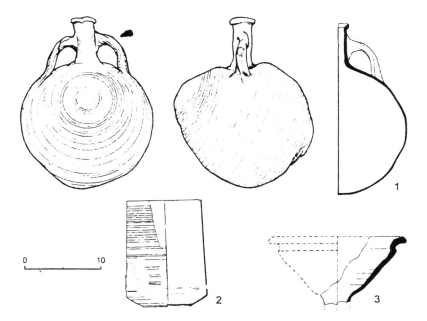

Figure X–8. Miscellaneous ceramic vessels.

well-defined nature of the assemblage (Killebrew 1999: 132–133, Fig. III.68–70). In many Jerusalem tombs only fragments of pottery were found.

The artifacts from the cemeteries comprise three main groups: (1) vessels dating to the first century BCE (in Jericho: placed in Type I, coffin burials); (2) pottery dating to the first century CE until 70 CE (placed with collected bone burials – Type II – and ossuary burials – Type III); (3) artifacts dating from the second half of the first century CE to the second century CE (placed with ossuary burials, such as Jericho tomb H and the mourning enclosure, Pl. X–5).

The deliberate breaking of grave goods used in the funerary ritual before being placed with the dead was a custom known in antiquity. The 'killing' of objects at funerals is explained in various ways: to reduce the risk of tomb robbery, abhorrence of using the objects again, fear of contamination (Grinsell 1961, 1973). The broken ceramic offerings could be explained as the breakage of the weak parts of vessels; only those shattered into pieces might indicate a ritual breakage ceremony (Anderson-Stojanovic 1987: 120). Broken pottery parts found in tombs that are irreparable may indicate some sort of funerary rite, to do with an expression of grief or pain (Rubin 1977: 220; Kloner 1980: 257).

Broken pottery found in graves at 'En el-Ghuweir are suggested to symbolized death (Bar-Adon 1977: 20). However, Yadin (1983, I:324, n. 64) maintains that the vessels that had become contaminated in the deceased's house before burial were broken and then placed in the grave. In Jericho most of the broken pottery was restorable. It follows that in Jericho most of the pottery was intact when it was deposited in the tomb.

B. VARIA

Grave goods other than pottery consisted of glass and wooden vessels, leather, iron, bronze, and stone objects; cosmetic utensils such as kohl stick, spatula, comb and accessories, spindle whorl, and jewelry.

Glass vessels

The majority of glass vessels, which are not commonly placed in tombs, are bottles; other vessels such as bowls seldom appear. Glass containers were found in only about 30 tombs. Two types of blown glass unguentaria are the most common (Figure X–9a–b): small pear-shaped bottles widespread in the first century and 'candlestick'-shaped ones that date to the late first-mid-third century CE (Zissu 1995: 162; Winter 1996: 96, Fig. 5.2, 5.4; Hachlili & Killebrew 1999: 134, Fig. III.71:2–5). Both these types belong to a group of Roman glass vessels that first appear during the second half of the first century CE (Barag 1972: 25–26). They have been recovered in funerary and domestic contexts and are found throughout the Roman Empire, especially in the eastern Mediterranean region.

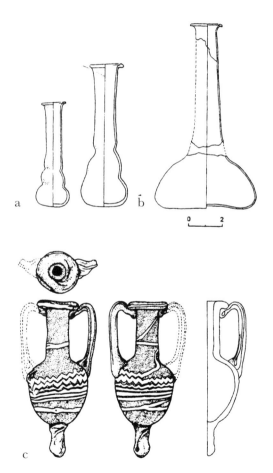

Figure X–9. Glass vessels.

A glass amphoriskos (Figure X–9c; Pl. X–6) was found in Jericho beside the feet of a child inside wooden coffin 104b (Hachlili and Killebrew 1999: 134, III.71:1, color Pl. III.3, Tomb D12–2). The amphoriskos originally had two handles, of which one is missing. It is of core-made dark blue glass, with an inlaid yellow thread wound around the vessel. It probably should be dated to the first century BCE. Comparable vessels have been found in Bari, Myrina, a necropolis of the third-second centuries BCE (Fossing 1940: Fig. 92, 93), and Cyprus (Harden 1968: 55–63, Pl. IV, B, g). Harden maintains that much of the Hellenistic core-made glass was produced on the Syrian coast, although other workshops may have existed in Alexandria, Rhodes, and perhaps Cyprus.

In some ossuaries the upper part of glass vessels are found (Tzaferis 1982: 51); the content may have been poured into the ossuaries and then the vessel was broken on the ossuary rim so that its upper part fell into the ossuary, its lower part to the floor.

Wooden Vessels

Various wooden containers were discovered in Jericho and 'En Gedi tombs. Bowls found there are associated with coffin burials: deep bowls were placed with deceased women in Jericho coffins (Hachlili 1999: Fig. III, 80:1; Coffin 59, Tomb D9–3; Fig. III.80:2, Coffin 104a; Tomb D12–2; and a bowl fragment in Coffin 128, Tomb D15). A small deep bowl was found with a child burial in Jericho coffin 104b, tomb D12–2 (Hachlili 1999: Fig. III.80:3). Similar bowls were found in coffins and tombs at 'En Gedi (Figure X–10; Pl. X–7): seven bowls were found in Tomb 1, two in Tomb 5; bowls and plates were found in tomb 6 (Hadas 1994: 51, 5*, Figs. 14:9–15; 50:16, 18; 61:7–17; Avigad 1962a: Pl. 18A). Similar wooden bowls were found in the Judean Desert Caves (Aharoni 1961: Pl. xxiii, 4; Benoit et al. 1961: Pl. X; Yadin 1963: Pl. 39:9, 10, 14). A comparable wooden box dated to the Bar-Kokhba period (second century CE) was found in the Cave of Horror (Aharoni 1962: Pl. 25, Fig. F). An unusual twisted fragment of wood was discovered in a Jericho coffin (Hachlili 1999: Fig. III.80:4; Coffin 104b, Tomb D12–2).

Other wooden vessels were recovered from Jericho and 'En Gedi: Handle (?) and box (?) decorated fragments were found in Jericho (Hachlili 1999: 138, Fig. III.80, 4, Tomb D2–6). At 'En Gedi wooden cosmetic vessels and a lid were found in Tomb 1, a wooden kohl

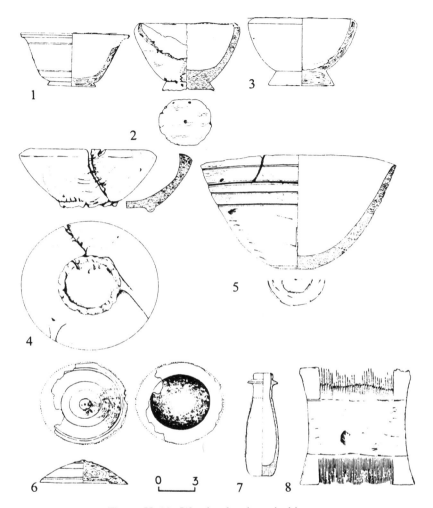

Figure X–10. Wooden bowls and objects.

tube in Tomb 5, a small wooden cosmetic bowl, a kohl tube, box, fragments of lids, and a tube (Hadas 1994: 51, 5*; Figs. 15:17–19; 50:19; 61:18–24). Two wooden decorated combs were found in tombs 1 and 6 (Hadas 1994: 51–52, 5*; Figs. 14:20; 61:25). The wooden vessels, except for the combs, were all produced on a lathe.

The wooden vessels recovered from the tombs (Tables X–4–6) might indicate two different burial customs: cosmetic articles placed with the deceased inside coffins and in the tombs were personal belongings, whereas the wooden bowls and plates possibly were made especially for burial (though they are considered table ware; however, no such vessels were found at sites as they usually did not survive).

Leather

A left foot three-layer leather sole (Figure X–11; Pl. X–8) was found under a woman's skull at the end of Jericho coffin 187; this is one of a pair of sandals placed one on top of the other (the second sole was found in bad condition). The three-layer sole was probably secured by stitching with thin leather thongs. The stitching (no thongs survived) was done along the edges of the soles and down a line in the center (Hachlili 1999: 136–137, Fig. III.76; Coffin 187, Tomb D27–6). Fragments of other sole layers were found placed in Jericho coffins (Hachlili 1999: 137, Fig. III.77; Coffin 103, Tomb D12–1; Coffin 104a, Tomb D12–2; Coffin 128, Tomb D15).

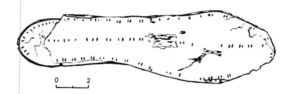

Figure X–11. Leather sandal from coffin 187, Jericho.

Similar sandals were found in an 'En Gedi – Naḥal David cave (Avigad 1962a: Pl. 19: 4–6) and in the Judean Desert, where they were dated to the second century CE (Aharoni 1961: Pl. XXII:1–4; 1962: Pl. 28B–D; Bar-Adon 1961: Pl. 15A; Benoit et al. 1961: Pl. XI; Yadin 1963: 165–168, Pl. 58). These were sandal soles with straps threaded through two slits on either side of the upper sole near the heel (Yadin 1963: 167). The Jericho sole layers showed no traces of slits or straps. They may have been destroyed, as in the damaged upper layer; alternatively the soles may have belonged to shoes rather than sandals (a child's shoe was found in the Naḥal Ḥever cave, Aharoni 1961: Pl. XXIII:5).

The sandals seem to have been placed in the Jericho wooden coffins as part of a funerary custom (they were usually placed with women and children). In the best preserved example the sandals were found under the woman's skull; placing the sandals under the

head, rather than beside the feet, may perhaps have had some meaning in connection with rites of grief or mourning. The Jericho sandals differ on two points from the sandals from the Judean Desert
Caves: they are earlier in date (first century BCE) and they were
found in wooden coffins in tombs, as part of Jewish burial customs.
The sandals from the Judean Desert were recovered in various parts
of the caves (Aharoni 1962: 195), and probably belonged to the people who found refuge there.

Fragments of shoes survived on a woman's legs at 'En Gedi (in
coffin 3, tomb 6, Hadas 1994: 34).

Some leather buttons and other fragments were found in Jericho
coffin 78, (tomb D12-pit), which may have belonged to sandals,
shoes (?), or leather garments (?). Leather fragments were found with
twigs in Jericho coffin 187 (tomb D27–6) indicating that the fragments may have belonged to a leather mattress (Hachlili 1999: 137,
Fig. III.79).

Cosmetic utensils, toilet vessels

Various cosmetic and toilet vessels were discovered in Jerusalem,
Jericho, and 'En Gedi tombs. They include bronze mirrors, kohl
sticks and tubes, a spatula, as well as spindle whorls, which are sometimes found with women's burials or often are considered to indicate women's interment (Table VII–1).

Bronze mirrors

Bronze mirrors were discovered in some Jerusalem tombs (Table
VII–1). Four were found in Jason's Tomb (Rooms A and B, Rahmani
1967: 91, Pl. 24C) and one at Giv'at Hamivtar (Tomb 28–4; Bahat
1982: 37, Pl. IX,6, Tomb A). A fragment of a bronze silver-plated
mirror was recovered from a Mount Scopus tomb (Zissu 1995: 20,
Tomb 1–36).

Bronze kohl stick

Bronze kohl sticks were discovered in several Jerusalem tombs (Pl.
X–5). The kohl stick was probably used to prepare cosmetics as well
as to apply them. The spatula was used to prepare creams or kohl
by braying it, as well as to spread cream and painting the eyes with
the color.

On Mount Scopus the kohl stick was buried with the bones of a woman inside ossuary 17 (Kloner 1980: 160–161, Fig. 30:1); another was recovered from a Mount of Olives tomb (Clermont-Ganneau 1899: 413–417; Kloner 1980: 161, tomb 3–24). The bronze kohl stick found with a mirror and a bone needle in *kokh* 1 of a tomb on Rehov Ruppin is considered an indication of a woman's burial (Rahmani 1961: 110, Pl. XVII:2). A bronze kohl stick from a tomb in East Talpiot (Kloner and Gat 1982: 74, Pl. XXIII:8) was elaborately decorated with incised rings and bands; a bronze kohl stick or spoon was found in a tomb in the Valley of the Cross (Sussman 1982: 69, Pl. XXII:1).

A bronze decorated kohl stick with a bead at its end was discovered inside Jericho coffin 78 (placed in the pit of tomb D12) with the primary burial of a woman and a child (Hachlili 1999: 22, 139, Fig. III.82). Two bronze kohl sticks were found at 'En Gedi (Hadas 1994: 11,40, Figs. 15:26, 62:31, Tomb 1 and Tomb 6).

Bone objects are seldom found in tombs, only several bone spatulas and spoons (Hachlili 1999: Fig. III.85; Coffin 78, Tomb D12 – pit; Kloner 1980: 183, Fig. 30:2,3; Tombs 26–9, 27–8).

Other cosmetic vessels were found at 'En Gedi (Hadas 1994: 5*, 51–52, Figs. 15:20; 61:20–25). They consist of wooden kohl tubes, a small container, a lid, a hairpin, and two combs (Figure X–10:6–8).

Spindle whorl

The spindle whorl was a small stone, clay, or glass disk with a hole pierced through the center into which a wooden stick was inserted. The spindle whorl (*pika* in Rabbinic Hebrew) served as the flywheel of the tool. This part of the object generally is preserved well and has been found in many of the tombs and sites all over the ancient world (Peskowitz 1997a: 164–165, 1997b: 112–115; Reich 2001: 149–150). The spindle whorl is mostly associated with women (see Chap. VII).

Spindle whorls were discovered in some Jerusalem tombs (Table VII–1): A hematite spindle whorl was found in Sanhedriya tomb 6 placed with a women (Rahmani 1961: 104, Pl. XIII:7, left), a basalt whorl was found in Jason's Tomb (Rahmani 1967: 90, Pl. 23C) and in other tombs (Sukenik 1930: 124, Pl. III,6; Zissu 1995: Tomb 13–33, Bilig 1995: 70–71). A fragment of a spinning hook was discovered in Jason's Tomb (Rahmani 1967: 91, n. 89).

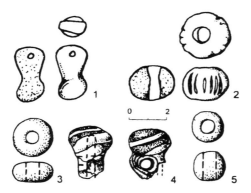

Figure X–12. Beads from tombs at Jericho.

Jewelry

Jewelry found in tombs includes mostly beads and rings (for a general study of Jewelry see Grossmark 1994). Beads of faience, glass, stone, bronze, and bone were found in Jerusalem tombs (Mount Scopus tomb, Reich and Geva 1982: 54, Fig. 6:10); glass, bronze, and bone beads were discovered in a tomb in Arnona (Bilig 1995: 70–71; Zissu 1995: 88, No. 13–33).

In Jericho single beads were found in coffins and in ossuary tombs (Hachlili 1999: 140–141, Fig. III.86).

At 'En Gedi, remains of bead necklaces were found in coffins 2, 4, 5, 8, tomb 1, in tomb 2 (8 beads), and in tomb 6 (88 beads). Most of these beads were made of glass, some of agate and carnelian; some of the 28 glass beads contained gold-leaf and some were granulated (129 beads) (Hadas 1994: 4–5, 11, 15, 55, 6*, Fig. 15:27, color Pl. 10).

Only single beads were placed with women in Jericho and many Jerusalem tombs. They were possibly an offering of grief, like other grave goods. Thrift may also have been a factor, as the buriers did not want to place whole bead necklaces there, which might have been expensive.

A few iron rings were found in Jerusalem tombs. An iron ring with a Carnelian gem set in was discovered in a Mount Scopus tomb; on the gem a boy's head is carved, possibly Apollo (Sussman 1992: 95, fig. 15). An iron finger-ring with glass oval bezel showing the bust of Fortuna-Tyche in profile and a cornucopia behind her

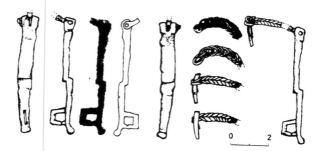

Figure X–13. Bronze clasp from Tomb D1 at Jericho.

shoulder was found in a tomb on Mount Scopus (Rahmani 1980: 53–54, Pl. VII:5,7). The use of a signet with a pagan deity depiction is unusual, although it is attested in some literary sources (M Avoda Zara 3:1; JT Avoda Zara 3, 42c). Rahmani contends that such ring gems possibly "were cut for the use of Jews, who though influenced by Hellenistic-Roman fashion, wished to keep, at least formally, within the boundaries of the Law".

Three copper alloy jewelry items, a finger ring, a fibula, and a plaque, were found inside ossuary 21 in a tomb on Mount Scopus, western slope (Vitto 2001: 91–2, Fig. 50).

Bronze items

Several items made of bronze were found in Jerusalem tombs (Tables X–1–3). In Jericho two pieces of a bronze clasp for a chest or box were found (Figure X–13; Hachlili 1999: Fig. III.81; Kokh 2, Tomb D1). A similar clasp was found in the Cave of Letters (Yadin 1963: No. 37, p. 90, Pl. 25, Fig. 32, dated to the Bar Kokhba period, second century CE).

A bronze broad ring (or cylinder?), two small bronze bell-shaped objects, and a bronze nail with round head were found in Jericho (Hachlili 1999: 138–139, Fig. III.83). Two bronze nails used to connect parts of the coffin were found in 'En Gedi, inside coffin 15, tomb 5 (Hadas 1994: 32). A bronze whistle was found in a Jerusalem tomb (Gershoni & Zissu 1996: 129, 57*, Fig. 33).

Iron objects

Various iron objects such as a shovel, a key, nails, chisels, and strigils were discovered in Jerusalem tombs: an iron shovel was found

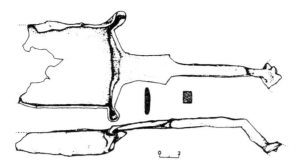

Figure X–14. Iron Shovel from a tomb at French Hill, Jerusalem.

among a heap of bones in the bone-repository chamber of a tomb on French Hill, Jerusalem. The shovel, which is a rare find in tombs, was probably used for handling the bones in the chamber (Mazar, A. 1982: 45, Fig. 2:12, Pl. XII:6).

A similar shovel was discovered in a Herodian Tomb in Geva (Sigelman 1988:36, Fig. 53)

Iron knives with bone or wooden handles were recovered among other objects in Jason's Tomb (Rahmani 1967: 91, Pl. XV:1) as well as in a tomb in Arnona (Bilig 1995: 70–71; Zissu 1995: 88, Tomb 13–33) and a tomb at Giv'at Shaul (Zissu 1995: 145, Tomb 30–44).

An iron key found in Jason's Tomb (*kokh* 10) was a personal belonging, which could be symbolic as cited in Sem. 8, 7: "The key and ledger of the deceased were hung up on his coffin because of intense grief". This implies that the object was placed in the tomb to arouse people's compassion or 'intense grief' (Rahmani 1961: 104, and n. 64; 1967: 96).

Iron chisels were recovered in the Goliath tomb at Jericho: one in the pit in chamber A and three in chamber B (Hachlili 1999: 140, Fig. III.84:1–3). They may have been used for carving inscriptions on the ossuaries. One of the iron chisels lay under ossuary XI in Chamber B (Hachlili 1999: 44).

Iron strigils found in two early questionably Jewish tombs in Jerusalem; a handle of a strigil and an iron knife were recovered from a first-century BCE tomb in the Valley of the Cross (Sussman 1982: 69, Pl. XXII:1). Another iron strigil was found in Mamila "Tomb 63" (Reich 1994: 117). Kurtz and Boardman (1971: 208, Fig. 44) state that strigils ("body scrapers for use after a rub-down with oil") are often found with oil bottles in burials of men and

children in the Classical period and later; the strigil characterizes
the dead person as an athlete. It was a sort of intimate personal
possession that was buried with its owner.

Iron nails were found in Jerusalem, Jericho, and 'En Gedi tombs
(Pl. X–6). In Jerusalem tombs the finds are two iron nails with
remains of wood, discovered in a Mount Scopus tomb (Tzaferis
1982: 51); a single iron nail discovered in Sanhedriya tomb 20, possibly for scratching names on ossuaries, or fixing the ossuary lid;
other nails found in Mahanayim Tomb; two nails in Jason's Tomb;
two small iron nails in a Mount Scopus tomb (Rahmani 1961: 100,
n. 35, 106; Rahmani 1967a: 91; Rahmani 1980: 53). An iron nail
was found in tomb C, Giv'at Hamivtar (Bahat 1982: 38, Fig. 5:2)
and an iron nail fragments was found in ossuary C2 at the Mount
Scopus Observatory (Weksler-Bdolah 1998: 51*).

At 'En Gedi, an iron nail was found in tomb 5 (Hadas 1994: 32)

The iron nails were probably wrought, forged by hand. Some
large angular nails with some iron fittings, angular iron parts, and
a lock were found in Jericho with wooden parts of coffin 113, tomb
D14 (Hachlili 1999: 67, 139–140; Figs. III.9, 84). They served to
reinforce several of the coffin parts.

Others nails were found in front of loculi or before the entrance
to Jericho coffin type tombs: two large angular nails with round
heads were found in tomb D27, in front of sealed *kokh* 3. Their location is unusual, and they seem to have been placed intentionally in
front of the sealed *kokh*. They may have been used for scratching
inscriptions, like the iron chisels, or they may have had a "magical"
function. Iron nails found in tombs were claimed to be in association with wooden coffins and ossuaries (Avigad 1967: 126, 1976a:
135; B. Mazar 1973: 222, fig. 17, Pl. 30:5). However, the find at
Jericho, where some of the iron nails were discovered in front of a
sealed loculus, possibly signify a special usage, perhaps connected
with the custom of placing nails in cemeteries or tombs, a magical
practice also known in Greek burials (Hachlili and Killebrew 1983a:
127–128; 1999: 169).

Bone items

Bone objects are seldom found in tombs. Some were cosmetic utensils (see above). A bone fork and die were recovered in Jason's Tomb

(Rahmani 1967a: 90, Pl. 24D). A bone object wrapped in a thin bronze sheet, possibly a whistle, was found in the repository of tomb II at Givʿat Shapira, Jerusalem (Gershuny and Zissu 1996: 55*, 129, Fig. 33).

Diverse objects

Many stone objects were recovered from Jerusalem tombs (Table X–1): stone 'measure cups' were found in a Sanhedriya tomb (Rahmani 1961: 104, Fig. 5) and in a tomb at Hizma (Avigad 1967: 139, Fig. 29). A stone vessel was found in Givʿat Hamivtar (Kloner 1980b: 222, Fig. 33); a stone bowl and a cup were recovered from the Mount Scopus Observatory (Weksler-Bdolah 1998: 51*, Figs. 33,17; 36,9). A round stone weight (?) was found, in the upper pool of the *miqveh* of the Jericho Goliath tomb. A basalt weight or grinding stone was found placed in Jericho coffin 78, tomb D12–pit (Hachlili 1999: 141, Figs. III. 87, 89). Two obsidian flakes (?) were found in Jericho coffin 78, tomb D12 (Hachlili 1999: 141, Fig. III.88). Small clumps of asphalt were retrieved from ʿEn Gedi tomb 1 (Hadas 1994: 7*). A fragment of a cotton hairnet was discovered in Jason's Tomb, near the entrance of Room B (Rahmani 1967: 93).

A folded lead plaque (fragmentary) was recovered from coffin 113, tomb D14 (Hachlili 1999: 141). Some folded lead plaques inscribed with curses, and sometimes pierced by a nail, have been found in Greek graves (Kurtz and Boardman 1971: 217, Pl. 45). A lead figurine of a naked headless male was found in a tomb at Ketef Hinnom, Jerusalem (Barkay 1994: 92).

Grave goods found inside coffins and ossuaries and in unusual placings in the tombs

Some of the personal effects were discovered in coffins in Jericho and ʿEn Gedi and inside ossuaries in Jerusalem (see Tables X–1–4). These include wooden objects, mainly bowls, glass containers, accessories and jewelry, beads, and bronze, iron, and bone objects. Leather sandals and shoes found in Jericho and ʿEn Gedi perhaps had some symbolic meaning in the funerary rites (Hachlili 1999: 31). The textile fragments recovered at ʿEn Gedi were probably burial shroud remnants (Hadas 1994: 56, 6*–7*).

Jesualem, Table X–1: Distribution of Artifacts in Jerusalem Burials*

Mt. Scopus, Western slope, Observatory

Tomb	Bibliography	Receptacles		Pottery						Glass vessel	Stone	Objects				
		Oss	Sarc	Cp	Jugl	Bowl	SJ	Ungun	Lamp			Iron Nail	Kohl stick	mirror	Fibula	Ring
1–1	Kloner 1980	9						3	3							
	Sussman 1982a															
1–2	Kloner 1980, 1982	5		1												
1–6	Vincent 1900	27														
1–7	Kloner 1980	12		1		1										
	Sukenik 1925															
	Kloner 1980															
1–8	Sukenik 1934	23		2	1			5	6							
	Kloner 1980															
1–10	Rahmani 1968	9														
	Kloner 1980															
1–11	Avigad 1971	14	2	1						1						
Nazarite Family	Kloner 1980															
1–12	Kloner 1980	4														
1–13, 14	Kloner 1980	7		2	2		1	9	3	3		2				
	Tsaferis 1982								2							
1–15	Kloner 1980	24		15	6	4	3	38	40	4		1			1	1
	Vitto 2000: 65–98											7				
												plaque				
1–16	Kloner 1980	8		+			+	+	2	1						
	Ben Arieh 1982a															
1–17, 18	Kloner 1980, 1993	38		6		1		4	3	3		5				
1–19	Kloner 1980	4		2	1			2	1							
1–20	Kloner 1980	3														
1–21	Kloner 1980	18		4		3		3	1	1						
1–22	Kloner 1980	1											1			
1–23	Kloner 1980	+						3								

Tomb	Reference														
1–24	Kloner 1980	+							1	+					
1–26	Sukenik 1928	10													
1–27	Kloner 1980 / Sukenik 1930b / Kloner 1980	13										100			
1–35, 36	Zissu 1995	7		+				+	+				1		
1–37	Zissu 1995	2						+	+	+					
1–39	Sussnan 1992 / Zissu 1995	18		+		+		+	+	+				1	1
1–40, 41	Zissu 1995	1													
1–42 A	Zissu 1995: 25–30	9		3	3	6	1	5	3	1	1			1	
Mt. Scopus Observatory	Weksler-Bdolah 1998														
1–43 B	Zissu 1995: 25–30 / Weksler-Bdolah 1998	4		2+	2	3		2	15		1				
1–44 C	Zissu 1995: 25–30 / Weksler-Bdolah 1998	11		4	3			8	8	2					
1–45 D	Zissu 1995: 25–30 / Weksler-Bdolah 1998	3		2			1	5	6						
1–47	Zissu 1995	10		1											
1–48	Zissu 1995	1													
1–49	Zissu 1995 / Abu-Raya and Zissu 2000	2		22	1	3	3	38	17	2					
1–50	Zissu 1995 / Abu-Raya and Zissu 2000	14		14	3	1	2	30	1			1			
1–52	Kloner & Zissu 2003	2													
1–53	Kloner & Zissu 2003	2													
Total		**301**	**2**	**83**	**22**	**20**	**14**	**152**	**112**	**16**	**4**	**117**	**1**	**2**	**2**

* The Jerusalem necropolis is divided into 30 areas following the Corpus published by Kloner (1980) and continued by Zissu (1995), finally published by Kloner and Zissu 2003 (with the same numbers). The tombs Nos. in the Tables follow this Corpus. Only tombs with ossuaries, sarcophagi and grave goods are recorded in these tables.

Mt. Scopus, East slope

Tomb	Bibliography	Receptacles		Pottery							Objects					
		Oss	Sarc.	Cp	Jugl	Bowl	SJ	Ungun	Lamp	Glass	Stone	Iron Nail	Ring	Bead Bone	Spindl whorl	Coin
2–1	Kloner 1980; Vitto 2000: 103–107	4		+	+		1	3								1
2–2	Kloner 1980; Vitto 2000: 107–109	4		+			1									
2–3	Kloner 1980; Vitto 2000: 99–103	3		5	7		1	2	1							
2–4	Kloner 1980			9				8	+		1					
2–5–9	Avigad 1967: 119–124	7	1	+	+				+			+				
Tomb of Nikanor	Kloner 1980															
2–10	Barag 1973; Kloner 1980	8														
2–11–15	Kloner 1980; Reich & Geva 1982	9		3				5	1							
2–16	Kloner 1980; Rahmani 1980	9		1	1			8	3		1		1 iron			
2–18	Kloner 1980	1		1					1							
2–19	Kloner 1980	1	3					3	3+		1	1				2
2–20	Kloner 1980	6														
2–21	Kloner 1980	1														
2–22	Kloner 1980			1	+			1	3+							
2–23	Sukenik 1932; Kloner 1980	13														
2–24	Sukenik 1942; Kloner 1980	3														
2–25	Kloner 1980	9														
2–29	Spoer 1907; Kloner 1980	1														

Tomb	Location	Bibliography	Total	Oss	Sarc.	Cp	Jug	Bowl	SJ	Ungun.	Lamp	Glass	Stone	Iron Nail	Jewelry	Misc
										Pottery			Objects			
				Receptacles												
2–33		Kloner 1980	1													
2–35		Kloner & Stark 1992; Zissu 1995	4													
2–36,37		Zissu 1995	1			+				+						
2–38, 39		Kloner & Zissu 2003; Edelshtein & Zias 2000: Tombs C, D	8					3	3	+		1	+		glass	1
2–40		Zissu 1995	1													
2–41		Zissu 1995	4													
2–42, 43		Kloner & Zissu 2003	10													
2–44		Kloner & Zissu 2003	1						+	+			+			
Total			**109**	**4**	**20**	**8**	**3**	**3**	**33**	**12+**	**+**	**3**	**1+**	**2**	**+**	**1** / 4

Mount of Olives

Tomb	Location	Bibliography	Oss	Sarc.	Cp	Jug	Bowl	SJ	Ungun.	Lamp	Glass	Stone	Iron Nail	Jewelry	Misc
			Receptacles						Pottery			Objects			
Dominus Flevit (DF)	Mount of Olives, Western slope	**Bagatti & Milik 1958; Kloner 1980: 21–25**													
3–1	DF 42–50	"	+		1				1		1	1			
3–2	DF 52–58	"	+		1					+	1				
3–3	DF 65–80	"	19		1		2		2		3				
3–4	DF 82–92	"	4				1								
3–5	DF 93–102	"	1							1	2				
3–6	DF 140–151	"	1				2								

Mount of Olives *(cont.)*

Tomb	Location	Bibliography	Receptacles		Pottery					Lamp	Glass	Stone	Objects		
			Oss	Sarc.	Cp	Jug	Bowl	SJ	Ungun.				Iron Nail	Jewelry	Misc
3–7	DF 280	"	2						1						
3–8	DF 282–284	"	1												
3–9	DF 294–301	"	17	2	3		2			2	2				
3–10	DF 310–313	"									1				
3–11	DF 331–336	"													
3–12	DF 355–369	"	15			1			2	1	3				
3–13	DF 370–376	"	1									1			
3–14	DF 384–389	"	6			2			1		3				
3–15	DF 425–426	"	2					1		1					
3–16	DF 427–438	"	25		2						1				
3–17	DF 438–452	"	7		1						2				
3–20		Kloner 1980	1												
3–24		Clermont-Ganneau 1989, I:413–417	+							1	1				spatula
3–27	Sisters of Zion	Kloner 1980 Vincent 1902	4												
3–28	A-Tur	Kloner 1980								+	+				
3–29	A-Tur	Kloner 1980	9										+	jewelry	
3–30		Avigad 1967: 135 Kloner 1980	3												
3–31		Clermont-Ganneau 1899, I:381–412	30+		1	1									cimbels
3–32		Kloner 1980	3												
3–35		Kloner 1980	1												
3–36		Clermont-Ganneau 1885: 99–102	6												

Tomb	Bibliography	Receptacles		Pottery						Objects			
		Oss	Sarc	Cp	Jug	Bowl	SJ	Ungun.	Lamp	Glass	Nail	Iron	Coin
3-37	Kloner 1980	+											
3-38	Kloner 1980	1											
3-41 A-Tur	Kloner 1980	2											
3-42 A-Tur	Kloner 1980	3+											
3-45	Kloner 1980	12											
3-46	Kloner 1980	5					1	3					
3-50	Allegretti 1982; Puech 1982a; Zissu 1995	8		6	3	6	5	6	1	1			
3-52	Kloner & Zissu 2003	2	2										
Total		**191**	**2**	**10**	**10**	**7**	**13**	**17**	**20**	**3**	**+**	**1**	**2**

Mount of Olives, East slope, Beth Phage, Beth 'Ania

Tomb	Bibliography	Receptacles		Pottery						Objects			
		Oss	Sarc	Cp	Jug	Bowl	SJ	Ungun.	Lamp	Glass	Nail	Iron	Coin
4-1	Orfali 1923; Milik 1924; Sukenik 1936; Kloner 1980	11											
4-2	Saller 1961: 220–232; Kloner 1980	5							+			1	1
4-5	Loffreda 1969; Kloner 1980				+				+				
4-6-9	Avigad 1967: 126–129; Kloner 1980	1											
4-15	Avigad 1967: 140; Kloner 1980	1		1				2	1	3			

Mount of Olives, East slope, Beth Phage, Beth 'Ania *(cont.)*

Tomb	Bibliography	Receptacles		Pottery						Objects		
		Oss	Sarc	Cp	Jug	Bowl	SJ	Ungun.	Lamp	Glass	Iron Nail	Coin
4–21	Saller 1957: 359 / Kloner 1980	1										
4–24	Kloner 1980											
4–27	Zissu 1995	1		1					1	1		1
Total		**20**		**2**	**+**			**2**	**2**	**4**	**1**	**2**

Upper Kidron Valley

Tomb	Bibliography	Recepteptable		Pottery						Objects		
		Oss	Sarc.	Cp	Jug	Bowl	SJ	Ungun.	Lamp	Glass	Jewlery	Coin
5–1 **Queen Helene of Adiabene**	Kon 1947 / Kloner 1980	+	3						1	+	+	+
5–10 / 5–14	Kloner 1980 / Zissu 1995	2							+	1		
Total		**2**	**3**						**1**	**1**	**+**	**+**

Kidron Valley (Rogel spring)

Tomb	Bibliography	Receptacles		Cp	Jug	Bowl	Pottery			Flask	Coin
		Oss	Sarc.				SJ	Ungun.	Lamp		
7–1	Kloner 1980	6									
7–2	Sukenik 1936; Kloner 1980	12									
7–5	Sukenik 1937; Kloner 1980	5									
7–8	Avigad 1962; Kloner 1980	11		1					1	1	
7–9	Avigad 1967: 127–132; Kloner 1980	8			3		2	8			
7–11	Sukenik 1945a: 26–31; Kloner 1980	18						1			
7–12	Sukenik 1945a: 23–26; Kloner 1980	5		1				5			
7–13	Mayer 1924; Savignac 1925; Kloner 1980	19									
7–20	Milik 1956; Kloner 1980	30		2				5	7		
7–21	Milik 1956; Kloner 1980	+						2			
7–36	Sukenik 1932; Kloner 1980	+									
7–38	Kloner 1980	+							+		1
Total		**114+**		**4**	**3**		**2**	**21**	**8+**	**1**	**1**

Akeldama (Avni and Greenhut 1996: 123–9; Kloner & Zissu 2003: Nos. 7–76–78)

Tomb	Receptacles		Pottery						Objects	
Akeldama	Oss.	sarc	Cp	Jug	Bowl	SJ	Ungun.	Lamp	Glass Bottle	coin
7–76–78										
Tomb 1										
Chamber A	4		15	13	9		2	10	28	9
Chamber B	3		1	1	1				19	
Chamber C	1		2				1	1	2	
Chamber D									2	
Tomb 2										
Chamber A	4									1
Chamber B	10	1								1
Chamber C	2							1	3	1
Unrecorded Chambers									1 bowl	
Tomb 3										
Chamber A	1		6		2		3		2	
Chamber B	3		1	1					5+	
Chamber C	1							1		
Chamber D	11									
Total	**40**	**1**	**25**	**15**	**12**		**6**	**13**	**62**	**12**

Areas 8, 9, 11: Valley of Hinnom, Abu Tor, Armon Hanazziv, Peace Forest

Tomb	Bibliography	Receptacles			Pottery						Objects	
		Oss	Sarc.	Cp	Jug	Bowl	SJ	Ungun.	Lamp	Glass	Iron Nail	Coin
8–4	Kloner 1980	1			3	2		23				1
9–2	Kloner 1980	2										
9–3	Kloner 1980	1										
9–4	Kloner 1980	7										
9–5	Kloner 1980	2										
11–39	Clermont-Ganneau 1899: 426–433	5										
11–41	Kloner 1980	1										
11–53	Greenhut 1992	12		6	4	4		5	2	1	2	1
Caiaphas Tomb	Zissu 1995											
Total		**31**		**6**	**7**	**6**		**28**	**2**	**1**	**2**	**2**

East Talpiyot

Tomb	Bibliography	Receptacle		Pottery					Objects	
		Oss	Sarc.	Cp	Jug	Bowl	SJ	Ungun.	Lamp	Bronze Kohl stick
12–2	Kloner 1980	13								
12–4	Avigad 1967: 133–135			2	5	1		8	1	
12–5	Kloner 1980			1	2		1			1

East Talpiyot (*cont.*)

| Tomb | Bibliography | Receptacles | | Pottery | | | | | Lamp | Objects |
		Oss	Sarc.	Cp	Jug	Bowl	SJ	Ungun.		Bronze Kohl stick
12-6	Kloner & Gat 1982 Zissu 1995									
	Kloner 1980				1			1	1	
	Kloner & Gat 1982 Zissu 1995									
12-44	Rahmani 1994: Nos. 712–735; Zissu 1995	24								1
12-45	Zissu 1995	7		4						
12-46	Rahmani 1994: Nos. 701–709; Zissu 1995	10								
12-47	Zissu 1995			1				3	1	
12-48	Zissu 1995			5	3			2		
Total		**54**		**13**	**11**		**1**	**14**	**3**	**2**

Talpiyot, Ramat Rachel, Beit Zafafa, Gilo

Tomb	Bibliography	Receptacles			Pottery					Glass	Iron nails Javelin knife	Spindle whorl	Objects				
		Oss	Sarc.	Cp	Jug	Bowl	SJ	Ungun.	Lamp				spoon	Bone	beads	earing	Coin
13–1	Sukenik 1947	14		4	3	1	2	4	5								1
13–2	Kloner 1980 / Bahat 1982		–	2		1		3	1								
13–3	Kloner 1980 / Ben Arieh 1982	4		1			1	2	1								
13–4	Kloner 1980 / Tsaferis & Berman 1982	6		1	2	1		3	3								7
13–8, 9	Stekelis 1934 / Kloner 1980	11		1	2	1		10	3	9	1	1			1 glass	gold earing	
13–10	Kochavi 1964: 74–82 / Kloner 1980		2							5	8 / 1 javelin						
13–11	Kochavi 1964: 70–73 / Kloner 1980	3															
13–32	Zissu 1995	2															
13–33	Bilig 1995 / Zissu 1995	11		28	2	4		27	11	1	2 knife	1 Bone	2	+			1
13– 40–89	Zissu 1998	1															
Beth Zafafa																	
Total		53		37	9	8	3	49	24	15	9	1	3	1	1	1	9

West and southwest of the Old City, Mamila, Ketef Hinnom

Tomb	Bibliography	Receptacles			Pottery							Objects			
		Oss	Sarc.	Cp	Jug	Bowl	SJ	Ungun.	Lamp	Misc.	Glass	Stone	Iron	coin	misc
14-1 Herod's Family Tomb	Vincent 1954; Kloner 1980		2												
14-2	Kloner 1980, 1985	+	+		+			+	+			+			
14-4	Avigad 1967: 125–6; Kloner 1980	5													
14-6	Zissu 1995														
14-7	Zissu 1995													1	
14-8	Reich 1994; Zissu 1995										+			1	
14-9	Reich 1994; Zissu 1995						1		+						
14-11	Reich 1994; Zissu 1995												1 Strigil		
14-13-31	Reich 1994; Zissu 1995									+	+				
14-32	Barkay 1994: Cave 34; Zissu 1995			1					1	seal	1	1		5+	figurine
14-33	Barkay 1994: Cave 51; Zissu 1995									+	+			6	
14-34	Barkay 1994: Cave 25; Zissu 1995							+	+		+	+			
14-35	Barkay 1994: Cave 13; Zissu 1995								1					1	
14-37, 38	Zissu 1995	2		+	+										
Total		7+	2+	1+	+		1	1+	2+	1+	1+	1+	1	14+	1

Areas 15–17: Malha, Giv'at Mordechai, Mt. Herzel, Kfar Shaul

Tomb	Bibliography	Receptacles		Pottery						Object
		Oss	Sarc.	Cp	Jug	Bowl	SJ	Ungun.	Lamp	Glass
15–15	Zissu 1995			+			+	2	2	
16–4	Kloner 1980	4		1	1			2		
16–7	Kloner 1980			4				1	1	2
17–1	Kloner 1980	2		1					2	
17–11	Kloner 1980	6			1			2		
17–15	Kloner & Eisenberg 1992; Zissu 1995	6		+	1	2	+	2		
Total		**18**		**6+**	**3**	**2**	**+**	**9**	**5**	**2**

Areas 19, 20: Romema, Meqor Baruch, North-west of the Old City

Tomb	Bibliography	Receptacles		Pottery						Objects					
		Oss	Sarc.	Cp	Jug	Bowl	Ungu	Lamp	Glass	iron Nail	Spindle Whorl	Mirror	Pin bone	Beads Bracelet	coin
19–1	Kloner 1980	2													
19–4	Sukenik 1930a; Kloner 1980	4				1	5	3	5	2+	1	1	1	2 bracelet	1
19–5	Baramki 1938; Kloner 1980	5					4	2	85					+	
19–6	Kloner 1980	1													
19–8, 9	Rahmani 1967b	23		+	+	1		4							1
19–13	Kloner 1980	3							+					1 bracelet	
19–14	Kloner 1980	2		1											
20–1	Kloner 1980	3							1						1
20–3	Kloner 1980	20													
Total		**63**		**1+**	**+**	**2**	**9**	**9**	**91+**	**2+**	**1**	**1**	**1**	**3+**	**3**

Valley of the Cross, Saker Park, University Giv'at Ram

Tomb	Bibliography	Receptacles		Pottery				Objects					
		Oss	Cp	Bowl	SJ	Ungun.	Lamp	Glass	Stone	Iron	Bronze	Kohl	Mirror Stick
21–1	Kloner 1980			1		3	1			1 Strigil knife	1 spatula			1
	Sussman 1982b												
21–7	Kloner 1980	3	+			+							
21–8	Kloner 1980	14	1	1		2	2						
	Bahat 1982b												
21–17	Kloner 1980	4						4					
21–	Rahmani	7	6		3	9	1						
18,19	1961: 110–114											1	
	Kloner 1980												
21–24	Zissu 1995	9											
22–1	Kloner 1980	2	1	+	1				1	2	2		
	Ben Arieh 1982b												
22–5	Zissu 1995	1											
Total		**40**	**8**	**3**	**4**	**14**	**4**	**4**	**1**	**3**	**3**	**1**	**1**

Areas 23–24: Rehavia, Kiryat Shemuel, Talbiya, Tel Arza to Shmuel Hanavi St.

Tomb	Bibliography	Receptacle			Pottery							Objects		
		Oss	Sarc.	pans	Cp	Jug	Bowl	SJ	Ungun	Lamp	krater	Glass	Iron	stone
23–3	Rahmani 1967a Kloner 1980			16	65	27	52	18	46	29		7		2
Jason Tomb														
23–4	Rahmani 1961: 114–6 Kloner 1980	4			3			3	6			4	1 nail	

		Objects										Organic Material				Coin
		Iron Nails	Key	Bronz	Bone	hooks	net	Ring iron	Spindle Whorl	Mirror	Knife iron	wood	Olive grain	Cotton Felt		
23–5	Kloner 1980, 1981			4						5					1
23–6	Zissu 1995		1	1							1				
23–13	Kloner 1980			4						5					
23–18	Hansler 1913			6											
Kalon Tomb	Kloner 1980														
23–19	Sukenik 1928; Kloner 1980			12											
23–23–25	Zissu 1995			3			1	7	2	1	1				
23–27, 28, 29	Zissu 1995			5				1	2	5	3	4			1 knife
	Greenhut 1996														
24–8	Lidzbarski 1908, II:191–197			8											
Habashmi Tomb	Kloner 1980														
24–9	Kloner 1980			3											
24–10	Kloner 1980			2		1		+		2	+				
24–12	Vincent 1901;														
Frieze Tomb	Macalister 1902; Kloner 1980				1										
Total		**52**	**1**	**16**	**70**	**35**	**55**	**25**	**70**	**34**	**4**	**12**	**2**	**2**	

Jason's Tomb, Rehavia

Tomb	Objects										Organic Material			Coin
	Iron Nails	Key	Bronz	Bone	hooks	net	Ring iron	Spindle Whorl	Mirror	Knife iron	wood	Olive grain	Cotton Felt	
Jason's Tomb 23–3	2	1	3	1	2	3	2	1	4	2	1	4	2 1	55

Sanhedriya

Tomb	Bibliography	Oss	Sarc	Cp	Jug	Bowl	SJ	Ungun.	Lamp	flask	Glass	Stone	Iron Nails	Spindle Whorl
								Pottery				Objects		
Shahin Hill	Rahmani 1961: 120			3	1	2	3	4	4					
Sanhedria 5 25–5	Rahmani 1961: 120 Kloner 1980			2										
Sanhedria 6 25–6	Rahmani 1961: 120 Kloner 1980			2								1 cup		1
Sanhedria 7 25–7	Rahmani 1961: 120 Kloner 1980		2	3			2	1						
Sanhedria 9 25–9	Rahmani 1961: 120 Kloner 1980													
Sanhedria 10 25–10	Rahmani 1961: 120 Kloner 1980			3		1		2		1				
Sanhedria 11 25–11	Rahmani 1961: 120 Kloner 1980	+		7		2	2	4	1	1				
Sanhedria 12 25–12	Rahmani 1961: 120 Kloner 1980			2				2	2					
Sanhedria 13 25–13	Rahmani 1961: 120 Kloner 1980	1		5	2	1	4	2	5			1 pendant		
Sanhedria 14 25–14	Rahmani 1961: 120 Kloner 1980	+	+	15	2	4	7	4	3	1				
Sanhedria 18 25–18	Rahmani 1961: 120 Kloner 1980			4			3	1						
Sanhedria 19 25–19	Rahmani 1961: 120 Kloner 1980			2										
Sanhedria 20 25–20	Rahmani 1961: 120 Kloner 1980			11	2	1	4	3	4				1	
R. Nisan Beq 25–22	Rahmani 1961: 120 Kloner 1980	7		1	1		2	1	1					
Mahanayim 25–23	Rahmani 1961: 120 Kloner 1980	8		4	1	1			5				1	
Total		**16+**	**2+**	**54**	**9**	**12**	**27**	**24**	**25**	**3**		**2**	**2**	**1**

Areas 26–27: Ramat Eshkol, Givʿat Hamivtar, Shderot Ashkol to Shmuel Hanavi st.

Tomb	Bibliography	Receptacles			Pottery			Ungun.	Lamp	Glass	Objects		
		Oss	Sarc.	Cp	Jug	Bowl	SJ				Spatula spoon	Kohl Stick	Coin
26–1	Kloner 1980	5											
	Tzaferis 1970: Tomb	5											
26–5	IV; Kloner 1980												
26–8 The Grape Tomb	Vincent 1899, Macalister 1900a, Kloner 1980	+						2					
26–9	Kloner 1980	2		3	2		1	2	3				
26–11	Kloner 1980	7								2	1	1	2
26–13	Zissu 1995	2											
27–1	Zissu 1995 Kloner 1980 Rahmani 1982 Zissu 1995	14	2	1			1						
27–3	Kloner 1980	24		1									2
27–5	Kloner 1980	14											
27–6	Kloner 1980 Zissu 1995	20		+		+	+	2					
27–8	Kloner 1980	2											
Total		**95**	**2**	**5+**	**2**		**2+**	**6**	**3**	**2**	**1**	**1**	**4**

Giv'at Hamivtar and Nahal Zofim

Tomb	Bibliography	Receptacles		Pottery							Objects			
		Oss	Sarc.	Cp	Jug	Bowl	SJ	Ungun	Lamp	Glass	stone	Spatula	mirror spoon	coin
28–1	Tzaferis 1970: I Kloner 1980	8		3	4			4	5					
28–2	Tzaferis 1970: II Kloner 1980			1				7						
28–3	Tzaferis 1970: III Kloner 1980	2		+	20			20	7					
28–4	Kloner 1980 Bahat 1982: A	9		3	1	1	2	3		1			1 bronze	1
28–5	Kloner 1980 Bahat 1982: B	3		1	1			1						
28–6	Kloner 1980 Bahat 1982: C			2		1		1		1				
28–7	Kloner 1980, 1981	17		2		1		15				1		
28–8	Kloner 1980	1		1				4						
28–9	Kloner 1980 Vitto 2000: No. 5	3		+				1	2		1			
28–12	Kloner 1980 Vitto 2000: No.6	2												
28–13	Kloner 1980 Bahat 1982: D	2		+	5	1	1	8	6					1
28–15	Tzaferis 1974 Kloner 1980	1												
Aba Tomb														
28–16	Macalister 1904: 246–48													
Umm el Amed														
28–17	Kloner 1980	2		1										
28–18	Kloner 1980	3		1+										
28–19	Zissu 1995							+						5
Total		**51**		**14+**	**31**	**4**	**2**	**64+**	**20**	**2**	**1**	**1**	**1**	**7**

French Hill

Tomb	Bibliography	Receptacles			Pottery							Objects						
		Oss	Sarc	Cp	Jug	Bowl	SJ	Ungu	Lamp	flask	Glass	Stone	Iron	Mirror	Kohl	Kohl stick	bead	misc
29–1	Kloner 1980	7																
29–3	Kloner 1980			+	+			+	+									
29–4	Kloner 1980 / Mazar 1982	4		1	9			4	4				shovel					
29–5	Kloner 1980	4		+			+		+									
29–6	Kloner 1980	7																
29–7	Kloner 1980	3		3				2	2									
29–9	Kloner 1980	7		1				2	3									
29–10	Strange 1975: Tomb 1 / Kloner 1980	2		2	1													
29–11	Strange 1975: Tomb 2 / Kloner 1980	7		2				4	1									
29–12	Strange 1975: Tomb 3 / Kloner 1980			5	1		1	3			1							
29–13	Strange 1975: Tomb 4 / Kloner 1980			26	7			3	8	1		1	1 (Iron nail)					
29–14	Strange 1975: Tomb 5 / Kloner 1980						1		1									
29–15	Strange 1975: Tomb 6 / Kloner 1980	7		8	1		10	3	2		1	1		1 bronze	1 bronze		2	2
29–16–18	Kloner 1980, 1980a			2	2	1		9	1									
29–19	Kloner 1980	2						2										
29–20	Kloner 1980	3		3	1	2		4	3									
29–21	Kloner 1980	2		2			1	5										
29–27	Kloner 1980	2																
29–28	Zissu 1995	14		5			1	9	9	1	1							
29–29	Gershuni & Zissu 1996: I / Zissu 1995 / Gershuni & Zissu 1996: II	16		7			+	24	3								1 bone	
29–36	Zissu 1995 / Gershuni & Zissu 1996: IX	3						1										flute
Total		**88**		**67**	**22**	**3**	**14**	**75**	**37**	**2**	**2**	**2**	**2**	**1**	**1**		**2**	**3**

Ramot, Shuʾafat, Givʿat Shaul, Neve Yaʿakov

Tomb	Bibliography	Receptacles			Pottery						Stone	Objects		
		Oss.	Sarc.	Cp	Jug	Bowl	SJ	Ungun.	Lamp	Glass		Iron	Bone	coin
30–1	Kloner 1980	6												
30–9	Clermont-Ganneau 1899, I: 448–50	6		+					2+	+				
	Kloner 1980													
30–12	Kloner 1980	2												
30–13	Abel 1913	25												
	Kloner 1980													
30–14	Kloner 1980	5		1	1			4	2	1				
	Vitto 2000: No. 7													
30–7	Kloner 1980	8												
30–18	Avigad 1967: 138–9	10									1 cup			
	Kloner 1980													
30–20	Zias 1982				2									
	Zissu 1995													
30–22	Zissu 1995			1			2							
30–23	Zissu 1995	6		2			1	5	3			Spatula or Kohl stick	1 bracelet	
	Wolff 1996													
30–25	Zissu 1995	4						1						
30–26	Zissu 1995				1	1								
30–44	Zissu 1995						2					1 knife		1
Total		72		4	4	1	5	10	7+	1	1	2	1	1

Table X-2: Distribution of Artifacts in Jerusalem Burials, Total

Tomb areas	Receptacles			Pottery						Objects								
	Oss	Sarc	Cp	Jug	Bowl	SJ	Ungu	Lamp	Misc	Glass	Stone	Iron	Mirror	Kohl stick	jewelry	Spindle whorl	coin	misc
1–1–53	301	2	83	22	20	14	152	112		16	4	117	1	1	4			
2–1–44	109	4	20	8	3	3	33	12		20	3	1			2	1	4	
3–1–52	191	2	10	10	10	7	13	17			3				1			2
4, 5	22	3	2				2	3	1	5							2	
7–1–78	154	1	29	18	12	2	27	21		62		1					13	
8, 9, 11	31		6	7	6		28	2		1		2					2	
12–	54		13			1	14	3						2				
13	53		37	11	8	3	49	24	1	15		9			2	1	9	3
14	7	2		9		1		2		1		1					14	1
15, 16, 17	18		6	3	2		9	5		2	1							
19, 20	63		1		2		9	9		91	1	2	1		4	1	3	
21, 22	40		8		3	4	14	4		4		3	1	1				3
23, 24	52	1	70	35	55	25	70	34	20	12	2	7	4	1	2	1	55	7
25	16	2	54	9	12	27	24	25	3		2	2						
26, 27	95	2	8	2			6	3		2				1			4	1
28	51		14	31	4	2	64	20		2	1		1				7	1
29	88		67	22	3	14	75	37	2	2	2	2	1	1	2			
30	72		4	4	1	5	10	7		1	1	2			1			3
Total	**1417**	**19**	**433**	**191**	**141**	**110**	**600**	**340**	**27**	**236**	**20**	**149**	**9**	**7**	**18**	**4**	**114**	**21**

Table X-3a: Distribution of Artifacts in Jericho Burials

Tomb	Receptacles		Pottery							
	Coff. wood	Oss.	Cp	Jug	Bowl	SJ	Ungun.	Lamp	Krater	Misc
A1		7		1					2	
A2		9	2			2	1	3	1	
A6		1	1		1	1				
B2		1								
D1		4	1	1	1	2		1		1
D2	6		4	1		2	3			
D2 Out						12		1	1	
D2/D3						1			1	
D3										
D4										
D6	4						1			
D8 Out			1		1	1				
D9	3				1	7				
D9 Out			2		1	1	4	1		1
D11	1									
D11 Out						8				
D12	7		4			4	3			
D12 Out			1	1	2	27	1	1	3	
D2/D12					1	3				
D13						3				
D14	1	4								
D14 front						5				
D12/D14						7				
D15	1									
D16	1					4				
D18						6		1		
D18 Out			1			6	1			
D21					1					

	30	50	105	71	109	250	64	18	19	9
D22	1		5	2	3	1	3			
D22 Out			1			2				
D25 Out			1			3				
D26 Out			1			1				
D27	5		3				1			
D27 Out			1			2				1 cup
F4			40	4	2	6	22			
F7			20		1	4	6			
G1							2			
G2							1			
Tomb H										
Courtyard+ Miqveh		1 lid	16	60	87	123	10	6	11	6 plates
Entrance								1		
Chamber A		10			2	6	5	2		
Chamber B		12		1	5					
H Outside		1								
Total	**30**	**50**	**105**	**71**	**109**	**250**	**64**	**18**	**19**	**9**

Table X–3b: Distribution of Artifacts inside Jericho Tombs

Tomb	Receptacles			Pottery						
	Coff. wood	Oss.	Cp	Jug	Bowl	SJ	Ungun.	Lamp	Krater	Misc
A1		7		1		2			2	
A2		9	2			1	1	3	1	
A6		1	1		1					
B2		1								
D1		4		1	1			1		1
D2	6		1			2	3			
D3						2				
D4							1			
D6	4									
D9	3				1	7	4	1		1
D11	1									
D12	7		4			4				
D13		4				3	3			
D14	1									
D14 front						5				
D12/D14						7				
D15	1									
D16	1					4				
D18			1			6				
D21					1			1		
D22	1		5		3	1	3			
D27	5		3				1			
F4			40	4	2	6	22			1 cup
F7			20		1	4	6			
G1							2			
G2							1			
Tomb H										
Chamber A		10			5		5	2		
Chamber B		12		1				1		
Total	**30**	**48**	**77**	**7**	**15**	**54**	**52**	**9**	**3**	**3**

Jericho, Table X–3c: Distribution of Artifacts inside Tombs (continue)

Tomb	Objects							Jewelery		Accessories		Misc	coin
	Glass	stone	wood	Leather	Iron Nail	Iron misc	Bronze Misc	Bead	Ring	Kohl Stick	Spatula bone		
A2							1	1					
A6	1								1				
D1			1 box										
D2						1	1 clasp						
D3													2
D9			1 bowl			1							
D12	1	2 flakes obsidian 1 basalt weight	3 bowl	2 sandals buttons	2	1		2		1	1	Grape seeds	
D14					5	5						1 Lead plaque Pecan	
D15			1 bowl	1 sandal									
D18					1								
D27				2+ sandal	2							matress	2
F7			1 frag.			1	2 bells	2					
Hill		Nefesh											
D-Surface													
Tomb H													
courtyard	2												
Chamber A	3		3 frag. charcoal		2+2	2	1 nail	2					
Chamber B						3							
Total	**7**	**4**	**10**	**6+**	**14**	**14**	**5**	**7**	**1**	**1**	**1**	**4**	**4**

Table X-4: Grave goods found inside Jericho Coffin

Coffin	Tomb	Individual	Pottery ungunt	glass	wood Bowl	Ring Bronze	Bead	Kohl Stick bronze	Iron Nail	metal	bone	Stone	Leather	Misc
59	D9–3	F + fetus			1	1								
78	D12– pit	F + child	3				1 glass	1	2	1	spatula	1 Weight 1 flake	buttons	hair
85	D12	M												rope
94	D12	M					1 faience							
103	D12–1	M											sandal	
104a	D12–2	F			1								Sandal+	
104b	D12–2	Child		amphriskos	2									rope
113	D14	M												
128	D15	M+F+ child			1								sandal	Pecan nut
185	D27–2	M+F												
187	D27–6	F											+ 2 Sandal Matrass +	
190	D27–4	M												
Total			**3**	**1**	**5**	**1**	**2**	**1**	**2**	**1**	**1**	**2**	**7+**	**4**

Table X–5: Distribution of Artifacts in Jericho Burials (Bennet 1965)

Tomb	Receptacles				Pottery					Objects				
	Coff. wood	Oss.	Cp	Jug	Bowl	SJ	Ungun.	Lamp	Bottle Glass	Bronze	Iron Nail	leather	Bead pendant	misc
G 2		2				1						pillow		
G 3	+							7					brooch	
G 5			1				2							
G 81	3		1	1	1		1							
H 23		1												
J 41		1												
K 23		2	3	1	11	16		10	15	4	10		1 Bead 1 pendant	1 shell 1 ring?
Q 1														
Total	3	6	5	2	12	17	3	17	15	4	10	1	3	2

Table X–6: Various Tombs, Distribution of Artifacts in Burials

Tomb	Reference	Oss	Pottery						Glass	Stone	Jewelry	Objects							
			Jug SJ	cup	Cp	Bowl	Ungun.	Lamp				Copper bronze	Key	Bone Spatula spoon	iron	Kohl stick	Spidle whorl	mirror	coin
Tel Goded Tomb1	Sagiv et al. 1998	8	6	1			1	3											
Tomb4		5	3	2		18	12	24	2										
Geva	Siegelman 1988		3		9			1		Bowl basalt	13 beads Gold earing Necklace beads	3 bowl +	1	1 1	Shovel sickle 7 rings nails	1 bone	5 glass 3 bone		
Horbat Zefiyya	Nahshoni et al. 2002	36	1		21	2		79	1										
Huqoq Tomb I	Ravani & Kahane 1961	3	3		1			8	12		18 beads	2 Band 2 vessel		1 spoon	2 nails			1	
Huqoq IV	"		2					1+	6						5 nails band				1
Total	Total	**52**	**18**	**3**	**31**	**20**	**13**	**116+**	**21**	**1**	**34**	**7**	**1**	**4**	**17**	**1**	**8**	**1**	**1**

Table X–7a: Distribution of Artifacts in 'En Gedi tombs (Hadas 1994: 62, Tables 1)

'En Gedi Tomb	Receptacles		Pottery				Objects				
	Coff. wood	Oss.	Cp	Bowl	Ungun.	Lamp	Glass	Stone	Wood Bowl	Wood misc.	Bronze
1	8		14	2	3	1		1	7	4	1
2	4		2		1	1					7
3	3		3	1	2	1					
4	4	1	2		4						1
5	15					1			2	1	5
6	5		2	1	2				9	7	1
7	+			1	2						1
8											
9											
Total	**39+**		**23**	**5**	**14**	**4**	**1**	**1**	**18**	**12**	**16**
Nahal David											
2	4			2	+	+					
3					+	+					
4	3								2		
5							1				
6								1			
Total	**46**		**23**	**7**	**14**	**4**	**1**	**2**	**20**	**12**	**16**

Table X–7b: Distribution of Artifacts in 'En Gedi Burials (Hadas 1994:62, Tables 1; Avigad 1962a:182–3)

	Objects		Accessories						Organic Material									Coin	Misc
'En Gedi Tomb	Iron Nail	Ladles	Bronze jug	Misc	Bead	Kohl Stick	Wooden Vessels	Comb	Basket	Rope	Belt	Textile	Papy	Mat	Nut	Palm	Leather shoes	Coin	Misc
1		2	1	2	129	1	11	1	1	+	+	+		+					Asphalt
2					8	1				+	+	+	+						
3	+																		
4				1 bell															
5	3	1		3 nail			3			+	+	+		+					
6					88	1	17	1		+	+	+		+					
7														+					
8															3	2		1	
9																			
Total	**3+**	**3**		**6**	**225**	**4**	**31**	**2**	**1**	**+**	**+**	**+**	**+**	**+**	**3**	**2**		**1**	
Nahal David																			
2		1																	
3		2																	
4									1						2		2		pomegr anates
5																			
Total	**3**	**6**	**1**	**6**	**225**	**4**	**31**	**2**	**2**						**5**	**2**	**2**	**1**	

Table X-8: Grave goods found inside 'En Gedi Coffins (Hadas 1994)

'En Gedi Coffin	individ	Objects			Pottery				Accessories				Organic Material					Clay lump
		Bead	Ladle	Bronze nail	CP	ungun	Lamp	Kohl Stick bronze tube wood	Albaster tube wood	Wooden Vessels	Comb	Basket	Rope	Mat	Textile	Nut	leather shoes	
Tomb 1																		
1	?							1 tube		2		1						
2	F+ child	+											+					+
3	2M+ child												+	+				
4	M+ child	+								2	1						2	+
5	?	+													+			+
6	2 child	+							1									
7	2 child	+																
8	2 child	37								2					+	+		
Tomb 3																		
1	5 skulls					1	1											
2	F, M, child				1	1	1											
3	2 children																	
Tomb 4																		
3					2													
Tomb 5																		
1	F+3M, 2? child				2	1				1		1			1			
11	2 F, 2 child			1														
15	M,+ ?				2			1 bronze 1 wood		1								
Tomb 6																		
2	F, M, 4 child									3					+			
3																	2	
Total	37+	1	2	5	3	3	3	1	11	1	2	+	+	1+	+	2	+	

Table X-9: Distribution of Artifacts in Second Temple Tombs Jerusalem, Jericho, 'En Gedi (Total)

Sites	Receptacles				pottery						objects					jewelry	Accessories			coin	misc
	Coff.	Oss	Sarc	Cp	Jug	Bowl	SJ	Ungu	Lamp	Misc	Glass	Iron	Stone	wood	leather		Spindle	Mirror	Kohl		
Jerusalem	–	1417	22	433	191	141	110	600	340	27	236	149	20			18	4	9	7	114	21
Jericho	33	54		110	73	121	267	67	35	28	22	36	4	7	7	11		1	1	9	12
'En Gedi/ Naḥal David	46			23		7		14	4		1	3	2	34	2	225			4	1	9
Total	**79**	**1471**	**22**	**566**	**264**	**269**	**377**	**681**	**379**	**55**	**259**	**188**	**26**	**41**	**9**	**254**	**4**	**12**	**9**	**124**	**40**

Finds inside wooden coffins

In Jericho, only few grave goods were placed inside coffins, but no objects were discovered inside ossuaries (see Table X–4). A small wooden bowl and a fragment of a large bronze ring were placed with the burial of a female with a fetus in coffin 59, tomb D9–3 (Hachlili 1999: 18). Tomb D12 contained several coffins with grave goods within; coffin 78 contained the primary burials of a woman and a child. Several objects placed next to the woman's head included a bronze kohl stick with a bead at its end, a basalt weight, a bone spatula, iron nails, leather fragments including some in the shape of flowers (buttons?), and a leather string. Coffin 94 contained the primary burial of a male with a faience bead. Coffin 103 contained the primary burial of a male with fragments of a leather sandal and grape seeds. Coffin 104a contained the primary burial of an adult female with fragments of a wooden bowl, leather fragments, and a sandal. Coffin 104b contained the remains of a young child, with a glass amphoriskos at his feet and next to it a wooden bowl, and some other wooden fragments (Hachlili 1999: 22, 24, Fig. II.43). Fragments of a sandal, a wooden vessel, and a pecan nut were recovered in coffin 128, tomb D15; the coffin contained the primary burials of three individuals: a male, a female, and child. Leather fragments were found in Coffins 185, 190, and 198, tomb D27; a leather sheet and twigs were found under the burial of a female, and two sandals under her head, in coffin 187, tomb D27; originally this was probably a leather mattress filled with twigs.

At 'En Gedi some grave goods were placed within the coffins in tomb 1 (Table X–6): coffin 1 (with a youth) contained textile fragments, a mat, a wooden bowl, chalice and a vessel, and a small clay lump. Coffin 2 (female and a child) contained textile fragments, a wooden vessel, and beads. Coffin 3 contained two adults and a child with textile fragments covering the deceased. Coffin 4 (with a male and a child) contained a wooden bowl, a box, a comb, textile fragments, leather shoe fragments, and a small clay lump. Above the coffin was a basket, which might have belonged to Coffin 7. Coffin 5 contained an adult with beads and a small clay lump with a wooden bowl under the coffin. Coffin 6 (with two children) contained beads, textile fragments, and an alabaster vessel. Coffin 7 (with two children) contained beads; under the coffin a wooden bowl and a small clay lump were found. Coffin 8 (two children) contained 37 beads, two wooden bowls, walnut shells, and a pine tree seed.

Items placed in ossuaries

Fragments of a cooking pot and other pottery fragments were found in ossuary 5, tomb 1–2, Mount Scopus, western slope (Kloner 1982: 58). A bronze kohl stick was found with a woman's bones in ossuary 17, tomb 1–21, Mount Scopus, western slope (Kloner 1980: 160). Several objects were discovered inside ossuaries placed in tomb 1–15, Mount Scopus, western slope: a glass tube-shaped bottle was found in ossuary 7; two flat based alabastra were found in ossuaries 10,11; three jewelry items made of copper alloy – a finger ring, a thin plaque, and a fibula – were discovered in ossuary 21 (Vitto 2000: 67, 87, 91, Fig. 50). Some items were found inside ossuaries placed in tombs 1–42–46 (Tombs A–D), Mount Scopus Observatory: fragments of an iron nail were found in ossuary C2 (an adult burial). A lamp nozzle was found in ossuary A7 (adult burial) and another one in ossuary D3 (with a woman's and children's burial) (Weksler-Bdolah 1998: 50–*51*). Glass bottles were found in ossuary 97, tomb 3–16, Mount of Olives (Dominus Flevit, 427–438; The 'Agra Family Tomb inscribed "Shalom the Proselyte"; Bagatti and Milik 1958: 18–19, 95). A glass bottle was placed in an ossuary with bones of a woman and child, tomb 4–27, Mount of Olives (Wadi Kadum; Zissu 1995: 50). A glass bottle, a lamp, and a glass bracelet were placed in the only ossuary in tomb 4–15, Mount Of Olives (Beth 'Aniya; Avigad 1967: 140; Kloner 1980: 35–6). Fragments of glass bottle necks were found in two ossuaries placed in tomb 1–13, 14, Mount Scopus, western slope (Tzaferis 1982: 51; Zissu 1995: 17). In an ossuary from a loculus tomb on Shemuel Hanavi St. Jerusalem (Rahmani 1994: 7–8, 126–127, No. 209) a small glass bottle dated to the first century BCE was discovered.

The recoveries of grave goods found inside the coffins seem to indicate that various personal items such as cosmetic objects and jewelry, mostly beads, were placed with the deceased. The wooden vessels might have been especially meaningful in burial rites, as it should be noted that wooden vessels were found at neither the Jericho nor the 'En Gedi settlement sites. These wooden vessels apparently have either not survived in the settlements or some of them were specially made for burial rites, particularly for placement with the dead in the coffins. Perhaps the same manufacturers that made the wooden coffins also produced the special wooden vessel used in burial. Sandals and leather fragments at Jericho were placed inside the coffins, frequently with burials of women, and usually next to the deceased's head, not the feet, which seems to indicate some custom connected with burial, possibly associated with some rites of grief or acts of mourning. Although in Jerusalem tombs no leather or wooden objects have survived due to the humid climate, organic items were presumably placed with the dead and the same rites were practiced.

The items found in the Jerusalem ossuaries were probably randomly collected together with the bones and might not have any significance in burial rites (but see Tzaferis 1982: 51).

Of special interest are some unusual placing of objects at Jericho tombs. Two pottery kraters were placed next to two ossuaries in a *kokh* in Tomb A1 (Hachlili 1999: 6, Fig. II.4), which seems to indicate a relation between the ossuaries and the kraters. A lamp was placed on top of the deceased's skull in tomb A2, *kokh* 5 (Hachlili 1999: 8).

In some cases cooking pots were placed either beside coffins or beside the sealed loculi; three cooking pots were found on the benches next to coffins 78, 84, one cooking pot was placed in front of sealed *kokh* 2 in tomb D12 (Hachlili 1999: 22, Fig. II.42). A cooking pot was discovered in front of sealed *kokh* 5, tomb D27 (Hachlili 1999: 29, Fig. II.57). Two whole cooking pots were found above a wooden coffin in tomb 4 at 'En Gedi, possibly thrown into the tomb shortly before the *kokh* was sealed (Hadas 1993: 21, 2*). The location of these cooking pots might indicate a rite associated with the placing of the objects in the tomb.

C. COINS

Although during the past century hundreds of tombs dating from the Second Temple down to the Late Roman period have been excavated or surveyed, coins are a rare occurrence. Only a scattering of coins have been found in various Jerusalem and Jericho tombs, most of them not in situ (Hachlili and Killebrew 1983c, 1986; Greenhut 1992: 71–72; Hachlili 1999: 135–6; Table X–7).

The largest collection of coins found inside a tomb of the Second Temple period is from Jason's Tomb, Jerusalem (Rahmani, 1967: 92–93); 42 of the 55 coins were found in room A, *kokh* 9. This is an unusual *kokh* in that it was dug into the floor of the tomb chamber; the sides were then built up with stones. Of the 42 coins, 36 were found at the foot of the deceased and another six were found nearby. The coins belong to the period spanning 5/6 to 30/31 CE (the Procurator period), with the exception of one coin, which dates to the time of Alexander Jannaeus (103–76 BC; Rahmani, 1967: 92–93, 96). The majority of the coins are later in date than the other artifacts discovered in the tomb. This led the excavator to suggest that the coins are associated with burial in *kokh* 9, and to conclude that this burial is later than the other interments in the tomb. In fact, it is not clear if the deceased was Jewish. In support of this suggestion Rahmani points out that the association of a large number of coins with the interred has rarely been discovered in Jewish tombs. Additional coins were found in room B, on the floor of the porch, or in the inner courtyard debris, but they cannot be related to any specific burial custom.

Some other coins discovered in relation to the deceased are notable.

A coin of Agrippa I was found in a woman's skull in Ossuary 8, from the Caiaphas Tomb, Jerusalem (Greenhut 1992: 70). A coin (No. 11) of the Jewish War (Year 2, 67 CE) was discovered in ossuary 9, chamber B, tomb 2, Akeldama (Avni and Greenhut 1996: 18). At Ketef Hinnom, Jerusalem, a coin was discovered next to the deceased's skull (Barkay 1994: 92–93; Zisso 1995: 96).

At "Dominus Flevit," Mount of Olives, numerous tombs of the Second Temple period have been excavated (Bagatti and Milik, 1958: 44, 163). Over a hundred coins were found in the debris of the tombs or in their vicinity. Only seven of these coins (one Hasmonean, one of Herod Antipas, and five of the Procurators) are dated to the first century BCE – first century CE.

A coin of Agrippa I was found in the debris of a Talpiyot tomb (Sukenik 1947: 21, Fig. 31). The coin, dating to year 6 of Agrippa I, is worn, and the reverse is only partly legible. The context of this coin lacks any significance and cannot be related to any of the burials. A bronze coin of the Year 2 of the revolt (67 CE) was recovered from a closed loculus of tomb A at Giv'at Hamivtar (Bahat 1982: 4*, 37, Pl. IX, 7).

Four coins were found in two rock-cut tombs at Jericho, two of them coins in tomb D18 (Tomb Type 1), dated to the second half of the first century BCE. One bronze coin of Herod Archelaus

(4 BCE–6 CE) (Pl. X–9) was found in the damaged skull of a coffin burial in Tomb D18 on the west bench of the chamber. The other, a Yehoḥanan Hyrcanus I coin (134–104 BCE) (Pl. X–10), seems to have fallen into the entrance debris of tomb D18 (Hachlili and Killebrew 1983a: 118; 1983c, 1986; Hachlili 1999: 135, Figs. III. 72, 73).

Two bronze coins were discovered in Jericho tomb D3 (Tomb Type II). The coins were found stuck together in a skull uncovered in *kokh* 1 (Pl. X–11). Both were coins of Agrippa I dated to his sixth year, 41–42 CE (Hachlili 1999: 135, Figs. III:74, 75).

At 'En Gedi, a bronze coin, Year 2 of the Bar Kokhba revolt, was found among the bones at the top of the repository in tomb 8, either belonging to the tomb's period of use or thrown in after the tomb was no longer in operation (Hadas 1994: 42, 3*).

Among tombs dating to later periods coins are only occasionally found. These are obviously later intrusions, and have no connection with the Jewish tombs of the Second Temple period.

Table X–10: List of coins found in Second Temple Jewish tombs*

Site	Coin	No. of coins	Reference
Jerusalem			
Akeldama	Herod	1	Bijovski 1996: 106
	1st War, Year 2	1	
	Romans	7	
Arnona	Procurators	1	Zissu 1995: 88, Tomb 13–33
Caiapas Tomb	Agrippa I	1	Greenhut 1992: 70
Dominus Flevit	Hasmonean	+	Bagatti & milik 1985: 163
	Herod Antipas	1	
	Procurators	5	
Gebel Mukaber	Pontius Pilate	1	Hachlili & Killebrew 1983b: 152
Giv'at HaMivtar	Alexander Jannaeus	1	Kloner 1980: 134, T. 28–12
Giv'at HaMivtar, Tomb A	2nd year, War	1	Bahat 1982: 4*, 37, Pl. IX,7
Giv'at HaMivtar	Hasmonean	3	Zissu 1995: 127, T. 28–19
	Procurators	2	
Giv'at Ram	Tiberius	1	Kloner 1980: 93
Giv'at Sh'aul	Procurators	+	Zissu 1995: 145
Jason's tomb	Hasmonean	7	Rahmani 1967: 91–93
	Herod	2	
	Procurators	46	
Ketef Hinnom, cave 13	Alexander Jannaeus	1	Zissu 1995: 97, 159

Table X–10 (*cont.*)

Site	Coin	No. of coins	Reference
Jerusalem			
Ketef Hinnom, cave 34	Hasmonean	1	Barkay 1994: 92; Zissu 1995: 158
	Seleucid; Nabatean	1+	
	Herod Agrippa,	+	
	Great Revolt	1	
Ketef Hinnom, cave 51	Hasmonean	5	Barkay 1994: 92; Zissu 1995: 158
	Seleucid	1	
Kidron Valley	Pontius Pilate	1	Kloner 1980: 54, T. 7–38
Mamilla-E. Botta St	Hasmonean	1	Reich
Mamilla-Haʿemek St. Tomb 5	Hasmonean	9	Reich
Mamilla- Haʿemek St. Tomb 8	Hasmonean	1	Reich
Meqor Ḥayyim	Roman	4	Tzaferis & Berman 1982: 70, 8*–9*,
	Nabatean		72–3; Pl. XXIII:1–7
Mt. of Olives, East	Pontius Pilate	1	Kloner 1980: 37
	Later Roman		
Samuel Hanavi St.	Procurators	2	Kloner 1980: 129, T. 27–3
Sharei Zedeq, south	Alexander Jannaeus	1	Sukenik 1930: 124
Talpiyot	Agrippa I	1	Sukenik 1947: 21, Fig. 31
Zikhron Moshe	?		Kloner 1980: 94
Jericho			
Tomb D3	Agrippa I	2	Hachlili 1999: 135
Tomb D18	Hasmonean	1	Hachlili 1999: 135
	Herod Archelaus	1	
ʿEn Gedi			
Tomb 8	Bar Kokcba, Year 2	1	Hadas 1994: 42, 3*

* updated list (see also Greenhut 1992: 71).

In addition to Jerusalem and Jericho, the use of coins in funerary ritual can be attested at only two other sites in the country: ʿEn Boqeq and Mampsis.

ʿEn Boqeq is the site of a second-century CE Roman fortress in the Judean Desert. The deceased was found in an excavated burial with two silver dinarii of Hadrian (ca. 133 CE) placed on his eye sockets (Gichon, 1970: 138, 141). Nearby a coin of the Bar Kokhba revolt was found. The excavator could neither determine the nationality of the deceased nor suggest whether he was a permanent resident; he assumed that he was not Jewish.

In the excavation of two tombs (100 and 117) in the Nabatean necropolis of Mampsis in the Negev, two silver dinarii of Trajan (ca. 117 CE) were found between the teeth of the deceased (Negev, 1971: 119, 128). This positioning was probably in line with the Greek custom of placing coins as payment to Charon.

A debate surrounding the use of coins in Jewish burial customs of the Second Temple period appears in published research, which has erroneously suggested that the custom of coin-on-eye was widespread among Jews of the Second Temple period (Rahhmani, 1980b; Hachlili and Killebrew 1983c: 149–151; 1986: 59–60 for further discussion).

Excavated skulls are mostly found in a damaged condition, so that coins might originally have been placed in any part of the skull. Two instances of coins in Jericho are associated with skulls (Hachlili 1999: 135), and a similar coin of Agrippa I was found inside the skull of a woman in the Caiaphas tomb in Jerusalem (Greenhut 1992: 70). The evidence indicates that the coins had been intentionally placed in the tombs at the time of burial. This might have been inspired by the pagan Greek custom, noted above, of placing a coin in the mouth of the deceased as payment to Charon (Charon's *obol*). In Greek mythology he is the ferryman who carries the spirits of the dead across the River Styx (Kurtz and Boardman, 1971: 211; Toynbee, 1971: 44, 49, 119, 124, 291). As Jews were often influenced by the surrounding Hellenistic culture, on occasion they adopted Hellenistic practices and customs (Hachlili and Killebrew 1983a: 127–128) without necessarily accepting their pagan significance. However, the rarity of this practice is obvious from the few finds of skulls containing coins. Rahmani (1993: 149–150) maintains that the two cases in Jericho and one in Jerusalem can hardly represent a custom practiced by Jews in Jerusalem and Jericho. Through rare, these instances are more likely manifestations of pagan influence on Jewish burial customs.

Recently published research, however, has misread the above data to indicate that the custom was widespread among Jews of the Second Temple period (Hachlili & Killebrew 1983c).

Bender (1894) traces the antiquity of the custom of *closing* the eyes of the deceased and cites the *Zohar*, a medieval Jewish manuscript, to support his claim; He also quotes two Jewish sources in Semahot 1.4, Mishnah Shabbath 23.5, which distinctly speak of the *closing of the eyes* of the deceased. But no mention is made of placing any object over the eyes. Bender (1894: 102–03) cites James Frazer (1886),

who discusses the practice of closing the deceased's eyes, setting forth
ancient and contemporary examples of this custom together. Nowhere
does one find mention of an ancient Jewish custom of placing coins
over the eyes of the deceased. The only reference by Frazer to the
placing of coins is with respect to the then modern-day Russians
Jews placed potsherds over the eyes.

Jumper, Jackson, and Stevenson (1978: 1350–57) examined the
image of the Shroud of Turin with an instrument known as the
Interpretation Systems' VP–8 Image Analyzer, and they discerned
an object resting on each eye. These objects were circular in shape,
flat, and nearly identical in size. Citing A.P. Bender as their source,
they state: "at the time of Jesus . . . it was customary for the Jews to
place objects (potsherds – pottery fragments – or coins) over the eyes
of the dead." From the material assembled in that article, there is
no basis for claiming that placing coins over the eyes of the deceased
was a prevalent burial custom among Jews of the first century CE.
(This mistake was repeated by Wilson 1978: 200.)

Several more misleading and false statements are used to support
the observation that coins are placed over the eyes of the image of
the Shroud of Turin, which consequently is considered as evidence
in the dating of the shroud. Virginia Borton (1980: 112) remarks,
with no reference whatsoever, that "Jews often used coins or pottery shards to close the corpse's eyes, believing they must not open
before glimpsing the next world".

Francis L. Filas (1981: 136) contends that the coin-on-eye custom
is mentioned in medieval times and later. In fact, as stated above,
this custom existed only during fairly recent times. It is impossible
to assume from these later sources that the coin-on-eye custom also
existed among Jews during the Second Temple period. Filas declines
to accept the fact that Jews of the Second Temple period could
practice a pagan custom such as placing coins in the mouth.

Rahmani (1980: 197; 1982: 6–7; 1993) correctly argues that the
subjective evidence Father Filas presents is not sufficient to identify
the spots found in the region of the eyes on the Shroud of Turin
as coins, specifically those of Pontius Pilate. He also stresses the lack
of evidence from first-century CE tombs to support the claim for a
coin-on-eye custom.

The placement of coins inside tombs was not usually part of the
burial ritual, particularly among Jews. Though the practice of plac-

ing coins in the mouth does sporadically appear, more rarely among Jews, the placing of coins over the eyes is reported in only one case at 'En Boqeq (furthermore, it is highly doubtful that the interred at 'En Boqeq was a Jew). Thus, the claim that placing coins over the eyes was a common Jewish burial practice during the Second Temple period cannot be substantiated either by the archaeological or literary evidence.

As a rule, most excavated skulls are found in a damaged condition, so that coins could have been originally placed in any part of the skull. The two cases of coins found in skulls in Jericho (Hachlili 1999: 135–136) and a similar coin of Agrippa I retrieved from the skull of a woman in ossuary 8 in the Caiaphas family tomb in Jerusalem (Greenhut 1992: 72; Horbury 1994: 34–35) were explained as coins placed in the mouth, as a payment for Charon (Charon's *obol*) for ferrying the deceased across the river Styx, mainly because that custom was well known in the Hellenistic world. The coin in Greek tombs was usually of bronze and found in the mouth, in the hand, or in the grave (Kurtz and Boardman 1971: 211; Toynbee 1971: 49, 119, 124, 219, n. 16; Stevens 1991). As Jews were often influenced by the surrounding Hellenistic culture, on occasion they adopted Hellenistic practices and customs (Hachlili and Killebrew 1983a: 127–128) without necessarily accepting the pagan significance of such practices. The rarity of this practice is obvious since only few skulls were at all associated with coins among the hundreds of skulls examined during the excavations of the Jerusalem and Jericho cemeteries; but see Rahmani (1993: 149–150, see also Zissu 1995: 158–9), who maintains that the two cases in Jericho and one in Jerusalem can hardly represent a custom that was practiced by Jews in Jerusalem and Jericho. However, it seems more probable that though rare, these are manifestations of pagan influence on Jewish burial customs. Thus, placing coins in tombs does not seem to have been part of the customary burial ritual, though it is occasionally evinced. It was no doubt an even rarer occurrence among Jews.

D. Conclusions

The funerary rite or practice of placing grave goods in tombs with the deceased was not a mundane custom. The grave goods placed in the graves are sparse, simple, everyday items, and the practice is to bury the body with only few, if any, personal belongings, frequently inexpensive objects. There is no definite sign of divergence between rich and poor tombs. Offerings were sometimes placed next to the burials, the coffins, and the ossuaries, but seldom within the coffin or ossuary; the grave goods in the Second Temple tombs were more often recovered from women and children's interments.

Second Temple tombs reveal the distribution of artifacts, which provides a valid assessment of their value to society and the objects' worth in the funerary context. The grave goods recovered from the tombs and their statistical analysis (Tables X–1–7) show a pattern. The most frequent items were pottery unguentaria vessels and cooking pots (see Table X–4). As for the former, the considerable number of them found in the graves reflects the extent of their use, functioning as a popular offering (Anderson-Stojanovic 1987: 120). Unguentaria vessels served several functions in the burial stages: they contained oil and perfumes brought into the tomb for funerary rituals. The body was cleaned, purified, and anointed with water and oil, and sprinkled with perfume in preparation for burial before being wrapping in shrouds. Funerary spices and perfume could add a pleasant scent and prevent the bad odor in the tomb; for fear of contamination, the vessels were left in the tomb or placed next to the bones. The liquid contained in the unguentaria could perhaps help decompose the body.

The function of the cooking pots in the funerary context is variously interpreted: (1) They reflect an early custom (later abandoned) of placing cooked food and drink in the tomb for the deceased; the cooking pots, being contaminated, were forbidden to be removed afterwards and were left in the tomb. (2) The cooking pots were brought as offering to the dead. They belonged to the deceased or to the mourners. (3) The cooking pots contained water to wash hands, or wine and oil that were poured onto the bones while the ossilegeum was being conducted. (4) The pots were used to heat water for various burial functions such as washing the deceased body. (5) Possibly a symbolic rite was associated with the cooking pots, indicated by the special places where they were positioned in the tomb or in the coffins.

Bowls and kraters might have contained liquids to wash, rinse, or anoint the body. Some storage jars found inside the grave may have held water used for the dead; other storage jars placed outside the tomb or next to the entrance might have symbolized some last rite, or the water in them was used for purification after the tomb was sealed.

Lamps were probably used mainly for lightning in the tombs, but they perhaps also had a symbolic meaning as designated by a lamp placed on a deceased's skull, implying both life and death. Lamps were found in lesser numbers inside the graves; the buriers might have taken them out after their task was finished.

A unique find is the written bowl recovered from a Jericho tomb, a ceramic small bowl similar to many such bowls found at sites and tombs in the country (Killebrew 1999: 117–118, Fig. III.56:4). This bowl is inscribed with the three-generation family genealogy and the origin, 'from Jerusalem', of Ishmael, who had placed the bowl close to the ossuaries of his father Shim'on and his grandfather Palt'a, all in the same loculus. The inscribed bowl seems to serve as a memorial to the family.

Personal objects and belongings were placed in the coffins, including wooden objects such as bowls, glass containers, jewelry – beads and rings, accessories, bronze, and iron and bone objects. Most of the items were common and cheap enough to leave in the tombs. Wooden items were found only in Jericho and 'En Gedi tombs, although it seems quite likely that similar objects were placed with the dead also in Jerusalem, where they did not survive because of the climate. The wooden objects might also have been used in everyday life, where they did not endure. Or perhaps these items, especially the wooden bowls, were produced by the same workshops that made the wooden coffins, intentionally crafted for burial as a type of mortuary production.

The evidence in some burials indicates an inclination to place certain vessels near specific parts of the body, usually the head and the feet. Leather sandals and lamps at times were so placed, perhaps bearing some meaning in the funerary rites. There is no indication that the offerings were put in the tombs randomly; their placement seems to have been deliberate. Many of the personal items were recovered with women's and children's interment in Jericho and 'En Gedi, occasionally positioned inside coffins. Jews quite rarely used items with pagan characters as grave goods: the examples consist mainly of ring gems and coins.

The grave goods recovered from the tombs seem to indicate that there was no distinctive concern that each item or vessel be unique. It was forbidden to remove grave goods: taking any object away was considered robbery of the dead (Alon 1976: 103; Rahmani 1961: 118). The wooden and metal items at 'En Gedi are suggested to be personal effects of the deceased, while the pottery vessels were left in the tombs by the buriers (Hadas 1994: 38, 7*). The grave goods might have originally belonged to the deceased, or conceivably to the family or to the mourners, though it is possible that particular personal possessions belonging to the deceased were placed with them.

CHAPTER ELEVEN

FUNERARY CUSTOMS AND RITES

The treatment of the dead comprises funeral ceremony, burial rites, mortuary practices, and rites of passage. The association between the living and the dead is articulated in literary sources, in material form consisting of archaeological evidence, and in social factors, which will affect the way death is seen in the framework of the community and its social relationships (see also Parker Pearson 1982: 110–112). The relation of the dead to the living is revealed in the separation and distance of the place of the living from that of the dead: Jewish custom positioned the cemetery outside the settlement. The relation between the living and the dead was emphasized also by the physical locating of the dead in receptacles and in tombs entirely detached from the living. The archaeological evidence shows some diversity among the deceased, and designates the roles of the family and the individuals as well as the rituals and customs expressed by the living toward death. The artifacts placed with the interred reveals their association with the dead. Some are an expression of grief, others might have been specially made for the grave, and various objects from the living are offered to the dead.

The significant manifestation of the relationship is provided by the building and erections of memorials to ancestors such as monumental tombs and the *nefesh*.

These aspects explain and interpret the burial practices and facilitate understanding of the symbolism of mortuary ritual, as well as surveying and evaluating the common and changing practices and their social association. Burial customs and funerary rites display social identity, status, gender, and place in society of the dead.

Reconstruction of ancient rituals and customs relies on analysis of written sources relating and illuminating them, and of the archaeological record of material remains such as the receptacles and the grave goods. It also has recourse to evidence found in the art created for burial rituals such as the architectural ornamentation, the decoration of the coffins, sarcophagi and ossuaries, and the wall paintings. These remains convey the beliefs of the living, of the buriers, about life and death as articulated in the burial practices and rituals.

A three-stage pattern was proposed for the *rite of passage* (Morris 1992: 8–10, Fig. 4): the first was 'the rite of separation', the second is a liminal status, and the third was the 'rite of aggregation'.

The Jewish funeral ritual and burial customs of the Second Temple period (first century BCE – first century CE) are mentioned in the writings of Josephus and in later rabbinical sources dealing with burial laws and describing or explaining the rituals.[1] Excavations of Second Temple Period tombs in Jerusalem have been an important source for the material remains of rituals and practices. However, only a partial and incomplete picture has emerged, due to the disturbed condition of the tombs and the poor preservation of the artifacts. As for the Jericho tombs, due to the isolated location of the area and the dry climatic conditions, their contents, including organic materials, are well-preserved (Hachlili & Killebrew 1999). Together with the data gathered from the Jerusalem tombs they provide a clearer and more detailed picture of the cemeteries, tomb architecture, burial types and chronology, burial containers, inscriptions, Jewish art, and funerary customs practiced by Jews during that period (Rahmani 1958; 1961; 1967a; 1967b; 1977, 1994; Avigad 1962a; 1967; 1971; Kloner 1980; Zissu 1995; Kloner & Zissu 2003).

The tomb architecture has the same general tomb-plan in each of the Second Temple necropoleis, consisting of a square chamber with several loculi or a single loculus. It continued in use throughout the Second Temple Period in Jerusalem, Jericho, and elsewhere in Judea (see Chapter II). Burials, both primary and secondary, were in loculi tombs hewn into the hillside, which served as family tombs with provision for the separate burial of each individual. A few graves dug into the earth were found in Jerusalem (Kloner 1980a: 244–246)

---

[1] The main contemporary sources are the works of Josephus, written in the latter part of the Second Temple period. His *Jewish War*, *Antiquities*, *Life*, and *Against Apion* reflect the ideas and customs of the time. Reference is also made to Rabbinical literature, codified from the second century CE onwards, which may at times reflect earlier Jewish customs of the Second Temple period. The subject of Jewish burial customs has been researched in the past, but it was based mainly on written sources rather than on archaeological evidence (Klein 1908; Meyers 1971; Safrai 1976). For a preliminary treatment of Jewish burial customs during the Second Temple period at Jericho, see Hachlili and Killebrew 1983a, 1999: 166–175.

and during Kenyon's excavations at Jericho (Bennett 1965: 516, 532–539).

The Jericho evidence proves conclusively that loculi tombs were initially designed and used for primary burials (i.e., permanent inhumation) in coffins, as is also indicated by the length of the loculus, which corresponds to the length of a coffin (Hachlili 1999: Tables II.5; III.1). The same loculus tomb plan continued to be used for ossuary burials as indicated by the tombs discovered in Jerusalem, Jericho, and elsewhere. An earlier claim that the *kokh* was "intimately" connected with secondary burial is unsubstantiated (Kutscher 1967: 279; Meyers 1971: 64–69; Avigad [1976a: 259] states: "For Jews the use of the *kokh* is associated with the custom of bone collection for secondary burial") as there was no need to prepare a *kokh* two meters long for the average ossuary, which was 70 cm long.

In addition to the single-chamber rock-cut tombs, an unusual monumental tomb, the Goliath tomb, was excavated at Jericho. It consisted of a large open courtyard with benches running alongside the north, south and to the west a two-chambered loculus tomb. Similar courtyards with benches are known from other contemporary monumental tombs in Jerusalem, such as the Tomb of Helene of Adiabene, Sanhedriya Tomb XIV, and Givʿat Shahin, which are usually smaller. Courtyards with benches are also found in the third-century CE Jewish necropolis of Beth Sheʿarim, and probably served a similar purpose (Avigad 1976a: 41–45, 81–82, Fig. 23–24, 35, 61, Pl. XXX:1). This courtyard was probably used for mourning and memorial services similar to the 'eulogy place' or house of assembly (Hachlili 1979: 58; Netzer 1982b: 110, 1999: 45–50, Figs. II.68, 78, 81, 82) mentioned in Jewish sources (BT BB 100b; see also Klein 1908: 51–52: Safrai 1976: 779). It could have accommodated a ceremony conducted at the grave on the day of burial, similar to the last libation and drink offering in Greek burial practices (Kurtz and Boardman 1971: 145). Comparable in plan, but differing in function, are the triclinia in the Nabatean cemetery at Petra (Horsfield 1938: 31–39, Pls. 64:2, 66, 67:2, 71, 73), which served as a gathering place for commemorative meals on the anniversary of the deceased's death. Some scholars argue that possible commemorative meals are indicated by some finds in tombs (see also Goodenough 1956 VI:169, 172, refuted by Lieberman 1965: 509, 511): ashes and soot scattered in the tomb and on some vessels at Givʿat Hamivtar tomb (Bahat 1982a; Zissu 1995: 125, 160, Nos. 28–13). A pile of ashes before the entrance to tomb 1 at Giv'at Shapira included blackened fragments of cooking pots (Gershuny and Zissu 1996: 46*). At Ras el-Jamiya, Isawiye (Kloner 1980: 18, No. 2–22), a cooking pot was found placed on ashes in a niche close to the courtyard stairs. However, no bowls or other vessels were found.

The Goliath monumental tomb at Jericho also contained a *miqveh* (ritual bath) constructed as an integral part of the courtyard. It was fed by the aqueduct running along the hilltops through the cemetery from 'En Duyuk (Na'aran) to ancient Jericho and the Hasmonean and Herodian palaces (Netzer 1977: 1).[2] In Jerusalem an aqueduct passed through the cemetery in close proximity to the tombs, and here and there actually cut into them. The role of the *miqveh* in a cemetery is intriguing, since according to the *Halacha* a person cannot be purified in a cemetery from contamination by the dead (Reich 1990: 119–121).

A. Burial Types: Jerusalem, Jericho, 'En Gedi, Qumran

Burial types and customs practiced in tombs in Jerusalem, Jericho, 'En Gedi, and Qumran are described. Each site varied in its customs.

Jerusalem Burial Types, Customs, and Chronology

Three different burial types and customs were practiced in Jerusalem tombs:

Type I – Primary burials placed on benches and in loculi, dated to the Hasmonean period. Interment in wooden coffins may also have been practiced, though no proof of coffins has survived; compare Jericho type I, wooden coffin burial.

Type II – Primary burial and the transfer of bones to a communal charnel, side loculi, or chambers, before the use of ossuaries, is evinced in Jerusalem; this custom is dated to Herodian times.

Type III – Reburial and bones collected into ossuaries; the later stage consisted of *Ossilegium*, namely collecting bones into ossuaries and it was used until the second half of first century BCE.

---

[2] For aqueducts in cemeteries see *Sem.* 14,1 in Zlotnick 1966: 85.165; M Yad. 4, 7; BT Hor. 13b; Meg. 29a and see Patrich 1980.

Type I

The earliest loculus tombs in the Jerusalem necropolis, which ceased to be used before *Ossilegium*, were identified by the appearance of the folded lamp (type A) and the early spindle bottle, typical of the second and first centuries BCE (Zissu 1995: 172–4). These early items were found in six loculus tombs with no ossuaries (Kloner & Zissu 2003): tombs 12–5 and 12–6 (Kloner and Gat 1982), 13–2 (Bahat 1982: 80–81), 14–37 and 21–1 (Sussman 1982: 69). On the basis of these two types of pottery, Zissu suggests that the earliest tombs in Jerusalem should be dated to the second or third century BCE. Several other Jerusalem tombs possibly belong to this type: a tomb on French Hill (Mazar, A. 1982: 42, Fig. 1), a tomb in the Kidron Valley (Sukenik 1930: 122, Mayer 1924: 50, pl. V); Givʿat Hamivtar, tomb IV (Tsafiris: 23, Fig. 5); Mount Scopus (Tzafiris 1982: 50–51, Fig. 1); Mount Scopus Observatory, tomb B (Weksler-Bdolah 1998: 52*, who suggests the tomb was hewn after the loculus tomb, and they both probably were used in the same period). This type of tombs might be a continuation of the First Temple tradition of burial evinced in first-century tombs in Jerusalem and Judea (Kloner 1980: 239–240; 1982; A. Mazar 1976).

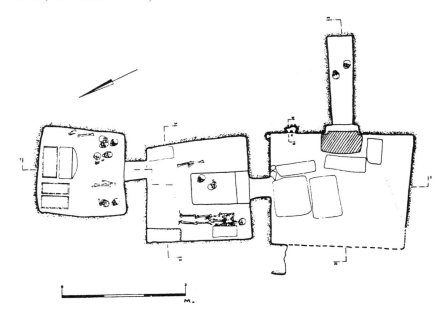

Figure XI–1. French Hill Tomb.

Types II and III attest to the development of the custom of collecting bones in Jerusalem.

Type II

The first stage of the collected-bones custom consisted of transferring the bones of the deceased into a repository, a communal charnel – sometimes with remains of their grave goods, which was left within the family tomb. This custom was practiced in the Second Temple period, during Hasmonean times until the rise of the Herodian dynasty; it continued an Iron Age II practice of a special cavity in the burial chamber for the removal of earlier burials and bones. This custom was replaced in a later stage, in Herodian times, by reburial in ossuaries. Occasionally the charnel was later converted into a room for the deposit of ossuaries, and in other cases the ossuaries were stored in a repository specially hewn for this purpose. The important principle was to keep the deceased within the tomb of their ancestors. A foremost example is Jason's Tomb, where chamber B is a charnel room that served for the collection of bones (Rahmani 1961: 105, 110, 117; 1967: 2, n. 3; 1994: 53; Mazar 1982: 45). In some tombs bone repositories were used before the introduction of ossuaries (Rahmani 1958: 104; 1981: 49–50; Kloner 1980a; 1993: 105–6, note 20; Mazar 1982: 5*, 45; Zissu 1995: 160, Fig. 97; Weksler-Bdolah 1998).

Several tombs in Jerusalem contained bones of earlier burials, which had been pushed aside into loculi or placed on benches (Rahmani 1961: 105, 107, 110, 117; Kloner and Gat 1982: 74–75; A. Mazar 1982: 41, 43, 45; Tzaferis 1982: 51). Rahmani maintains that the burials of collected bones or of bones from earlier burials, which had been pushed aside, "must precede the time when the owners of this tomb began to collect the bones for secondary burial in an ossuary".

A few Jerusalem tombs dated between the beginning of the first century and King Herod's reign have loculi for primary burial a communal charnel, and no ossuaries (Rahmani 1981: 46). In one instance the finds in Jason's Tomb indicate that bones from former burials were transferred from the loculi to the communal charnel on sheets and mattings (Rahmani 1967; 1981: 45). Another example is a Shahin Hill tomb that had two burial chambers, chamber A with five loculi and chamber B that was a communal bone charnel

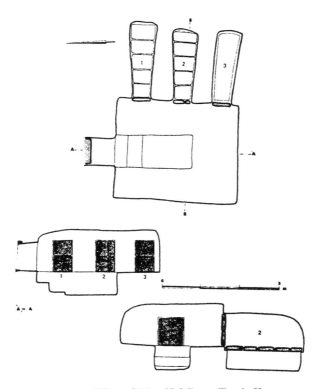

Figure XI–2. Giv'at HaMivtar Tomb II.

(Rahmani 1958: 101; 1981: 49, 105). The tomb had apparently been hewn for a family in Hasmonean times. Bones from chamber A and its loculi were moved into the special chamber B, sometimes with remains of their grave goods. Yet another case is Giv'at Hamivtar tomb II (Tzafiris 1970: 18–20, Fig. 3), which has a chamber and three loculi. In two of the loculi the graves cut into the floor were covered with stone slabs; no ossuaries were found. The pottery, a cooking pot, and seven complete spindle bottles are similar to the pottery from Jason's Tomb.

A tomb at French Hill (Kloner 1980a) consists of loculi for primary burial and an adjacent communal charnel, dated by the pottery from the late second century BCE to the mid-first century CE. The tomb consisted of a courtyard and two chambers, with primary burial in its early stages. Later, bones and pottery from loculi of Chamber A were brought into Chamber C, which originally might have been intended for secondary burial. Kloner contends that the deceased in

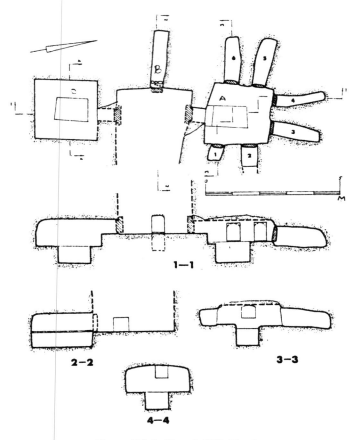

Figure XI–3. French Hill Tomb.

this tomb were first buried in the loculi of Chamber A with some
grave goods; later, after decomposition of the flesh, the bones were
collected and transferred to Chamber C with their associated grave
goods. Two or three generations were transferred in the second half
of the second century BCE. Some of the bodies were left in the loculi
of Chamber A in the final stages. The single *kokh* B might have been
the burial place of an important member of the family.

A different example is a tomb on Mount Scopus (Kloner 1980:
163–165, No. 2–4) where possibly burial in wooden coffins was practiced. Although Kloner contends that no remains of wooden coffins
have survived owing to the dampness of Jerusalem tombs, primary
burial in Jerusalem possibly was similar to that in Jericho. The dating of the tombs is also in question.

The location of the bodies and bones in these Jerusalem tombs, as well as the pottery associated with them, seem similar to the finds of coffin burials, i.e., type I tombs, in Jericho. This should indicate that at least some of the Jerusalem tombs lacking ossuaries might have contained burials in coffins, which, as conjectured, did not survive.

Type III

Ossilegium is the latest burial custom in Jerusalem tombs of the Second Temple period; the deceased's bones were intentionally collected and placed in special containers – the ossuaries, positioned in the family tomb (Pl. XI–1) (Kloner 1980: 241–243; 1982: 58, Rahmani 1994: 53; Zissu 1995: 95–98; Kloner & Zissu 2003: 50–52) (For more on Ossilegium rites see below).

The following Jerusalem tombs exemplify the practice of both bone collection and secondary burials in ossuaries, with the addition of some loculi or small chambers serving as the repository or storage rooms for ossuaries. A Mount Scopus tomb was possibly first used in late Hasmonean times (Rahmani 1980: 54); a generation or so later the earlier burials were collected into one or two *kokhim*. The later users of the tomb in the end of the first century BCE began to collect the bones of their ancestors in ossuaries, which were placed in one *kokh* and on the shelves of the chamber. Another tomb on Mount Scopus has a small lower burial chamber, which served as a repository or storeroom for collected bones and ossuaries (Taferis 1982: 51, Fig. 1). In yet another Mount Scopus tomb (Kloner 1980, Tomb 1–15; Vitto 2000: 98, No. 1, Fig. 1) three chambers and a pit served as repositories for ossuaries; 14 of the 24 ossuaries were stored in these four chambers. In a five-chambered tomb also on Mount Scopus, southern slope, 37 ossuaries were recovered (Kloner 1993: 81, 105–6). Bone collection was first practiced especially in loculi 6 and 8, which were used for that purpose only; later, ossuaries were placed all over the tomb, with Chamber C serving as a storage room for ossuaries in its final stages.

A tomb on Mount Scopus consisting of a single chamber with three arcosolia (Kloner and Stark 1991–2: 16) functioned as a store for ossuaries, as in the other tombs (Avigad 1954: 79–90; Macalister 1990: 54–61). In a one-chamber tomb in the Givʿat Shaul area, four *kokhim* were hewn; two (3 and 4) possibly served for primary burial, while the other two (1 and 2) were used for ossuary storage (Kloner

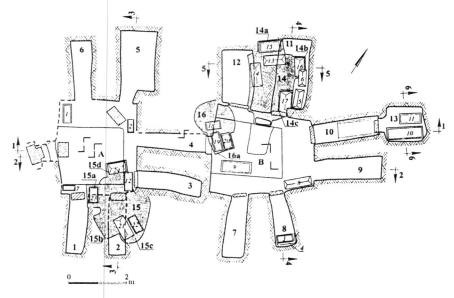

Figure XI-4. Tomb on Mount Scopus.

and Eisenberg 1992: 51*, Fig. 1). A rock-cut tomb in the Kidron Valley, with bones found on the benches and no ossuaries at all in chamber C, indicated to Mayer (1924: 56) that the dead were placed in this room until the flesh had decayed. Then the bones could be collected in the ossuaries in chamber B. At Mt. Scopus Observatory, Tomb C, Chamber CV was added and contained benches, a pit, and eight ossuaries. It served first as a benches chamber and in the last stage of the tomb's use it served for ossuary storage (Weksler-Bdolah 1998: 28*, 32*, 52*). At Giv'at Shapira Tomb I, *kokh* E, the loculi were converted into ossuary storage space (Gershoni and Zissu 1997: 45–46).

Scholars (Mazar A. 1976; 1982; Barkay 1994: 106ff.; Zissu 1995: 172; Kloner and Zissu 2002: 170) maintain that the custom in Jerusalem and Judea at the end of the First Temple period was primary burial on the tomb benches and collection of the bones in repositories hewn under the benches. They further claim that the Jerusalem bench tombs at Mamilla, Ketef Hinom, Mt. Zion, and others continue First Temple (Judean Iron Age) customs of first burial on benches and the usage of second burial in a repository. In the Jerusalem tombs bones continued to be collected in repositories and charnels at the end of the first century BCE. Sometime later, burial in loculi was practiced and ossilegium was applied for individual bone collection. In the first century CE in many expensive Jerusalem tombs arcosolia burial is found. The arcosolia were usually added to the loculus tomb, constituting the final stage of its development.

Jericho Burial Types, Customs and Chronology

Three distinct types of burials were discovered in Jericho (Hachlili & Killebrew 1983; 1999: 167–171).

Type I – primary burials in wooden coffins.
Type II – second burials of collected bones.
Type III – second burials of collected bones placed in stone ossuaries.

The Jericho tombs were hewn into the hillside and consisted of a square chamber, often with a square rock-cut pit in the floor. The *kokhim* (loculi) were cut into all the walls except the entrance wall, and they had roughly vaulted ceilings. Usually one to three loculi were hewn in each wall. In tombs with standing pits, benches were left along three sides of the chamber and the *kokhim* were hewn level with the tops of the benches.

Type I Primary burials in wooden coffins

Primary burial was in wooden coffins, which usually were placed one in a *kokh* (Figure XI–5; Pl. XI–2); in one case two coffins, of a woman and of a child, were placed side by side in the same *kokh*.

The coffin was a rectangular chest, approximately the length of a human body, constructed by mortising and pegging and decorated with red and black painting or incised geometric designs. The lids were either separate and gabled, sometimes decorated, or hinged to the chest. All parts of the coffins, including the nails, dowels, and hinges were made of wood. The most common species of timber used were cypress, sycamore, and christ-thorn.

The bodies were laid supine in the coffin, usually with the head to one side and the hands close to the sides: "Jews took pains to ensure that the body was interred with limbs unbent..." (Safrai 1976: 780; also Rubin 1977: 206–222). There are several instances of one or two deceased being added to an existing burial in a coffin, but no more than three individuals were found in any one coffin.

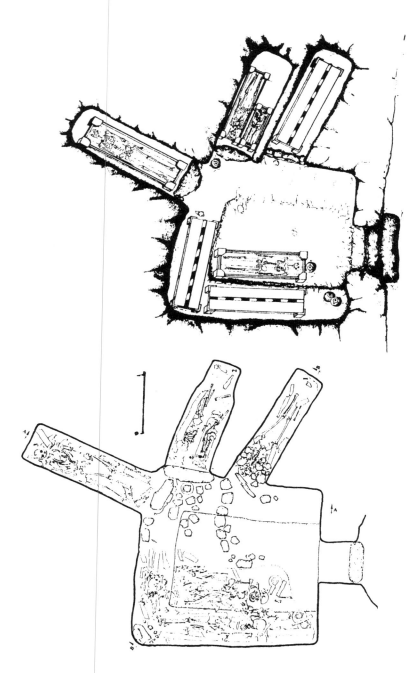

Figure XI–5. Jericho, Tomb Type I with wooden coffins.

These later deceased were probably placed in coffins because they were related to the person buried in it (Sem. 13, 8: "Two corpses may not be buried beside one another, nor a corpse beside bones, nor bones beside a corpse. Rabbi Judah says: whomsoever a person may sleep with when he is living, he may be buried with when he is dead": Zlotnick, 1966: 84, 164).

Orientation of the bodies in the loculus and in the tomb does not seem to have had any significance. No special marks were found on the coffins that might indicate the orientation of the head in the *kokh*. This is in contrast to the Qumran cemetery, where the orientation of most of the tombs was generally north-south (see below).

In Jericho the coffins were used only for primary, not secondary burials, unlike the case in 'En Gedi (Avigad 1962b: 180; Hadas 1994: 12, 18, 57, except for Tomb 1, Hadas 1994: 45), where wooden coffins were reused (like ossuaries?) for the burial of collected bones (see below).

Personal objects and belongings were placed in the coffins, sometimes consisting of several objects, and were usually placed near the head or feet of the deceased. They were found mostly with women and children, as is also the case in 'En Gedi tombs (Hadas 1994: 4, 27, 34) and the Dura Europos loculi tombs containing coffins (Toll 1946: 22, Figs. 21–24, 29, 37). These include wooden objects such as bowls, glass containers, jewelry – beads and rings, accessories, bronze, iron and bone objects, as well as leather sandals (see Tables X–1–8).

Most of the sandals and leather fragments were recovered from coffins in which women were buried, although two sandals were placed with males. The sandals were found usually next to the head of the deceased and not the feet, which seem to indicate some special burial custom, probably associated with rites of grief or acts of mourning. In the Jerusalem tombs no leather or wooden objects have survived due to the humid climate. Although similar sandals were found in second-century CE caves in the Judean Desert, they were not usually placed with burials, except at 'En Gedi (see below). Yadin (1963: 165–166, n. 19) discussing the form of the sandals and the relevant *Halakhoth* points out that the sandals found in the Cave of Letters were "fastened together exclusively by means of leather thongs, none bear any traces of nails." This is in compliance with the Mishnaic prohibition (Shab. 6:2) of wearing nail-studded sandals on the Sabbath, which most probably meant that people wore only sandals without nails.

Wooden bowls were found in the coffins, usually placed with burials of women and children. Similar wooden bowls and cups were found in a wooden coffin in 'En Gedi tombs (Table X–7–8; Avigad 1962a: 182, Pl. 18A; Hadas 1994: 5*, 51–52, 58). Note that no wooden bowls were found in excavations of settlements at Jericho or 'En Gedi. These wooden vessels have apparently not survived or they were specially made for funerary rites and placed with the dead in the coffins. Some intimate personal effects were placed in the coffins (see Tables X–3–4).

Utilitarian vessels for daily use were found on the floor or in the pit of the tomb. These include bowls, cooking pots, unguentaria, and folded lamps; the pottery vessels form a well-defined assemblage (for their special position next to the *kokh* sealing and coffins in tombs, see Chap. X). Storage jars were often discovered outside the tombs next to the entrance, and complete vessels were recovered outside some tombs.

This repertoire is distinct from that in tomb types II and III, and it is typologically earlier in date. The relatively large number and diversity of utilitarian ceramic containers found in association with coffin burials is in contrast to the limited number of ceramic vessels found with secondary burials.

The pottery assemblage found in the Jericho coffin tombs is identical to that used in daily life by Jews in the Second Temple period. However, certain vessels, such as cooking pots and unguentaria, appear frequently, while other types, such as bowls, were rarely placed in the tombs.

Type II

Secondary burials of collected bones were found in two large, disturbed Jericho tombs (D3 and F4; Hachlili 1999: Figs. II.27, 62) and three single-*kokh* tombs (D21, 23 and F7; Hachlili 1999: Figs. II.46, 64). They contained piles of collected bones in the *kokhim* and on the benches, without any traces of coffins or ossuaries (Figure XI–6; Pl. XI–3).

Large numbers of cooking pots and ceramic unguentaria, a few bowls and a cup had been placed with the bones of the deceased. Two coins of Agrippa I were found stuck together inside a skull recovered from tomb D3, *kokh* 1 (Hachlili & Killebrew 1983, 1986).

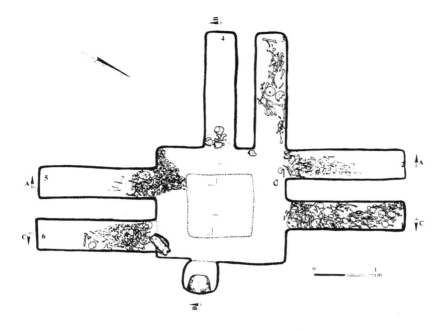

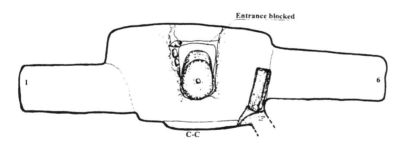

Figure XI–6. Jericho Tomb D3 with collected bones.

Type III

Burial type III consisted of second burial in stone ossuaries. The ossuaries were carved from a single limestone block, with a separate gabled, vaulted, or flat limestone lid, and were decorated with incised or chip-carved geometric or floral designs.[3] Occasionally inscriptions were carved on the ossuaries, giving the name and the family relationship of the deceased whose bones rested in the ossuary.

---

[3] It has been suggested that Roman funerary urns containing the remains of

The ossuaries were placed in the loculi or on the benches. The occupants of ossuaries placed in the same loculus were usually related, as can be deduced from the inscriptions. The ossuaries were sometimes placed on the benches or on the floor; however, this was not due to lack of space in the *kokhim*, as in many cases these were empty. The way the ossuaries were placed in the Jericho tombs indicates that burial in ossuaries was not due to a desire to save space (but see Avigad 1976: 259).

The bones were placed in the ossuary in a certain order: the long bones lay lengthwise at the bottom, with the bones of the arms and hands on one side and those of the legs and feet at the other (Pl. XI–4). The remaining bones of the body were placed on top, with the skull on top of all the bones at one end (Hachlili & Killebrew 1999: 170, Fig. VIII.2). Usually, each ossuary contained the bones of one individual, but in one tomb there were several instances of more than one individual in an ossuary (see Anthropological Table 2; Hachlili and Smith 1979: 68–69). Care was taken to place the bones in the correct ossuary. In Jericho, the inscriptions in the Goliath tomb mentioning the name and occasionally the age of the deceased correspond to the sex and age of the individual found in the ossuary (Tab. V–1; Hachlili 1999: Table IV.1 and Anthropological Table, App. I; Hachlili 1979a: Table 1; Hachlili and Smith 1979).

Fewer grave goods were discovered with ossuary burials, which is no doubt due in part to the tombs' disturbed condition. The finds, usually placed close to the ossuaries or in the pit, included bowls, kraters, a small number of ceramic unguentaria, juglets, a few lamps, glass unguentaria, and miscellaneous metal objects. Some of the pottery was decorated with red paint. This homogeneous repertoire of vessels is typical of first-century CE assemblages. A lamp placed on the head of the primary burial in tomb A2, *kokh* 5, may have been a symbol of grief. The practice of placing glass unguentaria in tombs was widespread throughout the eastern Mediterranean during the first century CE.

---

cremated burials may have influenced burial in ossuaries. However, these burials are vastly different in concept: the former consisted of the cremated remains of the individual immediately after his or her death (Toynbee 1971: 40–41, 50, 253–255), while the latter first entailed the primary burial of the individual and only after at least one year had passed, the gathering of his bones into a small rectangular container.

Numerous inscriptions, on ossuaries and on a bowl, were found in the Jerusalem and Jericho cemeteries. Quite often the inscription was repeated on the ossuary and several were bilingual. Such inscriptions usually gave the name of the deceased and his family relationship, making it possible to construct family trees, each usually consisting of three generations. An abecedary, consisting of nine letters of the Greek alphabet, was written in charcoal inside an ossuary lid (see below; Hachlili 1979a: 47–48). A stone slab inscribed with the names of the dead buried in the tomb was found in a tomb excavated north of Tell Jericho (Bennett 1965: 523–525, Tomb K23; Reynolds 1965: 721–722, Pl. XXIV).

Unusual burial customs. Three unusual burial practices, each of which occurs only once in the Jericho cemetery, differ from the burial customs described above:

(1) Bones transferred into a side *kokh* in the same tomb: this is tomb D27, where wooden coffins were placed on the benches and in the *kokhim*. *Kokh* 7 was probably used for the burial of the individuals removed from the coffins (Hachlili 1999: 29, 31, Fig. II.55). (2) Plastered-over *kokhim* containing primary burials in the first stage of the tomb, ossuaries placed later on the benches and in the pit (Tomb A2, Hachlili 1999: 6–8, Fig. II.5). (3) Heaps of bones placed in a special pit (Tomb H, Hachlili 1999: 37–38, Fig. II.71).

In the Jericho cemetery, collected-bone burials either were without a container and constituted a burial type (type II) exclusively practiced in some of the tombs (D3, D21, D23, F4, F7; Hachlili 1999: Figs. II.27, 46, 62, 64), or, as in tomb H, were placed in a *kokh*-pit specially hewn for the burial of the collected bones (Hachlili 1999: Figs. II.71, 72). The bones seem to have been purposely deposited and buried, rather than pushed aside. Presumably, gathering the bones from earlier burials, as in Jericho tomb D27, was practiced in Jericho because of lack of space in this particular tomb, and because the coffins were reused for other burials. This is in contrast to type II tombs, which contained only collected bone burials without a container. In tomb H, *kokh*-pit 9, which was specially hewn for collected bones burial at the end of the tomb's use, may have been utilized because ossuaries were unavailable at the time (perhaps because of the first Jewish War in 67–68 CE) or later, when ossuaries may not have been produced in Jericho.

Based on the stratigraphy of the Jericho tombs and the artifacts found in association with the deceased, type I burials are dated to the first century BCE and types II and III to the early first century CE, until *ca.* 68 CE (Hachlili and Killebrew 1983; 1999: 164–165).

ʿEn Gedi Burial types, Customs and Chronology

Nine tombs found and excavated at ʿEn Gedi (Hadas 1994) were used over an extended time in the Second Temple period (Figure XI–7):

Tomb 1. This contained primary burials in eight wooden coffins.

Tomb 2. This comprised a few primary interments in the pit and the benches, some originally in wooden coffins, of which fragments of only four survived. In secondary burials, most of the skeletal remains were found in heaps on the tomb floor, in the pit and a hewn repository, and in remains of a cedar-wood coffin (Hadas 1994: 12, 1*–2*, Plan. 2, Fig. 19).

Tomb 3. This contained secondary burial in two wooden coffins and a small wooden coffin (an ossuary, according to Hadas) and between them in the surviving section, which had mostly collapsed and was eroded (Hadas 1994: 18, 2*, Plan. 3, Fig. 27).

Tomb 4. The surviving section consisted of part of the floor and two loculi. Primary burials in two wooden coffins (1 and 3) and secondary burial in two other coffins (2 and 4) were found. The limestone ossuary was empty (Hadas 1994: 20–22, 2*, Plan. 4).

Tomb 5. The surviving chamber contained 15 wooden coffins (13 complete) with primary burials. A repository was packed with disarticulated skeletal remains (Hadas 1994: 24, 2*, Plan. 5).

Tomb 6. The surviving chamber yielded six wooden coffins, three of them fragmentary with primary burials. In coffin 3 bones were discovered. In the center of the tomb a woman was buried, without a coffin, probably originally in a basket or a mat (Hadas 1994: 34, 2–3*).

Tomb 7. A portion of the chamber and a repository in the annex survived; remains of four wooden coffins were found and bones lay in the repository (Hadas 1994: 41, 3*).

Tomb 8. Part of the chamber and a repository survived with remains of bones in the repository (Hadas 1994: 42, 3*).

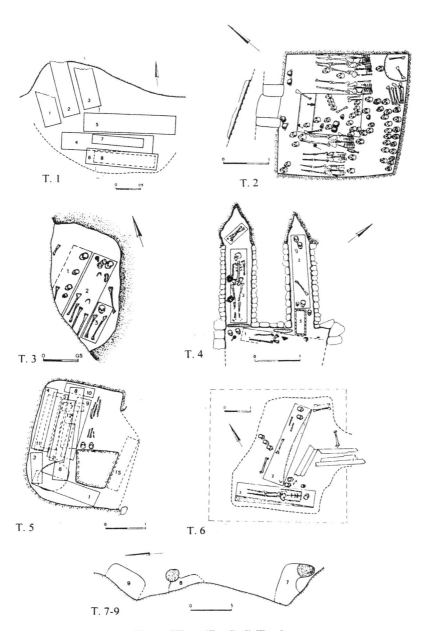

Figure XI–7. 'En Gedi Tombs.

Four distinct types of burials were discovered (Hadas 1994: 3*):

Type A. Primary burials in wooden coffins predominate in all tombs (except tomb 3). Large coffins were used for adults, small ones for children. All the coffins (1–8) in tomb 1 contained primary burials of an adult, sometimes with a child or only children. Primary burials were found in two of the wooden coffins of tomb 4, in all of the coffins in tomb 5, and in three coffins in tomb 6 (Hadas 1994: 63, App. A, Table 2).

Type B. This consisted of primary burials on the tomb floor, the bodies wrapped in mats or shrouds in tombs 5, 6, and 7 (Hadas 1994: 24).

Type C. This consisted of secondary burial in large wooden coffins (especially in the surviving section of Tomb 3, which had mostly collapsed and eroded (see also Avigad 1962) and in hewn repositories in tombs 2, 5, 7, and 8.

Type D. This consisted of secondary burials in one wooden ossuary in tomb 3 and one in tomb 4; a stone ossuary was found empty in tomb 4.

The various types of burial at 'En Gedi do not represent chronological differences. Dating of the tombs, based on pottery and other finds, is from the second–first century BCE to the late first century CE (Hadas 1994: 58, 7*–8*, App. table 2).

The burial containers were used for either primary or secondary burials. Most of the 'En Gedi wooden coffins were used for primary burials (type A); only in tomb 3 were the coffins used for secondary burials (type C). Possibly the bones were placed in these coffins shortly before the sealing of the tomb (Hadas 1994: 21, 2*).

Clearly, the 'En Gedi burials were mostly primary burials in wooden coffins (types A and B). Secondary burial of type C was either a last-minute resort or a transferred burial with the coffins being used as a repository. Type D is not confirmed, as the wooden ossuaries could have been small coffins. The chronological division between the primary and secondary burial types is not well distinguished at 'En Gedi: primary burials in wooden coffins on one hand, and the continuous use of some of the wooden coffins for secondary burial on the other, were the result of local factors. Furthermore, knowledge gathered from the badly eroded and destroyed 'En Gedi tombs is inadequate.

Tomb 4 seems to have been disturbed already in antiquity, as indicated by the placement of the stone ossuary in the loculus entrance, which prevented its sealing; coffin 1 obstructed access to the stone ossuary. Both could have been placed or moved only in the final stage of the tomb, especially as Hadas (1994: 21, 2*) states that two cooking pots were thrown in (above coffin 3, in the south loculus) shortly before the sealing of the tomb.

Grave goods found in the 'En Gedi tombs (Hadas 1994: 51–56, 3*–7*; Table 1) consisted of personal effects such as cosmetic vessels, personal toilet items, and beads; lathe-made wooden vessels were retrieved consisting of bowls, plates, kohl tubes, and combs. Metal objects consisted of a decorated bronze jug, two bronze ladles, two kohl-sticks, a section of a palm-made belt, a papyrus fragment, a basket and mats made of palm, and leather shoes. Linen textiles found are identified as burial shrouds. Pottery vessels found at 'En Gedi are mostly cooking pots and juglets (Tables X–5, 6; a few objects are comparable to the finds in Jerusalem and Jericho tombs).

The dating of the 'En Gedi tombs by the pottery from the mid-second century BCE to late first century CE might also explain the primary and secondary burial in the wooden coffins. The 'En Gedi pottery is similar to the finds from type I coffin burials in Jericho.

Qumran Burial Practices

The cemetery of Qumran, located east of the settlement, contained about 1,200 graves. The date is contemporary with the settlement dating. It was in use during the second half of the second century BCE until 68 CE. The cemetery is laid out in well-organized rows of single graves, usually oriented north-south. The Qumran tomb is a shaft, hewn as a rectangular cavity with a loculus at the bottom, usually under the east wall of the cavity. This was often covered by mud bricks or flat stones. The graves were marked by heaps of stones on the surface (Pl. XI–5) (de Vaux 1953, 1954, 1956, 1973: 45–48; 57–58; Humbert & Chambon 1994: 346–352; Hachlili 1993, 2000b; Eshel et al. 2002).

Several graves showed traces of wooden coffins (de Vaux 1973: 46–47, Tombs 17–19). Most of the excavated tombs contained individual primary burials (de Vaux 1953: 102, Fig. 5, Pls. 4b, 5a–b; 1973: 46, Pl. XXV–XXVI; Steckoll 1968; Bar-Adon 1977: 12, 16,

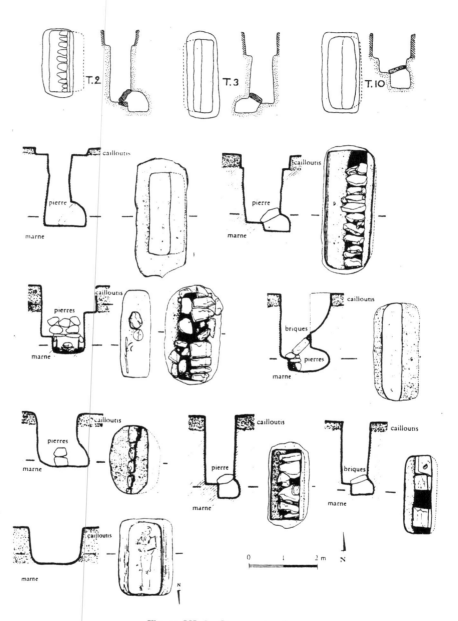

Figure XI–8. Qumran tombs.

Figs. 19–20), except for four tombs: T16 (two males), T24 (male and female), G6 (a woman and child) T35 (two women, the tomb is oriented east-west) (see Anthropological Table 6; Röhrer-Ertl et al. 1999: 47, Katalog; Eshel et al. 2002: Table V). Around the edges of this cemetery and in the smaller cemeteries of Qumran a few graves of women and children were uncovered (see Chap. VII; de Vaux 1956: 569, 575; 1973: 47, 57–58; Cross 1961a: 97–98).

The dead were placed supine, the head frequently oriented to the south or seldom to the north, with a headstone or a footstone or small stones beside it. The arms were usually crossed on the pelvis or stretched down the sides of body (Figure XI–8) (see tombs 3, 7, 9–13, 15, 18, 20–23, 28, 29; Humbert & Chambon 1994: 346–350, figs. 458, 466, pls. xxxv, xxxviii; For details see Eshel et al. 2002: Table IV).

A square building (de Vaux Building B,) was re-excavated (Eshel et al. 2002: 147–153, Pl. III; Broshi and Eshel 2003: 31–33, 71) at the eastern edge of the middle extension. The building is dated to the Second Temple period and argued to be a 'mourning enclosure' of the Qumran community compared to the structure at Jericho. In the building about 150 pottery body shards were found. In the southern part of the building a pile of human bones identified as two women in secondary burial were discovered and beneath it a male skeleton in primary burial oriented east-west was found, with a cooking pot above the legs and a couple of stones protecting the skull. The excavators date the burial of the two females and the male to the Second Temple period. The identification of the male skeleton as the *mevaqqer* (overseer) by Broshi and Eshel (2003: 31–33, 71) is highly speculative.

The finds in the tombs are extremely poor (de Vaux 1956: 570–572; Humbert & Chambon 1994: 346, 350–352): in tomb 4 a store jar was found, and in tomb 26 a Herodian lamp, both with burials of men aged 30–40. In tomb 32 (in the south extension) beads, an earring, and a bronze ring were found with a 30-year-old woman. Two earrings were discovered in tomb 33 (in the south extension) with a 30-year-old woman. In tomb 1 (in the south cemetery) 30 beads, an earring, and a bronze ring were found with a 30-year-old woman.

The pottery of the Qumran site, according to Magness (1994a, 1994b: 413–414; 2002: 89), is different from that of other Judean sites of that period. The Qumran types are limited and plain, while imported and fine ware is rare. The Qumran repertoire seems to indicate that the inhabitants preferred to create their own wares, suggesting a deliberate policy of isolation.

Several remnants of wooden coffins were discovered in the Qumran cemetery (in tombs 17, 19, 32, and 33, with male and female skeletons (de Vaux 1956: 572; 1973: 58; Humbert and Chambon 1994: 222, 224, 349). They are similar to the coffins customarily used for primary burial in Jericho and 'En Gedi. In the recent survey of the Qumran cemetery metal pieces (identified as zinc) deemed to be part of a coffin lid were discovered in a tomb (No. 978) in the eastern part of the Middle Finger. The use of zinc during this period was very rare. It is suggested that the person buried in the zinc coffin was brought to Qumran from abroad (Eshel et al. 2002: 143–147). There is no proof for the assumption by some scholars (Broshi 1992: 112; Kapera 1994: 108) that the coffins were used for moving the dead from other secondary burials areas, these persons being relatives of the Qumran inhabitants who had died elsewhere and were brought to be buried in Qumran. Jews did not begin to practice the custom of reinterment in the Land of Israel until the third century CE (Gafni 1981).

The survey of the male and female burials at Qumran is based on finds of human remains from graves dug by de Vaux, Steckoll and Eshel et al. (1956: 570; 1973: 37, 45, 69, 81, 96; Humbert & Chambon 1994: 350; Eshel et al. 2002: Table V; Broshi and Eshel 2003: 32). The data from graves in the cemeteries was recently re-examined and published revealing that the tombs contained 33 males, seven females, and five children. Only a few tombs included two individuals (Röhrer-Ertl et al. 1999: 47, Katalog; Eshel et al. 2002: Table V).[4] The age of most men found in the main cemetery is 30–45 years; exceptions are one-aged 16 years (T15), two aged 22–23 (T28, G5), and one aged 50 (T25). Two men are aged 65 years (Q.G.9).

Seven women (buried in the extensions of the main cemetery and in the south cemetery) are about 30 years old (T22, T24a, T32–35; TS1 in the south cemetery). Five children are 2–10 years old (T 36;

---

[4] In the questionable excavation conducted by Steckoll (1968: 335), in eleven tombs were found 11 skeletons: six men, four women, and one or two children (also Röhrer-Ertl et al. 1999: 47, Katalog).

TS2–4 in the south cemetery, G6b) (see Röhrer-Ertl et al. 1999: 47, Katalog; Eshel et al. 2002: Table V).

The anthropological research and its interpretation are controversial. Zias (2000: 225–230) argues that five tombs (T32–36) on the southeast margin of the Qumran cemetery, oriented along an east-west axis, and four anomalous tombs in the southern cemetery, with interment of men, women and children, are chronologically intrusive and thus are post-Byzantine, Islamic burials. He bases his argument mainly on the orientation, the beads found in tombs TS1 and T32 (49 beads), the shallowness of the burial, and the presence of marking stones for the head and feet (Zias 2000: 242, 248–253, Pls. 1, 2). He further claims that the Qumran cemetery reflects a celibate community of males. "[T]he only deviation from Jewish burial norm is the strict orientation of the graves along the north-south axis" in the main cemetery, which could be explained by "their opposition to the priestly class in Jerusalem whom they disdained" and by the fact that for the Essenes, Paradise and the New Jerusalem lay in the north (see Puech 1998: 29).

Zias (2000: 244) maintains that there are four shared criteria to categorize a cemetery as Essene: "orientation, tomb architecture, demographic disparity and few if any personal grave goods, all appearing in Qumran and 'En el-Ghuweir." He contends that only 55 individuals' remains are Essene (35 from Qumran and 20 from 'En el-Ghuweir). Zias excludes tomb 4 and tombs 32–36, which he identifies as Islamic burials. There are a few women and only one child (Zias 2000: Table 2). But see Zangenberg 2000a: 65–76, who disagrees with Zias and rejects his conclusions. He maintains that nothing in the anthropological data examined by Röhrer-Ertl et al., which came from all parts of the cemetery suggests two different ethnic groups. To the contrary, all the bones share the same features. Zangenberg (2000a: 72) concludes "There is nothing in the bones, nothing in the form and orientation of the graves and nothing regarding the grave finds that would compel us to assume that the tombs in the Southern Cemetery at Qumran were later intrusions or bedouin".

Eshel et al. (2002: 137–138, 140, 142) on the other hand "agree with Zias that fifty-four tombs oriented east-west should be identified as Bedouin tombs of the last centuries". Eshel et al assume that stone covering from several tombs were removed to cover over the later tombs. Magness (2002b: 95) agrees with Zias's conclusion. Magness

(2002b) discusses the archaeological evidence of the human remains from the cemeteries and the finds in the Qumran settlement; she further presents comparable evidence of 'gendered' finds from Qumran and those found at Masada and the Judean Desert Caves, and concludes (ibid., 108) that her examination of all the evidence verifies that the presence of females was only minimal at Qumran. But see Taylor (1999: 305, 309–310) who contends, "that females and males are found in all sectors of the Qumran cemeteries" . . . with . . . "a higher proportion of males buried in the western section of the large cemetery".

The evidence presented by most scholars confirms that a large number of men were interred in the main cemetery while a small number of women and children were found in the extensions and secondary cemeteries. Scholars argue that this circumstance attests the fact that Qumran community is composed of adult males and possibly of a celibate character (see also Chap. VII; de Vaux 1973: 45–47; Hachlili 1993: 251, and bibliography in note 9; Golb 1994: 58; Puech 1998: 27; Eshel at al. 2002; Magness (2002b: 108).[5]

Qumran is proven a Jewish settlement by the Hebrew inscriptions found on ostraca and jars at Qumran. The names יוחנן Yohanan (on a store jar from period Ib) and Josephus in Greek were found (de Vaux 1954: 229, Pl. XIIa); A similar name יהוחנן Yehohanan was inscribed on the shoulder of a storage jar found in tomb 18 at 'En el-Ghuweir (Bar-Adon 1977: 17, figs. 21:3, 23). These inscriptions and names are similar to the many ostraca and jar inscriptions at Masada (Yadin & Naveh 1989).[6]

Recent research and reexamination of the bones remains did not solve the controversy and riddle of the Qumran community, because of the small number of tombs excavated, and the even smaller number of human remains, which were available for the renewed research.

---

[5] The women's and children's skeletons found in the cemetery are problematic and difficult to explain for a Jewish garrison, as they are for a celibate community. Were the women also victims of the war?

[6] Golb acknowledges that the site is Jewish (1994: 65, n. 44): "The ostraca of Khirbet Qumran clearly prove nothing except that those inhabiting it when they were written ca. 50 BC–70 CE were Jews rather than Romans". He argues that the site was a fortress of a Jewish garrison (ibid., pp. 55, 66, 68), and he interprets the cemetery as graves dug for the Jewish warriors who fought at Qumran (ibid., p. 70).

The recent excavations at the Nabatean cemetery at Khirbet Qazone with similar shaft tombs add more fervor to the debate.

The Qumran burials are clearly not family tombs. They reveal individual burials of a community who elected to leave their families. The graves in these cemeteries are very well organized, carefully dug and thoughtfully arranged, and are solitary, one individual interred in each tomb. Though the number of excavated tombs is small, it is clear that the Qumran community practiced primary burial in individual graves during the period.

'En el-Ghuewir

In the 'En el-Ghuewir cemetery seventeen tombs were excavated (Bar-Adon 1977: 12–17).

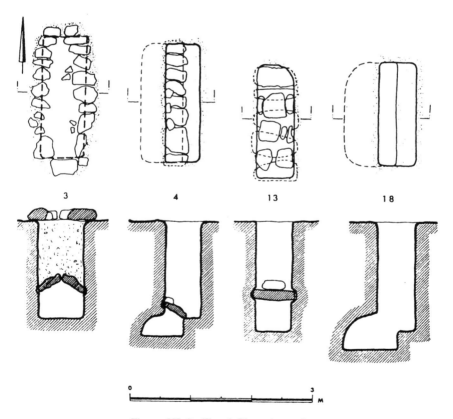

Figure XI–9. 'En el-Ghuweir tombs.

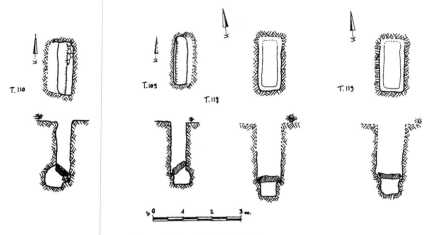

Figure XI–10. Beth Zafafa tombs.

The tombs are similar to those at Qumran, having a north-south orientation and a heap of stones marking each grave (Figure XI–9). In each tomb one interred individual lay supine. Remains of 13 men, seven women, and one child were found, with some broken vessels and potsherds. Among them was the above-mentioned jar inscribed with the Hebrew name Yehohanan. The dating of these tombs is first century BCE – first century CE, contemporary with the Qumran cemeteries.

Beth Zafafa, Jerusalem

The cemetery at Beth Zafafa has about 49 graves (Zisso 1996), of which 41 were excavated.

The graves are hewn shaft tombs, some oriented north-south, others east-west; most are marked by stone tablets (Figure XI–10). In most tombs one individual was interred. Forty-six interred persons were examined: 27 men, 16 women, and three children. The finds include 30 iron nails, two glass bottles, and a late glass bracelet. The tombs' form and size, as well as the custom of individual burial, are similar to the Qumran graves. The tombs date from the end of the Second Temple period to the Bar Kochba period (possibly some of the tombs were in use later during the Roman and Byzantine periods).

Several tombs discovered in other areas contained large coarse undecorated ossuaries (recorded in Rahmani 1994: Nos. 683–690, but see also Nos. 553, 858–859, 861–862 from the Hebron hills and

Asia Minor). This indicates that the custom of secondary burial in ossuaries might have survived until much later, namely the 4th century.

Burial practices at Qumran, Jerusalem, and Jericho: A Discussion

The burial customs practiced in the cemeteries of the Jewish mainstream, that is, Jerusalem and Jericho, in the Second Temple period should be equated with the Qumran cemeteries.

The description above shows that the cemeteries, burial customs, and burial forms at Qumran, and comparable shaft or dugout tombs discovered in 'En el-Ghuweir and other sites in the Judean Desert, as well as in Beth Zafafa, Jerusalem (Patrich 1994b: no. 10; Zisso 1996),[7] are fundamentally different from those of the Jews in Jerusalem, Jericho, and 'En Gedi.

Burial customs in the Jerusalem and Jericho cemeteries are similar. The Jericho excavations indicate that typologically, chronologically, and stratigraphically the loculus tombs can be classified into primary burial in wooden coffins, dated to the first century BCE, followed by secondary burials of collected bones, either placed in limestone ossuaries or piled up, dated to the first century CE. In Jerusalem, primary burials in wooden coffins did not survive owing to the poor preservation of organic material.

Grave goods were found in wooden coffins and ossuaries tombs, consisting primarily of personal possessions and everyday objects, usually placed in coffins or in the tomb itself.

The Qumran and 'En el-Ghuweir tomb, by contrast, is a shaft hewn as a rectangular cavity with a pit at the bottom, marked by heaps of stones on the surface. Most of the excavated tombs contained individual burials; only male interments were found in the main cemetery.

The burial practices of the Qumran sect have only a few elements in common with those of the Jerusalem and Jericho cemeteries (Hachlili 1993: 261–264; 2000). Coffin burials at Qumran, though later in date, can be compared to those found at Jericho. Grave goods were discovered with women and children, and at 'En el-Ghuweir remains of fabrics (shrouds?) and mattresses were also found

---

[7] The Jericho shaft tombs are reused MB tombs (Bennet 1965: 532–537).

(de Vaux 1973: 47; Bar-Adon 1977: 22). Broken store jars were
uncovered on top of the graves at ʿEn el-Ghuweir (Bar-Adon 1977:
16, Figs. 21:1–3, 22–23) and Qumran (de Vaux 1953: 103, Fig. 2:5,
Pl. VI). The placing of vessels on top of the grave corresponds to
the custom of placing store jars outside the tombs at Jericho.

The variations evident in these burial practices indicate differences
in religious philosophy and in attitudes to the dead among the Jews
of that time, and they reflect the separation of the Qumran community from the rest (Cross 1961a: 51ff.; de Vaux 1973: 126–138;
Yadin 1983 I:323–324; 342–343). The importance of the individual,
rather than of the family, is indicated by the individual burials found
in the graves at Qumran and ʿEn el-Ghuweir.

The Qumran cemetery was a central burial place for the community. The proximity of the cemeteries to the site at Qumran proves
that they belong together. The graves in these cemeteries are very
well organized, carefully dug, and thoughtfully arranged, and are
evidently not family tombs. These differences in grave form and burial customs reflect an out-of-the-ordinary distinctive community, that
no doubt deliberately used different customs.

The Temple Scroll, which contains the writings of a Judean Desert
sect (the Essenes?), lays down several rules regarding cemeteries (Yadin
1983 I:321–336) Cemeteries should be outside the town limits and
located between four settlements so as to avoid contamination of the
whole country. Yadin (1983 I:323–24), from his the interpretation
of later Rabbinical literature (M Oho. 17, 5; T Oho. 15), asserts
that these restrictions were formulated because in this period Jews
did bury within the town limits and the Essenes were attempting to
follow the stricter priestly laws. To date, however, no Jewish tombs
have been discovered within any town limits. In fact, the cemeteries at Qumran and ʿEn el-Ghuweir were located near, but outside,
the settlements. The Judean Desert cemeteries, then, cannot be distinguished by their location but rather by their type of primary burial in simple graves. Although most scholars observe that Qumran
is a desert site suitable for people seeking isolation, several have inter-
pretated it differently; one proposition is that the Qumran site was
a Jewish military fort (Golb 1990: 68; 1994: 69).

The well-organized cemetery seems to rule out Golb's argument
(1994: 70; 1995: 34) that the Qumran cemetery was dug at one single time on account of the somewhat uniform nature of this type of
graves, their layout, and their orientation. But these factors do not

necessarily point to a hastily dug cemetery all at once. This type of graveyard could just as well be the outcome of the community's laws and religious beliefs, which were noticeably different from the burial customs of mainstream Judaism of the period (Hachlili 1993: 257–261). Golb maintains that the graves were of the warriors of the fortress who fought at Qumran, as were the tombs of the same type elsewhere in the Judean Desert. He further contends that as some of the skeletal remains evince massacre and bones were broken and burnt, the tombs were dug in haste for a large group of people killed in connection with the first Jewish Revolt against the Romans (ca. 68 CE). However, some skeletons interred at Jericho, which display the same sort of wounds (Hachlili 1999: 16, 22, Fig. II.35, 41), are buried in a family loculus tomb; this would counter-indicate a hurried burial of warriors. Moreover, people who died during the revolt must have been buried in some kind of mass community grave (see, for instance, the special loculus at the Goliath tomb in Jericho; Hachlili 1999: 38, Fig. II.71). Nonetheless, a Jewish fortress would not have been permitted by the Romans (see Golb's discussion 1994: 71–72). The Qumran site interpreted by Golb as a fortress raises another question: are the unusual individual interments a burial custom at Jewish fortresses? Not unless it can be proven that burial at fortresses was individual in shaft tombs (but then it will be difficult to explain the cemetery at Beth Zafafa); up to now, no cemetery has been found at any of the Judean Desert fortresses.[8]

Other scholars posited that Qumran was the villa of wealthy Jerusalemites who lived there during the winter (Donceel-Voûte 1994; Donceel & Donceel-Voûte 1994; Hirschfeld 2003). Such an identification of Qumran is very difficult to accept as it differs from other palaces and villas discovered at Jericho, Herodium, Jerusalem, and various sites in Judea (Magness 1994b: 416–419; also Eshel 2003, Magen 2003). If Qumran had been a Jewish fortress or villa the burial customs would have followed the Jerusalem-Jericho form of loculus-family tombs and their burial customs.

---

[8] At Masada in the Cave of the Skeletons, a great heap of about 25 skeletons and bones (including women and children) was found, above objects such as pottery, fragments of mats, and remnants of food. They seem to have been tossed down haphazardly, probably at the end of the Masada siege in 73 CE.

The identification of Qumran with the Essenes is in dispute, and scholars base their arguments on two main interpretations: (1) Khirbet Qumran was an Essene settlement founded towards the end of the second century BCE and destroyed by the Romans in 68 CE. (2) The Dead Sea Scrolls found in caves 1–11Q belonged to the Essene settlement at Qumran, which was a study center where members could go to meditate, train, and study for a specific period of time or for the rest of their lives (Stegemann 1992: 96, 161–2; Eshel 2003, Magen 2003).[9]

Puech (1998: 21–36) explains the south-north orientation of the burial by the situation of Paradise in the north, according to the cosmology of the books of Enoch. Puech (2000: 519–520) concludes that "the practices of primary burial in invidual tombs at Qumran show a marked disdain for impure Jerusalem . . . The Qumran burial practices are in full agreement with the Essene belief in the afterlife written in the manuscripts found in the caves . . . that the inhabitans of Khirbet Qumran, who were Essenes, shared the belief in the afterlife, of the Pharisees . . . The Essene literature took over the same ideas and the Essenes adapted them to their everyday life, mainly to the burial practices . . ."

If the identification of the Qumran community with the Essenes is accepted, the graves found in Jerusalem could then belong to the Qumran inhabitants who moved to Jerusalem.[10] The Essenes lived in communities in cities and villages in Judea (Josephus *War* 2, 124; *CD* 12:10, 22) and possibly still retained their habits of life as a settled group, as well as their burial customs as indicated by the graves found at Beth Zafafa.

The finds at the cemetery reinforce the thesis that the Qumran community was a specific religious group, a separate Jewish sect, who fashioned their own divergent practices as well as some typical Jewish customs . . . The separate and isolated cemetery and the burial practices (also at 'En el-Ghuweir and Beth Zafafa), which deviate from the regular Jewish tradition, show a distinctive attitude to death and burial customs. The old Jewish tradition of burying the

---

[9] But see Golb 1994: 58–61; see also the arguments of Humbert (1994) about the early history of Qumran, refuted by Magness (1994b: 414–416).

[10] On the Essene community that lived in Jerusalem during the Second Temple period see the Essenes Gate and the relation between Herod and Menahem the Essene (Josephus, *War* 5, 144; *Ant.* 15:368–378; Yadin 1973: 129–130; Zisso 1996: 36).

dead with their ancestors was not followed by the Qumran community, where individual burial was stressed. The importance of the individual rather than the family is indicated by the burial customs at Qumran, which seem to testify that the residents of Qumran were not families and that it was a community cemetery. This might add proof to the identification of Qumran with one of the Jewish sects of the Second Temple Period.

An argument was put forward that loculus tombs – which are family tombs – are for the rich and affluent, while shaft tombs – which are individual burials – are for the poor. Taylor (1999: 312–313) maintains that apparently the Qumran community chose to be buried as poor people, which is a significant fact in establishing their sectarian nature. However, it is striking that they buried so poorly, whereas the skeletal research (Röhrer-Ertl et al. 1999: 13, 15, 19) suggests that the people of the cemeteries belonged to relatively high social class. Moreover, does it mean that not one of the Qumran community members was able to afford a rock-cut tomb plot for his family? It seems apparent that burial customs and the concept of death were the same for the entire Jewish population, rich and poor alike. However, it is reasonable to assume that a sect that separated itself from mainstream Judaism, such as the Qumran sect, would adopt different burial customs.

B. FUNERARY RITES, PRACTICES AND CUSTOMS

Literary testimony is the main source for funerary ceremony, burial rites, and practices, for the preparation of the dead and final burial. It is preserved in contemporary literature of the latter part of the first century: Josephus *War* 1.673, 3.437; *Ant.* 15.196–200; *Against Apion* 2.205; New Testament: Mark 15:46 (also Matthew 27:59–61) 16:1; Luke 23:56, 24:1; John 11:44; 19:39–40; Acts 5:6–10, 9:36–37. The tractate *Semahot* dedicated to laws of burial and mourning includes some early traditions (Zlotnik 1966). The Mishna and the Talmudic literature contain references to death practices and customs sometimes reflecting earlier Jewish customs of the Second Temple period (Safrai 1976: 773–787; Rubin 1997; Kraemer 2000).

Funerary ceremonies and rites upon death were crucial, and were administered to the dead by their relatives. The family indeed played the prominent part in the funeral, and most of the routine rites its members conducted in various stages were similar to Greek customs (Kurtz and Boardman 1971: 142–161). The family was responsible for the funeral, the coffins, women keeners, and pipers. Expenses were quite high for the execution of the rites, the funerary ceremony, and the burial.

Three stages in the treatment of the dead are suggested (Parker Pearson 1993: 204). (1) The presence of the corpse is contaminated, impure, and dangerous. (2) The corpse undergoes a transition to the ritual activities of the funeral. It is separated from the living by being purified and changed in appearance; grave goods might be broken or rendered unusable. (3) The corpse is moved into the liminal zone, a sacred area (the graveyard), separating the sacred from the profane. "Once the ritual activities have been completed, the dead pass into the 'other' world, which is anywhere other than the 'here and now'."

Preparations for the funeral and burial followed death immediately, as the deceased must be buried on the day of death. Preparation of the body for burial (usually the duty of women) consisted of bathing the corpse with water and anointing it (with oil and perfume). Then the body was wrapped in shrouds (see remains found at Jericho [Hachlili & Killebrew 1999: 169, Fig. VIII.1] and 'En Gedi [Hadas 1994: 6*]). The first arrangements including the rending of garments, which was obligatory for all family members and was the first sign of grief and lamentation. Candles were lit at the head or feet of the corpse out of respect for the dead (see the lamp found on a skull in Jericho Tomb A2, Hachlili 1999: 8).

Spices may have been placed in the shroud wrapped around the corpse, as well as being burned before the procession or sprinkled on the bier.

The deceased was probably treated and prepared at home, since inside the tomb it would be dark and work almost impossible; however, some funerary rites might possibly be conducted in the tomb's courtyard (perhaps in Jericho in the Goliath tomb courtyard).

In a Jerusalem tomb unique plastered bench in the main chamber was built around its walls (Mount Scopus Observatory tomb, Weksler-Bdolah 1998: 24–26*, 51*, 162). The excavator suggests that this plastered bench originally functioned as a place to prepare the deceased for burial.

The body was wrapped in a shroud and then placed in the coffin, as indicated by the imprint of woven material found on several bones and on a skull in tombs at Jericho (Hachlili and Killebrew 1983: 118; 1999: 169, Fig. VIII.1). At 'En Gedi, linen textiles found in several coffins and tombs designating burial shrouds. In coffin 4 of tomb 1 textile fragments were discovered around the skull and limbs, as well as a knotted piece above the deceased's right shoulder; a similar knot was found in coffin 2 of tomb 6 (Hadas 1994: 56, 6–7*, Figs. 15:24, 62–30, Color Pl. 9). The custom of wrapping the body in a shroud is mentioned in literary sources (M Kil. 9, 4; M Maas. 5, 12; T Ned. 2, 7; John 11:44; Safrai 1976: 777; Rubin 1977: 202–203). The Romans practiced the same custom (Toynbee 1971: 46).

The body was brought to the grave probably on some kind of bier (*kliva* or *dargash*; Safrai 1976: 778) or on a mattress, and placed in the coffin only at the cemetery (Rubin 1997: 115, 130). The remains of the twig-filled leather mattresses found in some of the Jericho coffins attest that the deceased was carried to the tomb on a mattress (perhaps the *kliva* – כ ל י ב א referred to in BT MQ 27b; T Nid. 9, 16; Safrai 1976: 778); but they were also buried on them and then placed in the coffin (Hachlili 1999: 31). Another possible explanation is that when persons died at home on their mattress they contaminated it. Instead of burning the mattress it was buried with the deceased in his or her coffin. Roman art portrays mattresses and pillows as common accessories in funeral processions (Toynbee 1971: 46, Pls. 9, 11). This may have been accepted practice among the Jews also. However, it is possible that the dead person was carried to the grave in a wooden coffin (Hachlili 1983a: Fig. on p. 122), which is not as heavy as a stone ossuary or sarcophagus.

Apparently no separation of men and women was practiced in burial customs; a man and wife were buried sometimes in the same coffin or ossuary. Sometimes each was interred in his or her own coffin or ossuary, and the two were placed in close proximity.

Keening over the deceased, in the presence of the body, was conducted to honor the dead through a display of sorrow; grieving could last for one or two days, whereas the rite of mourning had to go on for seven days (Ben Sira 22:11–12; 38:16–23; Kraemer 2000: 15–16).

The keening women began their lamentations already at the deceased's house, continuing along the route of the funeral procession.

Others in the community would join in, accompanying the deceased
to the grave.

After the deceased was laid in the grave the sealing stone was set
before the entrance of the loculi and the tomb. Returning home
from the funeral, the next of kin purified the house and everything
in it. On the third day they visited the tomb, perhaps bringing spices
and ointments for treatment of the body (Safrai 1976: 773–787;
Rubin 1997: 103–113; Kraemer 2000: 21).

In fourth-century Athens, "the body was laid out for the greetings
from family and friends (*prothesis*) within the house. Burial must take
place before sunrise on the day following the *prothesis*, the third day
from death . . . funeral procession would take place in daylight . . . The
funeral would end with a feast in the house of the heir . . . Further
commemorative rites were carried out on the ninth and thirtieth
days after death" (Humphreys 1980: 99–100). Similar rites and practices were performed in Jewish funerary process.

Written sources indicate that the more personal duties associated
with the burial of the deceased, such as carrying the coffin and its
orderly placement in the tomb, collection of bones in ossuaries,
mourning, and writing of inscriptions, were probably carried out by
relatives and friends: "The funeral ceremony is to be undertaken by
the nearest relatives . . ." (Josephus *Against Apion* 2.205). Contemporary
and later sources mention charitable societies, such as the town association (חבר עיר) which probably dealt with other duties involved in
the preparation of the body for burial (*Sem.* 12, 4–5; Zlotnick 1966:
80–81; Safrai 1976: 775; Schwabe and Lifshitz 1974: Inscr. No. 202;
Rubin 1977: 226ff., Weiss 1992: 362–363). Professional undertakers
were also known in Roman society (Toynbee 1971: 45). Another
example is the Dura Europos necropolis (Toll 1946: 20) where the
family did not even enter the tomb and the entire burial was carried out by gravediggers.

Josephus records the funerals of Herod and Aristoblus. He describes
spices carried in the procession at Herod's funeral and then buried
(*Ant.* 17.199, *War* 1.673). From this description and that of the funeral
of Aristoblus (*Ant.* 16, 61), as well as other sources, it seems that
certain families (not only kings) arranged a grand funeral, which
included impressive clothes, a bier, objects carried in the procession,
and a feast (*War* 2.1–3). However, Josephus describes how funeral
rites should be conducted in *Against Apion* 2.205: "The pious rites

which it provides for the dead do not consist of costly obsequies or the erection of conspicuous monuments. The funeral ceremony is to be undertaken by the nearest relatives, and all who pass while a burial is proceeding must join the procession and share the mourning of the family. After the funeral the house and its inmates must be purified" (on the funeral according to literary sources, see Rubin 1997: 130–133).

Burial Rites

Ossilegium

One of the main Jewish burial rites characterizing the Second Temple period is the *Ossilegium*, a deliberate procedure of gathering the skeletal remains of an individual after the decay of flesh and placing them in a special container, an ossuary, while retaining this individual burial within the family tomb to await the individual's physical resurrection (Rahmani 1994: 53–55). The gathering the bones were performed by close relatives of the deceased; occasionally near relatives were buried together as attested by ossuary inscriptions and skeletal remains. *Ossilegium* is burial practice type III, conducted in Jerusalem and Jericho.

It is not entirely clear how the bodies were prepared for secondary burial. First, the body was allowed to decay until only the bones remained, as attested in M Sanh. 6, 6: "... When the flesh is completely decomposed the bones were gathered and buried in their proper place"; Sem. 12, 7: "R. Akiba says: The bones may not be gathered until the flesh has wasted away" (Zlotnick 1966: 81). It has been suggested that the deceased was placed in a *kokh* in his or her family tomb, and that a year later his or her relatives gathered the bones and placed them in his or her ossuary (Rahmani 1961: 117–118; 1978: 104; Kloner 1980: 248–252). However, no evidence has yet been found in the Jericho cemetery to support this claim. Moreover, many years would have to elapse for a body to decompose inside a closed tomb in the dry Jericho climate. Perhaps there was a special structure where the deceased were placed, or an area where they were buried in shallow graves, until only the bones remained. Sem. 12, 9 reads: "... my son, bury me first in a fosse. In the course of time, collect my bones and put them in an ossuary..." (Zlotnick 1966: 82, 161–162); JT MQ 1, 5, 80c: "A man collects the bones of his father and mother because it is a joy unto him. First they interred them in the *mahamorot* ('pits' or 'valleys'?). When the flesh had decayed they collected the bones and buried them in a container [an ossuary?] . . ." (Lieberman 1962, V: 1235; Meyers 1971: 59–61; Hachlili 1979b: 35). Another possibility is that some special sort of spice was sprinkled on the body that accelerated decomposition and enabled the relatives to collect the clean bones sometime later. Literary sources indicated that the person gathering the bones of his or her relative mourned that day till the evening (M. Pesahim 8,8); in order to be in mourning for as short a time as possible it was customary to collect at dusk, to eat a funeral meal, and to praise the deceased (JT Moed Katan 1, 8, 74; Sem. 12,4; Rubin 1997: 153).

Commemoration of the dead was evidently needed to lessen the grief of family and friends, who might be comforted by the remembrance and memory of the dead (Park 2000: 128–134). As this was an important way of coping with death, with bearing the departure of the dead from the living, all kinds of memorials were used; the tomb itself with its additions is a memorial, especially the *nefesh* appearing as a standing stone grave marker (see Chap. VIII); the Jericho written bowl is a unique family memorial, as are some other inscriptions and epitaphs written by the living in reference to the deceased. Family and kin provided these commemorations.

Placement and purpose of grave goods

Several conclusions can be drawn regarding *the placement and purpose of grave goods* in the tomb; the placement of grave goods was random. No particular order is evident, and there seems to be no rule for the placing of the goods. Yet at times the arrangement of grave goods does seem intentional and occasionally the offerings are carefully placed. Store jars, some found *in situ*, were often placed outside the entrance of coffin tombs and may have contained water for purification. The most frequent objects placed in the tombs were cooking pots and unguentaria (see Tables X–1–6). Cooking pots were found in all types of tombs and various explanations for this have been proposed. It is possible that the cooking pots might have been placed inside the tomb and next to coffins or the deceased only as a symbol for the commemorative meals. Small unguentaria were apparently used for funerary spices and ointments (Josephus *Ant.* 15.61; 17, 199; *War* 1.673; Mark 16:1, Luke 23:56, John 19:39–40;

M Ber. 8, 6; Barag 1972; Basch 1972; Safrai 1976: 776, nn. 3–9; see also Patrich and Arubas 1989). The lamps found in the tombs may have been used to light the way for visitors or may have been lit and placed at the head of the deceased out of respect (Lieberman 1965: 509, n. 22; Rahmani 1967b: 96; Kurtz and Boardman 1971: 211; B. Mazar 1973: 210; Safrai 1976: 774, n. 4; Rubin 1977: 224–225; Kloner 1980a: 254–255).

Most of the pottery found in the graves is a selection of every-day assemblage, no luxury wares like Terra Sigilata or other imported vessels are found.

The practice of placing burial gifts with the dead was widespread throughout the Hellenistic and Semitic-Roman world, and sometimes connoted an offering to the dead for use in the afterlife. But also it met "an inner need to satisfy a sense of loss or reluctance to credit total separation from the dead" (Kurtz and Boardman 1971: 206). Similarly, as Lieberman (1965: 509) claims, Jews placed personal belongings in the tomb of the deceased not because he or she needed them, but because the scene aroused the grief of the onlookers (Zlotnick 1966: 16–17; Sem. 8, 7; Alon 1976: 99–105; Kloner 1980a: 257–258; Rahmani 1986: 98). In the Jericho tombs personal items were placed mostly with women and children. The wooden vessels recovered from Jericho and 'En Gedi tombs might designate two different burial customs: cosmetic articles placed with the deceased inside coffins and in the tombs were personal belongings, whereas the wooden bowls and plates were possibly made especially for burial.

In most cases only single beads were placed with the deceased in Jericho burials (Hachlili 1999: 140–141). This perhaps signified grief, as did other grave goods, though it might indicate thrift, for to place an entire bead necklace might have been much too costly.

Defective and broken objects

Several objects were defective when they were placed in the tomb, for instance a dented cooking pot (Killebrew 1999: Fig. III.58:4) and a glass amphoriskos with a broken handle (Hachlili & Killebrew: Fig. III.71:1). Though this may attest to a symbolic intention it is more likely that economic considerations were the cause.

Broken pottery found in graves at 'En el-Ghuweir symbolized death, according to Bar-Adon (1977: 20), while Yadin contends (1983, I:324, n. 64) that the vessels that had become contaminated in the deceased's house before burial were broken and then placed in the grave. The defective pottery as well as pottery fragments, whether because of contamination or thrift, may have been broken purposely or thrown into the tomb as an expression of pain, sorrow, or grief. As most of the broken pottery at Jericho was restorable, it follows that at Jericho pottery was intact when it was deposited in the tomb. Deliberate breaking of lekythoi took place in Greek cemeteries, but little is offered to solve the problem (Blegen et al. 1964: 82; see also Grinsell 1961, 1973).

Unusual funerary practices

Some unusual funerary practices should be noted:

Two Jerusalem ossuaries contained some soil that is different from the local soil, which may indicate that the deceased was brought for second burial from some other place with some of the land he or she was originally buried in (Kloner 1980: 194, Tomb 29–9; Kloner and Stark 1992). Several inscriptions on ossuaries cite the deceased's place of origin, in both the Land of Israel and the Diaspora (Rahmani 1994: 17).

In a tomb at Ramot, Jerusalem a large stone (24 × 15 cm) was placed on the chest of the deceased (Zissu 1995: 137, 160, No. 30–20); this might refer to some special rite.

Perforation of sarcophagi and ossuaries

Several examples of perforation in the bottom of sarcophagi and ossuaries were noted. A sarcophagus from the tomb of Queen Helene has four holes near the bottom of its front (Vincent 1954: Pl. XCIII:2). A sarcophagus from Mount Scopus, eastern slope (though it is recorded among the ossuaries), has on its left narrow side two small rectangular holes pierced at the center, near the base (Rahmani 1994: No. 668). In sarcophagus No. 1 from the Nazirite tomb, three small, square holes are pierced in its bottom sides; a small channel runs between two of the holes, sunk into the bottom of the interior (Figure XI–11a) (Avigad 1971: 192–194, Fig. 4, Pl. 38:B, 39:B).

Several ossuaries from Jerusalem had holes pierced through the base of the ossuary chest: an ossuary from the Kidron Valley had three round holes on its base (Figure XI–11b); on an ossuary from Schneller, one hole was pierced in its base; an ossuary from Romema has a hole near the base; an ossuary from Mount Scopus has irreg-

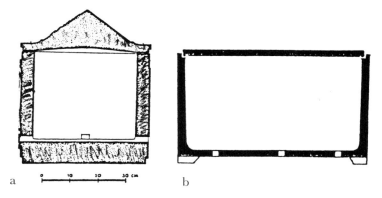

Figure XI–11. a. Nazarite sarcophagus No. 1; b. Kidron Valley ossuary.

ular spaced holes pierced into all the walls from the outside (Rahmani 1994: Nos. 85 [= Avigad 1967: 141–142, Fig. 35], 135, 304, 470).

These holes were apparently made for the drainage of body fluids. This interpretation is facilitated by a passage in the Jerusalem Talmud, Kilaim 9, 32b: "Don't abound in the shrouding, and let my coffin be pierced at the bottom"; a fifth-century CE commentary in Genesis Rabba (*Midrash Rabba* p. 1285:4 [ed. J. Theodor and Ch. Albeck, Berlin, 1928]) provides this version: "and let my coffin be pierced to the earth, on account of the fluid". The editors note that "the intent is that there be a perforation in the coffin so that the fluid issuing from the dead can drain off" (Avigad 1971: 193–194). Another interpretation is that the openings were meant to establish contact between the corpse and the soil. However, in ossuaries only dry bones were deposited, implying that this contact would have been symbolic rather than functional (Avigad 1967: 141–142; 1971: 193–194; Rahmani 1994: 9).

Impurity

Burying the dead is a contaminating activity, yet it is a duty that cannot be considered a sin. Biblical impure persons list includes persons who came in contact with a corpse-contaminated priest (Ezek. 44:26–27), Nazirite (Num. 6:9–12) and layperson (Num. 19:11–18) (Harrington 2000: 612–613, and n. 9: "Unlike the layperson, the priest and Nazirites can violate God's law by coming into contact with a corpse. The Nazirite nullifies his vow if he touches a dead body (Num. 6:11). The priest may only bury certain relatives and the high priest may not come into contact with death at all (Lev. 21:1–5, 11). According to Ezek. 44:27, the priest who buries even the allowed relatives must bring a purification offering").

Burial customs are mentioned in the Dead Sea Scrolls; the Temple Scroll deals with the commands of uncleanliness contracted from the dead (11QT, col. 51:10; see also 4Q512 col. XII, Harrington 2000: 615).

The discussion relates to: (a) burial grounds (col. 48:11–14); (b) the house of the dead person (col. 49:5–21); (c) uncleanliness of a grave (col. 50:5–9).

Yadin asserts that "this all seems to show that the main purpose of the commands in the scroll is to lay on all Israel the bans of uncleanliness contracted from the dead that were applied to the priests." The scroll bans random burials in dwellings and cities; it should be in one burial place assigned to every four cities (per tribe) so as not to pollute all the land and to prevent the situation whereby "a city surrounds a graveyard or is surrounded by one". The uncleanliness of the house, its people, and its contents, and its purification, are dealt in the Temple Scroll in detail. The house of the dead is impure for seven days (11QT, col. 49:11–13), as are all the vessels made of wood, iron, bronze, and stone, and foodstuffs (col. 49:14–15), clothing, sacks and skins; earthen vessels should be broken (col. 49:16). Anyone who entered the house or is in the house (col. 49:17) is also impure for seven days. The manner of purification and cleansing the house and its contents was by washing or bathing the occupants' clothing and vessels on the first, third, and seventh days, and sprinkling on the third and seventh days.

Uncleanliness occurs also by contact or by touching the bone or the blood of a dead person, or a grave. Yadin explains that according to the rabbinic laws "it is perfectly plain that people used to bury anywhere and everywhere, even inside houses in settled areas. The author of the Temple Scroll thus is challenging these customs." However, the archaeological findings do not prove these assumptions; the excavated cemeteries of Jerusalem and Jericho of the Second Temple period are hewn on hills outside the cities.

In sum, regulations regarding the impurity of the dead are dealt with in the Temple Scroll (Yadin I:45–17). It mentions the prohibition on the impure of entering Jerusalem, the city of the sanctuary, or only the Temple Mount (Schiffman 1990: 137); impurity was contracted by a dead person's house, by people, and by vessels (Yadin

1983 I:45.5–10; Schiffman 1990: 138–150). Schiffman (1990: 150–152) concludes that the impurity of the dead discussed in the Temple Scroll does not reflect any particular characteristics of sectarian life, and seems to have been part of the beliefs of other sects in the Second Temple period.

The Dead Sea manuscripts dealing with purity and defilement reveal no clear rules or laws. They seem to follow, as observed by Yadin and Schiffman, the regular Jewish laws with some deviations. The writings do not explain the significance of some of the Qumran burial customs, such as the marking of the graves by a heap of stones on top of each grave, the shaft grave, the stone under or beside the deceased's head, and the reason for individual burials.

C. PROTECTIVE MEASURES EMPLOYED AGAINST THE DESECRATION OF TOMBS, COFFINS, AND OSSUARIES

In ancient times the desecration of tombs for secondary usage or for plunder was a frequent occurrence. Ancient tombs, especially those of prominent or rich people, were supposed to contain valuable objects buried with the dead. During the Roman period an Imperial law (Avigad 1976: 256, note 15: *Supp. Epig. Graecum* III 1929: 13) was enacted to prevent the violation of tombs and the removal of bones from tombs in order to bury other bodies instead.

In Jewish tombs of the Second Temple period various measures were employed to avert intrusion by sealing wooden coffins and ossuaries. Wooden coffins were closed and fastened with ropes. Some ossuaries have pairs of drilled holes through the rim and lid, which served to secure the lid to the chest with rivets, strings or ropes. Some ossuaries have direction marks – incised or charcoal drawn lines usually in pairs – on the lid and on the chest to indicate the position of holes (Rahmani 1994: 18; cf. Sem. 12:8, 13:8). This step of securing the wooden coffins and ossuaries probably resulted from the wish to protect the remains of the deceased and the desire to prevent the mixing of their bones with those of others.

Lead coffins of the third-fourth century CE (some from Beth She'a-rim) had the lid soldered to the chest's rim or to both its long sides, or the closure is implemented with lead tongues (Rahmani 1999: 12–13).

Another preventive measure was Hebrew, Aramaic, and Greek inscriptions, which included curses and threats, with the affirmation that nothing of value was within the tomb. In addition, some of the epitaphs contain curses and warnings against tomb robbers or against secondary use of the tomb (Avigad 1953: 147; van der Horst 1991: 54–60; see also Strubbe 1994, listing 13 Jewish inscriptions from Asia Minor dating to the second and third centuries CE, with curses against the violation of the grave). The curse or threat is supposed to deter the tomb-violators, often depicting the outcome of violation as horrible death, bodily sufferings, punishment after death, and sometimes financial penalty. These inscriptions are common among pagans, Jews, and Christians throughout the ancient Near East.

Preventive measures employed against the desecration of tombs can be demonstrated by physical and symbolic evidence, as well as by the inscribed curse and warning formulae.

Physical evidence

Ropes binding wooden coffins

In Jericho a rope fragment, made of palm fiber, was discovered with wooden coffin 85, tomb D12 (Hachlili 1999: 22, Cat. no. 151). A leather string was found associated with coffin 78, tomb D12 (Hachlili 1999: 22).

A rope (unidentified) was found in wooden coffin 14, tomb D14 (Hachlili 1999: 24, Cat. no. 221). A string was found with one well-preserved reef knot across the lid of a coffin in Tomb G.81, presumably to hold it together (Bennett 1965: 532).

At 'En Gedi triple braided ropes (1 cm. thick) made of date-palm fibers were wound around almost all the closed wooden coffins. The rope was wrapped around once or more and tied in an overhand knot (Figure XI–12) (see coffins 5 and 8 from tomb 1; coffin 7 from tomb 5: Hadas 1994: 4*, fig. 4, coffin 8; fig. 12, coffin 5; figs. 33, 42, coffin 7).

Holes and direction marks on ossuaries

Some ossuaries from Jerusalem and Jericho have direction marks, namely lines incised or drawn with charcoal, on the rim and lid to indicate the position of holes. These pairs of holes drilled through

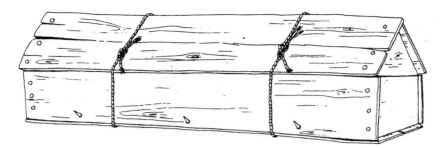

Figure XI–12. 'En Gedi wrapped wooden coffin.

the rim and lid of an ossuary were evidently intended as a means to secure the lid to the ossuary chest with strings, rivets, or ropes, and prevented its opening. These direction marks in the shape of crosses, which appeared on Jerusalem ossuaries, were once erroneously thought to be an early record of Christianity (Sukenik 1947: 12–15, 21–26, 30; refuted by Tzaferis 1970: 27; Smith 1974: 65; Rahmani 1982: 112; 1994: 19–21, Figs. 8–12; Weksler-Bdolah 1998: Ossuaries C7, C9, C11, D1). An ossuary lid with two notches on the handle probably suggests that the lid had originally been fastened by ropes (Vitto 2001: 73, 80, Ossuary 15, Fig. 32). Three ossuaries from Jerusalem have iron or lead rivets to attach the chest to the lid: one ossuary from a double-chambered acrosolium tomb on the south slope of Talbiyeh (Rahmani 1994: No. 70) has iron rivets through the outer edge of lid and the corresponding narrow side of chest. This ossuary also has the Aramaic inscription "Dostas, our father, and not to be opened" (see below), which emphasized the determination not to have the ossuary opened. Another ossuary (Rahmani 1994: No. 77) has incised marks and unfinished and unused holes in its upper, outer corners; an iron rivet is secured through rim of the chest and narrow outer edge of the lid. Fragments of lead rivets, which fastened the lid to the rim of the chest, appear on an ossuary from Arnona (Rahmani 1994: No. 196).

   Three ossuaries (nos. II, XV, XXII) from Jericho tomb H (the 'Goliath' family tomb) had drilled holes with incised lines or crosses as direction marks on the rim and lid, apparently to indicate the place for the holes (Hachlili 1999: 93, Figs. III.45, 49, 51). Ossuary II (Pl. XI–6) has six holes in the lid corresponding to six holes in the ossuary chest (two in each long side, one in each short side); ossuary XV (Pl. XI–7) has double drilled holes on the front, sides, and back and double holes on all four sides of the lid. Small ossuary XXII (Pl. XI–8) has four holes in each side of the lid and one hole in each side of the ossuary (Hachlili 1999: 93, 102, 108, 111, Figs. III.45, 49, 51). The sealing of these ossuaries was done with rope, iron, or lead rivets that have since disintegrated. The Jericho examples support the contention that the marks served to indicate the position of the lids on the ossuaries, since on or next to the marks were the holes, which served for fastening the lid to the ossuary with ropes or metal pieces.

The various measures employed to bind the wooden coffins and to facilitate closure of the ossuaries with strings or iron rivets were probably prompted by the wish to secure the coffin's or ossuary contents on the journey to the tomb, to guard the remains of the deceased, and to avoid the mixing of their remains with those of others (Rahmani 1994: 18; cf. Sem. 12:8, 13:8). However, it is also possible to interpret the closure practices as a form of defensive 'magic', to restrain hostile powers by preventing anything from leaving or entering the coffin or ossuary (also White 1997: 11; 1999: 87).

Nevertheless, it is quite difficult to explain why these measures were taken in so few instances. Were they employed especially for children? In Jericho the ossuary sealing was used only in tomb H (the 'Goliath' tomb); the skeletal remains in the ossuaries indicate that the they contained children, an infant, and a single 40-year-old woman (Hachlili 1999: 93, 102, 108, 111); the 'En Gedi wrapped coffins also contained children, and a male.

Symbolic evidence

Some symbolic implications could be observed in a double lid and graffiti on ossuaries, and a wooden coffin's iron lock, possibly designated as signs to protect the remains of the deceased and to prevent the ossuaries or coffins from being reopened. An ossuary from Jericho (Hachlili 1999: 102, Ossuary VIII, Fig. III.47 = Rahmani 1994: No. 789) was found with two lids (Pl. XI–9): a lower flat one, and placed on top of it an upper vaulted one. This double lid is unique.

An iron lock plate was found with Jericho wooden coffin 113 (Figure XI–13a); the lock has a perforated L-shaped opening, and it was probably attached to the long side of the coffin (Hachlili 1999: 67, Fig. III.8).

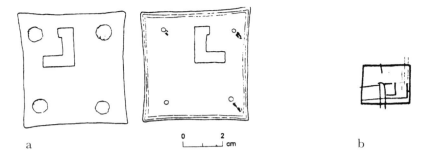

Figure XI–13. a. An iron lock plate of wooden coffin 113, Jericho;
b. a lock graffito.

A rough graffito of a similar lock (Figure XI–13b) appears on the flat sliding lid of an ossuary from Jerusalem; it was depicted next to a rivet, which firmly affixed the lid to the rim of the chest (Rahmani 1994: 20, No. 403). Both these locks may have implied that the coffin and the ossuary had been sealed. They could have been meant as symbolic protective marks.

A likely comparison is an engraved lock flanked by two disks decorating the front of a 'Sardis type' ossuary (Fraser 1977: Pl. 29; Thomas 1999: 551, Pl. 131:4).

Some lead coffins were encased in wooden casing or rarely in a stone sarcophagus (Rahmani 1999: 12–13, 17, 65–67, 79; Figs. 11–14; White 1999: 77–80, Figs. 12–15). Many of the lead coffins found in Jerusalem have a decorative element of running braided rope, twisted rope, cord, or cable in horizontal parallel lines or intersecting lines (Pl. XI–13); twisted cords and straps seem to appear tied down, with broad crossing straps arranged diagonally and horizontally along the coffin's central axis. These decorative and technical measures might have expressed a local concern for the security of the deceased's resting place.

The rope symbolizes the act of tying up and binding the coffin. The peculiar decoration on the Jerusalem lead coffins of crisscrossing ropes on the lid and on the long sides of the coffin creates the impression that the coffin was tied up with cord (Rahmani 1987: 136; 1999: 65; White 1997: 9, Fig. 10). The ropes decorating the lead coffins seem to be symbolic bonds, providing the coffin with the appearance of a firmly bound box.

The motif of the roped lead coffin could be clarified by the curse tablets made of lead or lead alloys, many of which were buried in graves, from the fifth–fourth centuries BCE onwards (White 1999: 85).

The figurine-like effigy (made of lead, mud, clay, or wax) of the victim was dropped into a grave as another way of targeting a curse. He may be shown mutilated and/or with his hands trussed up behind his back (Faraone 1991: 190, 200–291; Gager 1992: 15–16, 127–129, Figs. 2–3; White 1997: 10, fig. 13; 1999: 86, and notes 65–66). Examples include a lead figurine with hands bound placed in a lead coffin set in an Athens grave dated to the fifth century BCE (Kurtz and Boardman 1971: 217, Pl. 46).

Several similar figurines of later date were discovered in the Land of Israel: A lead figurine of a headless naked man with hands tied was found in a tomb in Ketef Hinnom, Jerusalem; its date is not clear, being Hellenistic to late Roman (Barkay 1994: 92–93). Sixteen similar lead figurines were discovered at Marissa (Bliss 1900: 332–334; Pl. 85; Zissu 1995: 162). At Tel Anafa a clay figurine of a man with hands tied on his back was found (Weinberg 1971: Pl. 19, D, E). A fragmentary folded lead plaque was discovered in Jericho in the wooden coffin of tomb D14 (Hachlili 1999: 141, Cat. No. 220).

Rope decoration on lead coffins symbolizes the act of binding or tying up the coffin. It might reflect a memory of a symbolic act of tying up and securing the coffin's contents. Avi-Yonah (1930: 310) took the motif of the rope loop on lead coffins for a symbol of immortality and resurrection, with the added significance of the binding of evil spirits. The lead coffins decorated with cord and rope, the curse tablets, and the curse figurines personified a way to avert something from either escaping from or entering the coffin (Rahmani 1987: 136; 1992: 82, n. 3; White 1997: 9; 1999: 77–80, 87–91). The purpose might have been to prevent the ghost of the deceased from escaping its chest to harm the living, as well as to protect the spirit of the dead from the powers of evil.

Epitaphs and inscriptions with curses and warnings

Warning and curses against tomb robbers or against reuse of the tomb appear frequently in inscribed epitaphs throughout the ancient Near East in various languages. Ancient tombs, in particular those of prominent people, were assumed to contain valuable objects buried with the dead (Avigad 1953: 147). As a deterrent measure the tomb inscriptions sometimes included curses and threats against would-be robbers, hostile spells, or spirits, and also affirmed that nothing of value was to be found within the tomb.

The term *defixiones* (*katadesmoi* in Greek) is used by Gager (1992: 3 and note 1) in the generic sense to designate curses, spells, and warnings inscribed on a variety of media in formulaic language. They . . ." illustrate the long and difficult debate about 'magic' and 'religion' in Western culture . . . Unlike ancient literary texts . . . they are intensely personal and direct". At present surviving examples exceeds fifteen hundred. They are inscribed primarily on thin sheets of lead, but also on ostraca, wax, and gemstones (Gager 1992: 25–26).

These curses were also common in Phoenician-Aramaic, Nabateans and Palmyreans funerary inscriptions from the eleventh to the fourth century BCE and are similar in structure and wording. They state that no valuables are present in the tomb, only the dead body; sometimes there is a warning against opening or plundering the tomb or sarcophagus, with the inclusion of a curse.

The following are formalized expressions, a wide variety of funerary inscriptions with curses and warnings, apparently installed for protection against robbers or hostile spells. Several examples are noted (Avigad 1953: 147–148):
• The 'Ahiram' Phoenician tomb-inscription (eleventh century BCE) contains: ". . . curses upon man who lays bare the sarcophagus".
• A seventh-century BCE Aramaic inscription of Agbar, priest of Sahar in Nêrab (Syria) states: ". . . Whosoever thou art that shalt injure and plunder me, may Sahar and Nikal make his death miserable, and may his posterity perish!"
• In a fifth- or fourth-century BCE Phoenician inscription on a sarcophagus from Sidon, Tabnit, the priest of Ishtar, declares: "Do not, do not open me nor disquiet me, for I have not indeed(?) silver, I have not indeed(?) gold nor any jewels of . . . only I am lying in this coffin . . . And if thou do at all open me and at all disquiet me, mayest thou have no seed among the living under the sun, not resting-place among the shades!"
• A formula of a vow and an oath appears on a fifth-century BCE Phoenician sarcophagus inscription of Eshmanezer (son of Tabnit) the king of Sidon: ז משכב אית יפתח אל אדם וכל ממלכת כל את קנמי . . . "For every prince and every man who shall open this resting-place . . .

may they have no resting-place with the shades, nor be buried in a grave, nor have son or seed in their stead . . ." (Avigad 1953: 148; Naveh 1992: 199).

• A Nabatean funerary inscription from Hager dated to the first century BCE (Cooke 1903: 217–220; Naveh 1992: 198).

• An Aramaic epitaph from Palmyra (second or third century CE) reads:

ואנש לא יפתח עלוהי נומחה דנה עד עלמא

"And let no man open over him this niche forever" (Sukenik 1935: 194; Avigad 1953: 149; 1967: 235).

Similar inscriptions with curse-formulae against those who do not leave the tomb untouched were common also in Asia Minor, in Phyrgia dating to the second–third century CE (van der Horst 1991: 54–60) and in Lycia dating to the fifth–fourth century (Bryce 1986: 116–120).

Protective Jewish inscriptions and curse-formulae in Aramaic, Hebrew, and Greek

The following protective inscriptions with curse, vow, and oath formulae appear on Jerusalem's ancient tombs and on ossuaries; early inscriptions such as inscription 1 (below) perhaps inspired the use of protective formulae on ossuaries. Some of the inscriptions were probably intended to prevent further handling of the remains in an ossuary, especially the burial of additional remains (Avigad 1953; 1967: 235; Rahmani 1994: 18–21).

The inscriptions are engraved or painted: above the door of a monolithic monument (No. 1), on a sealing stone (No. 2), on a stone slab (Nos. 3, 15), above a tomb loculus (No. 4), on a stone coffin lid (No. 7). Eight are carved on ossuaries (Nos. 3, 5, 6, 8–12), and six are painted on catacomb walls (Nos. 15–16, 18–21).

The inscriptions are dated to the eighth–seventh century BCE (No. 1), the first century CE (Nos. 2–14), and the third–fourth century CE (Nos. 15–22):

1. A Hebrew burial inscription above the door of a rock-façade small monolithic monument, from Silwan, Jerusalem, dated to the eighth–seventh century BCE, is worded as a curse (Figure XI–14):

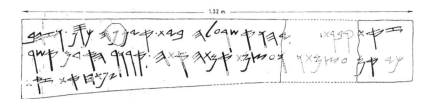

1

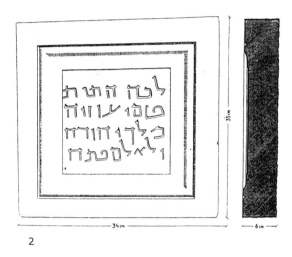

2

Figure XI–14. Inscriptions 1–2.

זאת [קברת . . .]יהו אשר על הבית אין פה כסף וזהב [כי] אם [עצמתו]
ועצמת אמתה אתה ארור האדם אשר יפתח את זאת

This is [the sepulchre of . . .]yahu who is over the house. There is no silver and no gold here but [his bones] and the bones of his slave-wife with him. Cursed be the man who shall open this [i.e., burial] (Avigad 1953).

The owner of the tomb was no doubt one of the king's ministers; he uses common formulae in sepulchral inscriptions.

2. On a sealing stone of a tomb loculus an Aramaic inscription of King Uzziah is engraved (Figure XI–14; Pl. XI–10) (Sukenik 1931a; Fitzmyer and Harrington 1978, no. 70; Naveh 1992: 194):

לכה החית טמי עוזיה מלך יהודה ולא למפתח

"Hither were brought the bones of Uzziah, king of Judah, and not to be opened". The inscription forbids the opening of the tomb, which apparently had belonged to King Uzziah. Avigad (1958: 78) dates the inscription to the mid-first century CE.

3. An Aramaic epitaph on a stone slab from the Kidron valley, in the collection of the Dormition Museum, Jerusalem, is inscribed with the formula (Pl. XI–11): אבהתנ[ה] ולא למפתח לעל[ם] "Our fathers, (It is) not (permitted) to be opened [forever]", or "Never to be opened" the last word being a new ending here (Spoer 1907: 358, No. 11; Sukenik 1935a: 195; Frey 1952: 1334; Fitzmyer and Harrington 1978: No. 71).

4. A dipinto, a red painted Aramaic inscription above the third loculus on the west wall of a tomb in the Kidron Valley, dated to the mid-first century CE, Reads (Pl. XI–12):

כוכה דנה עביד/לנרמי אבהתנה/ארך אמין תרתין/ולא למפתח עליהון

"This sepulchral chamber was made for the bones of our fathers. (In) length (it is) two cubits. (It is) not (permitted) to open them! (or Not to be opened!)". The inscription requests that the bones in the ossuary or the *kokh* not be moved again (Sukenik 1935a: 192–195, Fig. 3; Frey 1952: no. 1300; Avigad 1967: 235; Fitzmyer and Harrington 1978, no. 67; Naveh 1992: 194, fig. 133).

5. A brief Aramaic inscription on an ossuary from Talbiyeh, Jerusalem reads (Figure XI–15): דוסתס אבונה ולא למפתח "Dostas, our father, and not to be opened". The inscription prohibits the opening of an ossuary (Sukenik 1928: 113–121; 1929; Savignac 1925; Frey 1952: No. 1359b; Fitzmyer and Harrington 1978, no. 95; Rahmani 1994: No. 70). Iron rivets held the lid to the sides of the ossuary (see above), which means that the family was determined that the ossuary should not be opened. Park (2000: 65) following Horbury suggests that this "inscription may also express a concern for the integrity of the tomb".

6. An Aramaic protective formula on an ossuary lid from Ḥallat et-Turi (Milik 1956–1957: 235, Inscription A1, Figs. 2, 3; Fitzmyer 1959; Fitzmyer and Harrington 1978, No. 69; Naveh 1992: 198–199;

Rahmani 1994: 18, note 89; Benovitz 1995) reads (Figure XI–15):

כל די אנש מתהנה בהלתה דה קרבן אלה מן דבנוה

"Everything that a man will find to his profit in this ossuary (is) an offering to God from the one within it". This inscription does not follow the identification of the deceased person. The word קרבן *Qorban* is probably used in the inscription in the sense of "an offering to God" rather than "a curse of God" (Fitzmyer 1959: 65). The inscription has been widely discussed, and it seems that it is a sort of formula that warns against the secondary use of the ossuary; and that anything of value in the ossuary is an offering to God, and is not intended for any profane use. The language and formula of this inscription are comparable to Nos. 7 and 8.

7. On an ossuary from Arnona, Jerusalem (Bilig 2000; see also Benovitz 2002) a bilingual inscription in Aramaic and Hebrew was carved (Figure XI–15):

כל אנש מתחנא בה קרבן כל אש קרבן

"Everything that a man will find to his profit in this ossuary (is) an offering to God". The inscription and interpretation are similar to no. 6 (above).

8. An Aramaic inscription on a stone coffin lid reads (Figure XI–15):

סכר אמר די לא להשניה ולה יתקבר עמה בארנה דנה כול אנש

"Closed by the ram [or lamb]: It may not be changed and none entombed with him in this coffin" (Puech 1989; Rahmani's translation 1994: 18, note 89). The inscription means: the ossuary is closed, and by no means is it permitted to damage or open it, or to bury anybody else in it. Naveh (1992: 197, fig. 137, comparing with similar Nabatean burial inscriptions) proposes that אמרא "ram, lamb" refers to the daily burnt offering, here invoked as a binding conjuration.

9. On an ossuary lid, from Mount Scopus, eastern slope, Jerusalem, the Aramaic inscription reads (Figure XI–16): לא סכל אנש למעלה ולא אלעזר ושפירדה "Nobody has abolished his entering (the grave), not even Ele'azar and Shappira" (Rahmani 1994: no. 455, Pl. 66). Cross (1983: 245–6) interprets it in the sense of "can lift himself from the grave"; Puech (1989: 164*) understands it as forbidding any additional remains to be buried in this ossuary except for those of the persons mentioned, Ele'azar and Shappira. Naveh (1980; 1992:

דוקתס א בונה ולאלפיתה

דוסתס אבונה ולא למפתח Dostas, our father, and not to be opened

5

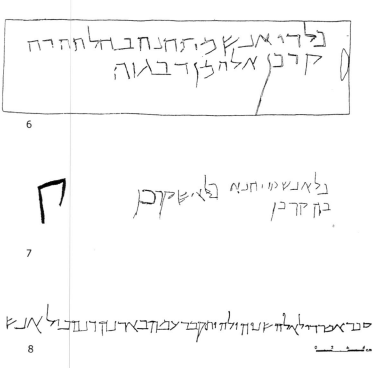

6

7

8

Figure XI–15. Inscriptions 5–8.

206–207) rejects both these interpretations and argues that the inscription is an Aramaic epigram, a consolatory burial inscription, only expressing loss and grief (see also Park 2000: 63–65).

10. An inscription on an ossuary from Ben Shemen, reads (Figure XI–16): בכנפיה מלשה בר לוי "Levi, son of Malosha, by himself" (Rahmani 1994: 18, No. 610).

11. On a lid of an ossuary the Hebrew inscription reads (Figure XI–16): בלבדא אחותי מרימ 'Miriam, my sister, by herself' (Avigad 1961).

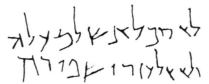

לא סכל אנש למעלה nobody has abolished his entering,

ולא אלעזר ושפירה not even El'azar and Shappira

9

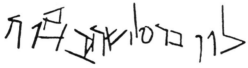

לוי בר מלשה בגפיה Levi, son of Malosha, by himself

10

11

Figure XI–16. Inscriptions 9–11.

The words as בגפיה or בלבדה meaning "himself" or "herself" on these two last inscriptions (Nos. 10 and 11) indicate that the ossuary was possibly intended for a single person's remains, or conceivably that it contained nothing worth taking.

12. A Greek formula on a Jerusalem (?) ossuary, reads (Figure XI–17): Ὁρκίζω/μηδένα ἄ/ραι Τερτιάν, "I adjure: let no one take away (of)

Tertian"; it is an admonition not to disturb the remains of the deceased (Rahmani 1994: No. 259).

13. A Greek protective inscription with a threat engraved on an ossuary from Qiryat Shemuel, Jerusalem, reads (Figure XI–17): Ρούφου ός δ ἀν/μετενένκη πα[ρ(έβη?)]/τόν ὁρκ/ον/αύ(του), "of Rufus, whoever/moves it/breaks his vow" (Rahmani 1994: No. 142).

14. A Hebrew and Greek inscriptions on an ossuary from French Hill, Jerusalem, read (Figure XI–17): a. מרים אשת מתיה "Maryam, wife of Matya"; b. Μαριεάμη Μαθίας/γυνή ὑ ἀντισκινής(ας)/αὐτά πάταξε αὐτου/ουρουν, "Maryame, wife of Mathia; who (soever) moves these (bones) away, may blindness strike him" (Rahmani 1994: No. 559). This formula is intended to protect the remains of the deceased with a threat against transgressors.

The language of the Greek inscriptions (Nos. 12, 13, 14) is vow and oath formulae. A similar type of formula was inscribed, for instance, on the Hellenistic tombs of Marissa (Peters and Thiersch 1905: 48, No. 17; Rahmani 1994: 18).

Similar Aramaic and Greek curse-formulae inscriptions were discovered at the necropolis of Beth She'arim, dated to the third-fourth century CE. These Aramaic inscriptions (Nos. 15–18) contain versions of explicit threats and retribution against transgressors; inscriptions 15 and 16 are unique in Aramaic epigraphy in the exceptional wording of their curses. The Greek inscriptions (Nos. 18, 19) express the protection of the tomb and include threats and belief in the immortality of the soul and the resurrection of the dead (Schwabe and Lifshitz 1974: 223–224).

15. On the back wall of arcosolium 3, room III, Hall A, Catacomb 12, an Aramaic dipinto in red reads (Figure XI–18):

כל מן דיפתחה הדא קבורתה על מן דבנוה ימות בסוף ביש

"Anyone who shall open this burial whoever is inside shall die of an evil end".

The Aramaic warning was apparently not sufficient, and it was repeated in Greek as well in a slightly altered formula: "Nobody shall open, in the name of the divine and secular law" (Avigad 1976: 23–25, 233; Inscription 1, Fig. 104, Pl. III:3, 4; Schwabe and Lifshitz 1974: 223, no. 134). The prohibition in this inscription against opening the tomb is based on the law of the Torah and of the state.

'Ορκίζω/μηδένα ἄ/ραι Τερτιάν I adjure: let no one take away (of) Tertian

12

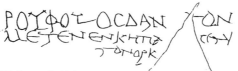

'Ρούφου· ὅς δ' ἂν/μετενένκη πα[ρ(έβη?)]/τὸν ὅρκ/ον/αὐ(τοῦ) of Rufus; whoever/moves it/breaks his vow

13

מרים אשת מתיה Maryam, wife of Matya

MAPICAMHMAΘIAC
ΓΥΝΗΑΝTIСKINHC
AΥΤΑΠΑΤΑΙСΑΥΤΟΥ
ΟΥΡΟΥΝ

Μαριεάμη Μαθίας/γυνή· ὑ ἀντισκινήσ(ας)/αὐτὰ πάταξε αὐτοῦ/ουρουν Maryame, wife of Mathia; who(soever) moves these (bones) away, may blindness strike him

14

Figure XI–17. Inscriptions 12–14.

Avigad notes, "the expression at the end of the inscription is unique and has no parallel in Aramaic or Hebrew epigraphy". This unique inscription demands protection for the deceased and addresses a warning in the name of both religious and secular laws. This inscription is elucidated by Schwabe as following the imperial edict (SEG, VIII,13) and is the only known epigraphic evidence which threatens punishment for the violation of graves, especially prohibiting the removal of the dead from their graves and their transfer elsewhere (Schwabe and Lifshitz 1974: 124 and n. 12).

16. An Aramaic painted inscription above the opening of the right kokh in the southern wall, room VIII, Hall A, Catacomb 12, states (Figure XI-18):

דקביר בהדין שמעון בר יוחנן ובשבועה דכל יפתח עלוי יהי מאית בסוף ביש

He who is buried here is Shim'on the son of Yoḥanan; and on oath whoever shall open upon him shall die of an evil end (Avigad 1976: 234–235; Inscription 2, Fig. 105, Pl. IV,4).

This inscription names the deceased and invokes the curse on whoever disturbs his rest; the wording is comparable to Greek inscription 129 from catacomb 11 (see below, No. 18). These two inscriptions are written in a formula "devised to warn people against touching the grave and disturbing the rest of the deceased and to threaten them with punishment otherwise . . . and threaten offenders with God's judgment or exclusion from eternal life. They are the only ones threatening a death penalty".

17. A painted Aramaic inscription on a fragment of a stone slab, Hall A, room VIII, Catacomb 12, reads (Figure XI–18): כל מן דיפתח "Anyone who shall open . . .". The stone slab either served to close a kokh or to cover one of the trough graves (Avigad 1976: 235; inscription 3, Fig. 106).

18. A Greek inscription painted on the front of arcosolium 2, room V, Catacomb 11, reads: οιὐμύρ[ι] Ἐγώ Ἡσύχις ἐνθάδε κῖμε σύν τή ἐμή συνβίω πάς τολμών ἀνύξε ἐφ [ἡ]μάς μή ἐχη μέρος εἰς τον [βίον] ἀόνιο[ν]. "I, Hesychios, lie here with my wife. May anyone who dares to open (the grave) above us not have a portion in the eternal life" (Schwabe and Lifshitz 1974: 113–114, no. 129; Pl. IV, 4).

The curse on this inscription is unusual, and "is the only example to date in which the share in eternal life is explicitly threat-

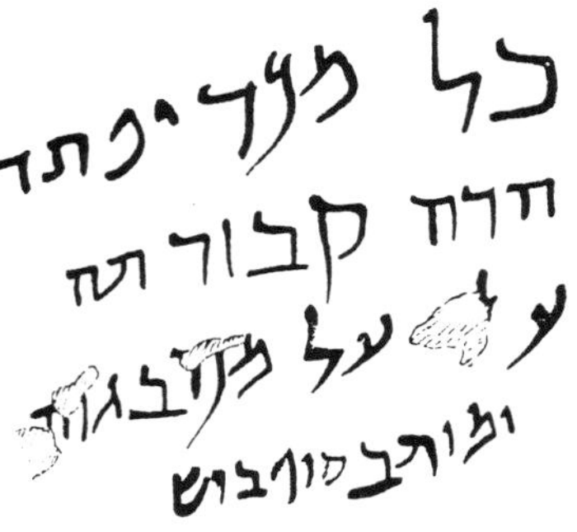

כל מן דיפתח
הדה קבורתה
על על מן דבגויה
ימות בסוף ביש

"Anyone who shall open this burial upon whomever is inside it shall die of an evil end."

15

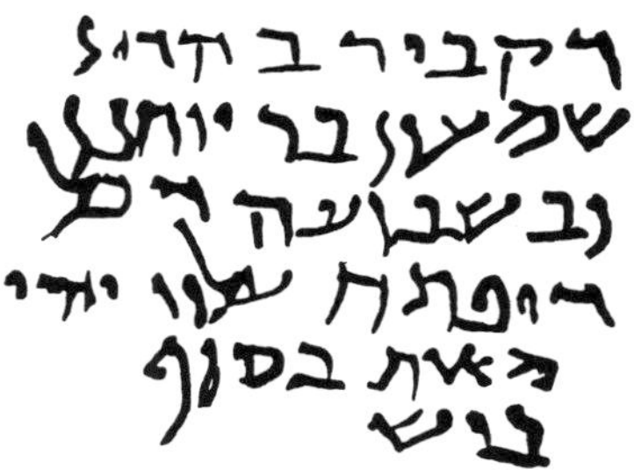

דקביר בהדין
שמעון בר יוחנן
ובשבועה דכל
דיפתח עלוי יהי 4
מאית בסוף
ביש

"He who is buried here is Shim'on the son of Yohanan; and on oath whoever shall open upon him shall die of an evil end."

16

כל מן דיפתח
"Anyone who shall open..."

17

Figure XI-18. Inscriptions 15–17.

ened ... The importance of this inscription is in the fact that it gives expression to the belief in eternal life ... it is not mere chance that explicit evidence of this belief is found in an inscription whose function is to protect a tomb".

19. A Greek inscription incised and red painted above the arch of arcosolium 1 in room II, Catacomb 13, reads:

Ος ἐάν μεταθή ταύτην ὁ ἐπανγιλάμενος ζωποιησε τούς νεκρούς αὐτός κρινε(ί).

Anyone who changes this lady's place [i.e., the woman buried in this grave], He who promised to resurrect the dead will Himself judge (him) (Schwabe and Lifshitz 1974: 139, no. 162; Pl. VI, 1).

The inscription warns against violation of the tomb and the peace
of the dead. Punishment by God Himself will befall those who do
not obey. The inscription's formula is unique; it constitutes definite
evidence of the current belief in the resurrection of the dead; it has
no parallel at Beth She'arim or other places in the country.

20. A fourth-century CE Aramaic inscription carved above the tomb
entrance of Ḥirbet Gomer reads:

אנה אלעזר בר אבה בר אבה מארי עבדת הדה קבורתה לאבה מארי בר בתה
חש[י]שתה שבועה

I, Elazar son of Abah Mari made this tomb for Abah Mari son of
Batha, warn against touching the tomb with a vow.

This inscription has a warning formula with a vow prohibiting the
opening of the tomb (Kloner 1985: 97–98; Naveh 1992: 196, Fig.
136).

The Beth She'arim and Ḥirbet Gomer inscriptions (Avigad 1976:
234–235; Schwabe and Lifshitz 1974: 162; also van der Horst 1991:
124–125) are written in a formula made as a warning to people
against touching the tomb or disturbing the rest of the deceased, as
well as threatening them with punishment. It is also meant to frighten
offenders with God's judgment or exclusion from eternal life. Two
of the inscriptions (Nos. 15, 16) also include a threat of the death
penalty. These warnings against tomb-violation comprise belief in a
judgment or post mortal punishment.

*

A popular belief on the coastal Levant under Roman administration
was that near the graves of persons whose lives had been cut short
by violence or accident ghosts hovered and sought retribution from
the living. Tombs, graves, and burial places were also believed to
be the potential haunt of ghosts and other evil spirits (Cumont 1962:
62–3; Toynbee 1971: 34–42; White 1999: 87). The ghosts of the
dead were regarded as evil spirits, which might harm the living; they
were feared especially at funerals and thereafter, when their evil powers had to be guarded against. The ghost of the dead was envisioned
as a hostile and dangerous spirit, hovering with malicious intent,
making demands or harming its living kin. It had to be dealt with
sensibly and watchfully so that the living might be safe from its anger
and malice. The attacks by these ghosts of the dead must be warded

off by various means and formulae; they must be appeased and their hostility placated (Morgenstern 1966: 141, 147, 185–186).

Binding and tying up the coffin, and sealing the ossuary, are associated with securing the coffin's or ossuary's contents on the journey to the tomb; they were also a preventive measure against the desecration of tombs for the purpose of plunder or secondary usage. The wish to protect the remains of the deceased and the need to prevent the mingling of the remains probably stimulated the various measures employed to bind the coffins, seal the ossuaries, and carve the inscriptions prohibiting the opening of a tomb or a receptacle.

The protective inscriptions had several types of formulae and probably various objectives: one was to prohibit the opening of a tomb, a loculus, or an ossuary (Inscriptions 1–9, 12–13). Another was to protect the remains of the deceased and warning against reburial and secondary use (Inscriptions 5–8, 10). They threatened those who disturbed the bones of the dead (Inscriptions 1, 7–8). Transgressors and those who disturbed the bones of the dead were explicitly threatened with curse-formulae and retribution (Inscriptions 1, 11, 12, 13, 15 and 16). Threats against transgressors and belief in the immortality of the soul and the resurrection of the dead are expressed in the Greek inscriptions of Beth She'arim (inscriptions 19, 21). Some of the inscriptions are warnings in general and do not mention the deceased's personal name (inscriptions 3, 4, 6–8, 17, 19).

The painstaking protective treatment of the dead (though only in a few instances) was realized by means of fastening coffin and ossuary chests and lids, special protective inscriptions, and marks and symbols. In addition, the sealing possibly reflected symbolic bonds. It might have implied a desire to prevent something from leaving or entering the coffin. The ropes or straps could also have represented symbolic tying and sealing to keep out evil spirits. The protective and curse inscriptions regularly include bodily sufferings, a terrible death, and punishment after death of the tomb disturber and his relatives; sometimes a financial penalty is threatened as a further deterrent.

D. 'Magic' Practice

Protective measures, beliefs and practices such as a Greek abecedarium inscription and iron nails might have had 'magical' intent and probably worked in some sense. Gager's introduction (1992: 22, 24–25) elucidates the treatment of 'magic' rightly: "No such category of magic exists . . . that is not to argue that some of the material in the ancient spells, defixiones and formularies – the sort of things customarily labeled as magical – do not derive from 'religious' (cultic) sources" (see also Versnal 1981).

Abecedaria inscriptions

Abecedaria have been found in some sites in Israel, several in a burial context (Hachlili 1984; Kloner 1986: 128–129; de Vaate 1994: 148–161).

A Greek abecedary inscription was written in charcoal on the inside of an ossuary lid (Figure XI–19; Pl. XI–13):

ΑΒΓΔ/ΕΖ/ΗΘ(?)/Φ

The lid belonging originally to Ossuary VI (Hachlili 1979: 47–48; 1984; 1999: 145, Fig. IV.2, Inscription 14) was placed in the northwest corner of the standing-pit of the Goliath family tomb (Tomb H) in Jericho. The inscription was set facing the tomb entrance (Hachlili 1999: Figs. II.73, 74). Sometime during the use of the tomb the lid was probably removed from the ossuary, the letters were written, and the lid was intentionally placed facing the entrance.

The inscription is a Greek abecedarium consisting of nine letters of the alphabet. Line 1: *alpha, beta, gamma, delta*; line 2: *epsilon, zeta* (or *nu?*), following the alphabetic sequence; line 3: *eta* and *theta* (an unusual form). Under a horizontal line across the width of the lid there is one letter, possibly a *phi* or a *psi*.

So far only one exactly similar inscription was found at Beth She'arim (third–fourth centuries CE) consisting of ΑΒΓΔΕΗΘ I, the first nine letters of the Greek alphabet; the inscription was carved on the passage arch between rooms II to IV, in Hall N, Catacomb 1 (Schwabe and Lifshitz 1974: No. 73). Two other inscriptions with abecedaria of the complete Hebrew alphabet were discovered in catacomb 25 (Mazar B. 1973: 122).

Other funerary abecedaria include a complete Hebrew abecedarium carved on the wall of the passage between two chambers of a loculus tomb at Ḥirbet 'Eitun (in the southern coastal plain of Judea). Four more graffiti inscriptions, one in Greek, were engraved above and below the abecedarium (Kloner 1986: 128–129).

ABΓΔ EZ HΘ(?) Φ

Figure XI–19. Jericho, abecedary inscription on the lid of an ossuary.

An ossuary from Reḥaviah, Jerusalem has a four-line inscription carved, each line containing three letters of the alphabet in sequence טיכך, it might have had a magical intent (Misgav 1996). In the Jerusalem Akeldama Tomb, Cave 1, Chamber D, stone slabs covering the arcosolia troughs had the first seven letters of the Hebrew alphabet (ז, ו, ה, ד, ג, ב, א) drawn in charcoal from left to right, one on each slab; the last slab had two letters (Avni and Greenhut 1996: 12, Fig. 1.21).

Two lines of abecedaria, one complete and one incomplete (*alef* to *mem*), were written in charcoal on the plaster of a bell-shaped cistern on the northern cliffs of Naḥal Michmas, dated to the first century CE (Patrich 1985: 157–158).

A number of incomplete Hebrew abecedaria from the Second Temple period have been found at various sites: a bilingual Hebrew and Greek abecedarium with five letters of the alphabet was found at Gezer (Macalister 1912: 277, fig. 425). Other incomplete abecedaria were discovered at Qumran and Herodium, and six alphabet-inscriptions were found in Murabbaʿat (de Vaux 1954: 229, Pl. Xa; Baillet,

Milik and de Vaux 1961: Nos. 10B, 11, 73, 78–80; Puech 1980; Hachlili 1984a: 28, nn. 7–9).

Several incomplete Hebrew abecedaria are known from earlier periods. They usually appear on seals (Hestrin and Dayagi-Mendels 1978: Nos. 127, 129), ostraca and pottery vessels (Hachlili 1979a: 47; 1984a: 28). A Hebrew abecedarium in triplicate was found at Kuntillat 'Ajrud, dating to the late ninth or early eighth century BCE (Meshel 1978: fig. 11). These abecedaria are usually interpreted as writing exercises (Demsky 1977: 16; Hestrin and Dayagi-Mendels 1978: 161; Naveh 1992: 64–67). Outside Israel, Greek abecedaria are known, but few have been found in tombs of the Roman period (Dornseiff 1922: 158–168, 163, No. 14; 165, No. 28; 166, No. 1; 168 No. 9; Coogan 1974: 62–63).

Interpretation

The Greek abecedarium found in the Goliath tomb in Jericho was purposely written inside an ossuary lid, placed facing the tomb entrance, and the Ḥirbet 'Eitun Hebrew abecedarium was engraved on the tomb's wall. These were apparently not a simple scribal exercise, but had a 'magical' significance intended to ward off intruders or the danger of desecration of the tomb, or perhaps they relate to the spirits of the dead (Hachlili 1979a: 48; 1984a: 30; Kloner 1986: 129; de Vaate 1994: 157–161; but see Rahmani 1994: 18, note 96). The Beth She'arim inscription, according to the authors (Schwabe and Lifshitz 1974: 46, No. 73) was also intended "... to serve as a spell against the evil spirits liable to disturb the peaceful repose of the deceased. They suggest that "the abecedaria had a magic and apotropaic value, based upon astrological and astral significance".

The inscriptions of nine Greek letters, which appear at the Jewish burials in both Jericho and Beth She'arim, are unusual. They might have signified or meant something that is now lost to us, or it was a coincidence.

There is evidence of the mystique of letters in the ancient world (Dornseiff 1922: 20–23), and from the second century CE on, the Jews were probably attentive to the Phythagorean concept of the creative powers of letters and numbers (Trachtenberg 1961: 82). The number of letters may differ; however, the 'magical' power is wielded irrespective of the number. It may now even be suggested that some of the incomplete Hebrew abecedaria on seals and ostraca be regarded as amulets rather than scribal exercises. Though proof is lacking for the 'magical' interpretation, it seems to be the most acceptable explanation for these unusual inscriptions.

Iron nails

Large iron nails probably forged by hand (Hodges 1964: 119) were found inside and outside several tombs at Jerusalem and Jericho, and seem to have been placed there on purpose.

Single large iron nails have been recovered in several tombs in Jerusalem (Rahmani 1961: 100, 106; 1980b: 53); in Jason's Tomb (Rahmani 1967a: 91) and the Caiaphas tomb (Greenhut 1992: 68). Many iron nails were discovered in the Tomb of Nicanor (Avigad 1967a: 124; however this tomb was already disturbed in antiquity). In a Mount Scopus tomb chamber, five iron nails were found (Kloner 1993: 85); in another Mount Scopus tomb one nail was discovered (Kloner 1980: 208, Tomb 2–18). Nine fragments of nails were found at Akeldama, in Cave 1, Chamber A.

Nails were found in the Jericho cemetery near the entrance of Tomb D18, and in the pit of Tomb 12. Two large angular nails with round heads found in Tomb D27, in front of a sealed Kokh; their location is unusual, and they seem to have been placed there intentionally. In the Goliath Tomb several nails were found, among them two angular nails (or key parts?) in front of loculi (Pl. XI–14; Hachlili 1999: Fig. III.84:4–6). These large iron nails, found both inside and outside the Jericho tombs, seem to have been placed there on purpose.

Some nails though large were used in the construction of wooden coffin 113 in Jericho (Hachlili 1999: 67, 139, Fig. III.9); two iron nails with remains of wood were discovered in a Mount Scopus tomb (Tzaferis 1982: 51).

Some of the nails recovered from the Jerusalem tombs were interpreted as belonging to disintegrated wooden ossuaries (Avigad 1967a: 124). However, from the discovery of wooden coffins at Jericho and 'En Gedi, usually constructed without nails, no longer could iron nails be taken as proof of wooden ossuaries (also Rahmani 1994: 4).

A similar practice was observed in ancient Greece. A dead man, in a fifth-century BCE grave at Camaria, had his coin for Charon and six nails in his hand. At Olynthus nails were found in rows at either side of the upper part of the body, or at the corners of the pit

(Robinson 1942: 159–160). Kurtz and Boardman (1971: 216) maintain that nails have a magical significance. Another 'magical' use of nails was to pierce folded lead plaques inscribed with curses found in graves in Greece, Sicily, Asia Minor, and Cyprus (Kurtz and Boardman 1971: 217, Pl. 45; Gager 1992: 18).

From Rabbinical sources we know that a nail or peg was sometimes placed to mark the permanent burial place of the deceased (Brand 1953: 71, n. 305). The Damascus Document XII, 16–18 (trans. Rabin 1954) mentions that "nail or peg in the wall that are with the dead person in the house shall become unclean in the same manner as the working tool". Hence, possibly some unclean nails were taken to the tomb and buried or placed with the dead. A later Rabbinical source which speaks of throwing iron between or inside tombs against spirits, may also support the 'magical' interpretation (T. *Shab.* 6, 10, 12; see Lieberman 1962 III:84, 88, for a discussion on the use of iron to frighten off spirits, for 'magic'; but see Rahmani 1986: 97). In Jericho the nails may have served all of these purposes.

The iron nails in these tombs may have had several different uses: to incise some of the inscriptions (Rahmani 1961: 100, 1982 IV:111; 1986: 97; 1994: 4; Greenhut 1992: 68) or to mark the place of burial; or they could have had a special meaning, possibly as a 'magical' practice (Hachlili and Killebrew 1983a: 127–128; Hachlili 1999: 173).

Red paint, found on the front, sides, and lids of ossuaries, may be related to the Greek 'magical practice of painting the inside of stone or clay sarcophagi red. The color red was sometimes used to symbolize blood or fire' (Kurtz and Boardman 1971: 217, n. on p. 364). A red painted ossuary from a tomb near Augusta Victoria, Jerusalem, was found with red stains beneath it; Sussman (1982: 5*–6*, 46, Pl. XIII:2) maintains that the ossuary was either painted inside the tomb, or carried in while the paint was still wet.

E. Evolution of Jewish Burial Customs

Primary burial in coffins and secondary burial in ossuaries were the two accepted forms of burial during the late Second Temple period, differing from earlier and later Jewish burial customs. To enhance understanding of these burial practices they will be compared with the earlier First Temple period burials (eighth–sixth centuries BCE) and with later, second–fourth centuries CE burials in the Jewish necropolis at Beth She'arim.

Rock-cut tombs of the pre-exilic period are known in Judah, many in the Jerusalem area (about 270 graves were discovered in Judah, 130 in the Jerusalem cemeteries: see Barkay 1994: 114–115; 2000: 244–248). The cemeteries were usually located in close proximity to the cities and villages, with no fences and no specific orientation. The necropolis of Jerusalem probably surrounded the city on all sides; at times some graves were attached to stone quarries.

The characteristic tomb usually consists of a small forecourt, a step or passage leading to a rectangular main chamber and a lateral chamber with benches and rectangular troughs. A repository pit for the transference of bones was often added. The dead were placed on the benches, several bodies at the same time with grave goods beside them. These items had been used throughout the deceased's life, and consisted of pottery bowls, jars, and cooking pots. The many unguenteria probably assisted in the decomposition of the bodies or in countering the smell; and there were lamps, jewelry, seals, etc. The objects found in the tombs and their use indicate a ritual of the dead (Barkay 1994: 152–155). The monumental tombs contained two to eight burial chambers. sometimes tombs were arranged around a central courtyard; troughs were a feature mainly in the monumental tombs of Jerusalem. Some hewn receptacles were found in the tombs serving as coffins, but this was not a common occurrence. A few graffiti were found on tomb walls and hardly any inscriptions (Loffreda 1965–6; 1968; Mazar B. 1971: 25–26; Barkai, A. Mazar and Kloner 1975; A. Mazar 1976; Davis and Kloner 1978; Barkay 1986: 19–20; Bloch-Smith 1992: 147–151; Ussishkin 1993; note especially Barkay's excellent 1994 article summarizing the subject).

Two stages define the burial practices in this period: the first was entering the deceased's body into the tomb; the second, which perhaps was the most important phase, was removing the bones and adding them to the bone pile of the deceased's ancestors located in the repository (Barkay 1994: 110–113).

Some similarities exist between the rock-cut tombs of the First Temple period in Jerusalem and those of the late Second Temple period. While the earlier Iron Age tombs were chamber tombs with lateral rooms, the rock-cut tombs of the Second Temple period had a chamber with loculi. Tombs of the Second Temple period served the immediate family, the loculi providing for the individual burial of each person. In the earlier Israelite tombs the individuals were laid on benches and later moved to the repository pit. Moreover the rock-cut tombs of the First Temple period served large numbers of people, probably an extended family or tribe, or in the case of the monumental tombs, only a small number of upper class individuals (Block-Smith 1992: 149–150; Ussishkin 1993: 328–331; Barkay 1994: 106–110). However, there is some typological continuation in the Jerusalem tombs: elements in the architecture, the tomb benches and repository chamber, troughs, and headrests carry Judean Iron Age burial customs on into the Second Temple period (Mazar A. 1982; Barkay 1994: 164).

The other Jewish necropolis relevant to this discussion is Beth She'arim, the central burial ground for Jews from the Land of Israel and the Diaspora in the third-fourth centuries CE. The burial customs differ from those of the Second Temple period: the dead were buried in large rock-cut catacombs consisting of halls, rooms and arcosolia, in which stone, lead, or clay sarcophagi containing primary burials of Jews from the Land of Israel or the reinterred remains of Diaspora Jews were placed. Burial had become a commercialized public enterprise, and was apparently directed by the Burial Society (*Hevrah Kadishah*), which sold burial places to any purchaser (Schwabe and Lifshitz 1974: 223; Avigad 1976a: 253, 265; Weiss 1992: 362–366). The Aramaic, Hebrew and Greek inscriptions found in these tombs mainly record the names of the tomb owner and their purpose was to identify the graves of the deceased to visitors (Avigad 1976a: 230; Schwabe and Lifshitz 1974:219). By the third century CE Beth She'arim burial customs had little in common with those of the Second Temple period and there was a return to primary burial in arcosolia, sarcophagi, etc.

Thus, the burial customs of the Second Temple period, and in particular burial in ossuaries, were short-lived and confined to Jews of this period, although sporadically continuing into the second and perhaps even third centuries CE in Galilee and parts of Judea.

F. Jewish Burial Customs and their Connections with the Pagan World

Jewish burial customs of the Second Temple period had connections with pagan customs, particularly those of the surrounding Greco-

Roman and Semitic cultures. As early as 300 BCE Hecataeus of Abdera, speaking about Jewish customs of his time, wrote: ". . . As to marriage and the burial of the dead he saw to it that their customs should differ widely from those of other men. But later, when they became subject to foreign rule, as a result of their mingling with men of other nations, many of their traditional practices were disturbed" (Stern 1974: 28, n. on p. 34).

Many of the burial customs of this period are prevalent throughout the entire region and seem to have been adopted by Jews living in the Land of Israel or in the Diaspora (Hachlili 1989). This influence is evident in tomb architecture, particularly in the rock-cut loculus tombs, adopted by Jews in Judea during the late Hasmonean period. The plan of the monumental courtyard tomb also had its roots in the Semitic world, paralleling the triclinia in the Nabatean cemetery at Petra. The wall painting in Jericho's Goliath Tomb is rare in Jewish funerary art, and was evidently influenced by Hellenistic practice.

Wooden coffins, which were a form of burial in the Hellenistic world, appear in the region during this period. Well-preserved coffins, dating to the fourth century BCE, have been found in Egypt and South Russia (Watzinger 1905) while less well preserved contemporary coffins have been discovered in Jericho and 'En Gedi. The 'magic' intention of the Jericho abecedarium, written on an ossuary lid and placed to face the entrance, may have served a similar magical purpose as found in other cultures. The iron nails found in the tombs may have had several different uses, among them to mark the place of burial, or as a 'magical' practice similar to the occurrence of nails in funerary contexts at Olynthus (cf. Robinson 1942: 159–160; Kurtz and Boardman 1971: 216).

Grave goods associated with the dead are found in tombs from nearly all periods and cultures. The leather sandals occasionally found in the Jericho tombs represent a custom probably borrowed from the Greeks, who often placed sandals with the dead as a necessary item for their 'last journey'. Pottery and Glass unguentaria, presumably receptacles for oil and perfumes, were commonly placed in tombs throughout the Roman Empire.

Coins, found at Jerusalem and Jericho, have also been found in Hellenistic tombs and were considered by the Greeks to be payment for Charon's ferry services. In this case, the pagan custom was apparently borrowed with the knowledge of its Greek significance.

The practice of placing store jars outside a tomb or on top of a grave, presumably filled with water for purification rites, appears not only in Jericho but also in Greek and Semitic cemeteries (Toll 1946: 21, and n. 20 on p. 104; Kurtz and Boardman 1971: 205). Niches for lamps are at times found in tomb walls, corresponding to the same practice in pagan tombs.

Although the presence of grave goods in Jewish tombs reflects pagan practices, they probably followed the ancient custom of funerary offerings due to an inner need of the living in connection with the dead (Kurtz and Boardman 1971: 206; Kloner 1980: 254–258; Rahmani 1986: 98).

Funerary inscriptions were a common occurrence in Jewish, Palmyrene, and Nabatean cemeteries. However, in the Jewish inscriptions the importance of the individual is evident. This is in contrast to the surrounding cultures, where only the name of the tomb owner and its architect were included. The grave marker, or *nefesh*, was evidently adopted from the surrounding Semitic world, where it was commonly used.

Evidently the surrounding cultures influenced Jewish burial practices of the Second Temple period, but their interpretation and combination produced burial customs unmistakably Jewish.

CHAPTER TWELVE

CHRONOLOGY AND CONCLUSIONS

A. Chronology

The absolute dating and chronological sequence of the Jewish cemeteries of the Second Temple period are based on several factors: (1) tomb architecture; (2) typology of tombs; (3) stratigraphic location of the tombs; (4) inscriptions; (5) grave goods found in association with these burials; (6) Chronology and geographic distribution of ossuaries; (7) historical evidence (Hachlili & Killebrew 1999: 164–165).

1. *Tomb Architecture*

The layout and plans of Jewish rock-cut loculi tombs of the Second Temple period are identical in the Jerusalem and Jericho tombs, and in the 'En Gedi tombs to some extent. The hewn tombs contain chambers, loculi, and frequently a standing pit. Rock-cut loculus tombs are well known from Egypt and Syria, as well as from several Nabatean sites dating from the first century BCE to the first century CE. They were probably adopted by Jews during the Second Temple period. The shaft hewn tombs recovered at Qumran, 'En el-Ghuweir, and Beth Zafafa are entirely different in plan and burial customs from the loculus tombs, though they are also characteristic of burial architecture of the Second Temple period.

2. *The classification and typology*

The tombs excavated in the Jerusalem, Jericho, 'En Gedi, and Qumran cemeteries are classified mainly according to the type of burial (i.e., primary or secondary), whereas the artifacts found in the tombs are helpful in the dating (Hachlili & Killebrew 1999: 59).

Type I: Primary Burial

Primary burials in wooden coffins was practiced in Jericho, 'En Gedi, and Qumran. In Jericho the coffins were placed in the rock-cut tombs, each loculus containing one wooden coffin (with the exception of one *kokh* with two coffins of a woman and a child). After the loculi were filled, additional coffins were deposited on the benches. Some coffins are placed in the pit of the burial cave or on the chamber floor. The grave goods recovered in association with the primary burials in wooden coffins include wooden vessels, leather objects, glass and pottery containers such as cooking pots, store jars, bowls, and lamps. Some of the 'En Gedi coffins were used for burial of several bodies or for collected bones. At Qumran only the remains of coffins were recovered, but they were used for primary burial on account of the design of the tombs.

Type II: Secondary/Collected Bone Burials

In Jerusalem the first stage of the custom of collecting bones consisted of transferring the bones of the deceased into a repository, a communal charnel within the family tomb. In Jericho the custom was to deposit piles of collected bones in the loculi and on the benches; no traces of coffins or ossuaries were found. The bones had been assembled systematically, with the skulls placed on top of the piles of bones (see also Rahmani, 1967a: 95). A much more limited repertoire of grave goods was recovered from these tombs.

Type III: Secondary Burial in Ossuaries

A large number of tombs containing secondary burials in ossuaries were recovered in Jerusalem and Jericho. The ossuary tombs were identical in their plan with the tombs of the other types. The ossuaries were found inside the loculi, on the benches, and in the standing pit. Some tombs appear to have been disturbed in antiquity, perhaps by members of the family, since some ossuaries had been moved out of their loculi. Tombs with ossuary burials contained various grave goods including bowls, kraters, unguentaria (mainly glass) and lamps.

Other Type

The hewn shaft tombs recovered at Qumran, 'En el-Ghuweir, and Beth Zafafa are a rectangular cavity with a pit at the bottom, often closed by mud bricks or flat stones. The graves were marked by heaps of stones on the surface. All the graves are dated to the Second Temple period.

3. *Stratigraphy*

In Jericho all three types of tombs were discovered on the same hill D. Type I tombs were hewn into the lower part of the hill, indicating that they were the earliest. Types II and III were found above Type I tombs, and in a few cases the tomb masons had slightly breached the earlier tombs. Some tomb pits of type III cut into two of the loculi of a lower tomb of Type I, or in another example, during the construction of a last *kokh* in Type II the tomb mason accidentally broke through the ceiling of the Type I tomb.

4. *Inscriptions*

The inscriptions on ossuaries and sarcophagi from the Jerusalem and Jericho tombs make it possible to reconstruct up to three generations of families buried in them. The inscriptions, together with the anthropological analysis of the skeletal remains in the ossuaries, indicate that the practice of burials in ossuaries existed for approximately 60–70 years. Furthermore, though not the most accurate method of dating, the palaeographic evidence corroborates the first century CE date (Hachlili 1979: 60, 62).

5. *Grave Goods*

The assemblages from the Jerusalem and Jericho tomb types include indicative forms dated to the first century BCE and the first century CE (Killebrew 1999: 115–133). Type I tombs contained vessels characteristic of the first century BCE, including sunburst and folded lamps, high-necked globular cooking pots, and store jars typically found on first-century BCE sites. Personal possessions, often found in the coffins together with the burial, include objects common in the first century BCE. In Jericho two coins found in association with coffin burials confirm the first century BCE date for burials in coffins.

Based on the grave goods associated with secondary collected bone burials, Type II tombs should be dated to the first century CE. Short-necked globular cooking pots, found in abundance with type II burials, appear in late first-century BCE and first-century CE contexts. These cooking pots, which have been placed inside the tomb, next to coffins or beside the deceased might have represented a symbolic act as a substitute for the commemorative meals.

Two coins of Agrippa I dated to his sixth year (41/42 CE) found inside skulls in collected-bone burials in Jericho provide further evidence for a first-century CE date.

A distinctive assemblage of vessels, characteristic of the first century CE (until 70 CE), has been recovered from secondary burials in ossuaries (Type III). These include bowls, kraters, lamps and unguentaria, especially glass bottles. Red-painted motifs on pottery vessels appear for the first time in Jericho ossuary tombs. This collection is typical of ossuary burials and of first-century CE assemblages at the sites of Jericho, Masada, and Herodium.

The grave goods found in the Jericho Goliath tomb and its courtyard complex date to the second half of the first century CE. The courtyard and its *miqveh* remained in use after the First Revolt and there is evidence that also the tomb was reopened, sometime after the destruction of Jericho, perhaps late in the first or early second century CE.

6. *Chronology and Geographic Distribution of Ossuaries*

Rahmani (1994: 21–25, Table 1) suggests three major periods of ossuary use, manufacture and distribution:

A. *20–15 BCE to 70 CE.* Ossuaries were introduced in Jerusalem ca. 20–15 BCE based on the dates of 'Herodian' lamps and moulded lamps. Rahmani further maintains that it took at least one generation for the custom of *ossilegium* to evolve in Jerusalem before spreading to Jericho. Thus, this date accords with the Jericho finds dating one generation later.

B. *70 to 135 CE.* The production of ossuaries ceased following the destruction of Jerusalem. The tombs in the Jerusalem vicinity contained some locally made ossuaries. The local ossuaries of the soft limestone variety were found in southern Judea on the Mediterranean coast (Group B2–3). Later ossuaries from the Hebron area (Group B4) are mostly plain, locally made and crudely fashioned. Ossuaries of Group B5 from Galilee are similar to Group B4b. Refugees from Jerusalem probably introduced ossilegium into these areas.

C. *Late-second to ca. mid-third century CE.* The custom of using limestone and clay ossuaries (Group C2), found in a few tombs was apparently as a result of waves of refugees to Southern Judea and Galilee after 135 CE.

7. *Historical Evidence*

An inscription found in the Goliath Tomb in Jericho (Inscription 3 on Ossuary VIII) provides an absolute date for the ossuary burials. The inscription mentions Agrippina, wife of the Roman Claudius, who reigned from 50–54 CE (Hachlili 1979: 60–62). The inscription states that Agrippina had freed Theodotos (Nat[an]el), whose remains rested in the ossuary, sometime during his adult life between 50 and 54 CE. Manumission probably occurred sometime during the reign of Agrippina, though it is difficult to determine when and for how long he was enslaved, and at what age he was manumitted. It is likely, however, that he was taken into slavery as an adult, and only after the birth of his daughter Mariah (the third generation buried in Tomb H). This inscription confirms a first-century CE date for secondary burials in ossuaries.

Based on the above evidence, the dating of the burial types found in the Jerusalem, Jericho, 'En Gedi, and Qumran cemeteries is as follows: primary burials in wooden coffins (Type I): first century BCE, perhaps continuing into the early first century CE. Secondary burials of collected bones (Type II) and secondary burial in ossuaries (Type III): early first century CE until the destruction of Jericho by the Romans in 68 CE. The dating of the Jerusalem tombs is similar, although no proof for primary burials in wooden coffins was discovered there. These dates correspond to the political events occurring in Judea at that time. In 6 CE the Jewish state lost its autonomy under Rome when Herod Archelaus, ethnarch of Judea, Samaria, and Idumea, was removed from power and Judea became a Roman province under the procurators. After the destruction of Jericho by the Romans in 68 CE (Jos. *War* IV 450–451) there is no evidence of the continuation of ossuary burials in the cemetery.

Research on Jewish burial customs in Jerusalem during the Second Temple Period has yielded different absolute dates for secondary burials in ossuaries. Rahmani (1961: 116; 1978: 111; 1982; 1986: 96; 1994: 21–25) suggests that the widespread practice of this burial custom began as early as 25–15 BCE in Jewish Jerusalem, reaching Jericho a generation later, and continued until 70 CE. This seems to me much too long a period for a custom from Jerusalem to reach Jericho, it could have taken at the most a couple of years or so. After the destruction of Jerusalem, this custom continued sporadically until *ca.* 135 CE (see also Kloner 1980a: 252–253 for similar dates).

In light of the discoveries in the Jericho cemetery, wooden coffins (although not preserved in Jerusalem) can be first dated in Jericho to the first century BCE. Thus, dates previously proposed for the beginning of ossuary burials in Jerusalem should be reconsidered. The close relationship evinced between Jerusalem and Jericho seems to indicate such a date – early first century BCE – for ossilegium at both sites.

B. CONCLUSIONS

The preceding chapters of this book examined and analyzed the theological and sociological aspects connected with ancient Jewish burial customs, the origins of funerary practices, as well as the evaluation of burial rites, their development, change, and continuation.

Burial practices are based on generations-long traditions, on beliefs which initiated communal rituals, as well as on the influence of surrounding cultures.

Burial customs and rites are described in contemporary literary testimony such as the works of Josephus *Jewish War, Antiquities, Life,* and *Against Apion,* written in the latter part of the Second Temple period, and the New Testament, reflecting the ideas and customs of the time. The tractate *Semahot* dedicated to laws of burial and mourning includes some early traditions. Rabbinical literature, codified from the second century CE onwards, refers to funerary practices and may at times reflect earlier Jewish customs of the Second Temple period.

The belief of individual physical resurrection, of the return from death, is reflected in Daniel (12:2) and later acknowledged in II Macc. 7 and 14:46; this idea might have developed following the Maccabean revolt and the influence of Hellenistic concepts pertaining to the individual. Some scholars maintain that this belief was adopted by the Pharisees and denied by the Sadducees (based on the writings of Josephus) and regard it as the basis for *ossilegium,* the new practice of the late Second Temple period (Rahmani 1994: 53–54). *Ossilegium* in fact means an extended process of death, grieving, and mourning; it represents two rites: the primary burial of the body, and about twelve months later, after the flesh has decayed, the gathering of the bones into the ossuary.

Funerary ceremonies and rites upon death were crucial. The prominent part in the funeral ritual was played by the family members, who performed in various stages most of the customary rites. The family was responsible for the funeral, the execution of rites, the funerary ceremony, and the burial.

Research of the Jerusalem, Jericho, and 'En Gedi necropoleis of the Second Temple period uncovered burials in rock-cut loculi tombs and revealed that two completely different burial customs, one chronologically following the other, were practiced by Jews of the Second Temple period.

The earlier custom, practiced during the first century BCE, was primary individual burials in wooden coffins (perhaps also individual interment in loculi first appeared among Jews at that time) (Hachlili & Killebrew 1999: 174–175). In the First Temple period no data of burial in coffins have been found. Nor do biblical references mention the word coffin (*aron*) except in the case of Joseph (Gen. 50:26) who died in Egypt and whose remains were transported to Canaan in a coffin (Hachlili 1979: 44; see also Terms, p). This isolated case can be explained as referring to the Egyptian burial practice of interment in coffins (Klein 1908: 32). The biblical concept of burial was "to be buried with his fathers", perhaps indicating a tribal burial. According to biblical accounts, after the settlement of the Israelite tribes in the Land of Israel a person was buried in a family tomb. The terms used in the Bible are: "to sleep with his fathers", (1 Kings 1:21, 11:43); "be gathered to your fathers", (Jud. 2:10); "gathered to his people" (Gen. 25:8; 49:29: Num. 31:2; Deut. 32:50); "buried with his fathers" (1 Kings 14:31; 15:24; 2 Kings 8:24). The concept of family burial was strong already at that time. Iron Age archaeological evidence (Loffreda 1968; Ussishkin 1993; Barkay 1994a) gives no indication that coffins were used at that time by the Israelites. However, coffins of this period are known in the Egyptian and Phoenician world.

Primary burials in wooden coffins have not been discovered so far in Jerusalem but this may be due to the poor preservation of organic material in the more humid Jerusalem climate and the disturbed condition of most of the tombs. But tombs containing primary burials have been uncovered where the bones had been transferred to repositories (Rahmani 1958: 104; 1967a: 94–95; 1977: 24) and one such tomb contained primary burials with pottery similar to that found in the Jericho coffin tombs (Kloner 1980b).

The second burial custom (types II and III) found in the Jerusalem and Jericho cemeteries, chronologically following on the coffin burials, is *ossilegium*, an intentional secondary burial of the bones, either placed in individual ossuaries or communal in nature (but see Rahmani 1986: 96, where both forms have been found together in Jerusalem). The ossuaries used in type III burials were carved from limestone, and similar motifs decorate both the Jericho and Jerusalem ossuaries. However, those from Jerusalem are frequently of better workmanship. This may be due to the relatively few ossuaries thus far discovered in Jericho, but it may also indicate that artisans of lesser standing resided and worked in Jericho.

The importance of individual burial as well as burial in a family tomb is evident in Jewish burial practices of the late Second Temple period. This is reflected in the plan of the loculus tomb, which provided for individual burial of coffins in loculi and at the same time allowed a family to be buried in the same tomb. The inscriptions found on tombs, sarcophagi and ossuaries reveal family relations and prove that the loculi tombs served as family tombs. The unique inscribed bowl found in a Jericho tomb traces the genealogy of a family and served as a memorial and commemoration for a family originating in Jerusalem. The concept of individual burial for the entire population and not just for the upper classes, as in the Israelite period, is probably related to the increasing importance ascribed to the individual in contemporary Hellenistic society as a whole (Kurtz and Boardman 1971: 273) and to the Jewish belief in the individual resurrection of the body. The concept of individual resurrection is reflected in sources as early as the second century BCE (Dan. 12:2; 2 Macc. 7:9–23; 12:38–45; 14:46; Jos. *Apion* II, 218; Finkelstein 1940: 145–159; Rahmani 1961: 117–118, n. 6: 1978: 102–103; 1981 I; 1982, III). Thus the importance of the family, combined with that of the individual in his family and society, is evident in the new Jewish practices of this period, namely the earlier type (I) of burial in coffins in Jericho and 'En Gedi.

This drastic change is difficult to explain. Unfortunately all the sources dealing with ossilegium describe only the custom itself, without giving any explanation for its sudden appearance.

Most of the burials, both primary and secondary, were in loculi tombs hewn into the hillside, which served as family tombs with provision for the separate burial of each individual. The same general tomb-plan, consisting of a square chamber with loculi or a single-

kokh, continued to be used throughout the Second Temple Period in Jerusalem, Jericho, as well as elsewhere in Judea. A few graves dug into the earth were found in Jerusalem and Jericho.

The Jericho data verifies decisively that loculus tombs were first planned and used for primary (i.e., permanent inhumation) burials in coffins, as is also indicated by the length of the loculus, which corresponds to the length of a coffin (Hachlili 1999: Tables II.5; III.1). The same tomb plan continued to be used for ossuary burials. Scholars have claimed that the *kokh* was "intimately" connected with secondary burial (Kutscher 1967: 279; Meyers 1971: 64–69; Avigad 1976a: 259: "For Jews the use of the *kokh* is associated with the custom of bone collection for secondary burial"). This claim is unsupported as there was no need to prepare a two-meter long loculus for the 70-cm long ossuary.

A few loculi tombs had a large open courtyard with benches such as monumental tombs in Jerusalem and the Goliath tomb at Jericho (Hachlili 1999: 37–44). These courtyards were probably used for mourning and memorial services similar to the 'eulogy place' or house of assembly mentioned in Jewish sources (BT BB 100b). Similar courtyards with benches dating to the third century CE were found in the Beth She'arim Jewish necropolis and probably served a similar purpose.

A *miqveh* (ritual bath) was constructed as an integral part of the Goliath tomb courtyard, fed by the aqueduct running along the hilltops through the cemetery. In Jerusalem an aqueduct passed through the cemetery in close proximity to the tombs and at times even cut into them.

In view of the homogeneous nature of burial customs in Jerusalem and Jericho, it is logical to assume that not only secondary burials in ossuaries but also primary burials in wooden coffins were practiced in both centers. Though Second Temple Period tombs with wooden coffins and collected bones burials were excavated at 'En Gedi (Hadas 1994), there is no conclusive evidence that these were Jewish burials.

The Qumran and 'En el-Ghuweir customs, however, differ considerably from the two forms that were the accepted Jewish burial practices in the Second Temple Period. The Qumran cemetery was a central community burial place, and the tombs are all oriented on the same north-south axis. The form is an individual burial in a

shaft grave, with or without a wooden coffin. The burials also lack
inscriptions. These are clearly not family tombs. The graves in these
cemeteries are organized and carefully dug out and arranged, which
seems to rule out the assumption by some scholars that the tombs
were dug in haste for a large group of dying people in connection
with the first Jewish revolt against the Romans (ca. 68 CE). Scholars
also are in dispute about the question of identifying the Qumran
community and cemetery with the Essenes. It seems that the burial
forms and customs at Qumran and ʿEn el-Ghuweir are fundamentally different from those practiced by normative Judaism in Jerusalem,
Jericho, and ʿEn Gedi; They indicate different attitudes to death and
burial practices, with the Qumran community separating itself from
mainstream Judaism.

Grave goods were placed with the deceased in tombs, coffins, and
seldom in ossuaries. They consisted of everyday items as well as personal possessions. Funerary grave goods found in tombs are of extreme
interest and importance, and the practices and rituals convey their
meanings.

The similar use of objects for everyday life and for funerary use
illustrates the connection between the dead and the living, while the
location of the cemetery and the purifying laws reveal the emphasis on the separation of the dead from the living.

Jewish art of the Second Temple period includes the ornamentation and embellishment of funerary structures such as tombs and
receptacles, sarcophagi and ossuaries. Jewish art of the Second Temple
period, though showing connections with the neighboring Greco-
Roman culture, withstood foreign influences by evolving strictly aniconic features. This art, together with the other arts of the period,
is characterized by highly skilled indigenous stonework, by plasticity
of carving, by the predominant Oriental elements of endless patterns, by the element of *horror vacui*, and by symmetrical stylization.
It is based on the ability and skill with which the artists related to
the needs and requirements of their clientele, whose demands were
mainly decorative. The strictly aniconic and non-symbolic art characterizing the Second Temple period is the outcome of Judaism's
struggle against paganism and idolatry. By the rigid observance of
the prohibition against animate images, the Jews retained their own
distinctiveness and identity.

The main question concerning burial rites in the Second Temple
period is what caused the change in the customs from primary buri-

als to *ossilegium*. In Jericho, burial customs were either primary burial in coffins or secondary in bone heaps or bones placed in ossuaries. Nowhere in Jericho were the deceased buried in coffins removed into ossuaries. These were two explicit, distinctive, dissimilar burial practices. In time one replaced the other.

Various hypotheses have been suggested for this major change in burial customs:

1. Economic factor: The need to economize on burial space included the removal of bones from primary burial to ossuaries because space for burial became more expensive (Bar Adon 1937). Rubin (1994: 262–269; 1997: 150–153) ascribes ossuary burial to the increased wealth in first-century Jerusalem and the abandoning of charnel burial. He further maintains that secondary burial in an ossuary is a local variation of an expression of economic-technical hardship??, and the justification is given to the custom as rationalization after the fact. Fine (2000: 73–74) adds that ossuary burial was dependent on the development and rise of local stone mason industry which produced the ossuaries.
2. Secondary burial in ossuaries was practiced by a wealthy section of Jewish society (Teitelbaum 1997: iii, 142–159, 151): "Its means allowed it to indulge in the luxury of the ultimate in individual safekeeping of its remains, thus identifiably guaranteeing memorialization by succeeding generations of visitors to the tomb."
3. Liturgical, political, and national elements were the reason for the changes in burial customs. The practice developed to facilitate resurrection of the complete dead body, and to expiate sins through decay of the flesh; it was perhaps connected with the Pharisaic beliefs in resurrection (Rahmani 1961: 117–118; 1977: 22; 1986: 99; 1994: 53–54). Theological motivation for the practice must have existed, although no evidence is found in literary sources. Fine (2000: 76) maintains there is no positive evidence to support it, neither literary nor archaeological.
4. Kraemer (2000: 22) argues that as death is a continuing process, and only the decomposed flesh will finally accomplish death; the deceased was then removed to the final rest to await resurrection.

It seems difficult to accept that economic and industrial means (nos. 1, 2) could be the explanations for such a radical change in burial practices. The evidence from the Jericho cemetery refutes these suggestions. In fact, more individuals were found buried in the coffin tombs at Jericho than in the ossuary tombs. Secondly, resurrection

of a complete body is more easily accomplished through primary
burial, and would be more difficult in second burial, since some of
the bones could be lost in the gathering of the skeletal remains after
the decay of the flesh. In many Jerusalem and Jericho tombs there
was room for many more burials: see for instance the Goliath tomb
at Jericho. The third suggestion is the most persuasive, being a logical extension of the belief that a person's sins reside in the flesh
and can be expiated after death through decay of the flesh. Rahmani
(1986: 99; 1994: 56–59) further claims that the custom of ossilegium
should be seen as Jerusalemite in origin, without any foreign influence.[1]

The question of what caused these changes remains unsatisfacto-
rily resolved by literary sources or by archaeological investigations.
Nonetheless, the changes could have been brought about by turmoil
in the society, perhaps as a result of historical events which affected
the religious beliefs of this period. The loss of Judea's political inde-
pendence after the expulsion of Herod Archelaus in 6 CE was followed by Roman procuratorial government until the destruction of
Jerusalem in 70 CE (Hachlili 1980: 239; 1994: 185–189). These events
may have led the Jews to feel that they were sinners and needed
expiation of their sins. They believed this could be achieved by let-
ting the flesh of the bodies decay first and than gather the clean
bones into ossuaries or piles, so that they might be pure for their
resurrection.

---

[1] It has been suggested that Roman funerary urns containing the remains of cremated burials may have influenced burial in ossuaries. However, these burials are
vastly different in concept: the former consisted of the cremated remains of the
individual immediately after his death (Toynbee 1971: 40–41, 50, 253–255), while
the latter first entailed the primary burial of the individual, and only after at least
one year had passed, the gathering of his bones into a small rectangular container.

ANTHROPOLOGY NOTES AND TABLES

Anthropological studies and examinations were conducted only in recent decades, with great difficulties entailed in recovering and determining data of skeletal remains. Some tombs were looted or disturbed and the skeletal remains dispersed, which added to the confusion. Parts of the same individual could be collected into more than one ossuary; remains belonging to the same individual could be recovered from an ossuary while others could be found in one of the tomb loculi, the pit, or the benches. Fractions of skeletal remains could be left in the loculi and others distributed among more than one ossuary (Smith and Zias 1980: 111; Zias 1992a: 78; 1992b: 97).

The skeletal remains found in many of the tombs were frequently in a disarray, and poorly preserved. Many of the samples were fragmentary and were represented only by some parts of the skeleton.

In some Jerusalem tombs previous burials had been thrust aside in order to provide space for an ensuing burial. The darkness in the tomb also caused some skeletal remains to be overlooked in the loculi during the removal to ossuaries or other parts of the tomb.

In several Jerusalem tombs (Mahanayim and Ruppin, Rahmani 1961: 105, 117) bones were pushed aside and were possibly collected into a sort of communal assemblage before the custom of burial in ossuaries (see Chap. XI). In Sanhedriya tomb 6 a woman's skeleton was found (Rahmani 1961: 96).

One or two generations are represented in Jason's Tomb, mostly by scattered bones, which were transferred, by means of mats or sheets, from *kokhim* in Chamber A and reposited in Chamber B, where about 25 burials were discovered (Rahmani 1967: 62–3).

A single undisturbed skeleton was found in *kokh* 9 with 42 coins, 36 of them at the foot the burial; some bones had been pushed aside for the skeleton's burial. The burial was probably completed at the time of the tomb's final sealing. There is no proof that this burial is Jewish or that it belonged to the family, though the menorah graffito may have been connected with this burial (Rahmani 1967: 99).

The skeletal remains from Giv'at HaMivtar present details recovered from 15 ossuaries containing 35 individuals: 11 males, 12 females, and 12 children (Haas 1970: 39–49, Table 1). Some of these interred people had died from illness or violence, and one showed evidence of crucifixion, according to this report (disclaimed by other researchers).

Skeletal remains from a group of French Hill tombs, Jerusalem (tombs 29–10–15; Arensburg & Rak 1975: 69, Fig. 2), are identified in a tentative result by age and sex: 45 adults and aged (17 males, 11 females, and 17 undetermined), five juveniles, six children, and eight newborn babies. The number of adult individuals in these tombs (70%) is high.

Most of the remains from the second group of tombs from French Hill (tombs 29–16–18; Smith and Zias 1980: 111) are of middle aged or older adults, while children and infants represent 27%.

Similar results of reported skeletal remains from other sites in Jerusalem and Jericho show groups in relatively good health with little pathology and a high life expectancy.

The close similarity and little variety indicate that these groups represent a typical, fairly homogeneous Jewish population of Second Temple period.

In the Caiaphas tomb child mortality is high (68%), suggesting that wealth or high status does not present health advantages (Zias 1992a: 79).

The bone remains from the Mount Scopus Observatory tomb (caves A–D; 1–42–45; Arieli 1998: 37, 41) were in poor preservation; the research identified at least 147 individuals: 66 adults (45%) including 20 males, 21 females, and 25 undetermined. They were 81 (55%) fetuses, infants, children, and adolescents. The highest mortality rate (25%) appeared among children aged one to three years, and the lowest (5%) among those aged 15–18.

A large percentage of the Jericho skeletal remains sample (Arensburg and Smith 1983: 133, Table 1) shows a survival rate of adults to age 50 years or older. In the sample more males (86) than females (52) were found; possibly the lighter and smaller female skeletons perished quicker. A low rate of child mortality was observed.

In one of the Jericho tombs (tomb A2, Hachlili 1999: 6) bones of children and infants were found in the lower level of the tomb's pit, which might indicate a unique burial of children. However, most children and infants were usually buried either with an adult, commonly the mother, or separately in their own ossuary.

The osteological findings in the Goliath family tomb corroborated data from the ossuary inscriptions (see Table V–1; Hachlili and Smith 1979: 67; Hachlili 1979: Table 1)

A preliminary report of the skeletal remains from the 'En Gedi tombs indicates that they belongs to a homogeneous assemblage (Arensburg and Belfer-Cohen 1994: 12*–14*; Table 1). The study examined remains recovered from communal burials and wooden coffins in five tombs (nos. 2, 5–8; see Anthropological Tables 3–4). Age and gender distribution is normal: the male-female ratio is 55.5:44.5 for adults and 49:51 for children and infants; age at death of males is slightly older; health was reasonably good, and the research found close genetic ties in this group.

The study of the Qumran human remains was accelerated in recent research (see Anthropological Table 6). The older study examined 43 individual remains from different parts of the cemetery (Vallois examined tombs 3–8, Kurth – T12–13, T15–19, TA–B, Haas and Nathan [1968] – G and Nagar – BE (See Anthropology Table 6; Taylor 1999: 298–310, Tables 1–4; Eshel et al. 2002: Table V; Magness 2002: 91–95; Sheridan 2002). "Only 39 exhumations have undergone modern anthropological analysis, representing approximately 3.5% of the total interred collection" (Sheridan 2002: 204). Röhrer-Etrl et al. (1999) reexamined twenty-two human remains identifying nine adult males, eight adult women and five children; the remains from the main cemetery he reexamined were identified as nine adult males and two adult females (from T22 and T24a; See Anthropology Table 6; Eshel et al. 2002: Table V). Zias (2000) disputed these results suggesting that the three identified females (from T7, T22, T24a) are actually males on the basis of their height, which exceeds the height for females in this period. He also argues that the remains of the women and children found in the Southern cemetery and the southern extension are recent Bedouin burials based on the tombs orientation (East-west) and the jewelry found in two of the graves (see Chap. VII). Human remains from tombs of De Vaux excavations (Tombs 3–8, 10, 11, 12, 13, 15, 16a, 16b, 17, 18, 19, A, B) were recently reexamined by Sheridan (2002: Table 5; see also Anthropological Table 6; Magness 2002: 94; Eshel et al. 2002: Table V). These tombs are oriented north-south, and are from the main cemetery, Tombs A and B provenance is not clear.

All the remains are identified as males except for three female found in T22 and T24a in the main cemetery and one female from

TA (probably in the northern cemetery). The women and children identified in the southern cemetery are probably recent Bedouin burials (see Chap. VII; Zias 2000; Magness 2002: 95; Eshel et al. 2002: 136, note 1; but see Zangenberg 2000: 65–72 for a rejection of this identification).

For a regional comparison of sex profile and the ratio of males to females, see Anthropology Table 7, also Sheridan 2002: Table 6.

The low figure of 30% child mortality in Jerusalem tombs in the French Hill cemetery has been explained by anthropologists in different ways: some found it possibly "indicative of differing cultural traditions regarding health care" (Arensberg and Rak 1975: 69). Others suggest that the lower infant mortality rate reflects the superior economic situation of Jerusalem middle and upper class families who were able to provide better health care and nutrition (Smith and Zias 1980: 112–113). In general, infant mortality in the Land of Israel at this time was lower than in other Mediterranean countries, and a higher percentage of individuals in the Israel population reached old age (Hachlili and Smith 1979: Table 1). These figures conform to those recorded for other Jewish remains of the period, with the mean age at death significantly higher than that observed in other contemporary Mediterranean populations.

The estimate of the population's stature shows an average of 1.67m for males and 1.46 m. to 1.57 for females (Hass 1970: 40–49; Arensburg & Rak 1975: 71; Arieli 1998: Table 5). At Qumran the average male height was 165.7 + −5.9 cm. and the average female height 158.3 + −3.3 cm. (Sheridan 2002: 235–241, 246). This estimate demonstrates a highly significant difference between the sexes. Note, however, the Goliath family, where four male individuals were extremely tall, judging from the length of the femora. The femora of the Goliath family father (Yeho'ezer son of Ele'azar) were 53 cm. long, giving an estimated stature of 188.5 cm., 20 cm taller than the mean stature for this period (Hachlili and Smith 1979: 67).

Special trauma-related data were found in Jerusalem and Jericho. For example, in a Jerusalem tomb on Mount Scopus a mutilated male adult (aged 18–21) was found in ossuary 18 (Zias 1992b: 101, Fig. 3), suggested to be the result of punitive measures inflicted on a captive. Decapitation is observed in several cases in Jerusalem tombs (Rak et al. 1985; Zias 1983) and at 'En Gedi (Arensburg and Belfer-Cohen 1994: 13*).

Two male skeletons with a triangular hole in their skulls were discovered in Jericho (Tomb D9–1, and in Coffin 84, Tomb D12, west bench). The shape of the holes seems to suggest arrowhead wounds (Hachlili 1999: 16, 22, Figs. II.35, II.41).

The Jerusalem sample show varying degrees of osteoarthritic conditions on individuals over 30, while the Jericho remains rarely demonstrate these changes; they also indicated a longer life span; more Jericho adults survived beyond the age of 50. The data show lower infant mortality (Arensburg and Smith 1983: 136, Table 4).

The data published in anthropological reports and the analysis of anthropological remains lacks accurate scientific data. It provides only the number of individuals, their sex, and sometimes the age of those interred in a tomb, an ossuary, or a coffin; they do not tell how many of the skeletal remains belonging to each of the individuals were found. It is clear that an ossuary could contain no more than a complete set of skeletal remains of one adult human or one adult with a child (see Hachlili & Killebrew 1983: fig. 11; 1999: fig. VIII.2). It is quite possible that in an ossuary a complete or nearly complete set of one individual's skeletal remains was found, with the addition of one or several bones, teeth, or a few remains of another individual. However, in the report two individuals will be registered, while properly it should state "one individual and several bones of a second". Otherwise all the data are unquestionably inaccurate. So we do not have a precise idea of how many individuals were buried in each ossuary (or coffin). See, for instance, the report on the human skeletal remains from a Mount Scopus tomb by Zias (1992: Table 2). He recorded remains in 18 ossuaries: four had only one male or one child, one had a male and a child. However, three had six individuals, at least three adults and three children; all their skeletal remains could not possibly fit into this one ossuary. The only case where details of the buried individuals are presented is the anthropological resume from Givʻat HaMivtar published by Haas (1970: 40–49; Tombs 28–1,2,3; 26–5).

To win credibility, the physical anthropology reports on skeletal remains should give precise scientific details (such as the number and description of the bones, skull, teeth) of the remains of every individual found in an ossuary, coffin, or loculus. Otherwise the data are sketchy, vague, and of only partial use.

Anthropological Table 1:
Identified Skeletal Remains from Jerusalem Tombs

Mt. Scopus, Western slope, Observatory

Tomb	Reference	No. of Individuals	Sex M	F	Child	?
1–1	Kloner 1980 Sussman 1982a	19				
1–4		20				
1–6	Vincent 1900 Kloner 1980	50				
1–7	Sukenik 1925 Kloner 1980	30				
1–8	Sukenik 1934 Kloner 1980	50				
1–12	Kloner 1980	10				
1–15	Kloner 1980 Vitto 2000: 65–98	70	4	2	12	52
1–17, 1–18	Kloner 1980, 1993	130	2		3	
1–21	Kloner 1980			1		
1–26	Kloner 1980	25				
1–39	Zias 1992b	88	15	24	38	10
Mt. Scopus Observatory						
1–42, cave A	Arieli 1998	37	8	4	15	10
1–43, cave B	Arieli 1998	15	3	3	7	2
1–44, cave C	Arieli 1998	59	5	11	34	4
1–45, cave D	Arieli 1998	37	2	3	25	7
1–49	Zissu 1995 Abu-Raya and Zissu 2000	9	1	3	2	3
1–50	Zissu 1995 Abu-Raya and Zissu 2000	24	4		5	15
Total		**673**	**44**	**51**	**141**	**103**

Mt. Scopus, East slope, Mount of Olives, East slope

Tomb	Reference	No. of Individuals	Sex M	F	Child	?	Comments
2–3	Kloner 1980 Vitto 2000: 99–103	6					
2–4	Kloner 1980		6	3			
2–16	Kloner 1980 Rahmani 1980	10				+	
2–18	Kloner 1980	29					

Table 1 (*cont.*)

Tomb	Reference	No. of Individuals	Sex M	Sex F	Child	?	Comments
2–35	Kloner & Stark 1992 Zissu 1995				2		
2–42	Zissu 1995 Edelshtein and Zias 2000: Tomb C	13	3	5	3	2	Woman with signs of violence
2–43	Zissu 1995 Edelshtein and Zias 2000: Tomb D	7	3	2	2		Head decapitated
4–27	Zissu 1995	2		1	1		
Total		**67**	**12**	**11**	**8**	**2**	

Kidron Valley, Akeldama

Tomb 7–76–78	Reference	No. of Individuals	Sex M	Sex F	Child	?
Tomb 1	**Avni and Greenhut 1996; 51–53, Table 2.1; Zissu 1995: Nos. 7–76–78**					
Chamber A	"	4	2	1	1	
Chamber B	"	35	1	4	20	10
Chamber C	"	41	4	5	17	15
Chamber D	"	2			2	
Tomb 2	"					
Chamber A	"					
Chamber B	"	24	1	4	12	7
Chamber C	"	2		2		
Tomb 3	"					
Chamber A	"	3			2	1
Chamber B	"	1				1
Chamber C	"					
Chamber D	"	2				2
Total	"	**114**	**8**	**16**	**54**	**36**

East Talpiyot, Ramat Rachel, Giv'at Mordechai, Kfar Shaul, Rehavia

Tomb	Reference	No. of Individual	Sex M	F	Child	?	Comments
11–53							
Caiaphas Tomb	Zias 1992a	64	11	7	43	3	
12–5	Kloner 1980 Kloner & Gat 1982; Zissu 1995	10			2	8	
12–6	Kloner 1980 Kloner & Gat 1982; Zissu 1995	10			1	9	
13–8,9	Stekelis 1934 Kloner 1980	14			4		Children bones found in pots
16–6	Kloner 1980	2					
16–7	Kloner 1980	6			3	3	
17–15	Kloner & Eisenberg 1992 Zissu 1995	18	5	1	6	3	
23–3							
Jason Tomb	Rahmani 1967	25		1			
23–19	Sukenik 1928 Kloner 1980	3				3	
23–27, 28	Zissu 1995 Greenhut 1996	5	1	3		1	
Total		**157**	**17**	**12**	**59**	**30**	

Ramat Eshkol, Giv'at Hamivtar

Tomb	Reference	No. of Individuals	Sex M	F	Child	?	Comments
26–5	Haas 1970: IV Kloner 1980	14	4	6	4		
28–1	Haas 1970: I Kloner 1980	17	6	6	5		One crucified?
28–3	Haas 1970: III Kloner 1980	4	1		3		
28–7	Kloner 1980	50?	4	2	1	2	
28–8	Kloner 1980 Vitto 2000: No. 5	3				3	
Total		**88**	**15**	**14**	**13**	**5**	

French Hill

Tomb	Reference	No. of Individual	Sex M	Sex F	Child	?
29–3	Kloner 1980	22	1		1	20
29–5	Kloner 1980	13	1		1	11
29–7	Kloner 1980	21	3	1	4	13
29–9	Kloner 1980	34	6	3	6	4
29–10	Kloner 1980 Arensburg & Rak 1975: Tomb 1	7	3		2	2
29–11	Kloner 1980 Arensburg & Rak 1975: Tomb 2	8	2	2	3	1
29–12	Kloner 1980 Arensburg & Rak 1975: Tomb 3	25	4	4	4	4
29–13	Kloner 1980 Arensburg & Rak 1975: Tomb 4	3	1		1	1
29–14	Kloner 1980 Arensburg & Rak 1975: Tomb 5	3	1		1	1
29–15	Kloner 1980 Arensburg & Rak 1975: Tomb 6	14	4	3	2	5
29–16–18	Kloner 1980, 1980a Smith & Zias 1980	33	10	8	10	5
29–19	Kloner 1980	6			3	3
29–20	Kloner 1980	10			1	4
29–28	Zissu 1995; Gershuni & Zissu 1996: I	26	3	5	13	17
29–36	Zissu 1995; Gershuni & Zissu 1996: IX	4	1	1	2	
Total		**225**	**40**	**27**	**64**	**91**

Ramot, Shuʾafat, Givʿat Shaul, Neve Yaʿakov

Tomb	Reference	No. of Individuals	Sex M	Sex F	Child	?	Comments
30–14	Kloner 1980; Vitto 2000: No. 7						
30–20	Zias 1982; Zissu 1995	9	3	3	3		Stone on the body
30–23	Zissu 1995; Wolff 1996	7	4			3	
30–25	Zissu 1995	12					
30–26	Zissu 1995	2					
Total		**30**	**7**	**3**	**3**	**3**	

Anthropological Table 2: Identified Skeletal Remains from Jericho Tombs
(Arensburg & Smith 1983: 133; 1999: 192–194)

Tomb	No. of Individuals in tomb, + coffin, +ossuary	No. of Individuals in coffin	ossuary	Sex M	F	Child	?	Comments
A1	6		4	2	1	2	1	
A2	17		2	5	3	9		+ Bones
A6								
B2	1					1		
D1	14		4	2	6	6		
D2	25	1		13	8	3	1	Spina bifida, osteoporosis
D3	49			15	11	8	15	Osteoporosis, osteophyles.
D6	8			6		2		Pathology in the pelvis
D9	17	6		1	9	6	1	Osteoporosis
D9 Outside	17			1	9	6	1	Osteoporosis
D10	Bones					1		
D11	1				1			
D12	8	8		4	2	2		
D13	1						1	
D14	1	1		1				Osteoporosis
D15	3	3		1	1	1		
D16	1						1	
D17	6			1	1	1	3	
D18	14			6	1	2	5	Spina bifida, osteoporosis
D21	Bones							
D22	5			3	1	1		
D23	Bones							
D27	35	7		14	10	8	3	Arthritis
F4	2					1	1	
F6	2			1	1			
F7	Bones							
Tomb H **Chamber A**	15 bones		15	5	3	7		Fused thoracic vertebrae Bones, tall, very tall, skull missing Bones of 5+ adults, Bones of 100+ individuals
Passage between Chambers A and B	1		1		1			
Chamber B	15 bones		15	6	3	4	2	Crippled, tall, Fused thoracic vertebrae, very tall, Bones.
Total	**264**	**26**	**41**	**87**	**72**	**71**	**35**	

Antropological Table 3: Identified Skeletal remains in 'En Gedi Tombs
(after Arensburg & Belfer 1994)

Tomb No.	Total In Tomb	Sex		Child
		M	F	
2	61	15	12	34
5	49	17	7	20
6	13	4	2	5
7	22	11	1	10
8	19	6	5	8
Total	164	53	27	77

Antropological Table 4: 'En Gedi, Distribution of Identified Skeletal remains in Coffins
(after Hadas 1994: Table 2)

Tomb No.	Coffin No.	No. of Individuals	Sex		Child	?
			M	F		
1	1	1			1	
	2	2		1	1	
	3	3	2		1	
	4	2	1		1	
	5	1	1			
	6	3			3	
	7	2			2	
	8	2			2	
3	1	5 Skulls				
	2	3	1	1	1	
	3	3	1		2	
4	1	1	1			
	2	5	1	1	3	
	3	3		1	2	
	4	2	1		1	
	Oss.					
5	1	5	1	1	1	2
	2	2				2
	3	1			1	
	4	3		2	1	
	5	4	1	2	1	
	6	7	1	2	1	3
	7	4		1	2	1
	8	5		3	1	1
	9	3	1	1	1	
	10	2			1	1
	11	3		2	1	
	12	2		2		
	13					
	14					
	15	2	1			1
	pit	8	1	4	2	1

Table 4 *(cont.)*

Tomb No.	Coffin No.	No. of Individuals	Sex M	F	Child	?
6	1	1	1			
	2	7	2	1	4	
	3	4	1	1	2	
	4					
	5					
	Total	**101**	**19**	**26**	**39**	**12**

Antropological Table 5: Identified Subadults in Selected Second Temple Period Tombs, Jerusalem and Jericho (after Arieli 1998: Table 7)

Tombs Site	Reference	MNI	No. of subadults	% of subadults
Jerusalem				
Akeldama	Zias 1996	113	54	48%
Caiaphas Tomb	Zias 1992a	63	43	68%
French Hill				
Arensburg & Rak 1975		64	18	28%
French Hill	Smith & Zias 1980	33	10	30%
Giv'at ha-Mivtar	Haas 1970	35	16	46%
Mt. Scopus	Zias 1992b	88	42	47%
Mt. Scopus Observatory	Arieli 1998	147	81	55%
Jericho Tombs	Arensburg & Smith 1983	225	58	26%
Jericho, Goliath Tomb	Hachlili & Smith 1979	31	13	42%

Table 6: Qumran, Identified Skeletal remains (after Rohrer-Ertl et al. 1999: Katalog; Taylor 1999: Tables 1–4; Eshel et al. 2002: Table V; Sheridan 2002: Tab. 5)*

Tomb No.	Sex M	F	Child ?	Orientation of tombs	Identified by	Comments
			Main Cemetery			**De Vaux excavations 1949–1956**
T1				N-S		
T2				N-S		
T3	x			N-S	Vallois; Sheridan	Sheridan et al.
T4	x			E-W	Vallois; Sheridan	
T5	x			N-S	Vallois; Sheridan	
T6	x			N-S	Vallois; Sheridan	
T7	x?	?		N-S	Vallois; Sheridan; Zias	Zias 2000
T8	x			N-S	Vallois; Sheridan	
T9		?		N-S	Vallois; Sheridan	

Table 6 *(cont.)*

Tomb No.	Sex		Child ?	Orientation of tombs	Identified by	Comments
	M	F				
T10	x			N-S	Vallois; Sheridan	
T11	x			N-S	Vallois; Sheridan	
T12	x			N-S	Kurth; Sheridan	
T13	x			N-S	Kurth; Sheridan	
T14				N-S	Kurth; Sheridan	
T15	x			N-S	Kurth; Sheridan	
T16a	x			N-S	Kurth; Sheridan	
T16b	x			N-S	Kurth; Sheridan	
T17				N-S	Kurth; Sheridan	
T18	x			N-S	Kurth; Sheridan	
T19	x			N-S	Kurth; Sheridan	
T20	x			N-S	Kurth; Rohrer-Ertl	Rohrer-Ertl et al. 1999
T21	x			N-S	Kurth; Rohrer-Ertl	
T22	x (1)	x(2)		N-S	(1) Kurth; Zias; (2) Rohrer-Ertl	
T23	x			N-S	Kurth; Rohrer-Ertl	
T24a	x (1)	x(2)		N-S	(1) Kurth; Zias; (2) Rohrer-Ertl	
T24b	x			N-S	Kurth; Rohrer-Ertl	
T25				N-S	Kurth;	
T26	x			N-S	Kurth; Rohrer-Ertl	
T27				N-S	Kurth;	
T28	x			N-S	Kurth; Rohrer-Ertl	
T29	x			N-S	Kurth; Rohrer-Ertl	
T30	x			N-S	Kurth; Rohrer-Ertl	
T31	x			N-S	Kurth; Rohrer-Ertl	
T32		x		E-W	Kurth; Rohrer-Ertl	Zias 1999 maintains the females in T32–T37 are Beduin burials
T33		x		E-W	Kurth; Rohrer-Ertl	
T34		x		E-W	Kurth; Rohrer-Ertl	
T35a		x		E-W	Kurth; Rohrer-Ertl	
T35b		x		E-W	Kurth; Rohrer-Ertl	
T36			x	E-W	Kurth; Rohrer-Ertl	
T37		x		N-S	Kurth	Three females?
Northern cemetery						Excavated by De Vaux 1955
TA		x		N-S	Kurth	
TB	x			N-S	Kurth; Sheridan	
Southern Cemetery						Excavated by De Vaux 1956
TS1		x		E-W	Kurth; Rohrer-Ertl	
TS2			x	N-S	Kurth; Rohrer-Ertl	
TS3a			x	E-W	Kurth; Rohrer-Ertl	
TS3b			x	E-W	Kurth; Rohrer-Ertl	
TS4			x	E-W	Kurth; Rohrer-Ertl	

Table 6 *(cont.)*

Tomb No.	Sex M	F	Child	?	Orientation of tombs	Identified by	Comments
G2	x				N-S	Haas and Nathan	G2–G11 excavated by Steckoll 1966–1967
G3a	x				N-S	Haas and Nathan	Haas and Nathan 1968
G3b	x				N-S	Haas and Nathan	
G4	x				N-S	Haas and Nathan	
G5	x				N-S	Haas and Nathan	
G6a		x			N-S	Haas and Nathan	
G6b			x		N-S	Haas and Nathan	
G7		x			N-S	Haas and Nathan	
G8		x			N-S	Haas and Nathan	
G9	x				N-S	Haas and Nathan	
G10	x				E-W	Haas and Nathan	
G11		x			N-S	Haas and Nathan	
BE2a		x			N-S	Nagar	
BE2b		x			N-S	Nagar	

* The table is based on the original skeletal studies done by Vallois, Kurth, Haas and Nathen; New studies were conducted by Rohrer-Ertl et al. 1999: Katalogue; Sheridan 2002; Eshel et al. 2002: App. A, Table V; App. C; Broshi and Eshel 2003. For different numbers, see Zangenberg 2000: 73–75; Zias 2000: 244–5, Table 2.

Antropological Table 7: Identified Skeletal Remains in Second Temple Tombs: Jerusalem, Jericho, 'En Gedi, 'En el-Ghuweir, Qumran

Jerusalem Cemetery area	No. of Individuals	Sex M	F	Child	?
1	673	44	51	141	103
2, 4	67	12	11	8	2
7	114	8	16	54	36
12, 13, 16, 17, 23	157	17	12	59	30
26, 28	88	15	13	14	5
29	225	40	27	64	91
30	30	7	3	3	3
Jerusalem Total	**1354**	**143**	**133**	**343**	**270**
Beth Zafafa	46	27	16	3	
Jericho	264	87	72	71	35
'En Gedi	164	53	27	77	
'En el-Ghuweir	20	13	6	1	
Qumran	54	30	14	6	11

ABBREVIATIONS

AJA	*American Journal of Archaeology*
ANRW	*Aufstieg und Niedergang der Römischen Welt*
ASR	Levine, L.I. (ed.) *Ancient Synagogues Revealed.* Jerusalem
BA	*Biblical Archaeologist*
BAIAS	*Bulletin of the Anglo-Israel Archaeological Society*
BAR	*Biblical Archaeology Review*
BASOR	*Bulletin of the American Schools of Oriental Research*
BCH	*Bulletin de Correspondance Hellénique*
BIES	*Bulletin of the Israel Exploration Society (YEDIOT)* (Hebrew) continuing
BJPES	*Bulletin of the Jewish Palestine Exploration Society (YEDIOT)* (Hebrew)
CA	*Cahiers Archéologiques*
DOP	*Dumbarton Oaks Papers*
DSD	*Dead Sea Discoveries*
EI	*Eretz Israel*
HA	*Hadashot Arkheologiyot* (Hebrew)
HTR	*Harvard Theological Review*
HUCA	*Hebrew Union College Annual*
IEJ	*Israel Exploration Journal*
INJ	*Israel Numismatic Journal*
JAC	*Jahrbuch für Antike und Christentum*
JAOS	*Journal of the American Oriental Society*
JBL	*Journal of Biblical Literature*
JFA	*Journal of Field Archaeology*
JJA	*Journal of Jewish Art*
JJS	*Journal of Jewish Studies*
JNES	*Journal of Near Eastern Studies*
JPOS	*Journal of the Palestine Oriental Society*
JQR	*Jewish Quarterly Review*
JRS	*Journal of Roman Studies*
JSQ	*Jewish Studies Quarterly*
JTS	*Journal of Theological Studies*
LA	*Liber Annuus*
NTS	*New Testament Studies*
PEQ	*Palestine Exploration Quarterly*
RAC	*Rivista di Archeologia Cristiana*
RB	*Revue Biblique*
RevQ	*Revue de Qumran*
ZDPV	*Zeitschrift des Deutschen Palästina-Vereins*

BIBLIOGRAPHY

Abel, F.M.
1913   Tombeau et ossuaires Juifs récemment découverts. *RB* 23:262–277.
1949   *Les Livres des Maccabees*. Paris.
Abu Raya, R., and Zissu, B.
2000   Burial Caves from the Second Temple Period on Mount Scopus. Atiqot
        40:1*–12* (Hebrew; English Summary p. 157).
Abu-Uqsa, H.
2002   Three Burial Caves at Kafr Kanna. In Gal. Z., (ed.) *Eretz Zafon, Studies in
        Galilean Archaeology*. Jerusalem: 153–161 (Hebrew; English Summary, p. *182).
Aharoni Y.
1961a   The Cave of Nahal Hever. *ʿAtiqot* (English Series) 3:148–162.
1961b   Expedition B, The Cave of Skulls, *IEJ* 11:11–64.
1962   Expedition B, The Cave of Horror. *IEJ* 12:186–214.
Allegretti, S.
1982   Una Tomba del Primo Periodo Romano sur Monte Oliveto. *LA* 32:335–354.
Alon G.
1967   *Studies in Jewish History* I. Tel Aviv (Hebrew).
1977   *Studies in Jewish History* II. Tel Aviv (Hebrew).
Amit, D.
1991   "Yatta", Survey. *Excavations and Surveys in Israel* 1989/1990, Vol. 9:165–167.
Amit, D., Seligman, J., & I. Zilberbod
2000   Stone Vessel Workshops of the Second Temple Period East of Jerusalem.
        In Geva, H. (ed.) Ancient Jerusalem Revealed (Reprinted and Expanded
        Edition). Jerusalem: 353–358).
Anderson-Stojanovic V.R.
1987   The Chronology and Function of Ceramic Unguntaria. *AJA* 91:105–122.
Archer, L.J.
1983   The Role of Jewish Women in the Religion, Ritual and Cult of Graeco-
        Roman Palestine. In Cameron, A. and Kuhrt, A., (eds.) *Images of Women in
        Antiquity*. London & Canberra: 273–287.
1990   *Her Price is Beyond Rubies. The Jewish Woman in Graeco-Roman Palestine*. JSOT
        Supp. Series 60. Sheffield.
Arensburg B. and Rak, Y.
1975   Skeletal Remains of an Ancient Jewish Population from French Hill, Jerusalem.
        BASOR 219:69–71.
Arensburg B. and Smith P.
1983   Appendix: The Jewish Population of Jericho 100 BC–70 AD. *PEQ* 115:133–139.
Arieli, R.
1998   Human Remains from the Har Hazofim Observatory Tombs. *Atiqot*
        XXXV:37–41.
Aviam, M.
1999   Yodfat: Uncovering a Jewish City in the Galilee from the Second Temple
        Period and the time of the Great Revolt. *Qadmoniot* 32:92–101 (Hebrew).
2002a   Finds from a Burial Cave at Daburria. In Gal. Z., (ed.) *Eretz Zafon, Studies
        in Galilean Archaeology*. Jerusalem 135–139 (Hebrew; English Summary p. *180).
2002b   A Burial Cave at Kabul In Gal. Z., (ed.) *Eretz Zafon, Studies in Galilean
        Archaeology*. Jerusalem: 141–145 (Hebrew; English Summary p. *181).

Aviam, M., and Stern, E.J.
1997   Burial in Clay Sarcophagi in Galilee during the Roman Period. *Atiqot*
          33:151–162.
Aviam, M., and Syon D.
2001   Jewish Ossilegium in Galilee. *What Athens Has to Do with Jerusalem*. Essays
          on Classical, Jewish and Early Christian Art and Archaeology in Honor
          of Gideon Foerster. Leuven: 151–185.
Avigad N.
1946–47   Architectural Observations on some Rock-Cut Tombs. *PEQ*: 112–122.
1950–51   The Rock-carved Façades of the Jerusalem Necropolis. *IEJ* 1:96–106.
1953   The Epitaph of a Royal Steward from Siloam Village. *IEJ* 3:137–152.
1954   *Ancient Monuments in the Kidron Valley*. Jerusalem (Hebrew).
1956   The Necropolis. In Avi-Yonah M. (ed.), *Sepher Yerushalayim*. Jerusalem:
          320–348 (Hebrew).
1958   The Palaeography of the Dead Sea Scrolls and Related Documents.
          Scripta Hierosolymitana 4:56–87.
1961   A Hebrew ossuary Inscription. *BIES* 25:143–144 (Hebrew).
1962a   A Depository of Inscribed Ossuaries in the Kidron Valley. *IEJ* 12:1–
          12.
1962b   Expedition A – The Burial Caves in Nahal David. *IEJ* 12:169–183.
1967a   Jewish Rock-cut Tombs in Jerusalem and in the Judean Hill Country.
          EI 8:119–142 (Hebrew).
1967b   Aramaic Inscription in the Tomb of Jason. *IEJ* 17, 101–111.
1971   The Burial-Vault of a Nazarite Family on Mt. Scopus. *IEJ* 21:185–200.
1976   *Beth She'arim III. Catacombs XII–XXIII*. Jerusalem.
1983   *Discovering Jerusalem*. Jerusalem.
Avi-Yonah M.
1930   Three Lead Coffins from Palestine. *JHS* 50:300–312.
1957   The Archaeological Survey of Masada, 1955–1956. *IEJ* 7:1–60.
1961   *Oriental Art in Roman Palestine* (Rome).
1981   Oriental Elements in the Art of Palestine in the Roman-Byzantine Period
          II, *Art in Ancient Palestine*. Jerusalem: 1–117.
Avni G.
1993   Christian Secondary Use of Jewish Burial Caves in Jerusalem in the Light
          of New Excavations at the Akeldama Tombs. In Manns F. and Alliata E.
          (eds.), *Early Christianity in Context. Monuments and Documents*. Jerusalem:
          265–276.
Avni G. and Greenhut Z.
1996   *Akeldama Tombs. Three Burial Caves in the Kidron Valley, Jerusalem (IAA Re-
          ports 1)*. Jerusalem.
Ayali M.
1984   *A Nomenclature of Workers and Artisans in the Talmudic and Midrashic Literature*.
          Tel Aviv (Hebrew).
Bagatti P.B.
1969   Nuovi apporti archeologici al Dominus Flevit (Oliveto). *LA* 19:194–236.
Bagatti P.B. and Milik J.T.
1958   *Gli Scavi del 'Dominus Flevit'*. (Monte Oliveto – Gerusalemme) I. *La Necropoli
          del Periodo Romano*. Jerusalem.
Bahat D.
1982a   Burial Caves on Giv'at Hamivtar. *'Atiqot* (Hebrew Series) 8:35–40 (English
          summary p. 4*).
1982b   Two Burial Caves at Sderot Ben-Zvi. *'Atiqot (HS)* 8:66–68 (English sum-
          mary p. 8*).
1982c   A Burial Cave in Talpiyot. *'Atiqot (HS)* 8:80–81 (English summary p. 10*).

Baillet M., Milik J.T., and de Vaux R.
1961   *Discoveries in the Judean Desert, II: Les Grottes de Muraabbaat*, Oxford.
1962   *Discoveries in the Judean Desert III: Les Petites Grottes de Qumran.* Oxford: Clarendon.
Bang M.
1910   Herkunft der römischen Sklaven. *Römische Mitteilungen* 25:223–251.
Bar-Adon P.
1937   On the Custom of Secondary Burial. *BJPES* 5:102–103 (Hebrew).
1961   Expedition C – The Cave of the Treasure. *IEJ* 12:215–226.
1977   Another Settlement of the Judean Desert Sect at ʿEin el-Ghuweir on the Dead Sea. *BASOR* 227:1–25.
Barag D.
1972   Two Roman Glass Bottles with Remnants of Oil. *IEJ* 22:24–26.
1973   A Jewish Burial Cave on Mount Scopus. *EI* 11:101–103 (Hebrew).
1978   Hanita, Tomb XV. A Tomb of the Third and Early Fourth Century CE. *ʿAtiqot [ES]* 13). Jerusalem.
2002   New Developments in the Research of the Tombs of the Sons of Hezir and Zecharias. *Qadmoniot* 123:38–47 (Hebrew).
2003   The 2000–2001 Exploration of the Tombs of the Benei Hezir and Zechariah. *IEJ* 53:78–110.
Barag D. and Flusser D.
1986   The Ossuary of Yehohanah Granddaughter of the High Priest Theophilus. *IEJ* 36:39–44.
Barag D. and Hershkovitz M.
1994   Lamps from Masada. In Aviram J., Foerster G. and Netzer E. (eds.), Masada IV. *The Yigael Yadin Excavations 1963–1965, Final Reports.* Jerusalem: 1–147.
Baramki D.C.
1935   An Ancient Tomb Chamber at Waʿr Abu es-Safa Near Jerusalem. *QDAP* 4:168–169.
Bar-Ilan M.,
1994   Patrimonial Burial among the Jews in Ancient Periods. In I. Singer (ed.). *Graves and Burial Practices in Israel in the Ancient Period.* Jerusalem: 212–229 (Hebrew).
Barkay G.,
1986   *Ketef Hinnom – A Treasure Facing Jerusalem's Walls (Israel Museum Cat. 274).* Jerusalem.
1989   Another Paleo-Hebrew Inscription. *IEJ* 39:201–203.
1994a   Burial Caves and Burial Practices in Judah in the Iron Age. In Singer I. (ed.), *Graves and Burial Practices in Israel in the Ancient Period.* Jerusalem: 96–164 (Hebrew).
1994b   Excavations at Ketef Hinnom in Jerusalem, In Geva H. (ed.), *Ancient Jerusalem Revealed.* Jerusalem: 85–110.
2000   The Necropolis of Jerusalem in the First Temple Period. In Ahituv S. and Mazar A. (eds.), *The History of Jerusalem, The Biblical Period.* Jerusalem: 233–270 (Hebrew).
Barkay G., Mazar A. and Kloner A.,
1975   The Northern Cemetery of Jerusalem in First Temple Times. *Qadmoniot* 30–31:71–76 (Hebrew).
Barthélemy D. and Milik J.T.
1955   *Discoveries in the Judean Desert I.* Oxford.
Baruch Y.
1997   A Burial Cave of the Roman Period on the Outskirts of el-Kirmil. *ʿAtiqot* 32:91–94 (English summary p. 42*).
Basch A.
1972   Analyses of Oil from Two Roman Glass Bottles. *IEJ* 22:27–32.

Ben-Arieh R. and Coen-Uzzielli T.
1996   The Pottery. In Avni G. and Greenbut Z. *The Akeldama Tombs, Three Burial Caves in the Kidron Valley, Jerusalem (JAA Reports* 1). Jerusalem: 73–93.
Ben-Arieh S.
1982a   A Burial Cave on Mount Scopus. *'Atiqot (HS)* 8:59–60 (English summary p. 7*).
1982b   A Burial Cave at Giv'at Ram. *'Atiqot (HS)* 8:65 (English summary p. 8*).
1982c   A Tomb in Arnona. *'Atiqot (HS)* 8:77–79 (English summary p. 9*).
Ben-Tor A.
1966   Excavations at Horvat 'Usa . . . *'Atiqot (HS)* 3:1–24 (Hebrew).
Bennett C.
1965   Tombs of the Roman Period. In Kenyon K. *Excavations at Jericho* II. London: 516–545.
Benoit P.
1967   L'inscription Grecque Du Tombeau de Jason. *IEJ* 17:112–113.
Benoit P., Milik J.T. and de Vaux R.
1961   *Les Grottes de Murabba'at (Discoveries in the Judean Desert II)*. Oxford.
Benovitz M.
1995   The Prohibitive Vow in Second Temple and Tannaitic Literature: Its Origin and Meaning. *Tarbiz* 64:203–228 (Hebrew; English summary p. VI).
2002   The Korban Vow and the Ossuary Inscription from the Arnona Neighborhood in Jerusalem. *Cathedra* 104:177–179 (Hebrew).
Bijovski G.
1996   The Coins. In Avni G. and Greenhut Z. *Akeldama Tombs. Three Burial Caves in the Kidron Valley, Jerusalem (IAA Reports 1)*. Jerusalem: 105–108.
Bilig Y.
1995   Jerusalem, Arnona. *Hadashot Archeologiyot* 103:70–71 (Hebrew).
2000   An Ossuary from Jerusalem Bearing *Qorban* Inscriptions. *Cathedra* 98:49–60 (Hebrew).
Blegen C.W., Palmer H. and Young R.S.
1964   *Corinth, The North Cemetery*, Vol. XIII. Princeton.
Bliss, F.J.
1900   Report on the Excavations at Tell Sandahannah. *PEFQSt* 32:319–341.
Bliss F.J. and Macalister, R.A.S.
1902   *Excavations in Palestine during 1898–1900*. London.
Bloch-Smith E.
1992   *Judahite Burial Practices and Beliefs about the Dead (JSOT Suppl. Series* 123). Sheffield.
Brand Y.
1953   *Ceramics in Talmudic Literature*. Jerusalem (Hebrew).
Broshi M.
1972   Excavations in the House of Caiaphas, Mount Zion. *Qadmoniot* 19–20: 104–109 (Hebrew).
2003b   A monastry Or a Manor House? A Reply to Yizhar Hirschfeld. *Cathedra* 109:63–68 (Hebrew, English Abstract pp. 191–192).
Broshi, M., and Eshel H.
1999   Residential Caves at Qumran. *DSD* 6,3:328–356.
2003   Whose Bones. *BAR* 29,1:27–33, 71.
Browning I
1982   *Petra*. London.
Brünnow R.E. and von Domaszewski, A.
1904–09 *Die Provincia Arabia*, I–III, Strassbourg.
Bryce T.R.
1986   *The Lycians in Literary and Epigraphic Sources*. Copenhagen.

Buchanan-Gray, G.
1896   *Studies in Hebrew Proper Names.* London.
1914   Children Named after Ancestors in the Aramaic Papyri from Elphantine
            and Assuan. In *Wellhausen Festschrift.* Giessen: 163–176.
Büchler A.
1966   *The Priests and Their Cult.* Jerusalem (Hebrew).
Burrell, B., and Netzer, E.
1999   Herod the Builder. *Journal of Roman Archaeology* 12:705–715.
Butler H.C.
1903   *Architecture and Other Arts.* New York.
1915–19   *Ancient Architecture in Syria*, Vols. V, VI, VII. Leiden.
Byatt A.
1973   Josephus and Population Numbers in First Century Palestine. *PEQ*
            105:51–60.
Cassuto-Salzmann M.
1954   Greek Names among the Jews. *EI* 3:186–90 (Hebrew).
Chaplin T.
1873   Letters from Dr. Chaplin, Jerusalem, Aug. 1st, 1873. *PEFQSt* 5, October:
            155–156.
Chapouthier F.,
1954   Les peintures murals d'un Hypogie funiraire pris de Massyaf. *Syria* 31:172–
            211.
Childs W.A.P.
1978   *The City-Reliefs of Lycia.* Princeton.
Clarke N.P.
1938   Helena's Pyramids. *PEQ* 71:84–104.
Clermont-Ganneau Ch.
1874   The Jerusalem Researches. *PEFQSt* 6:7–10.
1899   *Archaeological Researches in Palestine* I–III. London.
1903   Archaeological and Epigraphical Notes on Palestine. *PEFQSt* 35:125–
            140.
Clines D.J.
1972   X, X ben Y, ben Y – Personal Names in Hebrew Narrative Style. *Vetus
            Testamentum* 22:282–287.
Cohen N.G.
1974   The Greek and Latin Transliteration *Mariam* and *Maria. Lesonenu* 38:170–180
            (Hebrew).
1976   Jewish Names as Cultural Indications in Antiquity. *Journal of the Study of
            Judaism* 7:97–128.
Collignon M.
1911   *Les Statues Funeraires dans l'Art Grec*, Paris.
Contenau G.
1920   Mission archeologique a Sidon (1914), *Syria* I:xx–xx.
Coogan M.D.
1974   Alphabets and Elements. *BASOR* 216:61–63.
Cotton H.M. and Geiger J.
1989   *The Latin and Greek Documents. Masada I, The Yigael Yadin Excavations 1963–
            1965, Final Reports*, Jerusalem.
Cotton H.M., Geiger J. and Netzer E.,
1995   A Greek Ostracon from Masada. *IEJ* 45:274–277.
Cowley A. (ed.)
1923   *Aramaic Papyri of the Fifth Century* BC. Oxford.
Cross F.M.
1961a   *The Ancient Library of Qumran and Modem Biblical Studies.* New York.

1961b   The Development of the Jewish Script. In Wright G.E. (ed.), *The Bible and the Ancient Near East. Essays in Honor of William Foxwell Albright.* New York: 133–202.
1983   A Note on a Burial Inscription from Mount Scopus. *IEJ* 33:245–246.
Cumont F.
1962   *Afterlife in Roman Paganism.* New York (reissued).
Dalman G.
1908   *Petra und seine Felsheiligtumer,* Leipzig.
Dalman K.O.
1939   Über ein Felsengrab im Hinnomtale bei Jerusalem. *ZDPV* 62:190–208.
Davis D. and Kloner A.
1978   A Burial Cave of the Late Israelite Period on the Slopes of Mt. Zion. *Qadmoniot* 41:16–19 (Hebrew).
Demsky A.
1977   A Proto-Canaanite Abecedary Dating from the Period of the Judges and Its Implications for the History of the Alphabet. *Tel Aviv* 4:14–27.
2002   Hebrew Names in the Dual Form and the Toponym *Yerushalayim.* in Demsky A. (ed.), *These Are The Names, Studies in Jewish Onomastics,* Vol. 3. Ramat Gan: 11–20.
Domseiff F.
1922   *Das Alphabet in Mystik und Magie.* Leipzig-Berlin.
Donceel R.
2002   Synthèse des Observations faites en fouillant les Tombes des Nécropoles de Khirbet Qumrân et des Environs. *The Qumran Chronicle* 10.
Donceel R. and Donceel-Voüte, P.
1994   The Archaeology of Khirbet Qumran. In Wise M.O. et al. (eds.), *Methods of Investigation of the Dead Sea Scrolls and the Khirbet Qumran Site.* New York: 1–38.
Donceel-Voüte P.
1994   Les ruins de Qumran rinterprtes. *Archeologia* 298:24–35.
Driver G.R.
1953   Seals and Tombstones. *Annual of the Department of Antiquities of Jordan* 2:62–65.
Duff A.M.
1958   *Freedom in the Early Roman Empire.* Cambridge.
Dunand M.
1965   Tombe peinte dans la Campagne de Tyr. *Bulletin du Marie de Beyroath* 18:5–51.
Dussaud R.
1923   Comptes d'ouvriers d'une enterprise funéraire juive. *Syria* 4:241–249.
Edelstein G., and Zias J.
2000   Two Burial Caves with Ossuaries on Mount Scopus. *Atiqot* XL:13*–16* (Hebrew; English summary p. 158).
Edgar C.C.
1905   *Catalogue Général des Antiquité Égyptiennes du Musée du Caire. Graeco-Egyptian Coffins, Masks and Portraits.* Cairo.
Eldar A. and Nahlieli D.
1983   Tel Malhata. *HA* 80–81:39.
Elder L.B.
1994   Woman Question and Female Ascetics among the Essenes. *BA* 57,4:220–234
Eshel E.
1997   Personal Names in the Qumran Sects. In Demsky A. et al. (eds.), *These Are The Names, Studies in Jewish Onomastics,* Vol. 2. Ramat Gan: 39–52.
Eshel H.
1991   A Fragmentary Hebrew Inscription of the Priestly Courses from Nazareth? *Tarbiz* 61:159–161 (Hebrew).

2003   Qumran and the Scrolls – A Response to the article by Yizhar Hirschfeld. *Cathedra* 109:51–62 (Hebrew, English Abstract p. 191).

Eshel H., Broshi, M., Freund, R., and Schultz B.
2002   New Data on the Cemetery East of Khirbet of Qumran. *DSD* 9, 2:135–165

Eshel H. and Greenhut Z.
1993   Hiam el-Sagha, a Cemetery of the Qumran Type, Judean Desert. *RB* 100:252–259.

Eshel H. and Misgav, H.
1988   A Fourth Century BCE Document from Ketef Yeriho. *IEJ* 38:158–176.

Faraone C.
1991   Binding and Burying the Forces of Evil: The Defensive Use of 'Voodoo Dolls' in Ancient Greece. *Classical Antiquity* 10/2:165–205.

Faraone C. and Obbink D.
1991   *Magika Hiera: Ancient Greek Magic and Religion.* Oxford.

Ferron J.
1956   Un hypogée juif. *Cahiers de Byrsa* 6:107–109, Pls. 10–12.

Figueras P.
1983   *Decorated Jewish Ossuaries.* Leiden.

Fine S.
2000   A Note on Ossuary Burial and the Resurrection of the dead in First Century Jerusalem. *Journal of Jewish Studies* 51:69–76.

Finkelstein L.
1940   *The Pharisees* I–II. *The Sociological Background of Their Faith.* Philadelphia.

Fitzmyer J.A.
1959   The Aramaic *Qorban* Inscription from Jebel Hallet et-Turi and Mark 7,11; Matt. 15,5. *JBL* 78:60–65.
1992   Did Jesus Speak Greek? *BAR* 18:58–63.

Fitzmyer J.A. and Harrington D.J.
1978   *A Manual of Palestinian Aramaic Texts.* Rome.

Flusser D.
1992   Caiaphas in the New Testament. *Atiqot* 21:81–87.

Foerster G.
1978   Architectural Fragments from "Jason's tomb" Reconsidered. *IEJ* 28:152–156.
1998   Sarcophagus Production in Jerusalem from the Beginning of the Common Era up to 70 CE. In Koch, G. (ed.), *Akten des Symposiums "125 Jahre sarkophag-Corpus", 1995.* Mainz am Rhein: 295–310.

Fossing P.
1940   *Glass Vessels before Glass Blowing.* Copenhagen.

Frey J.B.
1952   *Corpus Inscriptionum Judaicarum* II. Rome.

Fritz V. and Deines R.
1999   Catalogue of Jewish Ossuaries in the German Protestant Institute of Archaeo-logy. *IEJ* 49:222–241.

Gafni Y.
1981   Reinterment in the Land of Israel: Notes on the Origin and Development of the Custom. *The Jerusalem Cathedra* 1:96–104.

Gager J.G.
1992   *Curse Tablets and Binding Spells from the Ancient World.* Oxford.

Gal Z. (ed.),
2002   *Eretz Zafon, Studies in Galilean Archaeology.* Jerusalem.

Gal Z., Hana B. and Aviam M.
2002   A Burial Cave at Zippori. In Gal Z. (ed.), *Eretz Zafon, Studies in Galilean Archaeology.* Jerusalem: 147–151 (Hebrew; English summary p. *181).

Galling K.
1936a   Die Nekropole von Jerusalem, *Palästina Jahrbuch des Deutschen evangelischen Instituts* 32:73–101.
1936b   Ein Etagen-Pilaster-Grab in Norden von Jerusalem. *ZDPV* 59:111–123.
Garland R.
1985   *The Greek way of Death.* Ithaca.
Gawlikowski M.
1970   *Monuments funéraires de Palmyre.* Warsaw.
1972   La notion du tombeau en Syrie romaine. *Berytus* 21:5–15.
Geraty L.T.
1975   A Thrice Repeated Ossuary Inscription from French Hill, Jerusalem. *BASOR* 219:73–78.
Gershuny L. and Zissu B.
1996   Tombs of the Second Temple Period at Giv'at Shapira, Jerusalem. *'Atiqot* 30:45*–59* (Hebrew; English summary, pp. 128–129).
Geva, H. and Avigad, N.
1993   Jerusalem, Tombs. In Stern M. et al. (eds.), *The New Encyclopedia of Archaeological Excavations in the Holy Land.* Jerusalem, Vol. 2:747–757.
Gibson S.
1983   The Stone-Vessel Industry at Hisma. *IEJ* 33:176–188.
Gibson S. and Avni G.
1998   The "Jewish-Christian" Tomb from the Mount of Offence (Batn Al-Hawa') in Jerusalem Reconsidered. *RB* 105:161–175.
Gichon M.
1970   Excavations at 'En-Boqeq. *Qadmoniot* 12:138:148 (Hebrew).
Ginzberg L.
1946   *The Legends of the Jews* I–VII. Philadelphia.
Glueck N.
1956   A Nabataean Painting. *BASOR* 141:13–23.
1959   *Rivers in the Desert.* London.
1965   *Deities and Dolphins.* New York.
Goitein S.D.
1970   Nicknames as Family Names. *JAOS* 90:517–524.
Golb N.
1990   Khirbet Qumran and the Manuscripts of the Judaean Wilderness: Observation on the Logic of Their Investigation. *JNES* 49 (1970): 108.
1994   Khirbet Qumran and the Manuscript Finds of the Judean Wilderness. In Wise, M.O. et al. (eds.), *Methods of Investigation of the Dead Sea Scrolls and the Khirbet Qumran Site.* New York: 51–72.
1995   *Who wrote the Dead Sea Scrolls?* New York.
Goodenough E.R.
1953–68   *Jewish Symbols in the Greco-Roman Period* I–XIII. New York.
Goor A.
1966   The History of the Grape-Vine in the Holy Land. *Economic Botany* 20:46–64.
Gordon M.L.
1924   The Nationality of Slaves under the Early Roman Empire. *Journal of Roman Studies* 14:93–111.
Govrin Y.
1997   Sarcophagus shaped ossuaries from south mount Hebron ("Daroma"). In Eshel Y. (ed.), *Judea and Samaria Research Studies, Proceeding of the 6th Annual Meeting, 1996.* Kedumim-Ariel: 203–216 (Hebrew).
Granger-Taylor, H.
2000   The textiles from Khirbat Qazone (Jordan). *Arcéhologie des textiles des origines au Ve siècle.* Montagnoc.

Greenhut Z.
1992   The 'Caiaphas' Tomb in North Talpiyot, Jerusalem. *'Atiqot* 21:63–71.
1996   Two Burial Caves of the Second Temple Period in Rehavia, Jerusalem.
        'Atiqot 29:41*–46* (Hebrew; English summary, p. 109).
Griffith F.L.
1890   *Antiquities of Tell el-Yahudiyeh.* London.
Grimme H.
1912   Inschriften auf Ossuarien aus Jerusalem. *Orientalistische Literaturzeitung* 12:530–534.
Grinsell L.V.
1961   The Breaking of Objects as a Funerary Rite. *Folklore* 72:475–491.
1973   The Breaking of Objects as a Funerary Rite, Supplementary Notes. *Folklore*
        84:111–114.
Grintz J.M.
1960   Jehoezer-Unknown Priest. *JQR* 50:338–345.
1974   The Giv'at Hamivtar Inscription. *Sinai* 75:20–23 (Hebrew).
Grossmark, T.
1994   *Jewellery and Jewellery-making in the Land of Israel at the time of the Mishnah and
        Talmud.* (Ph.D. Thesis, Hebrew University, Jerusalem; Hebrew, unpublished).
Haas N.
1970   Anthropological Observations on the Skeletal Remains from Giv'at ha-
        Mivtar. *IEJ* 20:38–59.
Haas, N., and Nathan, H.
1968   Anthropolical Survey on the Human Remains from Qumran, *RevQ* 6:342–352.
Habermann A.M.
1956   Ancient Hebrew and Aramaic Epistles and the Word 'Hela'. *EI* 4:133–137
        (Hebrew).
Hachlili R.
1978   A Jerusalem Family in Jericho. *BASOR* 230:45–56.
1979   The Goliath Family in Jericho: Funerary Inscriptions from a First Century
        AD Jewish Monumental Tomb. *BASOR* 235:31–66.
1979a   Ancient Jewish Burial Customs Preserved in the Jericho Hills. *BAR* 5:28–35.
1979b   A Jewish Second Temple Cemetery at Jericho. *Qadmoniot* 12:62–66 (Hebrew).
1980   A Second Temple Period Necropolis in Jericho. *BA* 43:235–240.
1981   The *Nefeš*: The Jericho Column-Pyramid. *PEQ* 113:33–38.
1983a   The Jewish Necropolis of the Second Temple Period at Jericho. *Jericho*
        (*Kardom Series* 28–31). Jerusalem: 120–131 (Hebrew).
1983b   Wall Painting in a Jewish Tomb at Jericho of the First Century. In M. Stem
        (ed.), *Nation and History: Studies in the History of the People of Israel.* Jerusalem:
        71–93 (Hebrew).
1984a   Did the Alphabet Have a Magical Meaning in the First Century CE? *Cathedra*
        31:27–30 (Hebrew).
1984b   Names and Nicknames of Jews in Second Temple Times. *EI* 17:188–211
        (Hebrew; English summary, pp. 9*–10*).
1985   A Jewish Funerary Wall-Painting of the First Century AD. *PEQ* 117:112–127.
1988   *Ancient Jewish Art and Archaeology in the Land of Israel.* Leiden.
1988a   *Jewish Ornamented Ossuaries of the Late Second Temple Period (The Hecht Museum,
        Catalogue* 4). Haifa.
1989   Greek and Roman Influence on Jewish Burial Customs of the Second
        Temple Period. In Kasher A., Fuks G. and Rappaport U. (eds.), *Greece and
        Rome in Eretz Israel, Collected Essays.* Jerusalem: 250–257 (Hebrew).
1993   Burial Practices at Qumran. *Revue de Qumran* 62:247–264.
1994   Changes in Burial Practices in the Late Second Temple Period: The Evidence
        from Jericho. In Singer I. (ed.), *Graves and Burial Practices in Israel in the Ancient
        Period.* Jerusalem: 173–189 (Hebrew).

1997	A Jericho Ossuary and a Jerusalem Workshop. *IEJ* 47:238–247.
1999	Chapters I–VI, in Hachlili R. and Killebrew A., *Jericho – The Jewish Cemetery of the Second Temple Period* (IAA Reports 7). Jerusalem: 1–163.
1999a	Names and Nicknames at Masada. *EI* 26 (Cross Volume): 49–54 (Hebrew).
2000a	Hebrew Names, Personal Names, Family Names, and Nicknames of Jews in the Second Temple Period". In van Henten J.W. and Brenner A. (eds.), *Families and Family Relations as Represented in Judaisms and Early Christianities:Texts and Fictions*. Leiden: 83–115.
2000b	The Qumran Cemetery: A Reconsideration. In Schiffman L.H. et al. (eds.), *The Dead Sea Scrolls, Fifty Years after Their Discovery*. Jerusalem: 661–672.
2000c	Cemeteries, in Schiffman L.H.and VanderKam, J.C. (eds.), *Encyclopedia of the Dead Sea Scrolls*, Oxford: Vol. 1, 125–129.
2002	Names and Nicknames at Masada. In Demsky A., (ed.), *These Are The Names, Studies in Jewish Onomastics* Vol. 3. Ramat Gan: 93–108.

Hachlili R., Arensburg B., Smith P. and Killebrew A.

1981	The Jewish Necropolis at Jericho. *Current Anthropology* 22:701–702.

Hachlili R. and Killebrew A.

1981	The House of 'Goliath'-A Family at Jericho in the First Century CE. *Qadmoniot* 14:118–122 (Hebrew).
1983a	Jewish Funerary Customs during the Second Temple Period in Light of the Excavations at the Jericho Necropolis. *PEQ* 115:109–132.
1983b	The Saga of the Goliath Family. *BAR* 9:44–53.
1983c	Was the Coin-on-Eye Custom a Jewish Burial Practice in the Second Temple Period? *BA* 46:147–153.
1986	The Coin-in-Skull Affair: A Rejoinder. *BA* 49:59–60.
1999	*Jericho – The Jewish Cemetery of the Second Temple Period* (IAA Reports 7). Jerusalem.

Hachlili R. and Smith P.

1979	The Genealogy of the Goliath Family. *BASOR* 235:67–74.

Hadas G.

1988/89	'En Gedi. *ESI* 7–8:51.
1994	*Nine Tombs of the Second Temple Period at 'En Gedi* ('Atiqot 24). Jerusalem (Hebrew; English abstract, pp. 1*–8*).
2002	Wood Industry in the Second Temple Period as reflected in 'En Gedi Finds. *Michmanim* 16:23–35 (Hebrew; English Abstract: 40*–41*).

Hänsler P.H.

1913	Die Ossuarien des Sionsmuseum. *Das Heilige Land* 57:85–95; 129–144.

Harden B.

1968	Ancient Glass I: Pre-Roman. *Archaeological Journal* 125:46–72.

Harrington H.K.

2000	The Nature of Impurity at Qumran. In Schiffman L.H. et al. (eds.), *The Dead Sea Scrolls, Fifty Years after Their Discovery*. Jerusalem: 610–616.

Heltzer M. and Ohana M.

1978	*The Extra-Biblical Tradition of Hebrew Personal Names from the First Temple Period to the End of the Talmudic Period* (*Studies in the History of the Jewish People and the Land of Israel Monograph Series* II). Haifa (Hebrew).

Hestrin R. and Dayagi-Mendels J.

1978	*Inscribed Seals. First Temple Period: Hebrew, Ammonite, Moabite, Phoenician and Aramaic*. Jerusalem.

Hestrin R. and Israeli Y.

1973	*Inscriptions Reveal. Documents from the Time of the Bible, the Mishna and the Talmud*. (Israel Museum Catalogue No. 100). Jerusalem.

Hirschfeld, Y.
2003   Qumran during the Second Temple Period: Re-evaluating the Archaeological Evidence. A Reply to Yizhar Hirschfeld. *Cathedra* 109:5–50 (Hebrew,
English Abstract p. 191).
Hodges H.
1964   *Artifacts. An Introduction to Early Materials and Technology.* London.
Hopkins K.
1983   *Death and Renewal.* Cambridge.
Horbury W.
1994   The Caiaphas Ossuaries and Joseph Caiaphas. *PEQ* 126:32–48.
Horsfield G. and A.
1938   Sela-Petra, the Rock of Edom and Nabatene. *QDAP* 7:1–42; 8:87–115;
9:105–204.
Humbert J.-B. and Chambon A.
1994. *Fouilles de Khirbet Qumrân et de An Feshkha I.* Fribourg.
Humphreys, S.C.
1980   Family Tombs and Tomb Cult in Ancient Athens: Tradition or Tradition-
alism? *JHS* 100:96–126.
Humphreys S.C. and King H. (eds.)
1980   *Mortality and Immortality: The Anthropology and Archaeology of Death.* London –
New York: 103–115.
Huntington R. and Metcalf P.
1979   *Celebrations of Death, The Anthropology of Mortuary Ritual.* Cambridge, MA.
Ilan T.
1984   *The Names of the Jews in Palestine in the Second Temple and Mishnaic Periods: A
Statistical Research.* M.A. Thesis, Hebrew University, Jerusalem (unpublished,
Hebrew).
1987   The Names of the Hasmoneans in the Second Temple Period. *Eretz Israel*
19:238–241 (Hebrew).
1989   Notes on the Distribution of Jewish Women's Names in Palestine in the
Second Temple and Mishnaic Periods. *JJS* 40:186–200.
1991/2   New Ossuary Inscriptions from Jerusalem. *Scripta Classica Israelica* XI:149–159.
1992   Man Born of Woman . . . (Job 14.1): The Phenomenon of Men Bearing
Matronyms at the Time of Jesus. *Novum Testamentum* 34:23–45.
1995   *Jewish Women in Greco-Roman Palestine. An Inquiry into Image and Status.* Tübingen.
1996   The Ossuaries and Sarcophagus Inscriptions. In Avni G. and Greenhut Z.
Akeldama Tombs. Three Burial Caves in the Kidron Valley, Jerusalem (IAA Reports 1).
Jerusalem: 57–72.
2001   *Integrating Women into Second Temple History.* Peabody, MA.
2002   *Lexicon of Jewish Names in Late Antiquity*, Part I. Tübingen.
Ingholt H.
1932   Quelques fresques recemment dicouvertes i Palmyre. *Acta Archaeologica* 3:1–20.
1935   Five Dated Tombs from Palmyra. *Berytus* 2:57–120.
1936   Inscriptions and Sculptures from Palmyra I. *Berytus* 3:83–128.
1938   Inscriptions and Sculptures from Palmyra II. *Berytus* 5:93–140.
1974   Two Published Tombs from the SW Necropolis of Palmyra, Syria. In *Near
Eastern Numismatics, Iconography, Epigraphy and History, Studies in Honor of G.C.
Miles.* Beirut: 43.
Isings C.
1957   *Roman Glass from Dated Finds.* Groningen.
Jacoby R.
1987   Jerusalem Ossuaries. In *Jerusalem Index of Jewish Art.* Jerusalem.
1989   The Ornamented Stone near the Fountain of the Qayatbay. *IEJ* 39:284–286.

Jashemski, W.
1979   The Gardens of Pompeii. New York.
Jastrow, M.
1926   A Dictionary of the Targumim. New York.
Jaussen J.A. and Savignac R.P.
1909   Mission Archéologique en Arabie 1. Paris.
Jeremias J.
1969   Jerusalem in the Time of Jesus. London.
Jones R.F.J.
1981   Cremation and Inhumation – Change in the Third Century. In King A. and Henig M. (eds.), The Roman West in the Third Century, Part i. Oxford (BAR International Series 109(i):15–19.
Kahane P.
1952   Pottery Types from the Jewish Ossuary Tombs around Jerusalem. IEJ 2:125–139; 176–182.
1953   Pottery Types from the Jewish Ossuary Tombs around Jerusalem. IEJ 3:48–54.
1961   Rock-Cut Tombs at Huqoq: Notes on the Finds. 'Atiqot (ES) 3:126–147.
Kane J.P.
1971   By No Means 'The Earliest Records of Christianity' – with an Emended Reading of the Talpioth Inscription ΙΗΣΟΥΣ ΙΟΥ. PEQ 103:103–108.
1978   The Ossuary Inscriptions of Jerusalem. Journal of Semitic Studies 23:268–282.
Kapera Z.J.
1994   Some Remarks on the Qumran Cemetery. In Wise M.O. et al. (eds.), Methods of Investigation of the Dead Sea Scrolls and the Khirbet Qumran Site. Present Realities and Future Prospects. New York: 97–111.
2000   Some Notes on the Statistical Elements in the interpretation of the Qumran Cemetery. The Qumran Chronicle 9, 2–4:139–151.
Kapera Z.J., and Konik J.
2000   How many Tombs in Qumran. The Qumran Chronicle 9,1:35–49.
Kasher A.
1978   The Jews in Hellenistic and Roman Egypt. Tel Aviv (Hebrew).
Kasowski C.J.
1972   Thesaurus Talmudis. Jerusalem: The Ministry of Education and Culture, Government of Israel (Hebrew).
Kelso J.L. and Baramki D.C.
1955   Excavations at New Testament Jericho and Khirbet en-Nitla (AASOR 29–30). New Haven.
Killebrew A.
1999   The Pottery. In Hachlili R. and Killebrew A., Jericho – The Jewish Cemetery of the Second Temple Period (IAA Reports 7). Jerusalem: 115–133.
Klein Samuel.
1920   Jüdisch- Palästinisches Corpus Inscriptionum. Vienna-Berlin.
1929   To the Study of Names and Nicknames. Lesonenu 1:325–350 (Hebrew).
1930   To the Study of Names and Nicknames. Lesonenu 2:260–272 (Hebrew).
Klein Siegfried.
1908   Tod und Begräbnis in Palästina zur Zeit der Tannaiten. Berlin.
Klein Y.
1992   The Origin of the Name Yerushalayim and its Meaning. Seqirah Hodshit 6 (Sept): 15–19 (Hebrew).
Kloner A.
1972   A Burial Cave of the Second Temple Period at Giv'at Ha-Mivtar. Qadmoniot 19–20:108–109 (Hebrew).
1975   A Painted Tomb on the Mount of Olives. Qadmoniot 29:27–30 (Hebrew).

1980	*The Necropolis of Jerusalem in the Second Temple Period*. Ph.D. Diss. Hebrew University, Jerusalem (Hebrew).
1980a	A Tomb from the Second Temple Period at French Hill, Jerusalem. *IEJ* 30:99–108.
1981a	A Burial Cave of the Second Temple Period at Givat Hamivtar, Jerusalem. In Oppenheimer A. et al. (eds.), *Jerusalem in the Second Temple Period*. Jerusalem: 191–224 (Hebrew).
1981b	Burial Caves in Ha'ari Street, Jerusalem, *EI* 15 (Aharoni Volume): 401–405.
1982	Burial Cave on Mount Scopus, *Atiqot* 8:57–58 (Hebrew; English summary p. 6*).
1984	The Cemetery at Horvat Thala. *EI* 17 (Brawer Volume): 325–332 (Hebrew; English summary: p. 14*).
1985a	A monument of the Second Temple Period West of the Old City of Jerusalem. *EI* 18 (Avigad Volume): 58–64 (Hebrew; English summary: p. 67*).
1985b	New Jewish Inscriptions from the "Darom". *Qadmoniot* 18:96–100 (Hebrew).
1986	Abecedary Inscriptions in Jewish Tombs in Light of Finds at H. Eitun. *Proceedings of the Ninth World Congress for Jewish Studies*, Div. A. Jerusalem. Pp. 125–132 (Hebrew).
1991	A Burial Cave from the Early Roman Period at Giv'at Seled in the Judean Shephelah. *'Atiqot* (ES) 20:159–163.
1993	Burial Caves and Ossuaries from the Second Temple Period on Mount Scopus. In Gafni Y. et al. (eds.), Jews and Judaism in the Second Temple, Mishna and Talmud Period. Jerusalem: 75–106 (Hebrew).
1994a	Burial Caves with Wall Paintings from the First Century CE in Jerusalem and Judea. In Singer i. (ed.). *Graves and Burial Practices in Israel in the Ancient Period*. Jerusalem: 165–172 (Hebrew).
1994b	An Ossuary from Jerusalem Ornamented with Monumental Façades. In Geva H. (ed.), *Ancient Jerusalem Revealed*. Jerusalem: 235–238.
1996	A Tomb with Inscibed Ossuaries in East Talpiot, Jerusalem. *'Atiqot* 29:15–22.
1998	Amphorae with Decorative Motifs on Ossuaries – Sources and Influences. In Baruch E. (ed.), *New Studies on Jerusalem. Proceeding of the Fourth Conference.* Ramat Gan: 48–54 (Hebrew).
2000	Survey of Jerusalem, The Southern Sector. Jerusalem.
2001	Survey of Jerusalem, The Northern Sector. Jerusalem.
2003	Survey of Jerusalem, The North Western Sector, Introduction and Indices. Jerusalem.

Kloner A. and Eisenberg, I.

1992	A Burial Cave from the Second Temple Period in the Givat Sh'aul area, Jerusalem. *'Atiqot* 21:51*–55* (Hebrew).

Kloner A. and Gat J.

1982	Burial Caves in East Talpiyot. *'Atiqot* (HS) 8:74–76 (Hebrew; English summary: p. 9*).

Kloner A. and Stark H.

1991–92	A Burial Cave on Mt. Scopus, Jerusalem. *BAIAS* 11:7–17.

Kloner A. and Zissu B.

2002	The "Caves of Shimeon the Just" and "the Minor Sanhedrin – Two Burial complexes from the Second Temple Period in Jerusalem. In Rutgers (ed.)., *What Athens Has to Do with Jerusalem*. Essays on Classical, Jewish and Early Christian Art and Archaeology in Honor of Gideon Foerster. Leuven: 125–185.

2003   *The Necropolis of Jerusalem in the Second Temple Period.* Jerusalem (Hebrew).
Kon M.
1947   *The Tombs of the Kings.* Tel Aviv (Hebrew).
Koch G. and Sichtermann H.
1982   *Römische Sarkophage.* Munich.
Kraeling C.H.
1961   Color Photographs of Paintings in the Tombs of the Three Brothers at Palmyra. *Les Annales Archiologiques de Syrie* 11:13–18.
Kraeling E.G.
1953   *The Brooklyn Museum Aramaic Papyri.* New Haven.
Kraemer D.
2000   *The Meanings of Death in Rabbinic Judaism.* London, New York.
Kurtz D.C. and Boardman J.
1971   *Greek Burial Customs.* London.
Kutscher Y.
1967   *Kwk,* and Its Cognates. *EI* 8:273–280 (Hebrew).
Lehmann Ph.W.
1953   *Roman Wall Paintings from Boscoreale in the Metropolitan Museum of Art* Cambridge, MA.
Le Lasseur D.
1922   Mission Archiologique a Tyr. *Syria* 3:1–26.
Levy J.
1876–89 *Neuhebräisches und chaldäisches Wörtbuch über die Talmudim und chaldäisches Midraschim.* Leipzig.
Lewis D.M.
1964   Leontopolis. In Tcherikover V.A., Fuks A. and Stern M. (eds.), *Corpus Papyrorum Judaicarum* III. Cambridge, MA. Pp. 145–163.
Lidzbarski M.
1902–09 *Ephemeris für semitische Epigraphik* 1–III. Giessen.
Lieberman S.
1962–63 *Tosephta Kifshua* (10 vols.). New York (Hebrew).
1965   Some Aspects of After Life in Early Rabbinic Literature. *American Academy for Jewish Research* 1:495–532.
1974   Notes on the Giv'at Hamivtar Inscription. *Praqim,* Jerusalem: 375–383 (Hebrew).
Lifshitz B.
1966   Notes d'epigraphie Palestinienne. *RB* 73:248–257.
Liphschitz N.
1996   Timber Analysis of 'En Gedi Wooden Coffins: A Comparative Study. *'Atiqot* 28:93–97.
Liphschitz N. and Waisel Y.
1975a   *Dendroarchaeological Investigations in Israel: Coffins from Jericho (Qarantal).* Mimeographed Report No. 38, Institute of Archaeology, Tel Aviv Univ. (Hebrew).
1975b   *Dendroarchaeological Investigations in Israel: Wooden Coffin of the Dayan Collection.* Mimeographed Report No. 37, Institute of Archaeology, Tel Aviv Univ. (Hebrew).
1976   *Dendroarchaological Investigations in Israel: Coffins from Jericho (Qarantal).* Mimeographed Report No. 44, Institute of Archaeology, Tel Aviv Univ. (Hebrew).
Littmann E.
1914   *Nabataean Inscriptions from the Southern Hauran.* Leiden.
Loffreda S.
1965–66 11 monolita de Siloe. *LA* 16:85–126.

1968 Typological Sequence of Iron Age Rock-Cut Tombs in Palestine. *LA* 18:244–287.

1969 Due Tombe a Betania presso le soure della Nigrizia. *LA* 19:349–366.

Luria B.Z.

1973 Towns of the Priests in the Second Temple Period. *HUCA* 44:1–18 (Hebrew).

Lyttelton M.

1974 *Baroque Architecture in Classical Antiquity.* London.

Macalister R.A.S.

1900 On a Rock Tomb North of Jerusalem. *PEQ* 33:54–61.

1901a The Nicophorieh Tomb. *PEFQst* 397–402.

1901b The Rock-Cut Tombs in Wady Er-Rababi, Jerusalem. *PEFQst* 145–226.

1902 The Newly Discovered Tomb North of Jerusalem *PEFQSt* 118–120.

1912 *The Excavation of Gezer*, II. London.

Magen Y.

1978 *The Manufacture of Stone Vessels and Jewish Law.* Jerusalem (Hebrew).

1994 Jerusalem as the Center of the Stone Vessel Industry during the Second Temple Period. In Geva H. (ed.), *Ancient Jerusalem Revealed.* Jerusalem: 244–256.

2002a *The Stone Vessel Industry in the Second Temple Period.* Jerusalem.

2002b Tombs Decorated in Jerusalem Style in Samaria and the Hebron Hills, *Qadmoniot* 123:28–37 (Hebrew).

Magness J.

1994a The Community at Qumran in Light of Its Pottery. In Wise, M.O. et al. (eds.), *Methods of Investigation of the Dead Sea Scrolls and the Khirbet Qumran Site.* New York: 39–50.

1994b A Villa at Khirbet Qumran. *RQ* 397–419.

1995 The Chronology of the settlement at Qumran in the Herodian Period. *DSD* 2:58–65.

1998 The Archaeology of Qumran: A Review. *The Qumran Chronicle* 8:49–62.

2001 Where is Herod's Tomb at Herodium? *BASOR* 322:43–46.

2002a *The Archaeology of Qumran and the Dead Sea Scrolls.* Cambridge.

2002b Women at Qumran, in Rutgers (ed.)., *What Athens Has to Do with Jerusalem.* Essays on Classical, Jewish and Early Christian Art and Archaeology in Honor of Gideon Foerster. Leuven: 89–123.

Maisler B.

1941 The House of Tobias. *Tarbiz* 12:121–122 (Hebrew).

Marcus D.

1975 The Term 'Coffin' in the Semitic Languages. *Journal of the Near Eastern Society of Columbia University* 7:85–94.

Margolioth M.

1973 *Encyclopedia of Talmudic and Geonic Literature, Being a Biographical Dictionary of the Tanaim, Amoraim and Geonim.* Tel Aviv (Hebrew).

Matz A.

1978 Die Jüdische Steindreherei in herodianischer Zeit. *Technik und Geschichte* 45:297–320.

Mayer L.A.

1924 A Tomb in the Kedron Valley, Containing Ossuaries with Hebrew Graffiti Names. *Bulletin of the British School of Archaeology in Jerusalem* 5:56–60.

Mazar A.

1976 Iron Age Burial Caves North of the Damascus Gate, Jerusalem. *IEJ* 26:1–18.

1982 A Burial Cave on French Hill. *'Atiqot* (HS) 8:41–45 (English summary, p. 5*).

Mazar B.
1971   *Excavations in the Old City of Jerusalem near the Temple Mount.* Jerusalem.
1973   *Beth She'arim 1. Report on the Excavations during 1936–1940. Catacombs 1–4.* Jerusalem.
1975   The Archaeological Excavations near the Temple Mount. In Y. Yadin (ed.), *Jerusalem Revealed.* Jerusalem. Pp. 25–40.
1978   Herodian Jerusalem in the Light of the Excavation South and South-West of the Temple Mount. *IEJ* 28:230–37.
McCown C.C.
1937   A Sarcophagus Inscription from Marwa. *BASOR* 66:19–20.
McKenzie J.
1990   *The Architecture of Petra.* Oxford.
Meshel Z.
1991   Naveh Yotvata. *Ariel* 78.
Meshorer Y.
1982   *Ancient Jewish Coinage* I, II. New York.
1990–91   Ancient Jewish Coinage, Addendum I. *INJ* 11:104–132.
1997   *A Treasury of Jewish Coins.* Jerusalem (Hebrew).
Metcalf P. and Huntington R.,
1992   *Celebration of Death.* Cambridge.
Meyer, E.A.
1990   Explaining the Epigraphic Habit in Roman Empire:The Evidence of Epitaphs. *JRS* 80:74–96.
Meyers E.M.
1971   *Jewish Ossuaries: Reburial and Rebirth. Secondary Burials in Their Ancient Near Eastern Setting.* Rome.
Milik J.T.
1954   Un Contrat juif de l'an 134 après J.C. *Revue Biblique* 61:182–90.
1956–57   Trois tombeaux juifs récernment decouverts an sud-est de Jerusalem. *LA* 7:232–267.
1971   Le couvercle de Bethpagé. In *Hommages à André Dupont-Sommer.* Paris: 75–96.
Minns E.H.
1913   *Scythians and Greeks.* Cambridge.
Misgav H.
1991   The Hebrew and Aramaic Inscriptions on Ossuaries in the late Second Temple Period. MA Thesis, Hebrew University, Jerusalem (Hebrew; Unpublished)
1995   Alphabetical Sequence on an Ossuary. *'Atiqot* 29:47*–49*, (Hebrew; English summary p. 110).
1997   Nomenclature in Ossuary Inscriptions. *Tarbiz* 66:123–130 (Hebrew; English summary p. VIII).
Morgenstern J.
1966   *Rites of Birth, Marriage, Death and Kindred Occasions among the Semites.* Cincinnati-Chicago.
Morris I.
1992   *Death-Ritual and Social Structure in Classical Antiquity.* Cambridge.
Mowry L.
1952   Settlements in the Jericho Valley during the Roman Period (63 BC–134 AD). *BA* 15:26–42.
Mussies G.
1976   Greek in Palestine and the Diaspora. In Safrai S. and Stern M. (eds.), *The Jewish People in the First Century.* Vol. II. Assen: 1040–1064.
1994   Jewish Personal Names in Some Non-Literary Sources. In Van Hanten J.W. and Van der Horst P.W. (eds.), *Studies in Early Jewish Epigraphy.* Leiden: 242–276.

Nahshoni P., Zissu B., Sarig N., Ganor A., Avganim A.
2002 A Rock-Cut Burial Cave from the Second TemplePeriod at Horbat Zefiyya, Judean Shephelah, *Atiqot* 43:49–71.
Nathan H.
1961 The Skeletal Material from Nahal Hever. *'Atiqot* 3:171–174.
Naveh J.
1963 Old Hebrew Inscriptions in a Burial Cave. *IEJ* 13:74–92.
1970 The Ossuary Inscriptions from Giv'at ha-Mivtar. *IEJ* 20:33–37.
1973 An Aramaic Tomb Inscription Written in Paleo-Hebrew Script. *IEJ* 23:82–91.
1978 *On Stone and Mosaic.* Jerusalem (Hebrew).
1979 Varia Epigraphica Judaica. *Israel Oriental Studies* IX:17–31.
1980 An Aramaic Consolatory Burial Inscription. *Atiqot* 14:55–59.
1990 Nameless People. *IEJ* 40:108–123.
1992 *On Shard and Papyrus. Aramaic and Hebrew Inscriptions from the Second Temple, Mishnaic and Talmudic Periods.* Jerusalem (Hebrew).
Naville E.
1890 *The Mound of the Jews and the City of Onias.* London.
Negev A.
1971 The Nabatean Necropolis of Mampsis (Kurnub). *IEJ* 21:110–129.
1976 The Nabatean Necropolis at Egra. *RB* 83:203–236.
Netzer E.
1975 Cypros. *Qadmoniot* 8:54–61 (Hebrew).
1977 The Winter Palaces of the Judean Kings at Jericho at the End of the Second Temple Period. *BASOR* 228:1–13.
1978 *Miqvaot* (Ritual Baths) of the Second Temple Period. *Qadmoniot* 42–43:54–59 (Hebrew).
1981 *Greater Herodium (Qedem* 13). Jerusalem.
1982 Ancient Ritual Baths, *Miqvaot*, in Jericho. In Levine L.I. (ed.), *The Jerusalem Cathedra* I. Jerusalem and Detroit. Pp. 106–111.
1991 *Masada* III. *The Yigael Yadin Excavations 1963–1965. Final Reports.* Jerusalem.
1999 Mourning Enclosure of Tomb H. (Goliath Tomb). In Hachlili R. and Killebrew A., *Jericho – The Jewish Cemetery of the Second Temple Period* (IAA Reports 7). Jerusalem: 45–50.
2001 *The Palaces of the Hasmoneans and Herod the Great. Jerusalem*
Netzer E. and Ben-Arieh, S.
1983 Remains of an Opus Reticulatum Building in Jerusalem. *IEJ* 33:163–175.
Noshy I.
1937 *The Arts in Ptolemaic Egypt.* London.
Noth M.
1928 *Die israelitischen Personennamen im Rahmen der gemeinsemitischen Namengebung (Beiträge zur Wissenschaft vom Alten und Neuen Testament Series III, 10).* Stuttgart.
Nylander C.
1970 *Iranians in Pasargadae, Studies in Persian Architecture.* Uppsala.
Orfali O.F.M.,
1923 Un hypogée juif à Bethphagé. *RB* 32:253–260.
Ory J.
1939 A Painted Tomb near Ascalon. *QDAP* VIII:38–44.
Ovadiah A.
1972 A Jewish Sarcophagus at Tiberius. *Israel Exploration Journal* 22:229–32.
Park J.S.
2000 *Conceptions of Afterlife in Jewish Inscriptions.* Tübingen.
Parker Pearson M.,
1982 Mortuary Practices, Society and Ideology: An Ethnoarchaeological Study. In Hodder I. (ed.), *Symbolic and Structual Archaeology*, Cambridge: 99–113.

1993 The Powerful Dead: Archaeological Relationships between the Living and the Dead. *Cambridge Archaeological Journal* 3:2:203–229.

Patrich J.

1980 The Aqueduct from Etam to the Temple and a Sadducean Halakhah. *Cathedra* 17:11–23 (Hebrew).

1985 Caves of Refuge and Jewish Inscriptions on the Cliffs of Nahal Michmas. *EI* 18:153–166 (Hebrew; English summary, pp. 70*–71*).

1994a Graves and Burial Practices in Talmudic Sources. In Singer I. (ed.), *Graves and Burial Practices in Israel in the Ancient Period.* Jerusalem: 190–211 (Hebrew).

1994b Khirbet Qumran in Light of New Archaeological Explorations in the Qumran Caves. In Wise M.O. et al. (eds.), *Methods of Investigation of the Dead Sea Scrolls and the Khirbet Qumran Site.* New York: 73–83.

Patrich J. and Arubas B.

1989 A Juglet Containing Balsam Oil (?) from a Cave near Qumran. *IEJ* 39:43–59.

Peleg Y.

2002 Gender and Ossuaries: Ideology and Meaning. *BASOR* 325:65–73.

Perrot G. and Chipiez Ch.

1885 *History of Art in Phoenicia and Its Dependencies* I. London.

Peskowitz M.B.

1997a *Spinning Fantasies, Rabbis, Gender and History.* Berkeley-Los Angeles-London.

1997b The Gendering of Burial and the Burial of Gender: Notes from Roman-Period Archaeology. *JSQ* 4:105–124.

Peters J.D. and Thiersch H.

1905 *Painted Tombs in the Necropolis of Marissa.* London.

Petrie W.M.F.

1892 The Tomb-Cutters' Cubits at Jerusalem. *PEFQSt* 28–35.

Piattelli D.

1987 Theodotos, Apeleutheros Dell'Imperatrice Agrippina, Nell' Inscrizione di Gerico. *Apollinaris* 60:657–666.

1990 The Jericho Inscription Concerning Theodotos, Apeleutheros of the Empress Agrippina. In Kasher A., Rappaport U. and Fuks G. (eds.), *Greece and Rome in Eretz Israel.* Jerusalem: 75–83.

Poleg Y.

2002 Gender and Ossuaries: Ideology and Meaning. *BASOR* 325:65–73.

Politis K.D.

1998a Rescue Excavations in the Nabatean Cemetery at Khirbat Qazone 1996–97. *ADAJ* 42:611–614.

1998b Khirbat Qazone. *AJA* 102:596–597.

1999 The Nabatean Cemetery at Khirbat Qazone. *Near Eastern Archaeology* 62, 2:128.

2002 Rescuing Khirbat Qazone. Minerva 13,2:27–29.

Porath Y. and Levy Y.

1993 Mughar el-Sharaf: A Cemetery of the Roman and Byzantine Periods in the Sharon. *'Atiqot* 22:29*–42* (Hebrew; English summary, pp. 153–154).

Powers, T.

2003 Treasures in the Storeroom, Family Tomb of Simon of Cyrene. *BAR* 29, 4:46–51.

Pritchard J.B.

1958 *The Excavations at Herodian Jericho 1951 (AASOR* 32–33). New Haven.

Puech E.

1980 Abécédaire et liste alphabétique de noms hébreux du début du IIᵉ s. AD. *RB* 87:118–126.

1982a Ossuaires inscrits d'une tombe du Mont des Oliviers. *LA* 32:355–372.

1982b   Les nécropoles juives palestiniennes au tournant de notre ère. *Les quatres fleuves* 15–16:35–55.

1983   Inscriptions funéraires Palestiniennes: Tombeau de Jason et ossuaires. *RB* 90:481–533.

1989   Une Inscription Araméenne sur un Couvercle de Sarcophage, *EI* 20:161*–165*.

1993   A-t-on redécouvert le tombeau du grand-prêtre Caïphe? *Le Monde de la Bible* 80:42–47.

1998   The Necropolises of Khirbet Qumran and Ain el-Ghuweir and the Essene Belief in Afterlife. *BASOR* 312:21–36.

2000   Immortality and Life after Death. In Schiffman L.H. et al. (eds.), *The Dead Sea Scrolls, Fifty Years after Their Discovery*. Jerusalem: 512–520.

Rahmani L.Y.
1958   A Jewish Tomb on Shahin Hill. *IEJ* 8:101–105.
1959   Transformation of an Ornament. *'Atiqot* (ES) 2:188–189.
1961   Jewish Rock-Cut Tombs in Jerusalem. *'Atiqot* (ES) 3:93–120.
1967a   Jason's Tomb. *IEJ* 17:61–100.
1967b   Jewish Tombs in the Romema Quarter of Jerusalem. *EI* 8:186–192 (Hebrew; English summary, p. 74*).
1968   Jerusalem's Tomb Monuments on Jewish Ossuaries. *IEJ* 18:220–225.
1973   Review of E.M. Meyers – Jewish Ossuaries: Reburial and Rebirth. *IEJ* 23:121–126.
1977   *The Decoration on Jewish Ossuaries as Representation of Jerusalem's Tombs*. Ph.D. Diss. Hebrew Univ. Jerusalem (Hebrew).
1978   Ossuaries and Bone Gathering in the Late Second Temple Period. *Qadmoniot* 11:102–112 (Hebrew).
1980a   A Jewish Rock-Cut Tomb on Mt. Scopus. *'Atiqot* 14:49–54.
1980b   The Shroud of Turin (Polemics and Irenics). *BA* 43:197.
1981/82 Ancient Jerusalem's Funerary Customs and Tombs I, II. *BA* 44:171–177; 229–235. III, IV. *BA* 45:43–53; 109–119.
1982   A Tomb and a Columbarium on Shemuel Hanavi St. *'Atiqot* 8 (HS): 61–64 (English summary p. 7*).
1986   Some Remarks on R. Hachlili's and A. Killebrew's 'Jewish Funerary Customs'. *PEQ* 118:96–100.
1987   More Lead Coffins from Israel, *IEJ* 37:135–136.
1988   Chip-Carving in Palestine. *IEJ* 38:59–75.
1992   Five Lead Coffins from Israel, *IEJ* 42:81–102.
1993   A Note on Charon's Obol. *'Atiqot* 22:149–150.
1994   *A Catalogue of Jewish Ossuaries in the Collection of the State of Israel*. Jerusalem.
1994a   Sarcophagi of the Late Second Temple Period in Secondary use. In Geva H. (ed.), *Ancient Jerusalem Revealed*. Jerusalem: 231–234.
1999   *A Catalogue of Roman and Byzantine Lead Coffins from Israel*. Jerusalem.

Regev E.
2001   The Individual Meaning of Jewish Ossuaries: A Socio-Anthropological Perspective on Burial Practice. *PEQ* 133:39–49.
2002   Family Burial in Herodianic Jerusalem and Its Environs and the Social Organization of Immigrants and Secterians. *Cathedra* 106:35–60 (Hebrew, English abstract, p. 204).

Reich R.
1990   *Miqwa'ot (Jewish Ritual Immersion Baths) in Eretz-Israel in the Second Temple and the Mishna and Talmud Periods*. Ph.D. Diss. Hebrew University, Jerusalem (Hebrew).
1992   Ossuaries Inscriptions from the 'Caiaphas' Tomb. *'Atiqot* 21:72–77.

2001   Women and Men at Masada, Some Anthropological Observations Based
            on the Small Finds (Coins, Spindles). *ZDPV* 117:149–163.
Reich R. and Geva H.
1982   Burial Caves on Mount Scopus. *'Atiqot (HS)* 8:52–56 (English summary,
            p. 6*).
Rènan E.
1864–71   *Mission de Phönicie* I, II. Paris.
Reynolds J.M.
1965   Inscribed Stone Slab from Tomb K23. In Kenyon K., *Excavations at Jericho*
            II. London. Pp. 721–722.
Richter G.M.A.
1926   *Ancient Furniture*. Oxford.
Rimon M.
1979   The Goliath Family in Jericho: Design of a Computer Program, Establishing
            the Family Relations of Individuals Buried in the Jericho Tomb. *BASOR*
            235:71–73.
Robinson D.M.
1942   *Excavations at Olynthus* XI. *Necrolynthia. A Study in Greek Burial Customs and
            Anthropology*. Baltimore.
Röhrer-Ertl O., F. Rohrhirsch and Hahn D.
1999   Über die gräberfelder von khirbet Qumran, inbesondere die Funde der
            Campagne 1956: I: Anthropologische Datenvorlage und Erstauswertung
            aufgrund der Collectio Kurth. *RevQ* 73:3–46.
Roller, D.W.
1998   *The Building Program of Herod the Great*. Berkeley
Rosenthal E.S.
1973   The Giv'at ha-Mivtar Inscription. *IEJ* 23:72–81.
Rostovtzeff M.
1919   Ancient Decorative Wall Painting. *JHS* 39:144–163.
Rothschild J.J.
1952   The Tombs of Sanhedria – I. *PEQ* 84:23–28.
1954   The Tombs of Sanhedria – II. *PEQ* 86:16–22.
Rubin N.
1977   *A Sociological Analysis of Jewish Mourning Patterns in the Mishnaic and Talmudic
            Periods*. Ph.D. Diss. BAR Ilan Univ. Ramat Gan (Hebrew).
1994   Secondary Burials in the Mishnaic and Talmudic Periods: A Proposed
            Model of the Relationship of Social Structure to Burial Practice. In Singer
            I. (ed.), *Graves and Burials Practices in Israel in the Ancient Period*. Jerusalem:
            248–269 (Hebrew).
1997   *The End of Life, Rites of Burial and Mourning in the Talmud and Midrash*. Tel
            Aviv (Hebrew).
Safrai S.
1972   The Holy Congregation in Jerusalem. *Scripta Hierosolymitana* 23:62–78.
1976   Home and Family. In Safrai S. and Stern M. (eds.), *The Jewish People in
            the First Century* II. Assen.
Sagiv N., Zissu B. and Avni G.
1998   Tombs of the Second Temple Period at Tel Goded, Judean Foothills.
            'Atiqot 35:7*–21* (Hebrew; English summary pp. 159–161).
Saller S.
1957   *Excavations at Bethany* (1949–1953). Jerusalem.
1961   Archaeological Setting of Shrine of Bethphage. *LA* 11:172–250.
Saller R.P., and Shaw B.D.
1984   Tombstones and Roman Family Relations in the Principate: Civilians,
            Soldiers and Slaves. *JRS* 74:124–156.

Sartre A.
1989   Architecture funéraire de la Syrie. In Dentzer J.M. and Orthmann W. (eds.),
        Archéologie et histoire de la Syrie. Saarbrücken: 422–446.
Saulcy F. de
1853   Voyage autour de la Mer Morte et dans les terre bibliques execute de
        decembre 1859 a avril 1851. Paris.
Savignac M.R.
1925   Nouveaux ossuaires juifs avec graffites (Mélanges) *RB* 34:253–266.
1929   Nouveaux ossuaires juifs avec inscriptions. *RB* 38:229–236.
Schick C.
1892   Recent Discoveries at the "Nicophorieh". *PEFQSt* 115–120.
Schiffman L.H.
1987   The Conversion of the Royal House of Adiabene in Josephus and Rabbinical
        Sources. In Feldman L.H. and Hata G. (eds.), *Josephus, Judasim and Christianity*.
        Detroit: 293–312.
1990   The Impurity of the Dead in the Temple Scroll. In Schiffman L.H. (ed.),
        Archaeology and History in the Dead Sea Scrolls (JSOT/ASOR Monographs 2). Sheffield.
        Pp. 137–156.
Schneller, L.
1905   Ein neuendecktes Grab mit handschriften aus der Zeit Christi. *Der Bote aus
        Zion* 21, 2:28–31.
Schrnidt-Colinet A.
1989   L'architecture funéraire de Palmyre. In Dentzer J.M. and Orthmann W.
        (eds.), *Archéologie et histoire de la Syrie*. Saarbrücken: 447–456.
Schreiber T.
1908   *Die Nekropole von Kom esch-S-chukafa, Ausgrabungen in Alexandria* I. Leipzig.
1914   Die ägyptischen Elemente der Alexandrinischen Totenplege. *Bulletin de la
        Societé Archéologique d'Alexandrie* 15:3–24.
Schuller E.M.
1994   Women in the Dead Sea Scrolls., In Flint P.W. and VanderKam J.C. (eds.),
        The Dead Sea Scrolls After Fifty Years: 117–144.
Schürer E., Vermes G. and Millar A.
1973   *The History of the Jewish People in the Age of Jesus Christ (175 BC–AD 135)*, I.
        Edinburgh.
1979   *The History of the Jewish People in the Age of Jesus Christ (175 BC–AD 135)*, II.
        Edinburgh.
1986   *The History of the Jewish People in the Age of Jesus Christ (175 BC–AD 135)*, III.
        Edinburgh.
Schwabe M.
1956   Greek Inscriptions. In Avi-Yonah M. (ed.), *The Book of Jerusalem*, Jerusalem
        and Tel Aviv: 358–368 (Hebrew).
Schwabe M. and Lifshitz B.
1974   *Beth She'arim* II. *The Greek Inscriptions*. Jerusalem.
Schwartz J.
1988   On Priests and Jericho in the Second Temple Period. *JQR* 79:23–48.
Sevenster J.N.
1968   *Do You Know Greek? How Much Greek Could the First Jewish Christians Have Known?*
        Leiden.
Seyrig H.
1940   Ornamenta Palmyrena Antiquiora. *Syria* 21:277–337.
Seyrig H. et al.
1975   *Le Temple de Bel a Palmyre*. Paris.
Shadmi T.,
1996   The Ossuaries and Sarcophagus. In Avni G. and Greenhut Z. *Akeldama*

Tombs. Three Burial Caves in the Kidron Valley, Jerusalem (IAA Reports 1). Jerusalem:
41–56.

Shanks H.
1999 Who Lies Here. Jordan Tombs Match Those at Qumran. *BAR* 25, 5:49–53.

Shaw, B.D.
1984 Latin Funerary Epigraphic and family Life in the Later Roman Empire.
Historia 33:457–497.
1991 The Cultural meaning of Death: Age and Gender in the Roman Family.
Chap. 4 in Kertzer, D.I., and R. P. Saller (eds.), The Family in Italy from
Antiquity to the Presest. New Haven: 66–90.
1996 Seasons of Death: Aspects of Mortality in Imperial Rome. *JRA*
86:100–139

Sheffer, A., and Granger-Taylor, H.
1994 Textiles, in *Masada IV*. Jerusalem: 151–256.

Sheridan, G.S.
2002 Scholars, Soldiers, Craftsmen, Elites?: Analysis of French Collection of Human
Remains from Qumran. *DSD* 9,2:199–248.

Shiloh Y.
1984 Excavations in the City of David, I, 1978–1982. *Qedem* 19. Jerusalem.

Siegelman A.
1988 A Herodian Tomb near Tell Abu-Shusha. In Mazar B. (ed.), *Geva, Archaeological
Discoveries at Tell Abu-Shusha, Mishmar Ha-ʿEmeq*. Jerusalem:13–41 (Hebrew).

Singer C., Holmyard E.J. and Hall A.R.
1956 *A History of Technology* II. Oxford.

Singer I., ed.
1994 *Graves and Burial Practices in Israel in the Ancient Period*. Jerusalem (Hebrew).

Slousch N., Sukenik E.L. and Ben Zvi Y.
1925 On the Discovery of a Tomb in the 'Mahanaim' Quarter, Jerusalem. *Qovetz*
1/2:96–102 (Hebrew).

Smith P.
1977 The Human Skeletal Remains from the Abba Cave. *IEJ* 27:121–124.

Smith R.H.
1973 An Early Roman Sarcophagus of Palestine and Its School. *PEQ* 105:71–82.
1974 The Cross Marks on Jewish Ossuaries. *PEQ* 106–53–66.
1983 Decorative Geometric Design in Stone. *BA* 46:175–186.

Spoer H.H.
1907 New Ossuaries from Jerusalem. *JAOS* 28:355–359.

Steckoll S.H.
1968 Preliminary Excavation Report on the Qumran Cemetery. *Revue de Qumran*
6:323–336.

Stegemann H.
1992 The Qumran Essens – Local Members of the Main Jewish Union in Late
Second Temple Times. in Trebolle Barrera, J. and Montaner V.L. (eds.),
The Madrid Qumran Congress. Leiden-New York-Köln: 83–166.

Stekelis M.
1934 A Jewish Tomb-cave at Ramath Rachel. *Qovetz 3, Journal of the Jewish Palestine
Exploration Society (Dedicated to the Memory of Dr. A. Mazie)*: 19–40 (Hebrew).

Stern, E., (ed.)
1993 *The New Encyclopedia of Archaeological Excavations in the Holy Land . . . Jerusalem.*

Stern M.
1960 Trachides – Surname of Alexander Yannai in Josephus and Syncallus. *Tarbiz*
29:207–209 (Hebrew).
1961 The Relations between Judea and Rome during the Rule of John Hyrcanus.
Zion 26:1–22 (Hebrew).

1966   The Politics of Herod and Jewish Society towards the End of the Second Commonwealth. *Tarbiz* 35:235–253 (Hebrew).

1974   *Greek and Latin Authors on Jews and Judaism.* I: *From Herodotus to Plutarch.* Jerusalem.

1975   The reign of Herod. In Avi-Yonah M. (ed.), *The Herodian Period* (*The World History of the Jewish People* VII). Jerusalem: 71–123.

1976   Aspects of Jewish Society: The Priesthood and Other Classes. In Safrai S. and Stern M. (eds.), *The Jewish People in the 1st Century*, vol. II. Amsterdam: 00–00.

Stevens S.T.

1991   Charon's Obol and Other Coins in Ancient Funerary Practice. *Phoenix* 45, 3:215–229.

Strange J.

1975   Late Hellenistic and Herodian Ossuary Tombs at French Hill, Jerusalem. *BASOR* 219:39–67.

Strubbe J.H.M.

1994   Curses against the Violation of the Grave in Jewish Epitaphs from Asia Minor. In van Henten J.W. and van der Horst P.W. (eds.), *Studies in Early Jewish Epigraphy.* Leiden: 70–128.

Strus, A.

2003   *Khirbet Fattir – Bet Gemal.* Roma.

Sukenik E.L.

1924   Notes on the Jewish graffiti of Bethphage. *JPOS* 4:171–174.

1925   The Tomb on the Premises of the Hebrew University. *Qovetz* 1:74–80 (Hebrew).

1928   A Jewish Hypogeum near Jerusalem. *JPOS* 8:113–121.

1929   Additional Note on a Jewish Hypogeum near Jerusalem. *JPOS* 9:45–49.

1930a   A Jewish Tomb in the North-West of Jerusalem *Tarbiz* I, 3:122–124 (Hebrew).

1930b   A Jewish Tomb on the Mount of Olives. *Tarbiz* I, 4:137–143 (Hebrew).

1931a   Funerary Tablet of Uzziah, King of Judah. *PEFQSt* 217–221.

1931b   *Jüdische Gräber Jerusalems um Christi Geburt*, Jerusalem

1932   Two Jewish Hypogea. *JPOS* 12:22–31.

1933–34 An Ancient Jewish Cave near the Jerusalem-Nablus Highway. *Bulletin of the Israel Exploration Society* 1:7–9 (Hebrew).

1934   A Jewish tomb-cave on the slope of Mt. Scopus. *Qovetz 3, Journal of the Jewish Palestine Exploration Society* (*dedicated to the Memory of Dr. A. Mazie*): 62–73 (Hebrew).

1935a   A Jewish Tomb in the Kidron Valley. *Tarbiz* 6:190–196 (Hebrew).

1935b   The Cave at Bethpage and Its Inscriptions. *Tarbiz* 7:102–109 (Hebrew).

1936   A Jewish Tomb Cave in the Kedron Valley near Silwan Village. In *Festschrift S. Krauss.* Jerusalem: 87–93 (Hebrew).

1937   A Jewish Tomb in the Kedron Valley. *PEQst* 69:126–130.

1942   A Jewish Tomb in the vicinity of Isawiyeh. *Kedem* 1:29–31 (Hebrew).

1945a   Jewish Tombs in the Kedron Valley. *Kedem* 2:23–32 (Hebrew).

1945b   Jewish Tombstones from Zoar (Ghor es Safi). *Kedem* II: 83–88 (Hebrew).

1947   The Earliest Records of Christianity. *AJA* 51:351–365.

Sussman V.

1982a   A Burial Cave near Augusta Victoria, *'Atiqot* 8:46–48 (English summary p. 5*).

1982b   A Burial Cave In the Valley of the Cross, *'Atiqot* 8:69 (English summary p. 8*).

1992   A Burial Cave on Mount Scopus. *'Atiqot* 21:90–95.

1999   A Sarcophagus Decorated with Personal Effects from the Collection of the Israel Antiquity Authority, Jerusalem. *New Studies on Jerusalem. Proceeding of the Fifth Conference.* Ramat Gan: 160–182 (Hebrew)

Taylor J.E.
1999   The Cemeteries of Khirbet Qumran and Women's Presence at the Site. *Dead Sea Discoveries* 6, 3:285–323.

Tcherikover V.A.
1970   *Hellenistic Civilization and the Jews.* New York.

Tcherikover V.A., Fuks A.F. and Stern M.
1964   *Corpus Papyrorum Judaicarum* I. Cambridge, MA.

Teitelbaum D.
1997   *The relation between Ossuary Burial and the Belief in Resurrection during the Late Second Temple Period Judaism.* MA thesis, Ottawa: Carlton University. (Ann Arbor: UMI, 1998).

Testa P.E.
1962   *Il simbolismo dei guideo-cristiani.* Jerusalem.

Thiersch H.
1904   *Zwei antike Grabanlagen bei Alexandria.* Berlin.

Thomas C.M.
1999   The Ephesian Ossuaries and Roman Influence on the Production of Burial Containers. In Brandt B. and Krierer K.R. (eds.), *100 Jahre sterreichische Forschungen in Ephesos.* Wien. Textband: 549–554.

Toll N.P.
1946   *The Necropolis in the Excavation of Dura Europos, Ninth Season 1935–36* III. New Haven.

Toynbee J.M.C.
1971   *Death and Burial in the Roman World.* London.

Trachtenberg J.
1961   *Jewish Magic and Superstition.* Philadelphia.

Treggiari S.
1969   *Roman Freedmen During the Late Republic.* Oxford.

Tsafrir Y.
1982   The Desert Fortresses of Judaea in the Second Temple Period. *The Jerusalem Cathedra* 2:120–145.

Tsuk T.
1993   The Jewish Community of Western Samaria in Light of Information from Burial Caves at Migdal Tsedek. In Tsuk T. and Kloner A. (eds.), *Niqrot Zurim* 19:67–76 (Hebrew; English summary p. 141).

Tzaferis V.
1970   Jewish Tombs at and near Giv'at Ha-Mivtar, Jerusalem. *IEJ* 20:18–32.
1974   The 'Abba' Burial Cave in Jerusalem. *'Atiqot (HS)*: 7:61–64. (Hebrew, English summary p. 9*).
1982   Rock-Cut Tombs on Mount Scopus. *'Atiqot (HS)*: 8:49–51 (Hebrew, English summary p. 6*).

Tzaferis V. and Yadin N.
1982   Burial Caves in Beth She'an. *'Atiqot* 8 *(HS)*: 12–15 (Hebrew, English summary p. 2*).

Tzaferis V. and Berman A.
1982   A Burial Cave in Meqor Hayim. *'Atiqot* 8 *(HS)*: 70–73 (Hebrew, English summary p. 8*).

Ussishkin D.
1970   The Necropolis from the Time of the Kingdom of Judah at Silwan, Jerusalem. *BA* 33:34–46.
1993   *The Village of Silwan. The Necropolis from the Period of the Judean Kingdom.* Jerusalem.

de Vaate Bij A.
1994   Alphabet-Inscriptions from Jewish Graves. In van Henten J.W. and van
        der Horst P.W. (eds.), *Studies in Early Jewish Epigraphy*. Leiden. Pp. 148–161.
van der Horst P.W.
1991   *Ancient Jewish Epitaphs: An Introductory Survey of a Millennium of Jewish Funerary
        Epigraphy (300 BCE-700 CE)*. Kampen.
1992   Jewish Funerary Inscriptions. Most are in Greek. *BAR* 18:46–57.
Van Gennep A.
1972   *The Rites of Passage*. Chicago.
Vaulina M.P.
1971   The Wooden Sarcophagus from the Yuz-Oba Barrow in the Hermitage
        Collection. *Cultura i Iskusstwo Antitchnogo Mira*. Leningrad: 56–62 (Russian).
Vaulina M. and Wasowicz A.
1974   *Bois Grecs et Romaines de l'Ermitage*. Warsaw.
Vaux R., de
1953   Fouilles de Khirbet Qumran-Rapport préliminaire. *RB* 60:83–106.
1954   Fouilles an Khirbet Qumran-Rapport préliminaire sur la deuxième cam-
        pagne. *RB* 61:206–236.
1956   Fouilles au Kbirbet Qumran-Rapport préliminaire sur les 4ᵉ et 5ᵉ cam-
        pagnes. *RB* 63:533–577.
1959   Fouilles de Feshkha. *RB* 66:225–255.
1973   *Archaeology and the Dead Sea Scrolls* (the Schweich Lectures of the British
        Academy 1959). London.
Vincent L.H.
1900   Hypogée Judeo-Grec decouvert au Scopus. *RB* 9:106–112.
1901   Hypogée Antique dans la necropole Septemtrionale de Jeusalem, *RB*
        10:448–452.
1902a   Nouveaux ossuaires Juifs. *RB* 11:103–107.
1902b   Le Tombeau a ossuaires du mont des Oliviens, *RB* 11:277–280.
1954   *Jerusalem de l'ancien testament*. Paris.
Vitto F.
2000   Burial Caves from the Second Temple Period in Jerusalem (Mount Scopus,
        Givʿat Hamivtar, Neveh Yaʿaqov). *ʿAtiqot* 40:65–121.
Waterhouse S.D.
1998   *The Necropolis of Hesban: A typology of Tombs*. Michigan.
Watzinger C.,
1905   *Griechische Holzsarkophage aus der Zeit Alexanders des Grossen (Wissenschaftliche
        Veroeffentlichung der Deutschen Orient-Gesellschaft 6)*. Leipzig.
1932   *Palmyra*. Berlin.
1935   *Denkmäler Palästinas. Eine Einfuhrung in die Archäologie des Heiligen Landes* II.
        Leipzig.
Weaver P.R.G.
1972   *Familia Caesaris. A Social Study of the Emperor's Freedmen and Slaves*. Cambridge.
Weiss Z.
1989   *The Galilean Jewish Cemetery in the Times of the Mishna and the Talmud. An
        Architectural Synthesis in Light of the Talmudic Sources*. MA Thesis. Hebrew Univ.
        Jerusalem.
1992   Social Aspects of Burial in Beth She'arim: Archaeological Finds and Talmu-
        dic Sources. In Levine L.I. (ed.), *The Galilee in Late Antiquity*. Jerusalem:
        357–371.
Weksler-Bdolah S.,
1998   Burial Caves and Installations of the Second Temple Period at the Har-
        Hazofim Observatory (Mt. Scopus, Jerusalem). *ʿAtiqot* 35:23*–54* (Hebrew;
        English summary pp. 161–163).

Werker E.
1994   Botanical Identification of Wood Remains from the ʿEn Gedi Excavations. In Hadas G., *Nine Tombs of the Second Temple Period* (*ʿAtiqot* 24). Jerusalem: 69–72 (Hebrew; English abstract, p. 10*).
Westermann W.L.
1955   *The Slave System of Greek and Roman Antiquity*. Philadelphia.
White D.,
1997   Of Coffins, Curses and Other Plumbeous Matters: the Museum's Lead Burial Casket from Tyre. *Expedition* 39/3:3–14.
1999   The Escatological Connection between Lead and Ropes as Reflected in a Roman Imperial Period Coffin in Philadelphia. *IEJ* 49:66–90.
Wilson I.
1978   *The Turin Shroud: The Burial Cloth of Jesus Christ?* New York.
Wolff S.R.
1996   A Second Temple Period Tomb on the Shuafat Ridge, North Jerusalem. *Atiqot* XXIX:23–28.
1997   An Inscribed Ossuary from Gophna. In Eshel Y. (ed.), *Judea and Samaria Research Studies, Proceeding of the 6th Annual Meeting, 1996*. Kedumim-Ariel: 149–156 (Hebrew; English summary, p. XVI).
Yadin Y.
1961   The Expedition to the Judean Desert, Expedition D. *IEJ* 11:37–38.
1962   The Expedition to the Judean Desert, Expedition D. *IEJ* 12:227–257.
1963   *The Finds from the Bar Kokhba Period in the Cave of the Letters*. Jerusalem.
1965   The Excavation of Masada 1963/64, Preliminary Report, *IEJ* 15:1–120.
1966   *Masada, Herod's Fortress and the Zealots' Last Stand*. New York.
1971   *Bar Kokhba*. Jerusalem.
1973   Epigraphy and Crusifixion. *IEJ* 23:18–22.
1977   Masada. In *Encyclopedia of Archaeological Excavations in the Holy Land*, III, Jerusalem: 811–812.
1983   *The Temple Scroll* I–III. Jerusalem.
Yadin Y. and Naveh J.
1989   *The Aramaic and Hebrew Ostraca and Jar Inscriptions. Masada II, The Yigael Yadin Excavations 1963–1965, Final Reports*. Jerusalem: 1–68.
Yellein, A.
1929   Notes and Comments on the Newly Discovered Jewish Ossuary Inscriptions, *JPOS* 9:41–44.
Zangenberg J.
1999   The "Final Farwell". A necessary Paradigm Shift in the interpretation of the Qumran Cemetery. *The Qumran Chronicle* 8,3:213–217.
2000a   Bones of Contention *The Qumran Chronicle* 9,1:51–76.
2000b   Qazone Tombs, Grave doubts. *BAR* 26, 1:66.
Zevulun U. and Olenik Y.
1978   *Function and Design in the Talmudic Period*. Tel Aviv.
Zias J.
1982   A Rock-Cut Tomb in Jerusalem. *BASOR* 245:53–56.
1992   Human Skeletal Remains from the Mount Scopus Tomb. *Atiqot* 21:97–103.
2000   The Cemeteries of Qumran and Celibacy: Confusion Laid to Rest. *Dead Sea Discoveries* 7, 2:220–253.
Zissu B.
1995   *The Necropolis of Jerusalem in the Second Temple Period. New Discoveries 1980*. MA Thesis, Jerusalem: Hebrew Univ. (Hebrew).
1996   Field Graves at Beit Zafafa: Archaeological Evidence of the Essene Community? *New Studies on Jerusalem* (ed. Faust, A). Ramat Gan: 32–37 (Hebrew).

1998 "Qumran Type" Graves in Jerusalem: Archaeological Evidence of an Essene Community? *Dead Sea Discoveries* 5, 2:158–171.
2002 Roman Period Burial Caves and Mausolea at Eshtemoa in Southern Judea. In Eshel Y. (ed.), *Judea and Samaria Research Studies* 11. Ariel: 165–174 (Hebrew; English summary p. XVIII).
Zissu B. and Ganor, A.
1997 Hurvat Burgin. *Excavations and Surveys in Israel* 16:117–120.
Zlotnick B.
1966 *The Tractate 'Mourning' (Semahot)*. New Haven.

INDEX OF SUBJECTS

INDEX OF SOURCES

PLATES

Plate I-1 Jericho, general view of cemetery

Plate I-2 Qumran view of the site and of the cemetery

Plate I-3 Qumran general view of the cemetery

Plate II-1 Jerusalem, Monumental Tombs in the Kidron Valley

Plate II-3 Tomb of Zechariah

Plate II-2 Bene Ḥezir Tomb

Plate II-4 Absalom Tomb

Plate II-5 Jason's Tomb

Plate II-6 Tomb of Queen Helene of Adiabene, Lintel

Plate II-7 Nazarite family Tomb

Plate II-8 Sanhedriya tomb, facade

Plate II-9 Sanhedriya tomb, interior

Plate II-10 Frieze tomb, Lintel

Plate II-11 Jericho loculi tomb

Plate II-12 Jericho mourning enclosure

Plate II-13 Jericho miqveh

Plate II-14a, b Jericho entrance and sealings

Plate II-15 Akeldama, Tomb 2, Chamber C

Plate III-1 Jericho, Tomb D14 with wooden Coffin 113   →

Plate III-2 'En Gedi wooden coffin

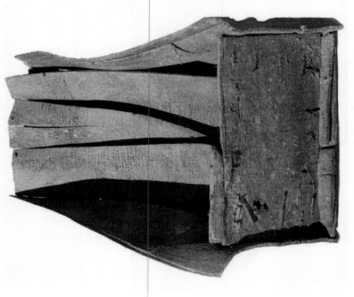

Plate III-3 Nahal David decorated wooden coffin →

Plate III-4 a-b Decorated ossuaries: Type I

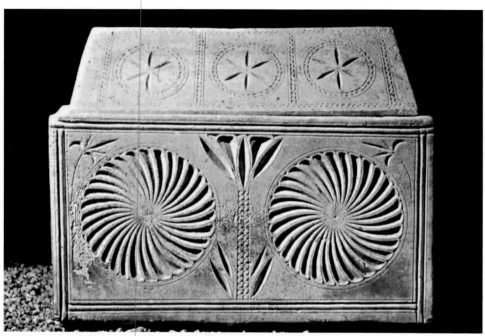

Plate III-5a, b Decorated ossuaries: Type II

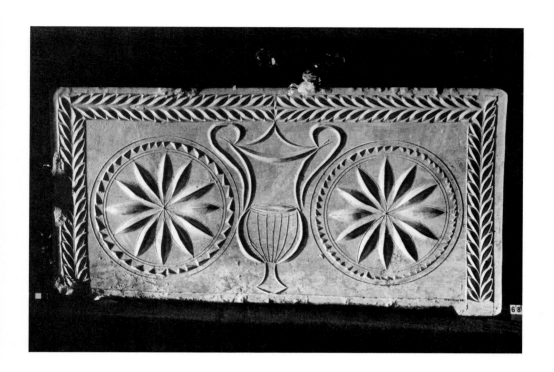

Plate III-5c-d Decorated ossuaries: Type II

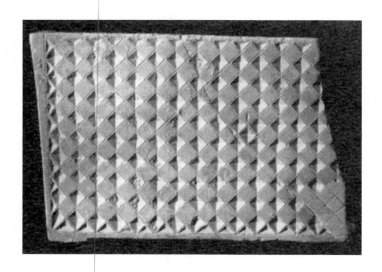

Plate III-6a, b Decorated ossuaries: Type III

Plate III-6c-d Decorated ossuaries: Type IV

Plate III-7a,b Decorated ossuaries with architectural motifs

Plate III- 8 Clay ossuaries

Plate III- 9 Sacophagus No. 1, Akeldama

Plate III-10 Sacophagus No. 2, Nazarite Sacophagus 1

Plate III-11a, b Sacophagus No. 4, Tomb of Herod's family

Plate III-12a, b Sacophagi Nos. 9, 10

Plate III-13a, b Sacophagus No. 12

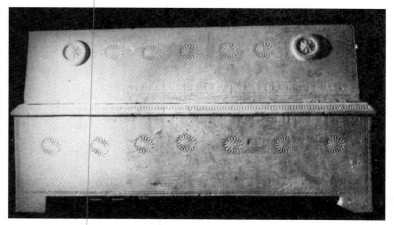

Plate III-14 Sacophagus No. 14

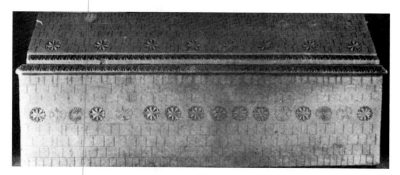

Plate III-15 Sacophagus No. 15

Plate IV-1a, b Masonry, Nazarite Tomb

Plate IV-2 Tomb of Jehoshaphat with pediment decoration

Plate IV-3 Jericho, Goliath Tomb wall painting, north wall

Plate IV-4 Jericho Goliath Tomb wall painting, north wall, detail

Plate IV-5 Jericho Goliath Tomb wall painting, south wall with birds

Plate IV-6 Akeldama, carved and painted architectural decoration

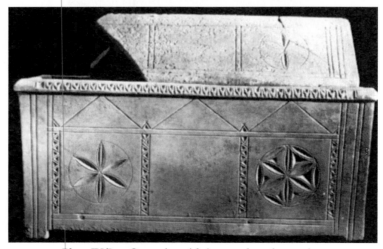

Plate IV-7a-c Ossuaries with incomplete decoration

Plate IV-7d, e Ossuaries with incomplete decoration

Plate IV-8a, b Ossuaries with incomplete decoration

Plate V-1a, b Abba Inscription

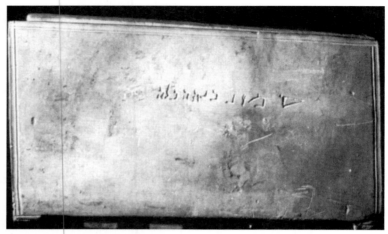

Plate V-2 'Simon builder of the Temple' inscription on ossuary front

Plate V-3 'Simon builder of the Temple' inscription on ossuary side

Plate V-4 Yehohana daughter of High Priest inscription

Plate V-5a Jericho, Goliath Family Inscription 12

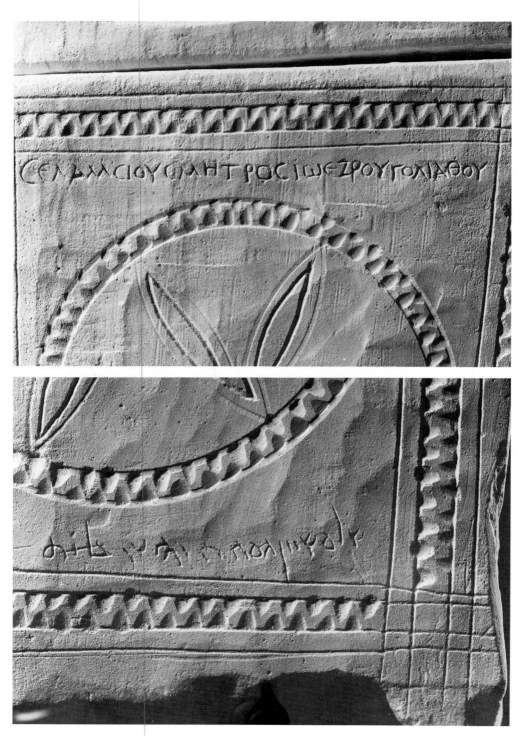

Plate V-6a, b Jericho, Goliath Family Inscriptions 11

Plate V-7a, b Jericho, Goliath Family Inscription 9

Plate V-8 Jericho Goliath Family Inscription 10

Plate V-9 Jericho Goliath Family Inscription 3

Plate V-10 Jericho Goliath Family Inscription 7

Plate V-11a, b Jericho Goliath Family Inscription a. Inscription 8; b. Inscription 13

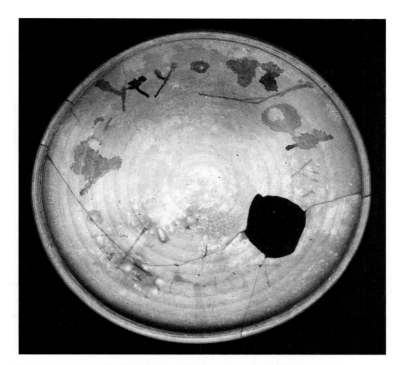

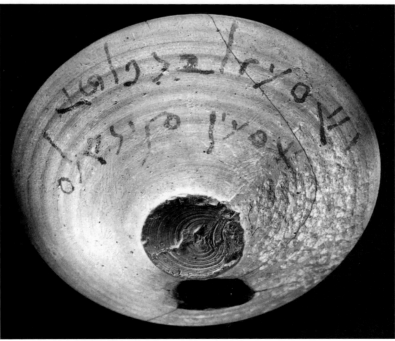

Plate V-12a, b Jericho memorial bowl inscriptions of family "from Jerusalem"

Plate V-13a, b selected inscriptions with nicknames: origin, title

Plate V-13c-d selected inscriptions with nicknames: honorific, positive

Plate VI-2 Ossuary (No. 17) from Akeldama, 'Eros' family Tomb

Plate VI-1 Ossuaries from Nazarite family Tomb

Plate VI-3a-c Goliath Tomb sealing

Plate VI-4a, b The Goliath family Tomb chambers: a. Chamber A; b. Chamber B

Plate VI-5 Ossuaries found in Goliath Tomb

Plate VI-6a, b Ossuaries XVIII, XX from the Goliath family Tomb

Plate VI-6c, d Ossuaries XIX, XXI from Goliath family Tomb, Jericho

Plate VI-7 Tomb D1 ossuaries and the written bowl

Plate VII-1 Ossuary with women's name, X daughter of Y

Plate VII-2 Ossuary with woman name + father+ husband

Plate VII-3 Ossuary with woman's name, wife

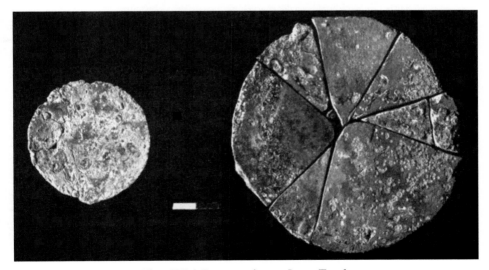

Plate VII-4 Bronze mirrors, Jason Tomb

Plate VIII-1 Jericho Nefesh stone

Plate VII-5 Wooden coffins of a woman and a child, Jericho Tomb D12

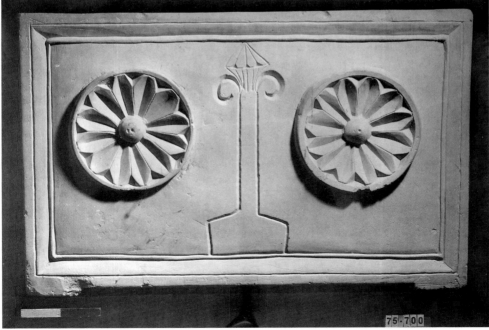

Plate VIII-2a, b Ossuaries with Nefesh

Plate VIII-3 Ossuary with Nefesh

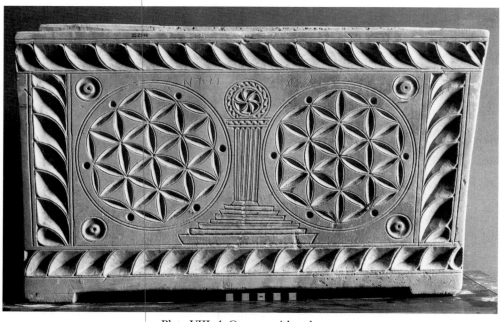

Plate VIII- 4 Ossuary with column

Plate VIII-6 Petra, Khasneh

Plate VIII- 5 Petra, Obelisk Tomb

Plate VIII-7 Petra, ed-Deir

Plate IX-1 Ossuary Group 1: Ossuary type A, with two columned
porch

Plate IX-2 Ossuary Group 1: Ossuary type A, with three columned porch

Plate IX-3 Ossuary Group 1: Ossuary type A, with columned porch and arrows

Plate IX-4a, b Ossuary Group 1: Ossuary with central motif type B

Plate IX-5a, b Ossuary Group I: Ossuary with central motif type B

Plate IX-6 Ossuary Group I: Ossuary with central motif type C

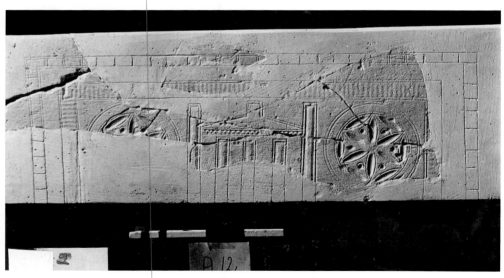

Plate IX-7 Ossuary Group I: Jericho Ossuary with central motif type C

Plate IX-8 Ossuary Group 2: Ossuary with central motif type A

Plate IX-9 Ossuary Group 2: Ossuary with central motif type B

Plate IX-10 Ossuary Group 2: Ossuary with central motif type B

Plate IX-11 Ossuary Group 2: Ossuary with central motif type C

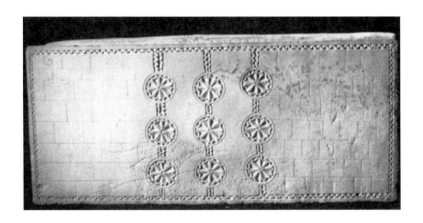

Plate IX-12a, b Ossuary Group 3: motif a

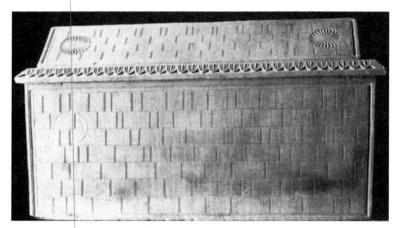

Plate IX-13 Ossuary Group 3: motif b

Plate IX-14 Ossuary Group 3: motif c

Plate X-1 bowl, Jericho

Plate X-2 krater, Jericho

Plate X-3 Cooking pots, ungunteria, and glass amphoriskos, Jericho

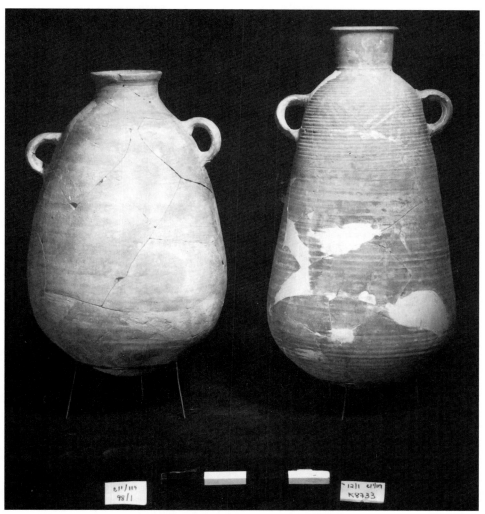

Plate X-4 Storage Jars, Jericho

Plate X-5 Grave goods from the Goliath Tomb, Jericho

Plate X-7 Wooden vessels from 'En Gedi tombs

Plate X-6 Glass amphoriskos, Jericho

Plate X-8 Leather sandal, Jericho

Plate X-9 Coin of Herod Archelaus, Jericho

Plate X-10 Coin of Yehoḥanan Hyrcanus I, Jericho

Plate X-11 Two coins of Agrippa I, Jericho

Plate XI-1 Jerusalem Burial Type III

Plate XI-2 Jericho Burial Type I

Plate XI-3 Jericho Burial Type II

Plate XI-4 Jericho Burial Type III

Plate XI-5 Qumran Burial

Plate XI-6a, b Jericho Ossuary II façade and lid

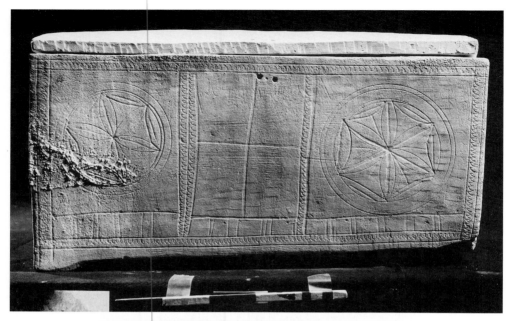

349—6

Plate XI-7a, b Jericho Ossuary XV façade and side

Plate XI-8 Jericho Ossuary XXII

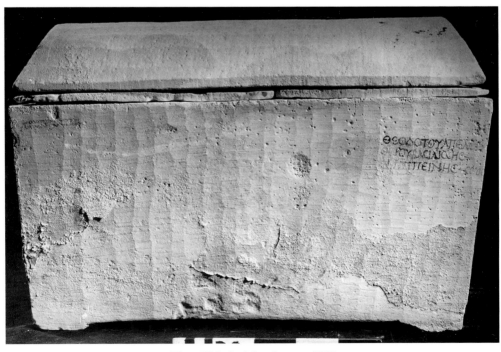

Plate XI-9 Jericho Ossuary VIII

Plate XI-10 Aramaic inscribed epitaph No. 2

Plate XI-11 Aramaic inscribed epitaph No. 3

Plate XI-12 Aramaic painted dipinto No. 4

Plate XI-14 Chisels and iron nails found in Goliath tomb, Jericho

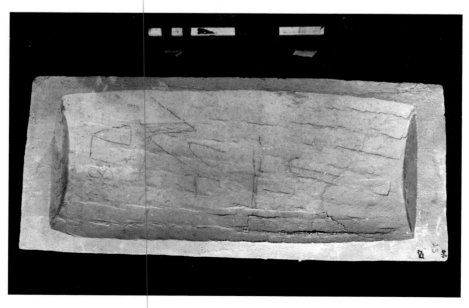

Plate XI-13 Greek abecedary inscribed on an ossuary lid, Jericho

SUPPLEMENTS

TO THE

JOURNAL FOR THE STUDY OF JUDAISM

49. LIETAERT PEERBOLTE, L.J. *The Antecedents of Antichrist*. A Traditio-Historical Study of the Earliest Christian Views on Eschatological Opponents. 1996. ISBN 90 04 10455 0

50. YARBRO COLLINS, A. *Cosmology and Eschatology in Jewish and Christian Apocalypticism*. 1996. ISBN 90 04 10587 5

51. MENN, E. *Judah and Tamar (Genesis 38) in Ancient Jewish Exegesis*. Studies in Literary Form and Hermeneutics. 1997.
ISBN 90 04 10630 8

52. NEUSNER, J. *Jerusalem and Athens*. The Congruity of Talmudic and Classical Philosophy. 1996. ISBN 90 04 10698 7

54. COLLINS, J.J. *Seers, Sibyls & Sages in Hellenistic-Roman Judaism*. 1997.
ISBN 90 04 10752 5

55. BAUMGARTEN, A.I. *The Flourishing of Jewish Sects in the Maccabean Era: An Interpretation*. 1997. ISBN 90 04 10751 7

56. SCOTT, J.M. (ed.). *Exile: Old Testament, Jewish, and Christian Conceptions*. 1997. ISBN 90 04 10676 6

57. HENTEN, J-.W. VAN. *The Maccabean Martyrs as Saviours of the Jewish People*. A Study of 2 and 4 Maccabees. 1997. ISBN 90 04 10976 5

58. FELDMAN, L.H. *Studies in Josephus' Rewritten Bible*. 1998.
ISBN 90 04 10839 4

59. MORRAY-JONES, C.R.A. *A Transparent Illusion*. The Dangerous Vision of Water in Hekhalot Mysticism: A Source-Critical and Tradition-Historical Inquiry. 2002. ISBN 90 04 11337 1

60. HALPERN-AMARU, B. *The Empowerment of Women in the* Book of Jubilees. 1999. ISBN 90 04 11414 9

61. HENZE, M. *The Madness of King Nebuchadnezzar*. The Ancient Near Eastern Origins and Early History of Interpretation of Daniel 4. 1999. ISBN 90 04 11421 1

62. VANDERKAM, J.C. *From Revelation to Canon*. Studies in the Hebrew Bible and Second Tempel Literature. 2000. ISBN 90 04 11557 9

63. NEWMAN, C.C., J.R. DAVILA & G.S. LEWIS (eds.). *The Jewish Roots of Christological Monotheism*. Papers from the St. Andrews Conference on the Historical Origins of the Worship of Jesus. 1999.
ISBN 90 04 11361 4

64. LIESEN, J.W.M. *Full of Praise*. An Exegetical Study of Sir 39,12-35. 1999.
ISBN 90 04 11359 2

65. BEDFORD, P.R. *Temple Restoration in Early Achaemenid Judah*. 2000.
ISBN 90 04 11509 9

66. RUITEN, J.T.A.G.M. VAN. *Primaeval History Interpreted*. The Rewriting of
Genesis 1-11 in the book of Jubilees. 2000. ISBN 90 04 11658 3

67. HOFMANN, N.J. *Die Assumptio Mosis*. Studien zur Rezeption massgültiger
Überlieferung. 2000. ISBN 90 04 11938 8

68. HACHLILI, R. *The Menorah, the Ancient Seven-armed Candelabrum*. Origin,
Form and Significance. 2001. ISBN 90 04 12017 3

69. VELTRI, G. *Gegenwart der Tradition*. Studien zur jüdischen Literatur und
Kulturgeschichte. 2002. ISBN 90 04 11686 9

70. DAVILA, J.R. *Descenders to the Chariot*. The People behind the Hekhalot
Literature. 2001. ISBN 90 04 11541 2

71. PORTER, S.E. & J.C.R. DE ROO (eds.). *The Concept of the Covenant in the
Second Temple Period*. 2003. ISBN 90 04 11609 5

72. SCOTT, J.M. (ed.). *Restoration*. Old Testament, Jewish, and Christian
Perspectives. 2001. ISBN 90 04 11580 3

73. TORIJANO, P.A. *Solomon the Esoteric King*. From King to Magus, Development of a Tradition. 2002. ISBN 90 04 11941 8

74. KUGEL, J.L. *Shem in the Tents of Japhet*. Essays on the Encounter of
Judaism and Hellenism. 2002. ISBN 90 04 12514 0

75. COLAUTTI, F.M. *Passover in the Works of Josephus*. 2002.
ISBN 90 04 12372 5

76. BERTHELOT, K. *Philanthrôpia judaica*. Le débat autour de la "misanthro-
pie" des lois juives dans l'Antiquité. 2003. ISBN 90 04 12886 7

77. NAJMAN, H. *Seconding Sinai*. The Development of Mosaic Discourse in
Second Temple Judaism. 2003. ISBN 90 04 11542 0

78. MULDER, O. *Simon the High Priest in Sirach 50*. An Exegetical Study of the
Significance of Simon the High Priest as Climax to the Praise of the
Fathers in Ben Sira's Concept of the History of Israel. 2003.
ISBN 90 04 12316 4

79. BURKES, S.L. *God, Self, and Death*. The Shape of Religious Transformation in the Second Temple Period. 2003. ISBN 90 04 12954 5

80. NEUSNER, J. & A.J. AVERY-PECK (eds.). *George W.E. Nickelsburg in Perspective*.
An Ongoing Dialogue of Learning (2 vols.). 2003.
ISBN 90 04 12987 1 (set)

81. COBLENTZ BAUTCH, K. *A Study of the Geography of 1 Enoch 17-19*. "No One
Has Seen What I Have Seen". 2003. ISBN 90 04 13103 5

82. GARCÍA MARTÍNEZ, F., & G.P. LUTTIKHUIZEN. *Jerusalem, Alexandria, Rome*.
Studies in Ancient Cultural Interaction in Honour of A. Hilhorst. 2003
ISBN 90 04 13584 7

83. NAJMAN, H. & J.H. NEWMAN (eds.). *The Idea of Biblical Interpretation*. Essays
in Honor of James L. Kugel. 2004. ISBN 90 04 13630 4

84. ATKINSON, K. *I Cried to the Lord*. A Study of the Psalms of Solomon's Historical Background and Social Setting. 2004. ISBN 90 04 13614 2

85. AVERY-PECK, A.J., D. HARRINGTON & J. NEUSNER. *When Judaism and Christianity Began*. Essays in Memory of Anthony J. Saldarini. 2004. ISBN 90 04 13659 2 (Set), ISBN 90 04 13660 6 (Volume I), ISBN 90 04 13661 4 (Volume II)

86. DRAWNEL, H. *An Aramaic Wisdom Text from Qumran*. A New Interpretation of the Levi Document. 2004. ISBN 90 04 13753 X. *In Preparation*

87. BERTHELOT, K. *L'«humanité de l'autre homme» dans la pensée juive ancienne*. 2004. ISBN 90 04 13797 1

88. BONS, E. (ed.) *«Car c'est l'amour qui me plaît, non le sacrifice …»*. Recherches sur Osée 6:6 et son interprétation juive et chrétienne. 2004. ISBN 90 04 13677 0

89. CHAZON, E.G., D. SATRAN & R. CLEMENTS. (eds.) *Things Revealed*. Studies in Honor of Michael E. Stone. 2004. ISBN 90 04 13885 4. *In Preparation*

91. SCOTT, J.M. *On Earth as in Heaven*. The Restoration of Sacred Time and Sacred Space in the Book of Jubilees. 2005. ISBN 90 04 13796 3

92. RICHARDSON, P. *Building Jewish in the Roman East*. 2005. ISBN 90 04 14131 6.

93. BATSCH, C. *La guerre et les rites de guerre dans le judaïsme du deuxième Temple*. 2005. ISBN 90 04 13897 8.

94. HACHLILI, R. *Jewish Funerary Customs, Practices and Rites in the Second Temple Period*. 2005. ISBN 90 04 12373 3.

ISSN 1384-2161